Women Across Cultures
A Global Perspective

Fifth Edition

Shawn Meghan Burn

California Polytechnic State University

Mc
Graw
Hill

WOMEN ACROSS CULTURES

Published by McGraw Hill LLC, 1325 Avenue of the Americas, New York, NY 10019. Copyright ©2023 by McGraw Hill LLC. All rights reserved. Printed in the United States of America. No part of this publication may be reproduced or distributed in any form or by any means, or stored in a database or retrieval system, without the prior written consent of McGraw Hill LLC, including, but not limited to, in any network or other electronic storage or transmission, or broadcast for distance learning.

Some ancillaries, including electronic and print components, may not be available to customers outside the United States.

This book is printed on acid-free paper.

1 2 3 4 5 6 7 8 9 LCR 27 26 25 24 23 22

ISBN 978-1-265-21969-7
MHID 1-265-21969-9

Cover Image: *Photography by Dusko Almosa/Moment/Getty Images*

All credits appearing on page or at the end of the book are considered to be an extension of the copyright page.

The Internet addresses listed in the text were accurate at the time of publication. The inclusion of a website does not indicate an endorsement by the authors or McGraw Hill LLC, and McGraw Hill LLC does not guarantee the accuracy of the information presented at these sites.

mheducation.com/highered

Contents

Preface *ix*

1 Introduction to Global Women's Studies 2

Theme 1: Global Women's and Gender Studies Sees Gender Inequality as a
Historical, Sociocultural Phenomenon 3

Theme 2: Global Women's and Gender Studies Is About
Activism and Empowerment 6

Theme 3: Global Women's and Gender Studies Takes
a Multicultural, Intersectional, Contextualized Approach 8
The Importance of Similarity 9
The Importance of Difference 9
The Challenge of Multiculturalism 10

Theme 4: Global Women's and Gender Studies Views Women's Rights as
Human Rights 12

Overview of the Book 17

Glossary Terms and Concepts 19

Study Questions 20

Discussion Questions 20

References 21

2 Women's Lower Status and Power 24

Men's Greater Economic Power 25

Men's Greater Political and Legal Power 26

The Higher Status of Boys and Men 28

Women and Girls as Objects and Property 31

Violence Against Women and Girls (VAWG) 35
Domestic or Intimate Partner Violence 37

Sexual Violence 41
Rape 41
Conflict-Related Sexual Violence 45

Conclusion 48

Glossary Terms and Concepts 49

Study Questions 49

Discussion Questions and Activities   50

Action Opportunities   51

Activist Websites   51

Informational Websites   52

References   52

3   *Reproductive Health and Reproductive Rights*   60

Maternal Mortality and Morbidity   64
  Maternal Mortality   64
  Maternal Morbidity   66

Female Genital Mutilation   67

Contraception, Reproductive Choice, and Reproductive Health   72

Abortion   75

The Agents That Control Women's Reproductive Choice and Health   77
  Government   77
  Men   80
  Corporations   81
  Religious Organizations   81
  Women   83

Conclusion   85

Glossary Terms and Concepts   86

Study Questions   86

Discussion Questions and Activities   87

Action Opportunities   87

Activist Websites   88

Informational Websites   88

References   89

4   *Women's Sexuality and Sexual Rights*   98

Sexual Rights as Human Rights   99

A Woman's Sexuality Is Often Not Her Own   101

Sexual Orientation, Gender Identity, and Human Rights (SOGI Rights)   104
  Gender Identity   105
  Sexual Orientation   106
  Lesbian and Bisexual Women's Invisibility   107

Sexual Orientation and Feminism   110
  Lesbian Feminism   111

Conclusion   114

Glossary Terms and Concepts   116

Study Questions   116

Discussion Questions and Activities   117

Action Opportunities   118

Activist Websites   118

Informational Websites   118

References   119

5 *Women's Work*   *126*

Women's Unpaid Care Work   127
  Explanations for Gender Inequalities in Unpaid Domestic and Care Work   128
  Why the Gender Gap in Unpaid Domestic and Care Labor Matters   131
  Reducing the Gender Gap in Unpaid Domestic and Care Work   133

Women's Paid Labor   134
  Effects of Paid Work on Women   134
  Maternity Protections and Child Care   135
  The Gender Wage (Pay) Gap: Explanations and Solutions   139
  The Glass Ceiling: Explanations and Solutions   145
  Sexual Harassment in the Workplace   150

Women in the Informal Labor Sector and Women's Entrepreneurship   154

Conclusion   157

Glossary Terms and Concepts   158

Study Questions   158

Discussion Questions and Activities   159

Action Opportunities   160

Activist Websites   161

Informational Websites   161

References   162

6 *Women, Development, and Environmental Sustainability*   *172*

Background   173
  Development Terminology   173
  Colonial History   175
  Women in Developing Nations (the Global South)   175
  Feminist Concerns with the Development Process   176
  *Traditional Development Programs Fail to Recognize Women's Economic
      Contributions   177*
  *Traditional Development Programs Have Not Reduced Women's
      Considerable Workloads   177*
  *Traditional Development Programs Focus on Men's Income
      Generation   178*
  *Traditional Development Programs Have Contributed to Erosions in
      Women's Status   179*

Women in Development Approach (WID)   180
  Income-Generating Projects   180
  Labor-Saving Technologies   181
  Improving Women's Access to Development Resources   181

Gender and Development Approach (GAD)   183

Women, the Environment, and Sustainable Development   187
  Environmental Sustainability Basics   187
  Women and Environmental Sustainability   190
  Global Women's Environmental Defenders   191
  Local Women Environmental Defenders   194

Conclusion   196

Glossary Terms and Concepts   198

Study Questions   198

Discussion Questions and Activities   199

Action Opportunities   200

Activist Websites   200

Informational Websites   200

References   201

7   *Women and Globalization*   208

The Effects of Globalization on Women   209

Women's Work in the Transnational Factory   212
  Stopping Sweatshop Labor   214

The Global Economy and Women's Migration   218
  Migrating for Domestic Work   219
  Migrating to Marry   223

Women and Girls' Labor in the Global Sex Trade   225
  Sex Tourism   226
  Sex Trafficking   227

Conclusion   231

Glossary Terms and Concepts   232

Study Questions   232

Discussion Questions and Activities   233

Action Opportunities   234

Activist Websites   234

Informational Websites   235

References   235

8   *Women and Religion*   244

Diversity and the Study of Women and Religion   245
  Religious and Spiritual Diversity   245

Religious Fundamentalism 246

Critiquing and Deconstructing Religion 249
  Masculine God-Language and Imagery 250
  Sexism in Religious Texts 251
  *Gender-Segregated Religious Practices and Traditions of Male Religious
    Leadership* 252

Reforming and Reconstructing Religion 253

Women and the World's Major Religions 255
  Islam 256
  Judaism 261
  Hinduism 265
  Buddhism 268
  Christianity 270

Intersectional Feminist Theologies 275

Feminist Spirituality 276

Conclusion 278

Glossary Terms and Concepts 279

Study Questions 280

Discussion Questions and Activities 280

Action Opportunities 281

Activist Websites 282

Informational Websites 282

References 283

9 *Women and Politics* 296

Women's Voting 298

Women Representatives in National Legislatures and Cabinets 300
  *Importance of Women Representatives in National Legislatures and
    Cabinets* 301
  *Explaining the Relatively Low Numbers of Women in National
    Legislatures* 302
  *Increasing the Number of Women Representatives in National Legislatures
    with Electoral Reforms* 306
  *Other Strategies for Increasing Women's Representation in National
    Legislatures* 309

Women Heads of State and Government: Presidents and Prime Ministers 311
  Paths to Power 312
  Gender Differences in Leadership 318
  Advocacy of Women's Issues 321
  Women Political Executives and Gender Stereotypes 322

Women in Informal Politics: Social and Protest Movements 324
  Women's Action Around Economic Issues 325

Women's Action Around Nationalist and Racial/Ethnic Issues 326
Women's Action Around Humanistic/Nurturing Issues 327

Conclusion 329

Glossary Terms and Concepts 330

Study Questions 330

Discussion Questions and Activities 331

Action Opportunities 332

Activist Websites 333

Informational Websites 333

References 333

10 *Women's Movements 340*

Diversity in Women's Movements 341
Different Strands of Women's Movements 341
Not All Women's Movements Are Feminist Movements 344

Forces Operating Against Women's Activism 346

Contextual Influences on Women's Movements 348
Local Political and Economic Conditions 349
Women's Movements Arising from Class Struggles 350
Women's Movements Arising from Nationalist Struggles 350
Women's Movements and Democratization 351

Women's Movements and State Feminism 356
Debate About the Role of the State 357
Factors Affecting the Success of State Feminism 359

Transnational Feminist Movements and Networks 359
TFNs and the United Nations' Four World's Women's Conferences 362
Transnational Feminist Movements and Women's Rights as Human Rights 364
Challenges to Women's Rights as a Human Rights Approach 365

Conclusion 367

Glossary Terms and Concepts 369

Study Questions 369

Discussion Questions and Activities 370

Action Opportunities 371

Activist Websites 371

Informational Websites 372

References 372

Appendix 380
Glossary 419
Index I-1

Preface

The cross-cultural study of women's issues and women's movements, the focus of this book, is fascinating and educational. It tells of the disadvantage of women and girls relative to boys and men and how that disadvantage arises from the greater male rights and privilege embedded in cultures, institutions, groups, and minds. Unfortunately, this truth can be disturbing at times. But I promise you that this book is also uplifting because it is equally about hope, resilience, and the power of people to fight and right social injustices. Throughout the book are many examples of actions to address women's issues and promote gender equality—ranging from the small grassroots effort addressing local women's issues to the use of international law for improving women's status. And while there is a long way to go, I have seen remarkable progress since the first edition of *Women Across Cultures: A Global Perspective* was published in 2000.

The global study of women is also about diversity and intersectionality and their importance for understanding the gendered human experience. Gendered discriminations are often heightened by their interaction with other discriminations such as those based on race, class, sexual orientation, age, and gender identity. The experiences and issues of women vary widely based on these and other intersections. Women's experiences as women are also strongly shaped by the particular political, social, and cultural contexts where they live, leading to diversity in women's lives and issues, and in their advocacy and activism. This diversity is true not only in our own country, but also globally. Documenting, studying, and appreciating this variety are hallmarks of global women's and gender studies and one of the major aims of this book.

I have many hopes for this fifth edition of *Women Across Cultures: A Global Perspective.* I hope my readers find the global study of women as captivating and inspiring as I do. I hope that after reading the book they not only better understand how the world works but that they also feel compelled to do their part for gender equality. I hope that readers will be struck by the scope of gender injustice but equally struck by the scope of women's resistance and the possibilities for change. I hope that the book helps readers better understand and appreciate feminism, diversity, and intersectionality, as they are so often caricatured, ridiculed, and negatively stereotyped. I hope that the book reflects and honors internationally oriented women's and gender studies scholarship and the many women's movements actors and organizations that advocate and serve women.

Pedagogy

There is a lot of information in the book from a variety of fields. As a long-time teacher and writer, I am sensitive to students' concerns about how to read and master textbook content. I strive to create a reader-friendly experience. To this end, I have included a number of pedagogical elements. Headings alert readers to upcoming content. Important terms and concepts appear in boldface in the text and appear in a glossary at the end of the book. To liven up and illustrate the often technical and factual textual material, many examples, thought-provoking quotes, and bits of women's history appear in the margins. Figures graphically depict text concepts to help students pull out key themes. Each chapter includes boxed examples of feminist thought and action from all over the world, including activist profiles of individuals and groups. Study questions are listed at the conclusion of each chapter. Students may use these to make sure they understand the major points of the chapter and to structure the study of text material. Discussion questions and activities follow the study questions. These are intended to stimulate critical and creative thinking and discussion. Instructors may use these as assignments or for class discussion. The book's chapters are organized by issues rather than by country or region, but an appendix provides an overall sense of women's status on a country-by-country basis using economic, educational, and health indicators. Students can use this information as the basis for country or regional reports on the status of women. This information may be enhanced by use of the end-of-chapter informational and activist organization websites.

Changes from the Fourth Edition

Our understanding of gender inequalities and progress toward gender equality is dynamic, so each chapter was updated to provide current examples, statistics, resources, and scholarship. For example, in this fifth edition, you will find a more comprehensive examination of sexual harassment, climate change, and the use of social media in women's activism. The study of global women's issues and equality is also complex and often technical, so I often rewrote and reorganized to promote readers' engagement and comprehension. Chapter 6, "Women and Development," for instance, was rewritten to better explain development concepts, and women's experiences in low-income countries.

Acknowledgments

This book is dedicated to my late colleague and global women's and gender studies mentor, Patrice Engle. Patrice was a shining example of the scholar-activist, and she literally saved lives through her work on maternal and child health. She left us far too soon. I must also thank all those who are working to bring about women's equality and all the great scholars (and journalists) whose work appears on the pages here—these are my heroes, and I feel I have been in the presence of greatness by reading their work and studying their efforts.

Writing a book is a time-consuming endeavor. It is also something that few of us can do without support. That includes the practical support provided by Emily Parrish, who recently completed her Master's in Library and Information Science. Emily did much of the research to update the statistics throughout the text, including the Appendix. I am also grateful to the reviewers who provided thoughtful feedback for this fifth edition, and I hope that they feel their suggestions were honored. These instructor-reviewers were Umme Al-wazedi, Augustana College; Habiba Boumlik, CUNY LaGuardia Community College; Ronald Carter, Northeast Community College; Marie Cartier, California State University Northridge; Jana Knibb, Community College of Rhode Island; Donnalynn Scillieri, William Paterson University of New Jersey; and Mandy Webster, Columbia Gorge Community College. Thanks also to Elisa Odoardi and Lisa Bruflodt (my editors at McGraw Hill), Susan Raley (my editor at MPS North America), and the team at MPS Limited.

Authors also benefit from emotional support, so an extra-big thank you to my husband, the always supportive and entertaining Gene Courter, and my son, the brilliant and talented artist Kane Lynch. I so appreciate their support of me, my writing, and their support for gender equality and feminism. And to my sister, Kevyn Burn, and my other women friends (special shout-out to Lois Petty), thank you for the support, the fun, and the sisterhood.

Proctorio

Remote Proctoring & Browser-Locking Capabilities

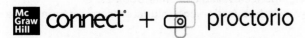

Remote proctoring and browser-locking capabilities, hosted by Proctorio within Connect, provide control of the assessment environment by enabling security options and verifying the identity of the student.

Seamlessly integrated within Connect, these services allow instructors to control students' assessment experience by restricting browser activity, recording students' activity, and verifying students are doing their own work.

Instant and detailed reporting gives instructors an at-a-glance view of potential academic integrity concerns, thereby avoiding personal bias and supporting evidence-based claims.

ReadAnywhere

Read or study when it's convenient for you with McGraw Hill's free ReadAnywhere app. Available for iOS or Android smartphones or tablets, ReadAnywhere gives users access to McGraw Hill tools including the eBook and SmartBook 2.0 or Adaptive Learning Assignments in Connect. Take notes, highlight, and complete assignments offline—all of your work will sync when you open the app with WiFi access. Log in with your McGraw Hill Connect username and password to start learning—anytime, anywhere!

Instructors: Student Success Starts with You

Tools to enhance your unique voice

Want to build your own course? No problem. Prefer to use an OLC-aligned, prebuilt course? Easy. Want to make changes throughout the semester? Sure. And you'll save time with Connect's auto-grading too.

65%
Less Time Grading

Laptop: McGraw Hill; Woman/dog; George Doyle/Getty Images

Study made personal

Incorporate adaptive study resources like SmartBook® 2.0 into your course and help your students be better prepared in less time. Learn more about the powerful personalized learning experience available in SmartBook 2.0 at **www.mheducation.com/highered/connect/smartbook**

Affordable solutions, added value

Make technology work for you with LMS integration for single sign-on access, mobile access to the digital textbook, and reports to quickly show you how each of your students is doing. And with our Inclusive Access program you can provide all these tools at a discount to your students. Ask your McGraw Hill representative for more information.

Padlock: Jobalou/Getty Images

Solutions for your challenges

A product isn't a solution. Real solutions are affordable, reliable, and come with training and ongoing support when you need it and how you want it. Visit **www.supportateverystep.com** for videos and resources both you and your students can use throughout the semester.

Checkmark: Jobalou/Getty Images

Students: Get Learning that Fits You

Effective tools for efficient studying

Connect is designed to help you be more productive with simple, flexible, intuitive tools that maximize your study time and meet your individual learning needs. Get learning that works for you with Connect.

Study anytime, anywhere

Download the free ReadAnywhere app and access your online eBook, SmartBook 2.0, or Adaptive Learning Assignments when it's convenient, even if you're offline. And since the app automatically syncs with your Connect account, all of your work is available every time you open it. Find out more at **www.mheducation.com/readanywhere**

> *"I really liked this app—it made it easy to study when you don't have your text-book in front of you."*
>
> - Jordan Cunningham, Eastern Washington University

Calendar: owattaphotos/Getty Images

Everything you need in one place

Your Connect course has everything you need—whether reading on your digital eBook or completing assignments for class, Connect makes it easy to get your work done.

Learning for everyone

McGraw Hill works directly with Accessibility Services Departments and faculty to meet the learning needs of all students. Please contact your Accessibility Services Office and ask them to email accessibility@mheducation.com, or visit **www.mheducation.com/about/accessibility** for more information.

Top: Jenner Images/Getty Images, Left: Hero Images/Getty Images, Right: Hero Images/Getty Images

OLC-Aligned Courses

Implementing High-Quality Online Instruction and Assessment Through Preconfigured Courseware

In consultation with the Online Learning Consortium (OLC) and our certified Faculty Consultants, McGraw Hill has created pre-configured courseware using OLC's quality scorecard to align with best practices in online course delivery. This turnkey courseware contains a combination of formative assessments, summative assessments, homework, and application activities, and can easily be customized to meet an individual's needs and course outcomes. For more information, visit https://www.mheducation.com/highered/olc.

Tegrity: Lectures 24/7

Tegrity in Connect is a tool that makes class time available 24/7 by automatically capturing every lecture. With a simple one-click start-and-stop process, you capture all computer screens and corresponding audio in a format that is easy to search, frame by frame. Students can replay any part of any class with easy-to-use, browser-based viewing on a PC, Mac, iPod, or other mobile device.

Educators know that the more students can see, hear, and experience class resources, the better they learn. In fact, studies prove it. Tegrity's unique search feature helps students efficiently find what they need, when they need it, across an entire semester of class recordings. Help turn your students' study time into learning moments immediately supported by your lecture. With Tegrity, you also increase intent listening and class participation by easing students' concerns about note-taking. Using Tegrity in Connect will make it more likely you will see students' faces, not the tops of their heads.

Test Builder in Connect

Available within Connect, Test Builder is a cloud-based tool that enables instructors to format tests that can be printed, administered within a Learning Management System, or exported as a Word document of the test bank. Test Builder offers a modern, streamlined interface for easy content configuration that matches course needs, without requiring a download.

Test Builder allows you to:

- access all test bank content from a particular title.
- easily pinpoint the most relevant content through robust filtering options.
- manipulate the order of questions or scramble questions and/or answers.
- pin questions to a specific location within a test.
- determine your preferred treatment of algorithmic questions.
- choose the layout and spacing.
- add instructions and configure default settings.

Test Builder provides a secure interface for better protection of content and allows for just-in-time updates to flow directly into assessments.

Writing Assignment

Available within Connect and Connect Master, the Writing Assignment tool delivers a learning experience to help students improve their written communication skills and conceptual understanding. As an instructor you can assign, monitor, grade, and provide feedback on writing more efficiently and effectively.

Create

Your Book, Your Way

McGraw Hill's Content Collections Powered by Create® is a self-service website that enables instructors to create custom course materials—print and eBooks—by drawing upon McGraw Hill's comprehensive, cross-disciplinary content. Choose what you want from our high-quality textbooks, articles, and cases. Combine it with your own content quickly and easily, and tap into other rights-secured, third-party content such as readings, cases, and articles. Content can be arranged in a way that makes the most sense for your course and you can include the course name and information as well. Choose the best format for your course: color print, black-and-white print, or eBook. The eBook can be included in your Connect course and is available on the free ReadAnywhere app for smartphone or tablet access as well. When you are finished customizing, you will receive a free digital copy to review in just minutes! Visit McGraw Hill Create®—www.mcgrawhillcreate.com—today and begin building!

1

Introduction to Global Women's Studies

We must be courageous in speaking out about the issues that concern us; we must not bend under the weight of spurious arguments invoking culture or traditional values. No value worth the name supports the oppression and enslavement of women.

—DR. NAFIS SADIK, Fourth World Women's Conference, 1995

The global study of women emphasizes how women's issues and activism are similar cross-culturally, yet different due to contextual and intersectional factors. Richard Ross/ Getty Images

This global women's and gender studies book is about women's issues and gender equality cross-culturally. The study of global women documents women's status worldwide. A key area of focus is the understanding of **gender inequality**, the disadvantage of girls and women relative to boys and men. Unfortunately, gender inequality is still extensive with enormous implications for women and girls everywhere. Global women's and gender studies links gender inequality to cultural practices that are embedded in social, economic, political, and legal systems and describes how these are targets of change. Considerations of diversity, and the intersections between gender and other variables such as region, race, class, and sexual orientation, are essential to global women's studies. An interdisciplinary endeavor, global women's and gender studies draws on research and theory from psychology, sociology, anthropology, economics, religion, political science, medicine, public health, geography, public policy, history, philosophy, and law.

The global study of women is rich and rewarding because it requires learning about different customs, religions, and forms of government and provides insights into women's diverse lives. Studying women's lives in other cultures also inspires a profound appreciation for women. The great strength possessed by women, and what they accomplish despite their customary lower status and power, are truly amazing. That said, the cross-cultural study of women is at times very difficult, shocking, and disturbing. You may be horrified, surprised, depressed, and angered at some of the gender-based abuses that continue today—in your own country as well as others. You might find that the material triggers a personal gender journey as you focus a gender lens on your own life and culture. The saying, "The truth will set you free, but first it will make you mad" (and I would add, sometimes sad), applies to the subject matter of this book. Fortunately, the bad news is tempered by courageous stories of activism and resistance, and evidence of hopeful progress. This is not just a tale of the victimization of women and girls. On the contrary, it is a tale of empowerment, activism, and change.

To provide you with a finer sense of what global women's studies is about, here are four key themes that characterize the field. These themes are illustrated throughout the book.

Theme 1: Global Women's and Gender Studies Sees Gender Inequality as a Historical, Sociocultural Phenomenon

It is hard to understand why girls and women are so disadvantaged economically, politically, legally, and socially relative to boys and men. Why, despite women's respected role as the bearers of children and caregivers, and their many cultural, historical, and economic contributions, are they often treated as second-class citizens? Why is gender equality so hard to achieve? Global women's and gender studies scholars typically answer these questions with materialist and sociocultural explanations.

Materialist explanations for gender inequality view the oppression of women as a social, historical, but alterable phenomenon (Khan, 2006). Family and

"The feminist movement challenges the very root of patriarchy, the idea that one person can be humanly superior to others and entitled to superiority over them."
Marilyn French

"Man was not made a tyrant by nature, but had been made tyrannical by the power which had, by general consent, been conferred upon him; she merely wished that woman might be entitled to equal rights, and acknowledged as the equal of man, not his superior."
Lucretia Mott, speaking at the Women's Rights Convention at Seneca Falls, New York, 1848

3

"To look for origins is, in the end, to think that we are something other than the product of our history and our present social world, and more particularly, that our gender systems are primordial, transhistorical, and essentially unchanging in their roots."
Michelle Rosaldo

"The oppression of women in any society is in its turn a statement of an economic structure built on land ownership, systems of inheritance and parenthood, and the patriarchal family as an inbuilt social unit."
Nawal El Saadawi

Sor Juana Inés de la Cruz (1651–1695) was a brilliant Mexican poet and intellectual. To avoid marriage and to continue her self-education, Juana entered a Catholic convent. When told by a bishop to give up her writing, she spiritedly defended the right of women to engage in intellectual pursuits, saying in a 1681 letter, "Who has forbidden women to engage in private and individual studies? Have they not as rational a mind as men do?" Ultimately, she lost her battle and was forced to give up her writing and her books.

social institutions that arose out of material forces such as the ownership of private property led to men's dominance and women's subordination and these materialist forces maintain gender inequality. For example, many societies and cultures are structured such that women are economically dependent on men, and this makes it difficult for them to leave situations of abuse. The idea that gender inequality is embedded in family, cultural, economic, and political social structures is sometimes referred to as **patriarchy**, and social systems that serve men's dominance over women are referred to as **patriarchal**. Materialist theorists, such as historian Gerda Lerner (1986), trace the development of patriarchy to the Neolithic period when agriculture developed and the labor of children was needed to increase production and further surpluses. At that point women came to be viewed as commodities—resources to be acquired, traded, and controlled.

Like materialist explanations, **social constructivist** and **sociocultural explanations** emphasize how gendered power relations are socially constructed. These explanations also assume that gender is *dynamic*—active and changing rather than permanently fixed. Sociocultural perspectives on gender inequality also explain *how* gender relations became embedded in culture and are passed on socially. The sociocultural approach also distinguishes between **sex**, which refers to inborn biological differences between girls/women and boys/men relating to reproduction and sex organs, and **gender**, which refers to the socially constructed roles, behavior, activities, and attributes a given society considers appropriate for girls/women and boys/men.

The sociocultural approach does not deny the relevance of differences in the bodies of girls/women and boys/men. Indeed, these differences create unique issues and inequalities for girls/women. For example, menstruation, pregnancy, and childbearing impact the lives of girls and women in important ways. Many girls worldwide lack access to safe and clean ways to manage their periods and experience educational disadvantage because they miss weeks of school, or drop out altogether. Where affordable contraception is scarce, women face unplanned pregnancies, which may lead to unsafe or expensive abortion. When women give birth without the presence of skilled medical professionals, they can experience lifelong disability resulting from obstetric fistula. Employment absences due to pregnancy and childbirth often affect women's salaries and career progression.

Some anthropologists and historians see gender inequality as originating in biological differences between women and men. Think about it this way. At one time, all cultures lacked reliable birth control and had no infant formula or convenient ways to manage menstruation. This, along with men's greater size and strength, made some types of work more suitable for women since they spent much of their adult lives pregnant, nursing, and menstruating. Women's work became concentrated in the **private sphere** or domestic domain of the home, and men performed the labor in the **public sphere** outside the home because they were not constrained by child care (Sanday, 1974). In other words, a gendered division of labor arose, and women ended up doing the work that was compatible with the unavoidable female life course of bearing and nursing children (Chafetz, 1990; Lerner, 1986). Once societies based on money evolved, men's labor appeared to have more value because it was more likely to be used in exchange for money or goods. Money-based economies also increased women's dependence on men because women's ability to make money was limited given their responsibilities in the private sphere. Men's dominance in the public sphere led to them having greater property rights and economic and political power, which they then used to further consolidate their power over women. Political and economic systems were constructed based on these traditional gender-role arrangements.

The sociocultural approach explains the mechanisms by which we learn to "do gender." Once a gendered division of labor arose and women and men had different roles (**gender roles**), people then constructed **gender stereotypes** (beliefs about the qualities of each gender) and **gender norms** (social rules regarding what is appropriate for each gender to do) that supported these divisions. These were passed on culturally through **gender socialization** (the process by which societal beliefs and expectations about gender are instilled in us). Parents, peers, myths, literature, media, religion, and so on teach children what is expected of them based on their gender in order to prepare them for adulthood and help them get along in society. Conformity to gender norms and gender roles is maintained by granting social status and approval to conformers and by ostracizing violators. A desire for social approval and fear of social rejection are partly why people choose gender conformity and may not rebel against gender-unequal cultural practices.

There is also a reciprocal relationship between gender stereotypes and gender roles—in other words, gender stereotypes lead to gendered roles but gendered roles also lead to gender stereotypes. This idea comes from social psychology's **social roles theory** (Eagly, 1987). People develop gender stereotypes about women and men from seeing them in different (gendered) roles, because we assume that if men and women are doing different things it must be because they are truly different. For example, if there are few women in leadership positions, people assume this is because women aren't suited for leadership.

According to social roles theory, once people develop gender stereotypes, these beliefs operate as expectations regarding appropriate roles for people from those groups—in this way gender stereotypes lead to gender roles. For example, if stereotypes suggest men are more suitable for leadership because they are more assertive and dominant than women (a gender stereotype), then men are more likely to be groomed and hired for leadership roles. These processes appear to operate in all cultures and explain how gender is socially constructed and maintained. Social roles theory maintains that because gender is socially constructed, it is dynamic and can be changed if gender stereotypes or gender roles change. For example, the stereotype that women aren't suitable for leadership roles is eroded when people see more women in leadership roles. Conversely, as this stereotype wanes, the number of women in leadership roles increases.

Cross-cultural and temporal (across time) variations in women's treatment testify to the large part culture plays in gender inequality. In many parts of the world, gender roles have changed rapidly, and as Rosenthal and Rubin (1982, p. 711) once said, these changes have occurred "faster than the gene can travel." Also, anthropological evidence tells us that gender inequality hasn't always been so. For example, today's anthropologists generally agree that in the foraging societies of early history, which covered much more time than the 120,000 years or so

"Female subordination runs so deep that it is still viewed as inevitable or natural rather than as a politically constructed reality maintained by patriarchal interests, ideology, and institutions."
Charlotte Bunch

"Men and women live on a stage, on which they act out their assigned roles, equal in importance. The play cannot go on without both performers. Neither of them 'contributes' more or less to the whole; neither is marginal or dispensable. But the stage set is conceived, painted, and defined by men. Men have written the play, have directed the show... assigned themselves the most interesting, heroic parts."
Gerda Lerner

Christine de Pizan (approximately 1365–1430), a Frenchwoman, was the most successful female writer of the Middle Ages. Furthermore, in her 1405 book *The City of Ladies*, she became one of the first to argue in writing against women's inferiority.

"The women we honor today teach us three very important lessons: One, that as women, we must stand up for ourselves. The second, as women we must stand up for each other. And finally, as women we must stand up for justice for all."
Michelle Obama, First Lady of the United States at the International Women of Courage Awards, which honored women from Afghanistan, Guatemala, Iraq, Malaysia, Niger, Russia, Uzbekistan, and Yemen who have stood up for women and human rights.

"I'm a little grayer than I was eight years ago, but this is what a feminist looks like."
U.S. President Barack Obama speaking in spring 2016

Sixty percent of American women and thirty percent of American men self-identify as feminist.
Washington Post/Kaiser Foundation Survey

from the Neolithic to the present, the genders were probably complementary and of equal importance (Ehrenberg, 1989). Even today there are some cultures with egalitarian gender relations (Bonvillian, 2001). Gender-egalitarian cultures were also common to hunter-gatherer and horticultural societies prior to colonization (Sanday, 1981), and there is some evidence from ancient times of matriarchies, societies in which women had greater power than men (cf. Bachofen, 1967; Diner, 1975; Gimbutas, 1991; Gross, 1996).

As you will see throughout the book, there is good evidence that gender inequality is in fact socially constructed and embedded in our legal, economic, political, and cultural practices. Our hope for change lies in our transformation of these human-created systems, beliefs, and practices.

Theme 2: Global Women's and Gender Studies Is About Activism and Empowerment

Although global women's and gender studies seeks a scholarly understanding of gender inequality cross-culturally, this is not an end in itself; the hope is that this will serve change toward gender equality and contribute to women's **empowerment** (their ability to advocate for their rights and have decision-making power in their public and private lives). The task of global women's studies is a positive one rather than a negative one. It is less about women as victims and more about what women (and their male allies) do to solve the unique problems faced by women due to their gender. It will quickly become apparent to you that wherever women's rights are violated, there are women that resist and rally for change, even in the face of social rejection and physical danger. Global women's studies illustrates that gender equality activism is not exclusively the domain of Western women. In fact, there is a long history of struggle for women's equality in the Middle East, Latin America, Asia, the Caribbean, and Africa. You will read about these efforts worldwide to increase the status of women throughout the book. Box 1.1 provides an example from Afghanistan.

Global women's and gender studies is a feminist endeavor and conceives of feminism as a commitment to changing the structures that keep women lower in status and power (Sen & Grown, 1987). That said, not all gender equality activists and organizations addressing women's issues identify as feminist (see Chapter 10). Also, despite general agreement that feminism is about social transformation and acting for gender equality, the truth is that feminist ideologies, identities, issues, strategies, and actions vary considerably. A truly **global feminism** recognizes this diversity and acknowledges diverse meanings of feminism, each responsive to the needs and issues of women in different regions, societies, and times. As you'll see later in this chapter (and throughout the book), acknowledging and appreciating this diversity is a key part of global women's studies.

Despite what some people say, we do not yet live in a post-feminist world where gender equality renders feminism obsolete. If you are not yet convinced of this, Chapter 2 highlights some important women's issues and gender disparities that will likely persuade you that there is still much to be done to achieve gender

---

BOX 1.1   *Activism Profile: Women's Human Rights Defenders in Afghanistan*

Afghan women's rights activists have been fighting for women's human rights for decades. In 1992, when the Taliban took over, the Revolutionary Association of the Women of Afghanistan (RAWA) drew international attention to the Taliban's oppression of women and ran secret schools to educate girls. In 2001, with the help of the United States, the Taliban was overthrown but it has battled the government forces ever since and still control parts of the country. Although the government is not under Taliban-control, many laws and cultural practices discriminate against women and girls. Despite danger, Afghan women's rights activists fight for women's rights to maternal health care, employment, and inheritance, and to increase girls' access to education. They fight against forced and underage marriage and violence against women and girls. In 2021, a campaign (#WhereIsMyName) started by Daughters of Rabia (named for Afghanistan's most famous poet), got a law passed requiring the inclusion of mothers' names on their children's birth certificates, which gives women parental rights that they didn't have. Activism has led to improvements in the twenty years since the Taliban were overthrown, but women's human rights defenders fear that their progress will soon be undone. Left out of peace negotiations between the Afghan government and the Taliban, they demand inclusion in peace talks and that women's rights not be bargained away.

---

equality, even in your own country, and despite notable progress. Box 1.2 talks about how feminism is often negatively stereotyped and misunderstood by those that seek to reduce its transformative power.

Global women's and gender studies emphasizes the important role of **nongovernmental organizations (NGOs)** and other collective action as agents of women's empowerment and equality. Governments can enact and enforce policies and laws that promote gender equality and address women's issues (a topic of this book), but they don't usually do this without sustained pressure from women's activism. Even once laws are in place, more action is usually needed to ensure their implementation and enforcement, and to educate women so they may exercise their rights. Much of the work of transforming women's legal and human rights into reality is done by women's nongovernmental organizations. For example, the International Center for Research on Women (ICRW) notes that laws to protect women's property rights now exist in most countries, and owning property is often a woman's ticket out of poverty. But many women don't know how to exercise their property rights. ICRW works with other NGOs to help women assert their legal rights to assets and property.

NGOs range from small, local grassroots organizations to large international organizations, including **WINGOs (women's international nongovernmental organizations)** and **GRSOs (women's grassroots support organizations)**. The activities of NGOs are varied. They include advocating for legal, societal, and cultural change to bring about gender equality. Some NGOs foster women's knowledge of their legal and human rights and empower women to advocate for themselves. Many NGOs provide services, resources, and programs to serve women's

BOX 1.2   *The "F" Word*

Are you hesitant to call yourself a feminist even though you believe in equal pay for equal work, gender equality in education, that sexual violence is a problem, that child marriage should be ended, that women should be able to control the number and spacing of their children, and that we need family-friendly employment policies? These are some of the things feminism is about. But because feminism is about challenging the privilege of some people relative to others, and because it's about transforming some long-held and cherished cultural practices and beliefs, efforts to discredit feminists and feminism abound. Type "anti-feminist" into a search engine and you'll find memes, quotes and even a "Men's Movement" suggesting that feminists are unattractive, whiny hypocritical manufacturers of self-imposed victimhood who discriminate against men. Given such stereotypes, it can take courage to identify as feminist.

All over the world, people call feminists "man-haters," "anti-family," and "lesbian." In some places, people cast suspicion by insisting feminism is a culturally insensitive Western import. In others, it's dismissed as only about the issues of privileged women. Given negative stereotypes of feminism, it's unsurprising that

many activists, organizations, and movements working on women's issues don't embrace the feminist label (see Chapter 10).

An American study found women that endorse feminist beliefs often hesitate to describe themselves as feminists because of negative stereotypes of feminists, such as "man-hating" (Anderson, Kanner, & Elsayegh, 2009). Ironically, that study found women that identified as feminists reported lower levels of hostility toward men than did nonfeminists.

Canadian research participants asked to provide adjectives describing feminists most frequently said: man-hating, lesbian, unhygienic, angry, behaves like a man, and unattractive (Bashir et al., 2013). The Canadian researchers also found these negative stereotypes led people to avoid affiliating with feminists and advocating for feminist causes. The researchers explained that people avoid association with stigmatized others so that they don't become targets of prejudice and social rejection. Fortunately, in my experience, once people learn more about gender inequality and feminism, their negative and inaccurate views fall away, and they are inspired to act on behalf of gender equality.

economic, health, and safety needs. WINGOs form international coalitions of women's NGOs to represent the interests of women and girls in intergovernmental agreements and policies. Websites of gender equality and women's issues NGOs are provided at the end of every chapter, beginning with Chapter 2. Also starting with Chapter 2, you will find a feature called "Action Opportunities," so that you can take action on issues that move you. Many of the websites listed at the end of each chapter also provide ways to help.

Theme 3: Global Women's and Gender Studies Takes a Multicultural, Intersectional, Contextualized Approach

The cross-cultural study of women and gender inequality requires a multicultural approach. **Multiculturalism**, or interculturalism, emphasizes helping people to understand, accept, and value the cultural differences between groups, with the ultimate goal of reaping the benefits of diversity (Ferdman, 1995). The goal is to both celebrate differences and emphasize the dimensions of commonality or inclusion that supersede these differences (Devine, 1995). Although it sounds contradictory, women are both the same and different cross-culturally and intra-culturally (within the same culture, country, or region), and this matters for our global study of women.

The Importance of Similarity

In some ways, women all over the world have a lot in common. Most live in patriarchal societies and cultures with legal, political, economic, and cultural structures that support gender inequality (see Chapter 2). The majority of women everywhere work extremely hard in both paid and unpaid labor, get married to men, structure their lives according to their children's needs, worry about unplanned pregnancies, experience gender discrimination, and are at some risk for gender violence such as rape, sexual assault, or domestic violence. The majority of women live in heteropatriarchal cultures where heterosexuality is expected and where bearing and caring for children are a chief source of status and identity for women. The shared biology of women also gives rise to commonalities such as menstruation, pregnancy, childbirth, and mothering that affect women everywhere.

Women's commonalities are an important topic of this book and create connection between diverse women as well as form the basis for **transnational feminist movements** and networks spanning across multiple nations. At the core of these movements is the belief that women are entitled to the same rights as men, regardless of where the women live, and their ethnicity, sexual orientation, religion, and social class. These movements involve the coming together of feminist NGOs to work across regional or international borders in coalitions and campaigns (Porter, 2007). However, transnational feminisms recognize diversity and acknowledge that there are diverse meanings of feminism, each responsive to the needs and issues of women in different regions, societies, and times. Diversity and difference remain central values in transnational feminisms, values to be acknowledged and respected, not erased in the building of alliances (Mohanty, 2003).

The Importance of Difference

Although women undoubtedly share certain experiences due to their gender, their experiences as women vary widely depending upon their race, class, ethnicity, social class, nationality, disability, age, sexual orientation, gender identity, region, and religion, whether they are refugees, immigrants, or natives, and so on. The interplay of these different social categories is referred to as **intersectionality** (Cole, 2009). Gender is "intersectional" because the way it is enacted and experienced depends on the way it interacts with other social categories and identities. Awareness of intersectionality is critical to an inclusive study of women globally, and global women's studies embodies an intersectional approach to gender.

"We…find it difficult to separate race from class from sex oppression because in our lives they are most often experienced simultaneously."
Combahee River Collective, a group of Black American feminists

"I am a Black feminist. I recognize that my power as well as my primary oppressions came as a result of my blackness as well as my womanness, and therefore my struggles on both fronts are inseparable."
Audre Lorde

In addition to awareness of intersectionality, it is also important to appreciate the role of context. To **contextualize** women's issues and activism means that to fully understand them, you have to consider the material contexts in which they are situated—cultural, social, political, historical, and economic. It also means that what's required for change and forms of activism varies greatly. For instance, gender inequality in politics is an important feminist issue, because worldwide men continue to hold the majority of political power. However, as Chapter 9, "Women and Politics," illustrates, the path to increasing women's political representation depends on a number of contextual variables, such as the electoral system specific to a country and the age and origins of its democracy.

> "The more diversity is affirmed, the more difficult inclusivity becomes, simply because human diversity is almost infinite."
> *Rita Gross*

Acknowledging intersectionality and contextualizing no doubt complicates global women's and gender studies. But a failure to do so ultimately restricts our understanding of women and reduces the usefulness of our study to promoting gender equality. Throughout this book, you will see that there are many differences in the issues facing women across countries and within countries (often based on intersectionality and context). Ideally, global women's and gender studies describes and reflects this diversity. However, you should understand that this is a small book that can't fully convey the diversity of women's lives worldwide or speak for all women everywhere. Given the enormity of the task and the fact that data is lacking on women in many parts of the world, the best this book can do is give you a sense of the great diversity of women's issues and activism and the contextual and intersectional influences on them.

> "The single story creates stereotypes, and the problem with stereotypes is not that they are untrue, but that they are incomplete. They make one story become the only story."
> *Chimanda Adiche*

Box 1.3 illustrates the concepts of intersectionality and context in understanding menstruation as a women's health issue.

The Challenge of Multiculturalism

As some of the more dramatic instances of women's lower status and power are chronicled, you should not become complacent about gender inequalities in your own country or feel that your culture is superior. Those cultural aspects that do not result in the oppression of women or others deserve our respect. Admittedly, multiculturalism is not always easy. It goes against our natural human tendencies to reject people and cultures that are different from our own and to defend our own cultural traditions. Humans have a general discomfort of diversity that is driven by a natural inclination to categorize people as one of "us," or one of "them," and to prefer those that are similar to us (social psychologists call this "ingroup-outgroup bias"). We like to believe that our culture's way of doing things is "right," and we like those things that are familiar to us. People are often **ethnocentric**—quick to think their culture's way is the right and only way, and quick to judge and reject the way other cultures do things. Our bias means that we may have trouble acknowledging the ways in which our own culture permits discrimination and suffering among identifiable groups of people and that we may be quick to negatively stereotype other cultures.

We have to override these tendencies because a multicultural approach to women's studies is not about judgment, cultural superiority, or the imposition of our ways on other cultures (what is sometimes called "cultural imperialism"). On the contrary, it is about understanding the influence of culture on women's issues and women's experiences while taking a critical look at our own culture. It

BOX 1.3   *Intersectionality and Context: The Case of Menstruation*

Coping with menstrual cramps, bloating, and messiness, and managing periods to avoid embarrassment, is something most girls and women worldwide can relate to. Healthy menstrual management for girls and women everywhere requires available, safe, and affordable materials, good sanitation and washing facilities, positive social norms, and safe and hygienic disposal (PATH, 2016). Despite these commonalities, intersectionality and context give rise to important differences in women's menstrual experiences across and within cultures. Here are some examples.

In some low-income regions, menstrual hygiene management (MHM) is so challenging girls miss entire weeks of school and sometimes drop out altogether. In Uganda, schoolgirls often lack access to sanitary menstrual products, bathroom privacy is lacking, and the means to wash up and discreetly dispose of used materials are often absent (Sommer & Mmari, 2015). This context means that addressing the MHM needs of Ugandan girls and women is not only about increasing access to affordable, hygienic materials, but also about addressing sanitation and water needs.

Whether a woman is from an urban or rural region, and whether she is of low, middle, or high income, may also affect her MHM. Families in rural Kenyan settlements are less likely to have private toilets, increasing women's risk of rape during menstruation. Rural Kenyan women and girls have little to no access to affordable commercial MHM products and use strips of cloth, cotton wool, pieces of mattress, mud, ash, or leaves, whereas middle and upper-middle class urban girls and women use premium, commercially made disposable menstrual pads (FSG, 2016).

In the United States, the high cost of period products creates a greater burden on homeless, incarcerated, and low-income girls and women. This is called "period poverty." A recent study found one in ten college women struggle to pay for menstrual products, with even higher rates for Black, Latina, immigrant, and first-generation college students (Cardoso et al., 2021). Activists and feminist legislators in the United States work to provide free tampons and pads in schools, jails, and other public restrooms, and to allow the use of flexible spending accounts (i.e., food stamps/welfare) for feminine hygiene products (Weiss-Wolf, 2016).

The restrictions placed on a menstruating woman also depend on religion and culture. For example, in parts of India and Nepal, norms require menstruating girls and women to avoid cooking, religious practices, bathing, and sexual intercourse while menstruating (PATH, 2016). Reproductive health NGOs are developing educational programs to reduce period stigma and promote MHM.

To some extent, menstruation is taboo everywhere, and in 2015 women started to speak out (Weiss-Wolf, 2016). For example, responding to a Hindu religious leader that said he looked forward to the day when a machine could ensure that no menstruating women came into temples, Indian college student Nikita Azad launched a social media campaign (#Happytobleed) intended to challenge Hindu period taboos (Panday, 2015).

is about bringing change in our own societies as we support the efforts of women's activists and organizations in other cultures.

We have to find ways to be critical of practices that are harmful to women, but understand that the issues of greatest concern to women in our country (or group) may not be the major issues of concern to women in other countries (or groups). While talking about women's lives in different cultures, we also must take care to acknowledge the wide range of women's experiences within any given culture. We want to be culturally sensitive and avoid assuming that our way is the right way and that the path to gender equality is the same regardless of culture. As

"Sisters are doing it for themselves."
Annie Lennox, singer/ songwriter/feminist

outsiders, we typically lack the understanding of the sociopolitical context that is crucial for effective action. We want to support gender equality movements everywhere while respecting the rights of women within particular countries to initiate their own movements in ways that work for them in their cultures.

Theme 4: Global Women's and Gender Studies Views Women's Rights as Human Rights

Some people suggest that cross-cultural women's studies cannot be done honestly because our own cultural biases inevitably lead to distortion. Others are uncomfortable with people from one culture making value judgments about the treatment of women in another culture when those judging cannot possibly understand the cultural context in which the treatment occurs. These concerns have some validity, and caution is clearly required. But sometimes people mistakenly assume that respecting cultural diversity requires that we accept all cultural practices (the idea that right and wrong are culturally determined is called **cultural relativism**). And yes, while it is true that just because a culture is different from our own does not mean that it is wrong, global women's and gender studies takes the position that culture should never be used to justify gender inequality.

"It is good to swim in the waters of tradition but to sink in them is suicide."
Mahatma Gandhi

Global women's and gender studies scholars and activists typically favor a human rights framework to help us determine when we should respect cultural practices and when we should work for their change. They approach women's rights from a human rights perspective. The idea behind the **women's rights as human rights perspective** is to wed women's rights to human rights, which are protected under international law and are monitored and enforced by the United Nations. This lends legitimacy to political demands because most governments already accept the protection of human rights, and there are established protocols for dealing with abuses (Friedman, 1995). Whether used in political lobbying, in legal cases, in grassroots mobilization, or in broad-based educational efforts, the idea of women's human rights has been a rallying point for women across many boundaries and has facilitated the creation of collaborative strategies for promoting and protecting the rights of women (Bunch & Frost, 2000). Coalitions of NGOs and local activists lobby governments, corporations, international financing institutions (like the World Bank), and regional and international intergovernmental bodies, to create the necessary political, economic, and human rights conditions for equality, sustainable human development, and social justice (Tripp, 2006). Throughout the book, you will see the women's rights as human rights approach in action.

At the heart of the women's rights as human rights approach is showing that women's rights follow from **universal human rights**. According to the concept of universal human rights, everyone has certain inalienable rights simply by virtue of being human. This means that all humans are born free and equal in dignity and rights, which no one, including governments, can deny them. In theory then, women have the same economic, political, civil, and social rights as men, and culture cannot be used to deny anyone these basic rights. The **Universal Declaration** of Human Rights (UDHR) adopted by United Nations (UN) member nations in 1948 is the foundational document of human rights. The **United Nations (UN)** is an international organization with 193 participating countries. Its purposes are international peace and security, human rights, and the correction of international economic, social, environmental, and humanitarian problems. Many UN agencies figure prominently in this book because of their work on behalf of gender equality.

The UDHR stipulates that by virtue of being human, we are all entitled to full and equal rights (Articles 6 & 7); everyone has the right to life, liberty and security of person (Article 3); no one should ever be tortured or held in slavery (Articles 4 & 5); everyone has the right to freedom of movement (Article 13); everyone has the right to own property and to participate politically (Articles 17 & 21); and everyone has the right to an education, to work for pay, and to be compensated fairly (Articles 22 & 23). Many of the situations described in this book are framed as violations of these and other basic human rights. For instance, domestic violence is a form of torture, and rape violates women's freedom of movement and their right to security. Although the principle of women's equality and nondiscrimination on the basis of sex was inscribed in the United Nations from the beginning through the UN Charter in 1945, and the Universal Declaration of Human Rights (UDHR) in 1948, this was the result of transnational feminist activism. Four women delegates attending the UN Charter Conference worked together with forty-two NGOs to ensure inclusion of sex in the antidiscrimination clause as well as to change "equal rights among men" to "equal rights among men and women." A similar effort was necessary in the drafting of the UDHR (Bunch, 2007; Jain, 2005).[1]

> "All human beings are born free and equal in dignity and rights."
> *United Nations Universal Declaration of Human Rights*

One of the most important human rights documents pertaining specifically to women is the United Nations' **Convention on the Elimination of Discrimination Against Women (CEDAW)**, basically an international bill of rights for women. The 1979 treaty defines discrimination against women as "any distinction, exclusion, or restriction made on the basis of sex which has the effect or purpose of impairing or nullifying the recognition, enjoyment or exercise by women, irrespective of their marital status, on a basis of equality of men and women, of human rights and fundamental freedoms in the political, economic, social, cultural, civil, or any other field." CEDAW consists of a preamble and thirty articles defining what constitutes discrimination against women and setting up an agenda for national action to end such discrimination. It is the only human rights treaty that affirms the reproductive rights of women and targets culture and tradition as influential forces shaping gender roles and family relations (DAW, 2009). It requires ratifying nations to eliminate discrimination against women in employment, education, and politics and to provide proof of progress (sadly, the United States, Iran, Somalia, Sudan, and Tonga have not yet ratified CEDAW).

> UN **conventions** are treaties, or legally binding agreements between countries; **declarations** are agreements that are not binding.

---

[1] The four women were Minerva Bernardino (Dominican Republic), Bertha Lutz (Brazil), Wu Yi-Fang (China), and Virginia Gildersleeve (United States).

Every four years, nations that have ratified the treaty are supposed to submit reports on their progress to the **CEDAW Committee**, a group comprised of twenty-three women's rights experts who monitor compliance with CEDAW and issue recommendations. NGOs are also encouraged to submit reports on their country's compliance with CEDAW, and many develop "shadow reports" documenting the gap between official government statements and the actual status of women (Hawkesorth, 2006). The UN offers technical report assistance to those countries that seem to have trouble meeting the report requirement. The Optional Protocol to CEDAW, adopted by the General Assembly in 1999, offers two mechanisms to hold governments accountable for their obligations under CEDAW: (1) a communications procedure that provides individuals and groups the right to lodge complaints with the Committee on the Elimination of Discrimination Against Women (CEDAW Committee), and (2) an inquiry procedure that enables the CEDAW Committee to conduct inquiries into serious and systematic abuses of women's rights. These procedures apply only to countries that have ratified the Optional Protocol. The Optional Protocol to CEDAW has been ratified by 109 nations as of May 2017. This is significantly less than the number ratifying CEDAW. This may be due to the Protocol's emphasis on accountability. It is one thing for governments to support women's rights in theory, but it is another thing for them to agree to take responsibility for women's rights violations in an international venue.

CEDAW is the most far-reaching convention specific to the rights of women, but there are other international human rights agreements that address women's rights. The **Beijing Platform for Action**, the product of the Fourth World Conference on Women (FWCW) held in Beijing, China, in 1995, is another important international agreement. The Platform, negotiated by 5,000 delegates from 189 countries, identifies "critical areas of concern" such as the feminization of poverty, inequalities in education, politics, and the economy, violence against women, and persistent discrimination against and violation of the rights of the girl child. It is called the Platform for Action because for each critical area of concern, it specifies strategic objectives and actions to be undertaken by governments. Throughout the book, you will read about these and other international conventions, declarations, and agreements that speak to women's rights.

Human rights are supposed to be protected under international law and monitored by the United Nations and human rights organizations, but human rights are also tools of activism. The potential of these tools can only be realized through vigorous leadership, difficult political dialogue among different groups of women, and women's political activity at all levels—from the global to the local. Throughout the book, you will see how women's rights activists work to ensure that women's rights are included in human rights instruments and mechanisms and how they use these to challenge gender inequalities. This is important because describing a particular discriminatory act as a human rights violation gives it more value than simply calling it unfair (Tomasevski, 1993). Once a government has signed on to an international human rights convention or declaration, activists can use that agreement to hold their government accountable for harms done and to pressure them to adopt, enforce, and implement consistent policies, programs, and laws. For example, women's rights activists use CEDAW as a tool to press

"The human rights of women and the girl-child are an inalienable, integral, and indivisible part of universal human rights. Gender-based violence and all forms of sexual harassment and exploitation, including those resulting from cultural prejudice and international trafficking, are incompatible with the dignity and worth of the human person, and must be eliminated."
Vienna Declaration and Programme of Action, 1993

their governments to adopt gender equality legislation and constitutional amendments and to petition courts for change. They use their country's CEDAW reviews to press for change. In Brazil (1988) and Colombia (1991), feminists used CEDAW to shape new national constitutions recognizing women's rights, and in India (1992), a group of women's NGOs successfully petitioned the Supreme Court to draft a sexual harassment law by arguing that the lack of one was in violation of CEDAW (Hawkesworth, 2006). Educating women about their human rights also motivates and empowers grassroots challenges to gender inequalities.

Framing discrimination against women as a violation of their human rights is not easy. In the United States, political conservatives object to international agreements like CEDAW, claiming they will give the UN too much power over U.S. laws. The notion of universal human rights (universality) is frequently undermined by the belief that respect for cultural and religious diversity provides exceptions to human rights law. Claims for universality are also sometimes rejected as imperialistic and as a way to uphold Western economic interests (Chinkin, 1999). This claim that international human rights are incompatible with respect for cultural diversity must be carefully considered. Cultural diversity and human rights must be balanced. Cultural diversity should not be used to excuse human rights violations; nor should a claim for universal values be used to justify the eradication of unique cultural practices that do not violate human rights. This issue is particularly acute in international law, which is concerned with transnational standards (Charlesworth, 1994).

Cultural relativists and human rights activists often disagree on women's rights, and at every international conference discussing women's rights, feminists and cultural relativists have battled (Coomarswamy, 1999). The most radical cultural relativists argue that there are no legitimate cross-cultural human rights standards and that the human rights endeavor, arising as it did out of the European Enlightenment, is, by its very nature, inapplicable to non-Western cultures (Coomaraswamy, 1999). In regard to women's rights, these cultural relativists suggest that Western condemnations of gender discrimination in other regions are insensitive and ethnocentric and are a version of cultural imperialism (Mayer, 1995a). This, however, ignores the long tradition of women's human rights writing and activism in non-Western cultures (Canetto & Burn, 2020).

Other cultural relativists are more selective, taking issue with only some of the rights specified in human rights documents or their interpretation (Coomaraswamy, 1999). For instance, cultural relativists often emphasize that the treatment of women is prescribed by a culture's religious practices; therefore calls for change are instances of religious intolerance (Jaising, 1995). Many of the countries that have ratified CEDAW did so only after registering "reservations" to those elements that they felt were contrary to important cultural or religious practices (indeed, CEDAW breaks the record for the most reservations recorded for an international human rights instrument). This problem for CEDAW symbolizes a problem that plagues the women's rights as human rights endeavor.

It is true that we shouldn't reject cultural practices just because they are not our own and that we should not presume to understand the experiences of those in another culture. And it is true that many cultural practices are nothing more than what Rachels (1993) calls "social conventions," which, objectively speaking, are neither right nor wrong and about which we should keep an open mind. But should

Rhonda Copelon (1944–2010) was a U.S. law professor and international human rights activist. She pioneered the use of international law to prevent and prosecute crimes against women such as war rape.

"Diversity and difference are central values here—to be acknowledged and respected, not erased in the building of alliances."
Chandra Talpade Mohanty

"Isn't it revealing that women's human rights need to be discussed?"
Isabel Allende

"The role of [Western] feminists is not to be in front, leading the way for other women, but to be in back supporting the other women's struggles to bring about change."
Kenyan Anthropologist Achola Pala-Okeyo

we accept cultural practices that obviously result in serious harm to large segments of a society out of respect for the existing culture or tradition? If this had been the case in the United States, slavery would not have been abolished, women would not have been allowed to vote, and civil rights legislation would not have been passed. As Rachels says, moral progress cannot occur if we take cultural relativism too far.

Another problem with the cultural relativist's position is that it implies that there is a homogeneous culture upon which there is agreement. However, "culture is not a static, unchanging, identifiable body of information," but rather is a "series of constantly contested and negotiated cultural practices" (Rao, 1995). For instance, Mayer (1995b) points out that contrary to the view of a monolithic Islamic position on human rights, Muslims actually espouse a wide range of opinions regarding international human rights. These range from the assertion that international human rights are fully compatible with Islam to the claim that international human rights are products of alien, Western culture and represent values contrary to Islam. Also, the claim that women's rights are in opposition to cultural rights overlooks the power dynamics that give men the right to define and defend their culture in ways that protect patriarchy (Canetto & Burn, 2020).

Some people doubt that it is possible to universalize feminism given the wide variety of women's experiences, and they question the usefulness of the international legal approach to women's rights. However, supporters of the international human rights approach point out that regardless of differences, women worldwide share the experience of patriarchy and the devaluing of women and all that experience encompasses (such as violence against women). They say we can respect cultural diversity *and* promote human rights as long as we recognize that cultural and class differences affect women's experience and how male domination can be contested. It is important to emphasize the separate identities and histories of groups of women based on religion, ethnicity, nationality, sexual orientation, and economic position while at the same time avoiding a dangerous fatalism of unbridgeable differences among women (Chowdhury et al., 1994). As Walter (2001) explains, culture determines the specifics of international human rights violations. For instance, she says that dowry violence is an Indian manifestation of the international problem of domestic violence. To address the problem, both the specific cultural context and the fact that they are a violation of women's human rights must be addressed. As noted throughout the book, this consideration of the cultural context is something that is best done by people in their own cultures. We can agree on human rights standards, but to be empowered and effective, people must be the architects of change within their own cultures.

In sum, advocating for women's human rights internationally and valuing cultural diversity are not mutually exclusive. Global women's and gender studies and transnational feminism require that we do both. The way to accomplish this is to recognize the cross-cultural variation in the challenges women face and to let women be the architects of change in their own countries. The best way to respect cultural diversity and advocate for women's rights is to focus on those practices of concern to women in their own countries and to support their efforts to do something about them. Besides, going into another country and telling people what to be concerned with and what to do about it almost always backfires; either because we lack the cultural understanding necessary to effectively bring about change, or because our efforts are met with accusations of cultural imperialism, which lead to a backlash (especially likely in countries with a history of colonization by western countries). Research shows that most credible advocates of gender equality are almost always members of the community whose practices are being challenged (Alexander & Welzel, 2015).

Of course that doesn't mean we can't be of service outside of our own culture and communities. We can contribute money to women's NGOs, respond to their "action alerts" in requested ways, network and share change strategies, help call international attention to abuses, lobby for international organizations to classify violations of women's rights as human rights violations, compare stories of struggle, and respect the rights of women to be the architects of change in their own cultures and societies. We must also remember that taking action that affects another society requires consulting local organizations regarding the advisability of a proposed strategy, its timing, how it is framed, and to make sure that it is guided by accurate information; otherwise, efforts may be disrespectful, ineffective, or even hurtful (Tripp, 2006). We must agree that regardless of culture, it is unacceptable to deny women their equal rights, yet we must acknowledge the diversity of women's experiences to make our efforts relevant. We must respect those cultural features that do not lead to the oppression of women (and others) so as to preserve and respect cultural diversity.

Overview of the Book

Chapter 2 begins the book with an overview of women's status in the world today. The chapter provides a summary of women's lower status and power, both politically and economically, and provides data on key women's issues globally. A major theme in the chapter is violence against women, women's sexual objectification, and how these relate to women's economic and political power.

The topic of Chapter 3 is reproductive health and reproductive rights. Reproductive health conditions are the leading cause of death and disability in women of childbearing age worldwide. Reproductive rights refer to the right to reproductive health care and the right to reproductive self-determination. These rights include women's ability to control the number and spacing of their children and their access to a range of birth control methods from which they may freely and knowledgeably choose. The relationship between women's reproductive rights and their status, power, economic situation, and health is emphasized in Chapter 3.

Chapter 4 is on the topic of sexuality and sexual rights. Women's sexual rights are important to gender equality—how free can people be if they cannot determine their sexuality? Unfortunately, a woman's sexuality is often defined in terms of men's sexual pleasure, and her family and community's honor. Sexual double standards and men's control of sexual decision-making affect women's health. Sexual rights also include rights based on sexual orientation and gender identity. These are important intersectional variables because they affect women's experiences as women, and because most societies discriminate against lesbian, bisexual, and transwomen. Chapter 4 also includes the topic of activism on behalf of women's sexual rights.

Using a feminist economic lens, Chapter 5 investigates the topic of women's work, both paid and unpaid, and in the formal and informal economic sectors. The ways in which women often experience discrimination in the world of work are highlighted with an examination of the gender pay gap, glass ceiling, and sexual harassment along with an examination of maternity protections and child care. The challenges that women face in balancing work and family are explored. Self-employed women are another focus. The undervaluing of women's unpaid labor and its relationship to women's status and power are key chapter themes as well.

Feminists generally believe that economic development should be an agent of women's empowerment. Chapter 6 takes a close look at women in low-income countries. The chapter begins by describing the lives and labor of women in low-income countries, and how traditional economic development approaches affect them. The chapter also explores feminist efforts to bring gender into the development process, and the important role of women in environmentally sustainable development—development that meets the needs of the present without compromising the future. The role of women's nongovernmental organizations (NGOs) in bringing about change is also featured.

Chapter 7 describes how a world economy dominated by transnational corporations affects women. The chapter begins by explaining what globalization is and how it impacts women. One major chapter topic is women's work in transnational factories (most are sweatshops). Another topic is women's migration to other countries to alleviate poverty and provide for their families. Migrant women's work in domestic service, sex work, and nursing and home health work are discussed, along with the phenomenon of "marriage migrants." The trafficking of women and girls into prostitution as part of the global sex industry is also presented as one of the effects of globalization.

Chapter 8 tackles the subject of women and religion. Many feminists view religion as part of the social systems that perpetuate gender inequality. The chapter provides feminist critiques of religion and includes an overview of women in the world's major religions. Of course, religion is profoundly important to many women, including many feminist women. Feminist efforts to reform existing religions or to create new women-centered religions are a major topic in Chapter 8.

Feminists agree that women's political activity is one key to their equality, and Chapter 9 examines women in national politics. This chapter explores women's representation in political parliaments, congresses, and cabinets and the factors that lead to greater numbers of women in formal politics. The chapter provides an analysis of women as heads of government—how do they come to occupy these positions and how does their leadership differ from that of men? Are they more likely to promote domestic policies favorable to women and children, and do they typically pursue feminist agendas? The chapter concludes with a discussion of women's political activity in social protest movements. When we consider this form of political activity, it is evident that women are more political than they might appear at first glance.

Chapter 10 investigates women's movements from the local to the global. The chapter begins by noting the many forces that operate against women's activism and how, despite these, women still frequently protest gender injustice. One of the main points of the chapter is that women's movements assume a variety of forms. In most countries you will find women's rights activist groups that focus on national policy, women's research groups that attempt to document the status of women and raise public awareness, and women's grassroots organizations that help women on a local level by providing shelter for battered women, providing credit for women-owned businesses, and so on. The chapter also includes transnational feminist movements spanning across multiple nations and how feminist NGOs work across regional or international borders in coalitions and campaigns.

Throughout each chapter, you will find quotes from women scholars and activists, as well as examples of "sheroes" and women's history. Bolded terms appear in the glossary toward the end of the book (there is also a list of glossary terms and concepts at the end of each chapter). In addition to the action opportunities and websites mentioned earlier, the end of each chapter provides study questions and discussion questions and activities. The study questions are intended to help you structure your studying of the information provided in the chapters. The discussion questions and activities are provided to stimulate your critical thinking on chapter topics. Finally, an appendix at the end of the book provides some key statistical indicators on women's status in the world's countries. These data remind us of the great diversity of women's status worldwide. However, information on the status of women is often hard to come by, as many governments do not compile accurate statistics, or, if they do, they may only release them periodically. This means that these statistics should be regarded cautiously, and it means that throughout the text, you will frequently find statistics that are several years old. You can also find *Women Across Cultures* on Facebook, where current news on women's issues and rights is posted.

Glossary Terms and Concepts

Beijing Platform for Action

CEDAW (Convention on the Elimination of Discrimination Against Women)

CEDAW Committee

Contextualize

Cultural relativism

Empowerment

Ethnocentric

Feminism

Gender

Gender inequality

Gender norms

Gender roles

Gender socialization

Gender stereotypes

Global feminism

Global women's studies

GRSOs (women's grassroots support organizations)

Intersectionality

Materialist explanations

Multiculturalism

Nongovernmental organizations (NGOs)

Patriarchy

Patriarchal

Private sphere

Public sphere

Sex

Social roles theory

Sociocultural explanations (social constructivist)

Transnational feminisms

United Nations (UN)

Universal Declaration of Human Rights (UDHR)

Universal human rights

WINGOs (women's international nongovernmental organizations)

Women's rights as human rights perspective

Study Questions

1. What are the four key themes that characterize global women's studies?
2. According to materialist approaches, what is the source of gender inequality?
3. What are the main features of sociocultural explanations for gender inequality?
4. What is the core idea behind feminism? How is global women's studies about action and empowerment?
5. What does it mean to say that women worldwide are "both the same and different"? What does this mean to the study of women cross-culturally?
6. What is intersectionality? What does it mean to contextualize our study of global women? Why are these so important to global women's studies?
7. What is multiculturalism? Why is it important to avoid ethnocentrism and to take a multicultural perspective when studying women cross-culturally? How does global or transnational feminism exemplify a multicultural approach?
8. What is the women's rights and human rights perspective? What is the Universal Declaration of Human Rights? What is CEDAW? Why are these and other international agreements important for gender equality?
9. What is the nature of the cultural relativist criticism that international human rights are incompatible with a respect for cultural diversity? How do "universalists" respond to cultural relativists' criticisms of the human rights approach?
10. How can we respect cultural diversity and advocate for women's rights internationally?

Discussion Questions

1. Do you call yourself a feminist? Why or why not? Do you agree with the chapter's claim that many people have a negative view of feminism but that most people agree with the aims of feminism? Does it matter whether we call ourselves feminists as long as we're doing our part to promote gender equality? Would we be more effective if we distanced ourselves from the feminist label?
2. Intersectionality is discussed as critical to global women's studies. Women's experiences vary widely because our experience of gender and the gender issues we experience depend on how gender intersects with other important social categories and identities such as race, religion, class, and sexual orientation. Thinking about this, how is your experience as a man or woman affected by intersectionality?
3. The chapter emphasizes multiculturalism when studying women cross-culturally but at the same time says that regardless of culture, women have basic human rights. Make a list of any cultural practices in regards to women in other countries that you are critical of. Should you override your ethnocentrism in regards to these, or are they violations of basic human rights?

4. According to the chapter, one of the risks of looking at some of the more dramatic instances of women's lower status and power is that it can foster feelings of cultural superiority. Why is this wrong, or is it?

5. The chapter makes the point that we should be careful in telling women in other cultures what to be concerned about and what they should do about it. What criticisms might an "outsider" make of your culture's treatment of women, and how would you feel about this outsider demanding change?

References

Alexander, A. C., and Welzel, C. 2015. Eroding patriarchy: The co-evolution of women's rights and emancipative values. *International Review of Sociology, 25,* 144-165.

Anderson, K. J., Kanner, M., and Elsayegh, N. 2009. Are feminists man haters? Feminists' and nonfeminists' attitudes toward men, *Psychology of Women Quarterly, 33,* 216-224.

Bachofen, J. J. 1967. *Myth, religion, and mother right.* Princeton, NJ: Princeton University Press.

Bashir, N. Y., Lockwood, P., Chasteen, A. L., Nadolny, D., and Noyes, I. 2013. The ironic impact of activists: Negative stereotypes reduce social change influence. *European Journal of Social Psychology, 43,* 614-626.

Bonvillian, N. 2001. *Women and men: Cultural constructs of gender,* 3rd ed. Upper Saddle River, NJ: Prentice Hall.

Bunch, C. 2007. Women and gender: The evolution of women specific institutions and gender integration at the United Nations. http://www.cwgl.rutgers.edu /globalcenter/charlotte/UNHandbook.pdf. Retrieved on October 28, 2009.

Bunch, C., and Frost, S. 2000. Women's human rights: An introduction. http:// www.cwgl.rutgers.edu/globalcenter/whr.html. Retrieved on March 10, 2003.

Canetto, S. S., and Burn, S. M. 2020. Whose culture? Challenging the idea of an opposition between women's human rights and the right to culture. In *The Cambridge handbook of psychology and human rights,* edited by N. S. Rubin & R. L. Flores, pp. 121-134. Cambridge, UK: Cambridge University Press.

Cardoso, L. F., Scolese, A. M., Hamidaddin, A., and Gupta, J. 2021. Period poverty and mental health implications among college-aged women in the United States. *BMC Women's Health, 21.* https://doi.org/10.1186/s12905-020-01149-5.

Chafetz, J. S. 1990. *Gender equity: An integrated theory of stability and change.* Newbury Park, CA: Sage.

Charlesworth, H. 1994. What are "women's international human rights"? In *Human rights of women,* edited by R. Cook. Philadelphia, PA: University of Pennsylvania Press.

Chinkin C. M. 1999. Cultural relativism and international law. In *Religious fundamentalisms and the human rights of women,* edited by C. W. Howland. New York: St. Martin's Press.

Chowdhury, N., Nelson, B. J., Carver, K. A., Johnson, N. J., and O'Loughlin, P. L. 1994. Redefining politics: Patterns of women's political engagement from a global perspective. In *Women and politics worldwide,* edited by B. J. Nelson and N. Chowdhury. New Haven, CT: Yale University Press.

Cole, E. R. 2009. Intersectionality and research in psychology. *American Psychologist, 64,* 170–180.

Coomaraswamy, R. 1999. Different but free: Cultural relativism and women's rights as human rights. In *Religious fundamentalisms and the human rights of women,* edited by C. W. Howland. New York: St. Martin's Press.

DAW (Division for the Advancement of Women). 2009. *Convention on the elimination of discrimination against women.* http://www.un.org/womenwatch/daw /cedaw/cedaw.htm. Retrieved on October 24, 2009.

Devine, P. G. 1995. Prejudice and out-group perception. In *Advanced social psychology*, edited by A. Tesser. New York: McGraw-Hill.

Diner, H. 1975. *Mothers and Amazons.* New York: Julian Press.

Eagly, A. H. 1987. *Sex differences in social behavior: A social role interpretation.* Hillsdale, NJ: Erlbaum.

Ehrenberg, M. 1989. *Women in prehistory.* Norman, OK: University of Oklahoma Press.

Elders, J. 2008, Summer. Sexual healing. *Ms.,* 79.

Ferdman, B. 1995. Cultural identity and diversity in organizations: Bridging the gap between group differences and individual uniqueness. In *Diversity in organizations*, edited by M. M. Chemers, S. Oskamp, and M. A. Constanzo. Thousand Oaks, CA: Sage.

Friedman, E. 1995. Women's human rights: The emergence of a movement. In *Women's rights, human rights: International feminist perspectives,* edited by J. Peters and A. Wolper. New York: Routledge.

FSG. 2016. *Menstrual health in Kenya: Country Landscape Analysis.* http:// menstrualhygieneday.org/wp-content/uploads/2016/04/FSG-Menstrual-Health -Landscape_Kenya.pdf. Retrieved on July 11, 2016.

Gimbutas, M. 1991. *The civilization of the goddess: The world of Old Europe.* San Francisco, CA: Harper and Row.

Gross, R. M. 1996. *Feminism and religion: An introduction.* Boston, MA: Beacon Press.

Hawkesworth, M. E. 2006. *Globalization and feminist activism.* New York: Rowman and Littlefield.

Jain, D. 2005. *Women, development, and the UN: A sixty-year quest for equality and justice.* Bloomington, IN: Indiana University Press.

Jaising, I. 1995. Violence against women: The Indian context. In *Women's rights, human rights: International feminist perspectives,* edited by J. Peters and A. Wolper. New York: Routledge.

Khan, T. S. 2006. *Beyond honour: A historical materialist explanation of honour related violence.* Oxford: Oxford University Press.

Lerner, G. 1986. *The creation of patriarchy,* Vol. 1. New York: Oxford.

Mayer, A. M. 1995a. Cultural particularism as a bar to women's rights: Reflections on the Middle Eastern experience. In *Women's rights, human rights: International feminist perspectives,* edited by J. Peters and A. Wolper. New York: Routledge.

Mayer, A. M. 1995b. *Islam and human rights: Tradition and politics,* 2nd ed. Boulder, CO: Westview Press.

Mohanty, C. 2003. *Feminism without borders: Decolonizing theory, practicing solidarity.* Durham, NC: Duke University Press.

Panday, G. 2015. Why are Indian women "Happy to Bleed"? *BBC News.* http://www.bbc.com/news/world-asia-india-34900825. Retrieved on July 11, 2016.

PATH. 2016. *Girls' and women's right to menstrual health: Evidence and opportunities.* http://www.path.org/publications/files/RH_outlook_mh_022016.pdf. Retrieved on July 11, 2016.

Porter, M. 2007. Transnational feminism in a globalized world: Challenges, analysis, and resistance. *Feminist Studies, 33,* 43–63.

Rachels, J. 1993. *The elements of moral philosophy,* 2nd ed. New York: McGraw-Hill.

Rao, A. 1995. The politics of gender and culture in international human rights discourse. In *Women's rights, human rights: International feminist perspectives,* edited by J. Peters and A. Wolper. New York: Routledge.

Rosenthal, R., and Rubin, D. B. 1982. Further meta-analytic procedures for assessing cognitive gender differences. *Journal of Educational Psychology, 74,* 706–712.

Sanday, P. R. 1974. Female status in the public domain. In *Women, culture, and society,* edited by M. Z. Rosaldo and L. Lamphere. Stanford, CA: Stanford University Press.

Sanday, P. R. 1981. *Female power and male dominance: On the origins of sexual inequality.* Cambridge, MA: Cambridge University Press.

Sen, G., and C. Grown. 1987. *Development crises and alternative visions.* New York: Monthly Review Press.

Sommer, M., and Mmari, K. 2015. Addressing structural and environmental factors for adolescent sexual and reproductive health in low-and-middle income countries. *American Journal of Public Health, 105,* 1973–1981.

Tomasevski, K. 1993. *Women and human rights.* London: Zed.

Tripp, A. M. 2006. The evolution of transnational feminisms: Consensus, conflict, and new dynamics. In *Global feminism,* edited by M. M. Ferree and A. M. Tripp. New York: New York University Press.

Walter, L. 2001. Introduction. In *Women's rights as human rights: A global view,* edited by L. Walter. Westport, CT: Greenwood Press.

Weiss-Wolf, J. 2016. Periods went public in 2015, here's what's next. *Ms. Blog.* http://msmagazine.com/blog/2016/01/05/periods-went-public-in-2015-heres-whats-next/. Retrieved on July 11, 2016.

Design Element: Abstract floral frame: Telnov Oleksii/Shutterstock

2 Women's Lower Status and Power

Although we are divided by race, class, culture, and geography, our hope lies in our commonalities. All women's unremunerated household work is exploited, we all have conflicts in our multiple roles, our sexuality is exploited by men, media, and economy, we struggle for survival and dignity, and, rich or poor, we are vulnerable to violence. We share our "otherness," our exclusion from decision making at all levels.

—PEGGY ANTROBUS, Caribbean feminist activist and scholar, founding member of Development Alternatives with Women for a New Era (DAWN) and the Caribbean Association for Feminist Research and Action (CAFRA)

All over the world, women act to reduce the sexual and domestic violence faced disproportionately by women and to assist women that experience it. This violence against women is only one indicator of women's lower status and power relative to men.
otnaydur/Shutterstock

I f you're uncertain that global women's and gender studies and global women's
rights are worthwhile pursuits, then perhaps this chapter will dispel your doubts.
It provides an overview of key global women's issues as well as some explanations
for women's lower status and power. As you will see, worldwide, girls and women
are generally lower in status and power relative to boys and men (see Figure 2.1). In
other words, there is gender inequality. In the sections that follow, pay attention to
the material conditions that gave rise to and perpetuate gender inequalities and how
societies are often patriarchal (structured in ways that foster and condone gender
inequality).

Men's Greater Economic Power

Money and property typically enhance status and power, and many feminists view
men's greater economic power to be at the heart of women's lower status and power.
Where women have little economic power, gender inequality is typically great (and
vice versa). Although there is widespread variation worldwide, men control more
economies, own more property, make more money, and occupy more positions of

FIGURE 2.1 *Evidence of Gender Inequality*

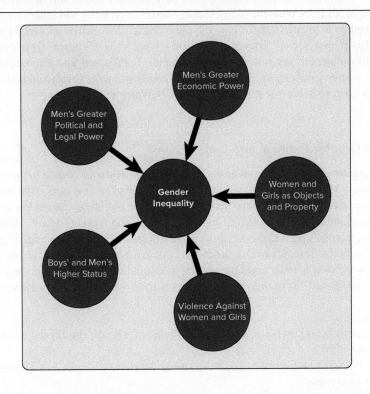

In China, women earn on average 36 percent less than men doing similar work.
Catalyst, 2020

In the United States, women earn on average 81 cents for every dollar men make, and the gender pay gap is even greater for women of color.

Women spend around 2.5 times more time on unpaid care and domestic work than men, and do three times more of it than men do.
UN Women, 2021

"When women participate in the economy, everyone benefits."
Hillary Clinton, former U.S. Secretary of State

In Liberia, one of the first laws passed following the election of President Ellen Johnson Sirleaf was a law criminalizing rape and making it a nonparole offense.

power in business and banking. And, in most countries, women earn on average only 77 percent of men's wages; the global average is women earn 23 percent of what men earn (UN Women, 2018[1]). Only part of this **gender wage gap** can be explained by differences in educational attainment, job experience, and part-time work. Women are also less likely to receive retirement pensions and to work in secure jobs (ILO, 2018). They are more likely than men to be unemployed, to work part-time, or to work in family businesses for no pay (ILO, 2018). All this translates into large lifetime economic gender inequalities for many women and increases women's vulnerability to poverty, especially widowed, separated, and single women with children (UN Women, 2018). Chapter 5, "Women's Work," discusses women's paid and unpaid labor in detail.

Men's greater control of economic resources and property relative to women matters because it increases women's dependence on men and gives men more power over them. Women's economic power is positively related to having a say in household decisions, their ability to leave situations of domestic violence, and their control over sexual relations (ICRW, 2016; UNICEF, 2006[2]). Children's nutrition, health, and education also improve when women have more economic power (UN Women, 2020).

Men's economic power also provides them with greater control of legal, justice, and political systems where gender inequality is often enshrined. For example, nineteen countries have laws requiring married women to obey their husbands, and in fourteen countries, married women do not have property ownership rights equal to their husbands (UN Women, 2020). Gender biases in property and inheritance laws leave women at greater risk for poverty, particularly when marriages end, or a husband dies (Open Society Foundations, 2016). Chapter 6, "Women, Development, and Environmental Sustainability" and Chapter 7, "Women and Globalization," discuss women's poverty in more detail. Redressing women's socioeconomic disadvantage is key to achieving gender equality (UN Women, 2020).

Men's Greater Political and Legal Power

Men's greater political and legal power provides more evidence of their higher status and power. Most of the world's politicians and lawmakers are men. That matters because it means our representative democracies are not so representative and because most men lawmakers are not inclined to think about sexual assault, domestic violence, women's reproductive rights and health issues, and women's labor in and out of the home. Equality before the law is critical for gender equality, but in many places, women have fewer legal rights than men and the law does not protect them from gender-based discrimination and violence. Even when gender-equal laws are in

---

[1]UN Women is the United Nations organization dedicated to gender equality and the empowerment of women.

[2]UNICEF (United Nations Children's Fund) works for children's rights, survival, development, and protection.

BOX 2.1   *Kuwaiti Women's Fight for Political Rights*

Kuwait, an oil-rich, predominantly Muslim country, is located in the Persian Gulf in the Middle East. By law Kuwaiti women are assured equal rights, but they were not granted the right to vote and run for political office until 2005, after almost a decade of women's activism. Kuwaiti women courageously smuggled food, weapons, and information to resistance fighters during the occupation by Iraq in 1990 and 1991. They expected that postwar they would be rewarded with their political rights. But there was fierce opposition from those that argued "the man speaks for the family" and politics "will take women away from their home and children." To win their rights, women demonstrated outside parliament chanting "Women's rights now!" and carried signs saying, "Our democracy will only be complete with women." The activists wore blue T-shirts with slogans like "Half a democracy is not a democracy." Wearing their blue shirts, they attended parliamentary sessions.

Although women won the right to vote, they are significantly underrepresented in elected office.

Since 2006, approximately 25 women have run in each parliamentary election and in spring 2009, women finally won four seats (6.2% of seats) in parliament, despite Islamists (fundamentalist Muslims) who encouraged people not to vote for women candidates. Islamists then tried to oust women who did not wear traditional dress but were overruled. In the most recent election (2020), only one woman was elected (Inter-parliamentary Union, 2021). In Kuwait, women cannot marry a partner without a male guardian's permission; the law requires obedience to husbands; a man who kills his wife, sister, or daughter for adultery receives only small fine or a maximum three-year prison sentence; a husband can prohibit his wife from employment and can marry up to four wives; and gender non-conformity is punished with heavy fines and jail time (Human Rights Watch, 2021). Kuwait law does not criminalize domestic violence but in 2020, after years of activism by Kuwaiti women, a law was passed to create domestic violence shelters and other services for abuse survivors.

place, male-dominated police and justice systems do not enforce them. Informal justice systems (also known as indigenous or traditional justice systems), which include forums of community representatives that decide on local disputes, usually consist of men that uphold customs and religious laws favoring men (UN Women, 2013).

In 2021, less than 10 percent of the world's countries had a woman heading their government as president or prime minister (Inter-parliamentary Union, 2021). Women are also underrepresented in parliaments and congresses, comprising only 25.5 percent of lawmakers in parliaments and congresses (Inter-parliamentary Union, 2021). Despite their somewhat poor representation in formal politics (parliaments, congresses, heads of state), women are often very political. In later chapters you will see that much of women's political influence comes from their activities in grassroots organizations that place pressure on formal political institutions. Increasing women's political participation and representation has long been a focus of women's activists. In the twentieth century, the focus was gaining women the right to vote (called **women's suffrage**). Saudi Arabia (2012) and Kuwait (2005) were the last countries to grant women suffrage. Box 2.1 discusses the efforts of Kuwaiti women to gain the vote and increase the numbers of women in parliament (Saudi women were awarded this right by the late King Abdullah).

"The concept of democracy will only assume true and dynamic significance when political policies and national legislation are decided upon jointly by men and women with equitable regard for the interests and aptitudes of both halves of the population."
Interparliamentary Union, 1994

Chapter 9 focuses on women in politics and how women gain political power. Another focus for activists is the reform of the legal and justice systems that allow the violation of women's human rights. This includes working for the passage and implementation of laws and constitutions that give women legal standing and guarantee women equal rights, increasing women's **legal literacy** (knowledge of their legal rights), improving women's access to legal advice and the courts, and reforming law enforcement institutions such that they are responsive to crimes against women such as sexual assault and domestic violence.

The Higher Status of Boys and Men

In many ways and in many places, boys and men are still more valued than girls and women and enjoy a higher social standing. Margaret Mead, the famous anthropologist and one of the first scholars to pay serious attention to the activities of women, noted, "Whatever the arrangements in regard to descent or ownership of property, and even if these formal outward arrangements are reflected in the temperamental relations between the sexes, the prestige values always attach to the activities of men" (1935, p. 302). Likewise, anthropologist Michelle Zimbalist Rosaldo (1974) said it is striking that male activities, as opposed to female activities, are always recognized as predominantly important, and cultures bestow authority and value on the activities of men.

Job prestige is one example of women's lower status. Jobs held predominantly by women are typically lower in status and pay than jobs traditionally held by men. Women's significant unpaid household and care labor is often overlooked or devalued. In most societies, high-status jobs such as those in science, engineering, and math (STEM) are stereotyped as male occupations with barriers to women's entry. Although the number of women in professional jobs has improved, and approximately one-third of managers are women, women are more likely to be employed in occupations considered "low-skilled" and to face worse working conditions than employed men (ILO, 2020). Even in athletics, boys and men's sports receive more funding, support, and media coverage than girls and women's sports. Semiprofessional and professional men athletes are typically paid far more than women athletes, and are admired more (Brewis, 2016).

Not only are male activities valued over female ones, but also in many countries, sons are valued over daughters in what is known as **son preference**. When Americans were asked in a 2018 Gallup poll, "Suppose you could have only one child. Would you prefer that it be a boy or a girl?," men preferred a boy by a 43 to 24 percent margin, whereas women showed no preference (Newport, 2018). Son preference is common globally, but in some South Asian, East Asian, Western Asian, and Central Asian countries, son preference is so strong that it means that significantly more boy babies are born and survive due to **gender-biased sex selection**. Gender-biased sex selection is sometimes classified as a form of violence against women and girls.

"Industries where women predominate tend to involve lower-paid and lower-status work than men. But, if you look historically at trends, it's not that women enter into low-paid, low-status professions. It's that, the more women populate a profession, the more low-paid and low-status it becomes." *Raina Brands, Professor of Psychology at London Business School*

"The most gifted and beautiful girl is not as desirable as a deformed boy." *Ancient Chinese proverb*

Prenatal sex selection, a form of gender-biased sex selection, involves using prenatal technologies to prenatally choose boys (it can also be used to choose girls, but this is less common). Methods include ultrasound, amniocentesis, chorionic villus sampling, blood or urine tests, and preimplantation genetic testing and sperm sorting prior to in vitro fertilization (IVF) (WHO, 2011). Parents are more likely to use prenatal sex selection after the first child or second child if they want a fixed number of children and have no sons (Jha et al., 2006; Zhu, Lu, & Hesketh, 2009). The highest rates of prenatal sex selection are found in countries where there is strong son preference, access to prenatal gender diagnosis, and low fertility (families have fewer children) (Bongaarts & Guilmoto, 2015). However, the practice of prenatal sex selection varies widely within countries. There are typically regional differences, rural versus urban differences, ethnic differences, and socioeconomic and religious differences (UNFPA, 2012).

Postnatal sex selection, which leads to higher death rates for girls under the age of five, is a nontech, passive method of sex selection. **Girl neglect**, where girls receive less food, supervision, and medical attention, is the most common form of postnatal sex selection (outright female infanticide is now rare). Child mortality data find evidence of girl neglect in Afghanistan, Bangladesh, China, Egypt, India, Jordan, Nepal, and Pakistan (UNFPA, 2020).[3] Fortunately, girl neglect has declined by as much as 50 percent since 1990 (when it was about 2 million annually). However, this is believed to be partly the result of increased access to prenatal sex selection (Bongarrts & Guilmoto, 2015).

> "Daughters are not for slaughter."
> *Indian women's movement slogan*

Understanding gender-biased sex selection requires a consideration of context. Poor economic conditions leading to a desire for smaller families is a contributing factor in Eastern Europe. In China, restrictive family planning regulations limiting families to one or two children increased the practice of sex selection (Zhu et al., 2009). Son preference is often rooted in traditional patriarchal practices and customs that vary between and within countries. In the Hindu and Buddhist religions, for example, sons have added value because they perform important rituals for deceased parents and for ancestors. These rituals are seen as essential for a good afterlife.

In some cultures, sons carry an economic advantage. When property inheritance is patrilineal (through the male line), male descendants are important to families. Where the family line and family name are carried on through sons, son preference is fueled. In many Asian cultures, custom requires that sons provide for elder parents. In contrast, daughters are expected to marry, leave the family, have children, and care for parents-in-law. Consequently, they do not have the potential to enhance the family's economic or social position the way sons do.

Son preference and the perception that daughters are an economic liability are aggravated in cultures with large dowry requirements (UNFPA, 2005). A **dowry** consists of money or goods paid by the bride's family to the groom or his

---

[3]The UNFPA (United Nations Population Fund) works to ensure universal access to family planning and sexual health.

family, mostly in the countries of Southeast Asia. Hundreds of years ago, dowries were property of the bride and provided her economic protection within the marriage. Women could not inherit land from their parents, and dowry was viewed as their inheritance. Dowry inflation is a problem in many countries, particularly in India, where some families with sons view dowries as a way to increase family wealth and acquire material things (Srinivasan & Bedi, 2007). One study in rural south India (Srinivasan, 2005) found that the expectation of a large dowry payment tops the list of causes for the undesirability of daughters.

At the family and individual level, son preference means that women often experience intense pressure to bear a son (Barot, 2012). Bearing sons affects a woman's status in the family, and a failure to produce sons sometimes carries the threat of violence or abandonment (Nanda et al., 2013). At the macro level, son preference has resulted in over 140 million "missing" women globally, a majority from China and India (Bongaarts & Guilmoto, 2015; UNFPA, 2020). There are 32.9 million more men than women in East Asia (mostly in China); 61.2 million more in South Asia (mostly from India); and 13.3 million more in West Asia (mostly from Saudi Arabia and the United Arab Emirates) (United Nations DESA, 2019). Distorted sex ratios at birth attributed to son preference are most profound in Azerbaijan, China, Vietnam, Armenia, Montenegro, North Macedonia, and Nepal (UNFPA, 2020).

Sex selection and consequent imbalanced sex ratios due to son preference are also linked to violations of women's human rights and higher levels of crimes against women (Edlund et al., 2013; UNFPA, 2012). Rather than increasing their status and power, a scarcity of women for marriage appears to put women at greater disadvantage for violence, forced marriage, polyandry (where brothers share wives), and trafficking (the recruitment, transportation, harboring, or receipt of people for the purposes of slavery, forced labor, and servitude) (WHO, 2011).

At the 1994 United Nations International Conference on Population and Development, representatives from 180 of the world's governments signed an agreement that included a commitment to "...eliminate all forms of discrimination against the girl child and the root causes of son preference, which result in harmful and unethical practices regarding female infanticide and prenatal sex selection" (paragraph 4.16 of the 1994 Programme of Action). Some countries have made efforts to eliminate the practice. Due to Indian women's activism, a national law was passed in 1994 banning the use of prenatal diagnostic techniques for sex selection, and an amended law was passed in 2002 prohibiting the determination and disclosure of the sex of the fetus, outlawing advertisements related to preconception and prenatal determination of sex, and prescribing punishments for violators. Other countries that ban sex selection include China, Great Britain, Australia, South Korea, Canada, Belgium, Spain, France, and Germany.

Four countries (China, Kosovo, Nepal, and Vietnam) ban sex-selective abortion (Citro et al., 2014). In the United States, concerns about sex selection in immigrant communities combined with anti-abortion sentiments have led to bans on abortions for purposes of sex selection in the states of Arizona, Kansas, Minnesota, North Carolina, North Dakota, Oklahoma, Pennsylvania, South Dakota,

BOX 2.2   *Reducing Son Preference in South Korea*

In the 1980s, sex-selection technologies became widespread in Korea, and by the early 1990s, Korea had one of the most lopsided sex ratios at birth in the world. Starting in 1991, Korea instituted a ban on physicians telling parents the gender of their unborn child (physicians could lose their medical license). Although physicians still found ways to skirt the law, for example, by using gender-stereotyped adjectives to describe the fetus, the law was more effectively enforced than similar laws in other countries (the ban was lifted in 2008).

A massive public awareness Love Your Daughter media campaign also focused on changing norms (WHO, 2011). Following campaigns from the women's movement, family laws were changed to give women rights and responsibilities in their birth family even after marriage, and recognizing women-headed households. An old-age pension system reduced parents' financial dependence on sons in old age. By the mid-2000s, surveys showed a decline in son preference, and the sex ratio returned to normal (Chung & Das Gupta, 2006).

Arkansas, Kentucky, Missouri, Texas, and Wisconsin (Guttmacher Institute, 2016, 2020). Because these state bans do not prohibit other sex-selection methods, such as preimplantation genetic testing prior to IVF, and because the need for them is questionable, they have not led to changes in sex ratios in those states (Citro et al., 2014; Guttmacher Institute, 2020). Sex-selection abortion bans are of concern because providers have no reliable way to determine a woman's reasons for abortion and because they may cause women to seek clandestine, unsafe abortions (Citro et al., 2014; WHO, 2011).

Laws banning prenatal sex selection have limited effectiveness because they are difficult to enforce and don't address the root causes of sex selection (WHO, 2011). For example, couples from countries where it is banned sometimes travel to clinics in countries where pregenetic screening for purposes of sex selection is legal. Clinics in the United States, Thailand, and Mexico all cater to parents from other countries seeking sex selection for "family balancing" in a practice known as reproductive tourism (see for example gender-baby.com, a website for a clinic in California). Box 2.2, on prenatal sex selection in South Korea, illustrates that reducing son preference requires multipronged approaches that include targeting son preferential social norms and changing laws and customs that make sons more economically advantageous.

Women and Girls as Objects and Property

When people are thought of as objects, commodities, or property, they are diminished and dehumanized and do not have the power to make their own life choices. In many ways, and in many places, girls and women are treated as objects to be ogled, traded, sold, and controlled.

"The sexual control of women has been a cornerstone of patriarchal power."
Andrea Parrot and Nina Cummings

StopStreetHarassment. org collects research studies and women's personal reports from all over the world as well as documenting and promoting activism (also see http://www .ihollaback.org).

"I am a social worker and I do my best to strive for a fair and free society. To me, wearing the veil does not mean being enslaved by a man. On the contrary, it means reappropriating the body and femininity."
Nawal Afkir, 25, Belgium

"Whether it's burkas or bikinis, the humiliation of women as property or sex objects is an affront to human dignity. It creates a market for women and girls who are traded like commodities."
Antonio Maria Costa, Executive Director of the UN Office on Drugs and Crime (UNODC)

One common form of women's objectification is **sexual objectification**, the reduction of women to bodies existing for men's pleasure. The sexual objectification of women and girls is evident in media (Galdi, Maass, & Candinu, 2014). It's also experienced daily by many women and girls in the form of **street harassment** (a form of sexual harassment involving unwanted sexualized comments, gestures, and actions forced on women in public places) and **objectifying gaze** (visual inspection of a woman's body by another person, including "leering," or looking a woman "up and down"). Street harassment and the objectifying gaze are common experiences for women worldwide.

Sexually objectifying environments are most likely where there is a male-favored power differential and when cultures prime men to view women as sexual objects. In more extreme cases, the sexual objectification of women leads to extreme restrictions on women's dress. For example, the Taliban of Afghanistan require women wear a *burqa*, a cumbersome garment that covers women from head to toe. Women in Saudi Arabia aren't allowed to wear clothes or makeup that shows their beauty, and most are expected to wear an *abaya* (a long cloak) and a headscarf (*hijab*). Religious police harass women that don't adhere to the dress code. (*Note:* Many women choose to wear the *abaya* and/or *hijab* as a personal expression of their religious faith. This is different than being required to and explains why bans imposed on the *abaya* and *hijab* in Western countries like France are often resisted by Muslim women and aren't supported by global feminists.)

Sexual exploitation involves sexual abuse for others' sexual gratification or financial gain, as in the case of prostitution and pornography. It is also considered a form of sexual violence. Barry (1995) summed it up well when she said that sexual exploitation objectifies women by reducing them to sex; this sexual objectification incites violence against women and reduces them to commodities for market exchange: "In the fullness of human experience, when women are reduced to their bodies, and in the case of sexual exploitation to sexed bodies, they are treated as lesser, as other, and thereby subordinated" (Barry, 1995, p. 24).

Prostitution is plainly about the sexual objectification of women, and it is clearly driven by economics. Although some women choose sex work as a profession and are not subservient or enslaved to their customers or to pimps (Chuang, 2005), the majority of women involved in prostitution are sexually exploited; this is a reflection of their lower worth in the world (Parrot & Cummings, 2006). Prostitution is most often about females as commodities to be bought and sold and about how poverty leads to prostitution. Activists say that cultural attitudes that consider prostitution a victimless crime, or that suggest women are sexual objects, must be changed.

Barry (1995) argues that prostitution is a form of sexual slavery because women and girls are held over time for sexual use and because getting out of prostitution requires escape. Although the prostitute herself typically earns barely enough to survive, an extended network of people profit from her body and her labor: The police and other government officials fine prostitutes or receive bribes to look the other way; pimps, bar, brothel, and hotel owners get a cut of her wages; airlines, travel agencies, and foreign customers also benefit. It is estimated that pimps control 80 to 95 percent of prostitution. These pimps find naive and needy young women, manipulate them into prostitution, and then take the majority of their money (Barry, 1995). The **trafficking of women and girls** for labor or sex is another instance of women as objects and property and is discussed in Chapter 7, "Women and Globalization."

Another example of women and girls as objects and property is that in many cultures, an unmarried woman has no choice about who she is to marry; this decision is made for her, without her input. Known as **forced marriage**, it occurs when one or both of the partners cannot give free or valid consent to the marriage. Forced marriage is sometimes classified as a form of sexual violence since many brides are too young to provide sexual consent and many brides are forcibly raped.

Forced marriages involve varying degrees of force, coercion, or deception, ranging from emotional pressure by family or community members to abduction and imprisonment. For example, in the Central Asian country of Kyrgyzstan, up to a third of ethnic Kyrgyz women are wedded in nonconsensual **bride kidnappings**, although the practice is illegal. A man seeking a wife abducts a woman he wants to marry with the help of other men and takes her to his home, where hours are spent pressuring her to accept the marriage. Women relatives of the prospective groom try to cover her head with a white scarf, symbolizing that she is ready to wed her kidnapper. Because a woman is considered impure once she's entered the man's home, around 84 percent of kidnapped women agree to marriage to avoid shame (Hayashi-Panos, 2013). In Tanzania, among the highly patriarchal Sukama tribe, the abduction, rape, and forced marriage of girls is so normal and men's entitlement to girls' bodies so accepted that no one even intervenes when they witness abductions (this is an example of what feminists call a rape culture). Rather than calling the police, parents seek out the "groom" so they can obtain a bride price and benefit from their daughter's marriage (Ellison, 2016).

Over 650 million women alive today were married before their eighteenth birthday, compared to 115 million boys and men (UNICEF, 2020). Over a 125-year period, child marriage rates (marriage before age 18), have declined 5 percent, to a global prevalence of about 21 percent (UNFPA, 2020). The highest rates of child marriage are in West and Central Africa, sub-Saharan Africa, Eastern and Southern Africa, and South Asia (30–40 percent) (UNICEF, 2020). However, while child marriage is more common in the least developed countries of the world, it also occurs in other parts of the world. Box 2.3 explains how recent activism has led to half of U.S. states enacting minimum marriage age laws.

Forced child marriage is most common when families are poor. To families living in poverty or financial difficulty, a daughter's early marriage may reduce financial strain. Indeed, poverty is the best predictor of early marriage. Forced marriages are also common where there is poverty in combination with **bride price** (sometimes called *bridewealth* or *lobala*). Bride price involves the groom giving money, goods, or livestock to the parents of the bride in return for her hand. Common in many African ethnic groups and parts of Papua New Guinea, India, and Afghanistan, it provides a financial incentive for parents to marry off their young daughters. Forced marriages of girls can also be used to settle men's debt.

"I have often heard men say that I had a choice, and I did, it was either work as a prostitute or starve to death."
Dawn, who became a prostitute at age 16 (Canada)

Approximately 12 million girls are married in childhood every year.

"I was on my way home from school. Together with three men, this boy caught me and tied me up. They carried me to the boy's house and locked me in a small room for three days. His parents brought alcohol and money to my brother's house. My brother accepted the price and I became the boy's wife."
12-year-old May, a member of the Hmong ethnic group from northern Vietnam's mountainous Ha Giang province

"I am a poor man, and this is how I can feed my large family. What else could I do? Many others are doing the same thing."
Afghan man that sold his 9- and 10-year-old daughters to wealthy opium poppy growers

BOX 2.3   *Child Marriage in the United States*

Americans are often horrified by child marriage in other countries but what they don't know is that it occurs in the United States. The *Tahirih Justice Center* and *Unchained At Last* are U.S. nonprofits (NGOs) working to prevent child and forced marriage in the United States and help women and girls leave such marriages. In the United States, over 200,000 children were married before the age of eighteen between 2000 and 2015, most of them girls married to adult men. Until 2016, child marriage was legal in 49 states with parental consent and no states required a determination of whether the child was pressured or coerced, a victim of human trafficking, or whether the marriage was statutory rape disguised as marriage. Only nine states had specific laws to prevent or punish forced marriage. Activism, led by the Tahirih Justice Center and Unchained At Last, has since led to the enactment of minimum marriage age laws in 25 states.

Sources: Portnoy, 2016; Tahirih Justice Center, 2020; Unchained At Last, 2016

"Choosing when and whom to marry is one of life's most important decisions. Child marriage denies millions of girls this choice each year."
UNFPA's Executive Director, Dr. Babatunde Osotimehin

"I was 16 and never missed a day at school. I had to leave it all as my parents had bartered me for a girl my elder brother was to marry."
Komal, a child bride in Madhya Pradesh/ Rajasthan, India

In Afghanistan, Pakistan's North West Frontier Province and the tribal territories, as well as in sub-Saharan Africa, girls are sometimes forced to marry in order to settle the debt of a father or brother.

Child marriage denies girls their childhood and is a human rights concern. According to the United Nations Declaration on Human Rights, Article 16, "Marriage shall be entered into only with the free and full consent of the intending spouses." Other human rights agreements, including the Convention on the Elimination of Discrimination Against Women (CEDAW), also specify that all people have the right to freely choose a spouse and to marry only with their full and free consent, that the minimum age of marriage for women be eighteen, and that governments take action to eliminate child marriage (UNICEF, 2015).

Child marriage is a human rights concern, but it is also a health and safety concern. Because girls tend to have little power compared to their husbands and in-laws, child brides are vulnerable to physical and sexual violence and sexually transmitted diseases, including AIDS (McFarlane et al., 2016). They are more likely to experience early pregnancy, which is associated with a greater risk of child mortality and the mother's death or disability (pregnancy and childbirth complications are the leading cause of death for girls aged 15–19 globally) (WHO, 2019). Early marriage is also associated with the curtailment of girls' education (ICRW, 2011; Singh & Anand, 2015).

Efforts to curb child marriage are underway. The International Center for Research on Women (ICRW, 2011) evaluated programs designed to reduce child marriage and identified five successful strategies: (1) Increase girls' access to quality education; (2) Educate families and community elders on the effects of child marriage; (3) Provide incentives and economic support to girls and their families (such as loans or income-generating skills) so the economic need to marry girls is reduced; (4) Encourage supportive laws and policies; and (5) Empower girls with information, skills, and support networks to advocate for themselves and aspire to alternatives to early marriage. On International Women's Day in 2016, the United Nations (the UNFPA and UNICEF) launched the Global Programme to Accelerate Action to End Child Marriage, which focuses on twelve countries with high rates of child marriage (Bangladesh, Burkina Faso, Ethiopia, Ghana, India, Mozambique, Nepal, Niger, Sierra Leone, Uganda, Yemen, and Zambia).

Violence Against Women and Girls (VAWG)

Violence is often "gendered" in that some types of violence, such as rape and domestic violence, are experienced disproportionately by women and girls because of their gender. The United Nations *Declaration on the Elimination of Violence Against Women* (1993) defines violence against women (VAW) as any act of gender-based violence resulting in, or likely to result in, physical, sexual, or mental harm or suffering to women, but we now use the term **violence against women and girls (VAWG)** to acknowledge sexual violence as a problem for both girls and women. VAWG has its roots in historical and structural inequalities in power relations between males and females and males' abuse of that power (UNICEF, 2013). Men's violence against women is neither natural nor inevitable. It arises from traditional gender stereotypes, norms, and roles that support male dominance, the sexual objectification of women, and that approve of, minimize, or ignore, violence against women and girls.

Figure 2.2 shows some of the many forms VAWG (also known as gender-based violence) may take. Keep in mind, however, that these often overlap. For example, **sexual assault** and physical and emotional battery may occur in the context of intimate relationships, forced marriage, sex trafficking, and conflict-related VAWG.

The World Health Organization (WHO) (2013) estimates that over 35 percent of women worldwide have experienced physical and/or sexual violence by an intimate partner or sexual violence by a nonpartner. The fact that VAWG is common, accepted (or at least ignored), and that police and legal systems frequently fail to intervene, is an indication of women's lower status and power.

Violence against women and girls occurs in every segment of society, but it is influenced by intersectionality. Race, class, disability, sexual orientation, gender identity, age, and religion all affect a woman's experience of gendered violence. Multiple intersecting forms of discrimination mean that some groups of women and girls experience higher rates of VAWG than do other women in the same country, region, or community. For example, migrant and refugee women, indigenous women, and lesbian, bisexual, and transgender women experience higher rates of gendered violence (OHCHR, 2016; UNICEF, 2013).

VAWG is recognized as a major public health problem since it results in injuries and deaths and negatively affects mother and child health, women's sexual and reproductive health, and women's psychological and emotional health (WHO, 2013). Women's ability to stay employed and their ability to care for their family are also impacted by VAWG (UN Women, 2016). VAWG is recognized as a violation of women's and girls' human rights and a form of gender discrimination.

"Cultural practices such as bride price, child engagements (where children are engaged before birth), exchange marriages (between girls from two separate families) and giving girls in baad (to solve a communal dispute), contribute to the high prevalence of child marriage and low value assigned to girls in Afghan society." *GirlsNotBrides.org*, an international partnership of over 1,000 organizations from more than 100 countries dedicated to ending child marriage.

"You cannot say: 'I will kill my wife, I will beat her to a pulp because that is culture.' We say because of culture we will allow that?" *Phumzile Mlambo-Ngcuka, Head of UN Women, 2016*

The OHCHR is the Office of the United Nations High Commissioner for Human Rights. The OHCHR represents the international community's commitment to promote and protect all human rights.

FIGURE 2.2 *Some Forms of Violence Against Women and Girls*

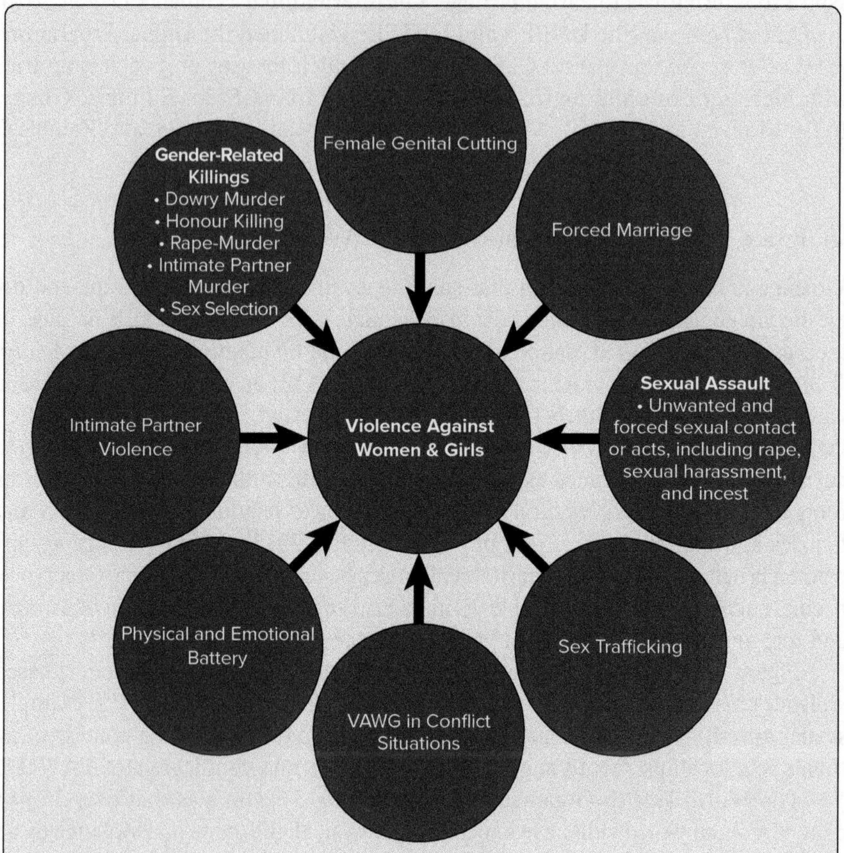

VAWG prevents women and girls from enjoying rights and freedoms equal to men and boys and denies them fundamental freedoms such as the right to life; the right not to be subject to torture or to cruel, inhuman, or degrading treatment or punishment; the right to liberty and security of person; and the right to equal protection under the law (OHCHR, 2016).

Studying violence against women shows us how women's social, political, and economic subordination are interrelated and influential in a variety of women's issues. For example, women's lack of political power means that legal and police protections against domestic and sexual violence are often absent or minimal. Women's lack of economic power means some are unable to leave abusive situations. Women's lower status and cultural norms lead to an acceptance of violence against them by families, communities, and authorities.

November 25th is International Day for the Elimination of Violence Against Women

Domestic or Intimate Partner Violence

Domestic violence or intimate partner violence (IPV) occurs in the context of an intimate relationship and may include physical violence (such as hitting, slapping, beating, burning), sexual violence (such as rape or being forced to engage in undesired sexual acts), and emotional abuse (such as being humiliated, insulted, intimidated, threatened). It may also include the destruction of property as means of coercion, control, revenge, punishment; other controlling behaviors, such as limiting a woman's ability to see family and friends and monitoring her whereabouts; stalking; control of a person's reproduction or sexual health; and cyber violence. According to the World Health Organization (2017), close to one-third of women who have been in a relationship have experienced IPV.

IPV exists in all regions, classes, and cultures, and women experience it at much higher rates than men. For example, in the United States, about 25 percent of women and 10 percent of men have experienced sexual violence, physical violence, and/or stalking by an intimate partner (CDC, 2021). Globally, 17.8 percent of ever-partnered women aged 15 to 49 have experienced IPV in the last year (UN Women, 2020). Box 2.4. shows the regional incidence of physical and sexual IPV.

People often ask, "Why don't victims of domestic violence just leave?", but it's important to understand that leaving isn't that simple. Psychological, social, legal, and economic chains often shackle women to abusive relationships. Abusers' psychological violence decreases women's confidence and self-esteem and convinces them they deserved the abuse and cannot survive outside the relationship. Many societies are structured such that women cannot leave because laws and cultural norms make it difficult for them to leave, they cannot support themselves and their children, and they have nowhere safe to go. Shame and embarrassment prevent women from seeking help where it's common to blame women for their abuse and violence against women is seen as justifiable. According to UN studies, acceptance of wife beating is the highest in Africa, Asia, and Oceania, and lower in Latin America and the Caribbean and developed countries (UN Women, 2016).

As women's status and power increase and a country progresses toward gender equality, IPV usually decreases. But in gender-unequal societies, women have few alternatives to staying in abusive relationships, legal and justice systems don't hold perpetrators accountable, and cultural beliefs, attitudes, and messages create a climate where VAWG is allowed.

In many countries, neither government laws nor the police protect women from IPV, as it is viewed as a private family matter and a husband's right. Activists work to get domestic violence laws passed, and they are making progress: 155 of 190 countries (81.6%) now have domestic violence laws, and 78 countries now have marital rape laws (World Bank, 2020). Most of these laws were enacted in the last twenty years, and they are only the beginning. Without activism and changes in patriarchal social norms, laws are often inadequate and unenforced. Papua New Guinea, a nation in the South Pacific near Australia and Indonesia, is a recent example. It's a patrilineal society where women have few resources of their own and husbands' paying of bride price is viewed by many as giving husbands the right to treat wives however they wish. Approximately two-thirds of women are victims of domestic violence, and rates of VAWG are estimated to be some of the highest and

According to the United Nations Broadband Commission Report, *Cyber Violence Against Women and Girls* (2015), almost three of every four women and girls online have been exposed to some form of cyber violence.

"Violence by men against women is tolerated in Japan, and this is particularly true of sexual violence. The whole of society has become so anesthetized to this that pornographic and other sexual items that many people overseas might find shocking are lined up even on the shelves of convenience stores, and so on, and nobody bats an eyelid."
Hiromi Nakano, whose nongovernment organization Shiawase-namida (Happy Tears) provides support for victims of sexual violence

"If he beats you, he loves you."
Well-known Russian proverb

BOX 2.4   *Regional Percentages of Women and Girls (Aged 15–49) Experiencing IPV in the Last Year*

Region	Countries Included in Sample	Average
Oceania	Cook Islands, Fiji, Kiribati, Marshall Islands, Micronesia, Samoa, Solomon Islands, Timor Leste, Tonga, Tuvalu	34.7
Central and Southern Asia	Afghanistan, Bangladesh, India, Kazakhstan, Maldives, Nepal, Tajikistan	23.0
Sub-Saharan Africa	Angola, Burkina Faso, Burundi, Cameroon, Cape Verde, Central African Republic, Chad, Comoros, Democratic Republic of Congo, Gambia, Ghana, Ivory Coast, Kenya, Liberia, Malawi, Mali, Mozambique, Namibia, Nigeria, Rwanda, Sao Tome and Principe, Senegal, Sierra Leone, Tanzania, Togo, Uganda, Zambia, Zimbabwe	21.5
Northern Africa and Western Asia	Azerbaijan, Armenia, Cyprus, Egypt, Georgia, Jordan, Turkey	12.3
Latin America and the Caribbean	Bolivia, Columbia, Ecuador, El Salvador, Guatemala, Haiti, Honduras, Jamaica, Mexico, Nicaragua, Panama, Paraguay, Peru, Trinidad and Tobago, Uruguay	11.8
Eastern and Southeastern Asia	Cambodia, Laos, Myanmar, Mongolia, Palau, Philippines, Vietnam	9.0
Europe and North America	Belgium, Bulgaria, Croatia, Czechoslovakia, Denmark, Estonia, Finland, France, Germany, Greece, Ireland, Latvia, Lithuania, Luxembourg, Malta, Netherlands, Poland, Portugal, Romania, Sweden, Slovenia, Spain, Ukraine, United Kingdom	6.1

Notes: Some country samples did not include the full age range, not all used the same definition of IPV, and some country samples only included married women.
Source: Data from UN Women (2020).

These countries have no laws against domestic violence or sexual harassment: Republic of Congo, Equatorial Guinea, Haiti, Iran, Kuwait, Libya, Mali, Mauritania, Micronesia, Myanmar, Oman, Qatar, Russia, Somalia, South Sudan, Sudan, Swaziland, Syria, United Arab Emirates, Uzbekistan, West Bank and Gaza, and Yemen.

the most vicious in the world outside of a conflict (war or civil unrest) zone (Doctors Without Borders, 2016). A 2013 family protection bill criminalizing domestic violence was passed in 2013, but women still have few options for the legal, social, medical, and protection assistance (Human Rights Watch, 2015b).

IPV is higher in countries with restrictive divorce laws that make it difficult for women to leave or keep their children (UNFPA, 2009; WHO, 2017). In the United Arab Emirates (UAE), Muslim men can initiate divorce by simply saying, "I divorce you" three times. But Muslim women can only initiate divorce if they can prove physical abuse (to do this a woman must provide at least two male witnesses, or a male witness and two female witnesses to attest to the injury). Alternatively, she can petition the Shari'ah court and pay compensation or return her dowry to her husband (in the UAE dowry is the woman's property). If she remarries, she may have to forfeit her children. Israeli women must be granted a *get*, a Jewish divorce writ that can only be granted by husbands; many will demand that she forfeit property, alimony, and child support in exchange. Activists in countries like these work to change these and other family laws that are discriminatory to women.

Women's economic dependence on the men in their lives also increases their risk and tolerance of domestic violence (Bornstein, 2006), as does women's social dependence on men (Carillo, 1992). In many cultures, women are socially dependent on men because women's status is tied to marriage. Unmarried, divorced, and even widowed adult women have very low status, and leaving one's husband, regardless of circumstances, is socially unacceptable. In patrilineal societies where women cannot own or inherit property and are excluded from the economic and political power bases of their society, their class position is tied to their relationships with men (Lerner, 1986). This increases women's dependence upon marriage and their husband's power over them.

Without a safety net, women cannot easily leave abusive situations. Shelters play a critical role in women's ability to leave IPV situations and most are started and run by women's NGOs. Women frequently need psychological services as they recover from trauma. They need legal, financial, and social services so they may become self-sufficient and do not have to return to their abusers. A safe secret place to stay is also required since many believe that their abuser will kill them or their children, or stalk them if they leave. This is not an unfounded fear. Globally, about two-thirds of victims of intimate partner homicides are women, and 34 percent of murdered women are killed by an intimate partner (UNODC, 2019). In 2017 alone, 50,000 women were killed by intimate partners or family members (UNODC, 2019).

On one day alone in 2014, 2,497 shelters in 46 countries reported serving 53,320 women and 34,794 children fleeing domestic violence. However, 7,337 women and 4,410 children were turned away due to limited resources and space (Global Network of Women's Shelters, 2015). Many shelters continuously struggle to stay open because they are dependent on voluntary contributions and insufficient and unreliable government funding that may be reduced due to economic downturns or changes in political leadership. Box 2.5 shares the story of Marina Pisklakova, founder of *Anna*, a Russian women's rights organization dedicated to preventing domestic violence and serving domestic violence victims in Russia.

Although women everywhere experience domestic violence, culture may shape the form that IPV takes. **Dowry violence**, for example, is a type of IPV that occurs in the Southeast Asian countries of Bangladesh, India, and Pakistan when husbands or in-laws use emotional, physical, or sexual violence to get a wife to extract more dowry from her family. In extreme cases, they murder the wife and stage it to look like suicide or an accident, in what is known as **dowry murder** or **dowry death**. Dowry murders usually occur when a woman's family is unable to provide the agreed upon dowry or the husband wants to remarry for another dowry or to produce a son. One of the most common methods is to splash a

"We spoke to woman after woman who told us really harrowing accounts...Too often police were simply ignoring their claims or telling them they should go back to their husbands."
Elaine Pearson, Human Rights Watch about women in Papua New Guinea

"Every woman thinking of leaving worries about finances. Women find themselves forced back into abusive marriages because they can't earn a living."
Ritsuko Nomoto, Japanese woman that opened a restaurant to give battered women jobs

"Survivors of gender-based violence need safe spaces, protection, empowering support, and access to justice."
Women Against Violence Europe

Help and services for domestic violence are available. The U.S. National Domestic Violence Hotline number is: 1–800–799–SAFE.

To find a gender-violence shelter or hotline in Europe, go to: https://www.wave-network.org/find-help/women-s-helplines-list

BOX 2.5   *Activist Profile: Russia's Marina Pisklakova*

It's estimated that 12,000 Russian women die every year from domestic violence. Although a law in 2016 made beating relatives a criminal offense, an amendment passed in 2017 decriminalized domestic battery as long as it isn't premeditated and the harm was unintentional. Despite the efforts of women's activists, there are still no specific laws criminalizing IPV or providing protections to victims.

In the early 1990s, Marina Pisklakova was coordinating a national survey on women's issues for the Russian Academy of Sciences when she practically stumbled upon the hidden problem of domestic violence. Soon after, she encountered a beaten wife, the mother of a school friend of her son's, who confessed that although her husband beat her, she would not leave as she had nowhere to go and no means of support. Pisklakova realized there were no services she could refer her to and in response, founded *ANNA* (Association No to Violence), an NGO devoted to the prevention of domestic violence in Russia. It became her life's work.

Before *ANNA*, there were no hotlines, shelters, laws, or advocacy campaigns in Russia, so she began a national domestic violence hotline, opened shelters, and created a media campaign to expose IPV and educate women about their rights. ANNA operates a network of 170 crisis centers across Russia and the former Soviet Union. Pisklakova continues to lobby for legislation banning domestic abuse (since the early 90s, over 50 proposed laws have been rejected), and to bring aid to victims and prosecution to criminals. In 2004 Pisklakova received the Human Rights Global Leadership Award. Although Pisklakova once said, "I am not an extraordinary person. Any woman in my position would do the same," the results of her action are truly extraordinary. ANNA has assisted over 100,000 women.

Sources: Gentleman, 2015; OpenDemocracy, 2020; Robert F. Kennedy Human Rights, 2016; Sebastian & Mortensen, 2017; Speak Truth to Power, 2016.

---

woman with kerosene, light her on fire, and then claim it was a cooking accident. According to the Indian government (National Crime Records Bureau, 2020), over 7,000 dowry murders occur every year (nearly twenty a day) in India, but it's estimated that the actual number may be three to four times higher since dowry deaths are often hard to prove (*Times of India*, 2013).

Honour-based violence (HBV), another form of IPV, occurs in cultures where a woman's virtuous behavior is believed to affect the honor and prestige of her male relatives who are in charge of her. The most extreme form is **honour killing**, a tradition whereby it is seen as morally justifiable to kill a wife, daughter, or sister for doing something that brings shame on her family or male relatives. Dishonorable acts include having premarital sex, being raped, engaging in marital infidelity (or suspected infidelity), seeking divorce, flirting, wearing makeup or nontraditional dress, dating or marrying without parental approval, or being lesbian. Honour killing differs from other forms of domestic violence in that it occurs in cultures where honor and morality are viewed as a collective family matter, and it frequently involves multiple family and community members that conspire to kill a woman because she has dishonored the family through disobedience and "immoral" behavior

"The purpose of honour crimes is to maintain men's power by denying women their basic rights to make autonomous decisions about marriage, divorce, and sexuality."
MADRE

(Chesler, 2009).[4] Gender-related killings of women and girls, like honour killings and dowry deaths, are sometimes referred to as "femicide."

The United Nations estimates that 5,000 women are killed each year in the name of honor, but this is likely an underestimate because they are often reported by families as accidents or suicides (Chesler, 2009; WHO, 2008). The highest incidence of honour killing is believed to be in Jordan, but honour killings also occur in Bangladesh, India, Pakistan, Afghanistan, Syria, Iraq, Egypt, Jordan, Morocco, Turkey, and Palestine. Honour killings also occur in North American and European countries like Canada, the United States, Sweden, and the United Kingdom, where immigrants have engaged in the practice, typically because their daughters have become too "westernized" and disobedient.

Before 1993, honour killings received little public attention or government action (Khan, 2006). Activists work to bring attention to the issue (see for example, the *Honour Based Violence Awareness Network*, founded by singer/filmmaker/activist Deeyah). They also work for the passage and enforcement of laws criminalizing honour killing. For example, in Palestine, Iraq, Pakistan, and Jordan, men that kill women in the name of honour receive short sentences, if they're even prosecuted. Women's rights groups also seek justice for slain women and open shelters for potential victims. After the 2016 honour killing of Pakistani social media star Qandeel Baloch by her brother, an international campaign was launched, Pakistani women's activists marched. They petitioned the government to close a legal loophole which allowed families to forgive perpetrators and avoid prosecution. A bill was finally passed but has yet to result in any convictions.

Sexual Violence

Sexual violence is any type of sexual contact or behavior without explicit consent of the recipient. Sexual violence is identified as a violation of women's and girls' human rights in many human rights documents. Its elimination is a target goal of the UN's 2030 Agenda for Sustainable Development. Women routinely experience sexual violence in ways that have no immediate parallels for men (Chowdhury et al., 1994). Figure 2.3 shows some of the forms of sexual violence identified by the World Health Organization (2014) and experienced disproportionately by girls and women. This is further evidence of gender inequality. If women and men were equal, rates of gendered sexual violence would be lower and legal and social consequences for offenders would be greater. More effort would be made to provide safe physical and social environments. Survivors would also have better access to support services.

Rape

The defining feature of **rape** is the lack of choice by a woman to engage in sexual intercourse (Koss, Heise, & Russo, 1994). **Non-normative rape** is rape that is both

---

[4] I use *honour crimes* instead of *honor crimes*, because this is the spelling and terminology used in the countries where these crimes are more common.

Pakistani activists estimate that there are about 1,000 honour killings every year.

"The right to life of women is conditional on their obeying social norms and traditions."
Hina Jilani, Pakistani lawyer and women's rights activist

"There is no honour in killing."
Kurdish Women's Action Against Honour Killing

Following the rape of her daughters by Roman soldiers, Boudicca Queen of Iceni (first century A.D.) rebelled and led a coalition of tribes on a revenge mission that destroyed ancient London.

"Everyone has a right to say no, regardless of the situation or the point in time. Even if a woman previously kissed the offender or has or used to have a sexual relationship with him, she has the right to say no at all times. In the event of rape, this right of girls and women is ignored. It is for this reason that the responsibility lies solely with the perpetrator."
The bff (the German association of rape crisis centers and women's counseling centers)

FIGURE 2.3   *Forms of Sexual Violence*

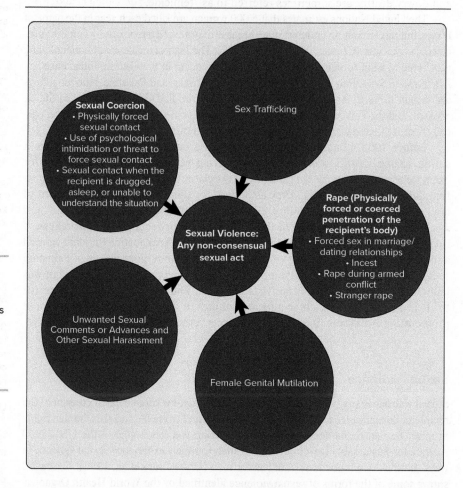

Every 23 seconds an American is sexually assaulted. Nine out of ten of those Americans are female.
RAINN, Rape Abuse Incest National Network

"Start by Believing"
Slogan of End Violence Against Women's campaign for supporting sexual assault survivors

"Over the last five years we are seeing a movement where women are breaking the shackles of shame, showing their faces and using their names, making it quite clear that they are not to blame for someone else's actions against them...this is promoting a paradigm shift in the culture."
Carol Tracy, executive director of the Women's Law Project

against a woman's will and in violation of social norms. Sadly, **normative rape**, rape promoted or allowed by a society, is common in many places (Koss et al., 1994).

Rape is a concern of feminists and women's rights activists for seven main reasons:

1. *Rape is a very real threat to women everywhere.* For instance, a national survey in the United States found that over one in five women (21.3%) experienced rape, 43.2 percent before the age of 18 (Smith et al., 2018). For Native American women, the rate is twice the national average. The UN estimates that worldwide, one in five women will become a victim of rape or attempted rape in her lifetime.

2. *Rape laws are poorly enforced.* About 97 percent of countries have national rape laws but only 57 percent of countries enforce them (WHO, 2020). **Victim blaming** (holding women responsible for the violence against them),

for example, by asking what they were wearing or doing that might have led to the assault, remains a barrier to justice. Police and judiciary systems often fail to investigate, and they interrogate victims in an accusatory manner because they don't believe them, or blame them.

Rape victims are frequently shamed and humiliated, which results in secondary victimization from family, the police, and the legal system. Meanwhile, research in the United States indicates that we should believe rape claims—on average, only 5 percent of allegations are false. In countries like Central African Republic, South Sudan, Nigeria, Somalia, and Myanmar, customary and tribal courts often require rapists marry their victim to reduce the shame experienced by the victim's family. In Afghanistan, rape is viewed as adultery, which means the victim may be charged with a crime, and in Yemen, women that report rape may be victims of honour killing (Stop Rape Now, 2016). Unsurprisingly, rape is one of the most underreported of all crimes worldwide.

Globally, you will find women's activists working to pass and strengthen rape laws and their enforcement. For example, in Pakistan, activism from women's rights groups led to a significant change in rape laws in 2006. Before changes to the law, women who were raped could be charged with the crime of having sex outside of marriage (Sattar, 2015). In 2016, the "No Means No" campaign of German women's rights activists led to a change in rape laws. The previous law did not count an assault as rape unless the victim physically resisted. Activists are already working for strengthening the new law since it requires a woman communicate lack of consent. The problem with the new law is that it fails to protect unconscious, drugged, or disabled people unable to communicate consent (BBC News, 2016).

Women's rights groups also advocate for police to investigate rape cases properly, take complaints seriously, and treat survivors sensitively. The ENDTHEBACKLOG project of the Joyful Heart Foundation (United States) is one example. Throughout the United States there are at least 700,000 untested rape kits containing forensic data collected from victims during an invasive 4- to 6-hour exam. The rape kit backlog, as it's known, means that many perpetrators remain unidentified and unprosecuted (DNA from the kits can be run through a criminal database to identify perpetrators). Joyful Heart volunteers, associates, and staff conduct research on where backlogs exist and how to eliminate them. They work for legislation and policies to hold law enforcement accountable for testing rape kits and keeping victims apprised of investigations. They also provide guidance to law enforcement on how to sensitively work with victims.

A recent victory occurred in the United States in 2016 when President Obama signed a sexual assault survivor's bill of rights. The Sexual Assault Survivors Act originated in the activism of 24-year-old Amanda Nguyen, an American rape survivor. Nguyen was angered to discover that rape kits were often destroyed without notifying victims. In some states women had to pay for their own rape kit. In her home state of Massachusetts, she had to file paperwork every six months to prevent her rape kit from being destroyed. She created a Change.org petition, which garnered over 140,000 signatures calling

Social media is being used by a new generation of activists to reduce victim blaming, challenge rape culture, and obtain justice. See for example #Thisdoesnotmeanyes, #SurvivorPrivilege, #It'sOnUs, #ProjectUnbreakable, #Rise4Revolution. In 2017, #Metoo went viral globally. Founder Tarana Burke has since created #ACTTOO, a platform for activism.

"If I could have one wish granted, it might well be a total end to rape. That means a significant weapon of war gone from the arsenal of conflict, the absence of a daily risk assessment for girls and women in public and private spaces, the removal of a violent assertion of power, and a far-reaching shift for our society."
Phumzile Mlambo-Ngcuka, UN Women Executive Director

Joyful Heart was founded by American actor Mariska Hargitay, who stars as a detective on the TV show *Law & Order: Special Victims Unit*. She was motivated by the show's topics as well as the heartbreaking fan mail she received from sexual assault survivors.

"Because of their constant fear of rape (conscious or not), women do things throughout the day to protect themselves. Whether it's carrying our keys in our hands as we walk home, locking our car doors as soon as we get in, or not walking down certain streets, we take precautions. While taking precautions is certainly not a bad idea, the fact that certain things women do are so ingrained into our daily routines is truly disturbing. It's essentially like living in a prison—all the time."
Jessica Valenti, from her book, Full Frontal Feminism

Help and services for sexual assault in the United States are available. Call the National Sexual Assault Hotline (U.S.) at 1-800-656-HOPE or go to https://hotline.rainn.org/online

for survivors' rights, and partnered with Funny or Die to create a humorous video to promote her cause. Jeanne Shaheen, a U.S. senator from New Hampshire, worked with Nguyen to create the legislation. Nguyen's NGO RISE now works at the state and federal levels to further strengthen survivors' rights.

3. *The threat of rape limits women's freedom of movement and denies them control over their sexuality.* More than any other crime, fear of rape leads women to restrict their movements and their life choices or, alternatively, to prepare for battle (Niarchos, 1995). Sexual assault awareness and prevention programs sometimes offer self-defense classes to prepare women to resist sexual attackers. However, it's important to recognize that teaching risk-reduction strategies does not mean that stopping rape is the responsibility of potential victims, or that those that are raped are at fault for their rape.

4. *Many of the victims of rape are girl children and adolescents, often raped by an adult relative or acquaintance.* The World Health Organization's study of violence against children (2020) estimates that, depending on the country, 8 to 32 percent of girls have experienced some form of forced sexual contact compared to 3 to 18 percent of boys. In some countries, girls experience much higher rates of sexual violence than boys. For example, in Uganda, 35 percent of girls and 17 percent of boys, and in Kenya, 32 percent of girls and 18 percent of boys. Girls are also more likely than boys to experience sexual violence while travelling to and from school, and young women in college are also vulnerable to sexual violence (UN Women, 2016).

5. *The fact that men can and do rape women, whereas the reverse is rarely true, intimidates women and gives power to men.* Some feminists, such as Brownmiller (1986), view the threat of rape as the basis of men's power over women. Rape is an expression of dominance, power, and contempt, a rejection of women's right to self-determination (Niarchos, 1995). The threat of rape also makes women dependent on fathers, brothers, or husbands to protect them. This places women in a subordinate position to men. Brownmiller (1986) suggests that, historically, marriage and women's subjugation by men arose because women needed men to protect them from other men. Furthermore, says Brownmiller (1986), the price a woman paid for this protection was her male protector's exclusive ownership of her body.

6. *Sexual assault is traumatic and has serious psychological, physical, and social costs.* **Sexual assault** includes any unwanted or forced sexual contact or acts including rape, sexual harassment, and incest. The World Health Organization (2020) reports that sexual violence is associated with sexually transmitted infections such as HIV/AIDS (forced sex results in greater abrasion, providing an avenue for the virus). Other physical effects include unintended pregnancies, gynecological problems, induced abortions, miscarriage, abdominal pain, and poor overall health status. Sexual violence is also associated with depression, anxiety, alcohol abuse, and posttraumatic stress disorder (enduring physical and psychological symptoms after an extremely stressful event). Women may be unable to work, or take care of themselves and their children. Rape is often associated with stigma and rejection of the victim, adding to its emotional

costs. In some countries, women may be rejected by their husbands or become unmarriageable due to the loss of their virginity. Sexual abuse as a child is associated with greater sexual risk-taking, substance abuse, and further victimization. Women's rights activists are instrumental in providing psychological and legal assistance to rape victims, largely through rape crisis centers and hotlines. Many governments also provide hotlines and resources for victims.

7. *The global prevalence and acceptance of* **rape cultures**, *where sexual assault is accepted, promoted, ignored, or minimized, is evidence of gender inequality.* In a gender-equal world, rape cultures would be dismantled. Rape and sex trafficking would be uncommon and not experienced disproportionately by women and girls. Laws, media, and traditions normalizing and excusing men's sexual violence against women would be few and far between. Men would be taught not to rape instead of women being taught how not to get raped. Rape wouldn't be something to joke about, and the media wouldn't romanticize or sexualize violence against women. Masculinities that sexually objectify women and condone nonconsensual sexual contact with women would be transformed. Victims of sexual violence would be believed, not blamed and tarnished. Rapists would be held accountable by law enforcement and justice systems. Gender norms supportive of male sexual entitlement would be changed. Worldwide, efforts are being made to call out rape culture (often on social media) and transform it.

In 2016, Stanford University student Brock Turner received only a six-month sentence for sexually assaulting an unconscious women. The judge (Aaron Persky) said he didn't want to ruin Turner's life with a stricter sentence. Women lit up social media in protect, collecting millions of signatures to recall the judge. Persky was ousted by California voters in 2018.

Conflict-Related Sexual Violence

Most civilians suffer when their communities are the scenes of armed conflict, but women and girls face heightened sexual violence due to their gender and low status. **Conflict-related sexual violence** includes rape, sexual slavery, forced prostitution, forced pregnancy, and other types of sexual violence directly or indirectly linked to a conflict (Stop Rape Now, 2016).

The rape of women during wartime is documented in writings as early as 420 B.C., but it is seen in modern history as well. During World War II, Moroccan soldiers raped Italian women, Japanese soldiers raped Korean women, and Nazi soldiers raped Jewish women. In the 1970s, Pakistani soldiers raped Bengali women. In the 1980s, war rapes occurred in El Salvador and Guatemala. Since 2000, hundreds of thousands of women and girls have experienced conflict-related sexual violence in Afghanistan, Burundi, Central African Republic, Columbia, Côte d'Ivoire, the Democratic Republic of Congo, Guinea, Iraq, Liberia, Libya, Mali, Myanmar, Nepal, Sierra Leone, Sri Lanka, Somalia, South Sudan, Sudan, Syria, Uganda, and Yemen (Stop Rape Now, 2009, 2016; UN Secretary-General, 2020). Figure 2.4 shows common features of conflict-related sexual violence.

During conflict, sexual violence is sometimes opportunistic, with men taking advantage of the breakdown of law and order to assault women, knowing they are unlikely to face consequences. But rape is also used as a weapon of war to defeat and terrorize. Women and girls are brutally raped, sometimes by gangs,

Men play an important role in sexual assault prevention. *Men Can Stop Rape* is an American organization whose mission is to mobilize men to use their strength for creating cultures free from violence, especially men's violence against women.

"It is more dangerous to be a woman than to be a soldier in modern conflict."
Patrick Cammaer, former Deputy Force Commander of the United Nations Mission to the Democratic Republic of Congo

FIGURE 2.4 *Conflict-Related Sexual Violence*

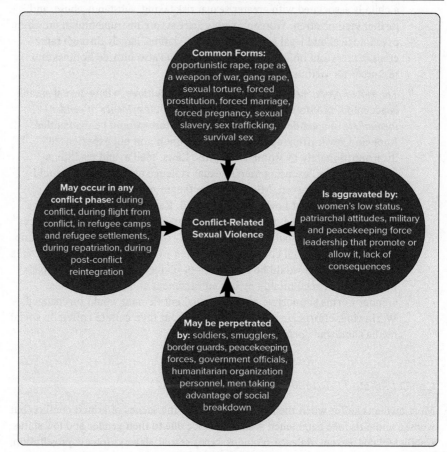

Rape is not incidental to warfare: it is a weapon. It is deliberately used to traumatize women and terrorize their entire communities. *MADRE, an international women's human rights organization that partners with community-based women's groups facing war and disaster*

The persistence and painstaking research of Yoshiaki Yoshimi, a Japanese history professor, as well as an international tribunal organized by transnational feminist networks, finally got the Japanese government to admit that Japanese soldiers had used thousands of girls and women from Korea and China as "comfort women." The Japanese government had covered up the situation for more than forty years.

and sexually tortured. Assaults are often committed in the presence of the victim's family, the community, or other victims. Women's human rights defenders are often targeted for sexual violence. Where women are viewed as the property of men, their rapes are used to punish their husbands or fathers. Sometimes the intent is genocide. In the 1990s, for example, Bosnian Serb soldiers raped between 20,000 and 50,000 Muslim women in the former Yugoslavia, their intention to impregnate Muslim women and destroy this ethnic group. Likewise, **genocidal rape** occurred in 1994 in Rwanda when Hutu men raped 250,000 to 500,000 Tutsi women and girls during a civil war in less than 100 days.

Forced prostitution is also common during wartime. Women and girls are kidnapped and forced to wash, cook, serve, and have sex with soldiers and militia. For example, during World War II, the Japanese enslaved between 200,000 to 400,000 Korean, Filipino, Chinese, Indonesian, and Dutch women in "comfort stations" for sexual use by Japanese soldiers (Copelon, 1995). Ninety percent of these women died in captivity. Currently, terrorist groups including ISIS, the Taliban, Al-Qaida, and Boku Haram abduct girls and women for sexual exploitation, forced marriage to their fighters, ransoms, trafficking, and trading. ISIS even runs competitions among its fighters with winners receiving sex slaves as prizes (Stop Rape Now, 2016).

Searching for safety and survival, civilians are often "displaced" within their home countries or become refugees in other countries where they reside in camps or urban settlements. According to the UN, 75 to 90 percent of displaced and refugee people are women and their children. While fleeing conflict, they are vulnerable to sexual attacks and sex trafficking at the hands of bandits, smugglers, border guards, and soldiers. Once in refugee camps, they are subject to sexual victimization by government officials, humanitarian workers, international peacekeeping forces, and male refugees, and are sometimes forced to trade sex for services or goods (**survival sex**).

Women and girls remain at risk for sexual violence in the post-conflict period due to ineffective or unstable new governments and undeveloped police and justice systems. For example, in Burundi, high levels of rape and sexual violence continued after the end of the civil conflict in 2003 (Amnesty International, 2007). Most women suffering injuries or illnesses caused by war rape and post-conflict instability do not have access to medical care or counseling and the means of rebuilding their lives. The stigma of rape sometimes leads to their abandonment by their partners or families. Fear of retribution prevents victims from reporting sexual violence perpetrated by the very authorities meant to provide protection (Stop Rape Now, 2016).

For most of human history, conflict-related sexual violence has been overlooked and ignored, but this is finally changing. One of the first signs of change occurred in 1998, when the majority of the world's governments agreed to form a permanent independent international organization called the International Criminal Court (ICC) to investigate and prosecute genocide, crimes against humanity, and war crimes. At first, the ICC's draft treaty initially did not acknowledge rape as a war crime. Women's activists and legal experts worked to have women's concerns incorporated into the treaty establishing the ICC (Frankson, 1998). In 2016, Jean-Pierre Bemba became the first person to be convicted for rape as a war crime and a crime against humanity. Bemba was the commander of a military militia in the Democratic Republic of Congo (DRC) that used rape as a war weapon (he later became vice-president of the DRC).

In 2007, UN Action Against Sexual Violence in Conflict (UN Action) was launched to unite the work of thirteen UN entities with the goal of ending sexual violence in conflict and post-conflict settings. UN Action works with affected countries to develop and implement strategies to combat sexual violence, to provide assistance to sexual violence survivors, and to prosecute perpetrators. Through their Stop Rape Now campaign, they raise awareness and foster outrage against the use of sexual violence as a tactic of war and an impediment to peace. UN Action also serves as a "knowledge hub" on sexual violence in conflict by conducting, supporting, and disseminating research (UN Action, 2015).

Many human rights and women's rights NGOs also work in concert with UN Action, or independently to end war rape and help survivors. For example, through their *Ending Rape as a Weapon of War* initiative, MADRE works with grassroots women's organizations to set up emergency shelters, hotlines, and

Masika Katsura (1966–2016) of the Democratic Republic of Congo (DRC) was a survivor of war rape, along with her two young daughters. Once she recovered, she turned her home into a support center for survivors and their children and traveled to remote areas to rescue victims of conflict-related sexual violence. "Mama Masika" helped thousands of women and children and continued her work even after she experienced multiple gang rapes as punishment. The organization she founded now operates 50 shelters for survivors of conflict-related sexual violence.

"Not only does sexual violence in conflict lead to devastating physical and psychological ramifications for survivors, their families and communities, it is a severe human rights violation constituting an act of torture, a war crime and/or crime against humanity."
Nobel Women's Initiative Report War on Women: Time for Action to End Sexual Violence in Conflict

"Whilst international law and the means by which it is enforced are far from perfect, they remain the best mechanism that the world has to challenge impunity, ensure accountability, and provide justice for victims of genocide, war crimes, and crimes against humanity."
Stephan Simanowitz, Amnesty International

"Rape in war is always a crime. We must send a clear signal that no military or political leader is above the law, and no woman or girl is below it."
Zainab Hawa Bangura, UN Special Representative of the Secretary-General on Sexual Violence in Conflict (Chair of UN Action)

"My body is not your battlefield."
MADRE

In 2016, the United Nations designated June 19th as the International Day for the Elimination of Sexual Violence in Conflict

escape routes. With OWFI (Organization of Women's Freedom in Iraq), and local activists, they run an underground railroad to help kidnapped girls and women held as sex slaves by ISIS. MADRE also partners with women's peace activists to hold governments accountable for their commitments to end war rape and to advocate for the victims of conflict-related sexual violence.

Conclusion

Gender inequality is a violation of women's and girls' human rights. This chapter documented girls' and women's lower power and status compared to boys and men and began our exploration of the intersectional nature of gender inequality. It's important to recognize the social construction of gender inequality. It is not men's nature to oppress women or to sexually harass and assault them, and of course, many men don't. But, as you will see throughout the book, men's individual, intentional acts of dominance over women are the reflections of cultures' overall systems of gender power relations. These can be changed to promote equality but this rarely happens without prolonged advocacy and activism.

Gender psychologist Hillary Lips (1999) once noted that the occurrence of many forms of routine oppression of women by men is mindless and unintentional, often unrecognized by either the perpetrator or the victim. Individuals, more or less unaware of the structure of power that surrounds them, participate in, maintain, and are limited by the power structures of their societies. For instance, many cultures define masculinity in ways that encourage the denigration of women and define femininity in terms of submissiveness and subordination to men. Both girls and boys are socialized into cultures that emphasize men's power over women and are taught to participate in traditionally gendered systems. It must also be acknowledged that many men actively support gender equality and many men do not personally perpetrate gender discrimination or violence against women. These male allies are greatly appreciated.

It is also important to realize that it is not uniquely male to create groups in which some individuals have greater power and status than do others. Women often discourage their girl children from challenging traditional gender relations, and they often participate in the social systems that oppress women. For instance, it is usually adult women that perform the physically traumatizing genital cutting of girls common in some countries. Similarly, the brokers that trick young women into sexual slavery are sometimes women, and women of the upper classes often exploit women of the lower classes (especially those of other ethnicities) for household labor. It generally takes a great deal of activism and vigilance to override the human inclination to exploit and dominate other humans and then justify it by seeing the victims as inferior and deserving of their fate.

Finally, to suggest that women have limited power and status in comparison to men is not to overlook their great strength. Women are really quite remarkable—carrying on, often under conditions of great adversity, in order to keep their families going. Although their lives are frequently hard, they find pleasure in their friends and family, and pride in their strength. Also, despite barriers to their political activity, they fight for their rights, and they have brought about significant change in the last hundred years through their efforts. This is impressive progress given the long history of patriarchy. The domination of women by men has been embedded in most societies' norms, roles, customs, religions, politics, and laws for hundreds—and in some cases, thousands—of years.

Glossary Terms and Concepts

Bride kidnappings
Bride price
Child marriage
Conflict-related sexual
 violence
Domestic violence or
 intimate partner vio-
 lence (IPV)
Dowry
Dowry murder (dowry
 death)
Dowry violence
Forced marriage
Gender wage gap

Gender-biased sex
 selection
Genocidal rape
Girl neglect
Honour killing
Honour-based violence
 (HBV)
Job prestige
Legal literacy
Non-normative rape
Normative rape
Objectifying gaze
Rape
Rape cultures

Sexual assault
Sexual exploitation
Sexual objectification
Sexual violence
Son preference
Street harassment
Survival sex
Trafficking of women
 and girls
Victim blaming
Violence Against Women
 and Girls (VAWG)
Women's suffrage

> The men who hurt women—they're not who we really are. They're dark shadows of ourselves, the aching parts of us projecting out our pain, harming ourselves and harming women. It's time to let in the light on those shadows, exposing them for the true fears they are. It's time to break the rules of that culture and make a new one.
> *Carlos Andrés Gómez, Author of "Man Up: Reimaging Modern Manhood"*

> The UN's Partners for Prevention Programme is implementing interventions in Vietnam, Cambodia, and Papua New Guinea to empower men to challenge harmful masculinities and become volunteers in their communities to lead and engage others in violence prevention.

> "It's not governments or superheroes that will change the world—it's ordinary people who realize that governments and superheroes aren't doing anything."
> *Lauryn Oates, age 20, Canadian Human Rights Activist*

Study Questions

1. What evidence does the chapter provide for the idea that women have less economic power than men? Why does this matter?

2. What evidence does the chapter provide for the idea that women have less political and legal power than men? Why does this matter?

3. What evidence does the chapter provide regarding the lower status of girls and women relative to boys and men?

4. What is gender-biased sex selection, what forms does it take, and where is it practiced? What are some of its effects? What works to combat it?

5. How are women and girls thought of as objects and property? How is this related to their lower status and power?

6. What is forced marriage and child marriage? Why is it a concern? Why does it happen? What is being done about it?

7. What is Violence Against Women and Girls (VAWG) and what forms does it take? Why is it a concern? What is the global prevalence? Why don't victims just leave? What are activists doing to aid victims and reduce it?

8. What are dowry violence and honour-based violence? Where do they occur? How do they illustrate the idea that culture influences IPV?

9. What is sexual violence, and what forms may it take? What is rape? Why is it a leading concern of feminists, and what are they doing in response?

10. What is conflict-related sexual violence, and what forms does it take? Who are the perpetrators? What are the contributors? What is being done about it?

Discussion Questions and Activities

1. In most cultures, it is expected that women will take their husband's name upon marriage, and most heterosexual women do (in the United States, about 80 percent do). Does this tendency reduce a female's value in her family of origin because she doesn't "carry on the family name"? Does this practice contribute to the perception that a woman is the property of her husband and secondary to him? What do you think of the practice of women taking their husband's name upon marriage? How about how fathers "give their daughters away" at the wedding and how the family of the bride is expected to pay for the wedding—is this suggestive of women as the property of their fathers to be given to a husband?

2. The chapter discussed the sexual objectification of women and rape culture. How do you think these concepts apply in your culture?

3. Some people might argue that women and girls have power and status but that it's just different from that of boys and men. After reading the chapter, what would you say if someone said this to you?

4. This chapter discussed women's status in generalities, when in fact there is great diversity not only across countries, but also within them based on geographic location, religion, ethnicity, and social class. Interview a woman from another culture using questions developed from the topics covered in this chapter. Make sure you ask her how long she lived in the other culture, whether where she lived was rural or urban, and what social class she is from, along with other intersectional questions. Share with her the general information about women's status in her country of origin (see the Appendix) and ask for her thoughts.

5. Using UN and human rights websites, identify current areas experiencing conflict-related sexual violence. Refer to Figure 2.4 and identify the form it takes, the phase(s) of conflict in which it occurs, and what is being done about it.

6. Where can women go in your community if they need to escape IPV or have experienced rape? The chapter says that most of these organizations are nonprofits started by local women's groups. What is the history of your community's domestic violence shelter and sexual assault prevention and treatment organizations? Are these services adequate given community needs?

7. The chapter identifies many reasons for the importance of rape as a critical women's issue. One was that fear of rape inhibits women's freedom of movement. What do you think about this? How is your freedom of movement (i.e., travel, going out at night) affected by your efforts to reduce your risk of rape? How are your answers influenced by your gender, sexual orientation, and gender identity? Do you agree that women's need for protection increases their dependency on men? Is that a problem?

8. The chapter briefly said that violence against women and girls is intersectional and some groups of women and girls face more violence than others. Use research to determine which groups of women and girls in your country experience higher rates of violence than others.

Action Opportunities

1. Volunteer at your community's or university's sexual assault prevention and recovery program, or your community's domestic violence shelter. Even if you don't have time to go through the training to be a counselor, you can help out with office duties or fundraising events.

2. Get involved with a "Take Back the Night" demonstration. Held annually around the country in April during Sexual Assault Awareness Month, and often organized by university's gender equity centers, these usually feature a nighttime walk followed by a rally with speakers. Contact your local women's center.

3. Contact your local domestic violence shelter and ask what types of donated goods they need. Common needs include toiletries and cleaning products. Giving people a list as they enter a store and requesting that they purchase one item to be dropped off to you when they leave is one strategy to easily collect these items.

4. Create wallet-sized cards that provide local statistics about violence against women and list local women's resources such as the local shelter and rape prevention and crisis center. Distribute in public places and get permission to leave small piles of them where they may be useful.

5. Use your social media tools and skills and to call out rape culture, reduce victim blaming, and promote justice.

6. Check out the activist websites below for activism opportunities.

Activist Websites

AHA Foundation (focuses on serving women at risk for forced marriage and honour violence in the United States) http://www.theahafoundation.org

ENDTHEBACKLOG http://www.endthebacklog.org/take-action

Girls Not Brides http://www.girlsnotbrides.org

MADRE https://www.madre.org

Men Can Stop Rape https://mcsr.org

Stop Street Harassment http://www.stopstreetharassment.org/toolkits/

Take Back the Night https://takebackthenight.org

UN Action Against Rape in Conflict http://www.stoprapenow.org/

UNiTE Campaign to End Violence Against Women https://www.unwomen.org/en /what-we-do/ending-violence-against-women/take-action

V-Day A Global Movement to End Violence Against Women and Girls http:// www.VDAY.org

Informational Websites

ICRW (International Center for Research on Women) http://www.icrw.org /research-programs/

Preventing Gender-Biased Sex Selection http://www.unfpa.org/resources /preventing-gender-biased-sex-selection

Sexual Violence in Conflict http://www.un.org/sexualviolenceinconflict

UN's Declaration on the Elimination of Violence against Women http://www.umn .edu/humanrts/instree/e4devw.htm

World Health Organization Violence Against Women https://www.who.int/health -topics/violence-against-women#tab=tab_1

The World's Women reports https://unstats.un.org/unsd/demographic-social /products/worldswomen/

References

Amnesty International. 2007. *Burundi: No protection from rape in war and peace.* http://www.amnesty.org/en/library/info/AFR16/002/2007/en. Retrieved on April 4, 2009.

Barot, S. 2012. A problem-and-solution mismatch: Son preference and sex-selective abortion bans. *Guttmacher Policy Review, 15,* 18–22.

Barry, K. 1995. *The prostitution of sexuality.* New York: New York University Press.

BBC News. 2016, July 7. 'No means no' law passed. http://www.bbc.com/news /world-europe-36726095. Retrieved on August 8, 2016.

Bongaarts, J., and Guilmoto, C. Z. 2015. How many more missing women? Excess female mortality and prenatal sex selection, 1970–2050. *Population and Development Review, 41,* 241–269.

Bornstein, R. F. 2006. The complex relationship between dependency and domestic violence. *American Psychologist, 61,* 595–606.

Brewis, K. 2016. Do women stand a sporting chance of closing the gender pay gap? *Newsweek.* http://www.newsweek.com/rio-2016-do-women-stand-sporting-chance-487295. Retrieved on August 4, 2016.

Brownmiller, S. 1986. *Against our will.* New York: Simon and Schuster.

Carillo, R. 1992. *Battered dreams: Violence against women as an obstacle to Development.* New York: UNIFEM.

Centers for Disease Control and Prevention (CDC). 2021. *Preventing intimate partner violence.* https://www.cdc.gov/violenceprevention/intimatepartnerviolence/fastfact.html. Retrieved on February 14, 2021.

Chesler, P. 2009. Are honor killings simply domestic violence? *Middle East Quarterly, Spring,* 61–69.

Chowdhury, N. 1994. Bangladesh: Gender issues and politics in a patriarchy. In *Women and politics worldwide,* edited by B. J. Nelson and N. Chowdhury. New Haven, CT: Yale University Press.

Chuang, J. 2005. The United States as global sheriff: Using unilateral sanctions to combat human trafficking. *Michigan Journal of International Law, 27,* 437.

Chung, W., and Das Gupta, M. 2007. Why is son preference declining in South Korea? The role of development and public policy, and the implications for China and India. *World Bank Policy Research Working Paper Series.*

Citro, B., Gilson, J., Kalantry, S., and Stricker, K. 2014. Replacing myths with facts: Sex-selective abortion laws in the United States. *Cornell University Law School Scholarship@Cornell Law: A Digital Repository.* https://napawf.org/wp-content/uploads/2014/06/Replacing-Myths-with-Facts-final.pdf. Retrieved on July 23, 2016.

Copelon, R. J. 1995. War crimes: Reconceptualizing rape in time of war. In *Women's rights, human rights: International feminist perspectives,* edited by J. Peters and A. Wolper. New York: Routledge.

Doctors Without Borders. 2016. *Return to abuser: Gaps in services and a failure to protect survivors of family and sexual violence in Papua New Guinea.* https://www.doctorswithoutborders.ca/sites/default/files/msf-pngreport-def-ir_0.pdf. Retrieved on February 18, 2021.

Edlund, L., Li, H., Yi, J., and Zhang, J. 2013. Sex ratios and crime: Evidence from China. *Review of Economics and Statistics, 95,* 1520–1534.

Ellison, M. 2016, July 12. Tales of a child bride: 'My father sold me for 12 cows.' *Aljazeera.* https://www.aljazeera.com/features/2016/7/12/tales-of-a-child-bride-my-father-sold-me-for-12-cows. Retrieved on June 8, 2021.

Frankson, J. R. 1998, May/June. Getting our day in court. *Ms., 7,* 19.

Galdi, S., Maass, A., and Cadinu, M. 2014. Objectifying media: Their effect on gender role norms and sexual harassment of women. *Psychology of Women Quarterly, 38,* 398–413.

Gentleman, A. 2015. Breaking the taboo: Moscow women taking a stand against domestic violence. *The Guardian.* https://www.theguardian.com/cities/2015/jun/10/moscow-domestic-violence-problem-russia. Retrieved on August 8, 2016.

Global Network of Women's Shelters. 2015. *2014–2015 Global Shelter Data Count Report.* https://gnws.org/wp-content/uploads/2020/06/gnws_2015_globaldatacount.pdf. Retrieved on March 1, 2021.

Guttmacher Institute. 2016. *Induced abortion worldwide.* https://www.guttmacher.org/fact-sheet/induced-abortion-worldwide Retrieved on September 14, 2016

Guttmacher Institute. 2020. *Banning abortions in cases of race or sex or sex selection.* https://www.guttmacher.org/evidence-you-can-use/banning-abortions-cases-race-or-sex-selection-or-fetal-anomaly. Retrieved on February 15, 2021.

Hayashi-Panos, N. 2013. Grab and run: Kyrgyzstan's bride kidnappings. *Newsweek.* http://www.newsweek.com/grab-and-run-1634. Retrieved on March 5, 2017.

Human Rights Watch. 2015a. *World report Kuwait: Events of 2014.* https://world-report/2015/country-chapters/Kuwait. Retrieved on July 28, 2016.

Human Rights Watch. 2015b. *Bashed up: Family violence in Papau New Guinea.* https://www.hrw.org/sites/default/files/report_pdf/png1115_4up.pdf. Retrieved on August 2, 2016.

Human Rights Watch. 2021. *World Report 2021.* https://www.hrw.org/sites/default/files/media_2021/01/2021_hrw_world_report.pdf. Retrieved on February 3, 2021.

ICRW. 2011. *Solutions to end child marriage: What the evidence shows.* http://www.icrw.org/files/publications/Solutions-to-End-Child-Marriage.pdf. Retrieved on July 29, 2016.

ICRW. 2016. *The issue: Women's assets and property rights.* http://www.icrw.org/what-we-do/property-rights. Retrieved on July 16, 2016.

International Labour Organization (ILO). 2018. *World Employment and Social Outlook: Trends for Women 2018: Global Snapshot.* http://www.ilo.org/wcmsp5/groups/public/–dgreports/–dcomm/–publ/documents/publication/wcms_619577.pdf. Retrieved on February 5, 2021.

International Labour Organization (ILO). 2020. *A quantum leap for gender equality: For a better future for all.* https://www.ilo.org/wcmsp5/groups/public/–dgreports/–dcomm/–publ/documents/publication/wcms_674595.pdf. Retrieved on February 18, 2021.

Inter-parliamentary Union. 2020. *Women in politics: 2020.* https://www.ipu.org/resources/publications/infographics/2020-03/women-in-politics-2020. Retrieved on January 28, 2021.

Inter-parliamentary Union. 2021. *Monthly ranking of women in national parliaments.* https://data.ipu.org/women-ranking?month=1&year=2021. Retrieved on January 29, 2021.

Jha, P., Kumar, R., Vasa, P., Dhingra, N., Thiruchelvam, D., and Moineddin, R. 2006. Low female-to-male sex ratio of children born in India: National survey of 1.1 million households. *Lancet, 367,* 211–218.

Khan, T. S. 2006. *Beyond honour: A historical materialist explanation of honour related violence.* Oxford: Oxford University Press.

Koss, M. P., Heise, L., and Russo, N. F. 1994. The global health burden of rape. *Psychology of Women Quarterly, 18,* 509–537.

Kuwait Society for Human Rights. 2015. *Report on* women's *rights in Kuwait: Submitted to the Committee on the Elimination of Discrimination against Women (CEDAW).* http://tbinternet.ohchr.org/Treaties/CEDAW/Shared%20 Documents/KWT/INT_CEDAW_NGO_KWT_21620_E.pdf. Retrieved on July 20, 2016

Lerner, G. 1986. *The creation of patriarchy,* Vol. 1. New York: Oxford.

Lips, H. M. 1991. *Women, men, and power.* Mountain View, CA: Mayfield.

McFarlane, J., Nava, A., Gilroy, H., and Maddox, J. 2016. Child brides, forced marriage, and partner violence in America. *Obstetrics and Gynecology, 127,* 706–713.

Nanda, P., Gautam, A., Verma, R., Kumar, S., and Brahme, D. 2013. *Masculinity, son preference, and intimate partner violence.* www.icrw.org/publications /masculinity-son-preference-intimate-partner-violence. Retrieved on July 23, 2016.

National Crime Records Bureau. 2020. Crime in India 2019: Statistics Volume 1. https://ncrb.gov.in/sites/default/files/CII%202019%20Volume%201.pdf. Retrieved on February 18, 2021.

Newport, F. 2018. Slight preference for having boy children persists in U.S. *Gallup.* https://news.gallup.com/poll/236513/slight-preference-having-boy-children -persists.aspx. Retrieved on February 12, 2021.

Niarchos, C. N. 1995. Women, war, and rape: Challenges facing the international tribunal for the former Yugoslavia. *Human Rights Quarterly, 17,* 649–690.

OHCHR (Office of the United Nations High Commissioner for Human Rights). 2016. *Informational series on sexual and reproductive health and rights: Violence against women.* http://www.ohchr.org/Documents/Issues /Women/WRGS/SexualHealth/INFO_VAW_WEB.pdf. Retrieved on July 31, 2016.

OpenDemocracy. 2020. Inside the fight over Russia's domestic violence law. https://www.opendemocracy.net/en/odr/russia-domestic-violence-law/. Retrieved on February 18, 2021.

Open Society Foundations. 2016. *Securing women's land and property rights: A critical step to address HIV, violence, and food security.* http://www.icrw.org/sites /default/files/publications/Securing-Womens-Land-Property-Rights-20140307 .pdf. Retrieved on July 19, 2016.

Parrot, A., and Cummings, N. 2006. *Forsaken females: The global brutalization of women*. New York: Rowman and Littlefield Publishers, INC.

Portnoy, J. 2016, July 3. Why 13-year-olds can no longer marry in Virginia. *Washington Post*. https://www.washingtonpost.com/local/virginia-politics /why-13-year-olds-can-no-longer-marry-in-virginia/2016/07/03/03849e46 -3ef9-11e6-a66f-aa6c1883b6b1_story.html?hpid=hp_local-news_vamarriage -1110am%3Ahomepage%2Fstory. Retrieved on July 28, 2016.

Robert F. Kennedy Human Rights. 2016. *Marina Pisklakova: Interview with Kerry Kennedy*. http://rfkcenter.org/what-we-do/speak-truth-power /defenders-curriculum/marina-pisklakova-lesson/. Retrieved on August 6, 2016.

Rosaldo, M. Z. 1974. Women, culture, and society: A theoretical overview. In *Women, culture, and society,* edited by M. Z. Rosaldo and L. Lamphere. Stanford, CA: Stanford University Press.

Sattar, A. 2015. The laws of honour killing and rape in Pakistan: Current status and future prospects. *AAWAZ Programme*. http://aawaz.org.pk/cms/lib /downloadfiles/1448430520v2%20Final%20AS%20Laws.pdf. Retrieved on August 9, 2016.

Sebastian, C., and Mortensen, A. 2017. Putin signs law reducing punishment for domestic battery. *CNN*. http://www.cnn.com/2017/02/07/europe/russia -domestic-violence-bill-putin/. Retrieved on March 18, 2017.

Singh, J., and Anand, E. 2015. The nexus between child marriage and women empowerment with physical violence in two culturally distinct states of India. *International Journal of Population Research, 2015*, 1–9.

Smith, S. G., Zhang, X., Basile, K. C. Merrick, M. T., Wang, J., Kresnow, M., and Chen, J. 2018. The National Intimate Partner and Sexual Violence Survey: 2015 data brief. https://www.cdc.gov/violenceprevention/pdf/2015data-brief508.pdf. Retrieved on February 20, 2021.

Speak Truth to Power. 2016. *Marina Pisklakova*. http://blogs.nysut.org/sttp /defenders/marina-pisklakova/. Retrieved on August 6, 2016.

Srinivasan, S., and Bedi, A. S. 2007. Domestic violence and dowry: Evidence from a south Indian Village. *World Development, 35,* 857–880.

Srinivasan, S. 2005. Daughters or dowries? The changing nature of dowry practices in south India. *World Development, 33,* 593–615.

Stop Rape Now. 2016. *Report of the Secretary-General on conflict-related sexual violence*. http://stoprapenow.org/uploads/advocacyresources/1464291095.pdf. Retrieved on August 12, 2016.

Tahirih Justice Center. 2020. Making progress, but still falling short: A report on the movement to end child marriage in America. https://1ttls613brjl37btxk4eg60v-wpengine.netdna-ssl.com/wp-content /uploads/2020/01/Reflection-Paper_Making-Progress-But-Still-Falling-Short _FINAL-with-map_May-13_2020.pdf. Retrieved on February 16, 2021.

Times of India. 2013, September 1. Dowry deaths: One woman dies every hour. http://timesofindia.indiatimes.com/india/Dowry-deaths-One-woman-dies-every -hour/articleshow/22201659.cms. Retrieved on August 6, 2016.

UN Action. 2015. *UN Action Against Sexual Violence in Conflict.* http://www .stoprapenow.org/uploads/advocacyresources/1451943991.pdf. Retrieved on August 13, 2016.

UN Secretary-General. 2020. *Conflict-related sexual violence: Report of the United Nations Secretary General.* https://www.un.org/sexualviolenceinconflict/wp -content/uploads/2020/07/report/conflict-related-sexual-violence-report-of-the -united-nations-secretary-general/2019-SG-Report.pdf. Retrieved on March 6, 202.

UN Women. 2013. *Informal justice systems: Charting a course for human rights-based engagement.* http://www2.unwomen.org/~/media/headquarters/attachments /sections/library/publications/2011/progressoftheworldswomen-2011 -executivesummary-en.pdf?v=1andd=20150402T222839. Retrieved on July 19, 2016.

UN Women. 2016. *Progress of the world's women 2015-2016: Transforming economies, realizing rights.* http://progress.unwomen.org/en/2015/pdf/UNW _progressreport.pdf. Retrieved on July 18, 2016.

UN Women. 2018. *Turning Promises into Action: Gender Equality in the 2030 Agenda for Sustainable Development.* https://www.unwomen.org/en/digital-library /publications/2018/2/gender-equality-in-the-2030-agenda-for-sustainable -development-2018. Retrieved on January 29, 2021.

UN Women. 2019. *World Survey on the role of women in development 2019.* https:// www.unwomen.org/-/media/headquarters/attachments/sections/library /publications/2019/world-survey-on-the-role-of-women-in-development-2019 .pdf?la=en&vs=2027. Retrieved on February 12, 2021.

UN Women. 2020. *Families in a changing world: Progress of the World's Women 2019-2020.* https://www.unwomen.org/-/media/headquarters/attachments /sections/library/publications/2019/progress-of-the-worlds-women-2019-2020-en .pdf?la=en&vs=3512. Retrieved on February 13, 2021.

Unchained At Last. 2016. *Laws to end child marriage.* http://www.unchainedatlast .org/laws-to-end-child-marriage/. Retrieved on July 29, 2016.

UNFPA (United Nations Population Fund). 2005. *State of the world popula- tion.* www.unfpa.org/swp/2005/english/ch1/index.htm. Retrieved on April 9, 2009.

UNFPA (United Nations Population Fund). 2009. *UNFPA report: Status of repro- ductive morbidities in Nepal.* http://www.un.org.np.sites/default/file/report /tid_67/2009-03-17-UNFPA-status-morbidity.pdf. Retrieved on September 4, 2016.

UNFPA (United Nations Population Fund). 2012. *Sex imbalances at birth.* http:// www.unfpa.org/publications/sex-imbalances-birth.

UNICEF (United Nations Children's Fund). 2006. *The state of the world's children 2007: Women and Children.* New York: United Nations Children's Fund.

UNICEF (United Nations Children's Fund). 2013. *Breaking the silence in violence against indigenous girls, adolescents, and young women.* http://www.unfpa.org /sites/default/files/resource-pdf/VAIWG_FINAL.pdf. Retrieved on August 4, 2016.

UNICEF (United Nations Children's Fund). 2015. *Child marriage, adolescent pregnancy and family formation in West and Central Africa.* http://www.icrw.org /sites/default/files/publications/Child_Mariage_Adolescent_Pregnancy_and _Family_Formation.pdf. Retrieved on July 28, 2016.

UNICEF. 2020. Child marriage. http://data.unicef.org/topic/child-protection/child -marriage. Retrieved on February 14, 2021.

United Nations Department of Economic and Social Affairs (DESA). 2019. *World Population Prospects 2019.* http://population.un.org.wpp/Download/Standard /Population/. Retrieved on February 16, 2021.

United Nations Office on Drugs and Crime (UNODC). 2019. *Global study on homicide: Gender-related killing of women and girls.* https://www.unodc .org/documents/data-and-analysis/gsh/Booklet_pdf. Retrieved on February 18, 2021.

United Nations Population Fund (UNFPA). 2020. *Against my will: Defying the practices that harm women and girls and undermine equality: State of the World Population 2020.* https://www.unfpa.org/sites/default/files/pub-pdf/UNFPA_PUB_2020_EN _State_of_World_Population.pdf. Retrieved on February 29, 2021.

WHO (World Health Organization). 2011. *Preventing gender-biased sex selection.* http://www.who.int/reproductivehealth/publications/gender_rights /9789241501460/en/. Retrieved on April 14, 2021.

WHO (World Health Organization). 2013. *Global and regional estimates of violence against women: Prevalence and health effects of intimate partner violence and non -partner sexual violence.* https://www.who.int/publications/i/item/9789241564625. Retrieved on June 30, 2021.

WHO (World Health Organization). 2017. Violence against women: Key facts. https://www.who.int/news-room/fact-sheets/detail/violence-against-women. Retrieved on February 18, 2021.

WHO (World Health Organization). 2019. *Trends in maternal mortality: 2000 to 2017.* https://apps.who.int/iris/handle/10665/327596. Retrieved on February 14, 2021.

WHO (World Health Organization). 2020. *Global status report on preventing violence against children 2020.* https://www.unicef.org/media/70731/file /Global-status-report-on-preventing-violence-against-children-2020.pdf. Retrieved on February 25, 2021.

World Bank. 2020. *Women, business, and the law 2020.* http://openknowledge. worldbank.org/bitstream/handle/10986/32639/9781464815324.pdf. Retrieved on February 18, 2021.

Zhu, W. X., Lu, L., and Hesketh, T. 2009. China's excess males, sex selective abortion, and one child policy: Analysis of data from 2005 national intercensus survey. *British Medical Journal, 338,* b1211.

Design Element: Abstract floral frame: Telnov Oleksii/Shutterstock

3

Reproductive Health and Reproductive Rights

". . . Good health is essential to leading a productive and fulfilling life, and the right of all women to
control all aspects of their health, in particular their
own fertility, is basic to their empowerment."

—United Nations Fourth World Conference for Women,
Beijing Platform for Action, para. 92

*This woman is from Ethiopia, a country in sub-Saharan Africa where women have
a life expectancy of age 67, female genital mutilation is prevalent, and maternal
mortality and disability are high. Women's reproductive health and rights are
critical issues worldwide although intersectionality and context lead to variation.*
hadynyah/Getty Images

The focus of this chapter is women's reproductive health and reproductive rights.[1] **Reproductive health** includes an array of topics and concerns including family planning, reproductive tract infections such as sexually transmitted diseases and HIV/AIDS, infertility, maternal mortality (pregnancy-related death), maternal morbidity (pregnancy-related illness and disability), unsafe abortion, reproductive tract cancers, and traditional harmful practices such as female genital mutilation/female genital cutting (FGM/FGC). Globally, HIV/AIDS is the leading cause of death for women of reproductive age (UNAIDS, 2020). Many of these deaths and health conditions are entirely preventable. **Reproductive rights** refer to the right to reproductive health care and the right to reproductive self-determination (Center for Reproductive Rights, 2006).

At the 1994 International Conference on Population and Development (ICPD), 179 countries agreed that sexual and reproductive health and reproductive rights are fundamental human rights. The ICPD Programme of Action (1994, para 7.3) proclaimed reproductive rights as including the right of all couples and individuals to decide freely and responsibly the number, spacing, and timing of their children and to have the information and means to do so, and the right to attain the highest standard of sexual and reproductive health. They also include the right of all to make decisions concerning reproduction free of discrimination, coercion, and violence. Reproductive rights are consistent with basic human rights agreed upon at major international and regional UN conferences by UN member nations and are incorporated into international development agendas, such as the Millennium Development Goals and the Sustainable Development Goals. For instance, Goal 5 of the UN's Sustainable Development Goals (Achieve Gender Equality and Empower All Women and Girls) includes Target 5.6, "Ensure universal access to sexual and reproductive health and reproductive rights as agreed in accordance with the Programme of Action of the International Conference on Population and Development and the Beijing Platform for Action." Activists often frame women's reproductive health and choice in terms of human rights agreements and human rights law to bring about legal and policy changes in their countries. Box 3.1 displays twelve human rights that are consistent with reproductive rights.

Reproductive rights mean having **reproductive control**. According to Jacobson (1992), a woman's reproductive control can be determined by her answers to the following questions: Can she control when and with whom she will engage in sexual relations? Can she do so without fear of infection or unwanted pregnancy? Can she choose when and how to regulate her fertility, free from unpleasant or dangerous side effects of contraception? Can she go through pregnancy and childbirth safely? Can she obtain a safe abortion on request? Can she easily obtain information on the prevention and treatment of reproductive illnesses?

Women's reproductive rights are a critical global feminist issue because for millions of women worldwide the answer to some or all of the above questions is "no," and

"When a woman is denied her reproductive rights—when she is denied obstetric care, birth control, the facts about reproductive health, or safe abortion . . . she is denied the means to direct her own life, protect her health, and exercise her human rights."
Center for Reproductive Rights

---

[1]The material in this chapter may also apply to people that do not identify as women, such as transgender men, and those who are intersex or nonbinary.

BOX 3.1   *Twelve Human Rights Key to Reproductive Rights*

1. The Right to Life

2. The Right to Liberty and Security of Person

3. The Right to Health, including Sexual and Reproductive Health

4. The Right to Decide the Number and Spacing of Children

5. The Right to Consent to Marriage and to Equality in Marriage

6. The Right to Privacy

7. The Right to Equality and Non-Discrimination

8. The Right to be Free from Practices that Harm Women and Girls

9. The Right to Not Be Subjected to Torture or Other Cruel, Inhuman, or Degrading Treatment or Punishment

10. The Right to be Free from Sexual and Gender-Based Violence

11. The Right to Access Sexual and Reproductive Health Education and Family Planning Information

12. The Right to Enjoy the Benefits of Scientific Progress

Source: Center for Reproductive Rights, *Reproductive Rights Are Human Rights.*

this affects women's status, power, economic situation, and health. Women cannot fully realize their human rights without their reproductive rights. Hundreds of thousands of women die or are seriously disabled every year because they lack reproductive control. Without reproductive control, women are at greater risk for sexually transmitted infections, unwanted pregnancy, and unsafe abortion. Lacking reproductive control, many women have multiple children in close succession and spend their adult lives in poverty while pregnant, nursing, and caring for their children. Their important maternal responsibilities limit their education and their participation in the paid labor force and in the formal political sphere, thereby contributing to their lower power and to gender inequality. Figure 3.1 shows the factors that constrain women's reproductive rights and health that are discussed in this chapter.

"Reproductive health and rights are cornerstones of women's empowerment."
United Nations Population Fund (UNFPA)

Although the focus of this chapter is women's reproductive health and rights, there are many ways in which health risks, experiences, and outcomes are different for women and girls compared to men and boys (WHO, 2007). Some of these **gender health disparities** are a consequence of gender inequality. For example, gender inequality leads to many health hazards for women, including intimate partner violence, sexual violence, and HIV/AIDS (WHO, 2009). Globally, moderate and severe food insecurity (going without eating, not having enough to eat, or not having the resources for healthy food) is significantly higher for women in comparison to men (Food and Agriculture Organization, 2021). In the United States, medical practice and research are disproportionately focused on men (Johnson et al., 2014). It is also important to recognize the role of intersectionality

FIGURE 3.1 *Common Factors Affecting Women's Reproductive Rights and Choice*

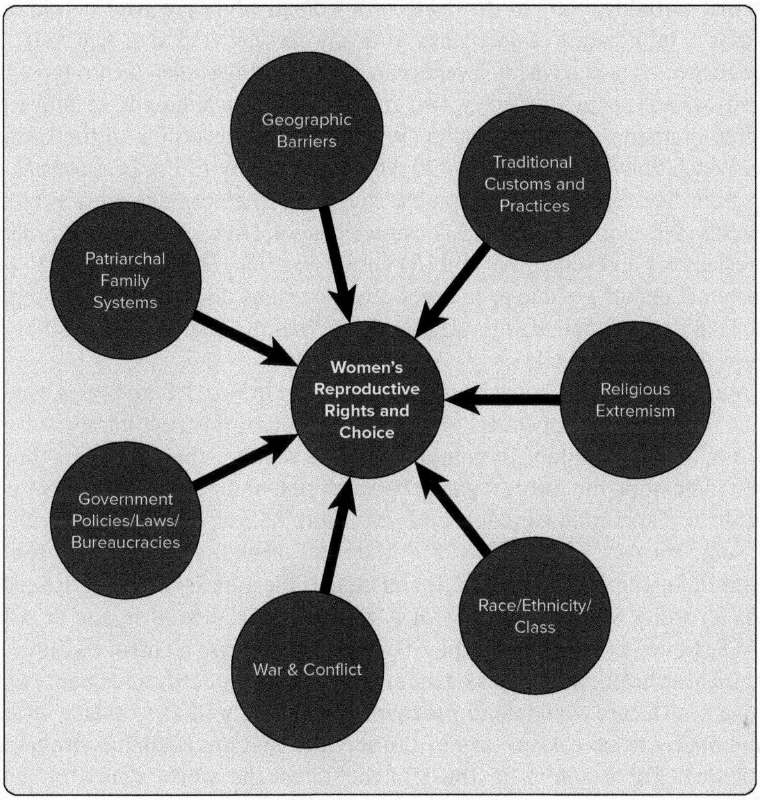

in women's health. Age, class, ethnicity, culture, region, sexual orientation, gender identity, and religion influence the health threats women face, their lifespans, and the availability and quality of their health care. In the United States, for example, Black and indigenous (Native American) women are almost three times more likely to die from pregnancy-related complications than white women and are twice as likely to have serious pregnancy complications (Center for Reproductive Rights, 2021a).

Although discussions of reproductive rights tend to focus on women because their health and equality are more affected in comparison to men's, it's important to recognize that reproductive rights and choice are not only women's issues. As sexual partners, husbands, fathers, and family members, women's reproductive choice and health significantly impact men (United Nations, 2014). Men also need family planning and reproductive health information not only for women's well-being, but also for their own and their family's well-being.

"Men have a stake in reproductive rights through their multiple roles as sexual partners, husbands, fathers, family and household members, community leaders, and gatekeepers to health information and services."
United Nations

Maternal Mortality and Morbidity

Maternal Mortality

Maternal mortality refers to the death of a woman while pregnant or within forty-two days of termination of pregnancy from any cause related to or aggravated by the pregnancy or its management. Every year, over 295,000 women die from pregnancy-related causes, about one every two minutes, leaving hundreds of thousands of children motherless and vulnerable (WHO, 2019a). According to the United Nations Population Fund (UNFPA, 2019b), the majority (75%) of maternal deaths arise from five direct and preventable causes: (1) hemorrhage (severe bleeding), (2) sepsis (systemic infection), (3) obstructed labor, (4) hypertensive disorders such as preclampsia and eclampsia, and (5) unsafe abortion. However, about 25 percent of maternal deaths are due to indirect causes such as diseases that are more likely to be fatal in combination with pregnancy, such as malaria, anemia, cardiovascular disease, diabetes, and AIDS.

"No woman should die giving life."
United Nations Population Fund (UNFPA)

Maternal mortality rates by region are shown in Box 3.2, and rates by country can be found in the Appendix. Maternal mortality ratios (the number of women that don't survive childbirth compared to the number that do) show that of all health indicators, the greatest gap is between rich and poor countries; 94 percent occur in low- and middle-income countries, with 86 percent in sub-Saharan Africa and Southern Asia (WHO, 2019a).[2] Maternal mortality rates also differ within countries. In the United States, for instance, the rate is 11.8 per 100,000 live births for white women and 31.7 for African American women, and in Arkansas it's 45.9, while in California it's 11.7 (Centers for Disease Control and Prevention, 2021). These health disparities occur mostly because quantity and quality of reproductive health care available to pregnant women—as well as women's knowledge of and ability to take advantage of the services that are available—are unequally distributed. For example, in the United States, the worst states for maternal health declined to expand Medicaid such that many lack health insurance. They have more abortion restrictions, fewer maternal health providers and programs, and more income inequality and racial segregation. Generally, wealthier nations, urban locations, and social groups with higher incomes and education have lower rates of maternal mortality (Dixon-Mueller, 1993).

The good news is that maternal mortality is 38 percent lower than it was in 2000. Since 1990, 172 countries and territories reduced maternal mortality and only 13 saw an increase (WHO, 2019a). The United States was one of the two high-income nations (the Bahamas was the other) that experienced an increase; from 2000 to 2017, maternal mortality in the United States increased by 19.3 percent (Centers for Disease Control and Prevention, 2021). Angola, Cambodia, Nepal, Rwanda, and Timor-Leste reduced maternal mortality by 66 percent. The dramatic global reduction in maternal mortality reflects a commitment made by

---

[2]Developing countries are countries with low standards of living and high poverty relative to countries with more developed economies. See Chapter 6 for a list of the world's least developed countries.

BOX 3.2   *Maternal Death Rates*

A woman's lifetime risk of dying due to maternal causes is:

- 1 in 37 in sub-Saharan Africa

- 1 in 260 in North Africa

- 1 in 250 in South Asia

- 1 in 320 in Southeast Asia

- 1 in 640 in Latin America and the Caribbean

- 1 in 690 in Oceania

- 1 in 56 in least developed regions

- 1 in 5,400 in high-income regions (in the United States, 1 in 3,000)

- 1 in 190 global lifetime risk

Source: World Health Organization (2019a), *Trends in Maternal Mortality: 2000 to 2017.*

United Nations Member States in 2000 to the **Millennium Development Goals (MDGs)**, the focus of which was to end poverty. These goals included a target of reducing maternal deaths by three-quarters by 2015, which resulted in many national, international, and grassroots programs and initiatives to improve maternal health. In 2015, world leaders committed to the **UN's Agenda for Sustainable Development for 2030**, which includes seventeen sustainable development goals (SDGs), each with multiple targets. One of these, Goal 3: Ensure Healthy Lives and Promote Well-Being for All At All Ages, includes a target of reducing the global maternal mortality ratio from the 2015 level of 216 per 100,000 births to less than 70 per 100,000 births by 2030.

Reaching the 2030 target requires both the will and the resources to address the causes of maternal death. Improved access to health care during pregnancy (known as **prenatal care** or **antenatal care**), skilled birth attendants, timely access to emergency obstetric care, and postnatal care are key to preventing maternal deaths. Evidence for this can be seen in the 44 percent drop in maternal mortality in developing countries from 1990 to 2015 (World Health Organization, 2015). For example, since 2000, the percentage of births attended by a skilled health professional has increased from 34 to 61 percent in the world's least developed countries (UNICEF, 2020a). Reducing child marriage also reduces maternal mortality, since child brides often become pregnant before their pelvises are fully developed (complications from pregnancy and childbirth are the leading cause of death among girls 15–19 in low- and middle-income countries; WHO, 2016). Access to safe, effective, and affordable contraception also reduces maternal death by allowing women to avoid multiple pregnancies in close succession and by reducing the need for women to seek unsafe abortions. Safe and legal abortion also reduces maternal death (this is discussed in more detail later in the chapter).

"Making motherhood safer is a human rights imperative."
United Nations Population Fund (UNFPA)

Maternal Morbidity

For each woman who dies as a result of pregnancy or childbirth, another twenty to thirty survive but suffer from health conditions or disability arising from pregnancy or childbirth (Firoz et al., 2013). The term for these pregnancy-related health conditions is **maternal morbidity**. A variety of such health conditions and disabilities negatively impacts women's well-being. These include **uterine prolapse**, a condition wherein the supporting pelvic structure of muscles, tissue, and ligaments gives way, and the uterus drops into or even out of the vagina. Also known as pelvic organ prolapse, the condition occurs due to giving birth at a young age, difficult prolonged labor, frequent pregnancies, inadequate obstetric care, and lack of rest and engaging in strenuous work during and soon after pregnancy. Often accompanied by back and abdominal pain, painful urination, defecation, and intercourse, the condition makes daily life uncomfortable and challenging. Many women live with the condition because they lack access to health care. Data is scarce but studies of pelvic organ prolapse in low- and middle-income countries find from 3 to 56 percent of women experience it, with a mean prevalence rate of close to 20 percent of women (Jokhio, Rizvi, & McArthur, 2020).

"Gender discrimination is the cause and consequence of uterine prolapse."
Amnesty International Report, Unnecessary Burden

Depression, anemia, and obstetric fistula are also common pregnancy-related disabilities. **Obstetric fistula**, a childbirth injury, is a current focus of activism and advocacy efforts. It arises from prolonged and obstructed labor, often in young women who are not physically mature or in those who have a small pelvis from nutritional deficits during childhood. Fistula occurs when tissues between the vaginal wall and the bladder or rectum are torn during childbirth, resulting in incontinence, infections, ulceration, and nerve damage (fistula can also arise from rape or other sexual violence). Access to medical care has virtually eliminated fistula in industrialized countries, but an estimated two million women live with fistula in developing countries, with an additional 50,000 to 100,000 new cases occurring annually (UNFPA 2016a). The babies usually die from the obstructed labor, and the women are often ostracized and abandoned because fistula makes personal hygiene difficult to maintain. Many are unaware that treatment is possible. Box 3.3 tells the story of *Agaicha*, a Malian woman who experienced fistula.

"I gave birth to my first daughter and after six days I went to bring millet from the farm. I was carrying a load of millet and I felt that something was coming out of my vagina."
Kesar Kala Malla, Mugu District, Nepal

"Obstetric fistula is one of the most devastating consequences of unequal access to health care during pregnancy and childbirth. Its persistence is a sure signal that health systems in many low-income countries are failing to meet the needs of women."
Campaign to End Fistula

The UNFPA's (United Nations Population Fund) Campaign to End Fistula operates in over 50 countries across Africa, Asia, the Arab region, and Latin America and emphasizes a variety of preventative measures, including increasing family planning services, improving access to maternal health care, reducing early marriage, and improving girls' nutrition. In addition to prevention, the UN and NGOs,

BOX 3.3　*Agaicha's Obstetric Fistula Experience*

Agaicha lives in Mali, a country in sub-Saharan Africa with a high maternal mortality rate (562 per 100,000 births). Over 50 percent of women are married and have their first child before age 18.

"When I was 15, my father arranged my marriage. Soon after I married, I was pregnant. I spent five days laboring in the hands of the village women, battling for my life and battling to give birth. On the sixth day, my uncle took me from the village to the nearest health center, 65 km (about 40 miles) away where an unskilled health provider pulled the baby out by force. My son was dead. The following day, my torment started: I could not control my bladder anymore.

After I came back from the health center, my friends and most of my in-laws family deserted me. At age 16, this rejection and isolation was more painful and destructive than my physical handicap. I thought that if my mother had been alive, she would have taken good care of me. But she had died of a massive hemorrhage while in labor. Things went on like this for two years. Then my father heard on the radio that it's possible to treat this sickness. He gave up everything he had to take me to Gao and stay with me there for 45 days.

When my husband heard that I was healed, he sent a delegation to pick me up, but I refused and fled. The manager of a nongovernmental organization (NGO) called Greffa took me in. Now, I help this NGO to help other women who are suffering from the same disease. I also raise awareness about this condition in villages."

———————
Fistula Care Plus https://fistulacare.org/stories-from-the-field/survivor-stories/Mali/agaicha/.

including the Fistula Foundation, One by One, WADADIA, Engender Health, and Amref Health Africa, offer and promote programs to repair physical damage through surgery (a simple surgery that costs about $400 can repair most fistulas) and treat emotional damage through counseling.

Female Genital Mutilation

Another source of reproductive health problems for women is the practice of **female genital mutilation** (FGM), also known as **female genital cutting** (FGC) and **female genital circumcision** (FC). The terminology is a matter of some debate, as some feel the label FGM is culturally insensitive. Others feel that FGC and FC are too mild in their connotations, and that FC suggests that the practice is equivalent to male circumcision when in fact it is far more severe. UNFPA and UNICEF currently use female genital mutilation (FGM).

FGM refers to all procedures involving partial or total removal of the external female genitalia or other injury to the female genital organs for cultural or other nonmedical reasons (UNFPA-UNICEF, 2020). In most cases, a midwife or practiced village woman performs FGM using various tools (knives, razors, scissors, rocks, glass) that may or may not be sterilized (UNICEF, 2013). Approximately

"In 1948, the Universal Declaration of Human Rights of the United Nations said: 'Everyone has the right to . . . medical care. Motherhood and childhood are entitled to special care and assistance.' Therefore, we also see fistula as a basic violation of human rights, a call to action to cry out against this injustice."
Worldwide Fistula Fund

May 23 is the International Day to End Obstetric Fistula (#FistulaDay), which promotes action toward treating and preventing obstetric fistula.

"Circumcision makes women clean, promotes virginity and chastity and guards young girls from sexual frustration by deadening their sexual appetite."
Female defender of FGM in Kenya

"You have one woman holding your mouth so you won't scream, two holding your chest and the other two holding your legs. After we were infibulated, we had rope tied across our legs so it was like we had to learn to walk again. We had to try to go to the toilet. If you couldn't pass water in the next 10 days something was wrong."
Zainab, who was infibulated at age 8

"FGM is one of the worst forms of violence against women."
Zipporah Kittony, Member of Kenya's Parliament

"I will circumcise my daughter because I don't want people to say that my girl is empty, I want her to be beautiful and her thing [to be] shiny like a mirror."
Somalian mother

1 in 4 FGM survivors were cut by health personnel. The growing medicalization of FGM is of concern because FGM is a human rights violation and has serious consequences for girls and women, whether it's performed by a health professional or not (UNICEF, 2020b).

There are four types of FGM (UNICEF, 2013; World Health Organization, 2020a):

- Type I: **Clitoridectomy**. Partial or total removal of the clitoris. Sometimes referred to as *sunna*.

- Type II: **Excision**. Partial or total removal of the clitoris and the labia minora, with or without excision of the labia majora.

- Type III: **Infibulation**. Narrowing of the vaginal opening through the creation of a covering seal formed by cutting and stitching the labia minora or labia majora, with or without clitoridectomy. The urethra and vaginal opening are almost completely covered.

- Type IV: Other forms involving no removal of tissue or alteration of the genitalia, such as pricking, piercing or incising, stretching, burning of the clitoris, scraping of tissue surrounding the vaginal orifice, cutting of the vagina. Sometimes called *symbolic circumcision*.

In some areas, FGM is carried out during infancy, but in others it occurs during childhood, at the time of marriage, during a woman's first pregnancy, or after the birth of her first child. It is usually performed before age 15, and about 50 percent of the time, before age 5 (UNICEF, 2013). More than 200 million girls and women alive today have undergone FGM and an estimated 4 million more each year is projected from 2019 to 2030 (UNFPA, 2020a; WHO, 2020a). Box 3.4 lists the countries where FGM is commonly practiced. Most of these are in sub-Saharan Africa, but FGM is also practiced in parts of the Arab countries of Iraq and Yemen, and in Southeast Asia in Indonesia. Due to international migration, the number of girls and women who have undergone FGM (or are at risk for it) has grown in Western Europe and in the United States, Canada, Australia, and New Zealand. Although religion is sometimes used to justify FGM, it is practiced by Muslims, Christians, Ethiopian Jews, and Copts, as well as by followers of certain traditional African religions (UNFPA, 2020a).

The negative health consequences of FGM are often significant, and it offers no medical benefits. Short-term medical consequences include severe pain, hemorrhage, infection, shock, and death. The long-term consequences of narrowing the vaginal opening include urinary retention and infections, difficulty menstruating, and difficulty having and enjoying sex (World Health Organization, 2020a). Genital infections, reproductive tract infections, and obstetric fistula are also long-term health risks (Berg et al., 2014). Women who have undergone FGM are at significantly higher risk for adverse obstetric outcomes such as Caesarean sections, hemorrhaging, prolonged labor, instrumental delivery, obstetric tears, infant trauma and death, and maternal mortality, with the risks especially great for those with more extensive FGM forms (Berg & Underland, 2013).

BOX 3.4   *FGM Prevalence: Percentage of Girls and Women Aged 15 to 49*

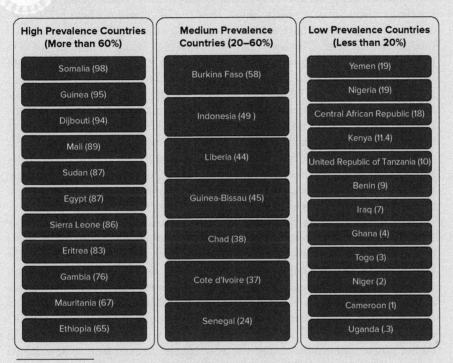

High Prevalence Countries (More than 60%)	Medium Prevalence Countries (20–60%)	Low Prevalence Countries (Less than 20%)
Somalia (98)	Burkina Faso (58)	Yemen (19)
Guinea (95)		Nigeria (19)
Djibouti (94)	Indonesia (49)	Central African Republic (18)
Mali (89)		Kenya (11.4)
Sudan (87)	Liberia (44)	United Republic of Tanzania (10)
Egypt (87)	Guinea-Bissau (45)	Benin (9)
Sierra Leone (86)		Iraq (7)
Eritrea (83)	Chad (38)	Ghana (4)
Gambia (76)		Togo (3)
Mauritania (67)	Cote d'Ivoire (37)	Niger (2)
Ethiopia (65)	Senegal (24)	Cameroon (1)
		Uganda (.3)

Source: UNICEF (2020). *Global data bases: Female Genital Mutilation*.

Efforts are underway to eradicate FGM and they are making a difference. According to the UNFPA (2019), in the last 25 years the prevalence of FGM fell from 49 percent to 31 percent in the countries where it is most frequently practiced. However, due to population growth, the number of girls and women affected has increased. The first campaigns were health risk approaches focused on educating about the harmful medical consequences of FGM. These campaigns had a limited effect and contributed to medicalization of the practice (UNICEF, 2013). Human rights approaches emphasize that FGM/FGC violates major international human rights such as the right to be free from all forms of gender discrimination, the right to be free from torture, the right to health and to bodily integrity, and children's right to special protections. FGM was first recognized as a human rights violation at the 1993 World Conference on Human Rights in Vienna where it was identified as a form of violence against women (UNICEF, 2013). In 2012, the United Nations General Assembly agreed on a resolution (67/146) urging UN Member States to pursue a comprehensive, culturally sensitive approach to eliminating FGM based

"Eradicating FGM does not take one single individual or organization; it's a collective effort by civil society, government, and young people. It's time we stood up for every girl. A world where women are not free is not a just world."
Amie Bojang Sissoho, GAMCOTRAP, Gambia

February 6 is the International Day of Zero Tolerance for Female Genital Mutilation #EndFGM

"Families expect other families to cut their daughters, and they believe other families expect them to cut their own daughters. They believe if they do not, they may be criticized or excluded, and their daughters may not be able to marry."
UNFPA Manual on Social Norms and Change

on human rights and gender equality principles. Goal 5 of the UN's Sustainable Development Goals, "Achieve gender equality and empower all women and girls," includes the target, "Eliminate all harmful practices, such as child, early and forced marriage and female genital mutilation by 2030" (UN DESA, 2021).

Legislative approaches focus on the passing of laws criminalizing or restricting the practice. Since the early 1990s, 26 of the 29 countries where FGM/FGC is commonly practiced have enacted laws, many resulting from grassroots and international activism. The laws vary, with penalties ranging from fines to life in prison. Thirty-three countries that receive immigrants from countries where FGM is practiced have also passed laws (UNICEF, 2013). For example, a 1996 U.S. law made it illegal to perform FGM/FGC. Activist Jaha Dukureh, a FGM/FGC survivor living in Atlanta (in the American state of Georgia) was instrumental in getting the law amended in 2012 to make it illegal to knowingly transport a girl outside of the United States for the procedure in what is known as "vacation cutting." For the most part though, police and judges fail to arrest and punish perpetrators, and families and practitioners conspire to keep their actions secret. In Egypt, for example, where 87 percent of women have undergone FGM, FGM was banned in 2008, but the first case to be prosecuted was in 2013 (Michaelson, 2016).

While health, human rights, and legal approaches are important for reducing FGM, they are increasingly acknowledged as incomplete because FGM occurs in a broader social context that influences its occurrence (UNICEF, 2013). For example, while laws are important, they alone can't change the social norms and traditional customs that support the practice. Cultural and social norms approaches acknowledge that FGM are entrenched cultural practices that are best understood and changed by the people in those cultures. These approaches consider FGM/FGC to be a social norm in the communities in which it's practiced. Like other social norms, people conform because they fear social rejection and want to be accepted members of their communities (and their children to be accepted as well). People also conform because they accept their community's beliefs about the desirability of a practice—in the case of FGM, people often believe myths that perpetuate the practice, for example, that it's necessary for hygiene, beauty, to control women's sexuality, or to preserve virginity, or that it's a religious requirement.

Social norms approaches target the social norms underlying the practice by mobilizing influential community members and groups to express their belief that the practice should change. Research finds that in most countries where FGM is practiced, a majority of girls and women, men and boys believe it should end, though there are educational and ethnic differences in attitudes toward FGM (UNICEF, 2013). People where FGM is practiced often believe it is more socially accepted and expected than it is and so don't share their own desires for change. They conform because they anticipate negative social consequences for their daughters and family such as ridicule, shame, or exclusion. Social norms approaches are intended to correct these social misperceptions that lead to pluralistic ignorance. Individuals and groups within a culture are encouraged to be catalysts for change by using their social networks to correct misconceptions about FGM and express support for its abandonment.

Programs targeting social norms can take a variety of forms, including enlisting the support of religious leaders, training midwives to educate women so they will choose not to cut their daughters, and public service announcements. Anti-FGM cyberactivism, including the provision of online multimedia tools, is also growing (Julios, 2019). *The Girl Generation: Together to End FGM*, supported by international NGO Equality Now, includes a social media campaign designed to highlight support for ending FGM. In Ethiopia, a UN program fostered the development of anti-FGM committees in six districts comprised of a village elder, the local clan leader, the community's religious leader, and a former FGM practitioner. These groups were successful in gaining community commitment to abandon the practice; 7,000 girls were spared between 2008 and 2013 (UNICEF, 2014).

Chapter 1 said it is important to avoid ethnocentricity and cultural superiority when studying global women. Cultural sensitivity is clearly important when it comes to FGM. African feminists often feel that Western feminists (feminists from Western Europe and the United States) are arrogant and demeaning in their study of and attitudes toward those who practice FGM. They remind us that although it is tempting to see cultures where FGM is practiced as barbaric and woman-hating, the practice is not intended to harm girls and women. It occurs because parents love their daughters and want them to be socially accepted so that they can have a good future and because parents believe that it is good for their daughters (Muteshi & Sass, 2005).

Some African feminists have accused Western feminists of focusing on FGM in Africa to make them feel culturally superior while failing to wage an equally vigorous fight against the abuse of the female body in their own countries (Nnmaeka, 2005). They have a point. After all, millions of Western women face mental and physical health difficulties due to social pressures that lead them to alter their bodies through surgery and unhealthy or restricted eating practices. Western women, especially American women, are preoccupied with weight and body image and have their bodies cut, shaped, stapled, waxed, and manipulated to conform to cultural beauty standards. In 2019 alone, almost 300,000 American women underwent cosmetic breast surgery, 265,000 got liposuction, 211,000 had cosmetic eyelid surgery, and over 123,000 had a "tummy tuck" (American Society of Plastic Surgery, 2019).

Some FGM defenders consider the criminalization of all forms of FGM to be a form of neocolonialism that destroys a culturally meaningful rite and symbol of ethnic identity. They say that the real problems are infibulation and FGM before the age of consent (La Barbera, 2009). Anti-FGM laws in western countries are also seen by some as denying adult migrant women's freedom of choice while supporting similar procedures chosen mostly by Euro American women, such as vaginoplasty and breast implants (Oba, 2008). These criticisms not only remind us to look at our own practices but also underscore the need for culturally sensitive approaches driven by the women that are affected. For example, in Kenya, Uganda, and Gambia, where the practice is an important rite of passage and initiation into womanhood, community-based women's groups have

"Together we will end the cutting of young girls!"
Tweeted by Maimouna Yade (age 25) President of AfriYAN Girl to more than 3,800 women in Senegal

"How can Western public health officials, global health institutions and feminist organizations maintain a straight face in condemning African female genital surgeries as FGM yet turn a blind eye to the performance of similar procedures on Western women under the guise of cosmetic surgery?"
Fuambai Sia Ahmadu, activist from Sierra Leone who advocates for the right of adult women to undergo female circumcision

"Circumcision in Maasai culture marks the transition from girlhood to womanhood, so in order to encourage people to move away from female genital cutting we have developed an alternative rite of passage, in which the girl experiences all the elements of the ceremony but is not cut...This symbolic ceremony is popular because we developed it in partnership with members of the community. It is not perceived as a threat to our culture."
Sarah Tenoi, Maasai woman (Kenya)

Margaret Sanger (1883–1966) founded the birth control movement in the United States. Despite harassment and arrest, she successfully pushed the federal courts to change laws preventing physicians from providing birth control information and devices. In 1921 she founded the organization that would later become Planned Parenthood. Sanger was an important figure in the history of women's reproductive choice but she was a supporter of eugenics, a movement to limit the reproduction of "undesirable" groups. Pro-life groups and politicians have used this to discredit the work of today's Planned Parenthood organization.

developed alternative rights of passage that have reduced the practice (Muteshi & Sass, 2005).

Contraception, Reproductive Choice, and Reproductive Health

When women have the option, they seldom choose to have as many children as biologically possible. The average woman must use some form of effective contraception for at least twenty years if she wants to limit her family size to two children, and sixteen years if she wants four children (Guttmacher Institute, 2008). Reliable and safe contraceptives (birth control) reduce maternal mortality and morbidity and decrease abortion rates. As early as the 1968 UN International Human Rights Conference, it was acknowledged that family planning is a human right—that is, couples should be able to freely decide how many children they want and the spacing of those children (Dixon-Mueller, 1993). Many human rights documents recognize the right of couples and individuals to decide freely and responsibly the number, spacing, and timing of their children and to have the information and means to do so. True reproductive choice and freedom require that women be able to make informed choices about a variety of birth control options (Hartmann, 2016).

The 1994 International Conference on Population and Development Programme of Action recommended that all countries provide universal access to a full range of safe and reliable family planning methods by 2015. Significant progress has been made toward this goal (UN DESA, 2019). The UN's 2030 Agenda for Sustainable Development sets a goal of universal access to reproductive health care services by 2030. Access to modern contraception has increased by 25 percent since 1994, but globally about 10 percent of women aged 15–49 who don't want to become pregnant don't use contraception (this is known as the **unmet need for family planning**) (UN DESA, 2019). However, progress is uneven. For example, while globally about 25 percent of women have unmet contraceptive needs, 45 percent of women in sub-Saharan Africa have unmet contraceptive needs (UN DESA, 2020). Box 3.5 provides a snapshot of unmet contraceptive need in low- and middle-income countries. Unmet contraceptive needs in these countries are almost double the unmet need in high-income countries.

One study of women in developing countries who did not want to become pregnant found the most common reasons for not using contraception were infrequent sex; concerns about side effects, health risks, or inconvenience of methods; they were breastfeeding and/or hadn't resumed menstruation after childbirth; or they or someone close to them opposed family planning (Sedgh, Ashford, & Hussain, 2016). Women in the United States who experienced unplanned pregnancies cited similar reasons for not using contraception (Mosher, Jones, & Abma, 2015). In most countries, unmet need is greater among women with less education, women living in rural areas, and low-income women, with the exception of West and Central Africa (United Nations, 2015). These reasons for unmet contraceptive need suggest that to avoid unintended pregnancy and promote reproductive health, women and men need comprehensive sex education so they can accurately assess their risk of becoming pregnant and make informed choices about contraception. They also need access

BOX 3.5   *Snapshot of Unmet Need for Contraception in Low- and Middle-Income Countries (LMICs)*

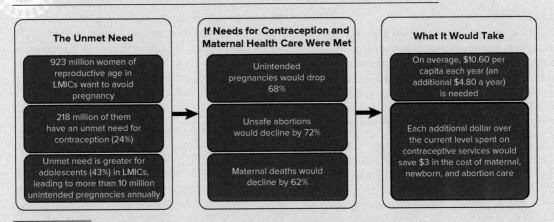

The Unmet Need

923 million women of reproductive age in LMICs want to avoid pregnancy

218 million of them have an unmet need for contraception (24%)

Unmet need is greater for adolescents (43%) in LMICs, leading to more than 10 million unintended pregnancies annually

If Needs for Contraception and Maternal Health Care Were Met

Unintended pregnancies would drop 68%

Unsafe abortions would decline by 72%

Maternal deaths would decline by 62%

What It Would Take

On average, $10.60 per capita each year (an additional $4.80 a year) is needed

Each additional dollar over the current level spent on contraceptive services would save $3 in the cost of maternal, newborn, and abortion care

Note: Low-income countries are those where the annual gross national income (GNI) is between $1,036 and $4,045. In middle-income countries, the GNI is between $4,046 and 12,536.
Source: Sully et al. (2020). *Adding It Up: Investing in Sexual and Reproductive Health.*

to a variety of contraceptive methods as well as new and improved contraceptive methods that balance effectiveness, safety, and convenience, and reduce side effects.

Box 3.6 provides an overview of the most common birth control methods, along with their advantages and disadvantages. Notice that the methods vary in effectiveness, ease of use, protection for sexually transmitted infections (STIs), and side effects, and that only two methods (vasectomy and the male condom) are male contraceptives.[3] Also keep in mind that the advantages and disadvantages of a method vary depending on a person's age, unique biology, and life situation as well as culture and region. Women need contraceptives that fit them and their particular circumstances. For example, heavy bleeding is a common side effect of the IUD (intrauterine device), but this may be a bigger issue for women living in areas with limited sanitation and for those whose religions restrict activities during menstruation. The best method may also depend on a woman's risk factors for sexually transmitted infections such as HIV, chlamydia, hepatitis B, HPV, trichomoniasis, syphilis, and gonorrhea. You should also know that although female sterilization and the male condom are the two most commonly used methods globally, there are large regional variations in the contraceptive methods used (UN DESA, 2019). For example, in Eastern and South-Eastern Asia, the IUD is the most common, in Europe and North America it's the pill, and in sub-Saharan Africa, injectables are the dominant method.

"When women are given a real choice, and the information and means to implement their choice, they will make the most rational decision for themselves, their community, and ultimately the world."
Dr. Mahmoud F. Fathalla, Egyptian gynecologist and former president of the International Federation of Planned Parenthood

"Women still face the dilemma that the safest contraceptives are not the most effective, while the most effective are not necessarily the safest."
Joni Seager

---

[3]STI is sometimes used interchangeably with the term *sexually transmitted disease* (STD). However, STI is starting to replace STD because it is considered a more accurate term (not all sexually transmitted infections have disease symptoms, especially early on), and because "infection" is less stigmatizing than "disease."

BOX 3.6   *Common Birth Control Methods*

Behavioral Methods

Abstinence—Continuous abstinence is not having sex play with a partner at all (vaginal, anal, or oral). It is 100 percent effective in preventing pregnancy and sexually transmitted infections (STIs). However, people may find it difficult to abstain for long periods of time, and women and men often end their abstinence without being prepared to protect against pregnancy or infection.

Outercourse—Sex play without vaginal intercourse, including oral sex, body rubbing, and mutual masturbation. Nearly 100 percent effective against pregnancy if semen (ejaculate or pre-ejaculate) isn't spilled in the vagina. Most methods of outercourse also carry a low STI risk.

Fertility Awareness (Natural Family Planning/Rhythm Method)—Uses calendars, cervical mucous, or temperature to chart the menstrual cycle; abstinence or barrier methods are then used during the woman's fertile period. Can be up to 88 percent effective with consistent and accurate monitoring, but this is difficult for many women, especially those with irregular periods or those who are breastfeeding. Apps (like Natural Cycles, Kindara, and Clue) are now available for period and fertility tracking and may increase effectiveness. Without a commitment to abstain or use barrier methods during the fertile period, this method is ineffective. Also, this method provides no protection against sexually transmitted diseases.

Withdrawal—An unreliable method requiring that the man withdraw his penis from the vagina before or when he feels he has reached the point when ejaculation is likely. It requires great control and experience on the part of the man. It does not protect against STIs and pregnancy may still occur due to the possibility of semen in pre-ejaculative secretions.

Barrier Methods

These methods prevent sperm from reaching an egg through the application of a barrier shortly before vaginal penetration. Many are used with a chemical that also kills sperm (a spermicide).

Diaphragm—A soft latex, shallow cup holding spermicide that is inserted by a woman over her cervix to block and kill sperm. Proper fitting requires the help of a health-care practitioner. It does not protect against STIs but is 88 percent effective in pregnancy prevention if used correctly and with spermicide.

Cervical cap—Similar to a diaphragm, this is a thimble-shaped, rubber cap that fits over the cervix. Like the diaphragm, it is used with a spermicide to block and kill sperm and must be fitted by a health-care practitioner. A similar product, the cervical shield, comes in only one size. The cap does not protect against STIs and is 71 to 88 percent effective for pregnancy prevention when used correctly and with spermicide.

Contraceptive sponge—A small, circular, polyurethane sponge containing spermicide inserted by a woman into her vagina that prevents sperm from entering the uterus. It has a dimple on one side that fits over the cervix and a loop on the opposite side to aid in removal. While it is 76 to 86 percent effective in pregnancy prevention with proper use, it does not reduce STI risk.

Male condom—Thin sheath, usually of latex, that covers the penis during sex. Condoms are highly effective (85–98 percent) in pregnancy prevention if used correctly and when they include lubrication and spermicide. Most also offer protection against sexually transmitted infections (STIs) such as HIV/AIDS (although natural/lambskin ones do not). However, some men's unwillingness to use them increases women's STI rates and unplanned pregnancies.

Female condom—Sheath made of rubber with two flexible rings at either end that is inserted by a woman into her vagina to prevent semen, vaginal fluid, and blood from being passed between sexual partners. It is the only female-controlled barrier method offering protection against STIs, including HIV/AIDS. Female condoms are 79 percent effective in pregnancy prevention; effectiveness is increased with use of a spermicide.

continued

Hormonal Methods

These methods deliver the hormones progesterone, estrogen, or both to suppress ovulation or thicken the cervical mucus, blocking sperm penetration. They are 91 to 99 percent effective in pregnancy prevention but offer no protection against STIs and may produce a variety of undesirable side effects. Some of the more common side effects are bleeding, weight gain or loss, breast tenderness, nausea, headache, change in sexual desire, and depression. Less common are blood clots in legs, lungs, heart, or brain; high blood pressure; and liver tumors, gallstones, and jaundice. Antibiotics and other medications may reduce effectiveness.

Oral Contraceptives (Birth Control Pills, the Pill)— Synthetic hormones a woman takes daily to prevent pregnancy, a prescription drug in most countries.

Contraceptive Implant—Synthetic hormones released gradually from match-size capsules inserted in a woman's arm by a trained professional. Prevents pregnancy for up to five years by inhibiting ovulation and thickening cervical mucus. Removal is tricky and requires a skilled health-care practitioner.

Contraceptive Injection (Depo-Provera)—An injectable contraceptive that prevents pregnancy for up to three months by inhibiting ovulation and thickening cervical mucus. Bone loss is associated with long-term use.

Contraceptive Patch—A woman places this thin, plastic patch on the skin of the buttocks, stomach, upper outer arm, or upper torso once a week for three out of four weeks.

Contraceptive Ring—A woman inserts this small, flexible ring into her vagina once a month, leaves it in place for three weeks, and takes it out for the remaining week.

Emergency Contraceptive Pills (EC, Plan B, or the "Morning After Pill")— A small dose of the hormone progestin (1 or 2 pills) taken within 72 hours of unprotected intercourse; useful for preventing pregnancy in the event of rape, barrier method failure (condom breaks or slips, etc.), or any other unprotected vaginal intercourse. It is not an abortion pill because EC *prevents pregnancy* by delaying ovulation, preventing fertilization, or inhibiting implantation of a fertilized egg in the uterus.

Intrauterine Devices (IUDs)

The most widely used form of reversible birth control in the world, the IUD is highly effective against pregnancy but provides no STI protection and has an array of possible negative side effects such as bleeding and infection. IUDs are small devices that fit in the uterus with a small string that extends into the upper vagina. Some contain copper or hormones. They prevent pregnancy until removal and must be inserted and removed by a qualified health-care practitioner. IUDs can be used as emergency contraception if inserted within five days after unprotected intercourse.

Permanent Methods—Sterilization

This highly effective and permanent form of birth control is achieved through surgery. Female sterilization is one of the most common contraceptive methods worldwide. It is generally safe with few negative side effects if performed by a skilled professional in a sterile setting. In women, the fallopian tubes are blocked or cut in a procedure called a *tubal ligation*, or a "micro-insert" is placed in the fallopian tube to block it. In men, a procedure called a *vasectomy* cuts the vas deferens so that sperm cannot mix with the seminal fluid. Sterilization provides no STI protection.

———————————

Source: Planned Parenthood, 2021.

Abortion

Unplanned pregnancies are a fact of life for almost 121 million women every year, and 48 percent of pregnancies are unintended (Guttmacher Institute, 2020a). Many unplanned pregnancies occur due to contraceptive unavailability or poor knowledge, but some happen because contraceptives fail, and others because sex was unexpected or nonconsensual, or using contraception was not within a woman's power. When women feel they

"I cannot understand anti-abortion arguments that center on the sanctity of life. As a species we've fairly comprehensively demonstrated that we don't believe in the sanctity of life. The shrugging acceptance of war, famine, epidemic, pain and life-long poverty shows us that, whatever we tell ourselves, we've made only the most feeble of efforts to really treat human life as sacred."
Caitlin Moran, English journalist

"The best and most acceptable way to reduce the incidence of abortion always has been and still is to reduce the need for it by lowering the rate of unintended pregnancy."
Andrea Rowan, Guttmacher Institute

"We make this journey in solidarity with all our Irish sisters who have gone before us."
Irish woman's live-tweet as she traveled to the United Kingdom for an abortion

cannot have a child at the time they become pregnant, about 61 percent choose to end their pregnancy—even when it's medically risky or illegal (Guttmacher Institute, 2020a).

Globally, 39 per 1,000 women age 15 to 49 have an abortion every year (73 million), but women in low-income regions have higher rates (38 per 1,000) than women in high-income regions (15 per 1,000) (Guttmacher Institute, 2020b). These differences occur because people in high-income countries have better access to sexual and reproductive health care (Bearak et al., 2020). The highest rates of abortion per 1,000 women of reproductive age are in the West Asia/ North Africa region (53) and in Central and South Asia region (46), while the lowest are in North America (17) and Western Europe (9) (Bearak et al., 2020). When abortion is supervised or performed by skilled health personnel, death, disability, and injury are rare but globally, 700 million women lack access to safe and legal abortion care (Center for Reproductive Rights, 2021b). About 44 percent of abortions (over 25 million a year) are unsafe (Ganatra et al., 2017).

Abortion laws vary considerably. Close to 34 percent of countries permit induced abortion without restriction as to reason; a little over 7 percent allow it on economic grounds; almost 29 percent to protect a woman's life or health; and about 34 percent prohibit it or allow it only to save the life of the mother (Center for Reproductive Rights, 2021b). Countries also vary in whether spousal or parental authorization is required; whether there are limits based on gestational age; whether exceptions are made in cases of rape, incest, or fetal impairment; whether medical abortion (abortion resulting from ingestion of medically supervised drugs) is permitted, and what to do with fetal remains. In Australia, the United States, and Mexico, there are within-country differences in legality and restrictions based on state law. In the United States, for example, federal law places no restrictions on abortion, but since 2011, states have legislated over 450 abortion restrictions (Donovan, 2020). Among other restrictions, 37 states now require parental involvement in a minor's decision to have an abortion, 25 states require a waiting period, and 18 require counseling intended to discourage abortion; 58 restrictions in 17 states were enacted in 2019 alone, though nine states took action to protect abortion rights (Nash et al., 2019; Guttmacher Institute, 2021a).

It's important to recognize that legal restrictions don't reduce abortions, nor do they increase them (Bearak et al., 2020). Abortion rates are similar in countries where abortion is restricted and those where it is not (Guttmacher Institute, 2020). That's because when women cannot attain legal abortions, they often get illegal ones or travel to where abortion is legal or services are available. For example, in the midwestern and southern United States, new laws have led to so many clinic closures and abortion barriers that some women travel to other states for abortion, or obtain and take drugs like misoprostol to induce abortion (Hennessy-Fiske, 2016; Zerwick, 2016). In Ireland, where abortion is only allowed when the mother's health is in danger, over 100,000 Irish women have travelled to Great Britain for an abortion since 1980 (O'Sullivan, 2016). Poland has a strict abortion law where abortion is only allowed in cases of rape or incest, or when the pregnancy threatens the woman's life, yet each year, 85,000 to 90,000 illegal abortions are performed there, and at least 100,000 Polish women travel abroad for abortion (Sethna & Davis, 2019; Teggarty, 2016). In Latin America and the Caribbean, more than 97 percent of women live where abortion is severely restricted or banned altogether. Despite this, 6.5 million abortions occur annually, and 760,000 women are treated for abortion complications every year (Guttmacher Institute, 2017).

Legality and restrictions do not affect abortion incidence but do affect abortion safety. In countries that prohibit abortion or only allow it to save a woman's life or health, 75 percent of abortions are unsafe (PRB, 2021). Evidence shows that removing abortion restrictions reduces maternal mortality from unsafe abortion (Latt, Milner, & Kavanagh, 2019). For example, after the reform of restrictive abortion laws in South Africa, abortion-related deaths fell 91 percent in 6 years (Guttmacher Institute, 2012). Countries with restrictive laws have more than four times as many unsafe abortions as countries with liberal abortion policies (Singh et al., 2018). Approximately 23,000 women die annually from unsafe abortion and more than 7 million are hospitalized due to complications, most in low- and middle-income regions like sub-Saharan Africa (Singh et al., 2018; WHO, 2020b). In Chile, where an outright abortion ban meant that both women and their doctors could be imprisoned, more than 300,000 Chilean women were hospitalized with abortion complications from 2006 to 2016 (Radwin, 2016).[4] The most common complications of unsafe abortion include incomplete abortion, excessive blood loss, and infection. Less common are septic shock, perforation of internal organs, and inflammation of the peritoneum (Guttmacher Institute, 2016b). Most unsafe abortions occur in low and middle-income countries (World Health Organization, 2020b).

> "Nearly every death and harm from unsafe abortion can be prevented through sexuality education, use of effective contraception, provision of safe, legal abortion and emergency treatment of abortion complications."
> *World Health Organization*

The Agents That Control Women's Reproductive Choice and Health

Male partners, governments, corporations, and religious organizations are major influences on women's reproductive lives. In the public sphere, corporations and governments sometimes make women's health concerns a low priority in the marketing and availability of contraception. Governments concerned with population control and corporations concerned with profit sometimes endanger women's health or, at the very least, restrict women's options. Powerful religious groups may also influence reproductive choice. Meanwhile, in the private sphere, women's reproductive choice is sometimes controlled by their male partners or husbands' families. However, women are also agents of reproductive rights and health, and advocacy and activism for reproductive rights are common globally.

Government

Because sex education is typically government funded, governments often determine reproductive knowledge. Governments pass and enforce abortion laws and policies and affect reproductive choice by approving and regulating contraceptives. For example, in the 1960s, Japan banned hormonal contraceptives, saying that they were unhealthy and promoted promiscuity. This finally changed in 1999 after 30 years of lobbying by women's activists.

---

[4]In August 2017, following years of activism, the Chilean constitutional court ruled in favor of a bill allowing abortion in case of rape, when a woman's life is at risk, or when the fetus is not viable. The bill was introduced by President Michelle Bachelet in 2015.

"The personal is
political."
*American Feminist
Slogan*

El Salvador has one of
the strictest abortion
laws in the world.
It is illegal under
any circumstances.
Women are sometimes
prosecuted for
aggravated assault
and homicide and
sentenced to prison.
Hospital employees
are pressured to report
suspected abortions to
authorities.

Through public funding of family planning and health care services, governments affect women's maternal and reproductive health and reproductive control. The limited contraceptives and services offered by government family planning programs often create racial and class disparities in reproductive health and choice. In the United States, the Title X national family planning program passed by Congress in 1970 is intended to fund Medicaid family planning services so that poor women have greater access to contraception. However, the 1977 Hyde amendment bans federal Medicaid funding for abortion; this makes abortion less available to poor women and women of color, who are more likely to rely on Medicaid insurance (Boonstra, 2016). Funding also varies depending on congressional and presidential administration. By the end of President George W. Bush's eight-year term, funding for low-cost, confidential family planning services was 61 percent lower in constant dollars than it was in 1980. President Obama's first budget in 2009 increased funding by $7.5 million (Jacobson, 2009). President Trump's Title X budget cuts reduced the capacity of federally supported family planning clinics by half, reducing access of an estimated 1.6 million women to reproductive health care (Dawson, 2020).

Government population policies aimed at shaping the composition, size, and growth of national populations also impact women's reproductive rights and health. These policies can impact women positively if they provide resources to expand women's reproductive empowerment and health, or impact them negatively if they violate human rights to control women's reproduction in the name of social needs or national interests. Countries with **coercive pronatalist policies** force people to have more children by reducing citizens' reproductive choice. For example, in the 1980s, following large casualties from war with Iran, the Iraqi government banned contraceptives. The Romanian government outlawed contraception in the 1970s and 1980s because it was feared that population growth was too low to keep up with projected labor needs. In contrast, **coercive antinatalism** is when a government is concerned about overpopulation and enacts strict policies to discourage childbearing—policies that infringe on reproductive and human rights.

China's one-child family policy, first instituted in the 1970s and ended in 2015, provides one of the more extreme examples of coercive antinatalism. In its early incarnation, parents were issued permits to have children, and those who had additional children could be fined; lose their jobs, land, or homes; or be demoted (Chow & Chen, 1994; Hartmann, 2016). There were also reports of forced abortion, and women could be fitted with an IUD after their first child and sterilized after their second. However, while the Chinese government has relaxed its one-child policy for the majority Han population, it has recently enacted coercive antitnatalist policies to curb its Muslim minority population (Associated Press, 2020). Governments usually claim that coercive antinatalism is necessary to reduce poverty and promote economic development, but there are other ways to achieve these goals. When women have higher status, when child mortality is low, and when women have access to information and a variety of ways to control their fertility, they have fewer children (Dixon-Mueller, 1993; Hartmann, 2016).

Many countries have a history of selective coercive antinatalism where the government targets groups of lower-income women or women from an ethnic group deemed undesirable by government officials. For instance, in 1976 it was revealed that the

U.S. government had sterilized 3,000 Native American women in a four-year period without obtaining adequate consent (Hartmann, 2016). The involuntary sterilization of Mexican immigrant women, African American women, and Puerto Rican women also occurred through the 1970s in the United States (Davis, 1990; Gutierrez & Fuentes, 2010). In the Czech Republic, Romany (Gypsy) women were sterilized without their consent as late as 2004 to limit the Roma population, a growing and unpopular minority (Amnesty International, 2008). From 1994 to 2000, the Peruvian government forced the sterilization of over 200,000 indigenous women; survivors still seek justice (Collyns, 2016; Moloney, 2021).

Fortunately, coercive antinatalism and coercive pronatalism are far less common than they once were. Research, along with women's and human rights activism, has led most governments to reject coercive antinatalist and coercive pronatalist policies. However, exceptions remain. From 2014 to 2017, the Islamic State (the fledgling government of ISIS/ISIL) had both coercive pronatalism and coercive antinatalist policies. In 2014, to boost their population and set down roots in their conquered territory, they banned contraception and shut down family planning services in Monsul, their stronghold in Northern Iraq (Sridharan, 2014). Meanwhile, they sexually enslaved women from the Yazidi religious minority, forced them to take contraceptives, raped them daily, and sold them to other men (Al-Dayel et al., 2020). According to ISIS's interpretation of ancient Islamic law, sexual slavery is allowed, but the owner of a female slave can have sex with her only if he is sure she is not pregnant (Callamachi, 2016).

Politics and political administration changes also significantly affect the reproductive choices available to women. Policies affecting women's reproductive rights are often made at the executive level, without legislative approval, and this means that when government leaders change, policies often change as well. The U.S. approval of Mifepristone, a chemical alternative to aspiration abortion used in early pregnancy, is a good example (the use of medicine to induce abortion is called medical abortion). Because surgical facilities are not needed for medical abortion, it can help make abortion more available and lower in cost. The drug became available in France in 1988, but activists opposed to abortion threatened to boycott its manufacturer Roussel Uclaf should it be marketed in the United States. By 1991, President George H.W. Bush put the pill on a list of medications banned by the United States. In 1993, newly elected President Clinton called on the FDA to test the drug. Roussel Uclaf gave the rights to the drug to a nonprofit group, the Population Council. This group had to raise millions of dollars to conduct clinical trials of the drug, because none of the major pharmaceutical companies was interested due to the controversial nature of abortion in the United States. Seven years later, the drug was approved for use in the United States, largely due to the efforts of activists who felt strongly that Mifepristone should be available to American women (Bernstein, 2000).

Where family planning programs receive foreign aid to fund family planning programs, the policies of the government of one country may affect the reproductive choices of women in other countries. A good example is the **Mexico City policy**, also known as the **Global Gag Rule**. First instituted by U.S. President Ronald Reagan in 1984, this federal policy prevents foreign nongovernmental organizations (NGOs) that

Nadia Murad, a Yazidi woman who escaped ISIS sex slavery, has won multiple human rights prizes for her global campaign to bring justice for sexual survivors of conflict-related sexual violence.

"The gag rule has done immense harm and caused untold suffering to millions around the world. It has undermined health systems and endangered the lives and health of the poorest and most vulnerable women on the planet by denying access to life saving family planning, sexual and reproductive health and HIV services and exposing them to the dangers of unsafe abortion."
Dr. Gill Greer, International Planned Parenthood Federation

receive USAID family planning funds from providing legal abortion services, lobbying their own governments for abortion law reform, and providing accurate medical counseling or referrals regarding abortion. This dramatically reduces funding for family planning and women's health services and reduces contraceptive availability, which increases unplanned pregnancies and abortions. For instance, after the reinstatement of the rule by the Trump administration, the International Planned Parenthood Federation lost 100 million dollars in funding, impacting health-care projects providing contraception, HIV tests, and prenatal care in 32 countries (Robbins, 2021).

Since 1984, the pattern is for Democratic presidents to repeal the global gag rule and restore funding and for Republican presidents to reinstate the rule and deny funding to the UNFPA. In his first act as President of the United States in 2001, George W. Bush reinstated the policy. The administration also attached abstinence-only program requirements to U.S. funding for international family planning and AIDS relief despite evidence that these programs are ineffective (Elders, 2008). As a result, the U.S. Agency for International Development (USAID) could no longer ship contraceptives to sixteen countries in sub-Saharan Africa, Asia, and the Middle East. In 2009, one of President Obama's first actions was to rescind the rule and promise increased funding for international family planning. On his first full day in office, President Donald Trump reinstated the rule and expanded it to include not just family planning agencies and programs but any organization that receives U.S. aid. One of the saddest things is that the policy is counterproductive: Research indicates that during the years the rule is in effect, abortion rates increase (Barot & Cohen, 2015; Brooks et al., 2019). After Trump's defeat, President Joe Biden, his successor, rescinded the rule in the first month of his presidency.

Men

Where men are considered the head of household and have higher status and power in their relationships with women, they are more likely to control sexual decision-making, including contraceptive use and abortion. As the family decision-makers in patriarchal cultures, men often decide the number and spacing of the children (Kabagenyi et al., 2014). In some cultures, men prefer large families, fear that birth control will result in infertility or costly side effects, or believe a woman who uses contraception will have sexual affairs (Mosha, Ruben, & Kakoko, 2013; Kabagenyi et al., 2014). On average, 9 percent of women from fifty-two African countries who weren't using contraception cited their male partner's opposition as the reason (Sedgh, Ashford, & Hussain, 2016). In Timor-Leste and Mali, almost a quarter of women cited this reason, in Krykyrgyzstan, 15 percent did, and in Nigeria, 36 percent of women provided this reason for contraceptive non-use (Lawani, Iyoke, & Ezeonu, 2015; Sedgh, Ashford, & Hussain, 2016). About 12 percent of American women cited males' unwillingness to use birth control as the reason for not using contraception (Mosher et al., 2015). A UN study of women in 57 countries found that only 55 percent of married/partnered women make their own sexual and reproductive health decisions (UNFPA, 2020b).

Men's sexual decision-making power over women is sometimes enshrined in law. Thirteen countries (Syria, the United Arab Emirates, Republic of Korea, Equatorial Guinea, Kuwait, Maldives, Morocco, Saudi Arabia, Japan, Taiwan, Turkey, Yemen, and Indonesia) require married women to have their husband's consent for an abortion (Center for Reproductive Rights, 2021b). Nine states in the United States have laws requiring spousal consent or notification, but these are unenforceable as a result of the 1994 Supreme Court decision *Planned Parenthood v. Casey*. In the next chapter, men's control of women's sexuality is linked to HIV/AIDS in women.

Corporations

Corporations play a large role in the reproductive technologies available to women, and they are motivated primarily by profit, not by concerns about women's reproductive choice or health. For instance, in the United States, the Today Sponge (250 million of which were sold from 1983 to 1995) was taken off the market when pharmaceutical giant Wyeth didn't want to pay for plant upgrades. The popular product was unavailable to American women until a small company bought the rights to it in 2003. It reappeared in 2005 under new ownership before being sold to another company that declared bankruptcy in late 2007, taking the Today Sponge out of production until a new company began selling it again in 2009 (Singer, 2009). In 2019, equipment failures stopped the production and availability of the sponge. In 2021, the producer of the sponge cited the Covid-19 pandemic as the reason production has not resumed.

Pharmaceutical companies also have a long history of emphasizing benefits and downplaying contraceptive side effects and risks. One recent case is Mirena, an IUD made by the Bayer Corporation, which has made the company billions of dollars. In 2009, the U.S. Food and Drug Administration sent a warning letter to Bayer claiming that Bayer overstated the benefits and safety of the device and made false and misleading advertising statements. Over 45,000 "adverse events," including uterine perforation, pelvic inflammatory disease, ectopic pregnancy, and device migration, have been reported to the FDA. Bayer was sued by thousands of women and in 2018 agreed to pay a total of 12.2 million dollars to settle 4,600 of the cases. Merck, another pharmaceutical corporation, paid out more than 100 million dollars in damages due to their NuvaRing product (used by women in 50 countries). Apparently, the company downplayed evidence that the device comes with an increased risk of blood clots and pulmonary embolism (Karlsson & Brenner, 2013). Unfortunately, the billions of dollars paid due to lawsuits since the 1970s have made corporations increasingly wary of investing in contraceptive development. This has slowed the development of new and improved contraceptive methods, and in the process, reduced reproductive choice (Schwartz, 2014).

Religious Organizations

Religious institutions, religious leaders, faith-affiliated and faith-inspired health services and workers, faith-based advocates, and international faith-inspired organizations may all affect women's reproductive health and reproductive choice. For instance, in the United States, Catholics and evangelical Christians act to create abortion restrictions and abstinence-only sex education and to decrease funding for family planning services that offer abortions or abortion information. Religion often

"Some of us are afraid of using FP methods without our husbands' consent. If we use FP methods and suffer from side effects, our husbands will not pay for our medical treatment. We could be left untreated . . . to die . . . we could be divorced, because we have gone against our husbands' wishes."
Woman from Mwanza, Tanzania

In the United States, 35 states require schools to stress abstinence when sex education is provided and nine states require teachers to portray LGBT+ people negatively, or prohibit teachers from mentioning them.

"Not in our name should any mother die while giving birth . . . Not in our name should a girl child be deprived of her education, be married, be harmed or abused. Not in our name should anyone be denied access to basic health care, nor should a child or an adolescent be denied knowledge of and care for her/his body. Not in our name should any person be denied their human rights."
From the "Call to Action" issued by a group of the world's religious leaders in a 2014 UN meeting on reproductive health, reproductive rights, and religion

influences reproductive law and services and shapes attitudes about contraception, abortion, and men's control of sexual decision-making. Some religions have beliefs about conception and when life begins that form the basis for opposition to contraception and abortion.

Human rights documents and agreements make clear that the freedom to practice religion is an important human right. However, international human rights law limits this right when it infringes on public safety, health, or the fundamental rights and freedoms of others (UNFPA, 2015). Women's and human rights advocates are concerned that despite this, the freedom of religion sometimes comes at the expense of reproductive rights and women's health. One example of this is the conscientious objection of health care providers and organizations. Due to their religious and moral beliefs, conscientious objectors refuse to provide reproductive health care services such as prescribing contraceptives and providing emergency contraception or performing sterilizations or abortions (even in cases of rape and incest, or when medically indicated).

Human rights bodies, such as the UN and global health organizations, affirm that health care is a human right. They also agree that conscientious objection to reproductive health care must be regulated to guarantee that refusals of care do not prevent or undermine women and girls' access to legal reproductive health care (Center for Reproductive Rights, 2021c). But conscientious objection to providing reproductive services is on the rise worldwide (Zampas & Andion-Ibaniez, 2012). For example, in Europe, 10 percent of UK OB-GYNs refuse to provide abortions, and in Italy, almost 71 percent of gynecologists are registered as conscientious objectors to abortion (Autorino, Mattioli, Mencarini, 2020; Chavkin, Leitman, & Polin, 2013). A 2014 U.S. Supreme Court decision (Burwell v. Hobby Lobby) allows companies to refuse health insurance coverage for contraceptive methods that violate the owner's religious beliefs. Health providers may refuse to provide abortion services in forty-six U.S. states and contraceptive services in twelve states; and in eighteen states, they can refuse sterilization (Guttmacher Institute, 2021b).

Not all religions pose barriers to reproductive rights and health, but some, like Catholicism, have exerted a considerable, negative global influence. With the exception of the calendar or rhythm method, the Catholic Church is officially opposed to the use of contraception and is strongly opposed to abortion. The Philippines, a largely Catholic country (80%), has one of the highest birth rates in Asia, and as many as 600,000 women have illegal abortions each year, with some 100,000 going to the hospital due to complications, and at least three dying a day (Esquerra, 2020; Hundley, 2013). The Church opposes access to modern contraception and until recently, successfully reduced contraceptive access by influencing government policy (contraception was even banned in the country's most populous city, Manila). Finally, in 2014, after a fourteen-year battle between women's rights activists and the Catholic Church, the Philippines Supreme Court upheld a reproductive health law passed in 2012. The law, which was supported by 70 percent of citizens, funds universal and free access to contraception, requires hospitals to treat post-abortion complications, and mandates family planning and sexuality education in schools. Abortion, however, remains punishable with up to six years in prison. In

2021, women's rights advocates, including the Philippine Safe Abortion Advocacy Network, launched a campaign to decriminalize abortion but face opposition from Catholic bishops (Esquerra, 2020).

Most of the countries that have the strictest laws on abortion are predominantly Catholic, and Catholic leaders exert pressure on governments to enact policies consistent with Vatican positions (for example, Poland, Ireland, the Philippines, Brazil, Chile, Nicaragua, and El Salvador). In 2009, public outcry ensued when a 9-year-old Brazilian victim of sexual abuse who was pregnant with twins was given an abortion (in Brazil, the procedure is legal only in cases of rape or to save the mother's life). A Brazilian archbishop excommunicated the child's mother and doctors from the Catholic Church (Adams, 2009). Anti-abortion groups led by the Roman Catholic Church have also been influential in countries like Poland, Slovakia, Lithuania, Italy, Nicaragua, Brazil, and Hungary. In the United States, anti-abortion efforts (called "pro-life" by their supporters) are led predominantly by white evangelical Protestants, and by the Roman Catholic Church.

"Each and every marital act must of necessity retain its intrinsic relationship to the procreation of human life."
Pope Paul VI in Humanae Vitae (Of Human Life), 1968 which banned contraception

Women

Because pregnancy and reproductive health are concerns of almost all women at some point in their lives, it's unsurprising that women often act to expand reproductive choice and advocate for safe contraception and reproductive health. All over the world, women's groups can be found working for legislation and policy changes, running nonprofit organizations that provide reproductive health care services, and working with governments and communities to increase reproductive choice. Large nongovernmental organizations like the Center for Reproductive Rights and the International Federation of Planned Parenthood and thousands of small, grassroots nongovernmental organizations are devoted to providing women (and men) with control over their reproductive lives.

One area of activism centers on contraception. In the 1970s, American women of Puerto Rican, Black, Chicana, and Native American descent waged a campaign against sterilization abuse. U.S. women's groups and feminist lawmakers also successfully worked to make emergency contraception available over-the-counter (2006) and to require health insurance to cover contraception and many reproductive health-care services without charging copayments or coinsurance (2010). Women's activists in China highlighted the conflicts between the government's family planning program and women's health care, the negative effects of certain contraceptive methods, abortion abuse, and the connections between the government's program and female infanticide (Zhang & Xu, 1995); the abandonment of China's one-child policy is due in part to their efforts. A recent example is Save the Women, a Polish women's rights group that fights for sex education, state-funded contraception, and the right to abortion.

Activism around the issue of safe, legal, and available abortion is also common. The number of countries legalizing abortion has grown dramatically in the last twenty years, largely due to women's activism. Most women know someone who had an abortion due to rape, incest, poverty, or youth, and most recognize the need for access to safe and affordable abortion. Where there are no safe and affordable abortions, almost all women have themselves experienced or know someone who has experienced the dangers of illegal abortion. In the 1970s, feminists in the United States and Western Europe worked for legalization by lobbying legislatures and staging demonstrations and speak-outs (they continue to fight abortion restrictions and the Hyde Amendment). The Family Planning Association of Nepal successfully worked for the passage in the Nepalese Parliament of a bill that would legalize abortion. Prior to its legalization in 2002, women were imprisoned for having abortions. Because of feminist activism, in 1998 South Africa passed one of the world's most liberal reproductive rights laws.

Some more recent campaigns for legalization or the removal of restrictions include those in Poland, Ireland, Argentina, India, and Nicaragua. In 2016, thousands marched in Dublin and 20 other world cities calling for the repeal of Ireland's strict anti-abortion law. The Irish public voted in 2019 to repeal the law banning abortion, but the law has many restrictions and anti-abortionists have deployed many tactics to block abortion access (Hogan, 2019).

In 2020, Polish pro-choice activists called for a "women's strike" after the government ruled that abortion in cases of fetal abnormality was unconstitutional. Over 400,000 people in more than 400 cities protested (Davies, 2020). The next year, following a near-total ban on abortion, tens of thousands marched in Warsaw, the country's capital, during the Covid-19 pandemic (BBC News, 2021).

In 2021, after years of activism and legal advocacy, and despite resistance from the Catholic Church, a law legalizing abortion was passed in Argentina, making it the first Latin American country to fully legalize abortion. However, abortion rights activists, known as the "Green Wave" for wearing green as a symbol of support for reproductive rights, battle court challenges to the law and to expunge the criminal records of hundreds of women prosecuted in the last decade for abortions or miscarriages (Politi, 2021).

In Europe in 2016, tens of thousands of Polish women protested a proposed anti-abortion bill, and thousands marched in Dublin and 20 other world cities to repeal Ireland's strict abortion law. In Nicaragua, a country that banned abortion completely in 2006, nearly a dozen women's rights groups fight for the reinstatement of legal abortion; they have sent 54 appeals to the Supreme Court to declare the law unconstitutional and have staged many street protests.

Women's health and rights activists also work for the end of inhumane abortion restrictions. These include laws that force girl and women victims of rape or incest to give birth to their assailant's child and laws that make women carry pregnancies to term even when the fetus will be stillborn, severely impaired, or will die soon after birth. Activists also target laws that subject women and those that help them to prosecution, make women who miscarry prove they did not self-abort, and make women fear seeking medical help for abortion complications. For example, in Argentina in August 2016, thousands of people marched in protest after an eight-year prison sentence was given to a woman (known as Belen) charged with murder after experiencing a miscarriage.

In the face of abortion illegality and unsafe abortion, some groups operate to provide safe abortion. *Women on Waves* is a Dutch NGO that promotes legal,

"Get your rosaries off my ovaries!"
Chant of Irish reproductive rights activists in 2019

"All pregnant children were raped."
Ad campaign slogan of Catholics for the Right to Choose in Nicaragua. The campaign organizers argue that it's cruel to force girls to have their sexual abuser's child, especially since they are only children themselves.

"For us, abortion isn't a discussion of morals or values. We aren't going to enter in the debate of when life starts or ends. But this is an issue of health, and a woman that wants to have an abortion must have all the information available to do so."
Carolina, an operator at Linea Aborto Libre

safe abortion by operating a mobile clinic on a ship that sails to countries where abortion is illegal. Their mission is to provide reproductive health services, provide sexual education, and support local initiatives to further women's reproductive rights. The NGO *Women on Web* is an online medical abortion service that helps women obtain the pills needed for a safe abortion (they also offer contraceptives for women without access to them). In Latin America, the Linea Aborto Libre (Abortion Liberty Hotline) gives callers information on how to induce a medical abortion up to twelve weeks of pregnancy.

Conclusion

This chapter illustrates the four global women's and gender studies themes identified in Chapter 1. It's evident that women's reproductive situations are not simply the result of biology. Sociocultural, political, and material factors all exert profound effects on women's reproductive choice and maternal and reproductive health.

Also evident is the multicultural and intersectional nature of global women's issues. Women's reproductive lives are similar globally in many ways, but women's reproductive rights and health vary greatly depending on multiple personal, social, political, and cultural factors. For example, within countries, lower income women, minority women, and transgender women usually have reduced reproductive choice and less access to reproductive health care, compared to other groups of women. Because of this diversity, change and change strategies have to be contextualized for the specific situation and the particular group of women affected. As we saw with the case of FGM, this complexity means that change is best driven by those affected by the "reproductive wrongs" in their own countries.

Human rights also featured prominently this chapter. Reproductive rights are consistent with basic human rights agreed upon at major international and regional UN conferences by UN member nations (United Nations, 2014). These rights include the right to life, the right to liberty and security of person, the right to health, including sexual and reproductive health, the right to decide the number and spacing of children, the right to consent to marriage and equality in marriage, and the right to be free from practices that harm women and girls. Framing women's reproductive health and choice in terms of human rights agreements and human rights law is often used as a tool for change.

Finally, the chapter underscored the theme of women's activism and empowerment. Gender equality is not possible without women's ability to control the number, spacing, and timing of their children and without their access to reproductive health services (United Nations, 2014). Women take action for reproductive health and reproductive choice. Activists and NGOs investigate and research, call out reproductive injustices, engage in a variety of protests, work for legislative change, and provide women's health resources, among other things. The diversity and range of women's reproductive rights activism are remarkable and have resulted in many advances in women's reproductive choices and health.

"Research by the World Health Organization has proven that an abortion with pills can be done safely at home by women themselves till 10 weeks of pregnancy. The health impact is similar to a miscarriage. Restrictive abortion laws will not keep women from accessing abortion pills, by ship, by mail, through the internet, drone or RC speedboat!"
Dr. Rebecca Gomperts from Women on Waves after an "abortion drone" and a speedboat delivered abortion pills to women in Northern Ireland.

"Reproductive freedom lies at the heart of the promise of human dignity, self-determination, and equality embodied in both the U.S. Constitution and the Universal Declaration of Human Rights."
Center for Reproductive Rights

Glossary Terms and Concepts

Abortion (Induced)
Agenda for Sustainable
    Development for 2030
Barrier contraceptive
    methods
Behavioral contraceptive
    methods
Clitoridectomy
Coercive pronatalism
Coercive antinatalism
Excision

Female genital mutilation
    (FGM)
Gender health disparities
Global gag rule (Mexico
    City policy)
Hormonal contraceptive
    methods
Infibulation
Intrauterine device
    (IUD)
Maternal morbidity
    (disability)

Maternal mortality
Obstetric fistula
Millennium Develop-
    ment Goals (MDGs)
Prenatal (antenatal) care
Reproductive control
Reproductive health
Reproductive rights
Sterilization
Unmet need for family
    planning
Uterine prolapse

Study Questions

1. What is reproductive health?

2. What are reproductive rights and reproductive control? Why are reproductive rights a critical global feminist issue?

3. What are gender health disparities? How are they affected by intersectionality?

4. What is maternal mortality? What percentage of maternal deaths are preventable? What are the causes of maternal mortality? How and why do maternal mortality ratios vary? How can it be reduced? How is reduction related to the UN's Millennium Development Goals and the Agenda for Sustainable Development Goals 2030?

5. What is maternal morbidity? What are some common types? What is being done to prevent and treat obstetric fistula?

6. What is female genital mutilation/cutting (FGM/FGC)? Where is it practiced? What is its purpose? What health problems does it create? What are the different approaches to stopping it? Why are social norms and cultural approaches to FGM/FGC eradication probably the best approaches?

7. Why is access to contraception an important human and reproductive right? What should be done to reduce unmet need? Why do people need access to a variety of contraceptive options? How does intersectionality relate to women's access to contraception and their experience of side effects?

8. How common is abortion? Approximately how many abortions are unsafe? How does legality and restrictions affect the incidence and safety of abortion? How do abortion laws vary cross-culturally?

9. In what ways do governments and politics affect women's reproductive choice? How can the policies of one country affect reproductive choice in another?

10. How do men sometimes control women's reproductive choice? Why should men care about reproductive rights?

11. What role do corporations and the global economy play in women's reproductive choice?

12. What influence does religion have on women's reproductive choice?

13. How do women act to promote their reproductive rights?

14. How does the chapter illustrate the four global women's and gender studies themes outlined in the book's introduction?

Discussion Questions and Activities

1. What do you think about African feminists' charge that Western women are quick to criticize African nations for FGM while failing to fight against the abuse of the female body in their own countries?

2. How is women's current reproductive choice in your culture affected by the government, men, and religion? Would your answer change if you were a different age, ethnicity, sexual orientation, gender identity, or religion?

3. Use the rights listed in Box 3.1 to explain why FGM, obstetric fistula, and uterine prolapse are violations of women's human rights.

4. Interview several people from another generation. Ask them about the contraceptive methods available when they were of childbearing age and ask what happened when unplanned pregnancies occurred. Were they able to decide how many children they wanted and the spacing of those children? How was this determined by sociocultural and material factors?

5. Explain how your reproductive choice is influenced by the factors identified in Box 3.1 and discussed in the chapter. Alternatively, do research to describe how these factors affect reproductive choice in another country.

6. The chapter suggests that women's reproductive health depends on many things, including knowledge. What kind of sex education did you receive? Was it effective in promoting reproductive health and reproductive choice? How did government and religion influence the education you received?

7. Do an Internet search to identify an example of a recent reproductive rights struggle. What do activists want and why do they want it? What kind of resistance do they face?

Action Opportunities

1. Do a project to increase women's reproductive choice or health in your community. For instance, distribute wallet-sized cards on public transportation with the locations and numbers of family planning clinics in your area, volunteer at a family planning clinic, or distribute condoms.

2. If you agree that women need access to safe and legal abortion with few or no restrictions, and your state or government has restrictive laws, participate in

efforts to increase abortion access. Alternatively, serve as an abortion clinic escort. In many places in the United States, women seeking an abortion face protestors who taunt them, yell at them, and even film them. Clinic escorts offer to walk women from their car to the clinic entrance and provide a buffer between protestors and patients.

3. Why do some women hesitate to ask men to use condoms? How can this be changed? Develop a program to help young women develop the skills to request that male sexual partners use condoms. Present your workshop in the dorms, at sorority meetings, or to at-risk teen girls.

4. Research gender disparities (or gender-and-race disparities) in reproductive health care or health-care coverage in your country, state, or community and take political action. For example, create a change.org petition, use social media, lobby your government leaders, or protest in a creative way that fits who you are.

5. Organize an awareness and fund-raising event to help prevent and treat obstetric fistula.

6. Take a look at the activist websites below and participate in the campaigns in the ways that most move you.

Activist Websites

Catholics for Free Choice www.catholicsforchoice.org

Engender Health https://www.engenderhealth.org

Equality Now End FGM www.equalitynow.org/end_fgm

Global Fund for Women www.globalfundforwomen.org/take-action/

International Day of Zero Tolerance for Female Genital Mutilation www.un.org /end/observances/female-genital-mutilation-day

International Women's Health Coalition www.iwhc.org

Pathfinder International www.pathfinder.org/get-involved/action-center

Population Connection Action Fund http://www.populationconnectionaction.org /what-can-i-do/

Safe Hands for Girls www.safehandsforgirls.org #ENDFGM

UNFPA Campaign to End Fistula www.endfistula.org/campaign

Women on Waves www.womenonwaves.org

Women on Web womenonweb.org

Informational Websites

Center for Reproductive Rights www.reproductiverights.org

Guttmacher Institute www.guttmacher.org

International Planned Parenthood Federation (IPFF) www.ippf.org

United Nations Population Fund (UNFPA) www.unfpa.org

World Health Organization's Department of Reproductive Health and Research www.who.int/teams/sexual-and-reproductive-health-and-research

---

References

Adams, G. 2009, March 9. Brazil rocked by abortion for 9-year-old rape victim; Church excommunicates mother and doctors—but not accused rapist. *The Independent (London)*, 20.

Al-Dayel, N., Mumford, A., and Bales, K. 2020. Not yet dead: The establishment and regulation of slavery by the Islamic State. *Studies in Conflict and Terrorism.* DOI: 10.1080/1057610X.2020.1711590

American Society of Plastic Surgeons. 2019. *Plastic surgery statistics surgery report.* https://www.plasticsurgery.org/documents/News/Statistics/2019/plastic-surgery -full-report-2.pdf. Retrieved on March 19, 2021.

Amnesty International. 2008. *Amnesty International International Report 2008.* http://archive.amnesty.org/air2008/eng/regions/europe-and-central-asia/czech -republic.html. Retrieved on March 31, 2009.

Associated Press. 2020. China cuts Uighur births with IUDs, abortion, sterilizations. https://apnews.com/article/ap-top-news-international-news-weekend-reads-china -health-269b3de1af34e17c1941a514f78d764c. Retrieved on July 7, 2021.

Autorino, T., Mattioli, F., Mencarini, L. 2020. The impact of gynecologists' conscientious objection on abortion access. *Social Science Research, 87:102403.* DOI: 10.1016/j.ssresearch.2020.102403

Barot, S., and Cohen, S. A. 2015. *The global gag rule and fights over UNFPA funding: The issues that won't go away.* https://www.guttmacher.org/about /gpr/2015/06/global-gag-rule-and-fights-over-funding-unfpa-issues-wont-go-away. Retrieved on September 17, 2016.

BBC News. 2021. Poland enforces controversial near-total abortion ban. https:// www.bbc.com/news/world-europe-55838210. Retrieved on March 21, 2021.

Bearak, J., Popinchalk, A., Ganatra, B., Moller, A., Tuncalp, O., and Beavin, C. et al. 2020. Unintended pregnancy and abortion by income, region, and the legal status of abortion: Estimates from a comprehensive model for 1990–2019. *The Lancet.* https://www.thelancet.com/journals/langlo/article/PIIS2214-109X(20)30315-6/fulltext. Retrieved on March 20, 2021.

Berg, R. C., and Underland, V. 2013. The obstetric consequences of female genital mutilation/cutting: A systematic review and meta-analysis. *Obstetrics and Gynecology International, 2013, Article ID 49654.* DOI:10.1155/2013/496564

Berg, R. C., Underland, V., Odgaard-Jensen, J., Fretheim, A., and Vist, G. E. 2014. Effects of female genital cutting on physical health outcomes: A systematic review and meta-analysis. *BMJ Open, 4, e006316.* DOI:10.1136/bmjopen-2014-0006316.

Bernstein, S. 2000. Persistence brought abortion pill to U.S. *Los Angeles Times,* 5 November, A1, A24.

Boonstra, H. D. 2016. *Abortion in the lives of women struggling financially: Why insurance coverage matters.* https://www.guttmacher.org/about/gpr/2016/07 /abortion-lives-women-struggling-financially-why-insurance-coverage-matters. Retrieved on June 23, 2017.

Brooks, N., Bendavid, E., and Miller, G. 2019. USA aid policy and induced abortion in sub-Saharan Africa: An analysis of the Mexico City Policy. *The Lancet.* https://www.thelancet.com/journals/langlo/article/PIIS2214 -109X(19)30267-0/fulltext. Retrieved on March 23, 2021.

Callimachi, R. 2016. To maintain supply of sex slaves, ISIS pushes birth control. *New York Times.* https://www.nytimes.com/2016/03/13/world/middleeast /to-maintain-supply-of-sex-slaves-isis-pushes-birth-control.html. Retrieved on March 21, 2021.

Center for Reproductive Rigths. 2021a. Center cheers reintroduction of the Black Maternal Health Momnibus Act in U.S. Congress. http://reproductiverights .org/story/center-cheers-reintroduction-black-maternal-health-momnibus-act-us -congress. Retrieved on March 26, 2021.

Center for Reproductive Rights. 2021b. *The World's Abortion Laws.* https:// reproductiverights.org/worldabortionlaws. Retrieved on March 21, 2021.

Center for Reproductive Rights. 2021c. *Law and policy guide: Conscientious objection.* https://reproductiverights.org/law-and-policy-guide-conscientious -objection. Retrieved on March 25, 2021.

Centers for Disease Control and Prevention (CDC). 2021. Pregnancy mortality surveillance system. https://www.cdc.gov/reproductivehealth/maternal -mortality/pregnancy-mortality-surveillance-system.htm. Retrieved on March 11, 2021.

Chavkin, W., Leitman, L., and Polin, K. 2013. Conscientious objection and refusal to provide reproductive healthcare: A White Paper examining prevalence, health consequences, and policy responses. *International Journal of Gynecology and Obstetrics, 123,* S41–S56.

Chow, E. N., and K. Chen. 1994. The impact of the one child policy on women and the patriarchal family in the People's Republic of China. In *Women, the family, and policy,* edited by E. N. Chow and C. W. Berheide. Albany, NY: State University of New York Press.

Collyns, D. 2016. Women vow to fight on in Peru after Alberto Fujimori absolved over forced sterilisations. *The Guardian.* https://www.theguardian.com /global-development/2016/aug/03/women-vow-to-fight-on-in-peru-after-fujimori -absolved-over-forced-sterilisations. Retrieved on September 17, 2016.

Davies, C. 2020. Pro-choice supporters hold biggest-ever protest against Polish government. *The Guardian.* https://www.theguardian.com/world/2020/oct/30 /pro-choice-supporters-hold-biggest-ever-protest-against-polish-government. Retrieved on March 23, 2021.

Davis, A. 1990. Racism, birth control, and reproductive rights. In *From abortion to reproductive freedom: Transforming a movement,* edited by M. Gerber Fried. Cambridge, MA: South End Press.

Dawson, R. 2020. *Trump administration's domestic gag rule has slashed Title X network's capacity by half.* Guttmacher Institute. https://www.guttmacher.org /article/2020/02/trump-administrations-domestic-gag-rule-has-slashed-title-x -networks-capacity-half. Retrieved on March 21, 2021.

Dixon-Mueller, R. 1993. *Population policy and women's rights: Transforming reproductive choice.* Westport, CT: Praeger.

Donovan, M. 2020. *After the latest Supreme Court ruling on abortion, the Women's Health Protection Act is more important than ever.* https://www.guttmacher.org /article/2020/07/after-latest-supreme-court-ruling-abortion-womens-health -protection-act-more. Retrieved on March 20, 2021.

Elders, J. 2008, Summer. Sexual healing. *Ms.,* 79.

Esquerra, A. 2020. Rights groups urge "emergency" decriminalization of abortion in Philippines. *Vice.* https://www.vice.com/en/article/v7gwx4/rights-groups-urge -decriminalization-abortion-philippines. Retrieved on March 21, 2021.

Firoz, T., Chou, D., von Dadelszen, P., Agrawal, P., Vanderkruik, R., Tunçalp, O. et al. 2013. Measuring maternal health: Focus on maternal morbidity. *Bulletin of the World Health Organization, 91,* 794–796.

Food and Agriculture Organization (FAO). 2021. *The state of food security and nutrition in the world 2020.* http://www.fao.org/documents/card/en/c /cb1447en/. Retrieved on March 9, 2021.

Ganatra, B., Gerdts, C., Rossier, C., Johnson, B. R. Jr., Tuncalp, O., Assifi, A. et al. Global, regional, and subregional classification of abortions by safety, 2010–2014. 2017. *The Lancet.* https://www.thelancet.com/journals/lancet/article/PIIS0140 -6736(17)31794-4/fulltext. Retrieved on March 20, 2021.

Gutierrez, E. R., and Fuentes, L. 2010. Population control by sterilization: The cases of Puerto Rican and Mexican-origin women in the United States. *Latino(a) Research Review, 7,* 85–100.

Guttmacher Institute. 2017. *Abortion in Latin America and the Caribbean.* https:// www.guttmacher.org/sites/default/files/factsheet/ib_aww-latin-america.pdf. Retrieved on March 20, 2021.

Guttmacher Institute. 2020a. *Unintended pregnancy and abortion worldwide.* https:// www.guttmacher.org/fact-sheet/induced-abortion-worldwide#. Retrieved on March 20, 2021.

Guttmacher Institute. 2020b. *New estimates show worldwide decrease in unintended pregnancies, abortion rates fall in regions where it is broadly legal.* https://www .guttmacher.org/news-release/2020/new-estimates-show-worldwide-decrease -unintended-pregnancies. Retrieved on March 20, 2021.

Guttmacher Institute. 2021a. An overview of abortion laws (United States). https://www.guttmacher.org/state-policy/explore/overview-abortion-laws. Retrieved on March 20, 2021.

Guttmacher Institute. 2021b. *Refusing to provide health services.* https://www
.guttmacher.org/state-policy/explore/refusing-provide-health-services. Retrieved
on March 21, 2021.

Hartmann, B. 2016. *Reproductive rights and wrongs: The global politics of population
control,* 3rd ed. Chicago, IL: Haymarket Books.

Hennessy-Fiske, M. 2016. Crossing the abortion desert: Women increasingly travel out of
their states for the procedure. *Los Angeles Times.* http://www.latimes.com/nation/la-na
-adv-abortion-traveler-20160530-snap-story.html. Retrieved on January 18, 2017.

Hogan, C. 2019. Why Ireland's battle over abortion is far from over. *The Guardian.*
https://www.theguardian.com/lifeandstyle/2019/oct/03/why-irelands-battle-over
-abortion-is-far-from-over-anti-abortionists. Retrieved on July 7, 2021.

Hundley. T. 2013, June 13. Philippines reproductive health law tests power of
Catholic Church as it lobbies Supreme Court. *Washington Post.* https://www
.washingtonpost.com/world/asia_pacific/philippines-health-law-tests-power
-of-catholic-church/2013/06/16/36bc3bdc-d36a-11e2-8cbe-1bcbee06f8f8_story
.html. Retrieved on October 1, 2016.

Jacobson, J. 2009. Yes we can: Ending eight years of frustration, the Obama administration has revived reproductive justice in just a few months. *Ms.,* Spring, 12–13.

Johnson, P. A., Fitzgerald, T., Salganicoff, A., Wood, S. F., and Goldenstein,
J. M. 2014. *Sex-specific medical research: Why women's health can't wait.*
http://www.brighamandwomens.org/Departments_and_Services/womenshealth
/ConnorsCenter/Policy/ConnorsReportFINAL.pdf. Retrieved on August 28, 2016.

Jokhio, A. H., Rizvi, R. M., and McArthur, C. 2020. Prevalence of pelvic organ
prolapse in women, associated factors and impact on quality of life in rural
Pakistan: A population-based study. *BMC Women's Health, 20.* https://doi.
org/10.1186/s12905-020-00934-6. Retrieved on March 11, 2021.

Julios, C. 2019. *Female genital mutilation and social media.* United Kingdom and
New York: Routledge.

Kabagenyi, A., Jennings, L., Reid, A., Nalwadda, G., Ntozi, J., and Atuyambe, L.
2014. Barriers to male involvement in contraceptive uptake and reproductive
health services: a qualitative study of men and women's perceptions in two rural
districts in Uganda. *Reproductive Health, 11.* DOI: 10.1186/1742-4755-11-21

Karlsson, J., and Brenner, M. 2013. Danger in the ring. *Vogue.* December 12.
http://www.vanityfair.com/news/politics/2014/01/nuvaring-lethal-contraceptive
-trial. Retrieved on September 22, 2016.

La Barbera, M. C. 2009. Revisiting the anti-female genital mutilation discourse.
Diritto and Questioni Pubbliche, 9, 485–507.

Latt, S. M., Milner, A., and Kavanagh, A. 2019. Abortion laws reform may reduce
maternal mortality: An ecological study in 162 countries. *BMC Women's Health,
19.* https://doi.org/10.1186/s12905-018-0705-y. Retrieved on March 21, 2021.

Lawani, L. O., Iyoke, C. A., and Ezeonu, P. O. 2015. Contraceptive practice after
surgical repair of obstetric fistula in southeast Nigeria. *International Journal of
Gynecology and Obstetrics, 129,* 256–259.

Michaelson, R. 2016, September 1. Egypt's tougher penalties for FGM will have little impact, say rights groups. *The Guardian*. http://theguardian.com /society/2016/sep/01/egypts-tougher-penalties-for-fgm-will-have-little-impact -rights-groups. Retrieved on September 4, 2016.

Moloney, A. 2021. Haunted by forced sterilizations, Peruvian women pin hopes on court hearing. *Reuters*. https://www.reuters.com/article/peru-women -sterilizations/haunted-by-forced-sterilizations-peruvian-women-pin-hopes-on -court-hearing-idUSL8N2JH4WB. Retrieved on March 21, 2021.

Mosha, I., Ruben, R., and Kakoko, D. 2013. Family planning decisions, perceptions and gender dynamics among couple in Mwanz, Tanzania: A qualitative study. *BMC Public Health, 13*. https://pubmed.ncbi.nim.nih.gov/23721196/. Retrieved on March 21, 2021.

Mosher, W., Jones, J., and Abma, J. 2015. Nonuse of contraception among women at risk of unintended pregnancy in the United States. *Contraception, 92*, 170–176.

Muteshi J., and Sass, J. 2005. *Female Genital Mutilation in Africa: An Analysis of Current Abandonment Approaches*. Nairobi: PATH.

Nash, E., Mohammed, L., Capello, O., and Naide, S. 2019. *State policy trends 2019: A wave of abortion bans, but some states are fighting back*. https://www .guttmacher.org/article/2019/12/state-policy-trends-2019-wave-abortion-bans -some-states-are-fighting-back. Retrieved on March 20, 2021.

Nnaemeka, O. 2005. African women, colonial discources, and imperialist interventions: Female circumcision as impetus. In *Circumcision and the politics of knowledge,* edited by O. Nnaemeka. Westport, CT: Praeger.

O'Sullivan, D. 2016, August 21. Irish women life-tweet journey to Great Britain for an abortion. *CNN*. http://www.cnn.com/2016/08/21/world/irish-women-live -tweet-abortion-journey/. Retrieved on June 24, 2017.

Oba, A. A. 2008. Female circumcision as female genital mutilation: Human rights or cultural imperialism? *Global Jurist, 8*, 1–38.

Planned Parenthood. 2021. *Birth control*. https://www.plannedparenthood.org /learn/birth-control. Retrieved on March 20, 2021.

Politi, D. 2021. Abortion is now legal in Argentina, but opponents are making it hard to get. *New York Times,* March 7. https://www.nytimes.com/2021/03/07 /world/americas/argentina-abortion-opposition.html?referringSource=article Share. Retrieved on March 21, 2021.

PRB. 2021. *Abortion: Facts and figures 2021*. https://prb.org/wp-content/uploads /2121/03/2021-safe-engage-abortion-facts-and-figures-media-guide.pdf. Retrieved on March 26, 2021.

Radwin, M. 2016, October 20. Chile's president wants to ease abortion ban, but opponents push back. *NPR Parallells*. http://www.npr.org/sections /parallels/2016/10/20/497983252/chiles-president-wants-to-ease-abortion -ban-but-opponents-push-back?sc=ipadandf=1001. Retrieved on October 20, 2016.

Robbins, C. P. 2021. End of US 'global gag rule' raises hopes for women's health-care at crucial time. *The New Humanitarian.* https://www.thenewhumanitarian.org/news/2021/1/28/global-gag-rule-abortion-access-biden-mexico-city-policy-haiti-namibia. Retrieved on March 23, 2021.

Schwartz, M. 2014, November 21. Where's better birth control? *New Yorker.* http://www.newyorker.com/business/currency/wheres-better-birth-control. Retrieved on October 1, 2016.

Scully, E., Biddlecom, A., Darroch, J. E., Riley, T., Ashford, L. S., Lince-Deroche, N. et al. 2020. *Adding It Up: Investing in Sexual and Reproductive Health.* https://www.guttmacher.org/report/adding-it-up-investing-in-sexual-reproductive-health-2019. Retrieved on March 19, 2021.

Sedgh, G., Ashford, L. S., and Hussain, R. 2016. *Unmet need for contraception in developing countries: Examining women's reasons for not using a method.* Guttmacher Institute. https://www.guttmacher.org/report/unmet-need-for-contraception-in-developing-countries. Retrieved on September 5, 2016.

Sedgh, G., Bearak, J., Singh, S., Bankole, A., Popinchalk, A., Ganatra, B. et al. 2016, May. Abortion incidence between 1990 and 2014: Global, regional, and subregional levels and trends. *The Lancet.*

Sethna, C., and Davis, G. 2019. *Abortion across borders: Transnational travel and access to abortion services.* Baltimore, MD: Johns Hopkins Press.

Singh, S., Remez, L., Sedgh, G., Kwok, L., and Onda, T. 2018. *Abortion worldwide 2017: Uneven progress and uneven access.* Guttmacher Institute. https://www.guttmacher.org/report/abortion-worldwide-2017. Retrieved on March 21, 2021.

Sridharan, V. 2014. *Iraqi Isis bans birth control in Mosul to boost population.* http://www.ibtimes.co.uk/iraqi-isis-bans-birth-control-mosul-boost-population-1477630. Retrieved on September 29, 2016.

Teggarty, N. 2016, September 15. Proposed bill deepens the rift in Poland's abortion debate. *News Deeply: Women and Girls Hub.* https://www.newsdeeply.com/womenandgirls/proposed-bill-deepens-the-rift-in-polands-abortion-debate/. Retrieved on September 24, 2016.

UN (United Nations). 2014. Reproductive rights are human rights: A handbook for national human rights institutions. http://www.unfpa.org/publications/reproductive-rights-are-human-rights. Retrieved on August 28, 2016.

UN DESA (Department of Economic and Social Affairs). 2019. *Contraceptive use by method 2019.* https://www.un.org/development/desa/pd/sites/www.un.org.development.desa.pdf. Retrieved on March 19, 2021.

UN DESA (Department of Economic and Social Affairs). 2021. *Sustainable development: Goal 5 Achieve gender equality and empower all women and girls.* https://sdgs.un.org/goals/goal5. Retrieved on March 11, 2021.

UNAIDS. 2020. *Women, adolescent girls and the HIV response.* https://www.unaids.org/en/resources/presscentre/pressreleaseandstatementarchive/2020/march/20200305_weve-got-the-power. Retrieved on March 9, 2021.

UNFPA. 2019. *Explainer: What is the ICPD and why does it matter?* https://www
.unfpa.org/news/explainer-what-icpd-and-why-does-it-matter. Retrieved on
March 19, 2021.

UNFPA. 2020a. *Female genital mutilation: Frequently asked questions.* https://www
.unfpa.org/resources/female-genital-mutilation-fgm-frequently-asked
-questions#religions. Retrieved on March 11, 2021.

UNFPA. 2020b. *Ensure universal access to sexual and reproductive health and reproductive rights: Measuring SDG Target 5.6.* https://www.unfpa.org/sites/default/files
/pub-pdf/UNFPA-SDG561562Combined-v4.15.pdf. Retrieved on March 27, 2021.

UNFPA (United Nations Population Fund). 2014. Implementation of the International and Regional Human Rights Framework for the elimination of female genital
mutilation. http://www.unfpa.org/publications/implementation-international
-and-regional-human-rights-framework-elimination-female. Retrieved on
December 28, 2017.

UNFPA (United Nations Population Fund). 2015. Religion, women's health, and
rights: Points of contention and paths of opportunities. https://www.unfpa.org/pcm
/node/15024. Retrieved on March 23, 2021.

UNFPA (United Nations Population Fund). 2016a. UN report on obstetric
fistula. http://www.endfistula.org/publications/un-report-obstetric-fistula-2016.
Retrieved on December 28, 2017.

UNFPA (United Nations Population Fund). 2016b. Universal access to reproductive
health: Progress and challenges. http://www.unfpa.org/publications/universal-access
-reproductive-health-progress-and-challenges. Retrieved on December 27, 2017.

UNFPA-UNICEF. *Measuring effectiveness of female genital mutilation elimination:
A compendium of indicators.* https://www.unfpa.org/sites/default/files/pub
-pdf/026_UF_CompendiumOfIndicatorsFGM_21-online_F.pdf. Retrieved on
March 11, 2021.

UNICEF. 2020a. *Global delivery care coverage and trends: 2014–2019.* https://data
.unicef.org/topic/maternal-health/delivery-care/. Retrieved on March 11, 2021.

UNICEF. 2020b. *Approximately 1 in 4 survivors of female genital mutilation
were cut by a health provider.* https://www.unicef.org/press-releases
/approximately-1-4-fgm-survivors-were-cut-health-care-provider. Retrieved
on March 11, 2021.

UNICEF (United Nations Children's Fund). 2013. *Female genital mutilation/cutting: A
statistical overview and exploration of the dynamics of change.* http://www.data.unicef
.org/resources/female-genital-mutilation-cutting-a-statistical-overview-and-exploration
-of-the-dynamics-of-change.html. Retrieved on September 4, 2016.

UNICEF (United Nations Children's Fund). 2014. *Voices of change: 2014
annual report of the UNFPA-UNICEF Joint Programme on Female Genital
Mutilation: Accelerating Change.* http://www.unfpa.org/publications/2014
-annual-report-unfpa-unicef-joint-programme-female-genital-mutilationcutting.
Retrieved on September 4, 2016.

WHO (World Health Organization). 2007. *What is a gender-based approach to public health?* http://www.who.int/features/qa/56/en/index.html. Retrieved on May 28, 2009.

WHO (World Health Organization). 2009. 10 facts about women's health. http://www.who.int/features/factfiles/women/en/index.html

WHO (World Health Organization). 2015. *Trends in maternal mortality 1990 to 2015.* https://www.who.int/reproductivehealth/publications/monitoring/maternal-mortality-2015/en/. Retrieved on March 11, 2021.

WHO (World Health Organization). 2016. Global health estimates. https://www.who.int/maternal_child_adolescent/data/causes-death-adolescents/en/. Retrieved on March 11, 2021.

WHO (World Health Organization). 2019a. *Trends in maternal mortality 2000 to 2017.* https://www.unfpa.org/sites/default/files/pub-pdf/Maternal_mortality_report.pdf. Retrieved on March 9, 2021.

WHO (World Health Organization). 2019b. *Maternal mortality*: Key facts. https://www.who.int/news-room/fact-sheets/detail/maternal-mortality. Retrieved on March 23, 2021.

WHO (World Health Organization). 2020a. *Female genital mutilation.* https://www.who.int/news-room/fact-sheets/detail/female-genital-mutilation. Retrieved on March 11, 2021.

WHO (World Health Organization). 2020b. *Preventing unsafe abortion.* https://www.who.int/news-room/fact-sheets/detail/preventing-unsafe-abortion. Retrieved on March 21, 2021.

Zerwick, P. 2016. The rise of DIY abortion. https://www.glamour.com/story/the-rise-of-the-diy-abortion. Retrieved on March 23, 2021.

Design Element: Abstract floral frame: Telnov Oleksii/Shutterstock

4

Women's Sexuality and Sexual Rights

No woman can determine the direction of her own life without the ability to determine her sexuality. Sexuality is an integral, deeply ingrained part of every human being's life and should not be subject to debate or coercion. Anyone who is truly committed to women's human rights must recognize that every woman has the right to determine her sexuality free of discrimination and oppression.

—PALESA BEVERLY DITSIE of South Africa, speaking at the 1995 Fourth World Conference on Women

A woman's sexuality is often not her own and belongs to her family, community, or male partner, but there is a growing global consensus that sexual rights are human rights that cultures cannot deny and must protect. Women's rights activism includes activism to promote the rights of nonheterosexual and trans women. Andrew Resek/ McGraw Hill

This chapter focuses on women's sexuality and **sexual rights.** Sexual rights are human rights related to sexuality—they are about the rights of people to make personal decisions about their sexuality and their sexual activity. Sexual rights also include rights based on sexual orientation, gender identity, and the rights of intersex people (sometimes called **LGBTQIA rights** or **SOGI rights**). Like women's reproductive rights, women's sexuality is often limited, restricted, and defined in the name of the national interest, the family, community, religion, or culture. In many places, women that challenge traditional gender and sexuality norms face hostility, condemnation, and violence.

Sexual Rights as Human Rights

Establishing that sexual rights are human rights is important. Being able to frame sexual inequalities in terms of human rights helps women assert they are human beings who demand and deserve respect and rights in regards to their sexuality, regardless of common cultural beliefs and practices. Casting sexual rights as human rights helps women reclaim their sexuality instead of it being defined solely in terms of its service to male partners, family, and community. Women's sexual rights also affect women's **sexual health**, a state of physical, emotional, mental, and social well-being in relation to sexuality (WHO, 2015). Box 4.1 lists some important sexual rights.

Fortunately, there is a growing global consensus that sexual rights are human rights that cultures cannot deny and must protect. But this acceptance is relatively new and tentative, the result of years of activism. Indeed, it was not until the 1990s that sexual rights were put on the human rights agenda, and not without struggle. In 1995 at the UN's World Conference on Women in Beijing, sexual and reproductive rights were hotly debated. Of particular concern to many countries was language in draft documents referring to sexual orientation. Ultimately, this language had to be dropped and women's sexual and reproductive rights were defined in the final Beijing Platform for Action as including the rights of women to

> . . . have control over and decide freely and responsibly on matters related
> to their sexuality, including sexual and reproductive health, free of coercion,
> discrimination and violence. Equal relationships between women and men in
> matters of sexual relations and reproduction, including full respect for the integrity
> of the person, require mutual respect, consent and shared responsibility for sexual
> behaviour and its consequences. (paragraph 96)

Since then, greater worldwide affirmation and expansion of sexual rights have occurred. NGOs such as OutRight Action International (formerly known as the International Gay and Lesbian Human Rights Commission or IGLHRC) worked to relate the rights of gays, lesbians, bisexuals, and transgender people to the Universal Declaration of Human Rights (UDHR) and other international treaties. For example, the UDHR specifies that everyone is entitled to equal protection under the law. OutRight pointed out that those who challenge sexual and gender norms regularly experience discrimination related to housing, social security, and employment, such as when they

"That's right. You heard me. Women's sexual rights. We have sexual rights including a right to ask for sex when we want it ('Come on baby I'm in the mood'); a right to say no ('Put that thing away, I'm tired'); a right to enjoy it ('Oh yeah! A little to the left!'); and a right to safe sex ("No glove, no love"). And guess what? These rights are enshrined in the Namibian Constitution and a host of other legally binding instruments including the AU protocol on the rights of women."
Trainer from Sister Namibia, Namibian Women's Rights Group

"Sexual rights are a fundamental element of human rights. Sexual rights include the right to liberty and autonomy in the responsible exercise of sexuality."
Health, Empowerment, Rights and Accountability (HERA), an international women's health advocacy group

BOX 4.1   *Some Important Sexual Rights*

Sexual rights include the right to:

- Choose one's own partner.

- Decide whether to be sexually active or not.

- Pleasurable and safe sexual experiences free of coercion, discrimination, and violence.

- Be free from sexually transmitted infections.

- Be free from negative sexual health consequences arising from sexual violence or FGM/FGC.

- Have access to sexual and reproductive health-care services.

- Comprehensive sexuality education.

- Protection from sexuality-related harm, including violence and abuse because of gender, gender identity, or sexual orientation.

Source: Derived from WHO, UN, IPFF, OutRight Action International, Yogyakarta Principles.

"In most communities, the option available to women for sexual activity is confined to marriage with a man from the same community. Women who choose options which are disapproved of by the community, whether to have a sexual relationship with a man in a nonmarital relationship, to have such a relationship outside of ethnic, religious or class communities, or to live out their sexuality in ways other than heterosexuality, are often subjected to violence and degrading treatment."
Radhika Coomaraswamy, former UN Special Rapporteur on Violence Against Women

are denied jobs because of their appearance or evicted from their homes because of their sexual orientation or gender identity. OutRight was part of an international team supported by the UN that developed the 2007 *Yogyakarta Principles on the Application of International Human Rights Law in Relation to Sexual Orientation and Gender Identity.* Named after an international seminar that took place in Yogyakarta, Indonesia at Gadjah Mada University in 2006, the principles clarify governments' human rights obligations in relation to sexual orientation and gender (Yogyakarta Principles, 2007). Figure 4.1 shows some rights from the Universal Declaration of Human Rights that are consistent with sexual rights.

In 2008, the International Planned Parenthood Federation released "The Declaration of Sexual Rights." According to the declaration, sexual rights encompass sexual activity, gender identities, and sexual orientation. Sexual rights require a commitment to "negative" rights such as protection from sexuality-related harm (violence and abuse of a physical, verbal, psychological, and sexual nature because of gender, gender identity, or sexual orientation). They also include "positive" rights such as the right to pursue sexual pleasure and to choose one's own partner. The same year, at the General Assembly of the United Nations, sixty-six countries from five continents agreed to a statement confirming that international human rights protections include sexual orientation and gender identity.[1] Then, in 2015, all twelve UN agencies, including UNWomen and the World Health Organization (WHO), issued a joint statement calling for an end to discrimination based on actual or perceived

[1]The annual UN General Assembly includes representatives from most of the world's countries and may draft conventions, resolutions, and treaties that when ratified are legally binding as part of international law. They may also draft and vote on declarations that are not legally binding, but serve as international guidelines and general commitments.

FIGURE 4.1   *Some Human Rights from the UDHR Relevant to Sexual Rights*

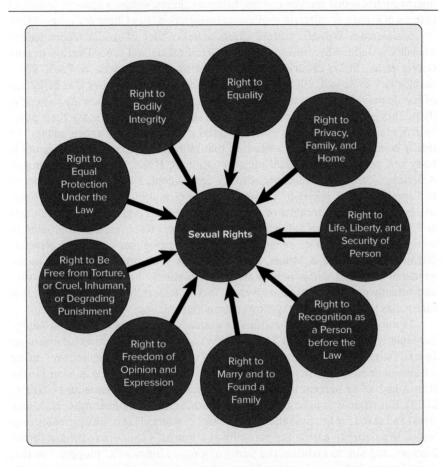

"Human rights are universal—cultural, religious and moral practices and beliefs and social attitudes cannot be invoked to justify human rights violations against any group, including LGBTI persons."
Joint UN Agency Statement Ending Violence and Discrimination against Lesbian, Gay, Bisexual, Transgender and Intersex People

sexual orientation, gender identity, and sex characteristics. The statement calls for repealing discriminatory laws and protecting individuals from discrimination. It promises support to UN member nations for changes that will protect, promote, and fulfill the rights of all LGBTQIA people (OHCHR, 2015).

OutRight Action International is one of the leading organizations documenting abuses of LGBTIQ people and advocating for their rights.

A Woman's Sexuality Is Often Not Her Own

A woman's sexuality is often not her own and belongs to her family, community, or male partner; this is a violation of women's sexual rights. Gender inequality often means that men's sexual rights supersede women's and that men can violate women's sexual rights with impunity. Sexual assault, forced marriage, FGM to control women's sexuality, and honour-based violence are examples from previous chapters. Many cultures have a **sexual double standard** where women's sexuality is defined in terms of monogamy, passivity, and receptivity to male partners, while men's sexual

"Proponents of sexual liberation and abstinence-until-marriage advocates appear to be on opposing ends of the sociopolitical spectrum; however, both are invested in the regulation of women's vaginas."
Casey Kelley and Kristen Hoerl, communications researchers

"Society is so concerned over women and girls' potential for promiscuity that we create dress codes, school curricula, even legislation around protecting women's supposed purity."
Jessica Valenti, American feminist and journalist/writer

"The concepts of honour and virginity locate the prestige of a man between the legs of a woman."
Fatema Mernissi, Moroccan feminist writer and sociologist

"I've been called a slut while I was still a virgin. I have been called a slut while I was in a committed relationship with my husband. So it really doesn't matter what you do in life, people can call you that name because they are uncomfortable with your sexuality. That's all it is."
Amber Rose, American activist, model, and media personality

urges are believed to be uncontrollable, such that they are not expected to be monogamous (Chant, 2003). Traditional masculinity norms in gender-unequal societies lead men to control sexual decision-making. In some cultures, women's sexuality is defined in terms of women as objects of men's sexual satisfaction (Bay-Cheng & Zucker, 2007).

Mainstream Western culture offers a heavy diet of media where female sexuality is defined by women's sexual objectification and subordination to men (Carta et al., 2021; Dworkin, 1987; Kilbourne, 2003; Nelson & Paek, 2005; Stankiewicz & Roselli, 2008). Some American women internalize this definition of female sexuality and go through great pain, discomfort, and expense to personify it. They wear uncomfortable high-heeled shoes and wax and shave their pubic hair. Some go so far as to get cosmetic genital surgery and whiten their anuses. All this is done to achieve body aesthetics that mimic the objectified pornographic body and privilege male sexual pleasure (Kelly & Hoerl, 2015). And, although American women are ostensibly sexually empowered, a sexual double standard still applies when it comes to having casual sex or multiple sexual partners (boys will be boys, but girls are sluts or whores). Men are still evaluated more positively and less negatively than women with similar sexual histories, and compared to men, women expect more negative judgment for casual sex (Allison & Risman, 2013; Conley, Ziegler, & Moors, 2012; Endendijk et al., 2020). In many cultures, gendered messages communicate that women should be sexually conservative and sexually passive (Abdolmanafi et al., 2018). Research finds that women that internalize these messages have lower sexual satisfaction.

In traditional patriarchal cultures, a woman's sexuality belongs to her family, particularly her male relatives. Her sexuality is confined to heterosexual marriage. In a UN study of 57 countries, 25 percent of women said they cannot say "no" to a husband or partner if they do not want to have sex; however, this number ranged from a high of 89 percent in Senegal to a low of 5 percent in Ecuador (UNFPA, 2020). Her virginity is to be guarded by her father (and sometimes other male relatives) and saved for her husband. This control of women's sexuality probably originated in a desire to ensure the paternity of a woman's children to protect family lineages, and also to maintain the purity of a future husband's "property" so that daughters would be marriageable. Honour-based violence (discussed in Chapter 2) is an example of how in some cultures a woman's sexuality serves as proof of her *family's* morality and righteousness.

The sexual purity of girls and women, including premarital virginity, is still highly valued in some cultures. Some prospective grooms (and/or their families) demand proof of a bride's virginity, particularly in parts of the Middle East and Asia. However, methods for determining virginity are ineffective, and often painful and traumatic (Olson & Garcia-Moreno, 2017; WHO, 2018). Virginity testing for cultural reasons has been documented in Afghanistan, Brazil, Egypt, India, Indonesia, Iran, Iraq, Jamaica, Jordan, Libya, Malawi, Morocco, Palestine, South Africa, Sri Lanka, Swaziland, Turkey, the United Kingdom, and Zimbabwe. Hymen restoration surgeries, which ensure bleeding on a woman's wedding night, are also on the rise, particularly in the Middle East (Ghanim, 2015). In some places virginity testing is forced on women suspected of having premarital sex (Afghanistan), women detained by police (Egypt, Libya, Jordan), or as a condition of employment (the Indonesian military), or for girls to receive a school scholarship (rural South Africa).

The costs to women of "failing" a virginity test can include physical punishment, honour killing, familial and social condemnation and banishment, fines, and education and employment discrimination (WHO, 2018). For example, in parts of Afghanistan, hundreds of girls and women are in jail for failing virginity tests because premarital sex is criminalized (Gharib, 2019). From a human rights standpoint, female virginity testing violates the right to nondiscrimination, the right to physical and psychological integrity, the right to respect for one's private life, and the right not to be subjected to cruel, inhuman, and degrading treatment (WHO, 2018). The World Health Organization calls for a global ban on the practice because there is no medical way to prove virginity, and virginity testing has high physical, psychological, and social costs for women and girls. From a feminist perspective, virginity testing is a form of women as objects and property. Remember that one example of women's and girls' lower status and power is that they are often treated as objects that are the "property" of men. Virginity testing is another example of this because male relatives (mostly fathers) control a woman's sexuality until she is married. Once married, her sexuality is controlled by her husband. It is considered a form of objectification by feminists, because a woman's value is reduced to her virginity and sexual purity.

Most religious frameworks emphasize women's sexual restraint, sexual duties to husbands, and sex for procreation. They do not acknowledge or affirm women's capacity for sexual pleasure, and the result is often guilt and shame about sexuality (Daniluk & Browne, 2008). Some conservative religions see women's sexuality as a dangerous and corrupting influence on men (see Chapter 8), and require that women keep their sexuality under wraps through modest dress and behavior. For example, the Taliban of Afghanistan require women be completely covered with only a small mesh screen through which to see. In Iran, women are legally required to cover their heads and wear modest dress, and police regularly hassle women they believe to be in violation. Meanwhile, in the United States at conservative Christian purity balls, girls pledge their virginity to their fathers for safekeeping until marriage, and thousands of girls sign virginity pledges rooted in religious teachings about sex and morality (Landor & Simons, 2014; Valenti, 2009).

Sexual double standards and male control of sexual decision-making (as well as a lack of comprehensive sexuality education) also significantly affect women's sexual health. For example, they impact women's risk for AIDS, an autoimmune disease resulting from infection with the Human Immunodeficiency Virus (HIV). **HIV/AIDS** in women is related to gender norms prescribing an unequal and more passive role for women in sexual decision-making that undermines women's autonomy, exposes many to sexual coercion in their relationships, and prevents them from insisting on monogamy or condom use by their male partners (UNAIDS, 2008). Early marriage, rape, sexual abuse, and sex work arising from economic hardship also put millions of girls and women at risk of HIV infection. Women and girls in these situations do not usually have the power to negotiate the terms of sex. Young women and girls are also at greater risk of rape, sexual coercion, and sex trafficking because they are perceived to be more likely to be free from infection, or because of the erroneous belief in some regions that sex with a virgin can cleanse a man of infection.

Where it is common for married men to have extramarital sex, the spread of HIV/AIDS is also fueled, especially when women are unable to negotiate the use of a condom or discuss fidelity with their partners without physical violence or the threat of violence (UNAIDS, 2008; 2016). Intimate partner violence is estimated to increase the rate of HIV infection by around 55 percent (UNAIDS, 2014). That's

"I can't go back, but I can give you this message as a culmination of my experiences: If you want to wait to have sex until marriage, make sure it's because you want to. It's your body; it belongs to you, not your church. Your sexuality is nobody's business but yours."
Samantha Pugsley, who regretted keeping a virginity pledge she made at age 10 because it inhibited her sexuality in adulthood

"Women's sexual autonomy and bodily integrity are core aspects of struggles for and against women's ability to exercise all of their human rights and to live lives of dignity."
Susana Fried, International Gay and Lesbian Human Rights Commission

"Women are not expected to discuss or make decisions about sexuality, and they cannot request, let alone insist, on using a condom or any form of protection."
World Health Organization

BOX 4.2   *Women and HIV/AIDS*

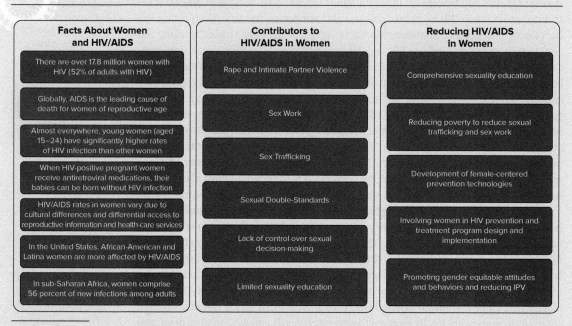

Facts About Women and HIV/AIDS	Contributors to HIV/AIDS in Women	Reducing HIV/AIDS in Women
There are over 17.8 million women with HIV (52% of adults with HIV)	Rape and Intimate Partner Violence	Comprehensive sexuality education
Globally, AIDS is the leading cause of death for women of reproductive age	Sex Work	Reducing poverty to reduce sexual trafficking and sex work
Almost everywhere, young women (aged 15–24) have significantly higher rates of HIV infection than other women	Sex Trafficking	Development of female-centered prevention technologies
When HIV-positive pregnant women receive antiretroviral medications, their babies can be born without HIV infection	Sexual Double-Standards	Involving women in HIV prevention and treatment program design and implementation
HIV/AIDS rates in women vary due to cultural differences and differential access to reproductive information and health-care services	Lack of control over sexual decision-making	Promoting gender equitable attitudes and behaviors and reducing IPV
In the United States, African-American and Latina women are more affected by HIV/AIDS	Limited sexuality education	
In sub-Saharan Africa, women comprise 56 percent of new infections among adults		

Sources: Centers for Disease Control and Prevention (2016), UNAIDS (2014), and UNWomen (2018).

because high levels of IPV often indicate the presence of traditional gender norms that support men's sexual dominance and reduce women's ability to say "no" to sex or insist on condom use or fidelity (Abramsky et al., 2014). You can see why the World Health Organization (2013) says that working with boys and men to promote gender equitable attitudes and behaviors and reducing IPV are critical to reducing HIV in women. Box 4.2 provides additional facts about HIV/AIDS and women.

Sexual Orientation, Gender Identity, and Human Rights (SOGI Rights)

Sexual orientation and gender identity (SOGI) are important to global women's and gender studies because they are intersectional variables that affect the lived experience of girls and women. In addition to the sexism (gender discrimination) commonly experienced by women, LBT (lesbian, bisexual, and transgender) women face added stigma and discrimination on the basis of their sexual orientation, gender identity, or gender expression. Because LBT women are gender-nonconforming women, their status is often lower than that of other women, leading to even greater inequality and disrespect of their human rights. Further demonstrating the diversity created by intersectionality, the SOGI-related stigma and discrimination a LBT woman experiences may also differ based on her class, religion, ethnicity, and where she lives, as well as whether she's lesbian, bisexual, or trans. For example, in the United States, lesbians of color often face a triple interacting burden of heterosexism, sexism, and racism (sometimes called triple jeopardy). Bisexual women often experience prejudice (biphobia or binegativity) from both heterosexuals and lesbians who question the legitimacy of the bisexual sexual orientation (Hayfield, Clarke, & Halliwell, 2014; Ross et al., 2018).

Gender Identity

Gender identity is a person's psychological sense of themselves as male or female; it is one's deeply held sense of gender. **Gender expression** is the way you express your gender through such things as your clothing, name, haircut, behavior, and body characteristics (OutRight Action International, 2016). In most places, "female/femininity" and "male/masculinity" are perceived as clear-cut, mutually exclusive categories, and gender norms and roles reflect this binary view of gender. Conformity to traditional gender norms and expectations is expected, and gender nonconformity is often discouraged and punished. Worldwide, this socially constructed gender binary contributes to norms supportive of stigmatization, harassment, discrimination, marginalization, and violence toward those with nonconforming gender identities and expressions. This minority stress negatively impacts the well-being of gender nonconforming and gender-variant people and is a violation of their human rights.

The truth is that gender identity and expression are considerably more diverse than the **gender binary** suggests. In fact, variability in gender identification and expression is normal and there have always been people whose gender identity and expression differ from cultural expectations associated with the sex/gender they were assigned at birth (World Health Organization, 2015). Furthermore, approximately 17 of every 1,000 (1.7%) of people are **intersex** and possesses chromosomal and anatomical features of both males and females (UN Free and Equal, 2016). Many gender scholars, like sociologist Judith Lorber (2000), call for dismantling the gender binary, deeming it a harmful and artificial social construction.

The term **transgender** or **trans** is used to describe people whose gender identity and/or expression differs from what is typically associated with their birth-assigned sex (**cisgender** refers to when a person's gender identity matches their birth-assigned gender). But people that don't fit the gender binary may prefer other labels such as "nonbinary" or "gender-queer," and terminology is evolving, so it's best to ask individuals what they prefer (OutRight Action International, 2014). **Trans girls** and **trans women** are people that identify as girls or women although they were labeled male at birth. Gender identity is not the same thing as sexual orientation, and trans women may be lesbian, bisexual, or heterosexual. Some trans women prefer simply to be called women while others identify as MTF or M2F (an abbreviation for male-to-female), or transfeminine. Labels may also vary by culture. Trans women are diverse. For instance, some trans women don't desire sex reassignment surgery, and some want it but don't have access to it (OutRight Action International, 2016). Intersectionality also applies to the experience of trans women and girls, many of whom experience even greater discrimination and violence depending on where they live and if they are also racial or ethnic minorities.

Transphobia is prejudice and discrimination against transgender people. Trans girls and women regularly experience violations of their human rights because of their nonconforming gender identity and expression. They experience high levels of

"It has become clear that human sexuality includes many different forms of behaviour and expression, and that the recognition of the diversity of sexual behaviour and expression contributes to people's overall sense of well-being and health."
World Health Organization

transphobic sexual and physical violence, harassment, and humiliation, and they face legal, economic, and social marginalization with little or no protection from their governments or support from their families (OutRight Action International, 2014; World Health Organization, 2015). This transgender bias has many negative impacts. For example, transgender women (trans women) have the highest rates of HIV infection because employment discrimination forces many into sex work, illicit silicone and hormone injections expose them to infection, and health-care discrimination means many lack access to HIV/AIDS prevention programs (Baral et al., 2013). Frequent experiences of harassment, discrimination, violence, and rejection also translate into significantly higher rates of suicidal behavior for trans women compared to the overall population (American Foundation for Suicide Prevention, 2014).

Sexual Orientation

At its most basic, **sexual orientation** is whether a person feels sexual desire for people of the other gender (heterosexual), the same gender (homosexual), or more than one gender (bisexual), though some people are asexual (for the most part, they don't feel sexual attraction to others). Although we'll use the sexual orientation terminology of *heterosexual/homosexual/bisexual/lesbian*, terminology varies considerably cross-culturally. In many places, there are no categories or concepts that include nonheterosexual sexuality, or only derogatory terms for people who don't fit traditional sexuality norms (Herdt, 1997; Laboy, Sandfort, & Yi, 2009). Often the term LGBTI is used as an inclusive term (lesbian, gay, bisexual, transgender, intersex), but some people use LGBTQI (adding "queer" to include those who eschew sexual categorization) and some use LGBTQIA where the "A" refers to "asexual." LGBT+ is also used as an inclusive term to refer to LGBT and related communities who may identify as asexual, pansexual, nonbinary, gender fluid, polyamorous, and more.

Some people insist that nonheterosexual sexual orientations are deviant or sick, but the majority of the world's psychologists, psychiatrists, and medical and health organizations disagree. Following significant lobbying activism from LGB political organizations, the American Psychiatric Association removed homosexuality from its list of mental disorders in 1974. Their current position is that it is no more abnormal to be homosexual than it is to be left-handed, which 15 percent of the population is. The World Health Organization removed homosexuality from its list of diseases in 1991. The simple fact of the matter is that people vary, not everyone is heterosexual, and nonheterosexuals are normal people deserving of their human rights just like everyone else. There is increasing recognition that forcing people to live as heterosexuals when they're not, trying to change their sexual orientations, and stigmatizing and discriminating against them due to their sexual orientation is a violation of their sexual rights, just as it would be were the reverse to be true.

Examinations of literature, art, and anthropology reveal that lesbians have been around forever. Scholars such as Lillian Faderman (1991; 1997; 2000) and Leila Rupp (1996; 1997) documented the lesbian relationships of western women such as Jane Addams, Emily Dickinson, and Eleanor Roosevelt, and the role of lesbian and bisexual women in America's history. Historian Vivien Ng (1996) has documented lesbians in Chinese history. Also, in the United States, there are the Lesbian

Barack Obama was the first U.S. president to use the words "transgender" and "lesbian" in a State of the Union address when he condemned the persecution of LGBTQ people. Between 2011 and 2015, the number of Americans who viewed transgender people favorably rose steeply from 26 percent to 44 percent.
Human Rights Campaign

"Transgender and gender nonconforming people face injustice at every turn: in childhood homes, in school systems that promise to shelter and educate, in harsh and exclusionary workplaces, at the grocery store, the hotel front desk, in doctors' offices and emergency rooms, before judges and at the hands of landlords, police officers, health-care workers and other service providers."
National Center for Transgender Equality (U.S.)

May 17th is the International Day Against Homophobia, Transphobia, and Biphobia.

Herstory Archives (LHA), the West Coast Lesbian Collections, and the Women's Collection held at the Northwestern University library. Cavin (1985) notes that it is ironic that lesbians are omitted from discussions of early society because their existence is documented in the earliest recorded history, art, and literature of Western society: lesbians in Sparta and Crete (400 B.C.E.) and among the Celts described by Aristotle. Lesbianism was also reported in Athens (450 B.C.E.) and in Rome (100 C.E.). Several ancient Chinese sexual handbooks also describe lesbian activities, and lesbian relationships are celebrated in a number of Chinese plays and stories dating from the tenth to the eighteenth centuries (Ruan & Bullough, 1992).

Anthropological accounts indicate that being lesbian was acceptable in a number of cultures prior to Western colonization (Allen, 1992; Blackwood, 1984; Greene, 1994). As Kendall (1998) says of her studies of lesbianism in Lesotho, an African country, "Love between women is as native to southern Africa as the soil itself, but . . . homophobia . . . is a Western import" (p. 224). According to Native American Paula Gunn Allen (1992), colonizers of Native American tribes tried to make Native American culture resemble the European patriarchy. The flexible and fluid sexuality found in many tribes did not fit this paradigm. Thus, colonization is linked to the growth of prejudice against lesbians (Allen, 1992). Anthropologists also believe that Native American women from the Mohave, Maricopa, Cocopa, Klamath, and Kaska tribes could marry other women and make love with other women without being stigmatized (Blackwood, 1984). Cavin (1985) examined anthropology's Human Relations Area Files and found evidence of lesbians in thirty different societies from all over the world. Lesbians did not appear to be more common to any one type of economy, family or household type, marriage form, stratification system, or marital residence. In other words, the lesbian sexual orientation reaches across a number of societies and social categories.

By the nineteenth century, nonheterosexual women were viewed as ill and in need of treatment. Confinements in mental asylums, clitoridectomy, and psychotherapy were commonly used to "treat" nonheterosexual women well into the twentieth century. In some places, the view that lesbians and bisexual women need to be "cured" remains. In Iran, for example, lesbians are often diagnosed with "gender identity disorder" and prescribed hormones and sex reassignment surgery (Outright Action International, 2016). Today, some American Christians coerce lesbian daughters into undergoing ineffective and traumatic conversion therapies intended to change their sexual orientation (National Center for Lesbian Rights, 2016).

Lesbian and Bisexual Women's Invisibility

The tendency for nonheterosexual women to live quiet, hidden lives and for societies to ignore or deny their existence is called **lesbian and bisexual invisibility**. Some people have suggested that bisexual invisibility may even be more pronounced than lesbian invisibility, because societies tend to dichotomize sexual relations as either homosexual or heterosexual, which obscures bisexuality (Bennett, 1992). Bisexual women may also be less visible because it is easier for them to "pass" as heterosexuals than people that are exclusively lesbian (Herek, 2009). Heteropatriarchal societies hide the existence of lesbians and bisexual women by portraying heterosexual womanhood as

In 2015, Nepal became the first Asian country, and one of a handful around the world, to provide constitutional protections for LGBTQ people when it adopted an inclusive new constitution.
Human Rights Campaign

The designation *lesbian* comes from ancient Greece and the life of the lyric poet Sappho, who lived on the island of Lesbos (600 B.C.E.). Some of her poetry described her strong love for women.

"The truth is that while the differences in sexual orientation and gender identity or expression are probably inborn— who would be so crazy to choose to be a lesbian in an extremely homophobic country?— the same cannot be said for homophobia, which is often the result of a certain time and context in history, a time and a context always marked by a strong inequality between men and women."
Renato Sabbadini, International Lesbian, Gay, Bisexual, Trans and Intersex Association (ILGA)

"Enforced heterosexuality is tied to women's lack of economic power and the restriction of female activity to the domestic sphere. Further, the embeddedness of sexuality with gender roles in Western societies proscribes homosexual activity and defines women as male sex objects."
Evelyn Blackwood, anthropologist

"A person's sexual orientation and/ or gender identity cannot be changed. What must change are the negative social attitudes that stigmatize LGBT people and contribute to violence and discrimination against them."
UN Free & Equal Campaign

"Being comfortable with homosexuality in societies that view your life as being not only abnormal but in fundamental opposition to patriarchal notions of the family, love, and heterosexual norms of desire is never an easy process, no matter where one lives."
Kaushalya Bannerji, Canadian poet

the only womanhood. Heterosexual marriage and romance are idealized in art, literature, media, and advertising as if this was the only form of sexuality (Rich, 1976). Anthropology and the social sciences have also contributed to lesbian invisibility (Blackwood, 1986; Blackwood & Wieringa, 1999; Cavin, 1985; Herdt, 1997). In some cultures, there isn't even a word for nonheterosexual women (Greene, 1994). At the UN's 1995 Fourth Women's World Conference, some country representatives balked at resolutions designed to protect lesbian rights, claiming there were no lesbians in their countries and that lesbianism was a Western cultural notion. However, if it seems that lesbianism is confined to Western white women, it is only because other lesbians face more obstacles to visibility (Bunch, 1995).

Worldwide, stigma and discrimination as well as a lack of government protection also contribute to invisibility because they lead LB women to hide their sexual orientation to protect themselves. In the majority of the world's countries, LB women do not have the same sexual rights as heterosexuals and do not experience equal protection under the law. Only 41 percent of the world's countries prohibit employment discrimination on the basis of sexual orientation (ILGA World, 2020). Only 14 percent of countries allow same-sex marriage, and less than 16 percent allow LGBT people to adopt children. In 35 percent of countries, same-sex sexual acts are illegal, and in eleven countries (Afghanistan, Brunei, Iran, Mauritania, Nigeria, Pakistan, Qatar, Saudi Arabia, Somalia, United Arab Emirates, and Yemen), criminal penalties may include death (ILGA World, 2020). In other countries, including Algeria, Egypt, Libya, Morocco, Nigeria, Somalia, Tunisia, Jordan, Kuwait, and Russia, propaganda and morality laws are used to harass and punish LGBTQ people who publicly express their sexual orientation or gender identity. In the United States, where 13 million people 13 and older identify as LGBT, 27 states do not protect LGBT people from discrimination in employment, education, public accommodations, or housing, and there is no federal law barring such discrimination based on sexual orientation or gender identity (UCLA School of Law, 2020).

Gender inequality and power relations within families and wider society put LB women at increased risk for family and community violence, and hate-motivated rapes and killings of LB women are reported in all societies (UNHCR, 2015). LB women are often punished by their families and communities for "betraying" their heritage, religion, and culture (OutRight Action International, 2016). In many countries, gender nonconforming women are expelled from their homes, disowned, subjected to physical and emotional abuse by their families, and forced to marry men. For example, in India, same-sex sexual relationships are against the law, and families often prevent their daughters from seeing their girlfriends and pressure them to marry men. Newspapers and LGBT organizations regularly report suicide pacts between lesbians who would rather die than live apart.

Research finds no relationship between a mother's sexual orientation and her child's mental health, no evidence that homosexual parents are more likely to be sexually inappropriate with their children, and no evidence that lesbians' parenting skills are worse than heterosexual mothers (American Psychological Association, 2005; Patterson & Goldberg, 2016). Despite this, lesbians are regularly denied their right to have children through artificial insemination and adoption and are refused custody of their biological children when they divorce their fathers (ILGA, 2016). Lesbians also remain closeted to protect their children from the stigma of having a lesbian parent (Shapiro et al., 2009). Figure 4.2 summarizes contributors to LBQ invisibility.

FIGURE 4.2 *Factors Contributing to Lesbian and Bisexual Invisibility*

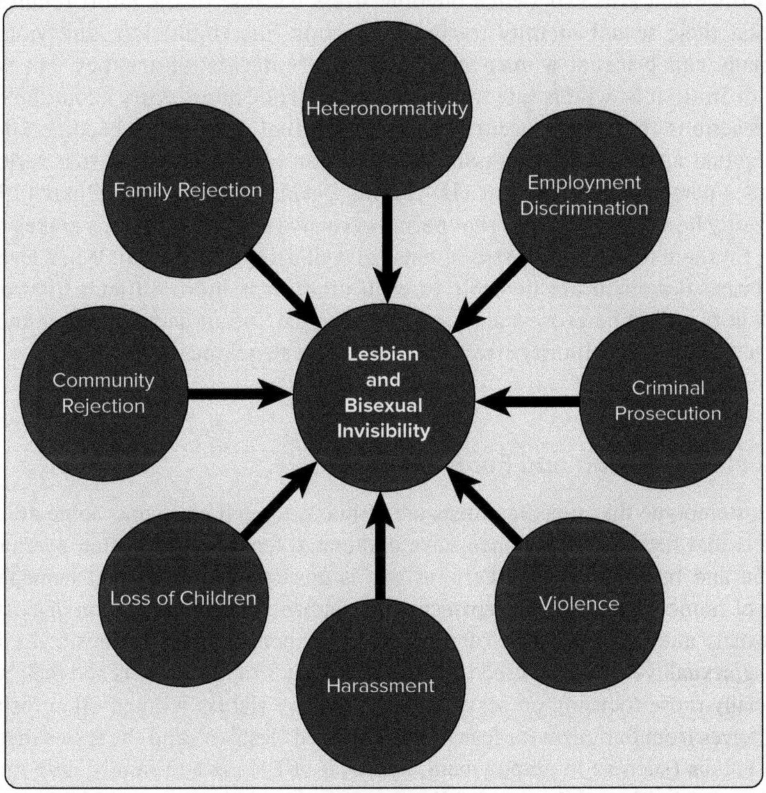

The stress and strain experienced by lesbian and bisexual women due to the pressure to conform to heteronormative expectations, and due stigma and discrimination, create what is known as **sexual minority stress** (Hequembourg & Brallier, 2009; Meyer, 2003). Sexual minority stress and the pressure to remain invisible have negative mental health consequences such as depression and anxiety (American Psychological Association, 2008; Hequembourg & Brallier, 2009). Rates of depression and anxiety are higher among LB women than heterosexual women and are linked to social stigma, discrimination, and denial of civil and human rights (Prell & Traeen, 2018; Salim, Robinson, & Flanders, 2019). LB women often experience psychological dissonance because of a conflict between their sexual orientation and the perceived ideals of society. Raised in heterosexist, heteronormative societies, they have often internalized the societal message that nonheterosexuals are bad. Consequently, they experience lowered self-esteem and shame, as well as guilt about maintaining a false image as a heterosexual (Friedman & Downey, 1995). Young lesbians who have never met another lesbian and are told that lesbianism is a sickness may experience self-directed

In the European Union, 20 percent of LGB people say they experienced sexual orientation discrimination while job hunting or at work, and in the United States, more than half of LGB employees hide their sexual orientation.

In 2003, the U.S. Supreme Court struck down laws making gay and lesbian sex illegal. The ruling voided laws in thirteen states that prohibited sex between same-sex partners.

"There have been many cases where women have been raped by their husbands, their brothers, even their fathers, in a bid to cure them. Some have been locked in a room for days and starved until they admitted it was all lies."
Betu Singh,
co-ordinator of the
Delhi India lesbian
support group Sangini

"The reason we have
to hide and pretend
all the time is that
society will hate us. The
only reason we live in
depression most of the
times and have suicidal
thoughts are that
we can't tell anyone
and not everyone is
courageous to come
out and face the
trouble."
*Annamika, 22-year-old
lesbian from India*

"I've always had
that feeling of being
oppressed, not being
able to tell who I
really am, lying about
myself to friends, and
disappointing my
mother if [I] came out...I
haven't come out for
22 years. I've taken it
for granted now to feel
this way."
*Ueki, 22-year-old
Japanese lesbian*

"If we come out, we
are more often than
not exiled by the
community. If we don't
come out, we still feel
that sense of exile
because we are unable
to share a very real part
of ourselves with them."
*Pratibha Parmar, British
filmmaker*

homophobia, which may lead to isolation, passive acceptance of persecution, exile, and even suicide (Dorf & Perez, 1995).

LB women also experience ongoing stress because of the effort required to conceal their sexual identity to avoid rejection, discrimination, and violence. Lesbians and bisexual women must continually decide whom they can safely confide in—that is, who is safe to "come out" to. They often worry about the negative reactions that might occur should their sexual orientation become known. This actual and expected harassment creates an emotional stress that seriously impedes personal development (D'Augelli, 1992). To paraphrase Pharr (1988), an overtly homophobic world that permits cruelty to LGBT+ persons makes it difficult for them to maintain a strong sense of well-being and esteem. When lesbians and bisexual women are invisible to each other, it is more difficult for women to identify as nonheterosexual women and be part of an accepting community, which ameliorates minority stress (Meyer, 2003; Penelope, 1990).

Sexual Orientation and Feminism

It is a stereotype that most feminists are lesbians, though of course, some are. The truth is that heterosexual women have dominated feminism and often overlooked lesbian and bisexual women. Perhaps this is unsurprising given that **homophobia** (fear of homosexuals) and **heterosexism** (prejudice and discrimination against homosexuals and bisexuals) are often used as weapons against feminism. **Lesbian-baiting/sexuality-baiting** are used to discredit women's rights activists and their work, especially those focusing on sexual or reproductive rights. Women often distance themselves from feminism for fear of being labeled "lesbian" and the losses that this label entails (such as in employment, approval of friends and family, community, children, and safety) (Currier & Migraine-George, 2016; Pharr, 1988). Feminists are called lesbians, whores, or bad mothers as a way of ostracizing and disempowering feminism. It is a way to keep women conforming to traditional gender roles and gender stereotypes (Greene, 1994).

It is interesting to consider this equation of feminism with lesbianism given that mainstream feminism is often guilty of ignoring the issues of nonheterosexual women. Lesbian activists from Chile, Colombia, Costa Rica, Hong Kong, Latvia, Mexico, Romania, the Philippines, Malaysia, Thailand, India, Germany, the United States, the United Kingdom, and Italy have all reported barriers to advancing lesbian rights within their feminist movements (Chant, 2003; Dorf & Perez, 1995; Mak et al., 1995; Nur, 1995; Rondon, 1995; Sharma, 2007). But women's movements vary significantly in the extent to which they address issues of sexual orientation (Basu, 1995). Sometimes heterosexual feminists are oblivious to these issues. Other times they want to enhance their credibility with the larger public and therefore distance themselves from lesbians (Currier, 2016). Basu (1995) notes that the stronger women's movements are, and the less worried they are about survival, the more likely it is that they will be inclusive and advocate for lesbian rights.

Just as it is true that most feminists are not lesbians, it is also true that most lesbians are not feminists. Yes, lesbianism can be a feminist political statement and identity, a point discussed below. But for most lesbians, lesbianism is a quiet, personal matter that arises out of a natural sexual attraction to women or from falling in love with a woman. In most cases, lesbianism is not intended as a political statement. Lesbians, like heterosexual women, are diverse in their feminism and vary in their awareness of women's issues and in their activism for women's equality.

Lesbian Feminism

Lesbian feminism is the variety of beliefs and practices based on the core assumption that there is a connection between an erotic and/or emotional commitment to women and political resistance to patriarchal domination (Taylor & Rupp, 1993). It is primarily a western ideology, embraced by educated, middle-class lesbian feminists in North America, Western Europe, and Australia (Ellis & Peel, 2010). A key focus of lesbian feminism is resisting the **compulsory heterosexuality** that essentially requires women to have heterosexual romantic relationships and deny or hide same-sex attractions and relationships. Compulsory heterosexuality is generally assured through **heteropatriarchy** (Penelope, 1990). Laws that outlaw homosexuality, religions that forbid it, police and justice systems that allow harassment and violence against lesbians and bisexual women, economic systems that make it difficult for women to live independently of men, and social norms that pressure women to marry men and define their lives in relation to them—are all features of a heteropatriarchal society.

Many lesbian feminists take the position that compulsory heterosexuality and its embedding in social structures (heteropatriarchy) is motivated by a desire to protect patriarchy. The idea is that lesbian existence involves the rejection of a compulsory heterosexual way of life and is a direct or indirect attack on the male right of access to women (Rich, 1980). As Adrienne Rich noted in her classic book *Of Woman Born* (1976), patriarchy could not survive without motherhood and sexuality in their institutional forms. If it was acceptable to live as a lesbian and women believed they could live independently of men, then men would be less able to exploit women's sexuality and to use them as a source of unpaid labor. In short, men would have less control over women and would have sexual and emotional access to women only on women's terms. Audre Lorde (1984) suggested that sexuality between women looks away from male power for valuation and provides an alternate base for the creation and proliferation of power. Likewise, Carla Trujillo (1991) proposed that the Chicano community finds lesbians threatening because lesbians challenge the cultural beliefs that women should define themselves in terms of men, and should be subservient to men. The existence of Chicana lesbians is a threat to the established order of male control and oppressive attitudes toward women. Ann Ferguson (1981) said, "The possibility of a sexual relationship between women is an important challenge to patriarchy because it acts as an alternative to the patriarchal heterosexual couple,

"Around the world, state and non-state actors intentionally deploy what they see as pejorative ideas about women's sexuality to discredit individual women, the organisations they work for, and their political agendas. This phenomenon, described as 'sexuality-baiting' and 'lesbian-baiting,' is a particularly potent method through which women's activism, advocacy and leadership are threatened."
Rauda Morcos, Aswat-Palestinian Gay Women

"When any woman curtails her freedom or fails to take an action or say what she believes out of fear of being labeled a lesbian, then homophobia has denied her independence and sapped her strength."
Charlotte Bunch, Human Rights Lawyer & Activist

"One distressing thing is the way men react to women who assert their equality: their ultimate weapon is to call them unfeminine. They think she is anti-male; they even whisper that she's probably a lesbian."
Shirley Chisholm, first Black woman elected to the U.S. Congress and the first major-party Black candidate for the President of the United States

"The one thing that most lesbians seem to have in common is the more or less conscious rejection of the social imperative that women must define ourselves in relation to men. In fact, it is the indifference to men that society finds so threatening."
Diane Griffin Crowder, American scholar and fiber artist

"Lesbian feminists translate their commitment to women and feminism into loving relationships with those who are the centre of their political lives and the force of their revolution, women, instead of members of the dominant class, men."
Sheila Jeffreys, political scientist, Australia

"For the lesbian of color, the ultimate rebellion she can make against her native culture is through her sexual behavior. . . . We're afraid of being abandoned by the mother, the culture, la Raza, for being unacceptable, faulty, damaged. . . . To avoid rejection, some of us conform to the values of the culture, push the unacceptable parts into the shadows."
Gloria Anzaldua, Chicana poet, writer, feminist

thus challenging the heterosexual ideology that women are dependent on men for romantic/sexual love and satisfaction" (p. 164).

As a political movement, lesbian feminism combines an interest in the liberation of women with an interest in the liberation of lesbians. The goals range from liberal lesbians' efforts to obtain lesbian civil rights within current patriarchal systems to the radical lesbian separatist goal of overthrowing world patriarchy in order to liberate all women (Cavin, 1985). According to Cavin (1985), lesbian feminism first emerged in Germany when lesbian feminists were politically active in both the early feminist and homosexual rights movements (1924–1935). Their activities continued until the Nazi regime sent them to the concentration camps, where they were forced to wear a pink triangle (now a symbol of lesbian and gay rights). Over 200,000 homosexuals died in Hitler's camps. In the United States, lesbian feminism emerged in the 1970s, stimulated in part by the neglect of lesbians by both the feminist and gay rights movements (Cavin, 1985).

Lesbian separatism, a radical form of political lesbian feminism, emerged in the United States and Britain in the early 1970s. The idea is that lesbian liberation requires women's noncooperation with the patriarchal system. This noncooperation ranges from a woman's choice not to be involved with men socially, emotionally, sexually, politically, or economically to physical separation from the institutions and jurisdiction of patriarchy (Cavin, 1985). Originally, lesbian "homelands"—free from sexism, racism, and ageism and embodying positive female values such as caring, compassion, and community—were seen as important in accomplishing these goals. In the 1970s and 1980s, some women lived in alternative separatist communities, but by the 1990s, these were all but extinct.

For many lesbian feminists, staying closeted is the core of lesbian oppression, so coming out—that is, being open about one's lesbian identity with others—is a political act. The strategy is that if everyone came out of the closet, lesbians and gays could not be oppressed because "they are everywhere" (Cavin, 1985). Because lesbianism is invisible, invalidated, and punished as a way of controlling women under patriarchy, proudly wearing the "lesbian" label is an assertive rejection of the heteropatriarchal order, and a commitment to women and other lesbians (Ellis & Peel, 2010). Staying invisible is also thought to perpetuate the notion that lesbians are inferior. For instance, when the existence of lesbians is acknowledged by the larger heterosexual culture, it is often portrayed negatively and inaccurately (Cath, 1995; Ishino & Wakabayashi, 1995; Lindau, 1993; Mak et al., 1995; Ruan & Bullough, 1992). Another benefit is that as more lesbians come out, the diversity of lesbians becomes more evident, and inaccurate stereotypes lose their power (Burn, Kadlec, & Rexer, 2005).

However, while coming out as nonheterosexual can be a potent political statement, an intersectional global feminism directs us to recognize that practically, respectfully, and humanely speaking, we should respect a nonheterosexual woman's decision about when, where, and to whom she comes out, and whether she adopts the lesbian label, another label, or no label. Coming out usually involves courage and risk. The potential costs are greater for some women than others depending on their families, communities, religions, regions, economic situation, and governments. And as Rupp (1997) points out, some non-Western lesbians find the lesbian label restrictive and disrespectful of cultural traditions that support woman-woman relationships without calling attention to them. Also, in some non-Western cultures, *lesbian* is viewed as a Western word. Its use reduces the credibility of nonheterosexual relationships since detractors claim that lesbianism is a Western import or the result of Western colonization (Currier & Migraine-George, 2016). In short, context matters when coming out as a political action.

In the 1980s, lesbian feminists of color spoke up about their invisibility and marginalization by white lesbian feminists. Chicana and Black lesbian feminists in the United States, including Audre Lorde, Rita Mae Brown, Gloria Anzaldua, Cherrie Moraga, and Barbara Smith, called attention to the fact that some lesbian women experience multiple interacting oppressions. Due to other overlapping identities, and cultural and social factors, lesbians aren't a monolithic, homogeneous group. Their differences make a difference; their issues as nonheterosexual women and their experiences of heterosexism vary (Greene, 2013). These feminist lesbians of color were on the forefront of recognizing the importance of intersectionality and of understanding interconnections between different oppressions (Smith, 1993). As the Combahee River Collective (1982), an American Black feminist lesbian organization active in the 1970s and 1980s stated, "We are actively committed to struggling against racial, sexual, heterosexual, and class oppression and see as our particular task the development and integrated analysis and practice based on the fact that the major systems of oppression are interlocking."[2] Box 4.3 describes tensions between lesbian feminists and bisexual feminists.

By the 1990s, lesbian feminism as a political ideology waned, and the popularity of **queer theory** grew. Queer theory opposes sexuality classifications as artificial, limiting, and inaccurate and instead focuses on challenging gender conformity and **heteronormativity** (the belief that heterosexuality is the one and only way to be human). "Queer" became accepted as an inclusive, unifying term for LGBTI people. Many political lesbian feminists joined the fight for SOGI rights, working with other discriminated-against sexual orientation and gender identity groups under the LGBTQI umbrella (Ellis & Peel, 2010). Their goal: attaining the human rights and freedoms accorded to heterosexuals and gender-conforming people—rights like safety and privacy, and sexual and legal rights. However, not all lesbian feminists are comfortable with this move from lesbian feminism politics to queer politics. The concern is that queer politics masks the unique forms of oppression faced by lesbians because they are women (Blackwood & Wieringa, 1999; Ellis & Peel, 2010).

"Woman-identification is a source of energy, a potential springhead of female power, violently curtailed and wasted under the institution of heterosexuality."
Adrienne Rich, American writer/poet

"Separatists begin with the assumption that the social injustices we live with are best understood as expressions of hatred enforced with violence. . . .choosing not to be violated is the objective of our action."
Jackie Anderson, Founder of Yahimba, a group for Black lesbians

"Probably the most serious deterrent to Black lesbian activism is the closet itself. It is very difficult and sometimes impossible to organize around Black lesbian issues, such as homophobic violence, child custody, and right-wing initiatives, when you do not want people to know who you are."
Barbara Smith, co-founder of Combahee River Collective and Women of Color Press

[2]The Combahee River Collective was named after a U.S. civil war guerilla mission in South Carolina led by Harriet Tubman in which 750 slaves were liberated from plantations. It remains the only military campaign in America planned and led by a woman.

BOX 4.3   *Tensions Between Lesbian Feminists and Bisexual Feminists*

Bisexual women often report feeling marginalized and invisible in both LGBTI and heterosexual communities. When they make themselves visible, the validity of their sexual identity is questioned or dismissed as a temporary phase, heterosexual attention seeking, or as really lesbian but hanging onto heterosexual privilege (Hayfield, Clarke, & Hallwell, 2014). Likewise, the relationship between lesbian feminists and bisexual feminists has been strained, although tensions have waned (Gerstner, 2006). For example, Sheila Jeffreys (1999) said that bisexual women undermine the power and resistance involved in the lesbian feminist decision to choose women as sexual partners as a form of political resistance to male dominance. Julie Bindel (2012) suggested that being bisexual is a "fashionable trend" and that if "bisexual women had an ounce of sexual politics, they would stop sleeping with men."

Bisexual feminists countered with charges of **biphobia** (fear and hatred of bisexuals), **monosexism** (placing greater value on romantic and sexual attractions to one sex), **mononormativity** (acting as though gay and straight are the only normal sexual orientations), and compulsory homosexuality (Hayfield et al., 2014; Sturgis, 1996). They pointed out that many women do not fit the sexual orientation binary that suggests people are either heterosexual or homosexual and nothing in between. They argued that being a bisexual woman is consistent with a feminist sex-positive sexuality where women authentically live their sexuality (Queen, 1991). Some bisexual feminists even suggested that bisexual feminists were better feminists than lesbian feminists because they were better able to change patriarchy from within (Elliott, 1992; Sturgis, 1996). Others criticized stereotyped media portrayals of bisexuality and called for a serious politics of bisexuality that acknowledges the reality of bisexual identities (Wilkinson, 1996).

"It is important to make a distinction between the secrets from which we draw strength and the secrecy which comes from anxiety and is meant to protect us. If we want to have the power for ourselves this silence must be broken. I want to encourage more and more women to identify themselves, to speak their name, where and when they can, and to survive."
Audre Lord, American poet and self-identified Black lesbian feminist

Conclusion

Women's sexual rights are an important part of gender equality. How free can a woman be if she does not have the power to determine her sexuality? Women are often unable to say no to sexual violence and to sex with men. Their rights to sexual pleasure, bodily integrity, and sexual self-expression are sometimes disrespected by patriarchal cultures that define their sexuality in terms of men's pleasure and heterosexual roles of wife and mother. Laws, policies, and cultural practices often restrict women's sexuality and punish gender nonconforming women.

Despite the fact that patriarchy and heteropatriarchy often make it difficult for women to challenge violations of their sexual rights, once again we see activism and empowerment, from the local to the global. Among other things, activists work for state, federal, and international laws prohibiting discrimination based on sexual orientation and identity. They organize and participate in political demonstrations to claim their sexual rights. They fight child marriage, sexual assault, honour crimes, and virginity testing and document abuses of women's sexual rights. They advocate for sexuality education and women's right to make their own decisions about their sexuality. They challenge sexual double standards via social media. As a result of activism, international human rights instruments now acknowledge that women's sexual rights are human rights.

This chapter once again demonstrates the global women's and gender studies theme of diversity. Although a human rights approach to women's sexuality suggests that women everywhere have the same sexual rights, women's sexuality varies cross-culturally. Sexuality is socially constructed because how it is perceived and experienced is influenced by legal, political, and cultural factors. For example, depending on the culture, premarital virginity may be a strictly enforced social requirement, desired but not necessary, or entirely optional. Culture also strongly influences same-sex practices between women; there is no single way to be a lesbian. This is so much so that the word "lesbian" does not have a coherent, unifying meaning across cultures, and great worldwide diversity in women's same-sex practices is found (Blackwood, 2007; Blackwood & Wieringa, 1999).

Sexuality is clearly intersectional—it varies based on a woman's age, religion, sexual orientation, location, disability, whether she's cisgender or not, and so on, and how these variables interact. Cultural and group identities such as class and ethnicity interact with nonheterosexual orientations to produce a variety of complex sexual identities. This means that even in the same country, experiences may differ. For example, in San Francisco, there is an open, vibrant lesbian community, but in most places in the United States, lesbian cultures are harder to identify. Lesbians from discriminated-against racial or ethnic groups may be triply marginalized by race, gender, and sexuality. For instance, the experience of Latin American, African American, and Asian American lesbians may be very different from those of Euro American lesbians because the Latin, African, and Asian American groups face racism from outside their communities and heterosexism within them. Unfortunately, invisibility makes it difficult for us to collect data and get an accurate picture of LB women's experiences worldwide.

Like other chapters, this chapter also points to the material roots of women's disadvantage. Women's economic and social dependencies on men often put them in a position where they have to conform to others' definitions of their sexuality. For instance, wage earning, the ability to live separately from kin, and lesbian bars and gathering places all seem to be preconditions for the development of a more political lesbianism where lesbians see themselves as an oppressed minority with a right to exist. Indeed, lesbian feminist communities and organizations are more common in modern capitalistic societies, and in those, are more common among urban, educated lesbians. Blackwood (1986) suggests that in societies where women do not have control over their productive activities, and may not gain status independently of men, lesbian behavior is more "informal." Sometimes female same-sex practices are even a normal part of some cultures, although they may not be labeled as lesbian (Blackwood & Wieringa, 1999). In general, the ability to express gender nonconformity and to assert one's sexual rights is greater for women who can survive economically and attain social status without heterosexual marriage. The role of economic power in bringing about women's equality cannot be underestimated. This is the focus of Chapter 5, "Women's Work."

"I do not call myself 'lesbian' and I do not want to be called 'lesbian' either. Life is too complex for us to give names not derived from us, dirty, conditioned words, to the deepest feelings within me."
Astrid Roemer,
Suriname poet

ILGA is a worldwide federation of 1,702 member organizations from 166 countries campaigning for lesbian, gay, bisexual, trans, and intersex rights. ILGA also tracks sexual orientation laws globally.

"Sexuality is a natural and precious aspect of life, an essential and fundamental part of our humanity. For people to attain the highest standard of health, they must first be empowered to exercise choice in their sexual and reproductive lives; they must feel confident and safe in expressing their own sexual identity."
Jacqueline Sharpe,
President of the
International Planned
Parenthood Federation

Glossary Terms and Concepts

Biphobia

Bisexual invisibility

Cisgender

Compulsory heterosexuality

Gender binary

Gender expression

Gender identity

Heteronormativity

Heteropatriarchy

Heterosexism

Homophobia

Intersex

Lesbian baiting/sexuality baiting

Lesbian feminism

Lesbian invisibility

Lesbian separatism

LGBTIQ rights

Mononormativity

Monosexism

Queer

Queer theory

Sexual double standard

Sexual health

Sexual minority stress

Sexual orientation

Sexual rights

SOGI rights

Trans girls/women

Transgender (trans)

Transphobia

Study Questions

1. What are sexual rights? What are some important sexual rights identified in the chapter? Why is it important to link sexual rights to human rights? How are sexual rights framed as human rights? What are "negative" and "positive" sexual rights?

2. What are the ways in which a woman's sexuality is often not her own? What examples of a sexual double standard were discussed in the chapter?

3. How many women are living with HIV/AIDS? How do sexual double standards and male control of sexual decision-making affect women's risk of HIV/AIDS? What else puts women at risk for HIV/AIDS? How can women's risk be reduced?

4. What are sexual orientation and gender identity? Why are they important to global women's and gender studies? How is SOGI-related stigma and discrimination affected by intersectionality?

5. What is the gender binary? How does it affect people who have gender nonconforming identities or expressions? How are trans women affected by anti-trans bias?

6. What is the evidence that sexual relations between women persist across time and culture?

7. What is lesbian and bisexual invisibility? Why do some people say that bisexual women's invisibility is even greater than lesbians' invisibility? What are the contributors to LB women's invisibility discussed in the chapter?

8. What are the consequences of the sexual minority stress experienced by LB women?

9. What is the relationship between mainstream feminism and lesbianism?

10. What are some of the core beliefs and practices of lesbian feminism? How can lesbianism be viewed as a challenge to patriarchy? What is lesbian separatism, and how common is it?

11. How did lesbian feminists of color challenge lesbian feminism? What is the relationship between bisexual feminism and lesbian feminism? What happened to lesbian feminism?

12. How is sexuality "socially constructed"? How is it "intersectional"?

Discussion Questions and Activities

1. The chapter suggests that women's sexuality is often not about their sexual pleasure or rights and is instead about women as objects of sexual satisfaction to men. It also suggests that women's virtue is equated with virginity and that there is a sexual double standard where men's sexual prowess is expected and encouraged and women's is negatively stereotyped. In what ways are these things true (or untrue) of your culture?

2. Using Box 4.1 and other chapter information on sexual rights as human rights, create your own "Declaration of Women's Sexual Rights." Make sure to include both "positive" and "negative" rights. Explain how your rights translate into sexual practice in regards to people like you.

3. How heteronormative and heteropatriarchal is your culture? Do lesbian and bisexual women face prejudice and discrimination? How visible are lesbian and bisexual women in the media and how are they portrayed? Do LGBT people have equal rights under the law? Does the law protect them from harassment, violence, and housing and employment discrimination?

4. What would the world be like if homosexuality, bisexuality, and nonconforming gender identities were not stigmatized? How would it affect children's play? How would it influence affection between those of the same sex? How would it affect what we wear? How would it affect what jobs we choose? How would it affect marriage?

5. Watch five videos from the United Nations' Free and Equal page and reflect on what you learned, relating it to chapter material. (https://www.unfe.org /videos).

6. Women's commonalities unite them, but intersectionality means their experiences as women are diverse. How does this apply to LBT women?

Action Opportunities

1. OutRight Action International volunteers work with local "Engagement Committees" to spread awareness about global LGBTIQ issues. They also hold periodic events and fundraisers to benefit activists and global LGBTIQ leaders in their communities. Start a group in your city or at your university. Email Development@OutRightInternational.org for guidance.

2. Volunteer for the Trevor Project (http://www.thetrevorproject.org/pages /volunteer), a U.S. suicide prevention hotline that provides information and support to lesbian, gay, bisexual, and transgendered youth.

3. Encourage your religious or school organization to reach out to LGBT members.

4. Participate in the U.S. campaign to end sexual orientation conversion therapy, organized by the Trevor Project and the National Center for Lesbian Rights (https://bornperfect.org).

5. Use strategies developed by the Gay, Lesbian and Straight Education Network to prevent heterosexism in the schools. Go to www.glsen.org for more information.

6. Participate in an LGBT+ advocacy campaign in your country. For example, in the United States, the National LGBTQ Task Force provides opportunities to take action (https://www.thetaskforce.org/current-task-force-actions.html).

Activist Websites

Amnesty International https://amnestyusa.org/issues/gender-sexuality-identity/

BiNet USA https://bi.org/en

Human Rights Campaign (USA) http://www.hrc.org

International Lesbian and Gay Association http://ilga.org

National Gay and Lesbian Rights Task Force (US) http://www.thetaskforce.org

OutRight Action International https://www.outrightinternational.org

UN Free and Equal http://www.unfe.org

Informational Websites

Bi.org https://bi.org/en

Global Action for Trans Equality (GATE) https://transactivists.org

Kinsey Institute for Research in Sex, Gender, and Reproduction https:// kinseyinstitute.org

Lesbian Herstory Archives https://lesbianherstoryarchives.org

National Center for Transgender Equality http://www.transequality.org

UNAIDS for women http://www.unaids.org/en/aboutunaids/unaidscosponsors /unwomen

World Association for Sexual Health http://www.worldsexology.org

World Health Organization on sexual health https://who.int/health-topics/sexual -health

Yogyakarta Principles http://www.yogyakartaprinciples.org

References

Abdolmanafi, A., Nobre, P., Winter, S., Tilley, T. J. M., and Ghorban, R. 2018. Culture and sexuality: Cognitive-emotional determinants of sexual dissatisfaction among Iranian and New Zealand women. *The Journal of Sexual Medicine, 15,* 687–697.

Abramsky, T., Devries, K., Kiss, L., Nakuti, J., Kyegombe, N., Starmann, E. et al. 2014. Findings from the SASA! Study: A cluster randomized controlled trial to assess the impact of a community mobilization intervention to prevent violence against women and reduce HIV risk in Kampala, Uganda. *BMC Medicine*, 12. DOI: 10.1186/s12916-014-0122-5

Allen, P. G. 1992. *The sacred hoop: Recovering the feminine in American Indian traditions*. Boston, MA: Beacon Press.

Allison, R., and Risman, B. J. 2013. A double standard for "hooking up": How far have we come toward gender equality? *Social Science Research, 42,* 1191–1206.

American Foundation for Suicide Prevention and the Williams Institute. 2014. *Suicide attempts among transgender and gender nonconforming adults: Findings of the National Transgender Discrimination Survey*. http://williamsinstitute.law.ucla .edu/wp-content/uploads/AFSP-Williams-Suicide-Report-Final.pdf. Retrieved on November 3, 2016.

American Psychological Association. 2005. *Lesbian and gay parenting*. https:// www.apa.org/pi/lgbt/resources/parenting-full.pdf. Retrieved on March 28, 2021.

American Psychological Association. 2008. *Answers to your questions for a better understanding of sexual orientation and homosexuality*. http://www.apa.org /topics/sorientation.pdf. Retrieved on March 29, 2021.

Baral, S. D., Poteat, T., Strömdahl, S., Wirtz, A. L., Guadamuz, T. E., and Beyrer, C. 2013. Worldwide burden of HIV in transgender women: A systematic review and meta-analysis. *The Lancet: Infectious Diseases, 13,* 214–222.

Basu, A. 1995. *The challenge of local feminisms: Women's movements in global perspective*. Boulder, CO: Westview.

Bay-Cheng, L. Y., and Zucker. A. N. 2007. Feminism between the sheets: Sexual attitudes among feminists, non-feminists, and egalitarians. *Psychology of Women Quarterly, 31,* 157–163.

Bennett, K. 1992. Feminist bisexuality: A both/and option for an either/or world. In *Closer to home: Bisexuality and feminism,* edited by E. R. Weise. Seattle, WA: Seal Press.

Bindel, J. 2012, June 12. Where's the politics in sex? *The Huffington Post.* http://www.huffingtonpost.com/julie-bindel/where-is-the-politics-in-_b_1589435.html. Retrieved on November 19, 2016.

Blackwood, E. 1984. Sexuality and gender in certain Native American tribes: The case of cross-gender females. *Signs, 10,* 27–42.

Blackwood, E. 1986. Breaking the mirror: The construction of lesbianism and the anthropological discourse on homosexuality. In *The many faces of homosexuality: Anthropological approaches to homosexual behavior,* edited by E. Blackwood. New York: Harrington Park.

Blackwood, E. 2007. Globalization, sexuality, and silences: Women's sexualities and masculinities in an Asian context. In *Women's sexualities and masculinities in a globalizing Asia,* edited by S. E. Wieringa, E. Blackwood, and Bhaiya, A. New York: Palgrave Macmillan.

Blackwood, E. and Wieringa, S. 1999. *Female desires: Same-sex relations and transgender practices across cultures.* New York: Columbia University Press.

Bunch, C. 1995. Transforming human rights from a feminist perspective. In *Women's rights, human rights: International feminist perspectives,* edited by J. Peters and A. Wolper. New York: Routledge.

Burn, S. M., Kadlec, K., and Rexer, R. 2005. Effects of subtle heterosexism on gays, lesbians, and bisexuals. *Journal of Homosexuality, 49,* 23–38.

Carta, A., Carraro, E., Martini, S.A., and Perasso, G. 2021. Fifty shades of pretty and thin: Psychological research on gender stereotypes in media and advertising. In *Handbook of Research on Translating Myth and Reality in Women Imagery Across Disciplines* (pp. 213–232). IGI Global.

Cath. 1995. Country report on lesbians in India. In *Unspoken rules: Sexual orientation and women's human rights,* edited by R. Rosenbloom. San Francisco, CA: International Gay and Lesbian Human Rights Commission.

Cavin, S. 1985. *Lesbian origins.* San Francisco, CA: Ism Press.

Centers for Disease Control and Prevention. 2016. *HIV among women.* http://www.cdc.gov/hiv/group/gender/women/. Retrieved on October 16, 2016.

Chant, S. 2003. *Gender in Latin America.* New Brunswick, NJ: Rutgers University Press.

Combahee River Collective.1982. *A Black Feminist Statement* (pp. 13–32). *Combahee River Collective.* http://americanstudies.yale.edu/sites/default/files/files/Keyword%20Coalition_Readings.pdf. Retrieved on November 13, 2016

Conley, T. D., Ziegler, A., and Moors, A. C. 2013. Backlash from the bedroom stigma mediates gender differences in acceptance of casual sex offers. *Psychology of Women Quarterly, 37,* 392–407.

Currier, A., and Migraine-George, T. 2016. "Lesbian"/female same-sex sexualities in Africa. *Journal of Lesbian Studies,* 1–18.

D'Augelli, A. R. 1992. Lesbian and gay male undergraduates' experiences of harassment and fear on campus. *Journal of Interpersonal Violence, 7,* 383–395.

Daniluk, J. C. and Browne. N. 2008. Traditional religious doctrine and women's sexuality: Reconciling the contradictions. *Women and Therapy, 31,* 129–142.

Dorf, J., and Perez, G. C. 1995. Discrimination and tolerance of difference: International lesbian human rights. In *Women's rights, human rights: International feminist perspectives,* edited by J. Peters and A. Wolper. New York: Routledge.

Dworkin, A. 1987. *Intercourse.* London: Arrow.

Elliott, B. 1992. Holly Near and yet so far. In *Closer to home. Bisexuality and feminism,* edited by E. R. Weise. Seattle, WA: Seal Press.

Ellis, S. J. and Peel, E., 2011. Lesbian feminisms: Historical and present possibilities. *Feminism and Psychology, 21,* 198–204.

Endendijk, J. J., van Baar, A. L., and Dekovic, M. 2020. He is a stud, she is a slut! A meta-analysis on the continued existence of sexual double standards. *Personality and Social Psychology Review, 24,* 163–190.

Faderman, L. 1991. *Odd girls and twilight lovers: A history of lesbian life in twentieth century America.* New York: Columbia University Press.

Faderman, L. 1997. Who hid lesbian history? *Journal of Lesbian Studies, 1,* 149–154.

Faderman, L. 2000. *To Believe in Women: What Lesbians Have Done for America: A History.* New York: Mariner.

Ferguson, A. 1981. Patriarchy, sexual identity, and the sexual revolution. *Signs, 7,* 157–172.

Friedman, R. C., and Downey, J. C. 1995. Internalized homophobia and the negative therapeutic reaction. *Journal of the American Academy of Psychoanalysis, 23,* 99–113.

Gerstner, D. A. 2006. Introduction. *Routledge International Encyclopedia of Queer Culture,* edited by D.A. Gerstner. United Kingdom: Routledge.

Ghanim, D. 2015. *The virginity trap in the Middle East.* United Kingdom: Palgrave McMillan.

Gharib, M. 2019. Why virginity tests are making news in the U.S. and Afghanistan. *NPR.* https://www.npr.org/sections/goatsandsoda/2019/12/06/785493554/why-virginity-tests-are-making-news-in-the-u-s-and-afghanistan. Retrieved on March 26, 2021.

Greene, B. 1994. Lesbian women of color: Triple jeopardy. *Journal of Lesbian Studies, 1,* 109–147.

Greene, B. 2013. Lesbians of color. In *Psychological Health of Women of Color: Intersections, Challenges, and Opportunities: Intersections, Challenges, and Opportunities,* edited by L. Comas-Diaz and B. Greene, pp. 203–218. ABC-Clio.

Hayfield, N., Clarke, V., and Halliwell, E. 2014. Bisexual women's understandings of social marginalisation: 'The heterosexuals don't understand us but nor do the lesbians'. *Feminism and Psychology,* 1–21.

Hequembourg, A. L., and Brallier, S. A. 2009. An exploration of sexual minority stress across the lines of gender and sexual identity. *Journal of Homosexuality, 56,* 273-298.

Herdt, G. 1997. *Same sex: Different cultures.* Boulder, CO: Westview Press.

Herek, G. M. 2009. Hate crimes and stigma-related experiences among sexual minority adults in the United States: Prevalence estimates from a national probability sample. *Journal of Interpersonal Violence, 24,* 54-74.

ILGA. 2016. *State sponsored homophobia.* http://ilga.org/what-we-do/state -sponsored-homophobia-report/. Retrieved on November 29, 2016.

ILGA World. 2020. *State-sponsored homophobia 2020: Global legislation overview update.* Geneva: IGLA.

Ishino, S., and Wakabayashi, N. 1995. Country report on lesbians in Japan. In *Unspoken rules: Sexual orientation and women's human rights,* edited by R. Rosenbloom. San Francisco, CA: International Gay and Lesbian Human Rights Commission.

Kelly, C. R. and Hoerl, K. E. 2015. Shaved or saved? Disciplining women's bodies. *Women's Studies in Communication, 38,* 141-145.

Kendall. 1998. "When a woman loves a woman" in Lesotho: Love, sex, and the (Western) construction of homophobia. In *Boy-wives and female husbands: Studies of African homosexualities,* edited by S. O. Murray and W. Roscoe. New York: St. Martin's Press.

Kilbourne, J. 2003. Advertising and disconnection. In *Sex in advertising: Perspectives on the erotic appeal,* edited by T. Reichert and J. Lambiase. Mahwah, NJ: Erlbaum.

Laboy, M. M., Sandfort, T., and Huso, Y. 2009. Introduction to Special Issue: Global perspectives on same-sex sexualities: Desires, practices, and identities: Part 1: Negotiating global sexual identities in local contexts. *Sexuality Research and Social Policy, 6,* 1-3.

Landor, A. M., and Simons, L. G. 2014. Why virginity pledges succeed or fail: The moderating effect of religious commitment versus religious participation. *Journal of Child and Family Studies, 26,* 1102-1113. http://doi.org/10.1007 /s10826-013-9769-3. Retrieved on May 4, 2021.

Lindau, R. 1993, June 10. A sexualized image of lesbians in Sweden. *Off Our Backs,* 20.

Lorber, J. 2000. *Gender and the social construction of illness.* New York: AltaMira Press.

Lorde, A. 1984. *Sister/outsider: Essays and speeches.* Freedom, CA: The Crossing Press.

Mak, A., Hui, K., Poone, J., and King, M. A. 1995. Country report on lesbians in Argentina. In *Unspoken rules: Sexual orientation and women's human rights,* edited by R. Rosenbloom. San Francisco, CA: International Gay and Lesbian Human Rights Commission.

Meyer, I. 2003. Prejudice, social stress, and mental health in lesbian, gay, and bisexual populations: Conceptual issues and research evidence. *Psychological Bulletin, 129,* 674–697.

National Center for Lesbian Rights. 2016. *#Hashtag Bornperfect: The truth about conversion therapy.* http://www.nclrights.org/bornperfect-the-facts-about -conversion-therapy/. Retrieved on October 29, 2016.

Nelson, M. R., and Paek, H. 2005. Cross-cultural differences in sexual advertising content in a transnational women's magazine. *Sex Roles, 53*, 371–383.

Ng, V. 1996. Looking for lesbians in Chinese history. In *The new lesbian studies: Into the twenty-first century,* edited by B. Zimmerman and T. A. H. McNaron. New York: Feminist Press.

Nur, R. 1995. Country report on lesbians in Malaysia. In *Unspoken rules: Sexual orientation and women's human rights*, edited by R. Rosenbloom. San Francisco, CA: International Gay and Lesbian Human Rights Commission.

OHCHR (Office of the United Nations High Commissioner for Human Rights). 2015. *Joint UN statement on ending violence and discrimination against lesbian, gay, bisexual, transgender and intersex people.*

Olson, R. M., and García-Moreno, C. 2017. Virginity testing: A systematic review. *Reproductive Health, 14,* 61. https://doi.org/10.1186/s12978-017-0319-0. Retrieved on May 4, 2021.

OutRight Action International. 2014. *Violence through the lens of lesbian, bisexual women, and trans people in Asia.* https://www.outrightinternational .org/sites/default/files/LBT_ForUpload0614.pdf. Retrieved on October 28, 2016.

OutRight Action International. 2016. *Human rights report: Being lesbian in Iran.* https://www.outrightinternational.org/sites/default/files/OutRightLesbian Report.pdf. Retrieved on October 28, 2016.

Patterson, C. J., and Goldberg, A. E. 2016. Lesbian and gay parents and their children. https://www.ncfr.org/sites/default/files/2017-01/ncfr_policy_brief _november_final.pdf. Retrieved on March 28, 2021.

Penelope, J. 1990. Introduction. In *Finding the lesbians: Personal accounts from around the world*, edited by J. Penelope and S. Valentine. Freedom, CA: Crossing Press.

Pharr, S. 1988. Homophobia: A weapon of sexism. In *Issues in feminism*, 3rd ed., edited by S. Ruth. Mountain View, CA: Mayfield.

Prell, E., and Traeen, B. 2018. Minority stress and mental health among bisexual and lesbian women in Norway. *Journal of Bisexuality, 18*, 278–298, DOI: 10 .1080/15299716.2018.1518180

Queen, C. 1991. The queer in me. In *Bi any other name: Bisexual people speak out*, edited by L. Hutchins and L. Kaahumanu. Boston, MA: Alyson Publications.

Rich, A. 1976. *Of woman born: Motherhood as experience and institution.* New York: Norton.

Rich, A. 1980. Compulsory heterosexuality and lesbian existence. *Signs, 5,* 631–660.

Robatjazi, M., Simbar, M., Nahidi, F., Gharehdaghi, J., Emamhadi, M., Vedadhir, A. A. et al. 2016. Virginity testing beyond a medical examination. *Global Journal of Health Science, 8,* 152–164.

Rondon, E. 1995. Country report on lesbians in Colombia. In *Unspoken rules: Sexual orientation and women's human rights,* edited by R. Rosenbloom. San Francisco, CA: International Gay and Lesbian Human Rights Commission.

Ross, L. E., Salway, T., Tarasoff, L. A., MacKay, J. M., Hawkins, B. W., and Fehr, C. P. 2018. Prevalence of depression and anxiety among bisexual people compared to gay, lesbian, and heterosexual individuals: A systematic review and meta-analysis. *The Journal of Sex Research, 55,* 435–456. https://doi.org/10 .1080/00224499.2017.1387755. Retrieved on March 29, 2021.

Ruan, F. F., and Bullough. V. 1992. Lesbianism in China. *Archives of Sexual Behavior, 21,* 217–228.

Rupp, L. J. 1996. Finding the lesbians in lesbian history: Reflections on female same-sex sexuality in the western world. In *The new lesbian studies: Into the twenty-first century,* edited by B. Zimmerman and T. A. H. McNaron. New York: Feminist Press.

Rupp, L. J. 1997. "Imagine my surprise": Women's relationships in historical perspective. *Journal of Lesbian Studies, 1,* 155–176.

Salim, S., Robinson, M., and Flanders, C. E. 2019. Bisexual women's experiences of microaggressions and microaffirmations and their relation to mental health. *Psychology of Sexual Orientation and Gender Diversity, 6*(3), 336–346. https://doi-org.ezproxy.lib.calpoly.edu/10.1037/sgd0000329. Retrieved on May 4, 2021.

Shapiro, D. N., Peterson, C., and Stewart, A. 2009. Legal and social contexts and mental health among lesbian and heterosexual mothers. *Journal of Family Psychology, 23,* 255–262.

Sharma, M. 2007. "She has come from the world of the spirits . . .": Life stories of working-class lesbian women in northern India. In *Women's sexualities and masculinities in a globalizing Asia,* edited by S. E. Wieringa, E. Blackwood, and A. Bhaiya. New York: Palgrave Macmillan.

Smith, B. 1993. *Ain't gonna let nobody turn me around.* Albany, New York: Suny Press.

Stankiewicz, J. M., and Roselli, F. 2008. Women as sex objects and victims in print advertising. *Sex Roles, 58,* 575–589.

Sturgis, S. M. 1996. Bisexual feminism: Challenging the splits. In *Bisexual horizons. Politics, histories, lives,* edited by S. Rose and C. Stevens. London, UK: Lawrence and Wishart.

Taylor, V., and Rupp, L. J. 1993. Women's culture and lesbian feminist activism: A reconsideration of cultural feminism. *Signs,* Autumn, 32–61.

Trujillo, C. 1991. Chicana lesbians: Fear and loathing in the Chicano community. In *Women images and realities: A multicultural anthology*, edited by A. Kesselman, L. D. McNair, and N. Schniedewind. Mountain View, CA: Mayfield.

UCLA School of Law (Williams Institute). 2020. LGBT people in US not protected by state non-discrimination statutes. https://williamsinstitute.law.ucla.edu /publications/lgbt-nondiscrimination-statutes/. Retrieved on March 28, 2021.

UN Free and Equal. 2016. *Fact sheet: Intersex.* https://unfe.org/system/unfe-65 -Intersex_Factsheet_ENGLISH.pdf. Retrieved on November 29, 2016.

UN Women. 2018. Facts and figures: HIV and AIDS. http://www.unwomen.org/en /what-we-do/hiv-and-aids/facts-and-figures#notes. Retrieved on March 27, 2021.

UNAIDS. 2008. *2008 report on the global AIDS epidemic.* Geneva, Switzerland: UNAIDS.

UNAIDS. 2014. *Uniting against violence and HIV.* https://www.unaids.org/sites /default/files/en/media/unaids/contentassets/documents/unaidspublication /2014/JC2602_UniteWithWomen_en.pdf. Retrieved on March 27, 2021.

UNFPA. 2020. *Ensure universal access to sexual and reproductive health and reproductive rights: Measuring SDG Target 5.6.* https://www.unfpa.org/sites/default/files/ pub-pdf/UNFPA-SDG561562Combined-v4.15.pdf. Retrieved on March 27, 2021.

UNHCR (United Nations High Commissioner for Refugees). 2015. *Discrimination and violence against individuals based on their sexual orientation and gender identity: Report of the Office of the United Nations High Commissioner for Human Rights.* (A/HRC/19/41).

Valenti, J. 2009, April 25. How 'virginity' is a dangerous idea. *The Toronto Star.*

WHO (World Health Organization). 2013. *Global and regional estimates of violence against women: Prevalence and health effects of intimate partner violence and non-partner sexual violence.* http://apps.who.int/iris/bitstream/10665/85239/1 /9789241564625_eng.pdf?ua=1. Retrieved on May 4, 2021.

WHO (World Health Organization). 2015. *Sexual health, human rights, and the law.* http://apps.who.int/iris/bitstream/10665/175556/1/9789241564984_eng .pdf?ua=1. Retrieved on October 22, 2016.

WHO (World Health Organization). 2018. Eliminating virginity testing: An inter-agency statement. https://apps.who.int/iris/bitstream/handle/10665/275451/WHO -RHR-18.15-eng.pdf?ua=1. Retrieved on March 26, 2021.

Wilkinson, S. 1996, June. Bisexuality "a la mode." *Women's Studies International Forum, 19,* 293–301.

Womenshealth.gov. 2016. *Lesbian and bisexual health facts sheet.* https://www .womenshealth.gov/publications/our-publications/fact-sheet/lesbian-bisexual -health.html. Retrieved on November 4, 2016.

Yogyakarta Principles. 2007. *The Yogyakarta principles and the Yodyakarta principles plus 10 (YP+10).* http://www.yogyakartaprinciples.org. Retrieved on November 29, 2016.

Design Element: Abstract floral frame: Telnov Oleksii/Shutterstock

5

Women's Work

All women are working women whether they are
engaged in market or nonmarket activities.

—MARY CHINERY-HESSE, former Ghanian judge and first
woman Deputy Director-General of the International
Labour Organization[1]

*This Mexican woman works in the informal economy. Women's paid and unpaid labor
is extremely important to societies and to women's status, power, and well-being, but it
is often undervalued and exploited.* Rodrigo Torres/Glow Images

---

[1]The International Labour Organization (ILO) is a United Nations agency that develops and
monitors international labor laws and agreements and promotes gender equality in work.

W omen have always worked, and work is a central part of women's lives all over the world. Most women work, and they work hard. The woman who enjoys a leisurely life paid for by her husband is a worldwide rarity. In fact, if you consider both the average number of hours spent per day in both paid work (work that earns a payment or makes a profit), and unpaid work (cooking, cleaning, shopping, child and elder care, etc.), women actually work as much, and usually more, than men (UN DESA, 2020).

Whether paid or unpaid, women's work is important. Women's paid labor is valuable because it reduces poverty. When women work for pay, they devote more of their income to family subsistence than do men, leading to better outcomes for children (Blumberg, 1995; World Bank, 2012). Women's labor also matters because of its relationship to gender equality and women's empowerment. This makes sense when you think about it—when women are economically dependent on men, they are less able to leave abusive situations, assert their reproductive and sexual rights, live independently, and challenge gender inequality. Indeed, many Marxist feminists view women's economic dependence on men as the primary basis of patriarchy (Chafetz, 1991). Women's unpaid labor, such as obtaining or growing food, food preparation, cleaning, laundry, collecting fuel for family consumption, and providing child care, sanitation, and health care to family members, is also essential to individual, family, community, and societal well-being.

Women's Unpaid Care Work

Worldwide, who does most of the laundry, shopping, cooking, and child care, and looks after the family's medical needs and aging parents? In countries where water and fuel must be gathered and families must grow much of their own food, who takes care of these tasks?

The answer is, of course, women. In every society, women do most of the daily, routine household labor (cooking, cleaning, shopping, dishes, laundry, etc.), and they are also the primary caregivers of children and sick or senior family members, regardless of labor force participation. We use the term **unpaid domestic and care work** to describe this type of unpaid work. Globally, women spend on average 3.5 to 4.8 hours daily on this unpaid work, while men spend between 0.9 and 2.2 hours (UN DESA, 2020). Overall, women spend three times as many hours a day on unpaid domestic and care labor (UN DESA, 2020). About 22 percent of working age women do this type of labor full-time, compared to 1.5 percent of men (ILO, 2019a). Gendered differences in unpaid domestic and care work begin early and follow women into adulthood. One study of thirty-three countries found that girls aged 7 to 14 spent significantly more time than boys doing household chores, including taking care of siblings and elders (ILO, 2016).

Time-use surveys, where research participants use 24-hour diaries to record how they allocate their time over different activities, are the preferred way to collect data on gender differences in labor. Box 5.1 provides time-use survey

"Most of the household and care work is done by women in all parts of the world, regardless of their employment status. As a result of this dual workload, women work longer hours than men, and have less time for sleep, education, leisure, and participation in public life."
UN Department of Economic and Social Affairs

BOX 5.1   *A Sampling of Daily Hours of Unpaid Domestic and Care Work by Gender*

Country	Women	Men
Australia	5	2.73
Austria	4.57	2.41
Belgium	3.81	2.42
Canada	3.5	2.3
Denmark	3.5	2.43
Estonia	4.13	2.58
Germany	3.94	2.5
Portugal	4.27	2.46
Japan	3.63	0.75
Korea	3.5	0.87
Mexico	7.09	2.34
South Africa	3.73	1.55
Turkey	4.6	0.89
United States	3.69	2.29

Source: Eurofound and ILO, 2019.

data on women's and men's weekly hours of unpaid domestic and care labor from fourteen countries. Notably, there is significant variation worldwide. For instance, in Qatar, women spend fourteen times the number of hours than men on domestic and care labor, and the unpaid labor gender gap is greater in low- and middle-income countries compared to high-income countries (ILO, 2019a; UN DESA, 2020). However, in every country, women still spend more time providing unpaid domestic and care labor than men (UN DESA, 2020).

Explanations for Gender Inequalities in Unpaid Domestic and Care Work

There are three common explanations for gender differences in household labor and care labor (see Figure 5.1). The **time availability perspective on unpaid domestic and care work** suggests that because women spend less time in the paid workforce, they have more time to perform household tasks (Bianchi et al., 2000). For instance, in Turkey, women average 276 minutes a day on unpaid domestic

FIGURE 5.1 *Explanations for Gender-Based Divisions of Unpaid Domestic and Care Work*

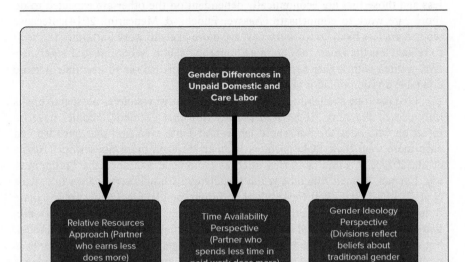

and care labor while men average 53 minutes, but only 34.5 percent of women are in the paid workforce, compared to 72 percent of men (UN DESA, 2020). In the countries of Colombia, Ethiopia, the Philippines, Uganda, and Zimbabwe, women spend 10 to 44 minutes less on care work for each hour of paid work (Rost et al., 2015). As wives' hours of employment rise, women's household and care labor decreases, and husbands' household labor contributions often increase (Bianchi et al., 2000).

But time availability is an incomplete explanation for gender differences in unpaid domestic and care labor. In some industrialized nations, women's unpaid labor relative to men's has shrunk not because men are doing so much more, but because women have reduced their in-home labor by lowering their standards, and when they can afford it, by outsourcing, such as buying prepared food and hiring home cleaning services (Bianchi et al., 2000; Horne et al., 2017; ILO, 2016a). Households with money often pay women and girls from lower income groups to do their household and care labor (Levtov, 2016). Also, research from a variety of countries indicates that employed women still do significantly more household labor than their male partners (Fuwa & Cohen, 2007). Many employed women work one shift in paid work and another unpaid second shift at home before or after paid work, in what is known as the **second shift** (Hochschild, 2003).

The **relative resources perspective on unpaid domestic and care work** emphasizes that the division of household labor reflects the relative economic power of women and men; whoever contributes more economic resources is able to better

"Before I leave home, I have to work. When I get home, I have to work."
Irene Ortega, Mexican woman who joined a one-day household labor strike. She normally puts in 10-hour days in the marketplace and does all the household labor.

avoid household labor (Bianchi et al., 2000). Partners share domestic duties according to their relative contributions to the household income; partners that earn less and those that are economically dependent on the other are expected to do more care work to compensate (Aassve, Fuochi, & Mencarini, 2014). Because women are less likely to work for pay, are more likely to work part-time, and tend to be paid less than men, they do more household labor. According to this perspective, women with higher earnings should have more power to negotiate a more equitable division of labor (Fuwa, 2004).

Like the time availability perspective, the relative resources perspective tells only part of the story. Some studies even find that partners' incomes have no effect on who does the household labor, and some even find that once women earn more than their male partners, women do even more housework (Horne et al., 2017). In some countries, such as Colombia, Ethiopia, the Philippines, and Uganda, women's income is not associated with decreased care work (Rost et al., 2015). This is likely the result of traditional gender ideologies that designate domestic and care labor as the work of females. According to the **gender perspective on unpaid domestic and care work**, also known as the "doing gender" model, household labor is a symbolic representation of gender relations, not merely a matter of who has time and who has the money (Bianchi et al., 2000). The idea is that men and women display culturally sanctioned gender roles through the activities they perform in the home. Unpaid domestic and care work is stereotyped as "women's work," and females are seen as naturally suited for it due to their nurturing and other-centered qualities. An ideology of intensive motherhood valorizes intensive and exclusive maternal care, especially of young children, and defines male caregiving as insufficient (Hook & Chalasani, 2008). Gender socialization in childhood reinforces this perception. Women's employed work is seen as secondary to their primary role as wife and mother, and men's higher status is such that they have refusal power (Blumberg, 1991). A twenty-country World Bank study found that making money for the family was the most common definition of "good husband," while domestic responsibilities were overwhelmingly seen as the main feature of being a "good wife" (Levtov, 2016).

Because gendered divisions of household labor and child care arise out of traditional gender ideologies, the gender perspective on unpaid domestic and care work predicts that more egalitarian beliefs about the genders should lead to more egalitarian divisions of household labor. Couples with gender-equal attitudes see housework as the responsibility of both partners and are thereby more likely to practice equitable divisions of household labor (Chesters, 2011). Indeed, cross-national studies find that gender empowerment (as measured by the number of women in government, administration, and professional careers) is related to more egalitarian divisions of household labor (Ruppanner, 2010).

All three explanations for gender differences in unpaid domestic and care work are supported by research. However, it appears that traditional gender ideologies often trump time availability and relative resources. For example, Fuma (2004) found that both the relative resources and time availability perspectives explained gender differences in household labor in gender-egalitarian societies like Sweden and Norway, but not in nonegalitarian countries such as Bulgaria and Japan.

An Australian study found that in dual-earner couples, men spend more time on care work, but traditional gender beliefs overrode this tendency (Chesters, 2011). Likewise, a study of European countries found that time availability and relative resources mattered less in countries that were less gender equal (Aasave et al., 2014).

Why the Gender Gap in Unpaid Domestic and Care Labor Matters

Women's greater responsibility for unpaid domestic and care labor is of concern. It is a sign of gender inequality that women's workdays are often longer than those of their male partners and that women frequently have less leisure time than men. Unpaid care work responsibilities also limit women's employment. Women's private sphere responsibilities, especially if they have children, reduce the time available for paid work, affect the types and quality of the employment available to them, and reduce their wages (Klugman & Melnikova, 2016; Matteazzi & Scherer, 2020; OECD Development Centre, 2014). This makes it more difficult for them to lift themselves and their children out of poverty and for them to accumulate retirement income and savings (Sepúlveda Carmona, 2013). The time and energy women spend on unpaid domestic and care work not only reduces women's earning power, it also limits women and girls' opportunities for education. Nearly two-thirds of illiterate people in the world are women, and girls are more likely to be kept out of school to take care of younger siblings and household tasks (UNICEF, 2019). Their disproportionate responsibility for unpaid household and care labor also limits women's political participation and increases their vulnerability due to their dependence on men's wage-earning (Levtov, 2016).

According to the ILO (2016a), work-family balance is the top work-related issue for women, and the greater burden of family responsibilities borne by women is a top barrier to women's leadership. The greater burden of balancing paid work and family responsibilities also means that women often experience greater stress from work-family conflict and have less time for recovery and relaxation (Baxter & Tai, 2016). In the United States, for example, 18 percent of mothers employed full-time say balancing work and family is very difficult for them compared with 11 percent of full-time employed fathers. While 50 percent of employed mothers report that being a parent has made it harder to advance in their career, only 39 percent of employed fathers say this (Pew Research Center, 2019; 2021).

Feminist economics is an economics framework that emphasizes gender analyses, including the economic value of unpaid domestic work and caregiving, the use of human well-being as a measure of economic success, and the importance of intersectionality in economics (Agenjo & Gálvez, 2019). Feminist economists note another problem: Because women's domestic and care labor is unpaid, it is unrecognized, undervalued, and unsupported (Waring, 1988). Considered "natural" for women, domestic and care labor isn't perceived and valued as work in the same way that paid labor is, and this contributes to gender inequality. Although the annual value of the unpaid work done by women is estimated at 10.8 trillion dollars, or 12 percent of the global GDP, governments do not measure it as economic activity or include it in the gross domestic product (GDP) (Klugman & Meinkova, 2016; Oxfam, 2020). Because national accounting figures guide policymaking, the undercounting of women's labor results in less government attention to programs

"Across the world, millions of women still find that poverty is their reward for a lifetime spent caring, and unpaid care provision by women and girls is still treated as an infinite, cost-free resource that fills the gaps when public services are not available or accessible." *Magdalena Sepúlveda Carmona, UN Special Rapporteur on Extreme Poverty and Human Rights*

"If you don't have equality at home, it will be an uphill battle to have it at work. That's where paternity benefits, child care and other work-family policies come in." *Shauna Olney, Chief of the ILO Gender, Equality and Diversity Branch*

"The international economic system constructs reality in a way that excludes the great bulk of women's work—reproduction (in all its forms), raising children, domestic work, and subsistence production." *Marilyn Waring, Feminist Economist*

BOX 5.2   *Feminist Economist Lourdes Beneria on Unpaid Labor*

Lourdes Beneria is a Spanish-American economist. A professor and researcher, she is the author of many books and articles and serves on the editorial board of the journal Feminist Economics.

The challenge of accounting for women's unpaid work first surfaced for me in 1978 when I visited the picturesque town of Chechaouen in northern Morocco while I was working at the International Labor Office. . . . Statistics showed that the labor force participation rate for men and women in Morocco differed widely—more than 75 percent for men and less than 10 percent for women. But what I saw in the streets of Chechaouen told me a very different story. I saw many women moving about the busy streets, some carrying dough on their heads to bake bread in public ovens, others

carrying wood on their backs or clothes to be washed in the brook bordering the town; still other women were carrying baskets or bags on their way to shopping, often with children at their side. The men were less busy—men were sitting outside the town's shops, idle and chatting, perhaps waiting for the tourist season to increase the demands for the beautiful crafts sold in the stores. I immediately thought something was wrong with the statistics I had seen. It was the first time I had thought about this type of discrepancy, but I soon found out how prevalent it was across countries and regions.

Source: Beneria, L. "On paid and unpaid work," *Radcliffe Quarterly.* Fall, 1998.

"Nearly 65 percent of people above retirement age without any regular pension are women. This means that 200 million women in old age live without any regular income from social protection (old age or survivors pension), compared to 115 million men."
Women At Work: Trends 2016 (ILO)

and policies addressing women's labor needs (SIDA, 2016). For example, many governments fail to invest in the water and sanitation infrastructures that would reduce women's unpaid labor. They do not provide affordable care services for child and elder care. They do not have policies that support work-family balance. Women that spend much of their lives doing unpaid domestic and care labor for their families usually receive no pensions. Box 5.2 highlights the early work of feminist economist Lourdes Beneria, one of the first economists to note the invisibility of women's work in government statistics.

Due to the advocacy of feminist economists like Marilyn Waring, Sakiko Fukuda-Parr, Devaki Jain, and Deniz Kandiyoti, and activities such as the Wages for Housework Campaign, many governments now collect data on unpaid household labor. However, these statistics remain outside the core statistics used to measure economic progress and activity (Saunders & Dalziel, 2016). Advocacy continues for greater inclusion of women's unpaid labor as part of government accounting systems and for valid and reliable time-use measures of unpaid care work. Collectively, these efforts are called the Accounting for Women's Work Project (Beneria, Berik, & Floro, 2015). Feminist economists also favor **gender-responsive budget analysis**, which examines how national budgets impact women and girls differently than men and boys. These analyses measure government commitment to women's specific needs and rights and include a focus on the unpaid care economy where much of women's time is spent.

Reducing the Gender Gap in Unpaid Domestic and Care Work

Recognizing, redistributing, and reducing unpaid care work are three interconnected ways to narrow the gender gap in unpaid care work and promote gender equality (see Figure 5.2). As noted above, measuring this unpaid work and its value to human well-being is important to increase its visibility and to monitor the effects of programs and polices intended to promote gender equity in divisions of family labor (Recognizing). Policies and programs directed at reducing the time needed for domestic and care labor, such as government-subsidized child and elder care and government investments in time-and-energy saving infrastructures, are also key (Reducing). Another strategy is to reallocate unpaid domestic and care work so that it is more gender-equal (Redistributing). For example, MenCare is a global fatherhood campaign to engage men as caregivers. Started in 2011 and active in 50 countries on five continents, MenCare includes programs and media to challenge traditional gender roles (men-care.org). Incentivizing

The Global Women's Strike (Huelga Mundial de Mujeres) is an international grassroots network calling for the return of military budgets to communities. One of their demands is payment and pensions for all care work. Their motto: Invest in caring, not killing.

FIGURE 5.2   *Reducing Gender Gaps in Unpaid Labor: Recognize, Reduce, and Redistribute*

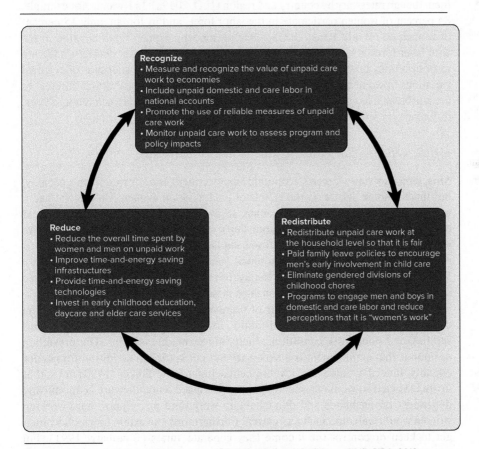

Recognize
• Measure and recognize the value of unpaid care work to economies
• Include unpaid domestic and care labor in national accounts
• Promote the use of reliable measures of unpaid care work
• Monitor unpaid care work to assess program and policy impacts

Reduce
• Reduce the overall time spent by women and men on unpaid work
• Improve time-and-energy saving infrastructures
• Provide time-and-energy saving technologies
• Invest in early childhood education, daycare and elder care services

Redistribute
• Redistribute unpaid care work at the household level so that it is fair
• Paid family leave policies to encourage men's early involvement in child care
• Eliminate gendered divisions of childhood chores
• Programs to engage men and boys in domestic and care labor and reduce perceptions that it is "women's work"

Sources: Klugman & Melinova, 2016; Levtov, 2016; Rost, Bates, & Dellipiane, 2015; SIDA, 2016.

"You see equality in my future. You are my father."
From a MenCare poster

men's early involvement in child care through paid paternal or parental leave is another redistribution strategy, since it involves men early in child care. Fathers who take leave, especially those that take off two weeks or more immediately after childbirth, are more likely to be involved with their young children (ILO, 2014). At least 94 countries currently provide paternity or parental leave policies that fathers can use after the birth of their child.

Feminist activists, organizations, and scholars pushed for the inclusion of unpaid domestic and care labor in the United Nation's 2015 Sustainable Development Goals (SDG) agreed upon by 193 world leaders (Institute of Development Studies, 2016). As a result, Goal 5 (Gender Equality) includes the target, "Recognize and value unpaid care and domestic work through the provision of public services, infrastructure and social protection policies and the promotion of shared responsibility within the household and the family as nationally appropriate" (UN DESA, 2021).

Women's Paid Labor

Globally, 47 percent of women are in the paid labor force compared to 74 percent of men, though rates vary by country and region (ILO, 2019a). In Rwanda, for example, 84 percent of women participate in the labor force, and in Jordan, only 15 percent of women do (World Bank, 2021a). One reason why women's participation in the paid labor force is lower than men's is because they have greater domestic and care responsibilities than men (ILO, 2019a). Box 5.3 provides a snapshot of regional variations in women and men's labor force participation. Cross-cultural differences are attributable to cultural factors such as traditional gender roles, economic factors, differences in fertility rates, and the demands of domestic and care labor.

By law, married women in Bahrain, Cameroon, Chad, Comoros, Egypt, Guinea-Bissau, Iran, Jordan, Kuwait, Mauritania, Niger, Qatar, Sudan, Syria, West Bank and Gaza, and Yemen must have their husband's permission to take a job.
World Bank, 2021

Effects of Paid Work on Women

Most feminists view women's economic empowerment as a key to women's equality, but there is some debate on the effects of paid work on women. On the one hand, earning money often empowers women. It gives them more "voice" in household decisions and in their intimate relationships, and may allow them to leave abusive relationships (UN Women, 2019). Some studies also find that women's earnings reduce domestic violence (Iregui-Bohórquez, Ramírez-Giraldo, & Tribín-Uribe, 2019). Women's earnings also decrease family poverty, and provide greater economic security in old age and when relationships dissolve (UN Women, 2019).

"Let our daughters go to school and get good jobs. The moment they will be independent from men in thinking and earning, they will have very good lives."
Tanzanian woman

On the other hand, the benefits of women's employment is often offset by the difficulties of balancing work and family, low wages, limited promotion opportunities, and poor work conditions, including sexual harassment. The prevailing opinion is that employment is a necessary but not sufficient condition for gender equality. Indeed, women and development scholar Irene Tinker (1990) notes that in some societies, women's social status is enhanced when they are economically dependent on husbands and don't have to work, and many poor, hard-working women would welcome such a situation. Furthermore, the extent to which women get to keep or control the income they generate varies (Blumberg, 1991). For example, in one study of 60 developing countries, 10 percent of women reported

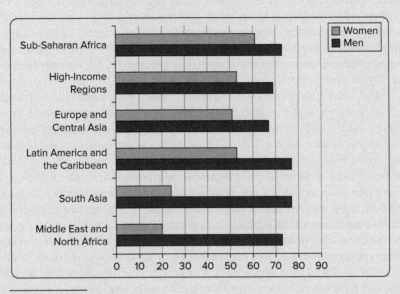

BOX 5.3   *Regional Variations in Gendered Labor Force Participation*

Source: World Bank (2021a).

having no say in how their income was used (UN Women, 2019). The more a society's political, economic, legal, and ideological systems disadvantage women, the less a woman gets her "hypothetical dollar's worth of economic power for every dollar she brings to the household" (Blumberg, 1995, p. 213).

Maternity Protections and Child Care

Maternity protections are policies and laws that ensure that expectant and nursing women will not face employment discrimination or be exposed to health hazards, that they will have time off to have children and return to the job without discrimination, and that they will be permitted breast-feeding breaks (ILO, 2016b). Maternity leave and child care are prerequisites for women's full participation in the labor force because it is common for women to get pregnant and have babies, and women have primary responsibility for children. Few countries provide adequate support for workers with family responsibilities. Government policies on child care and maternity leave are reflections of a society's views about the "proper" role of women in society and whether women's participation in the labor force is desired (Sjöberg, 2004).

In almost half of two-parent households in the United States, both parents work full-time, and in 40% of all families with children, the mother is the sole or primary breadwinner. *Pew Research Center*

"Expectant and nursing mothers require special protection to prevent harm to their or their infants' health, and they need adequate time to give birth, to recover, and to nurse their children. At the same time, they also require protection to ensure that they will not lose their job simply because of pregnancy or maternity leave."
International Labour Organization

Maternity leave policies are a maternity protection measure that provides time off for mothers following the birth of a child. These leaves are important for both women's health and for child development. The United Nations Convention on the Elimination of All Forms of Discrimination Against Women (CEDAW) affirms women's right to maternity protection. The **International Labour Organization (ILO)**, a division of the United Nations, brings together governments, employers, and workers representative of 187 member governments (states) to set labor standards, develop policies, and devise programs promoting decent work for all women and men. Its **Maternity Protection Convention**, 2000 (No. 183) is the most up-to-date international labor standard on maternity protection, but as of 2021, it has only been ratified by 37 UN member states (ILO, 2000; ILO, 2021).

The maternity protection convention has three minimum requirements: (1) At least 14 weeks of maternity leave; (2) A woman on maternity leave receive a cash benefit no less than two-thirds of her previous earnings (so that she can afford to take leave); and (3) To reduce the burden on employers and to reduce discrimination against employed mothers, maternity leave should be paid through social security (social insurance) or other public funds. Ratifying states also agree to ensure that a pregnant woman or nursing mother is not obliged to perform work that has been determined to be harmful to her health or that of her child. Employers are prohibited from terminating the employment of a woman during pregnancy or absence on maternity leave, except on grounds unrelated to pregnancy, childbirth and its consequences, or nursing. Women must be allowed to return to work in the same position or an equivalent position paid at the same rate and have the right to one or more daily breaks or a daily reduction of hours of work to breastfeed.

A large majority of women workers are not adequately protected by maternal protection legislation, and only about a quarter of the world's women receive paid maternity leave. Most countries now have federal laws guaranteeing women paid maternity leave (including parental leave), but six do not: the Marshall Islands, Micronesia, Palau, Papua New Guinea, Tonga, and the United States. However, the majority of maternity protection laws do not meet all three of the ILO's Maternity Protection Convention's minimum requirements. For example, the 14-week standard is only met by 36 percent of the countries with maternity protection laws and in 42 percent the leave is paid for by the employer (ILO, 2019b; World Bank, 2021b). Most countries with developed economies (Western Europe, Japan, and North America) require at least 14 weeks at two-thirds pay, funded by social security. The United States is an anomaly among the developed nations and stands out as having the worst maternal leave policies in the world (except for Papua New Guinea). In the United States, citizens that work for employers with more than 50 employees are guaranteed 12 weeks of unpaid leave, but this stipulation means that only 50 percent of American parents are eligible for legally mandated leave. However, employers may offer longer and paid leaves as employee benefits, and six states and the District of Columbia have laws granting paid maternity leave (California, Hawaii, New Jersey, New York, Rhode Island, and Washington). Box 5.4 shows some of the best and worst countries for maternity leave.

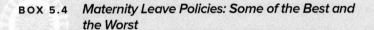

BOX 5.4   *Maternity Leave Policies: Some of the Best and the Worst*

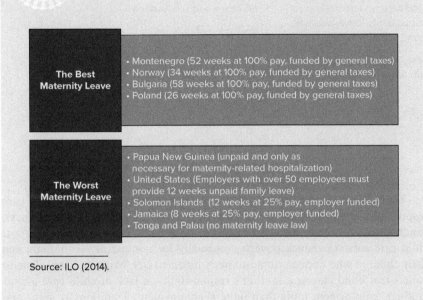

The Best Maternity Leave
- Montenegro (52 weeks at 100% pay, funded by general taxes)
- Norway (34 weeks at 100% pay, funded by general taxes)
- Bulgaria (58 weeks at 100% pay, funded by general taxes)
- Poland (26 weeks at 100% pay, funded by general taxes)

The Worst Maternity Leave
- Papua New Guinea (unpaid and only as necessary for maternity-related hospitalization)
- United States (Employers with over 50 employees must provide 12 weeks unpaid family leave)
- Solomon Islands (12 weeks at 25% pay, employer funded)
- Jamaica (8 weeks at 25% pay, employer funded)
- Tonga and Palau (no maternity leave law)

Source: ILO (2014).

The COVID-19 pandemic affected women's employment more than men's because it affected sectors where women's employment is high, and because more women than men had to take leave or quit their jobs due to increased household and care responsibilities. *World Bank*

It is important to consider that how family leave policies are structured is in some ways a two-edged sword as far as gender equality (Fuwa & Cohen, 2007). For one, most countries do not provide for paternity leave; this reinforces the assumption that mothers are the primary parents. Family leave and paternity leave policies that provide leave for fathers may be more successful in promoting both gender equality and fathers' involvement with their children. Also, because maternity leave encourages women to withdraw from the labor force at least temporarily (hurting career progression and wages) and often offers low or no monetary benefits, it may reinforce gender inequality in the market and in the family (Fuwa & Cohen, 2007). Extensive parental leaves, particularly in the absence of public or private supports for child care, may even encourage women to stay out of the labor force (Pettit & Hook, 2005). Laws that require lengthy maternity leaves may also reinforce perceptions that women are costly and unreliable, especially when employers are required to pay for them. It is also important to note that maternity protection laws are often poorly implemented, and women are often reluctant to take full advantage of their legal rights due to concerns about keeping their jobs (Probst et al., 2018). Box 5.5 summarizes gender-equality-friendly recommendations from the International Labour Organization to promote work-family balance and offset some of these limitations.

BOX 5.5   *Recommended Gender-Equal Family-Friendly Work Measures*

- Offering paternity leave and making parental leave, after the initial maternity or paternity leave, available to both men and women and nontransferable

- Making "normal" work more family-compatible: Flexible arrangements with regard to working schedules

- Short leave for emergencies

- Flex-time and teleworking

- Reduction of daily hours of work and overtime

- Availability of affordable and good-quality child and elder care

- More equal sharing of family responsibilities between men and women

---

Until child care needs are met by more equitable sharing of child care responsibilities by men, and by more support from governments and business, gender equality in paid work is unlikely (World Bank, 2021). Free or low-cost child care services reduce poverty, especially for non-partnered mothers and their children who depend on a mother's income (UN Women, 2016). Due to beliefs that child care is a mother's responsibility, a lack of child care affects mothers' employment more than fathers' employment. Traditionally, nonworking female relatives such as grandmothers provided child care and elder care, but due to women's increased labor force participation and migration, this support is waning (ILO, 2004). When child care is unavailable or too expensive and women must work for pay, they may leave their children alone, take older children (usually girls) out of school to care for younger ones, bring children to work with them (sometimes under unsafe conditions), and take on lower-paying or part-time work that makes poverty more likely (ILO, 2013). The ILO Workers with Family Responsibilities Convention, 1981 (No. 156) stipulates that UN member states develop community services such as child care and family services so that women and men have equality in employment. As of 2021, 45 countries have ratified it.

The provision of subsidized or publicly sponsored child care is associated with higher employment rates for women (World Bank, 2021a). Resources for child care may come from the family, government, nonprofit and religious organizations, and employers. In many countries, such as the United States, child care is viewed as the responsibility of parents, not the state. In such places, low-income and single parent households experience the greatest difficulties obtaining quality child care—ironically, those who need it the most (ILO, 2016a). Sweden, Norway, and the Republic of Korea have some of most affordable, large-scale, government-funded and operated childcare programs, while the United States, Turkey, and Ireland are examples of countries that rely almost entirely on privately provided childcare paid for by parents (World Bank, 2021a).

BOX 5.6   *Gender Wage Gaps in a Dozen Countries*

Country	Gender Wage Gap*
Korea	32.5
Japan	23.5
Israel	22.7
Mexico	18.8
Canada	17.6
Chile	12.5
Colombia	4.0
Costa Rica	4.7
Czech Republic	14.7
Denmark	4.9
Norway	5.0
United Kingdom	16

Source: OECD, 2021.

*Percent difference between the median earnings of men working full-time and the median earnings of women working full-time.

The Gender Wage (Pay) Gap: Explanations and Solutions

Women's economic power is diminished by the fact that they frequently receive less pay for their work than do men. This is known as the **gender wage gap** (the difference in average wages or earnings between men and women). Worldwide, the gender wage gap is 20 percent (18.8% when adjusted for factors like age, education, full or part-time, etc.). In other words, women's wages average 81 percent of men's (ILO, 2019a). But the gender pay gap varies by region, and by country, and within country depending on the type of job (ILO, 2018b). For example, the gap is about 22 percent in the Sub-Saharan African, Latin American, and the Caribbean regions, but in the North American region it is 15 percent, and in Western Europe it is 13 percent. In Pakistan, women earn on average 36 percent less than men, but in the Philippines, women earn about 10 percent more than men. In Norway, the gap rises from less than 5 percent for low-income jobs to 30 percent for high-income jobs. Box 5.6 provides a snapshot of the gender pay gap in a dozen countries. While the gender wage gap is narrowing, the ILO (2016a) estimates that at the current pace of change and without targeted action, gender parity in wages won't happen for another 250 years.

In the United States, the gender wage gap translates into $10,138 less per year in median earnings for women compared to men. *National Women's Law Center (U.S.)*

In yet another example of intersectionality, the gender pay gap also varies within a country based on ethnicity, motherhood, sexual orientation, gender identity, age, and disability. In the United States, for instance, Euro American men make more than all other demographic groups (except for Asian American men), but the size of the gender wage gap varies for different groups of American women. Euro American women working full-time year-round earn 82 cents for every dollar Euro American men earn, women with disabilities earn 80 cents, African American women earn 63 cents, Latinas earn 55 cents, and Native American women earn 60 cents. Mothers earn 70 cents for every dollar paid to fathers, lesbians earn 79 cents compared to heterosexual men and 80 cents compared to gay men (National Women's Law Center, 2020).

"If money talks, women do not have a loud voice."
International Labour Organization

International human rights laws and conventions call for gender equality in pay. For example, Article 11 of CEDAW (the 1979 convention on the elimination of discrimination against women ratified by 189 UN nations) affirms women's right to equal pay, benefits, and treatment, and requires governments to "take all appropriate measures to eliminate discrimination in employment." The ILO's **Equal Remuneration Convention**, 1953 (no. 100), ratified by 173 UN member states, requires states to ensure equal pay for men and women for work of equal value through laws, wage setting, and collective bargaining agreements between employers and employees. Goal 8 of the UN's Sustainable Development Goals ("Promote sustained, inclusive and sustainable economic growth, full and productive employment and decent work for all") also includes a target of equal pay for work of equal value.

On October 24, 2016, Icelandic women left their jobs 14 percent early (at 2:38 pm) to protest the 14 percent gender pay gap, as they had for the last 11 years. In November 2016, French women participated in a similar strike.

Why do employed women make less money than employed men? There are four main explanations: (1) Women are segregated and concentrated in lower-paying, female-dominated jobs (gender occupational segregation), (2) family responsibilities lead to more women than men working part-time, (3) women lack the experience and training for better-paying jobs (human capital), and (4) outright gender wage discrimination (see Figure 5.3).

One reason women earn less than men is their concentration in low paying, poor quality jobs (UN Women, 2016). In most societies, employed women and men tend to work in different jobs and employment sectors, and men hold the higher positions compared to women in the same job category. This is known as **gender job segregation** or **gender occupational segregation**. Women are overrepresented in the lowest paid occupations, and the higher the percentage of women in an occupation, the lower the pay for that occupation (Alonso-Villar & del Río, 2017; ILO, 2018b). Some studies indicate that the majority of the gender wage gap can be explained by gender occupational segregation (Blau & Kahn, 2016).

There are two types of gender occupational segregation: horizontal and vertical. **Horizontal occupational segregation** refers to the tendency for occupations mainly held by men to have substantially higher pay rates and status as compared to those mainly held by women. In other words, the greater the share of women working in an occupational category (the greater the degree of feminization), the lower the pay (ILO, 2018a). For example, in the United States, women make up nearly two-thirds of workers in the 40 lowest-paying jobs and only 37 percent of workers

FIGURE 5.3   *Contributors to the Gender Pay Gap*

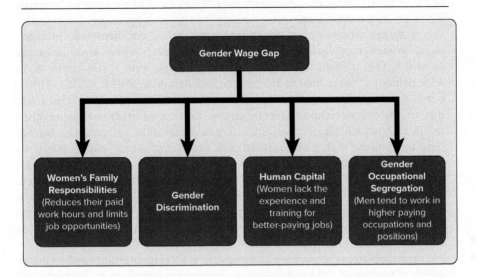

in the 40 highest paying jobs (National Women's Law Center, 2020). And in the United States, a university graduate working in a male-dominated occupation will earn $30 an hour versus $20 an hour if they work in a female-dominated occupation (ILO, 2018b). In Europe, working in a job with a mostly female workforce reduces wages by almost 15 percent (ILO, 2019a). Men are also more likely to be in core or salaried positions, whereas women are often in peripheral, insecure, less-valued positions (UN Women, 2016). Women generally work in service occupations like secretarial work, sales, and domestic and care services. Men generally work in better-paid industry, trades, plant and machine operations and managerial and legislative occupations (ILO, 2016a).

Due to women's increased levels of education and experience, changes in gender norms and stereotypes, and government equality policies, more women now work in higher-paying jobs traditionally held by men (Blau & Kahn, 2016). But horizontal segregation persists because many societies continue to believe that women and men are suited for different types of jobs and because gender socialization leads people to pursue jobs and education consistent with their gender role (Charles & Grusky, 2004). Gender differences in college major, for example, are an important determinant of gender pay gaps between college-educated women and college-educated men (Blau & Kahn, 2016). Jobs are often considered as "male" or "female" jobs, and this also affects whether women and girls are encouraged and choose to pursue those jobs, and whether they get hired when they do. There are often barriers to women's entry into better-paying, traditionally male occupations, such as discrimination in selection and gender

"In many countries young women are still encouraged to train in relatively low-skilled and poorly paid 'feminine' occupations with little prospect of upward mobility, while young men are encouraged to go into modern technology-based training and employment, which often pay better."
Geir Tonstol of the ILO Bureau for Gender Equality

stereotyping. Recruitment practices that favor men and barriers in the promotion or career development of women have the effect of excluding women or "segregating" them into certain jobs.

Although horizontal occupational segregation has declined, in many cases women receive lower pay than men do even when working in the same job. U.S. women in traditionally male occupations, for example, make 81.9 percent of what men in those occupations make (IWPR, 2020). This is partly due to gender wage discrimination (discussed a bit later), but also arises due to vertical occupational segregation. **Vertical occupational segregation** refers to how, within occupations, there is a hierarchy of jobs, and women tend to be more highly represented in lower-ranked, lower-paying positions than men are within the same occupation. For example, in the United States, only 20 percent of equity partners in law firms (the highest rank) are women, and on average, these women earn 14 percent less than male equity partners; this despite the fact that women start careers in private law firms at the same rate as men and work more hours than men (National Association of Women Lawyers, 2019).

As suggested earlier, women's unpaid care work responsibilities and an undersupply of health and child and elder care services also contribute to the gender pay gap. Women's family responsibilities often lead to part-time work and to gaps in employment that reduce work experience and seniority. Part-time work is synonymous with low status, low pay, and limited training and career opportunities (ILO, 2007). Worldwide, women are more likely to be in the workforce part-time, especially in middle- and high-income regions (ILO, 2018b). For example, in Canada, 51 percent of employed women work part-time compared to 35 percent of men, in Japan it is 48 to 19, in the United Kingdom it is 56 to 28, and in the Netherlands it is 75 to 39 (World Bank, 2021c; 2021d). Although part-time work is a desired choice for some women because it provides some income and time for family, it is important to recognize that for others, it a choice forced by lack of affordable child care and elder care, and unequal distributions of unpaid domestic and care labor. Employers also make hiring and promotion decisions based on stereotypical assumptions of the burdens imposed by families on mothers' time and energy, assuming, for example, that women are less committed to paid work than they are to their families (ILO, 2015a).

Women's unpaid domestic and care labor responsibilities typically increase when they have children, and in comparison to employed non-mothers, employed mothers make less money. In Mexico, for example, employed mothers earn 32 percent less than other employed women, and in China, the gap is 37 percent. In contrast, men are more likely to experience a fatherhood bonus in the form of increased wages (ILO, 2018b). The wage gap associated with motherhood is known as the **motherhood wage gap** (or the **motherhood wage penalty**) and is usually measured as the wage difference between mothers and women without children, or as the difference between the wages of mothers compared to fathers. The motherhood wage gap is also greater in developing countries than in developed ones but varies from country to country (Grimshaw & Rubery, 2015).

Another explanation for gender differences in pay is provided by the **human capital approach** (Blau & Ferber, 1987; Jacobsen, 2003). Human capital refers to any attributes a person has that contribute to her productivity and value as an employee. The idea is that women get paid less because they are less skilled, less educated, or less experienced workers than men typically are. These differences originate in gender discrimination in education and training, and also because many women enter and leave the workforce due to child bearing and rearing.

Gender occupational segregation, part-time work, and human capital only account for a small portion of the gender pay gap in most countries, leading the ILO (2018b) to conclude that the gap in most countries is due to direct and indirect gender discrimination. One U.S. study found the gender pay gap remains even when education, experience, hours worked, and occupational segregation are held constant (Blau & Kahn, 2016). This suggests that some of the gender wage gap is due to outright **gender wage discrimination** on the part of employers.

Gender wage discrimination appears to have three main sources. One is the traditional undervaluation of women's work (ILO, 2018b). In general, jobs designated as women's job pay less—work done by women is often devalued because it mirrors the unpaid domestic and care labor traditionally performed by women, and simply because women rather than men do it (ILO, 2019a). Second, in some cultures, it is assumed that a woman can be paid less because her income is merely a supplement to her husband's and that her paid job is secondary to her unpaid job as wife and mother (ILO, 2015a). Last, when employers can get away with paying women less, they sometimes do just that—because saving on women's wages increases employers' profits.

Eliminating the gender wage gap is crucial to achieving gender equality and reducing the poverty of women and their families. However, its multiple causes require multiple solutions. For example, it is clear that women's greater responsibilities for household and care labor must be addressed because they affect the types of jobs and the numbers of hours that women can work. Changing the gender stereotypes that lead to gender occupational segregation and the low wages for jobs traditionally held by women is also needed (ILO, 2015a). Because gender-based occupational segregation also reflects the difference between women and men in terms of their choice of education and vocational training, encouraging girls to study science and the technical subjects that lead to higher-paying work may also reduce occupational segregation (UN Women, 2016). Austria, Denmark, Finland, Germany, Iceland, and Sweden all have educational programs to encourage children to consider non-gender stereotypical occupations, and in Scotland, a program trains men for careers in child care and early childhood education (ILO, 2016a).

Improving the valuation of jobs traditionally held by women is also important for reducing the gap and for reducing occupational segregation (since more men may be attracted to these jobs if they are better paid). For example, a study of twelve developed and developing countries found that paid care workers are not

"The data show that even when women and men appear to have equal investments in their work (equal levels of education, similar occupations, etc.), they do not necessarily reap the equal outcomes in terms of pay that the human capital model would suggest."
Hillary Lips, Psychology professor, gender scholar (U.S.)

adequately compensated for their skills and experience in comparison to other workers (Buddig & Misra, 2010). Increasing the wages paid for care jobs, which are societally important but tend to be underpaid and held disproportionately by women, would make a difference (Rubery, 2016).

Combatting gender discrimination is also critical. Elimination of the gender pay gap requires government commitment to enacting and enforcing pay equity legislation, commitment to international conventions regarding pay equity, reducing gender occupational segregation, and providing family supports such as child care. By the early 2000s, most countries had ratified the ILO's Equal Remuneration Convention, 1951 (No. 100) and the accompanying Recommendation (No. 90). The Convention requires that remuneration rates (pay) are to be established without discrimination based on the sex of the worker and that men and women workers obtain equal remuneration for work of equal value, not just for the same or similar work. The implementation of this principle requires an objective comparison among jobs to determine their relative value (comparable worth). **Comparable worth** uses detailed classification systems to compare jobs on skill, effort, responsibility, and working conditions so that compensation can be fair, instead of being based on whether the job is customarily held by women or men (United Nations, 1994). Ratifying states are also supposed to work with businesses to ensure equal pay, provide job trainings and counseling to reduce horizontal occupational segregation, and provide services to meet the needs of women workers with family responsibilities (ILO, 2003). As of 2021, 173 countries have ratified the Equal Remuneration Convention, but 14 have not (Bahrain, Brunei Darussalam, Cook Islands, Kuwait, Liberia, Marshall Islands, Myanmar, Oman, Palau, Qatar, Somalia, Tonga, Tuvalu, and the United States).

Government commitment to equal pay for the genders can reduce the gender wage gap. Governments can make wage-setting policies that can help reduce the gap, such as implementing a minimum living wage (Rubery, 2016). In some countries, raising the minimum wage would also reduce the gender pay gap (and poverty) (ILO, 2020). In the United States, for example, almost two-thirds of minimum-wage workers are women, and 39 percent of Black working women and 46 percent of Hispanic working women earn under $15 an hour (Van Dam, 2021). Nearly 40 percent of single moms are minimum wage workers earning $7.50 an hour. Women working full-time for minimum wage earn just $15,080 annually.

Governments can also enact legislation or create policies requiring employers to identify and eliminate pay discrimination (a workplace-level approach). For example, some employers require employees to keep their salaries secret, making it difficult for women to know if they are paid less than similarly qualified men. Governments can prevent this by passing laws that require wage transparency (ILO, 2019a). They can pass pay equity laws as recommended by the ILO. The ILO Equal Remuneration Convention suggests that countries enact national laws prohibiting gender pay discrimination; approximately 47 percent of countries have such legislation (World Bank, 2021b). Unfortunately, equal pay legislation does not bring about gender pay equality when there is poor monitoring and

"The core argument for closing the gender pay gap is social justice for half the world's population."
Jill Rubery, Professor of Comparative Economic Systems, England

"Raising the minimum wage is even more critical than ever in the fight for equal pay for women."
Nancy Duff, co-president of the National Women's Law Center

"Pay inequality matters—both because it is a blatant injustice, and because it condemns millions of women and their families to live in a continuing cycle of poverty."
UN Women Executive Director Phumzile Mlambo-Ngcuka

enforcement or employer compliance is voluntary (as is often the case). Most laws are written narrowly and in ways that make enforcement challenging, discrimination difficult to prove, and cases hard to bring to court. A consistently well-funded equality agency that provides legal guidance and institutional support appears to be critical for the success of equal pay laws and policies (Charlesworth & McDonald, 2015).

The Glass Ceiling: Explanations and Solutions

Further evidence of gender inequality in paid employment comes in the form of a **glass ceiling**. This term refers to the various barriers that prevent qualified women from advancing into powerful decision-making positions in organizations and in politics. The glass ceiling in politics is discussed in detail in Chapter 9, "Women and Politics." Here we focus on women in decision-making positions in other organizations.

Compared to the past, women have made significant inroads into management positions. In a global survey of 70 countries, nearly half of companies ("enterprises") reported that women hold fewer than 30 percent of management positions (ILO, 2019c). It is worth noting that intersectionality applies to the glass ceiling. Consider that in many countries, some women face the dual burden of racism and sexism in organizations, leading to a **concrete ceiling** (Nkomo & Cox, 1989). For instance, in the United States, where women make up 40 percent of those in management occupations, only 10.7 percent are Latina, 5.8 percent are Asian American, and 8 percent are African American (United States Bureau of Labor Statistics, 2020). Where a woman lives also makes a difference. For example, the lowest average rates of women in management are found in the Middle East and North Africa (10.1%), Africa (20%), and Asia and the Pacific (20%) (ILO, 2019c).

The higher up the organizational ladder you go, the fewer women you find, a phenomenon known as the **leaky pipeline**. For example, in the United States, women make up 29 percent of chief executive officers and 7.4 percent of CEOs in Fortune 500 firms,[2] the latter figure a record high (Hinchliffe, 2020; U.S. Bureau of Labor Statistics, 2020). Globally, only 21.7 percent of CEOs are women and women comprise less than a third of corporate board members (ILO, 2019c). Latin America and the Caribbean have the largest percentage of women CEOs (29.7) and the Middle East and North Africa have the lowest (10%).

Voluntary gender diversity initiatives and targets are associated with reducing the glass ceiling but laws are sometimes needed to motivate increased gender diversity efforts. Norway's 2006 quota law requires that boards include 40 percent women. The quota increased the percentage of women on boards from 6 percent in 2006 to 40 percent by 2008 (ILO, 2019c). Other countries have also passed legislation intended to increase gender diversity in management. These include gender quotas for boards or management (France, Germany, Italy, India, Japan,

"Gender equality cannot be attained until women and men share leadership equally. With unfettered access of women to leadership, the policies of organizations and governments would balance the concerns of women and men more equitably."
Ronit Kark and Alice Eagly, gender and leadership researchers

---

[2]Fortune 500 companies are the 500 largest publicly traded companies in the United States. Fortune Global 200 and the Fortune 500 are the largest international publicly traded companies.

Gender diversity initiatives that increase the number of women in high-level leadership positions are associated with increased profits and productivity.
ILO, Women, Business, and Management

"The cracks might be bigger but the ceiling is still not shattered."
Kunyalala Maphisa, President of Businesswomen's Association, South Africa

Malaysia, the Netherlands, Panama, Spain) and requirements that companies disclose gender diversity and explain when gender diversity remains low (Canada, Switzerland, and the United Kingdom).

Leadership research does not support the idea that there are few women in higher-status positions because women's cognitive skills, personality traits, or behavior patterns make them less suited for managerial positions (Eagly & Carli, 2007; Heilman, Manzi, & Braun, 2015). Likewise, research finds that women and men are equally effective leaders (Paustian-Underdahl, Walker, & Woehr, 2014). Instead, the main culprits for the glass ceiling appear to be stereotypes that suggest that women are inappropriate for leadership positions, organizational barriers such as a lack of mentoring and training of women for leadership positions, and women's family responsibilities. The three common explanations for the glass ceiling are represented in Figure 5.4 and are discussed next.

When you think of a leader, what types of qualities do you imagine? In your culture, are these qualities typically associated with males or females? Gender stereotypes are one contributor to the perception that women are inappropriate for leadership and managerial positions—in other words, when people think leader or manager, they think male (Koenig et al., 2011). If it is believed that a woman's place is in the home or that women are ineffective as leaders and decision makers, then women will be denied leadership positions (Stevens, 2007). In general, leadership is more often associated with male rather than female stereotypes (Cuadrado, García Ael, & Molero, 2015; Garcia-Retamoro & López-Zafra, 2009; Koenig et al., 2011). Research also indicates that gender-stereotypic images of occupations correspond to sex segregation in employment (Carly et al., 2016;

FIGURE 5.4 *Three Contributors to the Glass Ceiling*

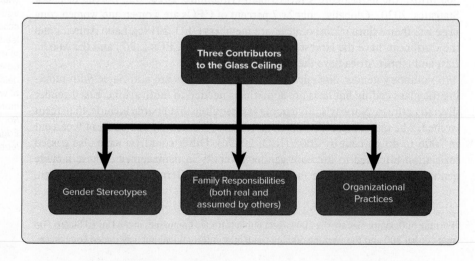

Cheryan, Handron, & Hudson, 2013; López-Sáez, Puertas, & Sáinz, 2011). Gendered leader stereotypes, combined with the fact that there are relatively few women in positions of power, may make it harder for some people to consider women as possible leaders and managers.

The incompatibility between the female gender role and the leadership role is described by **role congruity theory** (Eagly & Karau, 2002). The idea is that we are less likely to assign people to roles that call for qualities associated with the other gender. The agentic qualities associated with males (e.g., assertive, controlling, dominant, confident) are more consistent with the qualities expected of leaders compared to the communal qualities associated with females (e.g., helpful, nurturing, gentle, kind). These gender stereotypes lead to the conclusion that men are more suitable for leadership roles. Women are "agentically deficient" (presumed lacking in the qualities necessary for effective leadership), and this interferes with their leadership attainment. Meanwhile, they experience an "agentic penalty" (they are negatively judged when they act agentically) because they violate their communal gender role; this also interferes with their maintaining their leadership positions (Rosette et al., 2016).

Likewise, the **lack of fit model** proposes that there is a perceived lack of fit between the stereotypically based, nurturing and communal attributes and behaviors associated with women and the agentic, instrumental "male" attributes and behaviors believed necessary for success in powerful organizational positions; this incongruity leads to the perception that women are ill-equipped for these positions (Heilman & Okimoto, 2008). The concrete ceiling reflects greater negative stereotyping as a result of the combined effects of being female and from a negatively stereotyped ethnic or racial group. To the extent that both gender stereotypes and racial/ethnic stereotypes contradict "good leader" stereotypes, women from some groups may experience greater disadvantage (Rosette et al., 2016; Sanchez-Hucles & Davis, 2010).

Gender stereotypes are but one cause of the glass ceiling. A second explanation is that common organizational practices sometimes dictate the hiring and promotion of men rather than women into management positions. This is often a self-perpetuating artifact of the organization's history. In other words, if the organization has historically hired and promoted men rather than women into leadership positions, this becomes the standard operating procedure as managers follow organizational precedent (Eagly & Carli, 2007).

Another problem is that within the organization, that women may be structurally disadvantaged due to gender occupational segregation and other forms of institutionalized sexism (sexism embedded in organizational practices). For instance, until 2013, American military women were excluded from combat roles although these are typically a prerequisite for military career advancement. Generally speaking, women are more likely to be placed in jobs with less power and limited mobility, jobs that are less likely to lead to high-level positions in the organization (ILO, 2015b). In Japan, for instance, there is a two-track career system with a management track (with higher wages and opportunities for advancement) and a clerical track (with routine tasks and limited

> "In many cases, there is a "think leader, think male" stereotype that can disrupt our ability to build inclusive workplaces, and gender bias can become embedded in work processes and systems."
> *Dnika Travis and Julie Nugent, Catalyst*

advancement opportunities); women are more likely to be placed on the clerical track (Zacharias-Walsh, 2016).

Women are also more likely to be hired into "staff" positions rather than the "line" positions that provide the experience for top jobs (managers in *line jobs* direct and control essential organizational activities that directly advance key organizational goals, whereas managers in *staff jobs* provide support and expertise to line managers) (ILO, 2015b). Women are also less likely to be given the on-the-job experiences that prepare them for organizational leadership positions and allow them to demonstrate leadership capabilities (Catalyst, 2012; ILO, 2015b). To advance, women need to be in mission-critical roles and work on highly visible projects. One example of this is that women are over-represented as managers in support functions like human resources and administration, while men are over-represented in strategic management functions that are springboards to CEO and board positions (ILO, 2019c).The term **glass walls** refers to how gender segregation in management functions contributes to the leaky pipeline by reducing women's qualifications for top executive and CEO positions.

Yet another organizational barrier to women's progress is their relative lack of access to the political network. For instance, women managers in Hong Kong, Singapore, South Korea, Thailand, Japan, and India all report that the "old boys network" was a critical barrier to their career progress (Napasri & Yukongdi, 2015). A lack of mentoring is a related barrier. Mentoring occurs when a senior organizational member helps guide the career of a junior member by sharing knowledge about how to succeed in the organization. But because of their gender and concerns about intimacy and sexual attraction, women are often excluded from the informal social relationships shared by their male counterparts where power transactions and mentoring often occur (Napasri & Yukongdi, 2015). Also, both women and men may avoid a cross-gender mentoring relationship out of concerns it will be misconstrued as a sexual advance or sexual involvement and will affect their reputations or create problems with a spouse (Rockwell, Leck, & Elliott, 2013). Such concerns are an even greater issue in countries such as Afghanistan, Bangladesh, Cameroon, Pakistan, and Saudi Arabia, where it is considered inappropriate for women to interact closely with men who are not husbands or family members.

Finally, the third explanation for the glass ceiling is that women's responsibilities to home and family, real and perceived, may prevent upward mobility in the organization. Women often pay a **motherhood penalty** in both pay and promotion. **Family responsibility discrimination** occurs when an employer makes employment decisions about employees or prospective employees based on their assumed or real caregiving responsibilities (O'Connor, Kmec, & Harrris, 2015). When a woman is married and/or has children, employers often assume that her family responsibilities will interfere with her work productivity and commitment, and, consequently, they will not promote her into positions of responsibility (Abendroth, Huffman, & Treas, 2014). For example, in a U.S. study, mothers were expected to be less competent and were less likely to be kept in the

"To be selected for top management jobs, it is necessary to have diverse experience across different company areas. As long as women are boxed into certain roles, this will not happen—hence the need to break down glass walls before women can break through the glass ceiling to top management."
Sharon Bolton, Management Professor (Scotland)

running for advancement opportunities than were other female or male applicants who were applying for the same high-level managerial position (Heilman & Okimoto, 2008).

Women also remain disproportionately responsible for household labor and child and elder care, and these responsibilities are often incompatible with demands for the long hours, travel, and relocation required for advancement in the organization (Kark & Eagly, 2010). For example, in Japan, where women are almost entirely responsible for all outside-the-workplace labor, many women end up on the clerical track rather than the management track because they cannot devote themselves to the extremely long hours and travel required (Zacharias-Walsh, 2016). Because of the anticipated conflict between work and family, women in high-status careers (or pursuing them) frequently forgo or delay childbearing (Kincaid, 2015; Livingston, 2015). In a study of executives from North America, Latin America, and Asia, female executives were less likely than male executives to be married and more likely to delay or decide not to have children (Seager, 2009). Women's family obligations especially restrict their career advancement in well-paying jobs requiring long work hours and overtime (Cha, 2013).

As mentioned earlier in regard to the gender pay gap, childbearing and women's primary responsibility for child rearing also affect women's pay and promotion in the workplace because many women take leaves of absence from their jobs in the formal sector while their children are small. Employment interruptions reduce the seniority and accumulation of job experiences that lead to promotion and violate organizational norms regarding career advancement (Abendroth et al., 2014). For example, in Japan, advancement in the organization is highly dependent upon uninterrupted service to the organization and seniority. Japanese mothers generally do not participate in the paid sector because of difficulty reconciling the wife/mother role with the demands of paid employment (Zacharias-Walsh, 2016). As Tanaka (1995) points out, marriage is more costly to a woman's career because only women are called upon to reconcile the competing demands of work and family responsibilities. A 2015 ILO survey of 1,300 private sector companies in 39 developing countries found the number one barrier to women's leadership was the greater burden of family responsibilities borne by women in comparison to men (ILO, 2016a).

Because gender stereotyping appears to play a big role in the glass ceiling, it is important to reduce beliefs that women lack leadership skills and abilities. Progress is most evident in countries that have more gender-egalitarian beliefs. But changing gender-stereotyped leadership beliefs is not easy or swift—gender stereotypes often do not change until gender roles change, yet changing gender roles often requires changes in gender stereotypes. To jump-start this process, we need anti-discrimination legislation that bars discrimination in hiring and promotion and government policies and programs that reduce the structural disadvantages faced by women in organizations.

Organizations also need to do their part to increase the number of women in leadership. Leadership development theorists suggest that as much as

> "A robust "motherhood penalty" occurs toward working mothers who, compared to working fathers and (male or female) childless workers, experience discrimination in recommendations for hiring, salary, training, opportunities, and promotion."
> *Beatriz Aranda (Spain) and Peter Glick (United States), psychology researchers*

> "When a country does not enable women to combine work and family and has strong motherhood penalties, women are more likely to marry and have kids later in life."
> *Stephanie Coontz, US author, historian, professor*

70 percent of leadership development comes from on-the-job experiences—the "hot jobs" that provide challenging opportunities to develop and practice leadership skills (Catalyst, 2012). Organizations can employ measures to make sure that women receive the same on-the-job experiences that men do. They can implement targeted recruitment efforts and training and mentoring programs to increase the number of qualified women in the leadership pipeline, and they can consider gender as a "plus" factor in hiring or promotion. Over time, as the presence of women in leadership positions becomes more common, gendered stereotypes of leadership should ease and pave the way for more women in leadership, and such programs would become unnecessary. In Chapter 9, "Women and Politics," you'll learn that many of the countries with the highest numbers of women in politics used some of these methods. Changes in gendered divisions of household and care labor and family-supportive workplace and government policies would also clearly make a difference in eliminating the glass ceiling. In some countries, increasing educational parity between women and men is another key.

Sexual Harassment in the Workplace

"The señor wanted to take advantage of me, he followed me around . . . he grabbed my breasts twice from behind while I was washing clothes . . . I yelled, and the boy came out, and the señor left. I didn't tell the señora, because I was afraid. I just quit."
Maria Ajtún, domestic worker in Guatemala City

Women have long been exposed to workplace harassment of a sexual nature, but it wasn't until the 1970s that American women's activists gave it a name (**sexual harassment**) and demanded that it be recognized as sex discrimination under federal anti-discrimination legislation (Baker, 2005; McCann, 2005). Since that time, it is increasingly recognized as a global problem that reflects and reinforces women's inequality in the workplace.

Sexual harassment (SH) occurs when people are targets of unwanted sexual comments, sexual gestures, or sexual actions because of their actual or perceived gender, gender expression, or sexual orientation (Burn, 2019). Feminists consider it a form of sexual violence. Although workplace sexual harassment is the focus here, remember that sexual harassment also occurs on public transportation and in other public places, in educational and athletic settings, in homes, at social gatherings, and in online groups. Also keep in mind that sexual harassment may be conveyed in many ways including face-to-face interactions; via phone, text, social media, or email; through the display or "gifting" of materials or objects; or by tampering with personal territories and belongings. In the workplace, sexual harassers may be supervisors, peers, customers, or clients. For instance, restaurant workers experience high rates of sexual harassment from customers, hotel maids by hotel guests, and homecare and domestic workers by their employers (Nguyen, 2016). Unpaid workers such as volunteers, interns, job applicants, and job seekers also experience sexual harassment (Human Rights Watch, 2020).

The widely accepted **tripartite model of sexual harassment** (Fitzgerald, Swann, & Magley, 1997) identifies three behavioral dimensions of SH: gender harassment, unwanted sexual attention, and sexual coercion.

Gender harassment refers to crude sexual verbal and nonverbal behaviors conveying insulting, hostile, and degrading attitudes about one's gender, gender identity, or sexual orientation. Obscene sexual gestures, displaying sexual images or objects at work, and emailing or texting sexual images to a peer or coworker are all forms of gender harassment. Sexist or heterosexist language, jokes, or comments also fall under this heading. The ILO calls this form of sexual harassment "hostile work environment harassment."

Unwanted sexual attention includes making suggestive or positive and negative comments about a person's body, leering and catcalling, spreading sexual rumors about a person, and electronically sharing sexualized images of a person. Unwanted sexual touching, such as grabbing, pinching, groping, intentionally brushing up against another in a sexual way, is also considered unwanted sexual attention. This is also true of blocking another's path and following them in a sexual ("creepy") way; unsolicited, unwelcome, and unreciprocated sexual advances such as repeated requests for a kiss, a date, or sex; and attempted or completed rape.

Sexual coercion—also known as **quid pro quo sexual harassment**—refers to requiring sexual contact or sexual favors as a condition of receiving rewards or benefits such as employment, a promotion, favorable work conditions, assistance, or a good performance evaluation or grade. For example, an ILO study of women garment factory workers in Jordan, Indonesia, Haiti, Nicaragua, and Vietnam found that 23 percent of workers were offered work-related benefits in exchange for sexual favors or a sexual relationship (ILO/IFC, 2020). Although sexual coercion appears to be the most serious and least common form of SH, less intense but more frequent forms of SH may create ongoing stress and trauma detrimental to well-being (Sojo, Wood, & Genat, 2016; Thurston et al., 2017).

Sexual harassment is believed to be relatively common, though data are lacking because sexual harassment is underreported and understudied. Victims of sexual harassment are unlikely to report it due to its normalization, fear of reprisals, lack of effective reporting mechanisms, and victim-blaming (ILO, 2017). Estimates from anonymous or confidential surveys conducted away from the job site provide more accurate estimations. Rates differ depending on the sample, setting or industry sector, and how it is measured (Burn, 2019). One thing is clear: The majority of sexual harassment targets are women, and the majority of perpetrators are men. For example, a 2017 Pew Research Center study with a nationally representative American sample found that 22 percent of women and 7 percent of men reported personally experiencing workplace sexual harassment (Parker & Funk, 2017). In Australia, 39 percent of women and 26 percent of men said they experienced workplace sexual harassment in the last five years, and most (79%) said their harasser(s) were men (Australian Human Rights Commission, 2020). A study in the European Union found that 75 percent of women in managerial and professional jobs and 61 percent of women in service jobs said they experienced workplace sexual harassment (UN Women, 2016).

Sexual harassment is intersectional because it often has sexist, classist, heterosexist, transphobic, and racist elements. It reflects and contributes to gender and other social inequalities. For example, ethnic minority and migrant women are at increased risk for **racialized sexual harassment,** a combination of racial and sexual harassment infused by racial stereotypes (Clancy et al., 2017;

In 2015, hundreds of workers at Lexmark (a U.S.-based printer company) in Juarez, Mexico, participated in a series of protests against low wages, sexual harassment, and unsafe working conditions. Lexmark fired 120 workers for taking part in the protests.

"My executive manager came to the office and asked for my number and I gave it to him. I did not ask him why he wanted my number as he is a senior person. He then started touching my breast and private parts. I started feeling very uncomfortable and stopped him. I told him that I was going to report this to my supervisor. Even though I said I was going to report this, I felt I could not because I thought I could easily lose my job if I told."
Sisandra, a telecommunications worker in Durban, South Africa

ILO/IFC, 2020). Likewise, the sexual harassment experienced by LGBT+ people is frequently infused with heterosexism and transphobia (Grant, Mottet, & Tanis, 2011; Rabelo & Cortina, 2014). When sexual harassment reflects multiple oppressions and minority statuses or adds to them so that multiple forms of harassment are experienced, we call it **double jeopardy**. Double jeopardy increases the psychological distress of sexual harassment (Buchanan et al., 2018; Szymanski & Henrichs-Beck, 2014).

The ILO classifies sexual harassment as a version of sex discrimination and a violation of human rights because of its many negative effects on the equal opportunity, health, and well-being of workers. Victims (targets) perceive it as annoying, offensive, upsetting, humiliating, intimidating, embarrassing, stressful, and frightening (Fitzgerald et al., 1997). When sexual harassment diminishes, dehumanizes, and disempowers its targets, emotional and physical stress and stress-related mental and physical illnesses, including posttraumatic stress disorder, may result (Burn, 2019; Larsen & Fitzgerald, 2011). Sexual harassment can also reduce targets' sense of safety by conveying an implicit or explicit threat of further harassment or assault.

Sexual harassment can also deliberately or unintentionally interfere with performance and career aspirations by creating an intimidating, hostile, abusive, or offensive environment that erodes confidence and makes it harder to achieve (Jagsi et al., 2016). When people leave jobs due to sexual harassment, it may negatively affect their career progression and pay due to the loss of seniority and organization-specific work skills, difficult-to-explain gaps in employment, and trouble obtaining references from managers and coworkers (McLaughlin, Uggen, & Blackstone, 2017).

Feminists emphasize that sexual harassment is about power because it often arises from and reinforces the existing gender hierarchy where heterosexual men have more power and privilege. Consistent with this, women that threaten heterosexual male dominance and traditional hierarchies of power are common targets (Russell & Oswald, 2016). For example, women in authority positions, feminists (both female and male), sexual minorities, and women in traditionally masculinized spaces and industries are sometimes targets of sexual harassment by heterosexual male subordinates and peers (Holland & Cortina, 2016; Jagsi et al., 2016). Sexual harassment is frequently used to discourage women from running for office and reelection and to create obstacles to their effectiveness as legislators (Inter-Parliamentary Union, 2016).

Men's power and privilege also shields them from accountability, and targets are often members of groups that are not powerful or privileged (UN Women, 2019). Indeed, people low in sociocultural power and status (like women and racial and sexual minorities) and those with low organizational power (like migrant workers, those with temporary work visas or without legal immigration status, and those low in an organizational hierarchy) are more susceptible to sexual harassment by those with greater power. Occupational gender role segregation and the glass ceiling often give men greater organizational power. Traditional gender roles also give men greater sociocultural power relative to women such that men may harass women with equal or greater formal power than themselves (**contrapower**

Dolores Huerta (b. 1930) is the co-founder of the United Farm Workers Union in the United States. A mother of eleven, she has worked tirelessly for decades for the rights of farmworkers and against gender discrimination in the farmworkers' movement. She has focused attention on the rights of female farmworkers to work free of sexual harassment and assault and worked to get Latina women in leadership positions in unions and politics.

sexual harassment) (McLaughlin, Uggen, & Blackstone, 2012). From a sociocultural gender perspective, sexual harassment is also a consequence of gender-role socialization processes that promote male dominance, the sexual objectification of women (the reduction of women to heterosexualized bodies), and the cultural approval of violence against women (Burn, 2019).

The 2017 Harvey Weinstein case (United States) where dozens of aspiring actresses came forward to accuse the movie producer of decades of sexual harassment and assault, stimulated the explosion of the #MeToo movement started by Tarana Burke in 2006. Millions of women broke their silence by sharing on social media they had also been sexually harassed or assaulted. The MeToo movement and its global variations have pushed back on the cultural norms that minimize sexual harassment, blame victims, and allow men to sexually harass with impunity. By unmasking the frequency and harms of sexual harassment, lifting up victims, and demanding cultural and organizational change, the movements have changed attitudes and behaviors and increased accountability (though more cultural, organizational, and legislative change are obviously needed). In India, for example, registered cases of workplace sexual harassment increased by 80 percent since the advent of MeToo, and the number of countries that passed sexual harassment legislation increased (Arekapudi & Recavarren, 2020).

Changing the organizational climates and contexts that allow sexual harassment is one essential ingredient for reducing sexual harassment. In organizations that are tolerant of sexual harassment, complaints are not taken seriously, supervisors sexually harass, perpetrators are not meaningfully punished, and women who report sexual harassment face more harassment (Fitzgerald et al., 1997; Kakuyama et al., 2003). For example, 71 percent of people filing sexual harassment complaints with the Equal Opportunity Commission in the United States experienced retaliation for reporting (Frye, 2017).

Organizations that proactively develop, disseminate, and *enforce* sexual harassment policies and procedures have the lowest rates of workplace sexual harassment (Holland & Cortina, 2016). Clear anti-harassment policies and procedures can rein in sexual harassers and empower victims. Sexual harassment training can increase reporting and knowledge of organizational policies. Training can also increase sensitivity to sexual harassment, and reduce victim blaming and the minimizing of sexual harassment (Roehling & Huang, 2018). However, most workplaces globally do not have sexual harassment policies and trainings. In a study of 3,702 firms in 23 countries including the United States, Canada, Japan, France, Germany, Britain, and Australia, less than half of companies had sexual harassment policies (Elks, 2021). Furthermore, without strong support from leaders and managers, training and policies do little to reduce the problem (Cheung et al., 2017).

National and international prohibitions against sexual harassment are also important. Over the last twenty years, and especially following the MeToo and related movements against sexual violence, international and national efforts to reduce sexual harassment have increased. Global trade unions are increasing their

"Pervasive sexual harassment and other forms of violence in the workplace serve to reinforce and maintain existing hierarchies and gender power relations."
UN Women, 2015

"Sexual harassment at work is an issue which trade unions should actively deal with, as it is usually the result of power relations in the workplace, so the most vulnerable and least protected workers are most likely to be under threat."
ITUC

efforts to protect workers from sexual harassment (Human Rights Watch, 2020). The number of countries with laws prohibiting sexual harassment is also increasing. By 2020, 140 countries had laws prohibiting sexual harassment (World Bank, 2021b). Some countries have national laws specifically prohibiting sexual harassment and others recognize it as a form of sex discrimination prohibited under equality or anti-discrimination laws.

Of course, once again, laws are of limited impact when they are vague or unenforced, and this is definitely the case when it comes to sexual harassment law. In the countries that have laws, violations rarely make it to court. This is partly because sexual harassment laws are often more progressive than the societies in which they are enacted, meaning that they are not taken seriously. Sexual harassment law is also new and confusing, and legal systems are not yet prepared to handle sexual harassment complaints. This means that few attorneys are familiar with it, and that it is often unclear what legal evidence is necessary to prove harassment. Women often have difficulty finding legal counsel willing to take their cases. Some countries require that complaints first be registered through underfunded and backlogged government agencies. Women frequently see little point in pursuing legal avenues of redress given the high personal and financial costs. However, some courageous women pursue their cases despite this, and eventually their efforts may contribute to the reduction of organizational tolerance and the incidence of workplace sexual harassment.

In one of the largest sexual harassment settlements ever, news anchor Gretchen Carlson was paid $20 million. Carlson and other women at Fox News regularly experienced sexual harassment from Roger Ailes, the head of Fox News.

Sexual harassment is considered a form of sex discrimination and a type of violence against women by the Convention to Eliminate Discrimination Against Women (CEDAW), the UN Declaration of Violence Against Women, and by the ILO. The Beijing Platform for Action calls for its elimination. In 2019, the ILO adopted the first international standards aimed at ending workplace violence and harassment. This international treaty (the Violence and Harassment Convention No.190 and Recommendation No. 206) recognizes workplace harassment, including gender-based harassment and violence, as a human rights violation. The Violence and Harassment Convention also requires a commitment from ratifying countries to prohibit workplace harassment through law and policy and to adopt a comprehensive strategy to combat it (ILO, 2018a; ILO, 2019d). By 2021, five countries (Argentina, Fiji, Namibia, Somalia, and Uruguay) had ratified it.

"Workplace sexual harassment isn't inevitable. It flourishes when governments and employers fail to prevent it, protect survivors, and punish abusers."
Human Rights Watch

Women in the Informal Labor Sector and Women's Entrepreneurship

Women's earning often takes place in the **informal labor sector**. The Cuban woman who runs a beauty shop on the roof of her apartment building, the Peruvian woman who sells vegetables from her garden by the roadside, the South African woman who brews and sells her own beer, the Filipino woman who does others' laundry for pay, and the American woman who gets paid for watching her neighbor's children—are all women employed in the informal sector. In contrast to the **formal labor sector** where people get a salary or wages and pay taxes, this labor is "under the table" and "off the books" employment (ILO, 2017).

Globally, almost 60 percent of employed women are informally employed, but there are regional differences. For example, 95 percent of women's employment in sub-Saharan Africa (excluding the country of South Africa) is in the informal sector, and in Southern Asia, 91 percent of women are informally employed (Bonnet, Vanek, & Chen, 2019). Informal employment is considered **vulnerable employment** because it is economically precarious and usually lacks labor protections like maternity protections, social security, unemployment benefits, and unionization.

Women often choose this type of work because they can more easily balance it with their unpaid domestic and care labor responsibilities and/or because they lack opportunities in the formal sector. Informal sector work includes small enterprises, trading and selling at markets, domestic and care labor, and work done on a contract basis in the home. The ILO calls people that do this type of work **own-account workers**. Many women in the informal employment sector work in family-run enterprises; these workers are termed **contributing family workers** by the ILO. While men make up a greater percentage of own-account employment globally (36% to women's 26%), more women make up a greater percentage of contributing family workers (16.6%) compared to men (6.4%) (ILO, 2018c).

Women are also entrepreneurs, creating, organizing, and running their own income-generating enterprises. In the formal sector, about 34 percent of small, medium, and large businesses are owned by women; though of course, there are regional variations. In Latin America and the Caribbean 50 percent of business are women-owned, 47 percent in East Asia and the Pacific, 33 percent in Europe and Central Asia, 23 percent in the Middle East and North Africa, 29 percent in sub-Saharan Africa, and 18 percent in South Asia (Halim, 2020). But many women entrepreneurs operate what are known as **micro-and-small-scale enterprises (WMSEs)** in the informal labor sector. They return their profits to the family in the form of better food and living conditions.

Many women's businesses remain in the informal economy due to barriers preventing their formalization. Women entrepreneurs frequently have difficulty getting credit (loans) from banks, governments, and development agencies. One problem is lack of collateral. Women often do not have clear title to land or property due to the widespread practice of registering property in the man's name and inheritance systems that favor men. Bank practices, such as those that require a male cosigner, also discourage women. In addition, many poor women lack the literacy to complete the complicated loan application forms.

Legal barriers also inhibit women-owned businesses. A World Bank study (2021b) of 190 countries found that 108 (57%) have at least one legal barrier to women's businesses. These barriers include laws preventing women from traveling, signing a contract, owning property, opening a bank account, and registering a business. In 1974, the United States became the first country to

"I eat and drink from my business. I built a house so that I no longer rent. I bought my plot from my earnings. I have been able to educate my children. That is very important—an even better achievement than building a house." *Betty Nakiganda, 48, Ugandan widow with eight children who sells mangos*

Madam C. J. Walker (1867–1919), the first self-made woman millionaire in the United States, demonstrates the entrepreneurial spirit of African American women. She helped other women gain economic independence by hiring them to work at excellent wages for her hair-care products business.

BOX 5.7 *Activist Profile: Ela Bhatt of the Self-Employed Women's Association (India)*

Ela Bhatt, born in 1933 in India, is known as the founder of the Self-Employed Women's Association (SEWA). Bhatt's work as a lawyer for the textile industry brought her into contact with thousands of self-employed women workers such as street vendors and home-based piece rate workers. She realized that because the women were not organized, they were easily exploited, and because they worked in the informal labor sector, they could not appeal to the government for economic protections, and there were no unions to represent them. As Bhatt once said, "Personally, I don't think there can be any greater injustice to anybody in the world than to have one's work contribution negated. . . . Who is the backbone of any economy in the country? It's the poor! Yet they are not recorded as workers in the national census. They are described as non-workers!" Bhatt recognized that through organizing, these women could demand better pay and work conditions, and that by pooling their resources, they could provide loans to women microentrepreneurs without access to traditional business funding. With these goals, she founded SEWA in 1972. SEWA empowers women to have greater control of their economic lives and is the model for thousands of women's cooperatives worldwide.

"We may be poor, but we are so many. Why don't we start a bank of our own? Our own women's bank, where we are treated with the respect and service that we deserve." ("We may be poor, but we are so many" is now SEWA's slogan)
Chandaben, old clothes seller, Founder member, SEWA Bank

pass legislation barring gender discrimination in access to credit, but this would not have happened without House Representative Lindy Boggs (D-La.). She inserted language into the Equal Credit Opportunity Act to prohibit discrimination based on gender and marital status (originally it included only veteran status and age). She matter-of-factly told her male colleagues on the committee that she assumed they mistakenly left it out (Martin, 2013). Today, eighty-one countries have no legal restrictions on women's employment or entrepreneurship (World Bank, 2021b).

Self-employed women are resourceful and resilient, and some have organized to address their needs. For example, there are a number of self-employed women's unions such as the South African Domestic Workers' Union (SADWU) and the Union of Domestic Workers of Brazil. Perhaps the best-known self-employed women's union is SEWA (Self-Employed Women's Association) of India, begun in 1972. One of SEWA's principal activities is the organization of cooperatives through which labor problems are addressed and loans are made. For example, SEWA helped the "pushcart vegetables cooperative" to fight for women's right to receive vending licenses (Bhatt, 1995). As of 2018, SEWA had 1.5 million members, 160 different cooperatives, fifteen economic federations, three producer companies, and many self-help groups. The SEWA Cooperative Bank provides capital and banking services to self-employed women (and has a loan repayment rate of 96%). The SEWA Academy provides education and training, and SEWA's social security organizations provide health care, child care, and insurance to SEWA members. A brief biography of Ela Bhatt, founder of SEWA, appears in Box 5.7.

Conclusion

Human-made barriers stand in the way of gender equality in economic opportunity. Gender stereotypes, norms, and roles affect domestic and care labor responsibilities, workforce participation rates, the gender pay gap, sexual harassment, and the glass ceiling. Gender inequality in labor is also embedded in laws and cultural and organizational practices that allow, condone, and perpetuate gender discrimination in the world of work.

There are cross-cultural and intra-cultural differences in women's work and in the gender-based labor issues they face. For example, women everywhere are tasked with responsibility for domestic and care labor, but this labor is much greater where there are few laborsaving technologies, when it includes gathering fuel and water, and when it is strongly gender-stereotyped as women's work. Some groups of women are more disadvantaged relative to other groups of women, or have gender-based concerns common to a particular economic sector or job category. Intersectional variables such as race and class impact the experience of the gender pay gap, the glass ceiling, and sexual harassment. Effective policy and action for women's economic empowerment require consideration of intersectionality and context.

Women's rights are human rights, and international law acknowledges women's right to equality in work. For example, according to Article 23 of the Universal Declaration of Human Rights (UDHR, 1948), everyone has the right to work, the right to equal pay for equal work, and the right to payment that ensures an existence "worthy of human dignity." The 1979 Convention on the Elimination of Discrimination Against Women (CEDAW, 1979) not only commits member states to eliminate gender discrimination in employment, it says that men and women are equally entitled to work, employment opportunities, choice of profession, equal salary and wages, social security and paid leave, job security, promotions, and benefits. These agreements and others (such as four ILO conventions) have encouraged many nations to take steps towards gender equality in the world of work. Women's activism has been critical to many international agreements pertinent to gender equality in work and to getting governments to follow through on their commitments.

Women are disempowered by gender inequalities in both unpaid domestic and care labor and paid work, and there are campaigns all over the world to promote women's economic empowerment. When mainstream unions and governments are not responsive to their needs, women often empower themselves by forming self-employed women's unions, cooperatives, and other organizations to help one another (Cobble, 2009; Hernandez, 2014; Nadasen, 2016). To promote gender equality in the world of work, women also organize and go on strike, march and protest, file lawsuits, and lobby for legislation. Women's activism usually plays a key role in the passage of national legislation promoting gender equality in labor. For example, after a decade of women's activism, Japan passed equal employment legislation (Zharias-Walsh, 2016). Women also have a history of organizing and participating in labor strikes going back to the 1800s. Chapters 9 and 10 focus more on politics and activism. The next two chapters go into further depth on women in developing economies (Chapter 6) and how women are affected by globalization (Chapter 7).

Glossary Terms and Concepts

Comparable worth
Concrete ceiling
Contrapower sexual
  harassment
Contributing family
workers
Double jeopardy
Equal Remuneration
  Convention
Family responsibility
  discrimination
Feminist economics
Formal labor sector
Gender harassment
Gender job segregation
  (gender occupational
  segregation)
Gender perspective on
  unpaid care work
Gender-responsive
  budget analysis
Gender wage
  discrimination
Gender wage gap

Glass ceiling
Glass walls
Horizontal occupational
  segregation
Human capital approach
Informal labor sector
International Labour
  Organization (ILO)
Lack of fit model
Leaky pipeline
Maternity leave policies
Maternity Protection
  Convention
Maternity protections
Motherhood penalty
Motherhood wage gap
Own-account workers
Quid pro quo sexual
  harassment
Racialized sexual
  harassment
Relative resources
  perspective on unpaid
  care work

Role congruity theory
Second shift
Sexual coercion
Sexual harassment
Sexualized racism
Time availability
  perspective on unpaid
  care work
Time-use surveys
Tripartite model of
  sexual harassment
Unpaid domestic and
  care labor
Unwanted sexual
  attention
Vulnerable employment
Vertical occupational
  segregation
Women's micro- and
  small-scale enterprises
  (WMSEs)

Study Questions

1. Why is women's work important?

2. What is unpaid domestic and care labor? Why do women in low-income countries spend more time on unpaid domestic and care labor than other women? What is the gender divide of unpaid domestic and care labor? What three explanations were given for gender inequalities in unpaid domestic and care labor? Why does women's disproportionate responsibility for unpaid domestic and care labor? What can be done about it?

3. How common is women's participation in the paid labor force?

4. What does it mean to say that the effects of paid work on women are somewhat paradoxical? In what ways does working for pay benefit women?

5. What are maternity protections? Why are maternity leave and child care so important for gender equality in employment? What is the ILO's Maternity Protection Convention, and what does it recommend? How common are government maternity leave polices, and how are they paid for? How are we doing globally as far as meeting ILO minimum standards for maternity leave? Which countries have

the best policies, and which have the worst? How can maternity leave be a "two-edged sword" in regard to gender equality, and what can be done about this?

6. What is the gender pay (wage) gap? How large is it? What explanations for it were given in the chapter? Why is eliminating the gap important and how can this be done?

7. What is the glass ceiling? Worldwide, what is the percentage of women who hold senior management positions? What is the concrete ceiling?

8. How is the glass ceiling a function of gender stereotypes (role congruity theory and lack of fit theory)? What organizational practices contribute to it? What role do women's responsibilities to home and family play?

9. What is sexual harassment? What are the three main types according to the tripartite model? How common is it? How do power perspectives explain sexual harassment? How is it explained by the sociocultural perspective? What is being done to reduce sexual harassment?

10. What are WMSEs and "own account" workers? How common are these types of workers? What are some common difficulties facing self-employed women, and what have they done about them?

11. How do the global women's studies themes described in the first chapter apply to women and work?

Discussion Questions and Activities

1. The chapter suggested that government policies on child care and maternity leave may reflect a society's views about the "proper" role of women in society and whether women's participation in the labor force is desired. What do you think about this in regards to your country's maternity leave and child-care policies?

2. On International Women's Day (March 8) 2000, women in 60 countries took part in the first ever Global Women's Strike, demanding pay equity and wages for all "caring work." What would happen in your culture if women in hetero-sexual cohabiting or married relationships went on strike and refused to do any unpaid domestic and care labor for a day? Would women in your culture participate in such a strike? Why or why not?

3. How does your country (or state) fare in regards to the gender pay gap, glass ceiling, maternity leave policies, gendered divisions of domestic and care labor, and affordable child care? Does your country or state provide adequate policies and supports for women's equal participation in the paid labor force?

4. Describe what sexual harassment is using the chapter description and ask others whether they have experienced it. Ask them to describe the type of harassment, how it affected their productivity, and its emotional and physical effects. How did they handle it and why? How did the answers of females and males differ? Summarize your findings.

5. Interview a woman in high-level management using questions formulated from the chapter discussion on the glass ceiling.

6. If you grew up in a two-heterosexual-parent home, who did the majority of the household labor—your mother or your father? Which of the three explanations for gender-based divisions of household labor seem to best explain this? If your mother worked for pay, did she have a second shift? The gender perspective on domestic and care labor suggests that we unconsciously enact gender scripts for domestic and care labor. Do the unmarried heterosexual women and men you know seem to be doing this? What problems might this create as they become part of a dual-earner couple?

Action Opportunities

1. Hold a bake sale to draw attention to the gender pay gap. List your prices by gender (for example, in the United States, charge men $1.00 for each item and women $.82). Explain to puzzled customers that your pricing scheme reflects the fact that women make that percent of what men make. When they argue that your pricing is not fair, remind them that the gender pay gap is not fair either. Donate your proceeds to a worthy women's cause.

2. One reason women are paid less is gender occupational segregation where "men's jobs" pay less than "women's jobs." Put on a girls' career event that provides information and role models of high-status, well-paying careers. Alternatively, organize an event on pay negotiation for women (some research suggests that women college graduates sometimes lack salary negotiation skills compared to college men) or a "breaking the glass ceiling event" with local high-level professional women.

3. What is your university's policy on sexual harassment? What do students do to report sexual harassment? Educate your campus about what sexual harassment is and what to do about it. Write an article for your school newspaper, pass out information, design a social media campaign, or post your information on bulletin boards on campus.

4. Participate in a campaign to pass legislation intended to reduce the gender pay gap. For example, in the United States you can participate in the National Women's Law Center campaign (https://nwlc.org/issue/equal-pay-and-the-wage-gap/) or the Wage Project (http://www.wageproject.org).

5. Use your labor and ingenuity to create your own short-term microenterprise and donate all or part of your profits to The Global Fund for Women, an organization that uses monetary donations to fund women's microenterprises and empowerment all over the world. Learn more about the Global Fund for Women at http://www.globalfundforwomen.org. Explain what the project taught you about self-employed women.

6. Go to https://now.org/issues/economic-justice/ and take action on an economic justice issue that affects women.

Activist Websites

Canadian Women's Foundation https://canadianwomen.org/out-of-poverty/

Empower Women https://www.empowerwomen.org/en

Global Fund for Women http://www.globalfundforwomen.org

Global Women's Strike https://globalwomenstrike.net

MANA http://www.hermana.org/about (empowering Mexican American women)

MenCare: A Global Fatherhood Campaign http://men-care.org/about-mencare/guiding-principles/

metoo https://metoomvmt.org

National Association of Working Women (United States) http://www.9to5.org/

National Domestic Workers Alliance (United States) https://www.domesticworkers.org

SEWA (Self-Employed Women's Association) (India) http://www.sewa.org/

The Wage Project (United States) http://www.wageproject.org/

Informational Websites

AWP Network (African women entrepreneurs) https://awpnetwork.com/

Catalyst http://www.catalyst.org/

Counting Women's Work https://countingwomenswork.org

Directory of UN Resources on Gender and Women's Issues: Women and the Economy http://www.un.org/womenwatch/directory/women_and_the_economy_3006.htm

Equileap http://equileap.com

Feminist Majority Foundation https://feminist.org/news/category/money/the-economy/

International Federation of Business and Professional Women https://www.bpw-international.org/index.php

International Labour Organization http://www.ilo.org/global/topics/equality-and-discrimination/gender-equality/lang--en/index.htm

UN Women Economic Empowerment http://www.unwomen.org/en/what-we-do/economic-empowerment

U.S. Equal Employment Opportunity Commission https://www.eeoc.gov

Corporate Women Boards International (Globewomen) http://www.globewomen.org/

References

Aassve, A., Fuochi, G., and Mencarini, L. 2014. Desperate housework: Relative resources, time availability, economic dependency, and gender ideology across Europe. *Journal of Family Issues, 35,* 1000–1022.

Abendroth, A. K., Huffman, M. L., and Treas, J. 2014. The parity penalty in life course perspective motherhood and occupational status in 13 European countries. *American Sociological Review, 79,* 993–1014.

Agenjo, C. A., and Gálvez, M. L. 2019. Feminist economics: Theoretical and political dimensions. *American Journal of Economics & Sociology, 78,* 137–166.

Alawa, L., Lee, Y., Zhao, B., and Kim, E. 2016. Stereotypes about gender and science: Women ≠ scientists. *Psychology of Women Quarterly, 40,* 244–260.

Alonso-Villar, O., and del Río, C. 2017. The occupational segregation of African American women: Its evolution from 1940 to 2010. *Feminist Economics, 23,* 108–134.

Arekapudi, N., and Recavarren, I. S. 2020. Sexual harassment is serious business. *World Bank Blogs.* https://blogs.worldbank.org/developmenttalk/sexual-harassment-serious-business. Retrieved on April 16, 2021.

Australian Human Rights Commission. 2020. *Respect @ work: National Inquiry into sexual harassment in Australian workplaces.* https://humanrights.gov.au/our-work/sex-discrimination/publications/respectwork-sexual-harassment-national-inquiry-report-2020#P7FfE. Retrieved on April 15, 2021.

Baker, C. N. 2005. *The women's movement against sexual harassment.* Cambridge, UK: Cambridge University Press.

Baxter, J., and Tai, T. 2016. Inequalities in unpaid work: A cross-national comparison. In *Handbook on well-being of working women,* edited by M. L. Connerly and J. Wu. Netherlands: Springer.

Beneria, L. 1998. On paid and unpaid work. *Radcliffe Quarterly,* Fall.

Benería, L., Berik, G., and Floro, M. 2015. *Gender, development and globalization: Economics as if all people mattered.* United Kingdom: Routledge.

Bhatt, E. 1995. Women and development alternatives: Micro-and-small-scale enterprises in India. In *Women in micro-and-small-scale enterprise development,* edited by L. Divard and J. Havet. Boulder, CO: Westview Press.

Bianchi, S., Milkie, M. A., Sayer, L. C., and Robinson, J. P. 2000. Is anyone doing the housework? Trends in the gender division of household labor. *Social Forces, 79,* 191–229.

Blau, F. D., and Ferber, M. A. 1987. Occupations and earnings of women work. In *Working women: Past, present, future,* edited by K. S. Koziara, M. H. Moskow, and L. D. Tanner. Washington, DC: BNA Books.

Blau, F. D., and Kahn, L. M. 2016. *The gender wage gap: Extent, trends, and explanations.* Institute for the Study of Labor (IZA).

Blumberg, R. L. 1991. Income under female versus male control: Hypotheses from a theory of gender stratification and data from the Third World. In *Gender, family, and economy: The triple overlap*, edited by R. L. Blumberg. Newbury Park, CA: Sage.

Blumberg, R. L. 1995. Gender, microenterprise, performance, and power: Case studies from the Dominican Republic, Ecuador, Guatemala, and Swaziland. In *Women in the Latin American development process*, edited by C. E. Bose and E. Acosta-Belen. Philadelphia, PA: Temple University Press.

Bonnet, F., Vanek, J., and Chen, M. 2019. *Women and men in the informal economy: A statistical brief.* Women in Informal Employment: Globalizing and organizing (WIEGO)/ILO. https://www.wiego.org/publications/women-and -men-informal-economy-statistical-brief. Retrieved on April 18, 2021.

Buchanan, N. T., Settles, I. H., Wu, H. C., and Hayashino, D. S. 2018. Sexual harassment, racial harassment, and well-being among Asian American Women: An intersectional approach. *Women & Therapy,* 1–20.

Buddig, M. J., and Misra, J. 2010. How care-work employment shapes earnings in cross-national perspective. *International Labour Review, 149,* 441–460.

Burn, S. M. (2019). The psychology of sexual harassment. *Teaching of Psychology, 46,* 96–103.

Catalyst. 2012. Good intentions, imperfect execution? Women get fewer of the hot jobs needed to advance. http://www.catalyst.org/system/files/Good _Intentions_Imperfect_Execution_Women_Get_Fewer_of_the_Hot_Jobs _Needed_to_Advance.pdf. Retrieved on January 6, 2017.

Cha, Y. 2013. Overwork and the persistence of gender segregation in occupations. *Gender and Society, 27,* 158–184.

Chafetz, J. S. 1991. The gender division of labor and the reproduction of female disadvantage: Toward an integrated theory. In *Gender, family, and economy: The triple overlap,* edited by R. L. Blumberg. Newbury Park, CA: Sage.

Charles, M., and Grusky. D. B. 2004. *Occupational ghettos: The worldwide segregation of women and men.* Stanford, CA: Stanford University Press.

Charlesworth, H., and Macdonald, F. 2015. Australia's gender pay equity legislation: how new, how different, what prospects?. *Cambridge Journal of Economics, 39,* 421–440.

Cheryan, S., Play, V. C., Handron, C., and Hudson, L. 2013. The stereotypical computer scientist: Gendered media representations as a barrier to inclusion for women. *Sex Roles, 69,* 58–71.

Chesters, J. 2011. Gender convergence in core housework hours. *Journal of Sociology, 49,* 78–96.

Cheung, H. K., Goldberg, C. B., King, E. B., and Magley, V. J. 2017. Are they true to the cause? Beliefs about organizational and unit commitment to sexual harassment awareness training. *Group and Organization Management, 22,* 1–30.

Clancy, K. B., Lee, K., Rodgers, E. M., and Richey, C. 2017. Double jeopardy in astronomy and planetary science: Women of color face greater risks of gendered and racial harassment. *Journal of Geophysical Research: Planets, 122,* 1610–1623.

Cleveland, J. N., and McNamara, K. 1996. Understanding sexual harassment: Contributions from research on domestic violence and organizational change. In *Sexual harassment in the workplace: Perspectives, frontiers, and response strategies,* edited by M. S. Stockdale. Thousand Oaks, CA: Sage.

Cobble, D. S. 2009. *The other women's movement: Workplace justice and social rights in modern America.* New Jersey, NJ: Princeton University Press.

Cuadrado, I., García-Ael, C., and Molero, F. 2015. Gender typing of leadership: Evaluations of real and ideal managers. *Scandinavian Journal of Psychology, 56,* 236–244.

Eagly, A. H., and Carli, L. L. 2007. *Through the labyrinth.* Boston, MA: Harvard Business School Press.

Eagly, A. H., and Karau, S. J. 2002. Role congruity theory of prejudice toward female leaders. *Psychological Review, 109,* 573–598.

Elks, S. 2021. #MeWho? Global firms lag on sex harassment, women-friendly policy. *Reuters.* https://www.reuters.com/article/us-global-women-work-trfn/mewho-global-firms-lag-on-sex-harassment-women-friendly-policy-idUSKBN2AW1AD. Retrieved on April 19, 2021.

Eurofound and International Labour Organization. 2019. *Working conditions in a global perspective.* Office of the European Union, Luxembourg and International Labour Organization, Geneva.

Fitzgerald, L. F., Swann, S., and Magley, V. J. 1997. But was it really sexual harassment?: Legal, behavioral, and psychological definitions of the workplace victimization of women. In *Sexual harassment: Theory, research, and treatment,* edited by W. O'Donohue. Boston, MA: Allyn and Bacon.

Frye, J. 2017. Not just the rich and famous: The pervasiveness of sexual harassment across industries affects all workers. *Center for American Progress.* https://www.americanprogress.org/issues/women/news/2017/11/20/443139/not-just-rich-famous/. Retrieved on April 17, 2021.

Fuwa, M. 2004. Macro-level gender inequality and the division of household labor in 22 countries. *American Sociological Review, 69,* 69–92.

Fuwa, M., and Cohen, P. N. 2007. Housework and social policy. *Social Science Research, 36,* 512–530.

Garcia-Retamero, R., and López-Zafra, E. 2009. Causal attributions about feminine and leadership roles: A cross-cultural comparison. *Journal of Cross-Cultural Psychology, 40,* 492–509.

Grant, J. M., Mottet, L. A., and Tanis, J. 2011. *Injustice at every turn: A report of the National Transgender Discrimination Survey.* Washington, DC: National Center for Transgender Equality and National Gay and Lesbian Task Force.

Grimshaw, D., and Rubery, J. 2015. *The motherhood pay gap: A review of the issues, theory, and international evidence.* ILO.

Halim, D. 2020. Women entrepreneurs needed—stat! *World Bank Blogs.* https://blogs.worldbank.org/opendata/women-entrepreneurs-needed-stat. Retrieved on April 18, 2021.

Heilman, M. E., and Okimoto, T. 2008. Motherhood: A potential source of bias in employment decisions. *Journal of Applied Psychology, 93,* 189–198.

Heilman, M. E., Manzi, F., and Braun, S., 2015. Presumed incompetent: Perceived lack of fit and gender bias in recruitment and selection. In *Handbook of gendered careers in management: Getting in, getting on, getting out,* edited by A. M. Broadbridge. Cheltenham, UK: Edward Elgar Publishing.

Hernandez, S. 2014. *Working women in the borderlands.* Texas, TX: Texas A and M University Press.

Hinchliffe, E. 2020. The number of female CEOs in the Fortune 500 hits an all-time record. *Fortune.* https://fortune.com/2020/05/18/women-ceos -fortune-500-2020/. Retrieved on April 13, 2021.

Hochschild, A. 2003. *The second shift.* New York, NY: Penguin Books.

Holland, K. J., and Cortina, L. M. 2016. Sexual harassment: Undermining the wellbeing of working women. In *Handbook on well-being of working women,* edited by M. L. Connerly and J. Wu. Netherlands: Springer.

Hook, J. L., and Chalasami, S. 2008. Gender expectations? Reconsidering single fathers' childcare time. *Journal of Marriage and Family, 70,* 978–990.

Horne, R. M., Johnson, M. D., Galambos, N. L., and Krahn, H. J. 2017. Time, money, or gender? Predictors of the division of household labour across life stages. *Sex Roles, 78,* 731–743.

Human Rights Watch. 2020. *Two years after #MeToo erupts, a new treaty anchors workplace shifts.* https://www.hrw.org/world-report/2020/country-chapters /global-1#. Retrieved on April 19, 2021.

Institute of Development Studies. 2016. Unpaid care work and the new global goals. *Interactions.* http://interactions.eldis.org/unpaid-care-work/issues/global -goals. Retrieved on December 26, 2016.

ILO (International Labour Organization). 2000. *C183-Maternity Protection Convention, 2000 (No. 183).* http://www.ilo.org/dyn/normlex/en/f?p=NORMLE XPUB:12100:::NO:12100:P12100_ILO_CODE:C183:NO. Retrieved on April 9, 2021.

ILO (International Labour Organization). 2003. *Time for equality at work. Global report under the follow-up to the ILO Declaration on Fundamental Principles and Rights at Work. Report of the Director-General, 2003.* http://www.ilo.org/wcmsp5 /groups/public/--- dgreports/---dcomm/---publ/documents/ publication/wcms _publ_9221128717_en.pdf. Retrieved on July 27, 2009.

ILO (International Labour Organization). 2004. *Informational fact sheet: WF-1 Work and family responsibilities.* http://www.ilo.org/public/english/protection /condtrav/pdf/infosheets/wf-1.pdf. Retrieved on July 15, 2009.

ILO (International Labour Organization). 2007. *Equality at work: Tackling the challenges. Global report under the follow-up to the ILO Declaration on fundamental principles and rights at work. Report of the Director-General, 2007.* http://www .ilo.org/global/What_we_do/Publications/ILOBookstore/ Orderonline/Books /lang--en/docName--WCMS_ 082607/index.htm. Retrieved on July 14, 2009.

ILO (International Labour Organization). 2013. *Childcare: An essential support for better incomes.* http://www.ilo.org/wcmsp5/groups/public/-ed_emp/-emp_policy /documents/publication/wcms_210469.pdf. Retrieved on December 29, 2016.

ILO (International Labour Organization). 2014. *Maternity and paternity at work: Law and practice across the world.* http://www.ilo.org/wcmsp5/groups/public /-dgreports/-dcomm/-publ/documents/publication/wcms_242615.pdf. Retrieved on December 28, 2016.

ILO (International Labour Organization). 2015a. *Global wage report 2014/2015: Wages and income inequality.* http://www.ilo.org/wcmsp5/groups/public /-dgreports/-dcomm/-publ/documents/publication/wcms_324678.pdf. Retrieved on December 31, 2016.

ILO (International Labour Organization). 2015b. *Women in business and management: Gaining momentum.* http://www.ilo.org/wcmsp5/groups/public/-dgreports/-dcomm /-publ/documents/publication/wcms_334882.pdf. Retrieved on January 4, 2017.

ILO (International Labour Organization). 2016a. *Women at work: Trends 2016.* Geneva: ILO, 2016.

International Labour Organization (ILO). 2016b. *Maternity protection.* https://www .social-protection.org/gimi/ShowTheme.action?id=4425. Retrieved on April 5, 2021.

ILO (International Labour Organization). 2017. *World employment and social outlook 2017.* http://www.ilo.org/wcmsp5/groups/public/-dgreports/-dcomm /-publ/documents/publication/wcms_541211.pdf. Retrieved on January 13, 2017.

International Labour Organization (ILO). 2018a. *Ending violence and harassment against women and men in the world of work.* https://www.ilo.org/ilc/ILCSessions /previous-sessions/107/reports/reports-to-the-conference/WCMS_553577 /lang-en/index.htm. Retrieved on April 17, 2021.

International Labour Organization (ILO). 2018b. *Global wage report 2018–2019.* https://www.ilo.org/wcmsp5/groups/public/-dgreports/-dcomm/-publ /documents/publication/wcms_650553.pdf. Retrieved on June 1, 2021.

International Labour Organization (ILO). 2018c. *World employment social outlook: Trends for women 2018.* https://www.ilo.org/wcmsp5/groups/public /-dgreports/-dcomm/-publ/documents/publication/wcms_615594.pdf. Retrieved on April 18, 2021.

International Labour Organization (ILO). 2019a. *A quantum leap for gender equality: For a better future of work for all.* https://www.ilo.org/wcmsp5/groups /public/-dgreports/-dcomm/-publ/documents/publication/wcms_674831.pdf. Retrieved on June 1, 2021.

International Labour Organization (ILO). 2019b. *Ratifications of C183-Maternity Protection Convention 2000 (No.183).* https://www.ilo.org/dyn/normlex/en /f?p=NORMLEXPUB:11300:0::NO::P11300_INSTRUMENT_ID:312328. Retrieved on April 5, 2021.

International Labour Organization (ILO). 2019c. *Women in business and management: The business case for change.* https://www.ilo.org/wcmsp5/groups/public /-dgreports/-dcomm/-publ/documents/publication/wcms_700953.pdf. Retrieved on April 13, 2021.

International Labour Organization (ILO). 2019d. *Eliminating violence and harassment in the world of work: ILO Convention No. 190, Recommendation No. 206, and the accompanying resolution.* https://www.ilo.org/global/publications/meeting-reports/WCMS_721160/lang–en/index.htm. Retrieved on April 17, 2021.

International Labour Organization (ILO). 2020. *Global wage report: Wages and minimum wages in the time of COVID-19.* https://www.ilo.org/wcmsp5/groups/public/–dgreports/–dcomm/–publ/documents/publication/wcms_762534.pdf. Retrieved on April 13, 2021.

International Labour Organization/International Finance Corporation. 2020. *Sexual harassment at work: Insights from the global garment industry.* https://www.ilo.org/wcmsp5/groups/public/–ed_dialogue/–sector/documents/publication/wcms_732095.pdf. Retrieved on April 15, 2021.

Inter-Parliamentary Union. 2016. *Sexism, harassment, and violence against women parliamentarians.* https://www.ipu.org/resources/publications/reports/2016-10/sexism-harassment-and-violence-against-women-parliamentarians. Retrieved on April 17, 2021.

Iregui-Bohórquez, A. M., Ramírez-Giraldo, M. T., and Tribín-Uribe, A. M. 2019. Domestic violence against rural women in Colombia: The role of labor income." *Feminist Economics, 25,* 146–72.

IWPR (Institute for Women's Policy Research). 2020. *The gender wage gap by occupation 2019 and by race and ethnicity.* https://iwpr.org/iwpr-issues/employment-and-earnings/the-gender-wage-gap-by-occupation-2019/. Retrieved on April 12, 2021.

Jacobsen, J. P. 2003. The human capital explanation for the gender gap in earnings. In *Women, family, and work,* edited by K. S. Moe. Oxford, UK: Blackwell.

Jagsi, R., Griffith, K. A., Jones, R., Perumalswami, C. R., Ubel, P., and Stewart, A. 2016. Sexual harassment and discrimination experiences of academic medical faculty. *Journal of the American Medical Association, 315,* 2120–2121. DOI:10.1001/jama.2016.2188

Kakuyama, T., Tsuzuki, Y., Onglatco, M. L., and Matsui, T. 2003. Organizational tolerance as a correlate of sexual harassment of Japanese working women. *Psychological Reports, 92,* 1268–1270.

Kark, R., and Eagly, A. H. 2010. Gender and leadership: Negotiating the labyrinth. In *Handbook of gender research in psychology,* edited by J. C. Chrisler and D. R. McCreary. New York: Springer.

Kincaid, E. 2015, June 30. Why having kids later is really a big deal. *Business Insider.* http://www.businessinsider.com/why-delaying-parenthood-and-having-kids-later-is-a-big-deal-2015-6. Retrieved on January 16, 2017.

Klugman, J., and Melnikova, T. 2016. *Unpaid work and care: A policy brief.* https://www.empowerwomen.org/~/media/uploads/unwomen/empowerwomen/resourceimages/unpaid%20work%20%20carepolicy%20brief-20161130175412.pdf. Retrieved on December 12, 2016.

Koenig, A. M., Eagly, A. H., Mitchell, A. A., and Ristikari, T. 2011. Are leader stereotypes masculine? A meta-analysis of three research paradigms. *Psychological Bulletin, 137,* 616–642.

Larsen, S. E., and Fitzgerald, L. F. 2011. PTSD symptoms and sexual harassment: The role of attributions and perceived control. *Journal of Interpersonal Violence, 26*, 2255–2567.

Levtov, R. 2016. *Men, gender, and unpaid care: A background paper for the UN Secretary-Generaal's high-level panel on women's economic empowerment.* https://www.empowerwomen.org/en/resources/documents/2016/11/men-gender-and-inequality-in-unpaid-care?lang=en. Retrieved on December 24, 2016.

Livingston, G. 2015. For most highly educated women motherhood doesn't start until the 30s. *Pew Research Center.* http://www.pewresearch.org/fact-tank/2015/01/15/for-most-highly-educated-women-motherhood-doesnt-start-until-the-30s/. Retrieved on January 16, 2017.

López-Sáez, M., Puertas, S., and Sáinz, M. 2011. Why don't girls choose technological studies? Adolescents' stereotypes and attitudes towards studies related to medicine or engineering. *Spanish Journal of Psychology, 14*, 71–84.

Martin, D. 2013, July 27. Lindy Boggs, longtime representative and champion of women, is dead at 97. *New York Times.* http://www.nytimes.com/2013/07/28/us/politics/lindy-boggs-longtime-representative-from-louisiana-dies-at-97.html. Retrieved on January 15, 2017.

Matteazzi, E., and Scherer, S. 2020. Gender wage gap and the involvement of partners in household work. *Work, Employment, and Society.* DOI: 10.1177/0950017020937936

McLaughlin, H., Uggen, C., and Blackstone, A. 2012. Sexual harassment, workplace authority, and the paradox of power. *American Sociological Review, 77*, 625–647. DOI:10.1177/003122412451728

McLaughlin, H., Uggen, C., and Blackstone, A. 2017. The economic and career effects of sexual harassment on working women. *Gender & Society, 31*, 333–358.

Nadasen, P. 2016. *Household workers unite: The untold story of African American women who built a movement.* Boston, MA: Beacon Press.

Napasri, T., and Yukongdi, V. 2015. A study of Thai female executives: Perceived barriers to career advancement. *Review of Integrative Business and Economics Research, 4*, 108–120.

National Association of Women Lawyers. 2019. *2019 survey report on the promotion and retention of women in law firms.* https://www.nawl.org/page/2018survey. Retrieved on April 12, 2021.

National Women's Law Center. 2020. *The wage gap: The who, how, why, and what to do.* https://nwlc.org/wp-content/uploads/2019/09/Wage-Gap-Who-how.pdf. Retrieved on April 11, 2021.

Nguyen, F. 2016. Women workers fight back against sexual harassment and assault. *Women's Media Center.* http://www.womensmediacenter.com/feature/entry/women-workers-fight-back-against-sexual-harassment-and-assault. Retrieved on January 25, 2017.

Nkomo, S. M., and Cox, J. Jr. 1989. Gender differences in the upward mobility of black managers: Double whammy or double advantage? *Sex Roles, 21*, 825–839.

O'Connor, L. T., Kmec, J. A., and Harris, E. C. 2015. Giving care and perceiving discrimination: The social and organizational context of family responsibilities discrimination. *Research in the Sociology of Work*, *26*, 249–276.

OECD. 2021. *Gender wage gap (indicator)*. https://data.oecd.org/earnwage/gender-wage-gap.htm. Retrieved on April 12, 2021.

OECD Development Center. 2014. *Balancing paid work, unpaid work, and leisure*. https://www.oecd.org/gender/data/balancingpaidworkunpaidworkandleisure.htm. Retrieved on December 12, 2016.

Oxfam. 2021. *Time to care: Unpaid and underpaid care work and the global inequality crisis*. https://www.oxfam.org/en/research/time-care. Retrieved on April 5, 2021.

Parker, K., and Funk, C. 2017. *Gender discrimination comes in many forms for today's working women*. http://www.pewresearch.org/fact-tank/2017/12/14/gender-discrimination-comes-in-many-forms-for-todays-working-women/. Retrieved on April 17, 2021.

Paustian-Underdahl, S. C., Walker, L. S., and Woehr, D. J., 2014. Gender and perceptions of leadership effectiveness: A meta-analysis of contextual moderators. *Journal of Applied Psychology*, *99*, 1129–1145.

Pettit, B., and Hook, J. (2005). The structure of women's employment in comparative perspective. *Social Forces, 84,* 779–801.

Pew Research Center. 2019. *Despite challenges at home and work, most working moms and dads say being employed is what's best for them*. https://www.pewresearch.org/fact-tank/2019/09/12/despite-challenges-at-home-and-work-most-working-moms-and-dads-say-being-employed-is-whats-best-for-them/. Retrieved on April 5, 2021.

Pew Research Center. 2021. *The pandemic has highlighted many challenges for mothers, but they aren't necessarily new*. https://www.pewresearch.org/fact-tank/2021/03/17/the-pandemic-has-highlighted-many-challenges-for-mothers-but-they-arent-necessarily-new/. Retrieved on April 5, 2021.

Probst, I., Zellweger, A., Mercier, M. P. P., Danuser, B., and Krief, P. 2018. Implementation, mechanisms and effects of maternity protection legislation: A realist narrative review of the literature. *International Archives of Occupational and Environmental Health, 91,* 901–922.

Rabelo, V. C., and Cortina, L. M. (2014). Two sides of the same coin: Gender harassment and heterosexist harassment in LGBQ work lives. *Law and Human Behavior, 38,* 378–391.

Rockwell, B. V., Leck, J. D., and Elliott, C. J. 2013. Can e-mentoring take the "gender" out of mentoring? *Cyberpsychology: Journal of Psychosocial Research on Cyberspace, 7*. DOI: 10.5817/CP2013-2-5

Roehling, M. V., and Huang, J. 2018. Sexual harassment training effectiveness: An interdisciplinary review and call for research. *Journal of Organizational Behavior, 39,* 134–150.

Rosette, A. S., Koval, C. Z., Ma, A., and Livingston, R. 2016. Race matters for women leaders: Intersectional effects on agentic deficiencies and penalties. *The Leadership Quarterly, 27,* 429–445.

Rost, L., Bates, K., and Dellepiane, L. 2015. *Women's economic empowerment and care.* http://policy-practice.oxfam.org.uk/publications/womens-economic-empowerment-and-care-evidence-for-influencing-578732. Retrieved on December 13, 2016.

Rubery, J. 2016. *Tackling the gender pay gap: UN Women Policy Brief No. 6.* http://www.unwomen.org/en/digital-library/publications/2016/3/the-persistence-of-the-gender-pay-gap. Retrieved on June 1, 2021.

Ruppanner, L. 2010. Conflict and housework: Does country context matter? *European Sociological Review, 26,* 557–570.

Sanchez-Hucles, J. V., and Davis, D. 2010. Women and women of color in leadership: Complexity, identity, and intersectionality. *American Psychologist, 65,* 171–181.

Saunders, C., and Dalziel, P. 2016. Twenty-five years of counting for nothing: Waring's critique of national accounts. *Feminist Economics.* DOI: 10.1080/13545701.2016.1178854.

Seager, J. 2009. *The Penguin Atlas of women in the world,* 4th ed. New York: Penguin.

Sepúlveda Carmona, M. 2013. *Annual report of the Special Rapporteur on extreme poverty and human rights.* https://documents-dds-ny.un.org/doc/UNDOC/GEN/N13/422/71/PDF/N1342271.pdf?OpenElement. Retrieved on December 26, 2016.

Sex-ratios, sex-role spillover, and sexual harassment of women at work. *Journal of Social Issues, 38,* 55–74.

SIDA. 2016. *Unpaid care work: Entry points to recognize, reduce, and redistribute: Women's economic empowerment series.* https://www.oecd.org/dac/gender-development/47565971.pdf. Retrieved on December 12, 2016.

Sjöberg, O. 2004. The role of family policy institutions in explaining gender-role attitudes: A comparative multilevel analysis of thirteen industrialized countries. *Journal of European Social Policy, 14,* 107–123.

Smith, M., and Kauppinen-Toropainen, K. 1996. Sexual harassment types and severity: Linking research and policy. In *Sexual harassment in the workplace: Perspectives, frontiers, and response strategies,* edited by M. S. Stockdale. Thousand Oaks, CA: Sage.

Sojo, V. E., Wood, R. E., and Genat, A. E. (2016). Harmful workplace experiences and women's occupational well-being: A meta-analysis. *Psychology of Women Quarterly, 40,* 10–40.

Stevens, A. 2007. *Women, power, and politics.* New York: Palgrave Macmillan.

Szymanski, D. M., and Henrichs-Beck, C. 2014. Exploring sexual minority women's experiences of external and internalized heterosexism and sexism and their links to coping and distress. *Sex Roles, 70,* 28–42.

Tanaka, K. 1995. Work, education, and the family. In *Japanese women: New feminist perspectives on the past, present and future,* edited by K. Fujimura-Fanselow and A. Kameda. New York: Feminist Press.

Tinker, I. 1990. A context for the field and for the book. In *Persistent inequalities: Women and world development,* edited by I. Tinker. Oxford: Oxford University Press.

UN DESA (Department of Economic and Social Affairs). 2020. *World's women 2020: Economic empowerment.* https://worlds-women-2020-data-undesa.hub.arcgis. com/app/6f02cbbfb8d34cb7806d21f4bd14e826. Retrieved on April 4, 2021.

UN DESA (Department of Economic and Social Affairs). 2021. *SDG Indicators: Goal 5.41.* https://unstats.un.org/sdgs/indicators/database. Retrieved on April 4, 2021.

UNICEF. 2019. *Literacy among youth is rising, but young women lag behind.* https://data.unicef.org/topic/education/literacy. Retrieved on April 5, 2021.

UN Women. 2016. *Progress of the world's women 2015–2016: Transforming economies, realizing rights.* http://progress.unwomen.org/en/2015/pdf/UNW _progressreport.pdf. Retrieved on July 18, 2016.

UN Women. 2019. *What will it take? Promoting cultural change to end sexual harassment.* https://www.unwomen.org/-/media/headquarters/attachments/sections/library /publications/2019/discussion-paper-what-will-it-take-promoting-cultural-change-to -end-sexual-harassment-en.pdf?la=en&vs=1714. Retrieved on April 16, 2021.

U.S. Bureau of Labor Statistics. 2020. *Labor force statistics from current population survey.* https://www.bls.gov/cps/cpsaat11.htm. Retrieved on April 13, 2021.

Van Dam, A. 2021. Fewer Americans are earning less than $15 an hour, but Black and Hispanic women make up a bigger share of them. *Washington Post.* https:// www.washingtonpost.com/business/2021/03/03/15-minimum-wage-black- hispanic-women/. Retrieved on April 12, 2021.

Waring, M. 1988. *If women counted: A new feminist economics.* New York: Harper and Row.

World Bank. 2012. *World development report 2012: Gender equality and develop- ment.* http://siteresources.worldbank.org/INTWDR2012/Resources/7778105 -1299699968583/7786210-1315936222006/Complete-Report.pdf. Retrieved on December 8, 2016.

World Bank. 2021a. *Labor force participation rate, female (% of female population 15+).* https://data.worldbank.org/indicator/SL.TLF.CACT.NE.ZS. Retrieved on April 7, 2021.

World Bank. 2021b. *Women, business, and the law.* https://openknowledge. worldbank.org/bitstream/handle/10986/35094/9781464816529.pdf. Retrieved on April 6, 2021.

World Bank. 2021c. *Part-time employment, female (% of total employment).* https:// data.worldbank.org/indicator/SL.TLF.PART.FE.ZS?locations=AU-CA-JP-NZ -US-DE-IS-NL-CH-GB. Retrieved on April 12, 2021.

World Bank. 2021d. *Part-time employment, male (% of total employment).* https:// data.worldbank.org/indicator/SL.TLF.PART.MA.ZS?locations=AU-CA-JP-NZ -US-DE-IS-NL-CH-GB. Retrieved on April 12, 2021.

Zacharias-Walsh, A. 2016. *Our unions, ourselves: The rise of feminist labor unions in Japan.* New York: Cornell University Press.

Design Element: Abstract floral frame: Telnov Oleksii/Shutterstock

6

Women, Development, and Environmental Sustainability

Development was to be a liberating project—a project for removal of poverty and leveling of socioeconomic inequalities, based on class, ethnicity, and gender. While the dominant image of "development" persists as a class and gender-neutral model of progress for all, the experience of "development" has been the opposite, polarizing the dichotomizing society, creating new forms of affluence for the powerful, and new forms of deprivation and dispossession for the weak.

—VANDANA SHIVA, Indian Scholar, Activist, Author

Like many women in developing nations, this Liberian woman faces increased workloads due to environmental degradation. Efforts to help people in developing countries are frequently criticized for focusing on men and failing to acknowledge the role of women in development. MissiHibiscus/iStock/360/Getty Images

T his chapter focuses on women in developing countries and their important role in economic development, environmental sustainability, and poverty reduction. It emphasizes that women's empowerment is an instrument for successful development and that gender equality itself is an important development goal. The study of women and development is another story of successful activism. It took three decades of struggle by women's activists and scholars before gender empowerment and equality were finally acknowledged as an important and central part of sustainable development.

Background

Development Terminology

Globally, nearly 690 million people are in poverty, living on less than US$1.90 a day (World Bank, 2020).[1] Many of the world's poor live in **developing nations** in the Southern hemisphere. In these less-industrialized or non-industrialized nations of the **Global South**, poverty is the norm, health is poor, educational levels are low, and life expectancy is short. The United Nations identifies approximately 126 nations in Africa, Latin America, Asia, the Middle East, Central and Eastern Europe, and the Pacific as "developing." The 46 identified as "least-developed" (the poorest countries in the world with the lowest standards of living) are listed in Box 6.1. In these countries, the gross national annual income per capita is under US $1018, maternal mortality rates and mortality rates for children under age five are higher than in other parts of the world, and literacy rates and secondary school enrollments are lower. The least-developed countries (LDCs) also face many impediments to **sustainable development** (development that meets the needs of the present without compromising the ability to meet needs in the future). Not only are people in low-income and developing nations economically vulnerable, they are environmentally vulnerable. Some of the poorest nations in Sub-Saharan Africa and South Asia are particularly at-risk for natural disasters related to climate change (World Bank, 2020).

In a nation, **development** is the process of growth that may include the following: emphasis on large-scale economic growth; focus on small-scale community development projects aimed at increasing individuals' self-reliance; creation or improvement of national infrastructures such as roads; provision of credit, training, or services that enable people to participate more fully in the economic, political, and social lives of their communities; improvement in access to health care; mechanisms for increasing agricultural yield; increased access to education for women and children; and expanded opportunities for political development (Mermel & Simons, 1991).

Development programs and projects are intended to promote economic development and reduce poverty. The majority of development programs are funded through

---

[1]Poverty-reduction strategies have substantially reduced the number of people in poverty, from 36 percent of the world's population in 1990 to 8.7 percent in 2018. However, the World Bank estimates that due to Covid-19 pandemic, the number of people in poverty will rise by 150 million in 2021.

BOX 6.1 *Least Developed Countries (LDCs)*

Southern Asia
Afghanistan
Bangladesh
Nepal

Southeastern Asia
Cambodia
Laos
Myanmar
Timor-Leste

Oceania
Kiribati
Tuvalu
Solomon Islands

Northern Africa and Western Asia
Sudan
Yemen

Caribbean
Haiti

Sub-Saharan Africa
Angola
Benin
Burkina Faso
Burundi
Central African Republic
Chad
Comoros
Democratic Republic of Congo
Djibouti
Equatorial Guinea
Eritrea
Ethiopia
Gambia
Guinea
Guinea-Bissau
Lesotho
Liberia
Madagascar
Malawi
Mali
Mauritania
Mozambique
Niger
Rwanda
Sao Tome and Principe
Senegal
Sierra Leone
Somalia
South Sudan
Tanzania
Togo
Uganda
Zambia

Source: UN DESA (2021).

foreign aid, from the government of one country to the government of another country (called **bilateral aid**) such as that provided by USAID. **Multilateral aid** funded by the European Union, the World Bank, and the IMF (International Monetary Fund) and other UN agencies accounts for about 38 percent of the funding for development programs and projects (OECD, 2020). Nongovernmental organizations (NGOs) such as OXFAM and the Global Fund for Women, as well as foundations like the Ford Foundation, also fund development projects. The UNDP (United Nations Development Programme) works with countries to solve global and national development challenges, including poverty reduction. The program helps developing countries attract and use aid effectively and encourages human rights and women's empowerment. The UNDP also provides important global data on human development.

Colonial History

Many of the countries in the Global South spent years as colonies of countries in the **Global North**, some well into the twentieth century. For example, Sri Lanka (formerly Ceylon) is an island country off the coast of India. Europeans dominated it for more than 400 years, first the Portuguese in the sixteenth century, then the Dutch, and later the British, who controlled it until 1948. Only two countries in Africa were never colonies (Liberia and Ethiopia). Belgium, Britain, France, Portugal, Holland, Germany, and Spain controlled the other African countries until a lengthy decolonization period following World War II. Colonized countries were exploited as sources of cheap labor and resources. Typically, profits were not shared with the colonized people, and poverty increased. Colonization also permanently altered cultures, including language and economies.

One legacy of this colonial history is that development aid from the Global North is often viewed suspiciously. That includes efforts to promote gender equality as part of development, which are often resisted with the charge of Western cultural imperialism. Ironically, many feminist development scholars argue that colonization negatively impacted women's status and power by replacing egalitarian gender arrangements with traditional western gender roles. Colonizers (which were men) removed women from the political decision-making spheres, limited their access to and control over resources, and interfered with their legal rights and privileges (Boserup, 1970; Duley & Diduk, 1986; Sen & Grown, 1987). For example, Western patrilineal notions of land ownership contributed to a situation in which women own hardly any of the land in developing nations. Industrialization, which necessitated the movement of families into cities, increased women's dependence upon men for their livelihoods because offices and factories hire far fewer women than they do men, and urban work is often incompatible with traditional female roles.

Women in Developing Nations (the Global South)

Earlier chapters pointed to the greater challenges experienced by women in developing countries compared to women in the **developed** or **industrialized countries** in the Northern hemisphere (the Global North). For example, in developing nations, statuary and customary laws are more likely to restrict women's access to land and other assets, and their control over household economic resources is more limited. Child marriage is more common in developing nations, as are unmet needs for family planning and larger family sizes. Most of the countries that practice female genital mutilation are developing nations in sub-Saharan Africa where many of the least developed countries are located. The majority of the hundreds of thousands of women subjected to war and post-conflict rape in the last 20 years lived in one of the least-developed nations in sub-Saharan Africa.

Women in developing countries also have a higher incidence and higher death rates from HIV/AIDS, interpersonal violence, and cervical cancer. On average, they live 10 years less than women in the Global North. Most unsafe abortions and maternal deaths and disability occur in the Global South. Women in developing countries also work longer hours in both paid and unpaid labor and are more likely to work in the informal sector in low-paying, vulnerable jobs as own-account and unpaid family workers. The gender gap in unpaid care labor is also larger in the Global South. Many women in the least-developed nations lack convenient stores, cooking stoves (many cook over fires or with inefficient indoor stoves), fuel (some have to gather wood or other fuel daily) and on-site water (many have to travel long distances and carry it home). They often lack access to electricity, clean water, clean menstrual materials, and medical and sanitation services. This means that the unpaid care labor performed by women in developing countries is that much more difficult and time-consuming, and they experience unique threats to their health and safety.

Feminist Concerns with the Development Process

"It is not possible to address society's needs at any level while ignoring the perspectives, priorities, and knowledge of more than half of the world's population."
Roshina Wilshire, UNDP

Historically, most development programs focused on economic growth and a conversion to capitalist market economies and modern technology. This focus is commonly associated with **modernization theory**, so-called because urban-based market economies were viewed as modern and desirable. Modernization proponents believed if we transformed the economy of a developing country into a modern capitalist economy, then political and social development would follow. Unfortunately, modernization often increased income inequality and left social and political inequalities untouched.

"In the vast and ever growing literature on economic development, reflections on the particular problems of women are few and far between."
Ester Boserup

In 1970, Ester Boserup expressed serious concerns about the effects of traditional development programs on women. Her now-classic book, *Women's Role in Economic Development*, stimulated debate as the first major text in the women and development literature (Mosse, 1993). Boserup's research showed how contemporary development policies belittled women's economic contributions while relying on and exploiting their labor (Acosta-Belen & Bose, 1995). She also showed that economic development has a differential impact on men and women and that it often disrupted earlier, more egalitarian gender arrangements (Beneria & Roldan, 1987; Jaquette & Staudt, 2006). Boserup's book stimulated a number of feminist critiques of development programs, summarized into four categories below. These criticisms still apply to many development projects today, although things have improved significantly as a result of feminist development scholars and activists and "femicrats" (feminist bureaucrats) working for development organizations.

Traditional Development Programs Fail to Recognize Women's Economic Contributions

One common criticism is that development programs fail to acknowledge the importance of women's labor to the survival and ongoing reproduction of people in all societies and thus fail to meet important development goals such as poverty reduction and child mortality (Anand, 1993; Sen & Grown, 1987). For example, despite women's roles as providers of basic needs (food, fuel, water, health care, sanitation, and so on) and the relationship between women's empowerment and important development goals, women have more difficulties than men in gaining access to development resources. This gender disparity is important. Investing development resources in women is about empowering women. It is about gender equality in the distribution of development resources. Poverty is reduced when development increases women's ability to improve the health and education of their children. Investing in women also contributes to growth in local, regional, and national economies (Scott, 2020). Fortunately, this is increasingly recognized by most development funders and programs.

> "Greater gender equality contributes to economic efficiency and the achievement of other key development outcomes."
> *World Bank*

> "There is no tool for development more effective than the empowerment of women."
> *Kofi Annan, former Secretary-General of the United Nations*

Traditional Development Programs Have Not Reduced Women's Considerable Workloads

A second common criticism is that in most cases, development projects have not reduced women's considerable workloads. Women's work as primary household food producers and preparers and as water and fuel gatherers has gone largely unappreciated and unaided even as this workload grows because of resource depletion and pollution (Bryceson, 1995). For example, women in developing countries can spend up to 14 hours a day in unpaid labor because they lack time-saving infrastructure and devices, and unpaid domestic and care work is considered "women's work" (Oxfam, 2020). For example, almost 30 percent of the world's people do not have access to on-site water, and women and girls are responsible for collecting water in 80 percent of the households with off-site water (WHO/UNICEF, 2017). This is time that could be better spent on education, producing, earning, with family, politically participating, or contributing to the community, and rest and recovery (UN, 2020; UNDP, 2016). Women in low-income countries spend more time on unpaid work compared to other women due to:

- Traditional gender norms
- Larger families
- Inadequate access to water, sanitation, and electricity
- Fewer health care and social services
- Fewer labor-saving technologies
- Poverty, which increases the amount, intensity, and drudgery of unpaid care work as well as precluding its outsourcing
- Climate change, which impacts water and fuel availability and family member health

> "Unpaid care work is disproportionately distributed toward women and girls, which then restricts their freedom and participation in economic and social life, affects their health negatively and keeps them in this cycle of low income and poverty."
> *Deepta Chopra, Institute of Development Studies*

For example, in Rwanda, men's participation in the domestic tasks is generally stigmatized and made fun of by other men and by women. In Eastern Uganda, having a water source within 400 meters of the home saves women and girls more than 900 hours a year (Klugman & Melnikova, 2016). Each additional child under six increases the hours women are engaged in any care responsibility by 2 hours 35 minutes in Colombia, 43 minutes in the Philippines, and 1 hour 21 minutes in Uganda (Rost, Bates, & Dellipiane, 2015).

Development programs often provide tools and technologies to aid in men's work but not women's work. To address their time poverty, many women in developing nations could really use proper water and sanitation systems; energy-efficient, nonpolluting cook stoves; hoes and other hand-farming implements; and alternative fuel sources such as biogas and solar energy. For example, Oxfam found that improving access to water reduced women's labor by one to four hours a day in Uganda (Oxfam, 2018).

Box 6.2 gives you an idea of the average workday for a woman in the developing nation of Sierra Leone. You can probably readily think of development projects that could significantly reduce her work burden.

Traditional Development Programs Focus on Men's Income Generation

A third common criticism is that traditional development programs often assume a Western-style traditional gender-role arrangement in which men are breadwinners and women are homemakers. Consequently, they focus on fostering wage earning by male heads of household and on adult women in domestic homemaking roles. For instance, until the late 1970s, development efforts targeted at women viewed women primarily as mothers by focusing on mother–child health programs, feeding schemes, family planning, food aid, and so on (Moser, 1989). As Mosse (1993) points out, these programs did not do much to create independence and self-reliance among women, but they were politically safe in that they did not challenge women's traditional roles.

Article 14(9) of The UN's Convention on the Elimination of Discrimination Against Women (CEDAW) convention promises women the right to "have access to agricultural credit and loans, marketing facilities, appropriate technology and equal treatment in land and agrarian reform as well as land resettlement schemes." However, a gender gap exists for many assets, inputs and services for agricultural development (Johnson et al., 2016). Assuming that what benefits husbands will benefit women and children, and that men are the "real farmers," development resources are usually channeled through men (Manfre et al., 2013). Consequently, development programs typically increase men's but not women's access to important sources of agricultural development such as land, credit, cattle, labor, seeds, and extension services (services that provide information for innovation and to increase productivity), and thus create or maintain women's economic dependence on men. This also means that divorced, widowed, or abandoned women are particularly vulnerable to poverty because they often lack even indirect access to development resources (Bryceson, 1995). In sub-Saharan Africa, for instance, women head approximately 28 percent of rural households (UN DESA, 2019). The idea that progress involves

Sidebar (left margin):

"Women are most vulnerable to the effects of poor sanitation. One in three women worldwide risk shame, disease, harassment, and attack because they have nowhere safe to go to the toilet. Women and girls without toilets spend 97 billion hours each year finding a place to toilet."
WaterAid

I am told that the financial architecture is designed

So that abundance overflows from rich to poor, strong to powerless, man to woman

But all I can see in your architecture is bad plumbing

Clogged pipes everywhere

Congested with your investments

And my assortment of hard-earned debts

Excerpt from poem by Marwa Sharafeldin of Egypt 2013

BOX 6.2   *One Woman's Day in Sierra Leone*

4:00 A.M. to 5:30 A.M. Fish in local pond.

6:00 A.M. to 8:00 A.M. Light fire, heat washing water, cook breakfast, clean dishes, sweep compound.

8:00 A.M. to 11:00 A.M. Work in rice fields with four-year-old son and baby on back.

11:00 A.M. to 12:00 P.M. Collect berries, leaves, and bark, carry water.

12:00 P.M. to 2:00 P.M. Process and prepare food, cook lunch, wash dishes.

2:00 P.M. to 3:00 P.M. Wash clothes, carry water, clean and smoke fish.

3:00 P.M. to 5:00 P.M. Work in the gardens.

5:00 P.M. to 6:00 P.M. Fish in local pond.

6:00 P.M. to 8:00 P.M. Process and prepare food, cook dinner.

8:00 P.M. to 9:00 P.M. Wash dishes, then clean children.

9:00 P.M. to 11:00 P.M. Converse around the fire while shelling seeds and making fishnets.

11:00 P.M. to 4:00 A.M. Sleep.

Source: Food and Agriculture Organization, 2009.

the promotion of the male breadwinner/female homemaker roles also interferes with the provision of loan moneys to women entrepreneurs and women farmers. This is made worse by the fact that most development programs only lend to property owners when there is widespread discrimination against women inheriting, owning, or controlling property in many developing nations (World Bank, 2021).

Traditional Development Programs Have Contributed to Erosions in Women's Status

Finally, a fourth criticism is that by encouraging or assuming a Western version of gender-role arrangements, traditional development programs contributed to erosions in women's status. The notion that a male breadwinner and a female housewife is a desired goal pervaded national and international agents of development until the 1980s, and that, combined with local patriarchal beliefs, contributed to women's continued lower status and power relative to men. Rogers (1980), in a highly influential book called *The Domestication of Women*, argued that because development efforts failed to provide incentives for women as producers, development projects eroded what had been a source of power and status for women. For instance, in many developing nations, it is women who save, select, and use the seeds of traditional crops which are often better suited for local environments (Bajner, 2019). They play an important role in family food security and in maintaining biodiversity. However, this important role is undermined when development programs focus on supporting men's commercial farming, or when control over natural resources shifts from women's control to men's control for international markets (Montanari & Bergh, 2019). Likewise, many development projects resulted in women changing from being independent producers and providers to being housewives, economically dependent upon men as controllers of cash income. Furthermore, with cash, men gain access to banks and other modern institutions, leaving women further behind (Mosse, 1993).

"Without specific attention to gender issues and initiatives, projects can reinforce inequalities between women and men and even increase imbalances."
UNDP

Women in Development Approach (WID)

Feminist criticisms of traditional development programs had some impact. For example, in 1973, following considerable activism by American feminist development experts like Irene Tinker, the U.S. Congress enacted the Percy Amendment to the Foreign Assistance Act. It required that bilateral programs "give particular attention to those . . . activities that tend to integrate women into the national economies of foreign countries, thus improving their status and assisting the total development effort" (World Resources Institute, 1994–1995). In the 1980s, influenced by Boserup's critiques, the **women in development (WID)** approach emerged. This approach emphasized that directing development resources to women's remunerative (money-making) labor would improve food production and reduce poverty (Beneria, Berik, & Floro, 2015; Jaquette & Staudt, 2006).

WID demanded increased attention to women's development needs and emphasized women's productive labor. WID projects can be classified into three general types: (1) income-generating projects, (2) projects that provide labor-saving technologies, and (3) projects that improve women's local resource access (see Figure 6.1).

Income-Generating Projects

In the 1980s, development efforts began focusing on fostering women's economic participation in the public sphere. The typical income-generating project for women focused on traditional female skills such as sewing, embroidery, and handicrafts—all low in marketability and profit in comparison to the skills taught to men (Bryceson, 1995). The projects were often unsuccessful because they were not well thought out. Designers did not consider whether there was a market for the goods produced, and did not consider how the additional work would fit with women's already considerable domestic and care responsibilities (Momsen, 2020). Another problem is that this type of income-generating program frequently failed to include women in the project design process. Women were typically presented with the program instead of being asked to generate their own ideas. Involving women directly in the development process increases the likelihood that there will be a market for the item produced and that the item can be produced within the constraints of women's unpaid domestic and care labor. It also gives women organizational skills and a sense of empowerment that last long after the donor has left the area. Under these conditions, income-generating projects can positively contribute to women's status and power (Mosse, 1993).

Development programs sometimes still include small-scale income-generating development projects for women, particularly in rural areas, and many NGOs have these types of projects. Today, development agencies and programs are more likely to support income-generating projects that consider the specific context in which women live and work. There is also much more funding for women micro-and-small-scale entrepreneurs than there once was (discussed below). Also notable is that since the 1980s, bi-lateral aid (country-to-country aid) has often focused on the employment of women by transnational corporations. These corporations increase their profits by having product assemblywork done by low-waged factory workers and homeworkers in developing regions. You will learn in Chapter 7, "Women and Globalization" that women working for these corporations face difficult working conditions and usually do not earn enough to get out of poverty.

"Experience shows that investing in women is one of the most cost effective ways of promoting development. As mothers, as producers or suppliers of food, fuel, and water, as traders and manufacturers, as political and community leaders, women are at the center of the process of change."
Gro Harlem Brundtland, former Prime Minister of Norway and former head of the World Health Organization

Song of an African Woman

I have only one request.

I do not ask for money

Although I have need of it,

I do not ask for meat

I have only one request,

And all I ask is

That you remove

The road block

From my path.

From the Acholi poem, Song of Lawino by Okot p'Bitek

FIGURE 6.1 *Three Types of WID Projects*

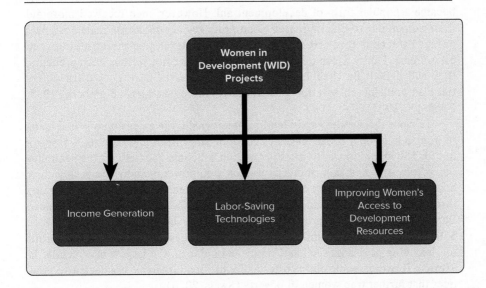

Labor-Saving Technologies

Labor-saving technologies can be a useful development strategy. A number of development projects have reduced women's labor loads by providing such things as grinding mills, pumps, or cooking stoves. The main criticism of these projects is that they have disseminated only a narrow range of devices that merely begin to address the reality of women's multitask responsibilities (Bryceson, 1995). Also, some donors and development agencies failed to consult women and consider the context. Consequently, the tools they provided were sometimes useless (Mosse, 1993).

Successfully addressing women's unpaid labor needs is context-specific. Women need solutions that are keyed to their unique sociocultural and geographic situations. For example, some water projects installed pumps without considering the height of traditional water vessels, or they provided water vessels that could not be carried on women's heads, assuming women could use a wagon. However, rocky and hilly terrain made transporting water by wagon impractical. Likewise, in theory, cookstoves that use clean-burning liquefied petroleum gas should save women hours of collecting and processing cooking fuel, but many women do not have the money to pay for the gas, or to repair cookstoves when they break. To some extent, this remains a problem.

Improving Women's Access to Development Resources

As mentioned earlier, development programs typically increased men's but not women's access to important sources of development such as land, credit,

"Women are community managers, farmers, water collectors, entrepreneurs, caretakers of fragile ecologies, and as mothers they daily create and maintain life. Only when their expertise and value are realized will development initiatives have half a chance of succeeding."
Julia Mosse

cattle, labor, seeds, and extension services providing information, tools, and training. In the 1980s and 1990s, aid in the form of small loans to individuals became a popular form of development aid. However, men received more aid than women due to discriminatory loan practices like requiring male cosigners or land ownership (only 10–20 percent of land in developing countries is owned by women). Faulty assumptions such as women are not serious entrepreneurs, they will default on their loans, and their businesses have no growth potential also contributed to a focus of these resources on men (Blumberg, 1995; Forrester, 1995).

To close this gender gap in lending, **microcredit**, the extension of small loans to women in poverty for small-scale economic enterprises and farming, was introduced. The intention was to increase women's income and help lift their families out of poverty, and contribute to women's empowerment by increasing their household decision power. Microcredit was adopted as a development strategy throughout Asia, Africa, and Latin America. NGOs like SEWA, the Grameen Bank, and Accion serve primarily women and provide microloans (as small as $50), business training, and other financial services. There are also for-profit microlending programs such as Compatamos Banco, the largest microlender in Mexico. However, some outfits offering for-profit micro-loans use deceptive practices that further trap women in poverty (Sweis, 2020).

Women's microcredit programs can benefit women and their families. However, microlending is not the hoped-for panacea to poverty reduction and women's economic empowerment. Although research finds that NGO microloans don't increase poverty due to increased debt burdens (a concern of some critics), microloans have mixed effects on women's household decision power and independence and only small effects on household income and living standards (Banerjee, Karlan, & Zinman, 2015). And, as noted by some feminist development scholars, microlending programs fail to bring about change in the historically masculinized domains of paid work and lending (Chant & Sweetman, 2012). Another criticism is that women-only microfinance fails to challenge patriarchy and nonegalitarian family norms (Chant, 2016).

"Alleviating poverty and enabling women to make some income can better lives, but the enabling environment that confirms the right to work, to property, to safety, to voice, to sexuality, and to freedom is not created by sewing machines or microcredit alone."
Hania Sholkamy

Micro-lending is one tool for women's economic empowerment in developing nations. But women also need more access to traditional financial services for gender equality of opportunity, and to raise themselves and their families out of poverty. A lack of access to traditional financial services, including credit and bank accounts, is a major barrier to the success of women entrepreneurs in developing economies. This is aggravated by their lack of collateral and, in some cases, their lack of control over family assets (Kende-Robb, 2019; World Bank, 2021). For example, in the majority of sub-Saharan countries, there are no laws prohibiting discrimination in access to credit. In some LDCs, like Equatorial Guinea and Guinea-Bissau, by law women do not have equal control of marital assets, and cannot register a business or open a bank account in the same way as men (World Bank, 2021). Increasing women's financial inclusion is receiving some attention from organizations like the World Bank, Women's World Banking, and UN Women.

Gender and Development Approach (GAD)

Critics of the WID approach pointed out that despite increased attention to women in development, development programs for the most part failed to increase women's status. As some put it, women were working for development instead of development working for women's equality and empowerment (Cornwall & Rivas, 2015). In the late 1970s and 1980s, this led to a new approach to women and development. Called the **gender and development approach (GAD)** or **empowerment approach**, it focused explicitly on improving women's status and power. GAD sees gender equality as a worthy development goal separate from its relationship to poverty eradication and children's well-being. The inclusion of the word "gender" in place of the word "women" reflects an emphasis on looking at the overall power relationships of women and men and their importance to development.

The GAD approach takes into account women's lives and labor, both inside and outside of the home. In addition, it emphasizes an approach in which women are not as much integrated into development as they are the architects of their own development. Projects based on a GAD approach encourage women to bring about positive change through women's organizations and activism. GAD differs from other approaches to women and development in that it sees the goals of development for women in terms of self-reliance, strength, and gender equality (Mosse, 1993). GAD emphasizes empowering women to work to change and transform the structures that contributed to their subordination (a bottom-up approach) (Moser, 1989).

Feminists from the south, particularly those in the organization DAWN (Development Alternatives with Women for a New Era), embraced GAD (Braniotti et al., 1994; Sen & Grown, 1987). DAWN, a transnational feminist network launched as a Global South initiative in 1984, includes representatives from Asia, Africa, Latin America, the Pacific, and the Caribbean. Many influential Southern Hemisphere feminists are members. DAWN's main purpose is to create a global feminist support network for equitable development and to use political mobilization, consciousness-raising, and popular education to promote women's empowerment and gender equality. DAWN is an example of a WINGO, a women's international NGO. WOCAN (Women Organizing for Change in Agriculture and Natural Resource Management) is another WINGO with a GAD focus. Among other things, WOCAN provides leadership training to empower women to become change agents. Box 6.3 summarizes the differences between the WID and GAD approaches.

In the 1990s, the leading development agencies began adding GAD-sounding rhetoric to their mission or goal statements, and **gender mainstreaming** emerged as the key mechanism for promoting women's empowerment and gender equality (Parpart, 2014). Identified as a strategy for promoting gender equality in the 1995 Beijing Platform for Action from the UN's Fourth World Women's Conference, gender mainstreaming is defined by the UN as "the process of assessing the implications for women and men of any planned action, including legislation, policies,

"No man, planning economic development for the developing countries, intended to empower women."
Irene Tinker

"We want a world where inequalities and discrimination based on gender and all other identities are eliminated from every country and from the relationships among countries and peoples; where development processes are founded on social solidarity and economic, political, ecological, social, and personal justice; where poverty and violence are eradicated; where human rights in their fullest and most expansive sense are the foundation of laws, public policies, and private actions."
From DAWN's vision statement

BOX 6.3   *Comparison of WID and GAD Approaches to Development*

Women in Development (WID)

Focus: Improving women's welfare.

How: By providing income-generating projects, labor-saving technologies, and access to development resources like credit and extension services.

Top-down approach: Services determined and offered by development organizations. Women are passive recipients of aid.

Criticisms: Usefulness impeded by failure to consult women. Does not increase women's status or empowerment.

Gender and Development (GAD)

Focus: Transform society to promote gender equality.

How: By encouraging women's empowerment through women's organizations and activism, participation in politics, and decision making.

Bottom-up approach: Women are architects of their own development. Women are active participants of aid.

Criticisms: Difficult to translate into specific policies and programs. Resistance due to its "revolutionary" nature.

"Systematic gender mainstreaming into policies and intervention ensures the empowerment of women and that both women's and men's knowledge, concerns, and experience are taken into consideration."
WEDO

or programmes, in all areas and at all levels. It is a strategy for making women's (as well as men's) concerns and experiences an integral dimension of the design, implementation, monitoring and evaluation of policies and programmes in all political, economic, and societal spheres so that men and women benefit equally and inequality is not perpetuated" (UN, 2002). Gender mainstreaming requires a gender analysis (sometimes called a gender audit) to make sure that gender equality concerns are taken into account in all developmental activities rather than being marginalized into specialized women's institutions (Charlesworth, 2005). It also requires women's active participation in the development process.

International feminist NGOs (WINGOs) such as the Women's Environment and Development Organization (WEDO) and the International Women's Development Agency (IWDA) promote gender mainstreaming. For example, along with partner organizations, IWDA developed a set of base criteria called "gender minimum standards" to inform their project planning, design, and implementation (Scothern & Brislane, 2016). These standards provide a system for conducting a power and gender analysis of all programs and projects. The goal is to ensure that projects and programs promote gender equality and women's and girls' meaningful participation in the decisions that affect them, as well as equal access to development resources and opportunities. InterAction, a coalition of nearly 200 U.S.-based development NGOs, found that organizations that conducted gender audits changed their approaches to better address the participation of women and reduced project structures that perpetuated inequalities and gender stereotypes (InterAction, 2010).

All UN bodies and agencies have formally endorsed gender mainstreaming, and most have corresponding statements, policies, programs, and activities. For example, the UNDP's 2008–2011 Gender Equality Strategy (UNDP, 2008) makes a specific commitment to address many of the gender problems associated with traditional development and provides a blueprint for doing so. The UNDP's gender mainstreaming tools advise programmers to incorporate gender specialists and representatives of women at all levels, to identify gender issues relevant to each project, to take all possible steps to ensure gender balance in project staff, and involve women's NGOs in project identification, formulation and appraisal. In July 2005, ECOSOC (UN's Economic and Social Council) adopted a resolution calling upon all United Nations' funds and programs to intensify their efforts to address the challenges involving the integration of gender perspectives into policies and programs. In 2011, the UN affirmed a commitment to gender mainstreaming and tasked the newly created UN Women (focused on gender equality and the empowerment of women and girls) with leading, coordinating, and evaluating these efforts. This commitment was reaffirmed in 2018.

Although GAD language and gender mainstreaming are popular "buzzwords" in development organizations and UN agencies, feminist development critics point out that it hasn't translated into a serious commitment to transforming power relations (Cornwall & Rivas, 2015; Parpart, 2014; Prugl & Lustgarten, 2006). For instance, the UN's Millennium Summit and Declaration, which was adopted by 189 nations in 2000, set gender equality as a Millennium Development Goal (MDG-3) and as a condition for the achievement of the other goals, but concrete goals were lacking (see Box 6.4 for the MDG goals). Instead of addressing gendered practices, social structures, and gender relations that undermine gender equality and maintain gender (and other racial, ethnic, and other) privileges, in practice gender mainstreaming has mostly promoted consideration of women's and girls' interests in the development process (Parpart, 2014). Including gender in program activities and projects does not necessarily serve women's well-being or gender equality (Beneria et al., 2015). For example, while the World Bank and other business and development agents say gender equality is an important goal, in practice their focus is on women as agents of poverty reduction and as producers and consumers that can drive economic growth, an approach called "smart economics" (Chant, 2016; Cornwall & Rivas, 2015; World Bank, 2012).

It doesn't help that GAD is often viewed with suspicion by Southern Hemisphere governments and communities who are uncomfortable with gender-role change and resist it with charges of cultural imperialism and cultural insensitivity (Adusei-Asante, Hancock, & Oliveira, 2015). But the problem also lies in development agencies. Development organizations with gendered hierarchies (including UN agencies where leadership is predominantly male) are not firmly committed to GAD strategies and goals (Charlesworth, 2005; Parpart, 2014). It is apparent that gender mainstreaming is not an "end-all-and-be-all" and must be complemented by gender activists and scholars who hold development agencies accountable (Prugl & Lustgarten, 2006).

After a gender audit, Heifer Zambia gave animals to women that previously had been taboo for their sex; trained the women in new areas of animal care, which increased nutrition and food security in those communities, and, through project contracts, enabled women to jointly own the animals and inherit them if their husbands died. *InterAction*

"When development is not 'engendered' it is endangered." *UNDP*

". . . governments and other actors should promote an active and visible policy of mainstreaming a gender perspective in all policies and programmes, so that, before decisions are taken, an analysis is made of the effects on women and men, respectively." *Beijing Platform for Action, Fourth World Conference on Women*

"Working on gender issues obliges organizations to set their own houses in order, and change aspects of the organizational culture which discriminate against women staff and women 'beneficiaries.'" *Caroline Sweetman,* editor of the international journal *Gender & Development*

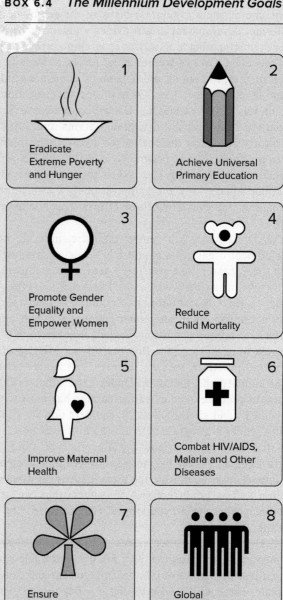

BOX 6.4 *The Millennium Development Goals*

1 Eradicate Extreme Poverty and Hunger

2 Achieve Universal Primary Education

3 Promote Gender Equality and Empower Women

4 Reduce Child Mortality

5 Improve Maternal Health

6 Combat HIV/AIDS, Malaria and Other Diseases

7 Ensure Environmental Sustainability

8 Global Partnership for Development

Source: United Nations (2009). http://endpoverty2015.org/goals.

Some feminist groups point out that if development organizations really want to support GAD, they should increase funding for women's rights groups and movements. Since the early 2000s, bilateral and multilateral organizations have increased funding to support gender equality, but still only a small fraction of development assistance is targeted towards gender equality as a primary or secondary objective (OECD Gendernet, 2021). As the Association for Women in Development (AWID) explains, gender power relations are best transformed by increasing women's formal rights under the law, increasing women's access to resources and income, and changing social norms and the internalized attitudes and beliefs of both men and women. Women's rights organizations and movements play a critical role in bringing about these changes and in defending, preserving, and maintaining them. Women's organizations need money not just to provide services, but to promote women's empowerment and gender equality through awareness raising, advocacy, campaigning, lobbying, leadership development, movement building and organizing, communications, and networking. While AWID applauds donor organizations' increased rhetoric supporting women and girls, their research finds that currently, less than 1 percent of the $48.7 billion of aid focusing on gender equality is going to women's rights organizations (Dolker, 2020).

"Women's rights organizations, with their grounding in diverse communities, in-depth analysis of problems of gender inequality and rights violations, history of experience and tested strategies to counter these problems, should be a priority partner for any donor interested in making sustainable change happen for women's rights and gender equality."
AWID

Women, the Environment, and Sustainable Development

In the mid-1980s, the United Nations, environmentalists, and policymakers concerned with the environment called attention to the environmental consequences of traditional development. Their main charge was that development, in both the north and the south, was unsustainable. Basically, **sustainable development** "meets the needs of the present without compromising the ability of future generations to meet their own needs" (World Commission on Environment and Development, 1987). This section explores the topic of women, gender, and sustainable development.

Environmental Sustainability Basics

Economic development is unsustainable when it has negative environmental consequences that significantly and negatively impact human health, well-being, and survival. Development has environmental impacts, and because the environment is an "*ecosystem*" comprised of many interlocking synergistic systems, environmental impacts often have cascading effects. Take the case of deforestation, the conversion of forested land to nonforested land as a direct result of human activities, a problem faced on almost every continent but especially in developing nations (Greenfacts, 2009). The main causes are industrial logging, clearing of forests for conversion of land for agriculture or cattle ranching, fuelwood collection, and forest fires aggravated by climate change. Trees hold soil in place and, consequently, deforestation contributes to soil erosion. Agricultural yields are significantly decreased when valuable topsoil washes away. But the animal waste often used for fertilizer is sometimes burned for fuel when there are no trees left. This means that petrochemical fertilizers must be used to increase agricultural yields. However, over time these build up and increase the salinity of the soil. This results in desertification, which means that nothing will grow. Runoff of agricultural fertilizers pollutes waterways,

"The poor are not living in industrialized countries where the environment is distant—where you have to go out to appreciate it. Our lives depend upon it."
Wangari Maathai of Kenya, winner of the 2004 Nobel Peace Prize (for her contribution to sustainable development, democracy and peace)

"The elimination of global poverty and the promotion of sustainable development are essential to a fair and equitable world. The current patterns of consumption and production are among the major causes of the degradation of the Earth's resources."
The Network of Women Ministers of the Environment

thus reducing the amount of drinkable water and killing fish. Deforestation also contributes to climate change. Trees are major consumers of carbon dioxide, a greenhouse gas, and their felling releases carbon dioxide. Climate change, discussed later in the chapter, is another example of how development can be unsustainable. A heavy diet of fossil fuels, which served the economic development and high standard of living in the United States and many other industrialized countries, is a major contributor to global climate change.

Because many environmental problems arising from economic development disproportionately impact low-income people in developing nations, this an environmental justice issue. These environmental problems include deforestation, the effects of climate change, air and water pollution from industry, pollution from toxic chemical and electronic wastes, depletion of natural resources, and biodiversity losses. The bottom-line: Development is frequently unsustainable and can aggravate social inequalities instead of reducing them. It can harm ecosystems and imperil people's present and/or future health, quality of life, and survival. Furthermore, impoverished people in developing countries often lack the power to resist harmful development and lack the money to escape its negative environmental impacts. To survive, they sometimes have little choice but to exploit already fragile ecosystems.

It might seem obvious that development should be sustainable. However, the role of the North in Southern development clouds the situation. Development in the Global South is often guided and in many cases controlled by the Global North countries that supply the capital for development. Guided by capitalism, they often strike deals with developing nations that benefit corporations from their country. Corporations based in these Northern countries open factories, develop large-scale agriculture or cattle operations, and resource harvesting operations (e.g., wood or petroleum) in developing nations. International trade agreements allow Northern countries to outsource the production of goods that degrade the environment (UNDP, 2011). The corporations benefit from higher profits from lower labor and materials costs, and weaker environmental laws. Consumers in Northern nations also benefit from lower priced goods. Meanwhile, the environmental costs are borne largely by the citizens of the Southern hemisphere countries, especially the poor. Some people consider this **neocolonialism** because even though the former colonial powers granted independence to the colonies, they continue to use the former colonies for raw materials, minerals, and cash crops and control the area's resources indirectly through the business corporations and the financial lending institutions they dominate (Ruether, 2008).

Initially it is hard to understand why a Southern country would accept this type of development, but the people most affected by unsustainable development lack the economic and political power to prevent it. They are "sold out" by people in their own countries and communities that stand to personally benefit. Some of the fault also lies at the doorstep of the economic development strategies encouraged by traditional development programs. These programs encourage the replacement of small, localized economies with market-based economies that produce crops, minerals, goods, etc. for export to generate cash. International development programs arrange large loans (sometimes in the millions and billions of dollars), but funding is based on projects' moneymaking potential, and environmentally sustainable development is often perceived as at odds with this goal. A related problem is that economic progress is typically measured in terms of short-run economic goals, such as increases in per capita income and gross national product. Developing nations must demonstrate this type of progress in order to receive more aid. To make matters worse, what has often happened is that the cash generated goes to pay the interest on the loans. A high debt burden results and is aggravated when international markets fluctuate and prices fall. To come up with the money simply to pay the interest on their loans, Southern governments are often forced to sell goods at rock-bottom prices and to exploit fragile natural resources.

A current concern in the development community is the effects of **climate change** on people in developing regions. Billions of people, particularly those in developing countries, are expected to face shortages of water and food and risks to health and life as a result of climate change (UNDP, 2020). Climate change results largely from human activities that lead to a build-up of greenhouse gases that trap heat near the earth's surface. Greenhouse gases from human activities include carbon dioxide from fossil fuel use (petroleum, natural gas, and coal), methane (from agricultural practices and livestock), nitrous oxide (from fertilizers, fossil fuels, and biomass burning), and chlorofluorocarbons (from industry) (NASA, 2017). Deforestation due to agriculture (forests are cut to plant crops or raise livestock), logging (trees are often worth more dead than alive), and building also contribute to climate change (National Geographic, 2017).

The effects of climate change are many. They include rising mean temperatures, more severe weather events and natural disasters, increased ecosystem stresses, shifting precipitation patterns and rising ocean temperatures affecting food and water security, pest and disease outbreaks, harsher storms, wildfires and droughts, rising sea levels and flooding, and increased conflict due to increased poverty and resource shortages (IPCC, 2018; UNDP, 2020; FAO, 2020).

> "A majority of deforestation today can be traced to four globally traded commodities: beef, soybeans, palm oil, and wood products."
> *Union of Concerned Scientists*

Not all people and groups are equally vulnerable to the effects of climate change. Some people, by virtue of where they live are more exposed to more of these threats, some are more sensitive to specific effects, and some have more resources to prepare, adapt, and recover to climate changes and climate-related disasters. Some of the worst impacts of climate change are expected to be experienced by already disadvantaged and vulnerable populations. For example, most of those vulnerable to coastal flooding from rising sea levels are in developing countries in Asia, and extreme temperatures are expected to be more frequent in developing countries than elsewhere (UNDP, 2020).

Although the consumer lifestyle and heavy fossil fuel use of people in most developed nations are the major contributors to climate change and environmental degradation, people in developing nations are more vulnerable to the effects of climate change (UNDP, 2020). People of the Global South are more likely to have livelihoods dependent on natural resources sensitive to climate change and to lack the technology, resources, and infrastructures to adapt and recover (UNDP, 2020). Climate instability has created more frequent and intense natural disasters; 98 percent of those killed and affected are from developing nations (UNDP, 2014). While in the Global North, climate change may mean adjusting thermostats, observing weather changes, and spending more on flood abatement, in the Southern hemisphere it means more hunger from crop failures and water shortages, increased workloads, migration, and more death and displacement from natural disasters (UNDP, 2020).

Women and Environmental Sustainability

Women in developing regions play an important role in environmental sustainability. They are often natural resource managers that live off the land even though they rarely own it (UNDP, 2020). For example, in many developing nations, rural and indigenous women collect fuel and water, harvest medicinal resources from local forests, fish, and grow small-scale crops to feed their families or sell at markets. This gives them local environmental knowledge and resource management skills, but it also affects their vulnerability to unsustainable development, including climate change.

We know that the effects of climate change and environmental degradation are not gender-neutral in developing regions. For example, due to gendered divisions of labor, climate change and environmental degradation impact women's labor in unique ways. In Nepal, for instance, forest destruction has reduced the availability of the non-wood forest products (such as grasses and medicinal plants) that women harvest to sell in the market (GGCA, 2016). Also, as you already know, women and girls are usually the primary collectors of fuel and water. When climate change reduces waterfall and increases drought, it can take girls and women many more hours to accomplish these tasks (UNDP, 2020). Contaminated water supplies (from fertilizers/pesticides, mining runoff, industrial pollution, or natural disasters resulting from climate change) increase women's workloads when they must travel farther for safe water. Polluted water also increases women's labor because women usually care for those who are sick with diarrhea and other water-borne diseases. Nearly half of people in low- and middle-income countries have one or more major diseases from polluted water and poor sanitation (Langer et al., 2015). Notably, increased workloads from climate change and environmental degradation interfere with the attainment of gender equality because they reduce women's time and opportunities for education, literacy, income-generation, and political activity.

Traditional gender norms and roles also affect women's ability to escape climate change–related natural disasters, like flooding. For example, social norms and customs can impede women's ability to escape rising water levels. In some places, girls and women aren't taught how to swim or climb trees. Women's traditional clothing can limit their mobility. Religious and cultural restrictions against women traveling without a male chaperone may prevent them from leaving. Consequently, in some developing nations, women's survival rates following natural disasters are lower than men's (Langer et al., 2015; Thomas et al., 2019; UNDP, 2020). For instance, parts of Bangladesh are already experiencing the effects of climate change in the form of cyclones, rising sea levels, and coastal and river flooding. But in Bangladeshi cultures where women's modesty is highly valued, women may not evacuate to shelters without separate facilities for women. Women may not even hear public evacuation warnings made in public spaces because cultural practices (like *purdah*), keep them close to home (Rahman, 2014).

Women's health in developing nations is also affected by climate change and environmental degradation. Carrying heavy loads of wood or water for longer distances, usually on their heads, leads to head, neck, and back injuries, and causes problems with childbearing (Langer et al., 2015). Traveling long distances for water increases exposure to heat and places women at risk for abuse (Sorenson, 2018). As the primary water carriers and managers, women have the most contact with polluted water and are therefore most vulnerable to water-related diseases (UNDP, 2009). Women are also more susceptible to some climate-related health impacts (Sorensen et al., 2018). Extreme heat, for example, can increase maternal morbidities including preeclampsia and preterm births, dehydration, and hyperthermia, especially when social norms require women to wear heavy traditional clothing. Ecological disasters linked to climate change displace more than 20 million people every year (UNHCR, 2020). In the aftermath of ecological disasters and relocation, women are at-risk for increased domestic violence, sexual assault, and sex trafficking (UNCC, 2019). Menstrual management and obtaining reproductive health care are also problems faced by women in these situations.

Empowering women is important in the mitigation of climate change and other environmental impacts. Climate change responses are more effective when they consider women's experiences, knowledge, and skills, and when they provide gender empowerment opportunities (UNEP, 2020). For instance, research in Nepal and Gujarat, India shows that gender equality in forest management benefits forest ecology and gender equality (Agarwal, 2010). But in patriarchal societies, gendered power imbalances can prevent women from having a say in the management of local environmental resources affected by climate change and environmental degradation even when they are directly affected (Nyukuri, 2016; UNEP, 2020).

Global Women's Environmental Defenders

Women's activism, both locally and globally, is largely responsible for the growing acknowledgment that women are important contributors to sustainable development.

Globally, transnational women's NGOs (we call these WINGOs) form global coalitions that ensure gender is included in intergovernmental environmental agreements (agreements between governments). WINGOs also promote gender mainstreaming in development programs and projects. Historically speaking, the 1991 World Women's Congress for a Healthy Planet organized by the Women's Environment and Development Organization (WEDO) laid the foundation for international women's environmental advocacy. There, 1,500 women from 83 countries prepared for the 1992 UN Conference on Economic Development (UNCED), sometimes called the Rio Earth Summit. Collectively they created and ratified the Women's Action Agenda 21 to guide their advocacy for the inclusion of women's concerns at the UN conference. Gender issues were given very little attention in the preparatory committees for UNCED (Brandiotti et al., 1994; Elliot, 1996). It took intense lobbying by a caucus of women's NGOs and transnational feminist networks before gender was considered. Ultimately, the Rio summit yielded "Agenda 21" which included a call for governments to strengthen the role of women in creating and implementing sustainable development strategies. In 2012, the UN Conference on Sustainable Development, known as Rio+20, was held. Once again, a coalition of over 200 women's organizations from around the world worked around the clock to maintain previous commitments to gender equality and sustainability. Unfortunately, they were unable to obtain additional commitments (WEDO, 2012).

One outcome of the 1992 Rio summit was the formation of the Women's Major Group (WMG), a coalition of organizations working for sustainable development with a focus on women's empowerment and equality. Today, the WMG is made up of more than 600 women's organizations and women's networks from all over the world. The WMG continues to contribute to intergovernmental negotiations on sustainable development and the environment. For example, in 2014, WMG participated in the development of the UN's Sustainable Development Goals (SDGs), also known as the 2030 Agenda for Sustainable Development. Governments are expected to incorporate the goals into their planning, policies, and strategies. Coordinated by WINGOs like WEDO, Women in Europe for a Common Future (WECF), and the Women Environmental Programme (WEP), WMG pushed (with some success) for adding a gender perspective throughout the 17 SDG goals and for including specific gender-responsive targets (each general goal includes multiple targets). The final SDGs include a specific goal (Goal 5) dedicated to achieving gender equality and the empowerment of all women and girls. Of the 169 goal targets across the seventeen goals, 19 (11.2%) relate to gender equality/inequality or to specific girl and women's issues. Box 6.5 shows the Sustainable Development Goals.

"Women's knowledge, agency and collective action has huge potential to improve resource productivity, enhance ecosystem conservation and sustainable use of natural resources, and to create more sustainable, low-carbon food, energy, water and health systems. Women should not be viewed as victims, but as central actors in moving toward sustainability." *Phumzile Mlambo-Ngcuka, Executive Director, UN Women*

The United Nations Fourth World Conference for Women's Platform for Action, adopted unanimously by 189 delegations in Beijing in September 1995, also includes a section on women and the environment. This too resulted from transnational feminist environmental advocacy. Three strategic objectives are detailed: (1) involve women actively in environmental decision-making at all levels; (2) integrate gender concerns and perspectives in policies and programs for sustainable development; and (3) strengthen or establish mechanisms at the national, regional, and international levels to assess the impact of development and environmental policies on women. However, some feminist environmentalists were disappointed because the terms "environmental justice" and "environmental racism" were left out. These terms would have clearly reflected the fact that a disproportionate share of the burden of environmental degradation is experienced by the poor and by ethnic and indigenous groups that are low in power. In 2008, the UN Commission on the Status of Women (also known as Beijing +10), adopted a resolution urging governments to integrate a gender perspective in national environmental policies. The resolution called for the full inclusion of women in environmental decision making, especially regarding climate change and the lives of women and girls.

Climate justice is about recognizing that some groups are more vulnerable to the impacts of climate change even though they have contributed to it the least. It demands that responses to climate change are fair and do not benefit some groups while harming others. It is about empowering people to craft a daptive local responses to mitigate and cope with the effects of climate change. Climate justice is also about involving people in the climate-change decision-making that impacts their lives. WINGOs operate across national borders to foster global climate justice coalitions of grassroots groups. For example, the Women's Earth and Climate Action Network International (WECAN) began at the 2013 Women's Earth and Climate Change Caucus's (WECC) International Women's Earth and Climate Summit. The summit was a meeting of over 100 women environmental leaders from around the world. Participants recognized the need for a long-term, diverse, decentralized mechanism for women's climate justice organizing and the WECC became WECAN.

BOX 6.5 *The 2015 Sustainable Development Goals*

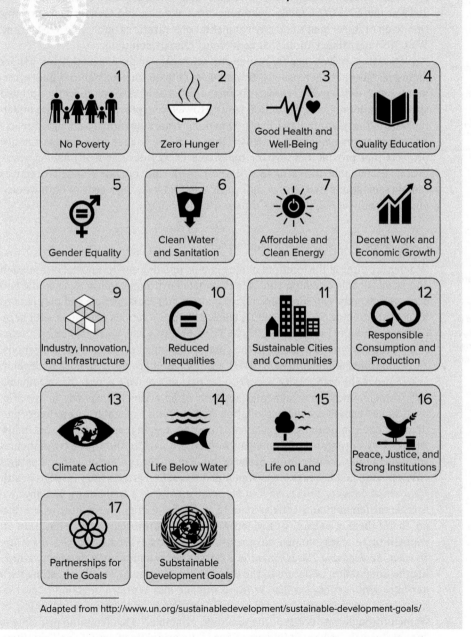

1 No Poverty	2 Zero Hunger	3 Good Health and Well-Being	4 Quality Education
5 Gender Equality	6 Clean Water and Sanitation	7 Affordable and Clean Energy	8 Decent Work and Economic Growth
9 Industry, Innovation, and Infrastructure	10 Reduced Inequalities	11 Sustainable Cities and Communities	12 Responsible Consumption and Production
13 Climate Action	14 Life Below Water	15 Life on Land	16 Peace, Justice, and Strong Institutions
17 Partnerships for the Goals	Substainable Development Goals		

Adapted from http://www.un.org/sustainabledevelopment/sustainable-development-goals/

In 2016, WECAN members attended the 2016 UN Framework Convention on Climate Change (UNFCC) COP22 talks where they marched in the streets, held public events and press conferences, and advocated for climate justice and women's leadership. WECAN also operates as a GRSO by supporting grassroots

The Global Gender and Climate Alliance (GGCA) is an alliance of 90 UN agencies and international organizations (including the Women's Environment and Development Organization). It was formed in 2007 to ensure climate change policies at the global, regional, and national levels are gender responsive.

GROs and working with GRO leaders to develop local climate change responses. The Women's Global Call for Climate Justice and Gender CC-Women for Climate Justice are two other WINGOs that focus on gender and climate justice. In 2019 at the UNFCC COP25 conference, the Women and Gender Constituency (made up of 33 women's and environmental organizations, including WEDO and WECAN) negotiated additional gender-just climate solutions.

Due to activism, gender-responsive language (including a call for gender mainstreaming) is increasingly common in climate change policies and agreements, and most major climate-financing mechanisms have recently adopted specific gender policies and action plans. However, in practice, women are under-represented in planning and decision-making regarding climate change impacts and other environmental problems. There is also evidence that climate finance projects that provide funding for renewable energy development, habitat restoration, sustainable infrastructure development, and climate-resilient practices remain men-dominated, and do not sufficiently address the needs of both women and men (Global Gender and Climate Alliance, 2016).

Local Women Environmental Defenders

"I will come back and I will be millions."
Bertha Càceres of Honduras, who led a fight against the Agua Zarca dam and was murdered in 2016 due to her efforts

"We regard the Earth as our human body. That stone is our bone. Water is our blood. Land is our flesh and the forest is our hair. If one of them is taken away, we are paralyzed."
Aleta Baun (Mama Aleta), Indonesia

Women are often at the forefront of movements resisting environmental degradation and unsustainable development. Men dominate environmentalism as scientific and economic experts, entrepreneurs, policy makers, and spokespeople and they tend to focus on technological and scientific climate change solutions consistent with hegemonic masculinity (MacGregor, 2010). Perhaps this is why much of women's activism for the environment occurs in the context of women's grassroots organizations.

Grassroots organizations (GROs), locally based groups that work to develop and improve the community, are a regular part of women's action for sustainability. Women's local environmental activism often arises in response to specific, local issues caused by the exploitation and pollution of natural resources, particularly environmentally unsustainable mining, logging, and agribusiness industries run by corporations. Some say women are usually the first environmental activists in their communities, because they are in direct contact with the natural environment, and because environmental degradation affects their family's health (Dobash & Seager, 2001). As Vandana Shiva (1988), a well-known Indian environmental feminist and activist said, "I know for certain, no matter where you go, that if there is a scarcity of water, women have protested; if there has been an over-felling of trees, women have resisted it." Shiva's 1988 book, *Staying Alive: Women, Ecology and Development* is a classic in ecofeminism, a perspective linking the domination of nature to the domination of women. That book, along with her later writings, argues that Western science and Western economic development have created both environmental destruction and the marginalization of women through the "death of the feminine principle." This feminine principle is "not exclusively embodied in women but is the principle of activity and creativity in nature, women, and men" (Shiva, 1988, p. 52).

The **Chipko movement** in the forests of Uttar Pradesh (now Uttarakhand), India, is a famous example of a GRO that developed due to concerns about unsustainable

---

BOX 6.6   *Activist Profile: Aleta Baun (Mama Aleta)*

Indonesia is a country in Southeast Asia with more than 300 ethnic groups. Until recently, Indonesia was considered a developing country. Aleta Baun, or "Mama Aleta" as she is known, lives on Indonesia's Timor Island. She is an indigenous Mollo woman. In the 1980s, mining companies began exploiting the lush forested mountains' rich reserves of oil, gas, gold, and marble with little consideration for environmental sustainability. This development resulted in landslides, deforestation, and polluted rivers—all resources critical to the survival of the indigenous Mollo people. When the mining companies set their sights on the sacred mountain Bukit Naususu, Mama Aleta had enough. She knew that mining operations on the mountain would destroy the water quality of the three rivers that met at the base of the mountain. She began traveling from village to village by foot with two other women, sometimes walking for 6 hours from one village to another. Her goals: educate about the effects of the mining operations and organize resistance. Despite intimidation and beatings by those wishing to stop her (at one point she had to go into hiding), the movement grew. It culminated in a peaceful protest. For a year, more than 150 women camped out at the entrance of an active marble mine (they called their group Pokja OAT). They brought their looms and wove their traditional tapestries while their husbands took care of things at home. Their protest brought the problem to the attention of the public and government officials. Finally, in 2010, the mining companies stopped operations. Mama Aleta's campaign won the Goldman Environmental Prize in 2013. Today Baun and Pokja OAT help local communities assert their rights to tribal forests so developers cannot take them without consent.

Sources: Cimons, 2016; Goldman Environmental Prize, 2013; Ramdas & Garcia, 2021.

---

development. In 1974, conflict escalated between logging companies supported by the state and the natives who depended upon the forest for food and fuel. The villagers were alarmed because they already suffered due to erosion and flooding caused by prior commercial logging. Village men were away on the day the contractors arrived to cut 2,500 trees, but village women took action. They wrapped themselves around the trees (*chipko* means "hug") and refused to move until the contractors left. The contractors left, and Chipko protesters continued their protests using a variety of techniques grounded in Mahatma Gandhi's concept of nonviolent resistance. In 1980, Indira Gandhi (the Prime Minister of India at the time) issued a 15-year ban on commercial logging in the forests of Uttar Pradesh. Many credit the Chipko movement for this and consider the Chipko movement to be the mother of the environmental movement in India (Ishizaka, 2013; Poonia, 2016). Box 6.6 tells the story of "Mama Aleta," who led a recent grassroots campaign against mining companies in Indonesia.

Women's environmental activism is sometimes perilous. In patriarchal societies, women face extra risks because they are defending not only the environment, but their right to speak up (UNEP, 2020). Box 6.6 tells the story of "Mama Aleta," who led a recent grassroots campaign against mining companies in Indonesia. Like many women environmental defenders, Aleta Baun faced threats of sexual violence and rape, and death. Men environmental defenders are also silenced with jail, threatened, and murdered (9 of 10 murdered environmental activists in 2020 were men). However, efforts to silence women environmental defenders also

"The forest nurtures us like a mother; you will only be able to use your axes on it, but you have to use them on us first."
Gaura Devi, an early leader of the Chipko movement

include sexual harassment and sexual violence (Global Witness, 2020). Despite these risks, women environmental defenders are active on every continent. Many are indigenous women like Aleta Baun, defending their ancestral lands and livelihoods.

Grassroots support organizations (GRSOs), nationally or regionally based development assistance organizations, usually staffed by professionals, also channel funds to grassroots organizations to help communities other than their own to develop. The **Greenbelt movement** in Kenya is a well-known example of the role of GRSOs in sustainable development involving women. Kenyan feminist, environmentalist, and national leader Wangari Maathai, in conjunction with the National Council of Women of Kenya, started the movement in 1977. By the 1970s, severe deforestation and soil erosion had created a shortage of fuelwood and food. The movement organized women to plant and manage trees for fuelwood and to guard against erosion. Maathai explained her focus on women by noting that it is women who use wood fuel for cooking and who also till the land (Katumba & Akute, 1993). As of 2015, more than 51 million trees have been planted, and the movement now includes over 4,000 community groups that promote sustainable environmental management and community empowerment as well as tree planting (Greenbelt Movement, 2015). The movement has been replicated in 12 other African countries including, Tanzania, Uganda, Malawi, Lesotho, Ethiopia, and Zimbabwe (Greenbelt Movement, 2009). Maathai died of ovarian cancer in 2011 and today, her daughter, Wanjira Mathai continues the work her mother started (Kirui, 2021). See Box 6.7 for an excerpt from Maathai's Nobel Peace Prize acceptance speech.

"Women are living on the frontlines of climate change, and are ready to be active partners in dealing with climate change. If the international community is serious about addressing climate change, it must recognize women as a fundamental part of the climate change solution."
Professor Wangari Maathai

Conclusion

This chapter reinforces the importance of a multicultural, intersectional approach to global women's and gender studies. Although women everywhere experience some of the same gendered inequalities, women in developing nations face additional gendered challenges to their health and survival. A lack of technology and infrastructure, along with the effects of environmental degradation and climate change, often lead to heavy workloads for women and girls. In some areas, patriarchal family structures and legal barriers to women's land ownership reduce their access to development resources and their input into development decisions. Effective development projects and programs take into account the local context, recognize that development is not gender-neutral, and involve both men and women in the development process. Likewise, gender and culture, as well as geography, affect climate change impacts and responses, and so should be considered for sustainable development.

The global women's studies' theme of activism and empowerment is evident in the study of women and development. Feminists generally favor the gender and development approach to development because it integrates development, gender equality, and women's empowerment. It also specifically emphasizes that gender equality should be part of development and that women should be empowered for effective development. Thousands of GRSOs advocate for gender mainstreaming

"Women do not want to be mainstreamed into a polluted stream. We want to clean the stream and transform it into a fresh and flowing body. One that moves in a new direction—a world at peace, that respects human rights for all, renders economic justice and provides a sound and healthy environment."
Bella S. Abzug, U.S. Congresswoman and Women's Environment and Development Organization (WEDO) co-founder

BOX 6.7 *Activist Profile: Wangari Maathai*

A founder of the Greenbelt Movement in Kenya, Maathai was the first woman in East and Central Africa to earn a doctorate degree (her specialty is veterinary anatomy). She is also the first African woman to garner a Nobel Prize and during her lifetime received dozens of international awards acknowledging her for promoting democracy, human rights, and environmental sustainability. She held a variety of positions, including professor, director of the Kenyan Red Cross, member of the Kenyan Parliament, and Assistant Minister of the Environment, Natural Resources and Wildlife. She was a leading global advocate for the cancellation of unpayable development loan debt for African nations. Professor Maathai died in 2011 at age 71 from ovarian cancer. Here is an excerpt from her Nobel Peace Prize acceptance speech in 2004.

> In 1977, when we started the GreenBelt Movement, I was partly responding to needs identified by rural women, namely lack of firewood, clean drinking water, balanced diets, shelter, and income.
>
> The women we worked with recounted that unlike in the past, they were unable to meet their basic needs. This was due to the degradation of their immediate environment as well as the introduction of commercial farming, which replaced the growing of household food crops. But international trade controlled the price of the exports from these small-scale farmers and a reasonable and just income could not be guaranteed.
>
> Through the GreenBelt Movement, thousands of ordinary citizens were mobilized and empowered to take action and affect change. They learned to overcome fear and a sense of helplessness and moved to defend democratic rights.
>
> It is 30 years since we started this work. Activities that devastate the environment and societies continue unabated. Today we are faced with a challenge that calls for a shift in our thinking, so that humanity stops threatening its life-support system. We are called to assist the Earth to heal her wounds and in the process heal our own— indeed, to embrace the whole creation in all its diversity, beauty, and wonder. This will happen if we see the need to revive our sense of belonging to a larger family of life, with which we have shared our evolutionary process.

Sources: Greenbelt Movement, 2009, 2015; Nobelprize.org, 2004.

in development, provide support to grassroots organizations, and form international coalitions to influence international policies and agreements. They work to ensure that women and girls are not forgotten in the development process and in intergovernmental development agreements. Hundreds of thousands of women's NGOs and courageous women organize locally to challenge and change their situations. This activism will continue because, to borrow a phrase from Jahan (1995), development agencies and organizations have only tinkered with the constraints on women's equality. They have yet to come forward with bold policies and adequate budgetary allocations. Networking and political pressure from a variety of women's organizations, which build on what happens at the local level, scale out the impact of women's NGOs at the grassroots level and scale up their impact on policy (Fisher, 1996).

Glossary Terms and Concepts

Bilateral aid

Development

Chipko movement

Climate change

Climate justice

Development programs
  and projects

Gender and development
  (or empowerment)
  approach (GAD)

Grassroots organization
  (GRO)

Grassroots support
  organization (GRSO)

Greenbelt movement

Least developed
  countries (LDCs)

Microcredit

Modernization theory

Multilateral aid

Neocolonialism

Gender mainstreaming

Global North (developed
  or industrial countries)

Global South (developing
  nations)

Sustainable development

Sustainable Development
  Goals (SDGs)

Women in development
  (WID)

Women's international
  nongovernmental
  organizations
  (WINGOs)

Study Questions

1. What are developing nations and the "Global South"? What are LDCs? What are development projects and programs, and who funds them?

2. How does a past history of colonialism affect development efforts?

3. What are some of the challenges faced by women in the Global South compared to women in the Global North?

4. Does modernization necessarily lead to increases in women's status?

5. What are the four common feminist criticisms of traditional development programs?

6. What is the "Women in Development (WID)" approach to development? What are the three types of typical WID projects? What criticisms are made of these? Why is the WID approach criticized?

7. How does the "Gender and Development (GAD)" or empowerment approach differ from WID?

8. What is gender mainstreaming, and why have development agencies adopted it? How has it worked in practice? What do feminists recommend that development agencies do if they really want to support the empowerment piece of GAD?

9. What is sustainable development? When is development unsustainable? How do neocolonialism and the high consumption rates of the Global North imperil sustainable development?

10. What is climate change? How do human activities and development contribute to climate change? What are the effects of climate change? Who is expected to bear the brunt of climate change impacts?

11. What does it mean to say the effects of climate change are not "gender neutral"? How are women in the Global South affected by climate change?

How does gender inequality affect impacts on women and women's participation in climate change adaptation and mitigation?

12. What are the roles of GROs, GRSOs, and WINGOs in promoting environmental sustainability?

Discussion Questions and Activities

1. Choose an LDC from the list provided in Box 6.1. Do research to answer these questions about your chosen country: How is the country impacted by climate change? Are some groups more affected by climate change than others? How does gender affect the experience of climate change? How has development impacted environmental sustainability? Are women's GRO or GRSOs acting on behalf of environmental sustainability and in response to climate change?

2. Do international development agencies have the right to promote gender equality as part of development? Is it morally wrong for them not to?

3. Consider this quote from DAWN's Peggy Antrobus: "We must never lose sight of the fact that the women's movement and the environmental movement are primarily *revolutionary* movements. If we give up that political challenge to the dominant paradigm, there is no hope for change." What do you think she means? Do you agree?

4. One theme in this chapter is the importance of including women in development. Gender is included in the UN's Sustainable Development Goals" shown in Box 6.5. Look at the SDGs and SDG targets (https://sdgs.un.org./2030agenda). Do you think the goals and targets sufficiently address gender equality and the empowerment of girls and women?

5. Find examples of development projects that reflect the WID and GAD approaches by visiting development agency or women's NGO websites (the list provided at the end of the chapter may be useful).

6. The chapter suggests that women's organizations play a key role in ensuring that women are included in development efforts. Do you think that eventually this may not be necessary? What would have to happen for their efforts to be no longer needed in this way?

7. Why should people in the Global North care whether their fossil fuel use, consumption patterns, and corporate practices impact people in the Global South? Why should they care about the significant challenges facing women in developing countries? What changes should they make if they care? What are the barriers to their caring and changing?

8. Write a short paper on an indigenous woman environmental defender like Bertha Caceres of Honduras. Show how their actions illustrate the importance of environmental activism and why it arises.

Action Opportunities

1. OXFAM is one of the world's leading NGOs and has a GAD focus. Join an OXFAM letter writing or fundraising campaign. (https://www.oxfam.org/en /take-action/campaigns).

2. One focus of this chapter was poverty. You can act locally or globally to reduce poverty. Locally, do a canned food drive for your local food bank, or volunteer at community organizations that serve low-income women. Globally, you can raise money for a NGO that recognizes the role of women's empowerment in alleviating poverty, such as The Hunger Project (https://thp.org).

3. The chapter indicated that nations of the Northern hemisphere are the biggest contributors to global warming. Do some research to determine how you, your household, or your workplace can reduce your contributions to climate change. Then create a sustainable behavior plan based on education (to motivate), reminders (to help people develop new habits), and modifications to your home or workplace to make the desired behaviors easier. Put it into action and monitor the results.

4. Join the Greenbelt movement's "Be a hummingbird" project with ideas from http://www.greenbeltmovement.org/get-involved/be-a-hummingbird.

5. Become a microlender with Kiva. Raise and donate money to support a women's small-scale enterprise at https://www.kiva.org/lend-by-category /women.

Activist Websites

Development Alternatives with Women for a New Era (DAWN) https://dawnnet.org

Gender Action (promotes gender justice in the World Bank and IMF) http://www .genderaction.org

Global Fund for Women https://globalfundforwomen.org/take-action

International Women's Development Association https://www.iwda.org.au

Pro Mujer (Latin American women's development organization) http://promujer.org

Women in Europe for a Common Future http://www.wecf.eu

Women's Environment and Development Organization http://wedo.org

WoMin (African Women Unite Against Destructive Resource Extraction) https:// womin.africa

Women's Organisation in Rural Development (WORD, India) http://www.wordorg.net

Informational Websites

AWID (Association for Women in Development) http://www.awid.org/

Gender & Development (the world's only journal focusing on international gender and development issues) http://www.tandfonline.com/toc/cgde20/current

Gender CC (Women for Climate Justice) http://www.gendercc.net/home.html

The Greenbelt Movement http://www.greenbeltmovement.org/who-we-are

United Nations Development Programme Human Development Report http://hdr .undp.org

UN Women (climate and the environment) https://www.unwomen.org/en/how-we -work/ingergovernmental-support/climate-change

UN Food and Agriculture Organization http://www.fao.org/gender/en/

United Nations Fourth World Conference on Women Platform for Action: Women and the Environment http://www.un.org/womenwatch/daw/beijing /platform/environ.htm

References

Acosta-Belen, E., and Bose, C. E. 1995. Colonialism, structural subordination, and empowerment: Women in the development process in Latin America and the Caribbean. In *Women in the Latin American development process*, edited by C. E. Bose and E. Acosta-Belen. Philadelphia, PA: Temple University Press.

Adusei-Asante, K., Hancock, P., and Oliveira, M. 2015. Gender mainstreaming and women's roles in development projects: A research study from Ghana. *Advances in Gender Research,* 20, 177–198.

Agarwal, B. 2010. *Gender and green governance: The political economy of women's presence within and beyond community forestry.* Oxford: Oxford University Press.

Anand, A. 1993. *The power to change: Women in the Third World redefine their environment.* London: Zed.

Banerjee, A., Karlan, D., and Zinman, J. 2015. Six randomized evaluations of micro-credit: Introduction and further steps. *American Economic Journal: Applied Economics,* 7, 1–21.

Benería, L., and Roldan, M. 1987. *The crossroads of class and gender: Industrial homework, subcontracting, and household dynamics in Mexico City.* Chicago, IL: University of Chicago Press.

Benería, L., Berik, G., and Floro, M. 2015. *Gender, development and globalization: Economics as if all people mattered.* United Kingdom: Routledge

Blumberg, R. L. 1995. Gender, microenterprise, performance, and power: Case studies from the Dominican Republic, Ecuador, Guatemala, and Swaziland. In *Women in the Latin American development process*, edited by C. E. Bose and E. Acosta-Belen. Philadelphia, PA: Temple University Press.

Boserup, E. 1970. *Women's role in economic development.* New York: St. Martin's Press.

Brandiotti, R., Charkiewicz, E., Hausler, S., and Wieringa, S. 1994. *Women, the environment, and sustainable development.* Santo Domingo, Dominican Republic: INSTRAW.

Bryceson, D. F. 1995. Wishful thinking: Theory and practice of western donor efforts to raise women's status in rural Africa. In *Women wielding the hoe: Lessons for feminist theory and development practice*, edited by D. F. Bryceson. Oxford: Berg Publishers.

Chant, S. 2016. Women, girls and world poverty: Empowerment, equality, or essentialism? *IDPR,* 38, 1–24.

Chant, S., and Sweetman, C. 2012. Fixing women or fixing the world? "Smart economics," efficiency approaches, and gender equality in development. *Gender and Development,* 20, 517–529.

Charlesworth, H. 2005. Not waving but drowning: Gender mainstreaming and human rights in the United Nations. *Harvard Human Rights Journal, 18*, 1–18.

Cimons. M. 2016. Women are the ones fighting the tough environmental battles around the world. *Think Progress.* https://archive.thinkprogress.org/women -are-the-ones-fighting-the-tough-environmental-battles-around-the-world -ed3c3a0e09e2/. Retrieved on June 3, 2021.

Cornwall, A., and Rivas, A. M. 2015. From gender equality and 'women's empow-erment to global justice: Reclaiming a transformative agenda for gender and development. *Third World Quarterly, 36*, 396–415.

Das, K., Pradhan, G., and Nonhebel, S. 2019. Human energy and time spent by women using cooking energy systems: A case study of Nepal. *Energy, 182*, 493–501.

Dobash, M., and Seager, J. 2001. *Putting women in place: Feminist geographers make sense of the world.* New York: Guilford Press.

Dolker, T. 2020. Where is the money for feminist organizing? New analysis finds that the answer is alarming. *AWID.* https://www.awid.org/news-and-analysis /where-money-feminist-organising-new-analysis-finds-answer-alarming. Retrieved on April 30, 2021.

Duley, M. I., and Diduk, S. 1986. Women, colonialism, and development. In *The cross-cultural study of women: A comprehensive guide*, edited by M. I. Duley and M. I. Edwards. New York: Feminist Press.

Elliot, L. 1996. Women, gender, feminism, and the environment. In *The gendered new world order*, edited by J. Turpin and L. A. Lorentzen. New York: Routledge.

Food and Agriculture Organization of the United Nations (FAO). 2009. *Gender and food security fact files: One woman's day in Sierra Leone.* http://www.fao .org/gender/en/Facte/FL9719-e.htm. Retrieved on August 6, 2009.

Food and Agriculture Organization of the United Nations (FAO). 2020. *The state of food and agriculture 2020.* http://www.fao.org/documents/card/en/c /cb1447en/. Retrieved on May 1, 2021.

Fisher, J. 1996. Sustainable development and women: The role of NGOs. In *The gendered new world order: Militarism, development, and the environment*, edited by J. Turpin and L. A. Lorentzen. New York: Routledge.

Forrester, A. 1995. From stabilization to growth with equity: A case for financing women in development programs. In *Women and the United Nations*, edited by F. C. Steady and R. Toure. Rochester, VT: Schenkman Books.

Global Witness. 2020. *Global Witness records the highest number of land and environmental activists murdered in one year—with the link to accelerating climate change of increasing concern.* https://www.globalwitness.org/en/press-releases /global-witness-records-the-highest-number-of-land-and-environmental-activists -murdered-in-one-year-with-the-link-to-accelerating-climate-change-of-increasing -concern/. Retrieved on May 4, 2021.

GGCA (Global Gender and Climate Change Alliance). 2016. *Gender and climate change: A closer look at existing evidence.* http://gender-climate.org/wp-content /uploads/2014/10/GGCA-RP-110616.pdf. Retrieved on February 22, 2017.

Goldman Environmental Prize. 2013. Aleta Baun. http://www.goldmanprize.org /recipient/aleta-baun/. Retrieved on March 2, 2017.

Greenbelt Movement. 2009. http://www.greenbeltmovement.org/w.php?id=3. Retrieved on August 1, 2009.

Greenbelt Movement. 2015. 2015 annual report. http://www.greenbeltmovement .org/sites/greenbeltmovement.org/files/GBM%202015%20Annual%20Report .pdf. Retrieved on March 2, 2017.

Greenfacts. 2009. *Scientific facts on forests.* http://greenfacts.org. Retrieved on August 9, 2009.

InterAction. 2010. The gender audit handbook: A tool for organizational self-assessment and transformation. https://www.interaction.org/sites/default/files/Gender%20 Audit%20Handbook%202010%20Copy.pdf. Retrieved on February 17, 2017.

Intergovernmental Panel on Climate Change (IPCC). 2018. *Global warming of 1.5°C: An IPCC special report on the impacts of global warming of 1.5°C above pre-industrial levels and related global greenhouse emission pathways, in the context of strengthening the global response to the threat of climate change, sustainable development, and efforts to eradicate poverty.* Geneva: World Meteorological Association.

Ishizaka, S. 2013. Reevaluating the Chipko (forest protection) movement in India. *The South Asianist,* 2, 9–27.

Jahan, R. 1995. Men in seclusion, women in public: Rokeya's dream and women's struggles in Bangladesh. In *The challenge of local feminisms: Women's movements in global perspective*, edited by A. Basu. Boulder, CO: Westview Press.

Jaquette, J. S., and Staudt, K. 2006. Women, gender, and development. In *Women and gender equity in development theory and practice: Institutions, resources, and mobilization*, edited by J. S. Jaquette and G. Summerfield. Durham, NC: Duke University Press.

Johnson, N. L., Kovarik, C., Meinzen-Dick, R., Njuki, J., and Quisumbing, A. 2016. Gender, assets, and agricultural development: Lessons from eight projects. *World Development, 83,* 295–311.

Katumba, R., and Akute, W. 1993. Greening takes root. *The Power to Change.* London: Zed.

Kende-Robb, C. 2019. To improve women's access to finance, stop asking them for collateral. *World Economic Forum.* https://www.weforum.org/agenda/2019/06/ women-finance-least-developed-countries-collateral/. Retrieved on April 29, 2021.

Kirui, D. 2021. How Wangari Maathai's daughter carries on her mother's bold fight for green spaces in Kenya. *Waging Nonviolence.* https://wagingnonviolence.org/2021/03/wanjira-mathai-green-belt-wagari-maathai/. Retrieved on May 4, 2021.

Klugman, J., and Melnikova, T. 2016. *Unpaid work and care: A policy brief.* https://www.empowerwomen.org/~/media/uploads/unwomen/empowerwomen/resourceimages/unpaid%20work%20%20carepolicy%20brief-20161130175412.pdf. Retrieved on December 12, 2016

Langer, A., Meleis, A., Knaul, F. M., Atun, R., Aran, M., Arreola-Ornelas, H. et al. 2015. Women and Health: The key for sustainable development. *The Lancet,* 386, 1165–1210.

MacGregor, S. 2010. A stranger silence still: The need for feminist social research on climate change. *The Sociological Review, 57,* 124–140.

Manfre, C., Rubin, D., Allen, A., Summerfield, G., Colverson, K., and Akeredolu, M. 2013. *Reducing the gender gap in agricultural extension and advisory services: How to find the best fit for men and women farmers.* MEAS discussion paper. http://dev.meas.illinois.edu/wp-content/uploads/2015/04/Manfre-et-al-2013-Gender-and-Extension-MEAS-Discussion-Paper.pdf. Retrieved on February 11, 2017.

Mermel, A., and Simons, J. 1991. *Women and world development: An education and action guide.* Washington, DC: OEF International.

Montanari, B., and Bergh, S. 2019. A gendered analysis of the income generating activities under the Green Morocco plan: Who profits? *Human Ecology, 47,* 409–417.

Momsen, J. 2020. *Gender and development,* 3rd ed. New York: Routledge.

Moser, C. 1989. Gender planning in the Third World: Meeting practical and strategical gender needs. *World Development, 17,* 1799–1825.

Mosse, J. C. 1993. *Half the world, half a chance: An introduction to gender and development.* Oxford: Oxfam.

NASA. 2017. *A blanket around the earth.* https://climate.nasa.gov/causes/. Retrieved on February 19, 2017.

National Geographic. 2017. *Deforestation.* http://www.nationalgeographic.com/environment/global-warming/deforestation/. Retrieved on February 19, 2017.

Nobelprize.org. 2004. https://www.nobelprize.org/nobel_prizes/peace/laureates/2004/maathai-facts.html. Retrieved on March 11, 2017.

Nyukuri, E. 2016. Gender approaches in climate compatible development: Lessons from Kenya. *Climate Development Knowledge Network.* https://cdkn.org/wp-content/uploads/2016/05/CDKN_KenyaGenderReport_Pr3Final_WEB-1.pdf. Retrieved on June 24, 2017.

Organisation for Economic Cooperation and Development (OECD). 2020. *Multilateral development finance.* Paris: OECD Publishing.

OECD Gendernet. 2021. *Financing women's economic empowerment.* https://www.oecd.org/development/gender-development/How-does-aid-support-womens-economic-empowerment-2021.pdf. Retrieved on April 30, 2021.

Oxfam. 2020. *Women and care work: Poor in time, choice, and voice.* https://www
.oxfam.org/en/women-and-care-work-poor-time-choice-and-voice. Retrieved on
April 25, 2021.

Parpart, J. L. 2014. Explaining the transformative potential of gender mainstreaming in international development institutions. *Journal of International
Development,* 26, 382–395.

Poonia, M. 2016. Reevaluating the Chipko movement of 1973. *International
Journal of Environmental Sciences,* 6, 839–845.

Prugl, E., and Lustgarten, A. 2006. Mainstreaming gender in international organizations. In *Women and gender equity in development theory and practice: Institutions, resources, and mobilization,* edited by J. S. Jaquette and G. Summerfield.
Durham, NC: Duke University Press.

Rahman, A. K. 2014. Women in natural disasters: A case study from the southern
coastal region of Bangladesh. *International Journal of Risk Reduction,* 8, 68–82.

Ramdas, K. N., and Garcia, L. 2021. Indigenous women are championing climate
justice. *Open Society Foundations: Voices.* https://www.opensocietyfoundations.
org/voices/indigenous-women-are-championing-climate-justice. Retrieved on
May 4, 2021.

Rogers, B. 1980. *The domestication of women: Discrimination in developing societies.*
New York: St. Martin's Press.

Rost, L., Bates, K., and Dellepiane, L. 2015. *Women's economic empowerment and
care.* http://policy-practice.oxfam.org.uk/publications/womens-economic
-empowerment-and-care-evidence-for-influencing-578732. Retrieved on
December 13, 2016.

Ruether, R. R. 2008. *Christianity and social systems: Historical constructions and
ethical challenges.* Lanham, MD: Rowman and Littlefield.

Scothern, A., and Brisbane, J. 2016. *Implementing gender minimum standards:
Approaches, tools, and lessons for the Solomon NGO Partnership Agreement
(SINPA).* https://www.interaction.org/sites/default/files/Gender%20Audit%20
Handbook%202010%20Copy.pdf. Retrieved on February 17, 2017.

Scott, L. 2020. *The double X economy: The epic potential of women's empowerment.*
New York: Farrar, Straus and Giroux.

Sorensen, C., Murray, V., Lemery, J., and Balbus, J. 2018. Climate change and
women's health: Impacts and policy directions. *PLoS Med,* 15. https://www
.ncbi.nim.nih.gov/pmc/articles/PMC6038986/. Retrieved on May 3, 2021.

Sweis, R. F. 2020. Microloans, seen as salvation for poor women, trap many in
debt. *New York Times.* https://www.nytimes.com/2020/04/08/world/middleeast
/microloans-jordan-debt-poverty.html. Retrieved on April 30, 2021.

Sen, G., and C. Grown. 1987. *Development crises and alternative visions.* New York:
Monthly Review Press.

Shiva, V. 1988. *Staying alive: Women, ecology and development.* London: Zed
Books.

United Nations (UN). 2020. *World survey on the role of women in development 2019: Why addressing women's income and time poverty matters for sustainable development.* https://www.unwomen.org/-/media/headquarters/attachments/sections/library/publications/2019/world-survey-on-the-role-of-women-in-development-2019.pdf?la=en&vs=2027. Retrieved on April 25, 2021.

United Nations Climate Change (UNCC). 2019. Climate change increases the risk of violence against women. https://unfccc.int/news/climate-change-increases-the-risk-of-violence-against-women. Retrieved on May 3, 2021.

UN (United Nations). 2002. Gender mainstreaming: An overview. http://www.un.org/womenwatch/osagi/pdf/e65237.pdf. Retrieved on February 17, 2017.

UN DESA. 2019. *Patterns and trends in household size and composition: Evidence from a United Nations dataset.* (ST/ESA/SER.A/433).

UN DESA. 2021. *Least developed countries.* https://www.un.org/development/desa/dpad/least-developed-country-category.html. Retrieved on April 24, 2021.

UNDP (United Nations Development Programme). 2008. *The gender equality strategy 2008-2011.* New York: Author.

UNDP (United Nations Development Programme). 2009. *Climate change affects all the MDGs.* http://www.undp.org/climatechange/climateMDGs.htm. Retrieved on August 6, 2009.

UNDP (United Nations Development Programme). 2011. *Human development report 2011: Sustainability and equity: A better future for all.* http://hdr.undp.org/sites/default/files/reports/271/hdr_2011_en_complete.pdf. Retrieved on February 20, 2017.

UNDP (United Nations Development Programme). 2014. *Human development report 2014: Sustaining human progress: Reducing vulnerabilities and building resilience.* http://hdr.undp.org/sites/default/files/hdr14-report-en-1.pdf. Retrieved on February 20, 2017.

UNDP (United Nations Development Programme). 2016. *Filling buckets, fuelling change.* Retrieved on February 11, 2017.

United Nations Development Programme (UNDP). 2020. *Human development report 2020: The next frontier.* http://report.hdr.undp.org. Retrieved on May 1, 2021.

United Nations Environment Programme (UNEP). 2020. *Gender, climate, and security: Sustaining inclusive peace on the frontlines of climate change.* https://www.unwomen.org/-/media/headquarters/attachments/sections/library/publications/2020/gender-climate-and-security-en.pdf?la=en&vs=215. Retrieved on May 3, 2021.

UNHCR (UN Refugee Agency). 2020. *Climate change and disaster displacement.* https://www.unhcr.org/en-us/climate-change-and-disasters.html. Retrieved on May 3, 2021.

WEDO (Women's Environment and Development Organization). 2012. *From the future we want to the future we need.* http://wedo.org/rio20-from-the-future-we-want-to-the-future-we-need/. Retrieved on February 25, 2017.

World Bank. 2012. *World development report 2012: Gender equality and development.* http://siteresources.worldbank.org/INTWDR2012/Resources /7778105-1299699968583/7786210-1315936222006/Complete-Report.pdf. Retrieved on December 8, 2016.

World Bank. 2020. *Poverty and shared prosperity 2020: Reversals of fortune.* Washington, DC: World Bank.

World Bank. 2021. *Women, business, and the law.* https://openknowledge. worldbank.org/bitstream/handle/10986/35094/9781464816529.pdf. Retrieved on April 25, 2021.

World Commission on Environment and Development. 1987. *Our common future.* Oxford, UK: Oxford University Press. http://www.un-documents.net /our-common-future.pdf. Retrieved on March 11, 2017.

World Resources Institute. 1994–95. *World resources: A guide to the global environment.* Oxford, UK: Oxford University Press.

World Health Organization (WHO) and United Nations Children's Fund (UNICEF). 2017. *Progress on drinking water, sanitation and hygiene 2017.* Geneva: World Health Organization (WHO) and United Nations Children's Fund (UNICEF).

Design Element: Abstract floral frame: Telnov Oleksii/Shutterstock

7

Women and Globalization

Global economic and trade policies are not "gender neutral." The failure of governments and intergovernmental organizations to formulate and evaluate trade policies from a gender perspective has exacerbated women's economic inequity.

—Women's Environment and Development Organization (WEDO)

Women's factory work for transnational corporations is one of the many gendered effects of globalization. This textile worker in Burma produces goods for foreign-owned companies. Many transnational factories employ primarily women and are exempt from labor, health, and safety laws and provide low wages and poor working conditions. Roberto Westbrook/Blend Images LLC

G lobalization refers to the integration of the world's economies, cultures, and societies through a global network of trade and communication. **Economic globalization** refers to the integration and rapid interaction of economies through production, trade, and financial transactions by banks and multinational corporations. Due to economic globalization, the goods consumed by people in one country are often grown, produced, or assembled in other countries, and economic crisis in one country is more likely to affect the economies of other countries. **Cultural globalization** refers to the transnational migration of people, information, and consumer culture. For example, people across the globe watch news and entertainment created in the United States and Western Europe. Global Internet and social media platforms create a global flow of information and provide rapid communication across national boundaries. This chapter discusses how globalization affects women's lives worldwide. It covers such topics as women's work in sweatshops for transnational corporations, women's international migration for work as maids and nannies, "mail-order brides," sex tourism, and sex trafficking.

The Effects of Globalization on Women

Globalization is to some extent a "dirty word" in the international women's rights community. That's primarily because economic globalization is based on **neoliberal economic policies** that emphasize free market corporate capitalism and balanced government budgets that often come at the expense of schools, social services, medical services, public transportation, and utilities (see Figure 7.1 for the basic features of neoliberalism). Neoliberal responses to economic recessions include cuts in wages and social services and rises in the costs of basic goods and services. These neoliberal policies have a greater impact on women because women are normally responsible for providing food, water, and health care for family members (Blumberg, 1995; Lorentzen & Turpin, 1996). Women's unpaid labor increases as government services are cut and women must provide more care for children, elderly parents, and the sick (Chang, 2000; Desai, 2002). Women struggle to feed their families because the prices of household goods, especially food, rise as government subsidies are removed to save the government money and when farmland is converted to commercial use. As pointed out by ethics of care feminists, neoliberalism prioritizes economic growth, efficiency, and profit over equality, human rights, environmental sustainability, and caring for others (Pakekh & Wilcox, 2014).

Due to neoliberal trade policies, corporations headquartered in one country can maximize profits by having their products manufactured in other countries. This economic globalization is associated with the creation of jobs for women in transnational factories. But many of the jobs created for women by globalization are not secure jobs—their availability depends on consumption patterns in northern countries and whether their country provides the most favorable conditions for corporate profit. This means that if demand for consumer products falls in northern countries or corporations can relocate to another country where labor

FIGURE 7.1   *Four Main Features of Neoliberalism*

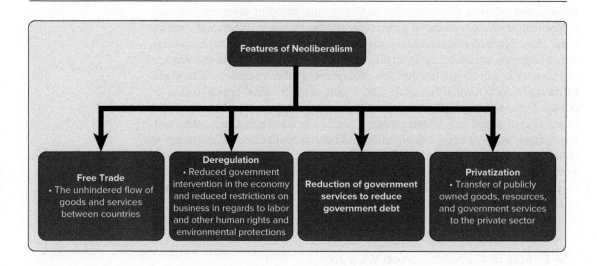

Features of Neoliberalism

Free Trade
• The unhindered flow of goods and services between countries

Deregulation
• Reduced government intervention in the economy and reduced restrictions on business in regards to labor and other human rights and environmental protections

Reduction of government services to reduce government debt

Privatization
• Transfer of publicly owned goods, resources, and government services to the private sector

"About 1,700 people used to work here, and all are unemployed now. Many women were pregnant, many are ill and are left with nothing. It's been three months since the factory closed and we haven't been paid anything, no severance, no social fund payments."
Ana Ruth Cerna, El Salvador

Human trafficking is a crime against humanity. It involves an act of recruiting, transporting, transferring, harbouring or receiving a person through a use of force, coercion or other means, for the purpose of exploiting them.
United Nations Office on Drugs and Crime (UNODC)

regulation is weaker, the jobs disappear. In times of economic downturns and transitions, women are often the first to lose their jobs. Women workers in export manufacturing, garments, electronics, and services (women constitute around 60%–80% of this workforce in developing countries) are especially hard-hit as global demand falls (Emmett, 2009). As will become apparent in this chapter, most of the jobs created by globalization for women are also poorly paid and offer difficult work conditions.

Globalization has also led to dramatic increases in women's migration to other countries for work, another topic of this chapter. When women are unable to sustain their families, they may have no viable option but to leave their families and migrate for work (Chang, 2000). In many cases, migrant women end up in vulnerable types of employment marked by low pay and poor working conditions, and prejudice against migrants prevents their full and equal participation in the host country. Many of the jobs are domestic and care labor jobs that replicate traditional gendered roles and allow more affluent women to participate more equally in the labor force while confining migrant women to low-status gendered roles. Women seeking migration to better their lives are also subject to human traffickers who trick and coerce them into situations of forced labor and sexual exploitation in a form of modern-day slavery. Cultural globalization means increasing global exposure to western media filled with sexually objectifying images of women and values supporting materialism and consumption.

Although these negative effects of globalization on women are real, women sometimes benefit from globalization. Throughout the book, you have read that employment has the potential to increase women's power and status, so you might expect that the creation of jobs for women is a positive benefit of globalization. There is some truth in this. Women in developing countries often cite the benefits of employment, such as the ability to earn independent income and spend it on desired purchases; the ability to save for marriage or education; the ability to help support their families and "repay" their debt to parents; the opportunity to delay marriage and childbearing and to exercise personal choice of a marriage partner; and the opportunity to enjoy some personal freedom, the companionship of other women, and to experience more of what life has to offer, such as a "widening of horizons" (Chant, 1997; Lim, 1990). Data from women of the Global South indicate that a woman's absolute and relative income is tied to increases in self-esteem and confidence, greater leverage in fertility decisions, and greater leverage in other household economic and domestic decisions (Blumberg, 1995). However, whether paid employment benefits a woman depends on whether she has control over the money she makes, whether her wages are sufficient to escape poverty, whether she is still responsible for the majority of household and care labor, and the work conditions. Migration can also benefit women and their families by reducing their poverty. It can allow women to escape patriarchal societies and abusive marriages.

To some extent, globalization has also benefited gender equality. Migration sometimes promotes gender role change—women abroad sometimes play a role in promoting gender equality back home (Ferrant & Tuccio, 2015; UNFPA, 2006). Globalization can expose women to ideas and influences that inspire them to question and challenge gender inequality where they live. Exposure to global media and the Internet can inspire action and change in traditional gender attitudes and roles. Notable, however, is that 300 million fewer women than men have access to mobile Internet technologies, a gender gap of 20 percent (Pangestu & Grandryd, 2020).

Transnational feminists point out that due to globalization, women can more easily draw global attention to their gender equality campaigns and garner international support, share change strategies, and form global and regional alliances and networks to exert pressure on intergovernmental agreements affecting women and girls. By opening up new spaces for resistance such as cross-border networks and transnational activism, globalization also makes possible new international women's rights organizations and movements (Moghadam, 2005). While transnational feminist solidarity networks of individuals, groups, and social movements enable "bottom up" action for change on important women's issues, globalization also supports "top-down" influences on gender equality. Global institutions, like the UN and European Union, draw attention to gender inequalities and develop global frameworks and agreements to address them (Pakekh & Wilcox, 2014). Likewise, when states that respect women's social and economic rights trade heavily with other states that do not, women's status in countries with poor respect for women's rights sometimes improves due to the transmission of transnational norms and policies supportive of increased gender equality (Powell & Schroeder, 2016).

Moving to a new country exposes women to new ideas and social norms that can promote their rights and enable them to participate more fully in society.
UNFPA, State of the World Population: Women's Migration 2006

"Entering the labor market for a woman does not automatically mean that she will have greater control over income; it may mean, instead, increased work burdens, greater drudgery, and multiple responsibilities as she is caught up in a global assembly line over which she has little control."
Gita Sen, Professor of Global Health (Harvard), coordinator for DAWN

"In my view, the singular achievement of globalization is the proliferation of women's movements at the local level, the emergence of transnational feminist networks working at the global level, and the adoption of international conventions such as the Convention on the Elimination of All Forms of Discrimination Against Women and the Beijing Declaration and Platform for Action of the Fourth World Conference on Women."
Valentine Moghadam, feminist sociologist

Intersectionality matters when considering the effects of globalization on women. In some ways, the answer to the question "How does globalization affect women?" depends on which group of women you are talking about. Nationality, geographic location, citizenship status, and socioeconomic position within the global economy are all intersectional variables that determine how globalization affects women (Pakekh & Wilcox, 2014). For example, it is women in the Global South that are most affected by global economic downturns (Gunewardena & Kingsolver, 2007). And in Northern countries like the United States, recessions and neoliberal economic policies also lead to cuts in services and subsidies, cuts that disproportionately affect poor women and children. Depending on where they live, women may also be affected when their governments become so desperate for foreign investment that they relax labor laws and allow pollution and the destruction of the natural resources women depend on to care for themselves, their families, and their communities. As discussed in Chapter 6, this impacts women who must travel farther for water and have less access to arable land to grow food for their families. In short, the costs of globalization fall more heavily on the shoulders of women already burdened by poverty.

Women's Work in the Transnational Factory

Transnational (multinational) corporations dominate the world economy in a globalized world, most of which are headquartered in the Global North. Of the world's top 200 global economic entities, 78.5 percent are transnational corporations rather than countries (Global Justice Now, 2018). As neoliberalism gained hold, corporations began moving production offshore and outsourcing manufacturing in search of low-cost labor and production opportunities (ILO, 2014). Knowledge-intensive aspects of the production process often remain in northern countries, but labor-intensive activities are subcontracted to factories in developing countries where cheap female labor is abundant (Naples, 2002). The United States was the first to relocate labor-intensive factory work such as garment making and production of footwear and electronics to lower-wage sites in the Caribbean, East Asia, and Latin America (United Nations, 1999).

The wealth and size of transnational corporations give them great power in influencing national and international legislation and trade agreements. This power is used to establish **export processing zones (EPZs)** in many cash-hungry low-income Southern nations (EPZs are also referred to as "free trade zones" and "special economic zones"). The ILO defines EPZs as "industrial zones with special incentives set up to attract foreign investors, in which imported materials undergo some degree of processing before being re-exported," but "imported material" also includes electronic data entry facilities and call centers (ILO, 2017a). In these zones, companies are generally exempt from labor, health and safety, and environmental laws and pay few, if any, taxes. The right to unionize and organize collectively to improve wages or working conditions is often banned in EPZs (ITUC, 2016). By 2018, there were over 500 special export zones in 147 countries, employing 90 to 100 million people,

85 percent in Asia (UNCTAD, 2019). Multinational corporations maximize their profits by having their products made by contractors and subcontractors operating in EPZs.

The vast majority of workers in EPZs worldwide are women, with a share of 70 percent, and in some cases 90 percent of the workforce, especially in the garment and electronics sectors (ILO, 2014). Young, poor women, many of them migrants from rural areas, dominate employment in most EPZs. They are often the preferred labor supply for low-skilled assembly work because they can be hired for lower pay with no benefits, they are considered fast, patient and dexterous, and they are less prone to organize in trade unions. Women in EPZs face many problems, including violence. It is also vulnerable employment (Otobe, 2015). Job losses are common during global economic downturns, and laborers are often hired on temporary contracts and are let go once an order is filled. Many women in EPZs have to undergo pregnancy tests when recruited. Most have no maternity protections. They are fired or forced to quit when pregnant or must work under the same difficult conditions as women that are not pregnant (ILO, 2017b).

Women laborers in developing nations are an important part of **global supply chains (GSCs)** where different pieces of production are spread across geographic locations. These complex chains often span multiple countries and involve many suppliers and subcontractors, many of which operate in EPZs. For example, transnational apparel corporations (most from the Global North) contract with multiple textile primary and subcontractors for yarn spinning, weaving, knitting, and fabric dyeing and printing and then contract with additional primary and subcontractors for garment designing, fabric cutting, sewing, ironing, and button holing. Pressures for cost reduction and short delivery schedules lead supplier firms in GSCs to resort to temporary labor, forced overtime, lowering wages, extending working hours, subcontracting, and minimizing investments in areas of health and safety at work (ILO, 2016; Otebe, 2015). Many factories in GSCs (especially those in EPZs) are little more than **sweatshops**—businesses that do not provide a living wage, require excessively long work hours, and provide poor working conditions with many health and safety hazards. In sweatshops, mistreatment of women workers (such as verbal, physical, and sexual harassment) is common, and those who speak out, organize, or attempt to unionize for better conditions are quickly shut down.

One advantage of GSCs to transnational corporations is that corporations can increase profits without taking responsibility for exploitative labor practices and poor pay and work conditions (Holdcroft, 2015). For example, over 9 million people (mostly women) work in Cambodian, Indonesian, and Vietnamese factories making apparel for leading sportswear brands, including Nike and Adidas, but they are not technically employed by these extremely profitable transnational corporations (ITUC, 2019). Nike's annual profit alone is over US$37 billion and Nike's CEO earns over $18 million a year (Clark, 2019). Disney officially employs 189,000 people but an estimated 1,450,000 work in their supply chains making Disney toys and apparel; the Disney CEO makes over $47 million annually (Goldsmith, 2021; ITUC, 2016). Meanwhile, Disney takes no responsibility for sweatshop conditions

"In the international women's movement, 'globalization' is a negative word because it has brought great harm to many women—by facilitating the systematic exploitation of women as a source of cheap domestic and migrant labor."
Jessica Neuwirth, founder of Equality Now, a women's human rights organization

"Women can be made to dance like puppets, but men cannot be abused in the same way. The owners do not care if we ask for something, but demands raised by the men must be given some consideration. So they do not employ male workers."
Bangladeshi factory worker

"The industrial structures of the advanced countries are intrinsically linked with networks of suppliers and workers across the world. A striking feature of contemporary globalization is that a very large and growing proportion of the workforce in many GSCs is now located in developing economies."
ILO, 2016

"In today's global economy, the clothes we wear will have been sewed by workers across an ocean and passed from one business to another before being sold for a tidy profit by a retailer whose name we all know. Companies throughout the supply chain bear a responsibility and have the power to ensure that workers are treated fairly."
Clean Clothes Campaign

in these factories because they do not own them (Dreier, 2019). The odds are good that the majority of your clothes, shoes, toys, and electronics were created with women's sweatshop labor in countries such as Bangladesh, Cambodia, China, the Dominican Republic, Haiti, Honduras, Indonesia, Guatemala, Jordan, Malaysia, Mexico, Myanmar (Burma), Nicaragua, the Philippines, Sri Lanka, and Vietnam.

Although it might seem that these jobs benefit women by reducing their poverty and that women are better off than they would be without the jobs, in most cases the wages are insufficient to escape poverty (Otobe, 2015). The fact that there are few better-paid jobs available for women is often used to rationalize their exploitation, but this is a poor excuse for taking advantage of them—it is hardly a choice when these are the only wage-earning jobs available to them. Some theorists argue that women's low-wage labor for transnational corporations fuels global production and is at the heart of corporate profits (Fuentes & Ehrenreich, 1983; Salzinger, 2003). For instance, women comprise at least 75 percent of garment workers in the export apparel industry. In Bangladesh, most earn the minimum wage, the equivalent of approximately US$100 a month when a living wage is close to $200 a month (Butler, 2019). Box 7.1 provides more on the consequences of poor working conditions in Bangladesh, looking specifically at the 2013 Rana Plaza Industrial Disaster.

"Why should garment workers endure poor wages and working conditions when they are contributing to the phenomenal profits of global brands?"
IndustriALL, a global union federation

One recent study found that none of the top twenty clothing brands pays enough for their factory workers in Asia, Africa, Central America, or Eastern Europe to escape poverty (Clean Clothes Campaign, 2019). The wages of Chinese apparel workers cover only 46 percent of a family's basic needs; in India, 36 percent; in Indonesia, 43 percent; in Turkey, 37 percent; and in Cambodia, 36 percent (Clean Clothes Campaign, 2019). Also notable is that most employers offer no health insurance or pensions despite occupational health risks worsened by noncompliance with health and safety requirements (ILO, 2020a). Sexual harassment is also a big problem in some factories (Human Rights Watch, 2019a; ILO, 2019). This is also vulnerable employment. As factories shift toward automation, companies leave for regions with even lower wages, or economic downturns reduce demand, women garment workers suddenly lose their jobs. For example, due to the COVID-19 pandemic, thousands of apparel factories closed (some permanently and some temporarily). Women garment workers were disproportionately affected and most were left without social safety nets, such as unemployment benefits (ILO, 2020b).

"If they think these wages are enough, they should try to live on them for a month and then decide whether they're OK."
Pakistani factory worker, 18

Stopping Sweatshop Labor

Box 7.2 summarizes some major needs of women working in the factories that contract with multinational corporations.

Unionization is one solution to labor and safety issues in GSC factories. When sufficient numbers of workers organize and act in solidarity to assert their rights, factory owners may have no choice but to negotiate with them. Although it is sometimes said that owners of GSC factories prefer female workers because they are cheap and docile, women workers regularly organize to advocate for a living wage, reasonable work hours, and safe working conditions (Chi & van den Broek, 2020). As Louie (2001) once said, they transform themselves from sweatshop workers

BOX 7.1   *Dying for Others' Affordable Fashion: The 2013 Rana Plaza Industrial Disaster*

Bangladesh is a densely populated country of 163 million in South Asia. It is among the least-developed countries globally. As the biggest earner of foreign currency, the ready-made garment industry is a backbone of the economy. Over 5,000 garment factories employing an estimated 4.2 million factory workers are part of the supply chains of multinational apparel corporations. Most workers are young women; about half are from rural and remote villages. The garment factories are notorious for pay below a living wage, poor work conditions, and the brutal treatment of workers that speak out or organize for better pay and conditions.

In 2013, it literally came crashing down outside of Dhaka, Bangladesh, when the Rana Plaza building crumbled. Inside: The 3,639 employees of five garment factories working 13 to 14 hour shifts making clothes for companies like Benetton (Italy), Bon Marche (UK), Cato Fashions (USA), The Children's Place (USA), El Corte Ingles (Spain), Joe Fresh (Canada), Kik (Germany), Mango (Spain), Matalan (UK), Primark (UK/Ireland), and Texman (Denmark). The owner of the building illegally added three floors to what was supposed to be a five-story building. On April 23, the day before the disaster, visible structural cracks appeared in the building, and a government inspector ordered everyone to leave. While a bank and shops on the bottom floors cleared out, the garment companies decided not to evacuate their employees. Early the next day, workers refused to go in, but the building owner hired thugs to make them. About an hour later, the building collapsed, and 1,138 workers were killed. Over 2,500 were injured, some permanently. Some victims were never found. The rescue took days. Many were trapped under tons of rubble and machinery. Some had to have their limbs amputated to free them. Following the Rana Plaza disaster, there were widespread protests involving thousands.

Protesters demanded justice and wages and compensation for survivors and families of the deceased. Only six months earlier, a fire from an electrical short at the Tazeen garment factory killed 112. Company bosses had padlocked all exits. Over 100 people escaped by jumping out of windows on the third and fourth floors.

If there is anything positive from these disasters, it is that soon after some Western companies, the Bangladesh government, factory owners, trade unions, and NGOs IndustriAll, the Clean Clothes Campaign, and the Workers Rights Consortium, came together to create the Accord on Factory and Building Safety in Bangladesh. The Institute for Global Labour and Human Rights established a fund for Rana Plaza survivors and relatives of the deceased.

But all is not well in the Bangladesh garment industry. Workers seeking to unionize are still punished with termination and violence. Little has been done to improve work conditions, especially at subcontractor factories. According to investigations by NGOs, the non-payment of wages and overtime, workplace discrimination against pregnant women, and physical and verbal abuse remain common. In 2016, hundreds went on strike in protest. Employers responded by locking out 200,000 workers. The government banned worker demonstrations and occupied the garment district with military forces. Over 50,000 Bangladesh garment workers went on strike again in 2019, this time for a living wage. Police fired water cannons, tear gas, and rubber bullets and violently raided homes. Employers fired thousands of workers when they returned to the factories. Meanwhile, the Accord expired in May 2021, and many fear that without its enforceable safety standards, workers are at risk for another disaster.

Sources: Clean Clothes Campaign, 2016, 2021; Farhana, 2014; Human Rights Watch, 2015, 2019b; Institute for Global Labour and Human Rights, 2016; Open Access Government, 2020.

to sweatshop warriors. Strikes and efforts to organize for better work conditions and pay are common in GSC factories but are often swiftly and harshly punished, and collective bargaining agreements remain rare. Organizers are fired, threatened with dismissal, intimidated in a variety of ways, and blacklisted such that they can't find work elsewhere. Strikes are shut down quickly, often with police help. When unions are formed, companies often close factories and move to friendlier locations.

BOX 7.2   *The Needs of Women Workers in Global Supply Chains*

- A living wage, above poverty level

- Reasonable working hours (no more than 48 hours a week plus 12 hours paid overtime)

- Reasonable production targets

- Respect for their right to freedom of association so they can organize with others for better working conditions and pay

- Healthy and safe workplaces

- Maternity protections and child care

- An end to sexual harassment and rape in their workplaces

- Sick leave, social security, and health care

- Protections for migrant workers in EPZs

- Noncorrupt, independent systems for reporting abuses that include protections against retaliation

"Whenever someone tries to form a union, the factory fires the person. Last Saturday a woman was fired because she was giving workers the CCAWDU [Coalition of Cambodian Apparel Workers Democratic Union] number."
Garment worker, Cambodia

"If workers had more of a voice, they might have been able to resist managers who ordered them to work in the doomed building a day after cracks appeared in it."
Phil Robertson, Deputy Director, Asia Division at Human Rights Watch, on the Rana Plaza disaster

Governments often participate in the suppression of labor organizing because of competition with other economically struggling countries for foreign investment. They feel they need the jobs and foreign currency to pay off loans and know that transnational corporations will move their operations to other countries that do not enforce labor regulations. In 2019, for example, tear gas, water cannons, police brutality, and imprisonment were used by the governments of Bangladesh, Cambodia, India, and Myanmar to punish striking garment workers and union members (Paton, 2020). However, these union-busting practices haven't stopped women from organizing for better pay and work conditions.

Cambodia is one example of how global supply chain laborers fight back despite obstacles. There, an estimated one million workers, over 80 percent women, produce over 8 billion dollars' worth of clothing, shoes, and textiles (Fashionating World, 2019; ILO, 2018a). The industry is rife with low pay, labor violations, pregnancy-related discrimination, sexual harassment, and "labor busting." Mass protests and strikes occurred in 2013 and 2014 despite arrests, firings, and killings of protestors. Ultimately, garment workers received a raise that increased their pay from $80 a month to $128 a month; but this was still not a living wage according to the government's calculations (Human Rights Watch, 2015). Labor protests and unionization have continued with some success, and some costs. In 2020, Cambodian garment workers were promised a $2 rise in the minimum wage (to $192), but this is still below the living wage of $588 (Blomberg & Dara, 2020). Meanwhile, the COVID-19 pandemic was used as an excuse to punish workers engaged in union activities, not only in Cambodia but in Bangladesh, India, and Myanmar (Blomberg & Dara, 2020; Paton, 2020).

Of course, it would also help if multinational corporations took more responsibility for what happens in their supply chains. We need a set of global norms and standards and ways to make corporations comply with them. Otherwise, corporate responsibility creates competitive disadvantage, leaving corporations unmotivated to comply. Although sweatshops are inconsistent with workers' human rights as defined by the ILO, this is customarily ignored due to a lack of accountability. For example,

Conventions 87 and 98 support the right of employees to organize for better wages and work conditions, yet many businesses operating in EPZs suppress and punish employee organizing and refuse to engage in collective bargaining. Conventions 29 and 105 require the elimination of all work that is forced or bonded or has elements of servitude or slavery. But sweatshop workers are routinely forced to work more excessively long hours without time off and are fired if they do not comply. They are sometimes denied wages due them. Forced confinement occurs in some sweatshops—workers are not allowed to leave the locked premises until supervisors release them. Migrant workers are sometimes trafficked, tricked, or coerced into migration and exploited through debt bondage. The majority of countries with EPZs that routinely violate these rights have ratified all or most ILO conventions relevant to work in transnational factories.

In 2011, the UN adopted the UN Guiding Principles on Business and Human Rights (GPs). These global standards emphasize the shared responsibility of government and businesses to protect human rights and remedy human rights violations in global supply chains. The UN also provides "protect, respect, and remedy" guidance (called the Guiding Principles Reporting Framework) for governments and corporations. In 2017, the UN released a report detailing how to integrate a gender perspective in GP implementation (UNDP, 2017). But these are called "guiding principles" for a reason: they do not include any enforceable international legal obligations, nor do they provide a way for people to file grievances and complaints (Dahan, Lerner, & Milman-Sivan, 2016). Consequently, they are criticized for not going far enough to make multinational corporations take responsibility for what goes on in their supply chains (Shetti, 2015). It is uncertain whether the GPs will result in significant change. However, many governments, investors, and corporations now reference or use the guidelines and framework to encourage the identification and remedy of human rights-related business issues (Ruggie, Rees, & Davis, 2021; Sherman, 2020; UN Guiding Principles, 2017).

International free trade agreements such as GATT (General Agreement on Tariffs and Trade), NAFTA (North American Free Trade Agreement), and CAFTA (Central American Free Trade Agreement) have aggravated poor labor conditions by making it easier for corporations to ask for and receive exemptions from laws that ostensibly interfere with free trade. Ideally, international trade agreements would require compliance with International Labour Organization core labor rights conventions and the Universal Declaration of Human Rights. This would ensure a level playing field such that companies and countries honoring worker's rights will not be at a competitive disadvantage. Some have also suggested that the World Trade Organization play a role in enforcement of these international labor standards in EPZs (Moran, 2002; Tyc, 2021). Governments of the United States, European Union, and Canada could also demand compliance with ILO Conventions and the UN Guiding Principles on Business and Human Rights as a condition of trade.

Nongovernmental organizations like IndustriALL, Human Rights Watch, and the Clean Clothes Campaign advocate for workers to be paid a living wage. They also document abuses, organize workers, mobilize shareholders and consumers to pressure corporations to clean up their act, and create standards of conduct for corporations. For example, the Netherlands-based Clean Clothes Campaign offers guidance to companies so they can eliminate abuses and better assess, implement, and verify compliance with labor standards in their supply chains. The Maquila Solidarity Network (MSN), a labor and women's rights organization, supports the efforts of workers in

> "The UN Guiding Principles make it explicit that brands are responsible for human rights violations all along their supply chain. If you profit from it, you must make sure no violations occur."
> *Clean Clothes Campaign*

> In 2017, the French parliament passed a law requiring French companies to ensure the respect of labor and human rights in their supply chains.

> "Solidarity among workers should cross the border as easily as companies move production."
> *Mary Tong, Director for the Support Committee for Maquiladora Workers*

global supply chains to win improved wages and working conditions. They work with women's and labor rights organizations in Mexico, Central America, and Asia and also bring change through corporate campaigning and engagement, networking and coalition building, and policy advocacy.

"Just don't buy it."
Slogan of the Global Exchange's Boycott Nike Program in the 1990s

Activism has led many corporations to develop their own corporate social responsibility policies, but these often allow corporations to look like they care while avoiding responsibility for what goes on in their supply chains (Lund-Thomsen & Lindgreen, 2014). For example, in the 1990s, many NGO investigations revealed sweatshop conditions and labor rights violations in Nike's supply chain, where women comprise 80 to 90 percent of workers. Following activism, including consumer boycotts, Nike became the first in its industry to disclose its subcontracted factory locations. Nike also instituted a Code of Conduct to address minimum wages, freedom of association, and gender and maternity discrimination. They employed independent monitors to assess code compliance (WEDO, 2009). However, as noted earlier, problems remain at many Nike subcontractors.

Lawsuits are another avenue for change, but many women lack the legal literacy, legal systems are not yet developed to support these types of complaints, and lawsuits require money and legal expertise often unavailable to affected women. However, in a victory for sweatshop activists, in 2004 the last of three lawsuits brought in 1999 by Sweatshop Watch, Global Exchange, Asian Law Caucus, Unite, and Saipan garment workers against dozens of U.S. big-name retailers and Saipan garment factories was settled (Bas, Benjamin, & Chang, 2004). The suits alleged violations of U.S. labor laws and international human rights standards in Saipan, an island in the U.S. Commonwealth of the Northern Mariana Islands. This island is home to a $1 billion garment industry, employing more than 10,000 workers. Most are young women from China, the Philippines, Thailand, Vietnam, and Bangladesh. Recruited with promises of high pay and quality work in the United States, the workers labored in sweatshop conditions to repay recruitment fees of up to $7,000. The retailers were also charged with misleading advertising by using the "Made in the USA" label and promoting their goods as sweatshop-free. The companies agreed to improve work conditions, to pay $20 million in back wages (the largest award to date in an international human rights case), and to create a monitoring system to prevent labor abuses in Saipan factories (Bas et al., 2004).

The Global Economy and Women's Migration

Driven by a desire to better the lives of themselves and their families, millions of women leave the familiarity of home and loved ones for work. Poor rural women may migrate to cities to work in factories or to work in the homes of affluent families. With few opportunities for economic advancement in their own country, poor women also migrate to other countries for work. Many women migrant workers leave children behind and rely on other women such as sisters, grandmothers, and cousins to care for them. For most, it is a choice made for family and arising from poverty. Some women consider labor migration to provide their only opportunity for the upward mobility of themselves and their families (Parreñas & Silvey, 2016).

There are approximately 68.1 million women migrant workers, about 42 percent of all migrant workers (ILO, 2018b). This section focuses on how globalization makes economic survival difficult in some countries and how this leads poor women to migrate to more affluent countries where there is a strong demand for low-wage workers. They typically send anywhere from half to nearly all of what they earn home to their families **(remittances)** and send a higher proportion of their earnings home than men do (UN Women, 2020). Governments in some countries encourage women's migration for work because the money sent home improves the standard of living for loved ones left behind and is a major source of capital for development (UNFPA, 2015). The top remittance-receiving countries include India (US$83.1 billion), China (US$68.4 billion), Mexico (US$38.5 billion), the Philippines (US$35.2 billion), and Egypt (US$26.8 billion) (UN Women, 2020).

The work that women migrants do in the global economy is often a reflection of traditional gender roles, and migrant women tend to work in traditionally "female" occupations marked by low wages and poor working conditions (UN Women, 2017). They are the janitors, maids, and nannies, "hostesses" and "entertainers" (sex workers), nurses, and home health workers. Ironically, globalization and migration push women into wage labor that could conceivably result in economic independence and increased status, but at the same time, the type of work they tend to do reaffirms traditional gender roles (Choi, Hwang, & Parreñas, 2018). Women also sometimes migrate to become brides where there are shortages of women due to son preference or migration, or shortages of women that will accept traditional gender-role arrangements.

Women migrants are among the most vulnerable to human rights abuses (OHCHR, 2015). Migrant recruitment agencies often enable poor women to migrate to become domestic or care laborers, factory workers, or brides but leave them in a position of indenture **(debt bondage)** as they work to pay off the fees (Choi, Hwang, & Parreñas, 2018). Criminal networks not only traffic drugs and guns, but they also use deception, coercion and violence to traffic women for prostitution, domestic work, and sweatshop labor in what the United Nations calls the "dark underside" of globalization (UNFPA, 2006; UNODC, 2017). During transit, women and girl migrants are often at risk for sexual harassment and physical and sexual abuse. Once they arrive, they often face multiple discriminations due to gender, race, class, and religion. Language, cultural barriers, and economic desperation interfere with migrant working women asserting their rights as women and workers and accessing services in cases of abuse. Undocumented workers without legal work papers and those who live where they work (like many nannies and domestics) are more likely to be exploited and to be physically or sexually abused since they face detention, deportation, or homelessness if they go to authorities (OHCHR, 2015).

"While migration can be an empowering experience for millions of people worldwide, when it 'goes bad,' migrants can find themselves trapped in situations of extreme exploitation and abuse. Trafficked women and domestic workers are two groups that are particularly susceptible to major human rights violations and slave-like conditions."
UNFPA, State of the World Population: Women's Migration 2006

Migrating for Domestic Work

Migrant domestic workers are international migrants whose main job is work performed in or for a household (ILO, 2018b). Cooking, cleaning, washing and ironing clothes, shopping, child care, eldercare, home health care, pet care, and gardening are examples of the work done by women migrant domestic workers. Domestic work is one of the largest fields of employment for female migrants, with a global estimate of 8.5 million domestic migrant women workers (UN Women, 2017). However, when "irregular" migrants are included (people that entered a country without authorization), that number grows to an estimated 17 to 25 million (OHCHR, 2015). The regions with the most women migrant domestic workers are Southeast Asia and the Pacific (24% of the world's migrant women domestic workers); Northern, Southern, and Western Europe (22%); and the Arab States (with 19%). In three regions (the Arab States, North America, and Northern, Southern, and Western Europe), between 65 and 73 percent of female domestic workers are migrants (ILO, 2015). Figure 7.2 provides a sampling of some source countries for migrant domestic workers and destination countries. Some women and girls are trafficked into domestic service, including forced domestic servitude (Human Rights Watch, 2016; UNODC, 2017).

The demand for these workers has grown and is driven by many factors. These include women's entry into the labor force. As middle- and upper-class

FIGURE 7.2   *Some Source and Destination Countries for Women Migrant Domestic Workers*

Sources: ILO, 2013, 2015; Tayah, 2016.

women enter the professional workforce, they seek help with traditional house-hold duties because in general, men have not compensated by increasing the time they spend on household and child-care tasks (Tayah, 2016). The demand for domestic workers is also because the governments of many industrialized nations do not provide or subsidize child care, after-school care, elder care, or paid maternity and family leave (or their support is inadequate). This leaves employed women with few options other than to rely on women migrant workers to help provide their families' care labor (Tayah, 2016; UN Women, 2017). In some places, increases in life expectancy in combination with the collapse of a system where extended family cared for sick and elderly relatives have increased the demand for domestic workers (Tayah, 2016). Migrant domestics are also common where the employment of domestic workers is a sign of social status (ILO, 2013).

> "It is hard to make a living back home. Working here and sending money home to my family is the only way I can take care of my family."
> *Dominique, New York City nanny from Trinidad*

Women migrant domestic workers (WMDWs) are part of **global care chains (GCCs),** a series of links between people across the globe based on the work of care (Hochschild, 2000). Global care chains include the grandmothers, sisters, cousins, and so on that care for WMDWs' children while they're gone. GCCs also include the state (governments of source and destination countries) and nonstate intermediaries (e.g., recruiters and traffickers) that coordinate the employment and travel of WMDWs. According to some, global care chains replicate global relations of inequality. Care resources are extracted from poor countries and transferred to richer ones. The costs are borne primarily by migrant mothers and the children they leave behind while the benefits are greater to the employer parents and their children who benefit from "surplus love" (Hochschild, 2000; Yeates, 2012). Many migrant women domestics have children and migrate as a means to support them (Hoang et al., 2015). They express guilt and remorse about leaving their own homes and children to care for the households and children of others (Hochschild, 2002).

> "The lifestyles of the First World are made possible by a global transfer of the services associated with a wife's traditional role—child care, homemaking, and sex—from poor countries to rich ones."
> *Barbara Ehrenreich and Arlie Hochschild, authors of Global Woman: Nannies, Maids and Sex Workers in the New Economy*

Although many domestic workers enjoy decent work conditions, others are denied a minimum wage, reasonable working hours, time off, and maternity leave and are expected to pay for employer-provided housing and food (ILO, 2013). Recruitment agencies facilitate employment but are known for incompletely disclosing the terms of employment such that migrants don't know what they're getting into (UN Women, 2016). As migrants from other countries, they are often viewed as "lesser" by prejudiced employers who do not treat them as fully human (Tayah, 2016). Some women endure a range of abuses, including nonpayment of salaries, forced confinement, food deprivation, excessive workload, and instances of severe psychological, physical, and sexual abuse (Human Rights Watch, 2016; ILO, 2013). Isolated in a household in a foreign country where they lack knowledge of local language and laws and often with precarious legal status, they are vulnerable to exploitation and abuse (ILO, 2013).

According to the ILO (2013), only 10 percent of the world's domestic workers are covered by general labor laws to the same extent as other workers, and more than a quarter are completely excluded from the scope of national labor laws. In Asia and the Pacific, about 60 percent of domestic workers have no legal labor protections. The situation is the worst in the Arab States, where 99 percent of domestic workers are excluded from labor protections (Jordan is the only one

BOX 7.3 *Slavery-like Conditions for Migrant Domestic Workers in Oman*

Oman, a Gulf state country, relies on approximately 154,000 migrant domestic workers. They come from countries including the Philippines, Indonesia, India, Bangladesh, Sri Lanka, Nepal, Tanzania, and Ethiopia. While some are paid adequately and treated well, many experience abusive employers and exploitative work conditions. If a worker is threatened, beaten or starved and flees her employer, she can be charged with "absconding" for leaving her job and faces imprisonment, a fine, and deportation. Human Rights Watch believes that Oman's legal framework, in combination with the government's lax enforcement of the country's already inadequate legal protections, gives rise to abuse. Here are some excerpts from interviews conducted by Human Rights Watch (2016) with 59 migrant domestic workers.

"I would start working at 4:30 a.m. and finish at 1 a.m. For the entire day they wouldn't let me sit. I used to be exhausted. There were 20 rooms and over 2 floors. He wouldn't give me food. When I said I want to leave, he said, 'I bought you for

1,560 rials (US$4,052) from Dubai. Give it back to me and then you can go.'"—*Asma K.*

"After a month they wouldn't give me my phone. I would cry and plead for my phone. My brother had an accident and his legs were injured. I managed to call my brother, but my boss said, 'This is not your brother.' They think I have a boyfriend. Then boss, madam, and their daughter beat me with sticks all over my body." —*Nalini H.*

"I sleep in the kitchen. I don't have a room." —*Anisa M.*

"I was working until late that night. I woke up at 3 a.m. to get something. The 27-year-old son grabbed and raped me."—*Mausumi A.*

"Madam would say all the time that I don't have a brain. That I'm dirty. That I don't know how to cook. They would call me 'ayb' (in Arabic, shameful or disgraceful)." —*Marisa L.*

Sources: Human Rights Watch, 2016, 2018.

whose labor legislation covers domestic workers). The *kafala* (sponsorship) system, which operates in Bahrain, Kuwait, Jordan, Lebanon, Oman, Qatar, United Arab Emirates, and Saudi Arabia, promotes abuse (ILO, 2015). Under the system, obtaining a work visa requires sponsorship by a local citizen or company employer. Because employers usually pay the costs of recruitment and sponsorship, they often feel that they own the migrant worker (Kagan, 2017). In most cases, migrants can't leave legally without the employer's permission. Migrants that try to flee abusive situations are considered "illegal" and are subject to detention and deportation. Practices include taking women's passports upon arrival and law enforcement agencies' refusal to investigate or prosecute abuses, resulting in the return of domestic workers to their employers (UNFPA, 2006; Human Rights Watch, 2016). Box 7.3 provides some excerpts from an investigation of abuse and exploitation of domestic migrant workers in Oman.

In addition to human rights organizations like Human Rights Watch, a number of migrant workers' organizations work to expose abuses, fight for workers' rights, and assist victims of abuse. These include Kalayaan (England and Wales), ASTRADOMES (Household Workers' Association) in Costa Rica and Nicaragua,

Migrant-Rights.org in the Middle East, and the Asia Migrant Domestic Workers' Alliance. Trade unions for domestic workers include the South African Domestic Workers Union, the Latin American and Caribbean Confederation of Domestic Workers, and the International Domestic Workers Federation, which has over 80 affiliate organizations. NGOs, unions, and the ILO (the UN's International Labour Organization) advocate for national labor laws and codes protecting migrant domestics' rights, criminal laws and penalties for abuses, accessible complaint mechanisms, and better resources for identifying and assisting victims. They also call upon the "labor-sending" countries to use diplomacy to improve conditions and to improve services at embassies and consular offices that would enable workers to leave abusive situations.

Following concerted activism by unions and NGOs, on June 16, 2011, ILO members adopted the first international standards on domestic work with the Domestic Workers Convention 2011 (No. 189) (ILO, 2011). The treaty requires ratifying states to take measures to respect and protect the right of domestic workers to organize and collectively bargain for better wages and work conditions. It also requires decent work conditions that respect domestic workers' privacy, and a safe and healthy work environment. According to the convention, workers get to keep their own travel and identity documents and must receive an employment contract that specifies such things as compensation, normal hours of work, annual leave, daily and weekly rest periods, and terms and conditions related to termination of employment. Led by International Trade Union Confederation (ITUC) and International Domestic Workers Federation (IDWF), trade unions in over 92 countries campaigned for ratification of the convention by UN member states. By 2021, over 50 governments had changed their laws to better protect domestic workers, but only 31 UN member states had ratified the convention. Box 7.4 highlights some of the UN's Sustainable Development Goals and targets that are relevant to women migrant workers. Recall that in 2015, world leaders committed to reaching these goals by 2030, and that the UN customarily provides guidance and support to countries to promote goal realization.

> "Providing domestic workers with stronger rights and recognizing them as workers would help to combat gender-based discrimination, and also discrimination on the grounds of race, national extraction or caste that often manifests itself in the sector."
> *ILO, 2013*

Migrating to Marry

Another example of women migrating due to poverty is the phenomenon of **marriage migrants** (also known as mail-order brides, Internet or cyber-brides, and commercial marriage migrants). Women in poor economic circumstances are marketed as brides to American, European, and Asian men seeking traditional marriages and to Asian men who seek wives due to "bride deficits" caused by son preference (Abrahamson, 2016; Starr & Adams, 2016). For example, China's recently ended one-child policy, along with son preference, created a women shortage that has led some men to turn to transnational brides (Abrahamson, 2016). Women are willing to migrate for marriage largely for practical reasons. They want to improve their economic and social status, though they may also hope for romantic love from their union, or to be able to support their families at home (Meszaros, 2017; Yeung & Mu, 2020). Sometimes women are under the impression that men in other countries will make better husbands and are less traditional than men in their country (Ryabov, 2016).

BOX 7.4   *The Sustainable Development Goals and Women Migrant Workers (WMWs)*

Goal 5. Achieve gender equality and empower all women and girls

- Mitigate vulnerabilities of WMWs to violence in the workplace (such as in Domestic Work) and WMDs in transit to COD (countries of destination).

- Recognize the value of global care chains in the countries of origin and destination.

- Identify the role and costs of transnational mothering.

- Challenge social constructions that undermine the value of the worker and the person by identifying all women migrants as workers with corresponding rights.

- Recognize the value and weight of social/political remittances of WMWs.

Goal 8. Promote sustained, inclusive and sustainable economic growth, full and productive employment and decent work for all

- Attention to and regulation of gender pay discrepancies/lack of decent work in feminized formal and informal sectors (entertainment and sex).

- Address the causes, organizations, and demands that generate and facilitate forced labour and trafficking of women.

- Protect WMWs' labour rights for the promotion of decent and dignified work.

Goal 10. Reduce inequality within and among countries

- Increase legal migration channels and opportunities for WMWs and formalize work that empowers WMWs and values their contributions at home and abroad.

- Gender inclusive social protection including transferability of benefits/pension for WMWs.

- Eliminating discrimination against WMWs in relation to costs (reduce the transaction costs of migrant remittances).

- Financial inclusion: bring awareness to the role of WMWs as sound agents of economic development.

Source: UN Women, 2017.

"The Russian woman has not been exposed to the world of rampant feminism that asserts its rights in America. She is the weaker gender and knows it."
Chance for Love Matchmaking Service Website

Technically speaking, the commonly used term "mail-order bride" is a misnomer because men don't simply pick women out of catalogues, send money, and receive a wife (Heston, 2016). Over 2,700 international marriage-brokering organizations (and over 400 in the United States) arrange introductions and facilitate marriages between women from one country and men in another (Starr & Adams, 2016). Today international marriage brokers (IMBs) have an online presence where they market prospective brides as sexy and exotic, traditional, and submissive. Some even tout that their women are unspoiled by feminism. By the 1990s, IMBs marketing women from the Philippines, India, Thailand, Eastern Europe, and Russia were established throughout Europe, the United States, Japan, and Australia. Potential customers can peruse hundreds of Internet mail-order bride sites and catalogues complete with photos and brief biographies of thousands of women. For additional fees, IMBs coordinate contact between men and women (for example, providing email addresses) and help with visas and marriage licenses once a match is made. Prospective grooms can go on package tours where groups of prospective grooms from one country are taken to meet groups of prospective brides in another country.

No firm statistics exist on the practice. However, in the United States alone, it is estimated that international marriage brokers arrange 4,000 to 15,000 marriages between American men and foreign women annually (Tran, 2012).

There is some evidence that these wives face a heightened risk for domestic violence, but governments typically do not collect specific data on violence against this group of women (Grosh, 2011). For example, in South Korea, marriage brokers arrange marriages between Korean men and women from Vietnam, the Philippines, Thailand, China, and Cambodia. A study by the Human Rights Commission of Korea found that 42 percent of foreign-born wives reported experiencing domestic violence (Hollingsworth, Seo, & Bae, 2020). Imbalances in power, cultural differences, linguistic barriers, isolation in a foreign country, and the marketing of prospective brides as submissive and deferential likely increase risk (Lindee, 2007; UNFPA, 2006) and exploitative marriages (UNODC, 2020).

The high fees paid to IMBs perpetuate men's feelings of entitlement or ownership of their wives, and the way women are marketed may attract men looking for women to abuse and exploit (Tahirih Justice Center, 2017). In one famous U.S. case, Indle King, a 39-year-old man with a history of domestic violence, murdered his wife of 2 years, Anastasia, a 20-year-old marriage migrant from Kyrgystan. It was later discovered that Indle, while planning Anastasia's murder, was already seeking a replacement. Some international marriage brokers participate in human trafficking (Barry, 1995; Lindee, 2007; UNODC, 2020). Not only do IMBs generally treat women as commodities to be "sold" to men, but also some international marriage brokers are merely covers for sex tourism operations and, in extreme cases, covers for prostitution rings that traffic recently immigrated marriage migrants (Lindee, 2007; UNODC, 2020).

Nongovernmental women's organizations act to protect commercial marriage migrants from abuse. For example, in the United States, the Tahirih Justice Center played a key role in getting the U.S. Congress to draft and pass the International Marriage Broker Regulation Act of 2005. Signed into law by President G.W. Bush in 2006, the act requires international marriage brokers to obtain criminal histories on their male clients, including any records from the National Sex Offender Public Registry, and provide a report to foreign women in their native language. It also requires that prospective brides receive an information packet with domestic violence resources. Unfortunately, implementation and enforcement of the law by U.S. agencies are lacking, and no IMBs have been prosecuted despite violations (Tahirih Justice Center, 2017). Gabriela, a Philippine-American women's organization, the Coalition Against Trafficking in Women (CATW), and the Global Alliance Against Trafficking in Women (GAATW) also work on this issue. Domestic violence shelters and NGOs serving migrants in regions where marriage migrants are more common are also adapting their services to help women escape abusive situations.

Women and Girls' Labor in the Global Sex Trade

Women have engaged in sex work for centuries, but globalization has shaped the economics and practices of sex work in some remarkable ways.

Sex Tourism

One effect of globalization is an increase in international tourism. In 2019 alone, there were over 1.5 billion international travelers (UNWTO, 2019). Easy global travel has changed the global sexual landscape, and travel for sexual purposes has grown with globalization. While tourism can create jobs and income-generating activities that empower women, for many poor women, the jobs it offers are as sex workers in the sex tourism industry.

The UN's World Tourism Organization (UNWTO, 1995) defines **sex tourism** as "trips organized from within the tourism sector, or from outside this sector but using its structures and networks, with the primary purpose of effecting a commercial sexual relationship by the tourist with residents at the destination." Sex tourism originates in the "entertainment sectors" developed in Thailand and the Philippines to serve American soldiers stationed in Southeast Asia from the 1950s through the 1970s. By the 1980s, it spread to other regions and countries such as the Caribbean, Kenya, Costa Rica, and Brazil, but instead of soldiers, it served mostly affluent men from Western Europe, North America, Australia, and Japan (Davidson, 2015). Today, destinations include South and Central America, the Caribbean, Thailand, the Philippines, with sex tourists from countries including Australia, Germany, the United States, England, and Korea (Lu et al., 2020; Simons, 2019). The nature of sex work in the global tourism industry varies based on region. In some places like Bangkok and Amsterdam, it is often a part of a formal tourism economy that includes brothels, but in other places, it is part of the informal economy. Services also differ depending on the region, with some areas offering more of a "girlfriend experience" while other regions offer sexual services of almost any sort (Brennan, 2002, 2004; Cabezas, 2002; Lu et al., 2020; Simons, 2019).

Sex tourism is another effect of globalization and is made possible by a globalized system of communication and transportation (Cabezas, 2002). It arises out of a globalized economy that makes sex work one of the only ways for some women to earn a living wage. The industry feeds on men from industrialized countries who stereotype foreign women as exotic and more submissive and available than women in their own countries (Enloe, 1989; Lu et al., 2020). Sex tourism is based on inequalities of power based on race, gender, class, and nationality (Brennan, 2004). Governments that need the money brought by international tourism are willing to encourage, or at least ignore, sex tourism due to the money it generates. Pimps, brothel owners, hotels, travel agencies, recruiters, and local police may all reap economic benefits from sex tourism (Baum, 2013). Sadly, the sexual exploitation of children in travel and tourism also occurs; it is a multibillion-dollar industry affecting over two million children a year (Hawke & Raphael, 2016; Kosuri & Jeglic, 2016; U.S. Department of State, 2016).

Eliminating sex tourism has proven challenging. When sex tourism destination governments clamp down to reduce supply, dedicated sex tourists often find new destinations. For example, Thailand's efforts to clean up their tourism industry led sex tourists to travel instead to Laos, Myanmar, and Bangladesh (Palet, 2016). These low-income countries are developing tourism as new sources of revenue and have a large supply of economically vulnerable people that are susceptible to sexual exploitation. Reduction of this "supply" depends on alleviating poverty and developing non-exploitative employment opportunities.

"Far too many men, in Sweden and the rest of the world, see women as objects, as something that can be bought and sold. . . . A woman's body is not the same as a glass of brandy or an ice cream after a good dinner."
Swedish Deputy Prime Minister Margareta Winberg

Mong La in Myanmar (Burma) is a sex tourist attraction. Hotel rooms are littered with ads for "newly arrived virgins," "mother-daughter combos," and "sassy 16-year-olds with large breasts."
Global Study on Sexual Exploitation of Children in Travel and Tourism

Some NGOs, like Human Rights Watch and Amnesty International, believe the best option is to legalize and regulate the sex trade (as done in Amsterdam). Otherwise, it is driven underground where sex workers are more likely to suffer from unhealthy, unsafe, and exploitative work conditions. Criminalizing those that travel for purposes of commercial sex is seen as a way to decrease demand and is a strategy employed in the Nordic countries of Sweden, Norway, and Iceland. NGOs like Equality Now focus on legal safeguards in the source countries of sex tourists, such as making it a crime to travel for sex tourism purposes. They also campaign to shut down and prosecute the sex tourism operators in high-income countries that market sex tourism.

Reducing demand requires more than a legal solution. While some sex tourists are hard-core sexual offenders (including pedophiles), those that are not might be less inclined to participate in sex tourism if they were more aware of its harmful and exploitative nature. Studies of male sex tourists (see for example, Katsulis, 2010; Neal, 2016; Thurnell-Reid, 2015) find that many rationalize, justify, and minimize their actions to reduce the dissonance (internal conflict) that results from their immoral behavior. It is also common for people to dehumanize the victims of their actions to resolve their dissonance due to immorality. We need to make it more difficult for sex tourists to maintain their view that they are good and moral people by emphasizing the harms of their actions, humanizing victims, and promoting empathy for sexually exploited people.

Sex Trafficking

The majority of sex workers are forced by economics and, often, by single motherhood, into prostitution—it is economics, not others, that forced them. In stark contrast are the millions of sex workers coerced or tricked and even sold into sexual slavery and taken away from their home countries. They are part of the multi-billion-dollar sex trafficking industry. **Sex trafficking** is a form of human trafficking. According to the UN Trafficking in Persons Protocol (which is part of the UN Convention Against Transnational Crime), human trafficking is the recruitment, transport, harboring, or receipt of persons by means of threat, deception, coercion, abduction, fraud, or abuse of power with the purpose of victim exploitation (UN Treaty Collection, 2017).

The **trafficking of women and girls** is often perpetrated by agents of local criminal networks. They first win the trust of women or the parents of girls and then they acquire and sell the victims to domestic or transnational criminal networks. Trafficking can be intraregional (within a country or region) or transregional (across regions). Sex trafficking occurs all over the world. The UNODC (2021) has identified over 534 "trafficking flows" (connections between origin and destination countries). Trafficking criminals target and exploit desperate people who are simply seeking a better life, as well as orphaned and poverty-stricken children.

The number of trafficked people is difficult to determine. However, human trafficking is a form of modern slavery and the ILO (2017b) estimates that 28.7 million girls and women are victims of modern slavery. Data indicate that the majority of trafficking victims are women and girls. For every ten detected victims, five are women and two are girls. Women comprise 46 percent of detected victims and girls comprise 19 percent, while men comprise 20 percent of detected victims and boys 15 percent (UNODC, 2021).

By 2018, sixty-three American men who traveled for purposes of having sex with a minor, or who ran child sex tourism businesses, have served prison time. They were prosecuted under the 2003 U.S. Protect Act. But most child sex tourists are not caught and prosecuted.

In 2016, American sex tourist David Strecker was the first to be convicted under a 2013 Costa Rican law prohibiting promotion of Costa Rica as a sex tourism destination. Known for blogging and writing about his sex tourism experiences in Central America and the Caribbean (and making money from it), he was sentenced to 5 years in prison.

If you are in the United States and believe someone may be a victim of human trafficking, call law enforcement (911) or the 24-hour National Human Trafficking Resource Center at 1-888-373-7888. Trafficking victims, including undocumented individuals, are eligible for services and immigration assistance.

BOX 7.5 *Percentage of Women and Girls Among Detected Trafficking Victims by Region*

Region	Percentage
North Africa	47
Sub-Saharan Africa	59
Middle East*	46
North America	84
Central America and the Caribbean	79
South America	74
East Asia and the Pacific	68
Eastern Europe	57
Central Asia	60
Central and Southeastern Europe	75
Western and Southern Europe	51

Source: UNODC, 2021 *Global Report on Trafficking in Persons 2020.*
*Data from Bahrain, United Arab Emirates, Saudi Arabia, Qatar, Oman, and Kuwait.

"The commodification of human beings as sexual objects, poverty, gender inequality, and subordinate positions of women and girls provide fertile ground for human trafficking." *Michelle Bachelet, UN Women Executive Director 2010–2013*

According to the UNODC (United Nations Office on Drugs and Crime, 2021), 77 percent of trafficked women and 72 percent of trafficked girls were trafficked for sexual exploitation, compared to 17 percent of trafficked men and 23 percent of trafficked boys. Detected women and girl victims are also trafficked for forced labor such as textile and domestic service work (14% of trafficked women and 21% of trafficked girls, compared to 67% of trafficked men and 66% of trafficked boys). Recent studies show that LGBTQI+ children are at high risk for being trafficked for sexual exploitation and forced labor because they are often forced to live on the streets when rejected by family. Although trafficking for sexual exploitation and forced labor are the most common forms of trafficking, people are also trafficked for other purposes including forced criminal activity, forced begging, forced marriage, organ removal, and baby selling. See Box 7.5 for regional differences in the percentage of girls and women among detected trafficking victims.

Trafficking agents, both women and men, are common. While 62 percent of convicted traffickers are men, 38 percent are women (UNODC, 2021). Women traffickers often operate as recruiters. Recruiters use the offer of work to entice poor women to illegally immigrate to other countries. Women might be told they will work as maids, waitresses, or entertainers. Sometimes women and girls are lured into false romantic relationships and false marriage offers (UNODC, 2014). Upon arrival, their agent, boyfriend, or "fiancé" sells them to a brothel or "club" or confines and prostitutes them under threats of violence or turning them over to the authorities for illegal immigration. Poverty-stricken parents sometimes knowingly sell their children into sexual slavery for cash or to settle debts (U.S. Department of State, 2016).

BOX 7.6 *Forced Prostitution: The Case of Grace*

Grace finished the tenth grade in Nigeria when an agent recruited her for work in Europe. Her poverty-stricken parents saw it as her destiny to go abroad and earn money for the family. The agent said her sister lived in Germany and Grace would work for the sister until Grace repaid the travel costs. After that, Grace could work as a babysitter or in a restaurant to send money back home. A man accompanied Grace and some other women to Europe. Once she arrived, she was told that her debt was 50,000 euro (US$67,000) and she would work as a prostitute in brothels (which are legalized in Germany). She was forced to have sex without a condom and abused if she didn't do everything she was told.

Seven months later, police raided the brothel and realized Grace's papers were false. They took her to an immigration detention center, where she became sick and they discovered she had HIV. The madam tracked her down and threatened her and her family if she did not return to pay off her debt. By then, she was working with SOLWODI*, and reported the madam and her accomplices to the police.

Source: Adapted from Equality Now (2017) "Trafficking Survivor Stories: Grace."
*SOLWODI (Solidarity for Women in Distress) is an NGO founded in Kenya in 1985 by a German woman, Sister Doctor Ackermann. SOLWODI now operates in Kenya, Rwanda, Germany, Romania, and Austria, providing counseling, legal aid, medical assistance, and other support for women and girl victims of trafficking.

According to Human Rights Watch, recruiters often take advantage of families known to have financial difficulties. Debt bondage is not uncommon as women and girls are forced to continue in prostitution through the use of unlawful "debt" purportedly incurred through their transportation or recruitment (UNODC, 2014; U.S. Department of State, 2016). They must first repay with interest the money given to their family or agent at the time of recruitment. This debt mounts as they are charged for food, shelter, and clothing. Should they try to leave without paying their debt, they are likely to experience physical punishment by the brothel owner or the police. To keep them there, they are threatened with harm to their parents and with being arrested as illegal immigrants. Lack of familiarity with the local language or dialect puts them at a further disadvantage. Because trafficked women are often in the country illegally, law enforcement agencies often respond to them as lawbreakers rather than as victims. To make things worse, they may be prosecuted for illegally leaving their own country should they attempt to return home. The case of Grace, a young woman from Nigeria, is described in Box 7.6.

Women forced into prostitution are exposed to significant health risks in the forms of violence and disease (Ottisova, 2016). Rapes and beatings are used to ensure compliance. Multiple daily clients, and the occasional sadistic client, inflict more pain. Trafficked women and girls are exposed to sexually transmitted diseases such as HIV/AIDS because they are forced to have unsafe sex with multiple clients. Many are also injected with drugs to foster compliance and may undergo clandestine abortions with unclean medical instruments (UNODC, 2017). Sex-trafficked women and girls face especially high risks of HIV infection (Goldenberg et al., 2013; WHO, 2015).

Stopping human trafficking is difficult because demand is high and there is a steady supply of potential victims to feed it—a supply sustained by poverty, ignorance, organized crime, and government and police tolerance and corruption. The Coalition Against Trafficking in Women (CATW) and Demand Abolition suggest that the best ways to reduce demand are to criminalize and penalize it and educate about the harms of sexual exploitation. As things currently stand, prostituted women are more likely to be arrested than the men buying sex. In many places, including much of the United States, trafficked women are prosecuted for prostitution or for illegal immigration. Many anti-trafficking organizations endorse the "Nordic Model," a demand reduction approach used in Sweden, Norway, and Iceland. It involves a set of laws criminalizing the demand for commercial sex while decriminalizing individuals in prostitution. Reduction of supply will only be accomplished through a lessening of poverty, educating potential victims, and the dismantling of criminal trafficking networks.

Due to globalization and sophisticated criminal networks, international cooperation is essential. The Protocol to Prevent, Suppress and Punish Trafficking in Persons, especially Women and Children, was adopted by the UN General Assembly in 2000, and by 2020 had been ratified by 178 member nations (making it legally binding in those countries) (UN Treaty Collection, 2021). Often referred to as the **Palermo Protocol**, it requires a "comprehensive international approach in the countries of origin, transit and destination that includes measures to prevent such trafficking, to punish the traffickers and to protect the victims of such trafficking, including by protecting their internationally recognized human rights" (p. 41). It is the first global legally binding instrument with an agreed definition on trafficking in persons.

Objectives of the Palermo Protocol are to prevent and combat the trafficking of women and children; to protect and assist the victims of trafficking; and to promote cooperation among governments to achieve these objectives. The UNODC coordinates international investigations and prosecutions. The UNODC also offers the "Toolkit to Combat Trafficking in Persons." The toolkit provides guidance, resources, and strategies to policymakers, law enforcement, judges, prosecutors, victim service providers, and NGOs. The Protocol stimulated the passage of national legislation criminalizing human trafficking, and over 90 percent of countries now have such laws. However, many do not cover all forms of human trafficking or comply with the Protocol's recommendations (UNODC, 2014; 2017). The UN's Sustainable Development Goals also include a target specific to the trafficking of women (see Box 7.4).

There are many NGOs (nongovernmental organizations) working on the issue. The Coalition Against Trafficking in Women-International (CATW), a GRSO (grassroots support organization) that works with NGOs all over the world, was founded in 1988. CATW was the first international nongovernmental organization to focus on human trafficking, especially sex trafficking of women and girls. They have many programs, projects, and campaigns. CATW united over 140 NGOs to shape the Palermo Protocol to protect all victims of trafficking. GRSOs such as the Global Fund for Women and Shared Hope International provide money and technical assistance to NGOs working to prevent trafficking, aid victims, and

---

"The most efficient approach to ending sexual exploitation is targeting sex buyers: when they stop buying, the entire system of degradation collapses. No buyers, no business."
Demand Abolition, American NGO working to eradicate illegal commercial sex

"When I was in the sex industry, I prayed that someone would take me away. If men would be charged, given severe punishments, it would stop."
Grace, trafficked from Nigeria to Germany

Josephine Butler (1828–1906) of Great Britain was one of the first Northern women to organize against prostitution and the trafficking of women. Despite threats of violence against her, she proved that the state-licensed brothels were participants in white slave traffic and the sale of children for prostitution throughout Europe.

achieve justice. GROs like Shakti Samuha in Kathmandu, Nepal, help survivors. Shakti Samuha established the first shelter run by and for trafficking survivors in South Asia. NGOs like the Safe House for Women in Yugoslavia and Safe Horizon in the United States rescue women and provide them with medical treatment and counseling.

Conclusion

In this chapter, you learned that globalization has had mixed effects for women and girls. Although it has increased women's paid employment and consequently benefited some women, the costs of economic globalization are also often disproportionately borne by women—especially women who are already poor. Such women are hit harder by economic downturns and are more likely to directly experience the effects of environmental degradation. Because they have few economic choices, they are vulnerable to exploitation in the global labor marketplace and by human traffickers. This is another example of how women's disadvantage arises out of material, economic forces.

Globalization has also created a number of violations of women's human rights. We need to ask, as Hochschild (2002) suggested, what kind of a world globalization has created when working in a sweatshop, sex work, migration to work as a domestic, and becoming a marriage migrant are rational economic choices. These may appear to be individual choices, but they are not really free—they are the result of economic globalization and poverty. This chapter also illustrates intersectionality because how globalization affects women depends on their race, region, and socioeconomic class.

Like other chapters, this one illustrates the global women's studies theme of activism and empowerment. Once again, we saw that where there are gendered wrongs, there are people working for women's rights. Despite risks, women organize and act to end abuses in transnational factories and fight for a living wage. GROs (grassroots organizations) provide services for trafficked and migrant women. NGOs create and advocate for legislative solutions and push for law enforcement. GRSOs unite diverse organizations to influence international agreements. They also fund GROs serving migrant and trafficked women.

Fueled by the dynamics of globalization itself, women all over the world fight the negative effects of globalization and use the transnational political stage to press for social, economic, environmental, and political justice (Cabezas, 2002; Desai, 2007). Transnational networks of activists play an increasing role in international and regional politics and may have progressive effects on policies regarding women, human rights, and the environment (Karides, 2002). They can expose injustices in an international arena. This is globalization from below, rather than from above. They use electronic communication and international and regional conferences to share information and expand political participation.

Globalization is relevant to our next topic of women and religion. Under conditions of economic stress and cultural globalization, people often seek certainty and a return to a romanticized past. Traditionally masculine men who feel threatened by gender equality and cultural globalization are often more open to conservative and fundamentalist religious ideas that are detrimental to women's status. Just as women's

"It is a fundamental human right to be free of sexual exploitation in all its forms. Women and girls have the right to sexual integrity and autonomy."
Coalition Against Trafficking in Women (CATW)

Despite threats to his life, Oluremi Banwo Kehinde has helped over 250 Nigerian women escape criminal sex trafficking networks in Russia.

organizations join together across borders to influence international agreements, so do fundamentalist religions. They form alliances to resist sexual orientation and gender identity (SOGI) rights, women's rights, and gender equality (Imam, 2016).

Glossary Terms and Concepts

Cultural globalization	Global supply chains	Remittances
Debt bondage	Globalization	Sex tourism
Economic globalization	Marriage migrants	Sex trafficking
Export processing zones	Migrant domestic workers	Sweatshops
(EPZs)	Neoliberal economic	Trafficking of women
Global care chains	policies	and girls
(GCCs)	Palermo Protocol	

Study Questions

1. What is globalization?

2. What are the positive and negative effects of globalization on women? How are the effects of globalization on women influenced by intersectionality?

3. What are neoliberal economic policies, and how are women affected by these policies?

4. What are EPZs? What percentage of workers in these zones are women? How is women's work in EPZs part of global supply chains? How do multinational corporations benefit from women's work in global supply chains?

5. What are sweatshops, and why do women work in them? Do jobs in transnational factories help women get out of poverty? What is being done and what needs to be done to reduce women's sweatshop labor?

6. How does globalization influence women's migration? What does it mean to say "the work women migrants do is often a reflection of traditional female roles and stereotypes"? Why are migrant women vulnerable to human rights abuses?

7. Why has the demand for migrant women domestics risen? How are they part of a global care chain? What types of abuses have been documented? What is being done and what should be done?

8. What are mail-order and Internet brides? Why do women migrate to marry foreign men? Why do men seek such brides? What is the role of international marriage brokers? Why are such wives at greater risk for domestic violence?

9. What is sex tourism? How is it related to the differential effects of globalization based on gender, class, and race? Who are these "sexual tourists" and what are their destinations? What can be done to reduce sex tourism?

10. What is human trafficking? What different things are women and girls trafficked to do, and how does this compare to the trafficking of men and boys? How are victims usually recruited?

11. What is sex trafficking? How does it work? How is debt bondage used to keep women enslaved? What are the effects on women? What is being done and needs to be done to stop it?

Discussion Questions and Activities

1. How is your life affected by globalization?

2. How do migrant women contribute to your community? Which countries do they come from? What are the economic conditions in those countries that contribute to their migration? Are they a part of global care chains? What types of work do they do—is it the domestic and care work traditionally done by women?

3. Interview a recent woman migrant using questions developed from the chapter.

4. Where were your clothes made, and who made them? Choose an article of your clothing and research the garment industry in that country. Frame your report using concepts from the chapter.

5. Cheap clothing and electronic products and large corporate profits (which mean good stockholder returns) are partly due to women's work in sweatshops. Is this free-market capitalism at its best or at its worst? How comfortable are you with Northern people receiving more of the benefits due to this feature of economic globalization?

6. Locate websites that advertise marriage migrants (just type "mail-order brides," "internet brides," "international marriage agency," or "international marriage broker," into a basic search engine and you'll find hundreds of sites). What countries do most potential "brides" come from? What are the economic conditions in those countries? Do the sites appear to cater to men seeking traditional gender-role relationships?

7. The chapter discusses how sex workers are victims of economics and a commercial sex industry that uses coercion and force to exploit them. However, some feminists and human rights organizations (like Amnesty International) argue that rather than eliminating sex work, we should work for sex workers' legal, political, and labor rights. They say this honors the choice of some women to choose sex work as an economic advancement strategy and will reduce the domination of sex work by criminal pimps and organized crime. They emphasize that there is a big difference between sex trafficking and sex work (where sexual services are negotiated between consenting adults with the terms of engagement agreed upon between the seller and the buyer). Meanwhile, others, such as the international Coalition Against Trafficking in Women, strongly disagree. They argue that prostitution is always abusive and exploitative. What do you think? Can sex work be non-exploitative? Can sex work be

conceptualized as a form of legitimate work and regulated so that sex workers have decent work conditions and their human rights are respected? Would this stop sex trafficking?

8. The chapter notes that there are regional differences in the trafficking of women and girls. Conduct research to describe the trafficking of women and girls in a specific region and what is being done about it. You may want to start with the most recent UNODC trafficking in persons report.

Action Opportunities

1. Go to Green America https://www.greenamerica.org/take-action-our-current -green-economy-campaigns or the Clean Clothes Campaign https://cleanclothes .org/action and participate in an anti-sweatshop campaign.

2. Take action to educate others and inspire change on sex trafficking. Use resources from the UNODC's "Blue Heart Campaign" (https://www.unodc.org/blueheart/), Coalition Against Trafficking in Women (http://www.catwinternational .org/), and Stop the Traffik (http://www.stopthetraffik.org/resources/).

3. Help your local domestic violence or sexual assault prevention and recovery program develop a program to reach out to migrant women who experience abuse from male partners or employers.

4. Join one of Equality Now's campaigns to stop sex trafficking and sex tourism (http://www.equalitynow.org/end_sex_trafficking).

5. Visit the International Domestic Workers Federation to take actions for migrant domestic workers (https://idwfed.org/en/take-action).

Activist Websites

Clean Clothes Campaign http://www.cleanclothes.org/

Coalition Against Trafficking in Women https://catwinternational.org/action/

Global Modern Slavery Directory (a comprehensive directory of groups in the world tackling aspects of human trafficking and modern slavery). http://www .globalmodernslavery.org

Maquila Solidarity Network https://www.maquilasolidarity.org/

Polaris Project https://polarisproject.org/take-action/

Shared Hope International http://www.sharedhope.org

Tahirh Justice Center http://www.tahirih.org/

United Nations Office of Drugs and Crime's (UNODC) Have A Heart campaign for victims of human trafficking https://www.unodc.org/blueheart/

Informational Websites

Corp Watch http://www.corpwatch.org/

Equality Now https://www.equalitynow.org/end_sex_tourism

Human Rights Watch http://hrw.org

UNODC Trafficking Resources https://www.unodc.org/unodc/en/human-trafficking/recent-publications.html

ILO Migrant Domestic Workers http://www.ilo.org/global/topics/labour-migration/policy-areas/migrant-domestic-workers/lang–en/index.htm

References

Abrahamson, P. 2016. End of an era? China's One Child Policy and its unintended consequences. *Asian Social Work and Policy Review, 10*, 326–338.

Barry, K. 1995. *The prostitution of sexuality.* New York: New York University Press.

Bas, N. F., Benjamin, M., and Chang, J. C. 2004. Saipan sweatshop lawsuit ends with important gains for workers and lessons for activists. http://www.cleanclothes.org/about-us/617-saipan-sweatshop-lawsuit-ends-with-important-ga. Retrieved on August 17, 2009.

Baum, T. 2013. *International perspectives on women and work in hotels, catering, and tourism.* ILO: Geneva. http://www.ilo.org/wcmsp5/groups/public/–dgreports/–gender/documents/publication/wcms_209867.pdf. Retrieved on January 12, 2018.

Blomberg, M., and Dara, M. 2020. Will Cambodia's garment sector rebound after 'horror year'? *Reuters.* https://www.reuters.com/article/us-cambodia-garment-workers-feature-trfn-idUSKBN28S007. Retrieved on May 18, 2021.

Blumberg, R. L. 1995. Gender, microenterprise, performance, and power: Case studies from the Dominican Republic, Ecuador, Guatemala, and Swaziland. In *Women in the Latin American development process,* edited by C. E. Bose and E. Acosta-Belen. Philadelphia, PA: Temple University Press.

Brennan, D. 2002. Selling sex for visas: Sex tourism as a stepping stone to international migration. In *Global woman: Nannies, maids, and sex workers in the new economy,* edited by B. Ehrenreich and A. R. Hochschild. New York: Metropolitan Books.

Brennan, D. 2004. *Transnational desires and sex tourism in the Dominican Republic: What's love got to do with it?* Durham, NC: Duke University Press.

Butler, S. 2019. Why are wages so low for garment workers in Bangladesh? *The Guardian.* https://www.theguardian.com/business/2019/jan/21/low-wages-garment-workers-bangladesh-analysis. Retrieved on May 15, 2021.

Cabezas, A. L. 2002. Tourism, sex work, and women's rights in the Dominican Republic. In *Globalization and human rights,* edited by A. Brysk. Berkeley, CA: University of California Press.

Chang, G. 2000. *Disposable domestics.* Cambridge, MA: South End Press.

Chant, S. 1997. Female employment in Puerto Vallarta: A case study. In *Gender, work, and tourism,* edited by M. T. Sinclair. London: Routledge.

Chi, D. Q., and van den Broek, D. 2020. Gendered labour activism in the Vietnamese manufacturing industry. *Gender, Work, & Organization, 27,* 1145–1164.

Choi, C., Hwang, M. C., and Parreñas, R. S. 2018. Women on the move: Stalled gender revolution in global migrations. In *Handbook of the sociology of gender* (pp. 493–506), edited by B. Risman, C. Froyum, and W. Scarborough. Switzerland: Springer, Cham.

Clark, E. 2019. Mark Parker's pay day: The Nike CEO's compensation rose 48 percent last year. *WWD.* https://wwd.com/fashion-news/fashion-scoops/nike-ceo-mark-parker-compensation-1203225959/. Retrieved on May 15, 2021.

Clean Clothes Campaign. 2016. *Rana Plaza: A manmade disaster that shook the world.* https://cleanclothes.org/ua/2013/rana-plaza. Retrieved on March 30, 2017.

Clean Clothes Campaign. 2019. *Tailored wages 2019: The state of pay in the global garment industry.* https://cleanclothes.org/news/2019/major-brands-are-failing-on-living-wage-commitments. Retrieved on May 12, 2021.

Clean Clothes Campaign. 2021. On Bangladesh Accord's anniversary, brands should commit to new binding safety agreement to safeguard its work. https://cleanclothes.org/news/2021/on-bangladesh-accords-anniversary-brands-should-commit-to-new-binding-safety-agreement-to-safeguard-its-work. Retrieved on May 21, 2021.

Dahan, Y., Lerner, H., and Milman-Sivan, F. 2016. The Guiding Principles for Business and Human Rights: Labour violations and shared responsibility. *International Journal of Comparative Labour Law and Industrial Relations, 32,* 425–447.

Davidson, J. O. 2015. Sex tourism (male). In *The international encyclopedia of human sexuality,* edited by P. Whelehen and A. Bolin. Chichester, West Sussex, and Malden, MA: John Wiley and Sons.

Desai, M. 2002. Transnational solidarity: Women's agency, structural adjustment, and globalization. In *Women's activism and globalization: Linking local struggles transnational politics,* edited by N. A. Naples and M. Desai. New York: Routledge.

Desai, M. 2007. The messy relationship between feminisms and globalizations. *Gender and Society, 21,* 797–804.

Dreier, P. 2019. Disney is not the greatest place on Earth to work. *The Nation.* https://www.thenation.com/article/economy/disney-iger-labor/. Retrieved on May 15, 2021.

Emmett, B. 2009. *Paying the price for the economic crisis.* http://www.oxfam.org.uk/resources/policy/economic_crisis/downloads/impact_economic_crisis_women.pdf. Retrieved on August 14, 2009.

Enloe, C. 1989. *Bananas, beaches, and bases: Making feminist sense of international relations.* Berkeley, CA: University of California Press.

Farhana, K. 2014. Ready-made garments in Bangladesh: No longer a forgotten sector. *OECD Observer.* http://oecdobserver.org/news/fullstory.php/aid/4368/Ready-made_garments_in_Bangladesh:_No_longer_a_forgotten_sector.html. Retrieved on March 30, 2017.

Fashionating World. 2019. *Cambodia's GTF exports increase by 13.18%.* https://www.fashionatingworld.com/new1-2/cambodia-s-gtf-exports-increase-by-13-18. Retrieved on May 18, 2021.

Ferrant, G., and Tuccio, M. 2015. South–South migration and discrimination against women in social institutions: A two-way relationship. *World Development, 72,* 240–254.

Fuentes, A., and Ehrenreich, B. 1983. *Women in the global factory.* Boston, MA: South End Press.

Global Justice Now. 2018. *69 of the richest 100 entities on the planet are corporations, not governments, figures show.* https://www.globaljustice.org.uk/news/69-richest-100-entities-planet-are-corporations-not-governments-figures-show/. Retrieved on May 10, 2021.

Goldenberg, S. M., Engstrom, D., Rolon, M. L., Silverman, J. G., and Strathdee, S. A. 2013. Sex workers, perspectives on strategies to reduce sexual exploitation and HIV risk: A qualitative study in Tijuana, Mexico. *PloS One, 8,* p.e72982.

Goldsmith, J. 2021. Disney executive chair Bob Iger sees pay package plunge as he and CEO Bob Chapek forgo bonuses for pandemic-struck 2020. *Deadline.* https://deadline.com/2021/01/disney-executive-chair-bob-iger-sees-pay-package-plunge-as-he-and-ceo-bob-chapek-forgo-bonuses-for-pandemic-struck-2020-1234676578/. Retrieved on May 15, 2021.

Grosh, O. (2011). Foreign wives, domestic violence: US law stigmatizes and fails to protect mail-order brides. *Hastings Women's LJ, 22,* 81.

Gunewardena, N., and Kingsolver, A. 2007. Introduction. In *The gender of globalization: Women navigating cultural and economic marginalities,* edited by N. Gunewardena and A. Kingsolver. Santa Fe, NM: School for Advanced Research Press.

Hawke, A., and Raphael, A. 2016. *Offenders on the move: The Global Study Report on Sexual Exploitation of Children in Travel and Tourism.* Bangkok, Thailand: ECPAT International.

Heston, L. V. 2016. Mail order brides. In *The Wiley Blackwell encyclopedia of gender and sexuality studies,* edited by N.A. Naples, R.C. Hoogland, M. Wickramasinghe, W. Ching, and A. Wong. Malden, MA: Wiley-Blackwell.

Hoang, L., Lam, T., Yeoh, B., and Graham, E. 2015. Transnational migration, changing care arrangements, and left-behind children's responses in Southeast Asia. *Children's Geographies, 13,* 263–277.

Hochschild, A. R. 2000. Global care chains and emotional surplus value. In *On the edge: Globalization and the new millennium,* edited by T. Giddens and W. Hutton. London: Sage Publishers.

Hochschild, A. R. 2002. Love and gold. In *Global woman: Nannies, maids, and sex workers in the new economy,* edited by B. Ehrenreich and A. R. Hochschild. New York: Metropolitan Books.

Holdcroft, J. 2015. Transforming supply chains in industrial relations. *International Journal of Labour Relations, 7,* 92–104.

Hollingsworth, J., Seo, Y., and Bae, G. 2020. South Korean authorities encourage men to marry foreign women. But their brides often become victims of abuse.

CNN. https://www.cnn.com/2020/08/02/asia/foreign-wives-south-korea-intl-hnk -dst/index.html. Retrieved on May 24, 2021.

Human Rights Watch. 2015. *Whoever raises their head suffers the most: Workers' rights in Bangladesh's garment industry.* https://www.hrw.org /report/2015/04/22/whoever-raises-their-head-suffers-most/workers -rights-bangladeshs-garment. Retrieved on March 30, 2017.

Human Rights Watch. 2016. *"I was sold": Abuse and exploitation of migrant domestic workers in Oman.* https://www.hrw.org/report/2016/07/13/i-was-sold/abuse-and -exploitation-migrant-domestic-workers-oman. Retrieved on April 8, 2017.

Human Rights Watch. 2018. *Respect the rights of the domestic workers that Oman depends on.* https://www.hrw.org/news/2018/01/18/respect-rights-domestic -workers-oman-depends. Retrieved on May 21, 2021.

Human Rights Watch. 2019a. Combatting sexual harassment in the garment industry. https://www.hrw.org/news/2019/02/12/combating-sexual-harassment -garment-industry. Retrieved on May 15, 2021.

Human Rights Watch. 2019b. *Bangladesh: Investigate dismissal of protesting workers.* https://www.hrw.org/news/2019/03/05/bangladesh-investigate-dismissals -protesting-workers#. Retrieved on May 20, 2021.

ILO (International Labour Organization). 2011. *C189-Domestic Workers Convention, 2011 (No. 189).* http://www.ilo.org/dyn/normlex/en/f?p=NORMLEXPUB:12100 :0::NO::P12100_INSTRUMENT_ID:2551460. Retrieved on April 19, 2017.

ILO (International Labour Organization). 2013. *Domestic workers across the world: Global and regional statistics on the extent of legal protection.* http://www .ilo.org/wcmsp5/groups/public/--dgreports/--dcomm/--publ/documents /publication/wcms_173363.pdf. Retrieved on April 8, 2017.

ILO (International Labour Organization). 2014. *Wages and working hours in the textiles, clothing, leather, and footwear industries.* http://www.ilo.org/wcmsp5 /groups/public/@ed_dialogue/@sector/documents/publication/wcms_300463. pdf. Retrieved on March 28, 2017.

ILO (International Labour Organization). 2015. *ILO global estimates on migrant workers.* http://ilo.org/wcmsp5/groups/public/--dgreports/--dcomm/documents /publication/wcms_436343.pdf. Retrieved on April 6, 2017.

ILO (International Labour Organization). 2016. *Promoting decent work global supply chains in Latin America and the Caribbean.* http://www.ilo.org/wcmsp5 /groups/public/--americas/--ro-lima/documents/publication/wcms_503754.pdf. Retrieved on March 28, 2017.

ILO (International Labour Organization). 2017a. *How to promote decent work and workers' rights in export processing zones.* https://www.ilo.org/global/about-the -ilo/newsroom/news/WCMS_599888/lang--en/index.htm. Retrieved on May 10, 2021.

ILO (International Labour Organization). 2017b. *Global estimates of modern slavery.* https://www.ilo.org/wcmsp5/groups/public/--dgreports/--dcomm /documents/publication/wcms_575479.pdf. Retrieved on May 26, 2021.

ILO (International Labour Organization). 2018a. *Cambodia garment and footwear sector bulletin.* https://www.ilo.org/wcmsp5/groups/public/—asia/—ro-bangkok /documents/publication/wcms_663043.pd. Retrieved on May 18, 2021.

ILO (International Labour Organization). 2018b. *ILO global estimates on international migrant workers.* https://www.ilo.org/global/publications/books /WCMS_652001/lang–en/index.htm. Retrieved on May 21, 2021.

ILO (International Labour Organization). 2019. *Sexual harassment at work: Insights from the garment industry.* https://www.ilo.org/wcmsp5/groups/public /—ed_dialogue/—sector/documents/publication/wcms_732095.pdf. Retrieved on May 15, 2021.

ILO (International Labour Organization). 2020a. Understanding the gender composition and experience of ready-made garment (RMG) workers in Bangladesh. https://www.ilo.org/wcmsp5/groups/public/—asia/—ro-bangkok/—ilo-dhaka /documents/publication/wcms_754669.pdf. Retrieved on May 16, 2021.

ILO (International Labour Organization). 2020b. *The supply chain ripple effect: How Covid-19 is affecting garment workers and families in Asia and the Pacific.* https://www.ilo.org/wcmsp5/groups/public/—asia/—ro-bangkok/documents /briefingnote/wcms_758626.pdf. Retrieved on May 18, 2021.

Imam, A. 2016. *The devil is in the details: At the nexus of development, women's rights, and religious fundamentalisms.* Toronto: AWID.

Institute for Global Labour and Human Rights. 2016. *Factory collapse in Bangladesh.* http://www.globallabourrights.org/campaigns/factory-collapse-in -bangladesh. Retrieved on March 30, 2017.

ITUC. 2016. Inside the global supply chains of 50 top companies. http://www.ituc-csi .org/IMG/pdf/pdffrontlines_scandal_en-2.pdf. Retrieved on March 26, 2017.

ITUC. 2019. *Foul play: Sponsors leave workers (still) on the sidelines.* https://cleanclothes. org/news/2018/06/11/adidas-and-nike-pay-record-breaking-amounts-to-footballers-but -deny-decent-wages-to-women-stitching-their-shirts. Retrieved on May 15, 2021.

Kagan, S. 2017. *Domestic workers and employers in the Arab states: Promising practices and innovative models for a productive working relationship: ILO white paper.* Beirut: International Labour Organization, 2017.

Karides, M. 2002. Linking local efforts with global struggle: Trinidad's national union of domestic employees. In *Women's activism and globalization: Linking local struggles and transnational politics*, edited by N. A. Naples and M. Desai. New York: Routledge.

Katsulis, Y. 2010."Living like a king": Conspicuous consumption, virtual communities, and the social construction of paid sexual encounters by US sex tourists. *Men and Masculinities, 13,* 210–230.

Kosuri, M. D., and Jeglic, E. L. 2016. Child sex tourism: American perceptions of foreign victims. *Journal of Sexual Aggression.* DOI: 10.1080/13552600.201.

Lim, L. Y. C. 1990. Women's work in export factories: The politics of a cause. In *Persistent inequalities,* edited by I. Tinker. Oxford: Oxford University Press.

Lindee, K. M. 2007. Love, honor, or control: Domestic violence, trafficking, and the question of how to regulate the mail-order bride industry. *Columbia Journal of Gender and Law, 16,* 551–602.

Lorentzen, L. A., and Turpin, J. 1996. Introduction: The gendered new world order. In *The gendered new world,* edited by J. Turpin and L. A. Lorentzen. New York: Routledge.

Louie, M. C. Y. 2001. *Sweatshop warriors.* Cambridge, MA: South End Press.

Lu, T. S., Holmes, A., Noone, C., and Flaherty, G. T. 2020. Sun, sea, and sex: A review of the sex tourism literature. *Tropical Diseases, Travel Medicine and Vaccines, 6.* https://doi.org/10.1186/s40794-020-00124-0. Retrieved on May 26, 2021.

Lund-Thomsen, P., and Lindgreen, A. 2014. Corporate social responsibility in global value chains: Where are we now and where are we going? *Journal of Business Ethics, 123,* 11–22.

Meszaros, J. 2017. American men and romance tourism: Searching for traditional trophy wives as status symbols of masculinity. *Women's Studies Quarterly, 45,* 225–242.

Moghadam, V. M. (2005). *Globalizing women: Transnational feminist networks.* JHU Press.

Moran, T. H. 2002. *Beyond sweatshops: Foreign direct investment and globalization in developing countries.* Washington, DC: Brookings Institution Press.

Naples, N. A. 2002. Changing the terms: Community activism, globalization, and the dilemmas of transnational praxis. In *Women's activism and globalization: Linking local struggles transnational politics,* edited by N. A. Naples and M. Desai. New York: Routledge.

Neal, M. 2016. Dirty customers: Stigma and identity among sex tourists. *Journal of Consumer Culture, 18,* 1–18.

OHCHR (Office of the United Nations High Commissioner for Human Rights). 2015. *Behind closed doors: Protecting and promoting the human rights of migrant domestic workers in an irregular situation.* http://www.ohchr.org/Documents/Publications /Behind_closed_doors_HR_PUB_15_4_EN.pdf. Retrieved on April 7, 2017.

Open Access Government. 2020. *The cost of fashion: 4.1 million Bangladeshi garment workers.* https://www.openaccessgovernment.org/bangladeshi-garment -workers/89939/. Retrieved on May 15, 2021.

Otobe, N. 2015. *Export-led development, employment and gender in the era of global-ization: Working paper no. 197.* Geneva: ILO.

Ottisova, L., Hemmings, S., Howard, L. M., Zimmerman, C., and Oram, S. 2016. Prevalence and risk of violence and the mental, physical and sexual health problems associated with human trafficking: An updated systematic review. *Epidemiology and Psychiatric Sciences, 25,* 317–341.

Pakekh, S., and Wilcox, S. 2014. Feminist perspectives on globalization. *Encyclopedia of Philosophy.* https://plato.stanford.edu/archives/win2014/entries /feminism-globalization/. Retrieved on March 25, 2017.

Palet, L. S. 2016. January. This is the new sex destination. *Ozy.* http://www.ozy.com /fast-forward/this-is-the-new-sex-tourism-destination/61036. Retrieved on January 11, 2018.

Pangestu, M. E., and Granryd, M. 2020. Equal access to digital technologies: A key to resilient recovery. *World Bank Blogs.* https://blogs.worldbank.org/voices/equal -access-digital-technologies-key-resilient-recovery. Retrieved on May 10, 2021.

Parreñas, R. S. 2008. *The force of domesticity: Filipina migrants and globalization.* New York: New York University Press.

Parreñas, R. S., and Silvey, R. 2016. Domestic workers refusing neo-slavery in the UAE. *Contexts, 15,* 36–41.

Paton, E. 2020. Union garment workers fear 'an opportunity to get rid of us'. *New York Times.* https://www.nytimes.com/2020/05/08/fashion/coronavirus -garment-workers-asia-unions.html. Retrieved on May 18, 2021.

Powell, J. M., and Schroeder, T. M. 2016. Friends in low places? The conditional influence of trade on the status of women. *Studies in Comparative International Development, 51,* 169–188.

Ruggie, J. G., Rees, C., and Davis, R. 2021. Ten years after: From the UN Guiding Principles to multi-fiduciary obligations. https://corpgov.law.harvard.edu /2021/05/13/ten-years-after-from-the-un-guiding-principles-to-multi-fiduciary -obligations/. Retrieved on May 20, 2021.

Ryabov, I. 2016. Post-migration experiences of female immigrant spouses from the former Soviet Union. *Journal of Intercultural Studies, 37,* 286–302.

Salzinger, L. 2003. *Genders in production: Making workers in Mexico's global factories.* Berkeley, CA: University of California Press.

Sherman, J. 2020. The story of the UN Guiding Principles on Business and Human Rights. *Harvard Kennedy School.* https://www.hks.harvard.edu/sites/default/files /centers/mrcbg/files/CRI_AWP_71.pdf. Retrieved on May 20, 2021.

Shetti, S. 2015. Corporations have rights. Now we need a global treaty on their responsibility. *Amnesty International.* https://www.amnesty.org/en/latest /campaigns/2015/01/corporations-have-rights-now-we-need-a-global-treaty -on-their-responsibilities/. Retrieved on March 30, 2017.

Simons, M. 2019. 'Do you ever think about me?': The children sex tourists leave behind. *The Guardian.* https://www.theguardian.com/society/2019/mar/02/children -sex-tourists-leave-behind-fathers-visited-philippines. Retrieved on May 24, 2021.

Starr, E., and Adams, M. 2016. The domestic exotic: Mail-order brides and the paradox of globalized intimacies. *Signs: Journal of Women in Culture and Society, 41,* 953–975.

Tahirih Justice Center. 2017. *International marriage brokers.* http://www.tahirih.org/what -we-do/policy-advocacy/international-marriage-brokers/. Retrieved on April 17, 2017.

Tayah, M. 2016. *Decent work for migrant domestic workers: Moving the agenda forward.* ILO. http://www.ilo.org/global/topics/labour-migration/publications /WCMS_535596/lang–en/index.htm. Retrieved on April 7, 2017.

Thurnell-Read, T. 2015. 'Just blokes doing blokes' stuff': Risk, gender and the collective performance of masculinity during the Eastern European Stag Tour Weekend. In *Men, Masculinities, Travel and Tourism,* edited by M. E. Casey and T. Thurnell-Read. Basingstoke, UK: Palgrave Macmillan.

Tran, T. 2012. Mis-matched: Taking a state approach to enforcing the growing international matchmaking industry. *Family Court Review, 50,* 159–174.

Tyc, A. 2021. *Global trade, labour rights, and international law.* Abingdon, UK: Routledge.

UN (United Nations). 1999. *World survey on the role of women in development: Globalization, gender and work.* New York: Author.

UN Guiding Principles. 2017. Reporting framework: Users and supporters. https://www.ungpreporting.org/about-us/support-and-users/. Retrieved on May 20, 2021.

UN Treaty Collection. 2021. *Protocol to Prevent, Suppress and Punish Trafficking in Persons, Especially Women and Children, supplementing the United Nations Convention against Transnational Organized Crime.* https://treaties.un.org/pages/ViewDetails.aspx?src=TREATYandmtdsg_no=XVIII-12-aandchapter=18 andclang=_en. Retrieved on May 25, 2021.

UN Women. 2016. *Progress of the world's women 2015-2016: Transforming economies, realizing rights.* http://progress.unwomen.org/en/2015/pdf/UNW_progressreport.pdf. Retrieved on July 18, 2016.

UN Women. 2017. *At what cost? Women migrant workers, remittances, and development.* http://www.unwomen.org/-/media/headquarters/attachments/sections/library/publications/2017/women-migrant-workers-remittances-and-development.pdf?vs=5146. Retrieved on April 6, 2017.

UN Women. 2020. Migrant women and remittances: Exploring the data from selected countries. https://www.unwomen.org/en/digital-library/publications/2020/06/policy-brief-migrant-women-and-remittances-exploring-the-data-from-selected-countries. Retrieved on May 21, 2021.

UNCTAD (United Nations Conference on Trade and Development). 2019. *World Investment Report 2019: Special export zones.* https://unctad.org/webflyer/world-investment-report-2019. Retrieved on May 10, 2021.

UNDP (United Nations Development Programme). 2017. *Gender dimensions of the Guiding Principles on Business and Human Rights.* https://www.ohchr.org/Documents/Issues/Business/BookletGenderDimensionsGuidingPrinciples.pdf. Retrieved on May 20, 2021.

UNFPA (United Nations Population Fund). 2006. *State of the world population 2006: A Passage to hope—women and international migration.* https://www.unfpa.org/publications/state-world-population-2006. Retrieved on May 20, 2021.

UNFPA (United Nations Population Fund). 2015. *Migration.* http://www.unfpa.org/migration. Retrieved on April 7, 2017.

UNODC (United Nations Office on Drugs and Crime). 2014. *Global report on trafficking in persons 2014.* Vienna: UNODC.

UNODC (United Nations Office on Drugs and Crime). 2017. *Global report on trafficking in persons 2016.* Vienna: UNODC. http://www.unodc.org/documents /data-and-analysis/glotip/2016_Global_Report_on_Trafficking_in_Persons.pdf. Retrieved on April 18, 2017.

UNODC (United Nations Office on Drugs and Crime). 2020. *Interlinkages between trafficking in persons and marriage.* https://www.unodc.org/documents /human-trafficking/2020/UNODC_Interlinkages_Trafficking_in_Persons_and _Marriage.pdf. Retrieved on May 24, 2021.

UNODC (United Nations Office on Drugs and Crime). 2021. *Global report on trafficking in persons 2020.* https://www.unodc.org/documents/data-and-analysis /tip/2021/GLOTiP_2020_15jan_web.pdf. Retrieved on May 25, 2021.

UNWTO (United Nations World Tourism Organization). 1995. *WTO Statement on the prevention of organized sex tourism.* https://www.e-unwto.org/doi/ pdf/10.18111/unwtodeclarations.1995.05.06. Retrieved on August 17, 2021.

UNWTO (United Nations World Tourism Organization). 2019. *International tourism growth continues to outplace the global economy.* https://www.unwto.org /international-tourism-growth-continues-to-outpace-the-economy. Retrieved on May 24, 2021.

U.S. Department of State. Trafficking in persons report. 2016. https://www.state .gov/documents/organization/258876.pdf. Retrieved on January 12, 2018.

WEDO (Women's Environment and Development Organization). 2009. *Challenging Nike to deliver on worker rights.* https://wedo.org/challenging -nike-to-deliver-on-workers-rights/. Retrieved on May 20, 2021.

WHO (World Health Organization). 2015. *A technical brief: HIV and young people who sell sex.* http://www.unodc.org/documents/hiv-aids/2015/WHO _HIV_2015.7_eng.pdf. Retrieved on April 14, 2017.

Yeates, N. 2012. Global care chains: A state of the art review and future directions in care transnationalization research. *Global Networks, 12,* 135–154.

Yeung, W. J., and Mu, Z. 2020. Migration and marriage in Asian contexts. *Journal of Ethnic and Migration Studies, 46,* 2863–2879.

Design Element: Abstract floral frame: Telnov Oleksii/Shutterstock

8 *Women and Religion*

Now what about Islam? And what of the other great religions? When we think about religions in general, it seems to me that, more or less, they are the same. They all have a general human call for the equality of people—regardless of color, race, or sex. One finds this conception of equality in all of the religions, as well as in Marxism or existentialism. But when we come to the specifics, when we come to the daily lives of men and women, rich and poor, one race and another, this general sense of equality does not seem to be in evidence. Here we find oppression, including the oppression of women. So we must not have illusions about religion, because religion is used, and it is used often by those in power.

—NAWAL EL SAADAWI, Egyptian feminist writer and activist, physician

Religious feminists seek to reform and reclaim religion so that it supports women's equality. This photo shows Israeli members of the liberal Jewish religious group Women of the Wall carrying a Torah scroll during prayers in the women's section of the Western Wall, in the Old City of Jerusalem on November 2, 2016. The group fights for equal prayer rights at the site. MENAHEM KAHANA/AFP/Getty Images

This chapter focuses on women and religion and feminist theology. Religion is profoundly important to many women worldwide and can be a source of women's empowerment, or their disempowerment. Inequalities based on gender, race, class, and sexuality can be seen as incompatible with a just, loving God and can motivate activism. Women's religious and spiritual leadership and participation in sacred rituals can strengthen them. Religious affiliation may also empower women by giving them strength and hope in the face of patriarchal family structures and harsh economic conditions (Avishai, 2008). Unfortunately, though, religions are sometimes agents of gender inequality, presenting patriarchy as inevitable, inescapable, and correct (Daly, 1978; Sered, 1999). Religious feminists call attention to the ways that their religions contribute to gender inequality and work for reform in their religions to promote women's empowerment. Some religions have been transformed by feminism, and other religions (like goddess spirituality) have arisen out of feminism (Braude, 2006).

Diversity and the Study of Women and Religion

One of the challenges for global women's studies and the study of religion is that the great diversity of religious and spiritual traditions makes it hard to generalize about women and religion.

Religious and Spiritual Diversity

The relationship between religion and gender inequality is complex and depends on which religion you are talking about, the role it plays in a society or culture, and the role it plays in an individual's life. Even within a religion, there are variants, some of which support gender equality more than others. Likewise, the gendered practices of a religion can vary widely based on local norms. Research finds that the sexism associated with religion is accounted for by specific aspects of some religions, rather than by religion in general (Maltby & Hall, 2014). However, while contextualizing religion and its effects on women is enormously important for this chapter, you should be aware that it is difficult given the immense variability of religions, religious contexts, and religious practice.

This chapter focuses on the world's four major religions. Christians comprise the largest religious group in the world (31%), followed by Muslims (24.1%), Hindus (15.1%), and Buddhists (6.9%) (Pew Research Center, 2017). Although the primary focus of this chapter is the world's major religions, it is important to keep in mind that smaller indigenous religions (religions in small-scale, kinship-based communities) often give women a greater role than do the world's major religions. In many indigenous traditions, there are strong female mythological figures, female rituals, and no doctrine of male superiority and dominance (Gross, 1996; Sered, 1994, 1999). For example, in many traditional African religions, women play active roles as *diviners* (who foretell the future) and *healers* of physical and psychological illnesses (Mbon, 1987). In nonmainstream religions, women often have more power and autonomy (Agadjanian, 2015; Gross, 1996). Sered (1994) examines twelve contemporary,

"Unquestionably 'religion' or 'spirituality' defined by and in the service of patriarchy is a force against freedom, vitality, and survival. But patriarchy's definition of religion is not the only one."
Sheila Ruth, feminist religious studies scholar, author of "Take Back the Light"

BOX 8.1   *Some Contemporary Woman-Centered Religions*

Afro-Brazilian Religions (Brazil)

These combine elements of African tribal religions, Amerindian religions, Catholicism, and Kardecism (French Spiritism). Their main features are curing and public rituals where female mediums are possessed by spirits. They coexist with Catholicism.

Black Carib Religion (Central America)

This religion is centered on numerous rituals to honor and appease ancestral spirits and to protect the living against evil spirits and sorcery. Old women are the spiritual leaders. Most Black Caribs are also Roman Catholic.

Burmese Nat Religion (Upper Burma)

This religion focuses on the appeasement of spirits called *nats*. These *nats* are also called upon to prevent and cure illness and to bring good luck. Women perform most rituals, and almost all shamans are women as well. The religion exists alongside Buddhist practices.

Christian Science (United States)

Mary Baker Eddy founded this religion in the nineteenth century. Christian Scientists believe that healing comes about through study and prayer.

Korean Household Religion

Korean women make offerings to gods for the well-being of their households and consult female shamans for guidance. This religion coexists with Buddhism.

Sande Secret Society (West Africa)

Adolescent girls are initiated into the societies at lengthy all-female retreats where they are taught about childbirth and other skills women are expected to know. Sande societies also control the supernatural and sacred realm. This religion coexists with male secret societies called *Poro*.

Za–r (parts of Africa and the Middle East)

Za–r are spirits that attack and possess women. Women then join za–r cults in which they participate in rituals to appease the possessing spirit and turn it into an ally. Women's za–r activities often serve as a counterpart to men's involvement in official Islamic practices.

Feminist Spirituality Movement

This is discussed at the end of the chapter.

_____

Source: Sered, 1994.

woman-dominated religions in depth (Box 8.1 gives a sampling of her research). These religions are interesting in that they often exist alongside mainstream religions and frequently emphasize the appeasement of spirits for purposes of healing and bringing good tidings.

Religious Fundamentalism

As Ruether (2002) points out, it is a mistake to think that religiousness is authentically represented only by patriarchal, misogynist religious traditions; there are progressive, egalitarian principles within religious traditions. It is primarily the conservative and fundamentalist strains of the world's religions that most vociferously promote traditional roles for women and attempt to limit women's rights. Indeed, it is important to recognize that fundamentalisms have emerged out of all of the world's major religious traditions, including Buddhism, Christianity, Hinduism, Islam, and Judaism (UN Special Rapporteur in the Field of Cultural Rights, 2017).

Religious fundamentalisms are committed to the authority of ancient scriptures and believe them to be infallible; hold religion to provide a total worldview inseparable from politics; idealize a past when gender spheres were separate; require women to be modest and subordinate and regulate their sexuality; reject norms of universal human rights and multiculturalism; and have an "us versus them" mentality (UN Special Rapporteur in the Field of Cultural Rights, 2017). These religions see men and women as essentially different. They justify gender inequality as divinely mandated and use religious scriptures to support traditional views of gender roles (Daly, 1985; Glick, Lameiras, & Castro, 2002; Gross, 1996). They often condemn and resist feminism. Research confirms the idea that fundamentalism is a stronger predictor than religiosity in discriminatory attitudes toward women (Hannover et al., 2018; Hunsberger, Owusu, & Duck, 1999; Kirkpatrick, 1993; Mangis, 1995). See Figure 8.1 for a summary.

"No religion is inherently fundamentalist nor should fundamentalist views be imputed to all adherents of any religion."
UN Special Rapporteur in the Field of Cultural Rights

FIGURE 8.1 *Features of Fundamentalist Religions Affecting Women's Rights*

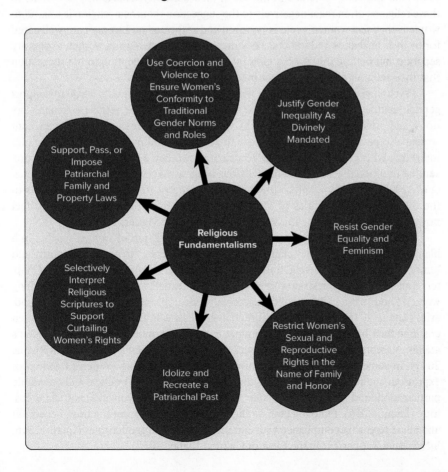

Research on sexism and religion finds that the gender stereotypes and ideologies associated with religion are primarily "benevolent" rather than "hostile," although this relationship may differ depending on the particular religious form (Burn & Busso, 2005; Maltby & Hall, 2014; Mikołajczak & Pietrzak, 2014; Taşdemir & Sakalli-Uğurlu, 2010). **Benevolent sexism** is a belief that characterizes women "as pure creatures who ought to be protected, supported, and adored and whose love is necessary to make a man complete" (Glick & Fiske 2001, p. 109). Benevolent sexism has three domains: *Protective Paternalism* (i.e., men should protect and provide for women); *Complementary Gender Differentiation* (i.e., women are naturally suited for traditional female-specific gender roles); and *Heterosexual Intimacy* (i.e., heterosexual romantic relationships are essential) (Glick & Fiske, 2001). These domains are characteristic of conservative and fundamentalist religious ideologies and are found in scriptures selectively interpreted as the literal word of God.

Benevolent sexism is evident in fundamentalist and conservative religious strains. Adherents usually express great concern and respect for family, motherhood, and childrearing. And although they place men as the family head, restrict religious leadership to men, and expect women to submit to male authority, men are expected to be kind and compassionate in the use of their authority. This is why adherents to these religions often react negatively to the suggestion that their religion is unkind to women—they feel women's role is honored and respected and women are well-cared for by their husbands and fathers. They may admit that men's and women's roles are separate, but believe this is what God intended and take exception to the suggestion that their religion promotes gender inequality.

Psychologists point out that the net effect of benevolent sexism is still to support gender inequality. After all, it justifies traditional gender roles, restricts women's options, and privileges a gender hierarchy where men have greater power. Benevolent sexism also pacifies women's resistance to gender subordination by masking gender inequality with chivalry, appearing to celebrate women's traditional role, and presenting traditional gender roles as religious imperative (Glick & Fiske, 2001; Glick et al., 2002). The way religious fundamentalisms construct gender often appeals to the threatened masculinities of men who are excluded from elite groups and feel powerless due to economic injustice (Imam, Gokal, & Marler, 2017).

Fundamentalist religions frequently wrap the restriction of women's rights in a blanket of benevolence. They claim restrictions are necessary to protect the purity and honor of females and to defend traditional family and cultural values. As seen in Chapters 3 and 4, they often restrict women's sexual and sexuality rights. Indeed, controlling women's bodies is a hallmark of fundamentalist ideology that crosses religious boundaries (Imam, 2016). When religious fundamentalists gain political power, they often enshrine their beliefs in gender discriminatory laws and policies and restrict women's sexual and reproductive rights (UN Special Rapporteur in the Field of Cultural Rights, 2017). In some cases, they support laws and practices limiting women's freedom of expression and movement, as well as their rights to education, political and economic participation, and rights to citizenship, property, inheritance, divorce, and child custody (Imam, 2016). Fundamentalist religions sometimes support the use of coercion and abuse to ensure compliance with extremely traditional gender roles (Imam, 2016; UN Special Rapporteur in the Field of Cultural Rights, 2017).

In fundamentalist religions, benevolent sexism often coexists with **hostile sexism**, the perception of women as enemies or adversaries and as inferior in ways that justify men's control of them. As will become evident later in this chapter, there are elements in most fundamentalist religions that suggest women are temptresses that threaten men's religious study, men's relationships with the divine, and men's enlightenment, and consequently suggest that women have to be controlled. The coexistence of both benevolent and hostile sexism is known as **ambivalent sexism** (Glick & Fiske, 2001).

The heterosexual intimacy and complementary gender differentiation components of benevolent sexism also support heteropatriarchy. Religious fundamentalisms reinforce not only male authority over women, but also rigid heteronormative relationships (Imam, 2016). Although many religions now welcome LGBTQI+ persons, some fundamentalist and conservative religions condemn homosexuality and compel followers to view it as a sickness to be overcome through spiritual practice. Scripture is read selectively to justify discrimination against LGBTQI persons. For example, many Christian denominations have excommunicated and oppressed LGBTQI+ persons, using the Sodom and Gomorrah narrative (Genesis 19: 1-29) to justify their actions. In the United States, conservative Christian denominations have been instrumental in fighting against the right of lesbians and gays to marry, claiming that it's wrong because the Bible says that marriage is between a man and a woman. All over the world, conservative and fundamentalist religions are on the forefront of passing legislation that criminalizes homosexual behavior and denies SOGI rights (Imam, 2016). Fundamentalist and conservative religions do not ordain gays and lesbians or permit them to serve in religious leadership roles, and contest their right to marry.

Before we go on, it is important to note that women actively interpret religious gender norms and beliefs (they have "agency"). In other words, religious women are not victims that blindly follow the gendered expectations of their religion (Leamaster & Einwohner, 2018). They respond in different ways to their religion's sacred version of femininity and how to perform it. Their responses can range from acceptance and compliance, to reinterpretation, to resistance (Avishai, 2016; Di, 2020). Also notable is that feminism does not require the rejection of religion. As you will soon see in this chapter, many religious women identify as feminists, and many that do not explicitly identify as feminist still reject and resist patriarchal aspects of their religion.

Critiquing and Deconstructing Religion

According to Peach (2002), almost all religions are patriarchal in origin, development, leadership, authority, and power. Feminist critiques of religion propose that the majority of the world's religions depict men's greater power and status relative to women as appropriate and acceptable. Feminist theologians are scholars of religion that reinterpret and resist the patriarchal aspects of their religions. **Feminist theology** reconsiders the traditions, practices, scriptures, and theologies of religion from a feminist perspective with a commitment to transforming religion for gender equality (Watson, 2003). A feminist lens is used to critique, deconstruct, and

FIGURE 8.2 *Common Feminist Critiques of Religion*

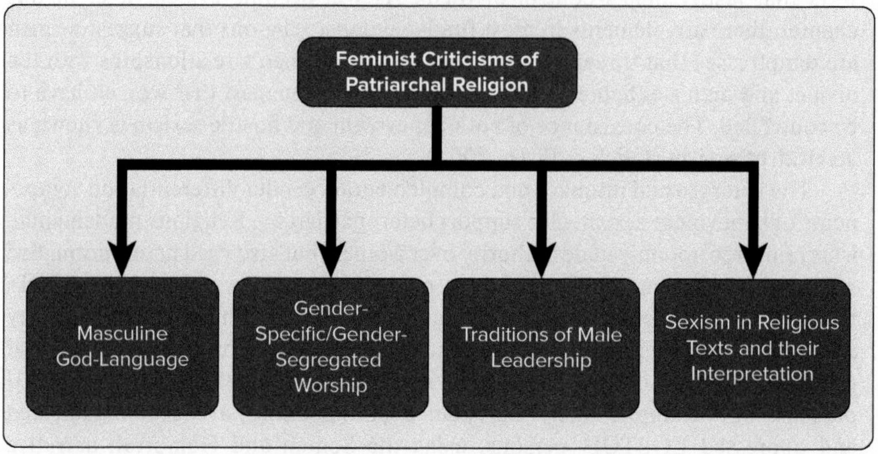

reconstruct religion. Feminist theology suggests that gender inequality is legitimized and reinforced by the common presentation of God as male, by traditions of male leadership, by the exclusion of women from major religious rituals, and by religious texts that leave out the female experience and validate men's authority over women (see Figure 8.2). In this chapter, these concerns are first described generally, and then later in regards to each of the world's major religions.

Masculine God-Language and Imagery

Feminist critics of religion often cite the male imagery used by so many of the world's religions as both a source and a reflection of patriarchy. For instance, God or Allah is typically presented using **masculine God-language,** androcentric language arising from the patriarchal historical contexts in which the world's major religions emerged (Hidayatullah, 2014; Schüssler Fiorenza, 1992). The language used daily in worship and prayer, such as "Our Heavenly Father" and "He," gives the impression that God is thought of in exclusively masculine terms (Pagels, 1976). The concern is that this deifies male power because if God is exclusively male, then male is God and male dominance is legitimized through cosmic means (Daly, 1973; Plaskow & Christ, 2014; Whitehead, 2012). Many feminists also object to conceptions of God as a stern, male father/ruler when God could as easily be conceptualized as having feminine, motherly qualities (Ramshaw, 1995; Ruth, 1995). Masculine God-language, along with the fact that the many religions portray God as male and God's main messengers on earth as male—Jesus (Christianity), Muhammad (Islam), and the Buddha (Buddhism)—also contributes to common cultural views that spiritual leadership and "family headship" are the domain of men, and it is men that mediate our relationship with God. Some feminist theologians feel that the sexist and masculine focus of so many religions contributes to women's acceptance of male dominance by grounding it in the Divine (Daly, 1973; Ruth, 1995).

"Consider the impact on your self-image of being 'in the likeness of God,' like Jesus, the Pope, and the 'Brothers of the Church' and contrast it with never finding yourself reflected in the sacred pronoun. Utter: God, He . . . ; God, Him. Now say: God, She. . . . Imagine the experience of seeing oneself reflected in the sacred images of power."
Sheila Ruth, feminist religious studies scholar, author of Take Back the Light

Some religious leaders argue that masculine God-language does not mean that God is gendered, nor does it imply the superiority of the male over the female. However, that it is frequently considered daring, degrading, or alienating to speak of God using female pronouns and imagery suggests that referring to God in gendered terms is important in many religious traditions (Gross, 1979). Also, studies on gendered language (for example, using "he" or "man" to refer to all people) indicate that the generic masculine is not so generic after all and evokes male imagery (Hamilton, 1988, 1991; Hardin & Banaji, 1993). One study (McMinn et al., 1993) found that presenting God as male brought to mind the conception of God as "powerful" while presenting God as female brought to mind God as "merciful." Studies find that masculine images of God are associated with conservative gender ideologies (Slee, 2014; Whitehead, 2012). Fundamentalist and conservative religions (such as evangelical Christianity) especially embrace the idea that masculine God-language and imagery reflect the true nature of God, and they believe this supports male religious leadership and male headship of the family. To them, questioning masculine God-language is to question the truthfulness of the scriptures as the literal word of God.

> "If we do not mean that God is male when we use masculine pronouns and imagery, then why should there be any objections to using female imagery and pronouns as well?"
> *Rita Gross, Buddhist feminist theologian*

> "If Jews believe that all of us, male and female are created in the divine image, then why doesn't our liturgy reflect this basic theological conviction?"
> *Ellen Umansky, Jewish feminist theologian*

Sexism in Religious Texts

Another focus of feminist criticism of religion is sexism in religious texts. Historically, in all major religions, it is men who have composed, transmitted, and interpreted the sacred writings. Over time these writings and their interpretations increasingly reflected men's activities, achievements, and power, as well as societal views of male superiority (Holm, 1994). Religious stories and texts often contain these five messages that perpetuate women's lower status and power: (1) Female sexuality is potentially dangerous; (2) female religious figures are subordinate to male religious figures (they are typically portrayed in relationship to males); (3) females should be subservient wives, mothers, and homemakers; (4) men and women have fundamentally different "natures" (essentialism); and (5) women's lower status is punishment for their sinful nature.

Feminist theologians are also concerned about the relative absence in scriptures of women and girls and their experiences. As Ruether (1985) suggests, although women's experience may be found between the lines of religious texts, for the most part the norm presented for women is one of absence and silence. When women are portrayed, it is as objects praised for obedience or admonished for disobedience to men. Contemporary Christian, Jewish, and Islamic feminist theologians are also critical of the assumption that men are the normative recipients of revelation and the common representation of God as male (Hidayatullah, 2014; Smith, 2009). Additionally, most scriptures also sacralize patriarchy (present it as sacred) (Daly, 1985; Gross, 1996). Feminist theologian Mary Daly (1985) notes that the endorsement of traditional gender roles in religious texts makes women feel guilty or unnatural if they rebel against the role prescribed to them, and this condemns women to a restricted existence in the name of religion.

"Societal parity for women will never be fully realized until women are spiritually integrated into every major faith tradition in the world."
Kate Kelly, founder of the Ordain Women movement in Mormonism

Gender-Segregated Religious Practices and Traditions of Male Religious Leadership

A number of the world's religions have different rituals and forms of worship based on gender—that is, they have **gender-segregated religious practices.** In general, the religious practices of men are more public (for example, in the church, temple, or synagogue), and the practices of women are conducted in the home (for example, they prepare ritual and religious holiday meals).

Another instance of gender-segregated religious practices is that leadership roles in religions are usually reserved for men. Women ministers, bishops, priests, rabbis, gurus, mullahs and imams, and sadhus (holy people) remain rare or nonexistent in most religious traditions, even today (Eck & Jain, 1987). As Gross (1996) suggests, this is not the only important indicator of women's religious equality, but it is a way to quickly assess the status of women in a given religion. The exclusion of women from religious leadership positions is also important because it limits women's ability to introduce more gender-equal interpretations of scripture and reform patriarchal religion (Audette, Kwakwa, & Weaver, 2017).

Passages in religious texts are often used to justify why women should not hold religious leadership positions. Many religions also keep women theologically illiterate, thus ensuring that they are unqualified to hold high positions within the religion. For instance, women may not be permitted to study key religious texts, attend important religious ceremonies, or have access to theological education. Likewise, higher rates of illiteracy among females, and the lack of schooling in the languages of the texts, are in some cases obstacles. In most of the world's major religions (for instance, Christianity, Islam, and Buddhism), God's messengers on earth are male, and it is often said that only males may represent them. Some religions also maintain that women are spiritually inferior to men and that they are therefore unsuitable for religious leadership.

"If God had not intended that Women shou'd use their Reason, He wou'd not have given them any, for He does nothing in vain. If they are to use their Reason, certainly it ought to be employ'd about the noblest Objects, and in business of the greatest Consequences, therefore in Religion."
Mary Astell (1666–1731), English feminist philosopher

Many religious women maintain that just because women's role in religion is largely a private one, it is not a lesser one. Ahmed (2002) suggests that women's limited public role in Islam means that "women's Islam" is more spiritual and mystical than the "men's Islam" that focuses on religious texts and what some male religious leader says. It is also interesting that in virtually every culture, the heart of the religious tradition, at the local level and in the home, is performed, maintained, and transmitted by women (Eck & Jain, 1987). For instance, in most American Christian homes, it is the mother who gets the children ready for church and who prepares all religious holiday meals. Women's religious roles frequently provide the support necessary for the growth and maintenance of the tradition (Peach, 2002). Religious women often have a sense of importance in their religions from the knowledge that without them, those parts of religious traditions that take place in the home would not occur. Even in many highly patriarchal cultures, women sacralize their domestic lives through food preparation. In many cultures, food is one of the few resources controlled by women, and it plays a central role in women's religious lives (Sered, 1994). Plaskow (1987) suggests that one benefit of the sex-segregated nature of religion is that it provides women with a common life, or **womanspaces**, where power and integrity come from their shared experiences and visions as women.

Reforming and Reconstructing Religion

Feminist theologian Ursula King (1994) once said that feminist theology has two tasks. The negative task is the critique of and struggle against the oppression of women, whereas the positive task is one of reform and reconstruction. In other words, feminist theology deconstructs and then reconstructs religion. Although there is great diversity in how feminists reform and reconstruct religion, reformists assume that although it is generally the case that religion has contributed to the oppression of women, this does not have to be so. Reformers argue that feminist reforms bring religion closer to its true heart and core of equality and freedom (Gross, 1996). Hartman (2007) argues that feminism and religion are not incompatible. We must be careful, she says, not to blur the distinction between the people in power who make decisions and speak in religion's name and the intangible, unbounded spiritual-human root of religion itself. There are four main reformist efforts (summarized in Figure 8.3). These are described generally next and later illustrated within discussions of each of the world's major religions.

One common reformist effort centers on the changing of God and prayer language to be more inclusive. For example, Jewish, Christian, and Muslim feminists have tried, with some success, to de-masculinize God-language. These efforts include avoiding the use of gendered pronouns altogether and not referring to God as the "Father" or alternating gendered pronouns and using God as

FIGURE 8.3 *Reformist Efforts in Feminist Theology*

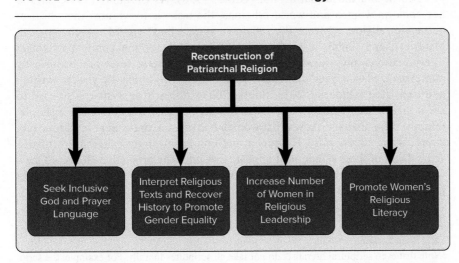

"The first step in the elevation of woman to her true position, as an equal factor in human progress, is the cultivation of the religious sentiment in regard to her dignity and equality, the recognition by the rising generation of an ideal Heavenly Mother, to whom their prayers should be addressed, as well as to a Father."
Elizabeth Cady Stanton, The Women's Bible, 1895

the "Mother" as well as the "Father." The idea is that without de-emphasizing the masculine face of God, women cannot be fully equal in the religious community.

Key to the feminist challenge and reform of patriarchal religion is hermeneutics. **Hermeneutics** is the theory and practice of interpretation for the sacred texts of a religion (Schüssler Fiorenza, 2015). It is important to realize that it is not the scriptures themselves that lead to women's subordination; rather, it is how people interpret them and which scriptures they focus on that is the problem. For example, one hermeneutic is to interpret a text literally (as the word of God), and another is to interpret a text allegorically (as stories from which moral lessons are to be learned). A historical hermeneutic interprets a text as a reflection of the time in which it was written or translated and is important to feminist theology. Hermeneutics matter because the same religion can be very different depending on the lenses of the interpreters.

As noted earlier, fundamentalist strains are more likely to interpret texts as the literal word of God. They also use a patriarchal hermeneutic that leads them to select and interpret scriptures to justify gender inequalities and men's greater power. Therefore, the traditional relationships between men and women found in the scriptures are seen as prescriptions for modern life as well.[1] More liberal strains of the same religion will look at scriptures metaphorically and consider the historical context in which they were written. This hermeneutic provides more room for gender equality; passages that condone women's subordination can be seen as historical reflections rather than as role models for current gender relationships.

Feminist theologians call for the interpretation of sacred texts in light of women's life experiences and the recovery of the stories of significant women figures in early religious history (Hidayatullah, 2014; Smith, 2009). They also distinguish between those aspects of the tradition that support women's empowerment and those that do not (Gross, 1996). As Carmody (1979) says in her book on women and world religions, the task "is to winnow the wheat of authentic religion. . . from the religion's sexist chaff" (p. 14). Archeological, historical, and linguistic study are used to challenge inaccurate patriarchal interpretations and translations. Divine and prophetic texts are historically contextualized—analyzed in regard to the times in which they were written and translated (Duderija, 2015; Smith, 2009). Historic analysis is also used to show that women's current low status in religion arose over time. For example, feminist scholars have shown that women had greater status in at least four religions (Islam, Christianity, Hinduism, and Buddhism) in the religions' formative years. In all of these religions, it appears that once the original leaders died, new writings and interpretations emerged that justified the continuation of existing patriarchal traditions.

---

[1]Note that even scriptural literalists do not take all scriptures literally. For example, the scriptures of Christianity, Judaism, and Islam all have passages supporting slavery (Gross, 1996).

Feminist hermeneutics have the task of changing scriptural interpretation by viewing religious scriptures and texts through feminist and liberation lenses instead of patriarchal ones. The point is to give people the tools for reclaiming their scriptures for empowerment instead of simply accepting the interpretations offered by traditional religious leaders. These hermeneutics are intended to deconstruct the politics of inequality and subordination found in religious texts while reconstructing new interpretations supportive of justice and equality. In this way, feminist hermeneutics are a type of **liberation theology.** Feminist hermeneutics contextualize religious texts (consider them within a historical context) and are interpreter-centered in that they acknowledge that interpreters do not simply retrieve the meaning of the text but play an important part in creating meaning (Duderija, 2015).

Feminist biblical scholar Elisabeth Schüssler Fiorenza (1995, 2015) suggests a number of feminist hermeneutics. A *hermeneutics of suspicion* means that religious texts are not taken at face value. Instead of the typical hermeneutics of obedience that leads to acceptance of submission, texts are critically examined for how they serve the interests of domination. A *hermeneutics of proclamation* analyzes religious texts for their oppressive or liberating potential and to proclaim the power of the Divine for liberation. A *hermeneutics of remembrance and historical reconstruction* means that scriptures are read with an effort to reconstruct women's history, while a *hermeneutics of creative actualization* involves a creative reading, interpretation, and envisioning of women in religious texts to dream of a world of justice and well-being. It may include poetry, drama, and dance (see for example, Bechmann, 2014). Some feminist hermeneutics are intersectional in nature. A *hermeneutics of domination and social location* asks us to consider how our social, cultural, and religious location shapes our experience with the scripture and how we react to it. To reveal the liberating presence of God, a *hermeneutics of experience* calls on us to explore the experiences of struggle and liberation of the marginalized and colonized in scripture, through an intersectional lens of gender, race, culture, class, age, and ethnicity.

So they are not dependent on male interpretations of scriptures that may be biased by patriarchal lenses, feminist theologians and activists advocate for women's theological literacy. Feminist theologians promote women's access to scriptures and encourage women to read them for themselves. Reformists also work for women's ordination and leadership within their religious traditions as well as their rights to read sacred texts and perform sacred rituals. For many women, the realization that they are unequal in the eyes of their religions is experienced as a betrayal of deeply felt spiritual and ritual experience (Christ & Plaskow, 1979). Women who felt called to religious leadership and found themselves barred from these vocations have been instrumental in the fight for the right to become religious leaders (Christ & Plaskow, 1979).

"I heard the gospel long before I heard of the women's movement." *Nancy Hatch Wittig, one of the first women to be ordained as an Episcopal Priest in 1974 on "being called" to the priesthood.*

Women and the World's Major Religions

So far you have learned that religion can be an agent of gender inequality. Religious scriptures and texts (a religion's **canon**), gender-segregated religious practices, and masculine God-language contribute to traditional gender ideologies and are sometimes used to support the subordination of women. You have also learned that many women do not believe that God, or the founders of their religion, intended for their religions to be used to justify gender inequality. These women, along with supportive men, seek to reform their religions. This next section applies these ideas to each of the world's five main religions.

Islam

Islam is the fastest growing religion in the world. It originated in the Middle East and is now a major religion not only there, but also in Asia (such as in Bangladesh, Indonesia, Pakistan, and Malaysia) and Africa (including Algeria, Comoros, Djibouti, Mali, and Morocco).[2] Muhammad is seen as the final prophet of God, the last of a lineage beginning with Adam, and including Moses, Abraham, and Jesus (Peach, 2002). All Muslims are expected to observe the "Five Pillars of Islam": (1) to profess faith in God's oneness and to accept Muhammad as God's prophet, (2) to pray five times a day, (3) to fast during the holy month of Ramadan, (4) to give alms, and (5) to make a pilgrimage to Mecca at least once. Islam began in the eighth century C.E., when Muhammad recorded the **Qur'an** (also spelled Koran). People that practice Islam are called Muslims. There are different forms of Islam, including Sunni, Shiite, and Sufi.

The Qur'an is considered to be the primary source of Islam, but there are other sources to which Muslims refer. These include the *Sunna* (everything Muhammad said or did) and the Hadith. The **Hadith** is the report of the Sunna, the collective sayings attributed to Muhammad and what he approved (a single report attributed to him is called a "hadith"). Developed over several centuries, some hadith are of questionable authenticity. Hadith often form the basis of the religious law called **shari'ah,** the collectivity of laws that Muslims govern themselves by. In practice, shari'ah varies from place to place depending on the community of Muslims and the consensus of their religious leaders on how to define it. These definitions vary depending on culture and theological interpretation.

Although Islam opposes gendered imagery for the Divine, Allah (God) is typically referred to as "He." Like many religions, there are scriptures that seem to support gender equality and others that do not. For example, in the Qur'an, Muhammad said, "Men and women are equal as two teeth on a comb," but another passage reads, "Men shall protect and maintain women because God has made some of them excel others, and because they support them from their means. Therefore the righteous women are obedient, guarding the intimacy which God would have them guard. As for those women whose rebellion you justly fear, admonish them first; then leave their beds; then beat them."

Religious practice is gendered in Islam, and women and men are expected to show their devotion to God in distinctly different ways. Women play an important role in the practice of religious rituals in the home. Also, unlike men, many women show devotion through Islamic dress. Some wear the *hijab,* a headscarf

> "The Qur'an establishes that God is unique, hence beyond representation, and also beyond gender."
> *Asma Barlas, Muslim feminist theologian*

---

[2]The CIA Factbook provides data on the world's countries, including religion. https://www.cia.gov/the-world-factbook/

that allows no hair to show (sometimes called a veil), or the *abaya,* a long dress or coat and a headscarf. (It should be noted that controversy about whether Islam truly calls for veiling has occurred for over 100 years. Although there are clearly cases where Islamic dress has been oppressively imposed on women, some women choose it as an expression of faith and appreciate that it frees them from sexual objectification.)

Almost all Muslim mosques are segregated by gender so that men and women are not distracted from prayer. Customarily, the women's areas are smaller with separate entrances. In some places, like parts of India and some of the Gulf states, women are not allowed to worship in mosques. Also interesting is that menstruation restricts participation in some religious practices. For example, a woman cannot enter a mosque or touch the Qur'an until her period is over and she has had a ritual bath (the Ghusl).

Women were important leaders in early Islam. Khadija, Muhammad's first wife, was the first person to accept his prophetic mission. After Khadija's death, Muhammad married A'isha and clearly said that she was to be accepted as an authority on the hadith ascribed to him (Hassan, 2003). She and her daughter Fatima carried the word of Muhammad long after his death. Women's authority as scholars and teachers of Islam was accepted and respected in early Islam (Shaaban, 1995). Rabi'a, a female saint, is also an important figure in early Islam.

Despite women's importance as spiritual leaders in early Islam, there are still relatively few opportunities for women's leadership outside of female groups that worship together. In general, women are not allowed to act as imams, or leaders of prayer services, although there are some exceptions. One exception is the Uighur Muslims, an ethnic and religious minority in China. Uighur Muslims have a history of all-female mosques led by women going back to the eighteenth century (Steinkopf-Frank, 2020).

But women imams are rare globally and are not part of mainstream Islam. Their intention is not to rewrite the Qu'ran but to return to the essence of Islam, which they argue is not fundamentally patriarchal but rather made so over time by men. They usually claim the imam role with little or no support from the male leadership of the Muslim community where they live. For example, Jamida Beevi of Kerala, India, made history in 2018 as the first Muslim woman to lead a mixed-gender prayer service, and faced death threats as a result (Dhillon, 2019). Western Europe is also seeing a small movement toward women-led mosques. Sherin Khankan and Salina Khankan of Denmark serve as imams in a woman-led mosque they opened in 2016 (Taylor, 2018). In 2019, efforts were underway in England and France to build women-led mosques (Wemare, 2019). In the United States, the first women-led mosque (the Women's Mosque of America) opened in Los Angeles in 2015.

Imams are not the only religious leaders in Islam. A hierarchy of *mullahs* (low-level religious officials) and *mojaheds* (high-ranking religious officials) serve as religious leaders and with only a few exceptions worldwide, these are men (Peach, 2002). This matters since religious leaders are the ones that determine shari'ah (religious law) through their interpretation of the Qur'an and the Hadith. There are some women clerics, or *ulema* (experts in Islamic sacred law and theology), but

Amina Waddud, an African American Muslim feminist theologian, and Asra Normani, an Indian American Muslim journalist, both led mixed-gender prayer services in the first decade of the twenty-first century. Although there is evidence that women led prayers in the time of the Prophet Mohammad, Waddud and Normani's actions were considered scandalous.

"If women's rights are a problem for some modern Muslim men, it is neither because of the Koran nor the Prophet, nor the Islamic tradition, but simply because those rights conflict with the interests of a male elite."
Fatima Mernissi, Moroccan feminist sociologist

their numbers and influence are small in comparison to the male clerics that commonly issue *fatwas* (religious proclamations). However, in 2017, the first women's ulema congress was held on Java Island, Indonesia with a goal of amplifying their voices. Hundreds of ulema (most of them Indonesians) issued two important religious edicts relevant to girls and women. One fatwa called on Muslims to end child marriage, and another forbids marital rape (Ross, 2017). In Morocco, hundreds of women have trained with governmental support to work as *mourchidat* (clerics that teach Islamic law and practice), but they are not allowed to act as imams (Steinkopf-Frank, 2020).

How Islam affects women's equality depends partly on how it blends with other cultural practices. It is important to recognize that it is the fundamentalist strains of Islam that are the most oppressive to women. Like other fundamentalist religions, they use a patriarchal hermeneutic to justify gender inequality. They seek religious states that rule according to an unreformed version of shari'ah (Islamic religious law) from the seventh century, which they see as divine law. Muslims with these conservative ideas are sometimes called **Islamists** or Islamic fundamentalists, and the process by which states become governed by conservative forms of Islam is called **Islamization.** This is a trend in many Muslim countries including Pakistan, Afghanistan, Algeria, Sudan, Egypt, Nigeria, Yemen, Syria, and Iran.

Pointing to the problems of Westernized cultures (e.g., promiscuity, divorce, unwed mothers), fundamentalist Muslim leaders promote separating the genders, extremely modest dress for women, early marriage, and men's power over women. They selectively choose and interpret the Hadith to create shari'ah supportive of patriarchy. For example, in 2016, mullahs in the Islamic Republic of Iran banned women from riding bikes in public, wearing boots with pants, letting their hair come out of their headscarf or veil, wearing bathing suits, wearing tight and short winter coats, and entering sports arenas (NCRI, 2016). State-sanctioned shari'ah law in Sudan leads to the arrests and punishment of thousands of women annually for immodest conduct or clothes (Salih, 2015). In Afghanistan, a national shari'ah based law requires women to obtain permission from their husbands to leave their houses, gives husbands the right to deny food to their wives if their sexual demands are not met, grants guardianship of children exclusively to their fathers and grandfathers, and allows rapists to avoid prosecution by paying "blood money" to a girl or woman injured when he raped her (Human Rights Watch, 2009; Lozano, 2009). In 2015, a woman named Farkunda was brutally murdered by a mob of men for studying the Qur'an, and prominent mullahs supported them (Nawa & Nomani, 2015). Defying a shari'ah ban on women from attending burials, over two-dozen women (many of them women's rights activists) carried her coffin to the cemetery and buried her.

The jihadist terrorist group ISIS (also known as ISIL or the Islamic State) practiced a particularly regressive form of shari'ah in their conquered territories in Iraq and Syria from 2014 to 2019. Earlier in the book, you read about a system of organized rape and sexual assault, sexual slavery, and forced marriage by ISIS forces against Yezidi women in Iraq (Yezidis are a non-Muslim religious minority). But Muslim women also saw restrictions of their rights in ISIS territories in Iraq and Syria. For instance, by law women were required to stay in their homes (leaving only in cases

"Muslim women represent a diverse and heterogeneous sociological group. While they may confront similar challenges or find common ground in some areas, the lived experiences of Muslim women vary considerably, depending on the socio-historical and political contexts in which they lead their lives."
Women's Islamic Initiative in Spirituality and Equality (WISE)

of necessity) (Callimachi, 2016). Women had to be completely covered, including their eyes (with the *niqab*, a thin black cloth film) and their hands and feet. Violators are fined or physically punished. Women's main role was to procreate to grow the Islamic State. Human rights organizations documented incidents of rape, forced marriage, and other forms of violence against Muslim women, particularly those that tried to escape ISIS rule (Human Rights Watch, 2017). Although ISIS was largely defeated, they are still a force in Iraq, Syria, and Somalia (CNN Editorial Research, 2020). Many Muslims worldwide feel that Muslim fundamentalists are hijacking Islam and using religion to gain political power.

Muslim feminists and feminist theologians challenge conservative Islamic interpretations that are oppressive to women. They seek to revive a more woman-inclusive version of Islam in a broader struggle for gender justice (Agugideiri, 2014). Egypt's Nawal el Saadawi, who died in 2021, spent most of her life challenging patriarchal interpretations of Islam despite being fired, receiving death threats, and being imprisoned (Abraham, 2015; Misdary, 2021). Because their efforts for gender equality are often greeted with charges that they are "Westernized" and untrue to Islam, Muslim women working for change in their religion typically ground their arguments in Islam rather than the language of human rights or social justice values (Moghadam, 2003). Those pursuing a more gender-equal Islam emphasize the religious heritage of Islam and that Muhammad intended equality and dignity for women as well as men (Barlas, 2002; Hassan, 1991, 1999, 2003; Mernissi, 1987). They point to Khadija, Ai'sha, Fatima, and Rabi'a, early women leaders of Islam, and show how Muslims came to read inequality and patriarchy into the Qur'an to justify patriarchy. They note that there is nothing in the Qur'an that says women cannot lead a congregation and that while some hadith suggest this, others suggest that women can, or at least that they can lead other women in prayer.

Hermeneutics are key to unlocking the potential of the Qur'an for redressing Islamic patriarchy and its tradition of misogyny (Agugideiri, 2014). Muslim feminist theologians, such as Asma Barlas (2002) and Riffa Hassan of Pakistan (1999, 2003), Aysha Hidayyatullah (2014), and Amina Wadud of the United States (1999, 2006), interpret the Qu'ran to show it is compatible with gender equality. They retranslate Arabic phrases and terms in the Qu'ran for precise meanings, and place Qu'ranic passages in historic context. Some Muslim women work for women's literacy, feeling strongly that women's dependence on men for the interpretation of texts interferes with their ability to know their rights under Islam. They emphasize that early Islam stressed women's right to education and literacy. Egyptian Muslim feminist Leila Ahmed (2002, p. 120) put it this way: "Just because they were powerful, privileged in their societies and knew how to write, does this mean they have the right to forever to tell us what Islam is or what the rules should be?" As Nilofar Ahmad, the director of Daughters of Islam, a women's organization in Pakistan, said, "If I have any message for Muslim women it is that they must study their religion for themselves, learn what it really says, not accept someone else's idea. Only then will they be able to fight for their rights with the very weapon currently used against them—the Koran" (in Goodwin, 1994, p. 75).

Many Muslim women are concerned about fundamentalist movements and the reduction of women's rights in the name of Islam, and they take action. For example,

"To accept the authority of any group and to resign oneself to its misreading of Islam not only makes one complicit in the continued abuse of Islam and the abuse of women in the name of Islam, but it also means losing the battle over meaning without even fighting it."
Asma Barlas, Muslim feminist theologian

BOX 8.2   *Activist Profile: Shirin Ebadi of Iran*

"The discriminatory plight of women in Islamic states, whether in the sphere of civil law or in the realm of social, political, and cultural justice, has its roots in the patriarchal and male-dominated culture prevailing in these societies, not in Islam."

Shirin Ebadi

Shirin Ebadi is the first Iranian and first Muslim woman to win the Nobel Peace Prize. She is one of the founding members of the Nobel Women's Initiative (nobelwomen-sinitiative.org), which unites women Nobel Peace Prize laureates to promote women's grassroots organizations and movements globally. The award was made for her years of legal work advocating on behalf of Iranian political activists, religious and ethnic minorities, women, and children. A lawyer, Ebadi became Iran's first female judge in 1970 and in 1980s began battling for the rights of women and children and the unjustly detained and imprisoned. Ebadi defended many of the democratic activists that protested against the government in 1999 and served jail time for publicizing evidence that the government attacked pro-democracy forces. She was instrumental in the successful drive to get women to elect candidates favorable to women's equality, including President Mohammad Khatami in 1997. Ebadi grounds her arguments for women's equality in the law and in the Qur'an. She insists that the true spirit of the Qur'an is consistent with women's rights. Harassed and intimidated by government forces, she went into exile in 2009. In 2016, Ebadi published an autobiography *Until We Are Free: My Fight for Human Rights in Iran.* Today, Ebadi calls for regime change in Iran. She says it is now clear that the government does not respect human rights, especially women's human rights, and reform is unlikely.

Sources: Angel, 2019; Gibson, 2016; Mostaghim & Daragahi, 2009; nobelprize.org, 2003.

"Islam was revealed into a context dominated by patriarchy, but it also provides a route beyond patriarchy. It is the duty of Muslims to follow this route and challenge patriarchy within our societies. It is also our duty to challenge the notion from outside Muslim culture that Islam does not have the tools to move beyond patriarchy."
Amina Wadud, Muslim feminist theologian

in 1994, the Algerian feminist organization Rassemblement Algerien des Femmes Democrates (RAFD) organized a protest involving tens of thousands of Algerian women. They were responding to the increased violence against women that rose with fundamentalism. Unveiled women, women living alone, and feminist activists were attacked and in some cases killed, apparently with the support of the government (Moghadam, 2003).

Protests following the arrest and prosecution of women under shari'ah also occur. In 2009, three Sudanese women arrested for wearing pants decided to go to trial to challenge the law. One of them, Sudanese journalist Lubna Hussein, said the law is un-Islamic and oppressive and used her trial to rally support to change it. Sudanese police fired tear gas and beat women protesting outside the court, and some women quietly protested by attending the trial wearing pants. Found guilty, Lubna Hussein chose to protest this misuse of Islam and serve her jail time rather than pay a large fine, but her fine was paid by someone seeking to quell the negative publicity. More recently, in Iran, three women were sentenced to five years in prison. Their crime: Handing out flowers in a public space without headscarves and encouraging women to protest the mandatory hijab (Begum, 2019). Their lawyer, Nasrin Sotudeh, a well-known human rights activist, was given 38 years in prison and 148 lashes for defending them (Rezaiah, 2020). Box 8.2 profiles Shirin Ebadi of Iran who, in 2003, won the Nobel Peace Prize for her women's rights and democracy work in Iran. She exemplifies those devout Muslim women who, despite high personal costs, use the Qu'ran to show that Islam is compatible with women's rights.

Transnational feminist organizations also join together against fundamentalist Islam. WLUML (*Women Living Under Muslim Laws*) is an international solidarity network formed in 1984. This transnational network monitors laws affecting Muslim women and publicizes gender-related acts of violence and oppression due to shari'ah, along with campaigns for justice. WISE (*Women's Islamic Initiative in Spirituality and Equality*) is an American-based Muslim women's GRSO. They work with Muslim women's organizations globally to address a variety of issues, including stoning, women's religious education and leadership, domestic violence, separation and divorce laws, and women's court testimony. Through their "Muslim Women: Past and Present" project, they document how Muslim women have always been community leaders. Musaweh ("equality" in Arabic) is a transnational organization that arose from the Sisters of Islam global meeting in 2009. They apply feminist and human rights lenses to Islam with the goal of promoting gender equality and global activism.

Judaism

Judaism is the world's oldest western religion. By 700 C.E., the Jewish tradition achieved most of the major features that it has today (Peach, 2002). Jews are found all over the world, but the largest Jewish communities are found in Israel, Europe, and the United States. The two most important Jewish texts are the *Torah* (the first five chapters of the Bible's Old Testament) and the *Talmud* (a sixty-three volume of legal and theological teachings centering on the meaning of the Torah and the practice of Judaism). Reconstructionist Judaism is the most progressive in regard to women's equality, followed by Reformist Judaism, Modern Orthodox Judaism, and finally ultra-Orthodox Judaism (referred to as *Haredi*, it is a fundamentalist religion).

> In Israel, Orthodox Judaism is the official state religion.

Masculine God-language and imagery is the norm in Jewish texts and liturgy[3] (Hartman, 2007). One of the best-known Jewish feminist theologians, Judith Plaskow, once said, "Half of Jews have been women, but men have been defined as normative Jews, while women's voices and experiences are largely invisible in the record of Jewish belief and experience that has come down to us. Women have lived Jewish history and carried its burdens, but women's perceptions and questions have not given form to the scripture, shaped the direction of Jewish law, or found expression in liturgy" (1991, p. 1). The keeping of the Torah's commandments is the pride of Jewish life, yet very few of the 613 religious injunctions in the Torah apply to women (Carmody, 1994). The religious life of Jewish men is the central concern of the *mitzvot,* the commandments of the Torah and the Talmud (Heschel, 2003). Parts of the Talmud can be interpreted to suggest that women's study of the Torah and their public religious worship should be restricted, and parts also portray women as sexual temptresses who distract men from prayer (Heschel, 2003). Indeed, the Talmud says: "Let the words of Torah rather be destroyed by fire than imparted to women."

> "The fact that, in traditional Judaism, women are not counted in a *minyan* (quorum required for public prayer) or called to the Torah amounts to our exclusion from the public religious realm."
> *Judith Plaskow, one of the first Jewish feminist theologians*

Judaism is also based on various other texts, stories, and prayers not found in the Bible, and these often contain negative images concerning women. For instance, a legend from *Genesis Rabbah* in the Midrash (a record of rabbis' biblical exegeses

---

[3]*Liturgy* refers to a religion's public forms of worship and ritual.

from 200 to 600 C.E.) explains that menstruation is one of women's punishments for Eve's sins (Schulman, 1974). One Orthodox Jewish prayer is the male's daily morning prayer: "Blessed art thou, O Lord our God, King of the Universe, who has not made me a woman." Heschel (2003) points out that although there are Jewish prayers for all sorts of bodily experiences, there is no prayer for giving birth. She provides this as an example of how the theological literature of Judaism was composed by men concerned primarily with the religious life of men, not women.

"Not counting as a person standing before God is the deepest offense you can lodge at a person. You know, when some guy starts counting heads and you are standing right there, you literally do not exist. Your body. Your soul. Invisible."
Jewish feminist writer and researcher Dr. Elana Sztokman

Gender-segregated religious practices are common in Judaism, but this is less true of progressive variants and truer of Orthodox Judaism. Haredi Judaism excludes women from the majority of religious activities that take place outside of the home. The spiritual domain belongs to men; women participate by following the labor-intensive laws required to ensure the ritual purity of their homes. These include keeping the laws of family purity, such as the ritual bath seven days after menstruation (the *niddah*), preparing kosher food, and doing the ritual work for home-centered religious holidays and the weekly Sabbath dinner. Married women in Haredi communities cover their hair with hats or wigs, dress modestly, and on average have more children than other Jewish women. Women's exclusion from the public religious realm is also apparent in Orthodox Judaism in the fact that women do not count as members of the *minyan,* the quorum of ten males required for public religious services. Women are also segregated from men in orthodox synagogues. Women's sections are typically in the back, separated from the men by a wall or curtain. Services are conducted on the men's side. Orthodox Judaism also does not permit the ordination of women as rabbis, and women cannot lead group prayers because they are not supposed to read from the Torah.

"What is it after all that Jewish women seek? They do not ask to be excused or exempt. They do not wish to turn their backs on the tradition, to wash their hands of it and walk away. Rather, they desire to enter it more fully. They long to share a greater part of the tradition, to partake of its wealth of knowledge, to delight in the richness of ritual. For these reasons, their efforts should be welcomed, not scorned."
Blu Greenberg, one of the best-known Jewish Orthodox feminists and a founder of the Jewish Orthodox Feminist Alliance, a major source of information and activism

Over the last 40 years, Jewish feminists have brought significant reform in their religion, especially in the non-Orthodox versions of Judaism. In many non-Orthodox synagogues, masculinist religious language has been changed. "Blessed Are You, Lord Our God, King of the Universe" has become "Let us bless the source of life," and the names of the foremothers Sarah, Rebecca, Leah, and Rachel have been added to those of the forefathers Abraham, Isaac, and Jacob in Jewish prayer books (Cantor, 1995; Gross, 1996; Umanksy, 1999). They have also created feminist liturgies and rituals (Heschel, 2003; Umansky, 1999) and re-envisioned parts of the Talmud. For example, Judith Plaskow (1979, 2005) reconceived the story of Lilith from one in which Lilith is a female demon and the first wife of Adam, spurned because she acted equal to him, to one in which she is a model for women's empowerment. Jewish feminists show how the Talmud supports gender equality, pointing out that it contains protections against the exploitation of women and advanced the status of women over what was common when it was written (Heschel, 2003). Jewish feminists use history to show that women held important roles as prophets, judges, and leaders during early Judaism (Heschel, 2003; Peach, 2002). They emphasize the strong female figures in the Old Testament such as Deborah, Jael (Yael), Esther, and Naomi (see Niditch, 1991 for a discussion).

In the United States, where the greatest numbers of Jews live, women now participate equally in most non-Orthodox synagogues. Following decades of struggle, most branches of Judaism now allow women to be rabbis. In the United States, this began in 1972 with Reform Judaism, followed by Reconstructionist Judaism in 1974, and Conservative Judaism in 1985 (Nadell, 2009). The reform, reconstructionist, and conservative Jewish traditions also permit women to be cantors (directors of music and prayer in the synagogue). However, it should be noted that women rabbis and cantors still face sexism in hiring and promotion. The 1990s and early 2000s also saw the first women rabbis in many countries, including Brazil, Italy, France, Poland, Norway, Austria, and Israel.

The battle to ordain Orthodox women as rabbis continues (Samuel, 2014; Jewish Telegraphic Agency, 2017). In 2009, Sara Hurwitz broke the gender barrier in Orthodox Judaism when she became the first Orthodox woman to complete the rabbinical studies and exams necessary to become a rabbi. She studied privately for 5 years with Rabbi Avi Weiss, who initially conferred upon her the title of "Maharat" (spiritual leader and educator) rather than Rabbi. Soon after, she opened a religious rabbinical school for women (Yeshivat Maharat) and changed her title to Rabba, a feminine form of rabbi. By 2014, five women had been ordained after graduating from her school, but with the title of Maharat, rather than Rabba, to quell controversy. But controversy remained. In 2015, following the ordination of six women who opted for the title "Rabba," the Rabinnical Council of America passed a resolution reaffirming that women could not be ordained as Orthodox rabbis. Following concerns that four Orthodox synagogues employed women in some clergy roles, in 2017 the Orthodox Union released a new policy barring women from serving as clergy or performing clergy-like tasks at its 400 member congregations across the United States. By 2021, thirty-nine women had graduated from Yeshivat Maharat but only a few lead synogogues of their own.

Orthodox feminists work for changes in religious laws that are detrimental to women, in particular, the one that allows only a man to initiate and grant a divorce. To be divorced under Jewish law, the husband must grant a *get* (also known as *gett*), a Jewish Bill of Divorce document that is unobtainable without the husband's cooperation. In Israel, even non-Orthodox women are subject to this divorce requirement, and in U.S. Orthodox communities, a *get* is also required for divorce. Under Jewish law, when a husband refuses to grant a *get*, his wife is considered *agunot* or an *agunah* (a chained woman) and cannot move on with her life and cannot remarry. While many Orthodox men grant the get, abusive husbands sometimes withhold it to punish their wives or as a means for extortion. Organizations like the Center for Women's Justice in Israel consider the agunah to be marital captives and the withholding of a get to be a form of domestic abuse. Other organizations, like GETTOUT UK, and the Organization for the Resolution of Agunot (based in New York), offer support and legal counsel to agunah. In 2021, a grassroots movement began when American Chava Herman, an agunah waiting since 2011 for a divorce get, messaged Dalia Oziel, a 25-year-old Israeli Orthodox woman singer and social media influencer. She asked Oziel to share a post calling for her husband to provide the get. Oziel complied (#freeChava). Within weeks, thousands of Orthodox women globally reposted in support, many sharing their own stories, and helping others shame resistant husbands into granting gets. The resulting grassroots movement also includes advocacy for sweeping changes, including the standardization of religious prenups to protect women in case of divorce, demands for rabbis and rabbinic courts to shut down husbands' extortion of their wives in exchange for divorce, and recognition of refusal as abuse (Chizhik-Goldschmidt, 2021; Jaskoll, 2021).

The first ordained woman rabbi was Regina Jonas, ordained in Germany in 1935. She served the Jewish community in Berlin until she was deported to a concentration camp. She died in Auschwitz, and her story forgotten until 2014 when a group of women rabbis and scholars traveled to Germany to retrace her journey.
Jewish Women's Archive

BOX 8.3 *Activist Profile: Women of the Wall*

The Western Wall (or the Kotel) in Jerusalem, Israel, is considered one of the holiest sites in Judaism. Custom has traditionally separated men and women at the Kotel and allowed only men to read from the Torah and pray as a group there. In 1988, a group of 70 Jewish women from Israel, the United States, Europe, South America, and Australia from Orthodox, Conservative, Reform, and Reconstructionist forms of Judaism, went to the women's section of the Wall and prayed as a group and read from the Torah. They were immediately harassed and threatened but left unharmed. Committed to the quest for equal access to this holy site, the "Women of the Wall" (WOW) returned in early 1989, but this time Haredi men threw heavy metal chairs and canisters of tear gas at them over the high barrier that separated men from women.

At the time, there was no law prohibiting what the women were doing, but the violence escalated, so they asked the Israeli Supreme Court for protection for their peaceful, religiously lawful prayer services. The Supreme Court issued a temporary injunction barring women from praying at the Kotel with a Torah and tallit (a prayer shawl). WOW followed the injunction; however, the ultra-Orthodox then asked the court to enforce the religious law prohibiting women from praying out loud because "kol b'isha erva" (the voice of woman is lewd). The Ministry of Religion and the Ministry of Justice declared that "any religious ceremony at a holy place that is not in accordance with the custom of the holy site and which offends the sensitivities of the worshipers at the place" is prohibited. The penalty for violating this regulation is six months in jail and/or a fine. WOW fought back in the courts.

After a decade of delays, a law passed in 2000 designated a separate women's area at the Wall, but it was still illegal for a woman to take out a Torah scroll and read from it (the punishment: 7 years in prison). In 2003, following numerous appeals, the Court gave WOW permission to have its prayer groups in an area next to the Wall called Robinson's Arch, claiming that this does not violate women's right to pray at the Wall since it is so close to the Kotel. Robinson's Arch opened in 2004. In the ensuing years, dozens of WOW members and supporters are arrested, detained, harassed, interrogated, and banned from the Wall for wearing tallits and carrying the Torah. In 2013, five women were arrested during WOW services for reciting the Kadish prayer, a sacred, but common, Jewish ritual. Judge Sharon Larry Bavly reviewed the case. She stated there is no cause for arresting the women and the women of WOW are not disturbing the public order with their prayers. Police now protect WOW worshippers from protestors. WOW holds services once a month (on Rosh Chodesh, the monthly women's holiday) in the women's section of the Western Wall plaza.

But the issue is hardly decided. In 2016 the government approved a plan to expand the non-Orthodox prayer area for mixed-gender prayer but under pressure from the ultra-Orthodox community, they shelved it. In 2019, thousands of young ultra-Orthodox women and men disrupted WOW's 30th anniversary service at the Wall, following direction from their rabbis.

Sources: BBC News, 2019a; Chesler, 2008; Raday, 2005; Shalev, 1995; Women of the Wall, 2017.

The Jewish Orthodox Feminist Alliance (JOFA), based in New York City, and Kolech in Israel, offer tools and resources to help women increase their participation in religious rituals. They advocate for increased leadership opportunities for women in synagogues and communities, and engage in activism to resolve the agunah problem. Modern Orthodox Jewish feminists like Blu Greenberg and Tova Hartman, and Rabbis Avi Weiss, Rabbi Daniel Sperber, Rabbi Daniel Landes, and Rabbi Herzl Hefter, also advocate for change, but there is controversy regarding their efforts and fierce resistance in some Haredi communities. However, there are now some Modern Orthodox communities that allow women to study and teach the Torah, study the Talmud, and who have synagogues where the women's section is on par with the men's section (Greenberg, 2000). There are even some Haredi synagogues that hold women-only prayer groups and allow the Torah processional to pass through the women's section (Kress, 2009). Some Orthodox women in the United States and Israel lead Talmud studies for women. And in 2020, an estimated 3,000 Orthodox women gathered in Israel for the first large-scale Talmud celebration conducted by and for women (Estrin, 2020).

In Israel, Orthodox and non-Orthodox women have protested sexist policies initiated by the Haradein (ultra-Orthodox), who exert considerable political power. For example, they have fought gender-segregated public transportation, gender separated hours for government medical clinics, the exclusion of women from government ceremonies, the requirement that women stand separately from men in public cemeteries, and the harassment of girls and women by Haredi men for "immodest" dress (Sommer & Lithwick, 2013). Box 8.3 describes the activism of "Women of the Wall," a group seeking equal worship rights at a holy site in Jerusalem.

Hinduism

Hinduism, practiced primarily in India for 6,000 years, is the only major polytheistic religion in the world and the only one in which goddess worship is prominent and normal (Gross, 1996, 2009). Key concepts of Hinduism are *dharma*, a natural cosmic balance that exists in everything, and *karma*, the idea that one's present life is the result of actions taken in previous lives. Hinduism has no single founder or single prophet—no male Son of God such as Jesus or male prophet such as Muhammad. Although the **Vedas** (written from 1750 to the sixth century B.C.E.) are the primary Hindu scriptures, there is no single authoritative scripture, no one sacred text (Carmody, 1991; Narayanan, 1999). One difficulty in defining Hinduism is the wide diversity of practices, beliefs, and cultural groups that emphasize different gods and goddesses, different scriptures, and have differing rituals (Lucia, 2014). Relative to many other religions, local customs, festivals, and rituals are far more important to the practice of Hinduism than the scriptures, which are written in Sanskrit, a language that most Indians cannot read (Narayanan, 2003). Drama, dance, and music are vehicles for religious expression and religious teaching (Narayanan, 2006).

Masculine God-language and exclusive male God-imagery are not issues in Hinduism as they are in the world's other major religions—there are both gods and goddesses. In this way Hinduism appears to affirm the spiritual equality of men and women. While the Hindu trinity consists of male gods Brahma, Vishnu, and Shiva, their power cannot be enacted without *Shakti*, the power of Hindu goddesses. That said, how different goddesses are interpreted and whether they are centralized or marginalized in Hindu practice varies considerably based on local norms and the strain of Hinduism. In more progressive strains of the religion, goddesses are sources of power for women. These goddesses include *Durga,* who rules strength and protection and is believed by some devotees to be the Supreme Being; *Sarasvati,* Goddess of Learning; *Lakshmi,* Goddess of Prosperity; and *Kali,* "the Dark One." Many Hindus celebrate and honor the goddesses Lakshmi, Saraswati, and Durga during a ten-day fall festival called *Navaratri* (Narayanan, 2003, 2006).

"Like other major religions, Hinduism is marked by a heritage of patriarchal hierarchy, but it also contains a strong matriarchal mythology."
Riva Joshee and Karen Sihra, Hinduism scholars

However, men have often construed the power of Shakti as necessitating the control of women. Goddesses are envisioned in ways that reinforce traditional gender ideologies (specifically, women's role as obedient wife) (Ross, 2008). They are seen as dangerously passionate, capable of giving and taking life, and needing the control of male gods so that they do not produce chaos (Carmody, 1989). The unmarried goddesses are generally considered the most dangerous ones. The married ones, such as Savitri, Sita, Parvati, and Lakshmi, are viewed as more virtuous and are more likely to be held up as models for women. For example, in the Hindu epic the *Ramayana,* Sita is kidnapped from her husband Rama by the demon Ravana. She is twice victimized—first, by the terror of abduction and captivity, and again, when she is rescued by Rama and must prove to him that she remained pure and faithful to him. She steps into a sacrificial fire but emerges unscathed because she was virtuous. Sita risked death to protect the honor of her husband and for that she is often held up as the ideal Hindu woman (Joshee & Sihra, 2013; Robinson, 1985).

> "These are man-made traditions. God does not differentiate between man and woman."
> *Trupti Desai, leader of the Bhumata Brigade, a women's rights group challenging temples' bans on women*

Like other religions, Hindu religious rituals differ depending on gender (Gold, 2008). Women perform various life cycle and calendrical rituals at home, in public places, and in temples, on behalf of their families' well-being (Gold, 2008; Narayanan, 2006). The theme of *pativratya,* or husband devotion, is important to the practice of Hinduism, as many conservative and fundamentalist Hindus see a woman's highest religious duty as being to her husband. Many believe that good karma comes to those women who are good and loyal wives. Men gain good karma, and therefore a higher level of rebirth, through the study of the Vedas and through meditation (Carmody, 1989). Traditionally, ideal Hindu wives ended their lives by throwing themselves on their husband's funeral pyre, a practice called *sati* or *suttee.* Although outlawed during the British colonial era, some Hindu fundamentalists have defended the practice and attempted to legalize it (Ross, 2008). Some Hindu fundamentalists still practice *purdah,* which requires that women stay indoors and segregated from all men other than their husbands and sons.[4]

Hinduism does not technically bar women priests, but male priests are the norm and perform almost all Hindu temple rituals and rites of passage. Most Hindu teachers (gurus) are also male (Kaur, 2008; Young, 1987). The classical Hindu texts, especially the *Vedas* and early *Upanishads,* seem to suggest that women could receive religious education and perform religious ceremonies, but as time went on, these were closed to women (Carmody, 1991; Narayanan, 1999). In some areas of India, there are restrictions on women's study of the *Vedas,* and some temples ban women entirely from Hindu temples (Kaur, 2008; Naidu, 2013). Because Hinduism views women to be polluted when menstruating, more conservative and fundamentalist strains restrict their full participation in public sphere religious activities such as those in temples (Narayanan, 1999).

In India, fundamentalist Hinduism (Hindutwa) has gained power in recent decades. The Hindu nationalist group RSS (Rashtriya Swayamsevak Sangh) seeks a Hindu State. Like other fundamentalist religions, they believe their religion is the one true version and use political and social means to impose it on others. Hindu

---

[4]Some Muslims in Afghanistan and rural and tribal areas of India and Pakistan also practice purdah.

BOX 8.4   *Hindu Women Challenge Temple Restrictions Limiting Women's Access*

Each Hindu temple is devoted to a specific god or goddess and is considered the deity's home on Earth. Historically, Hindu temples were the exclusive domain of men. Women were not allowed, presumably because menstruation is "polluting" and threatens the purity of holy sites. By the 2000s most sites allowed women. However, limitations on women's access remained common. These included denying women access to a temple's inner shrine (the most holy part) and denying women access to the site when they are on their periods.

In the last decade, Hindu women and women's groups like Bhumata Brigade (Women Warriors of Mother Earth) have challenged temple bans and restrictions on women. They have led public protests and marches, and used social media—for example, #Happytobleed, a movement against banning menstruating women from temples. They have also used the courts, who so far have ruled that entering temples is a fundamental right of Indian women.

But the power of the courts and the power of tradition are at odds as shown by the case of the Sabarimala temple, a popular Hindu pilgrimage site in

the Indian state of Kerala. Since 1991, only boys and men, girls under 10, and older women who were no longer menstruating, were allowed. In September 2018, a Supreme Court ruling gave women the right to enter the Sabarimala temple. When three young women attempted to enter the temple a few months later, they were stopped by thousands of angry male devotees of Ayyappa, the temple's celibate deity.

What followed was one of the largest gender equality protests in Indian history. On the day of the January 2019 protest, an estimated three to five million women lined up to form a 385-mile wall of protest along the state's main highway. The next morning, two women were able to enter Sabarimala, but massive protests followed and at least one person was killed. Meanwhile, the court agreed to revisit the case after receiving dozens of challenges to the landmark judgement, and women's access is still restricted.

Sources: BBC, 2019b; Nair, 2019; Pandey, 2016; Poonam, 2019; Schouten, 2016; Thiagarajan, 2019.

---

nationalists are responsible for attacks on Muslims (who comprise about 14% of the India population) and on women who violate traditional gender norms, for example, drinking in bars (Imam, 2016). As far as Hindu nationalists are concerned, modern problems are partly due to the destruction of the Hindu family system. Therefore, women need to return to their exalted place as modest and submissive mothers, daughters, and wives in the private sphere; men are the stronger sex and are to protect them (Singh, 2016). At militaristic camps run by Durga Vahini (named after the Hindu Goddess that protects society from evil), the women's wing of RSS, young women are taught to fight for the nationalist cause and to embrace traditional gender roles while Westernization and Islam are blamed for increased sexual violence against women (Jain, 2019; Nashrulla, 2014).

Hindu women who seek to reform their religion often look to the epic figure Draupadi, who does not allow men to dictate to her, and to the goddess Kali, who inspires terror and awe and is a model of female power (Gupta, 1991; Sugirtharajah, 1994). They recast Hindu goddesses and religious figures as spiritual beings that show their devotion independent of husband devotion (Narayanan, 1999). They aim to rescue Shakti (feminine divine power) from its patriarchal prison (Singh, 2016). They resist Hindu fundamentalism and its demands that women be restricted to their roles as wives and mothers, and its insistence that women not read the Vedas.

> "Hindu fundamentalism is a contradiction in terms, since Hinduism is a religion without fundamentals; there is no such thing as a Hindu heresy. How dare a bunch of goondas shrink the soaring majesty of the Vedas and the Upanishads to the petty bigotry of their brand of identity politics?"
> *Shashi Tharoor, Indian politician*

"Although Hindu traditions are portrayed, and quite correctly in some instances, as being patriarchal, the system has built-in mechanisms to allow for dynamic reinterpretation."
Vasudha Narayanan, Hinduism scholar

They refer to the evidence that women contributed to the development of Hinduism, for example, composing hymns, poems, and performing rituals in the Vedic period (Peach, 2002). They study the ancient texts that support women's equality and point out how it was only over time that Hindu texts came to support the subordination of women. For example, they explain that it was the introduction of the Laws of Manu (200 B.C.E.-100 C.E.) that removed women from the educational and religious spheres and put almost exclusive emphasis on the destiny and role of women as wives and mothers (Joshee & Sihra, 2013). Many point out how British colonization gave Hindu texts supportive of male power greater legal precedence than those that were more liberal in their attitudes toward women (Narayanan, 1999). Some Hindu women challenge temple limits on women's entrance (see Box 8.4 for some recent examples).

Hindu women seeking reform also work toward women's inclusion as spiritual leaders. Early Hinduism was more supportive of women's equality than later Hinduism. Until recently, one barrier to women's leadership in Hinduism was that only males could study Sanskrit, the language of the religious texts. Women gurus remain relatively uncommon but are growing in number, especially in Hindu communities in the United States and Canada (Lucia, 2014; Narayanan, 2006). One of the most famous global gurus is an Indian woman called "Amma" (Mother). Born Mātā Amrtānandamayī in 1953 in Kerala, India, Amma's spiritual gift is hugging people, and her spiritual mission is to spread love and compassion and to serve others. With a huge following, including celebrities, she has hugged over 40 million people, worldwide. Although she is not without controversy, her global charities (collectively called Embracing the World) have aided millions.

"My Dream: A vision of a world in which women and men progress together, a world where men respect the fact that, like the two wings of a bird, women and men are of equal value."
Amma

Buddhism

Buddhism began in India in the fifth or sixth century B.C.E. after Siddhartha Gautama attained enlightenment and became the "Buddha" or the "awakened one" (Peach, 2002). Very generally, Buddha counseled that spiritual enlightenment requires devoting oneself to understanding and ending suffering, getting rid of ego and desire, seeking spiritual depth, and behaving morally (e.g., no killing, stealing, lying, gossiping, no intoxicants). Death and rebirth occur until enlightenment is reached. Countries with a high proportion of Buddhists (55%-97%) include Burma (Myanmar), Bhutan, Cambodia, Laos, Mongolia, Thailand, Sri Lanka, and Tibet. However, there are also large Buddhist populations (10%-36% of a country's population) in China, Hong Kong, Japan, Macau, Malaysia, Nepal, Singapore, South Korea, Vietnam, and Taiwan.

There are two main forms of Buddhism. *Theravada* (Hinayana) Buddhism is more likely to view women as obstacles to spiritual progress and to suggest that women are inferior spiritual beings. Theravada denies the possibility of a female Buddha (a Buddha is a person who has achieved a state of perfect enlightenment and has been released from the cycle of birth and death). It is the dominant Buddhist form in Cambodia, Laos, Myanmar (Burma), Sri Lanka, and Thailand. In contrast is *Mahayana* (Zen) Buddhism, which stresses that all human experience, male and female, is the source of enlightenment and that all things share one life because nothing can stand on its own. This is known as the Supreme Wisdom, *Prajnaparamita*, or the feminine principle (Bancroft, 1987). Mahayana Buddhism is more common in Bhutan, China, Korea, Japan, Mongolia, Taiwan, Tibet, and Vietnam.

Although the Buddha is male, in Buddhism there are no gendered Absolute or Supreme Beings and no masculine God-language. However, most Buddhist archetypes of enlightenment are male. Like the world's other major religions, we find evidence of hostile sexism in some Buddhist scriptures that describe women as filled with evil desires and as harmful obstacles to men's attainment of enlightenment (Uchino, 1987). Buddhist popular thought often regards women as impure (due to menstruation and childbirth), as having a more sinful karma than men (thus their poor situation), and as being unable to attain Buddhahood (the highest level of enlightenment) unless they are reborn as a man (Gross, 1999, 2003; Uchino, 1987). Women improve their karma by being good wives and mothers. As far as religious practice is concerned, women are expected to show devotion through their domestic duties as wives and mothers, in lay devotional practices, and by feeding monks (monastic rules prohibit monks from farming or handling money). There are also scriptures that suggest the genders are essentially different (Gross, 2003). However, like other major religions, there is also scriptural support for women's equality.

A glass ceiling is evident in Buddhism, as it is in most religions. Men hold most positions of authority and prestige in the majority of Buddhist organizations (Halafoff & Rajkobal, 2015). In traditional Buddhism, the main religious leaders are the male monks, or *bhikkhu*. The female counterpart is the *bhikkhuni*, sometimes translated as "nun," although it is really the female form of the word *bhikkhu*. According to some historical accounts, women's right to enter the monastic order was granted by the Buddha following protest; 500 women with shaved heads and saffron robes walked 100 miles to plead with the Buddha, who relented after their third protest (Goonatilake, 1997). Ultimately, the Buddha ordained over 500 women (Halafoff & Rajkobal, 2015). But Buddhist nuns have not fared as well as Buddhist monks anyplace in any period of history (Gross, 2003). Although there is some improvement, in general there are fewer monasteries for bhikkhuni, fewer opportunities for economic support, and less family and social support. The ordination process is often made more difficult for nuns, their lives are more closely regulated than monks' lives, and the monks usually have authority over nuns.

Mahayana (Zen) Buddhism gives women greater equality in religious practice and leadership. In Taiwan, Buddhist nuns have their own monasteries and enjoy social and financial support from the public. In Japan, nuns are ordained and may even perform some priestly duties in some sects. Women's ordination is also common in the United States, Canada, and Europe, which are growing their own versions of Buddhism to fit their culture. In some countries—such as Cambodia, Laos, Tibet, Thailand, Nepal, Bhutan, and Burma—there are no orders of fully ordained *bhikkhuni*, even where there once were. Most of these countries practice Theravada, which does not ordain nuns, or does so under limited conditions (Bancroft, 1987; Barnes, 1994). For instance, in Thailand, women may become *bhikkhuni* (nuns) or *mae chii* (female monks), but they are not fully

"When men know that spiritually we are the same as they are, they will have to judge us on our merits and our ability and not on what someone said thousands of years ago." *Reverend Master Jiyu Kennett Roshi ("Roshi" means Zenmaster), woman founder of the Order of Buddhist Contemplatives (with chapters in the U.S., U.K., the Netherlands, Canada, and Germany)*

"Let's face it, Burma has a male-dominated, patriarchal society, which means religious life is also dominated by men. The patriarchy is deep-rooted here." *Keta Mala, Burmese nun*

"The weightier texts, stories, and teachers argue that dharma is neither male nor female. There have always been important Buddhist thinkers that clearly said discrimination against women in Buddhism is inappropriate and un-dharmic."
Rita Gross, Buddhist theologian

"The Lotus Sutra teaches that all living beings possess the world of Buddhahood. There is not even a hint of discrimination toward women. If there are men who deny the enlightenment of women, they are denying the possibility of their own attainment of Buddhahood."
Soka Gakkai International, the world's largest Buddhist practitioner's organization

ordained, receive no public or governmental support, and are marginalized within the religion (Carr, 2016; Falk, 2008). Nuns in Burma, home to over 60,000 bhikkhunis, are not allowed to formally teach the dharma, are unable to be fully ordained, and must bow to bhikkhus and sit below them (Rigby, 2017).

Buddhist women's activism for equal rights within their religion has a long history (Boucher, 2006; Falk, 2008; Goonatilake, 1997; Lavine, 2006). Buddhist women theologians argue that Buddhist *dharma* (the central truth or spiritual path) does not support patriarchy. Rita Gross's work (1993, 1996, 1999, 2003) is an excellent example. Using a historical hermeneutic, Buddhist theologians discredit the orthodox Theravada view of women's inferiority by showing that the scriptures were not written down until 200 to 400 years after the Buddha's death and have changed over time (Findly, 2014; Derris, 2008). They argue that Buddhism was co-opted by politics and patriarchy and use history to show that the Buddha did not intend to restrict women's participation (Falk, 2008; Findly, 2014). They recover and reimagine scriptures and use essential Buddhist teachings to show that women and men have equal potential for enlightenment. They draw attention to stories and texts supporting gender equality (Derris, 2008).

Women also work to break the glass ceiling in Buddhism. They question the authenticity of the eight extra rules for women seeking ordination, which allegedly came from the Buddha and are used to limit women's ordination (Halafoff & Rajkobal, 2015). They use the Buddhist canon to show that the Buddha acknowledged the importance of women's religious leadership and point out that it includes the *Therigatha*, a volume of writings by female disciples of the Buddha (Boucher, 2006, Neumaier, 2016). Action is both local and global. For example, in Thailand and Burma, *bhikkhunis* advocate for full recognition as spiritual leaders of their faith (Carr, 2016; Rigby, 2017). Meanwhile, globalization and the Internet have fostered a transnational feminist Buddhism dedicated to equality in all Buddhist traditions. *Sakyadhita* (Daughters of the Buddha) is an international association of Buddhist women that challenges gender disparities in Buddhism. They educate teachers of Buddhism and have created an international communication network of Buddhist women. They hold international conferences and conduct research on Buddhist women's history and contemporary issues (Halafoff & Rajkobal, 2015). They also work for women's ordination, once convincing the Theravada male clergy in Sri Lanka to reestablish women's ordination (not since the eleventh century had they had this right) (Boucher, 2006; Falk, 2008). Box 8.5 showcases the a Thai mother and daughter who have led the modern movement to ordain Theravada Buddhist women.

Christianity

Christianity arose out of Judaism around the first century C.E. and is based on the life, death, and resurrection of Jesus of Nazareth. The main text of Christianity is the **Bible,** both the Old and New Testaments. The New Testament tells of Jesus and his followers and was composed between 50 C.E. and 90 C.E., long after Jesus's death (Gerhart, 2003). Most Christians believe that Jesus is the Son of God, and God personified on Earth. Christianity is the main religious practice of people in Europe, the South Pacific (including Australia and Papua New Guinea), North America, South

BOX 8.5 *Thai Mother and Daughter Blaze Trail for Buddhist Women Monks*

Thailand is a predominantly Buddhist country with approximately 40,000 Buddhist temples and 300,000 Buddhist monks. But as recently as 2014, the monks' highest leadership body (the Supreme Sangha Council) affirmed the 1928 Sangha Act that forbids the ordination of women by Thai monks. Although women may become Buddhist nuns in Thailand, nuns have lower status than male monks and are often relegated to housekeeping tasks in temples.

This was not enough for Voramai Kabilsingh. In 1956, she adopted the saffron robes of the ordained and founded the Songdammakalayani Temple, an all-female monastery outside of Bangkok. Unable to become ordained in the Thai Theravada tradition, she travelled to Taiwan in 1971 where she was ordained in the Mahayana tradition and became known as Ta Tao Fa Tzu. Because her ordination was not in the Theravada tradition, her ordination posed little threat and went largely unnoticed in Thailand. Three decades later, her daughter, Chatsumarn Kabilsingh, an author and professor, felt called to the monastic life. Sri Lanka was now ordaining women and unlike her mother,

Chatsumarn could be ordained there in the Theravada tradition. But when she returned to Thailand from Sri Lanka after ordination in 2003 as a Theravada monk, clergy protested and Dhammananda Bhikkhuni, as she was now known, was criticized, and ridiculed.

Today Dhammananda Bhikkhuni is in her 70s and abbess of the monastery her mother founded. She remains dedicated to reestablishing the Theravada bhikkhuni lineage in Thailand and increasing the number of women monks in Thailand and Asia. The Songdammakalayani monastery ordains women novices (becoming a novice is the first step in preparing for ordination) but cannot fully ordain women because in Thailand this requires ten male monks. However, women can begin their studies there and travel abroad for ordination. There are now approximately 300 women monks in Thailand. Dhammananda says, "Ordination is given to us by the Buddha. It's our heritage. I'm not fighting for equality; I'm fighting for my right."

Sources: Lewis, 2019; Rasicot, 2019; Tanakasempipat, 2019

America, Central America, the Caribbean, and many African countries including Angola, Botswana, Burundi, Cabo Verde, Democratic Republic of Congo, Ethiopia, Liberia, Rwanda, and South Africa.

Disagreements over biblical interpretation and practice led to three main forms of Christianity: Catholic, Protestant, and Orthodox. The Catholic Church and the Orthodox Church emphasize women's role as wife and mother and deny them most leadership roles. The official position of the Catholic Church is to prohibit abortion, contraception, and sterilization; to limit divorce and remarriage; to deny the rights of gays and lesbians; and to deny women's ordination, although many Catholics do not agree with these positions (Pew Research Center, 2014).

In some versions of Christianity, most notably Latin American Roman Catholicism, Jesus's mother, Mary, is an important religious figure and model of womanhood. Mary is also presented as the perfect mother and a spotless virgin, ideals that some Catholic women have noted are difficult to live up to (Cisernos, 1996; Drury, 1994). Mary is also very important in Orthodox Christianity, which has a period of fasting dedicated to her as well as numerous feasts and festivals.

"Patriarchy is not God's dream for humanity. It never was and never will be."
Sarah Bessey, author of Jesus Feminist

There are also a number of female saints in Catholicism and Orthodox Christianity. However, the stories told about these saints by male clerics typically depict them as exemplars of an all-giving sacrificial femininity that supports traditional gender power relationships (McPhillips, 2017).

"Feminism is a reality check on the Gospel message of equality among all people in the eyes of God."
Rev. Winnie Varghese, Episcopal Priest

There are dozens of different Protestant denominations. These vary considerably in their promotion of patriarchy; some are far more liberal about women's roles than are others. For instance, most evangelical and fundamentalist Christianities are explicitly antagonistic to feminism and use scriptures to justify the traditional patriarchal family. There are evangelical churches among Baptist, Methodist, Lutheran, Presbyterian, Pentecostal, Anglican, Episcopal, and Congregational denominations as well as nondenominational evangelical churches. Feminism is disdained by these religions not only because most feminists support abortion rights and contraceptive access, but also because feminists suggest that traditional gender roles and patriarchy are socially constructed and in need of change. Evangelical Christians generally share a belief that gender roles and gender differences are God-given and biblically mandated. They believe in "complementarian" marriages with the husband as head of the household and the wife as submissive to him (Green, 2014). The Russian Orthodox Church also subscribes to this view (Chernyak, 2016).

There are also fundamentalist strains that seek a Christian state, such as the Lord's Resistance Army, founded by self-proclaimed prophet Joseph Kony in Uganda in 1987. Kony's fighters have killed more than 100,000 people, displaced more than two million, and abducted more than 20,000 children to use as soldiers, servants, or sex slaves; fortunately, the army has shrunk and is no longer considered a major threat in the region (Baddorf, 2017). In the name of "pro-family values," American fundamentalist Christian organizations (like the Christian Coalition and the Family Research Council in America) and evangelical Christian legislators actively work for public policies limiting women's reproductive rights and sexuality education, penalizing nontraditional families, and legalizing discrimination against LGBT people. Some of the most patriarchal of Christian religions are fundamentalist Evangelical Christian cults and movements. Men rule over women and control women's sexuality. Women are restricted to the home sphere where they produce and homeschool children and perform care labor. Patriarchy is sold to followers as God's will. Box 8.6 describes two fundamentalist Christian groups that put their own extreme religious twist on patriarchy.

"Jesus first reminded His followers that in the very beginning, God made humanity in His own image, male and female. Men and women are different, yet complementary; specifically designed by God to complete each other."
Focus on the Family, American Christian organization

Because the Bible uses masculine God-language and the majority of biblical stories are the stories of men, many feminists view the Bible as a patriarchal document of a patriarchal society. But hermeneutics vary among Christian denominations. Evangelical Protestant Christian denominations and conservative denominations like Church of Jesus Christ of Latter-Day Saints (Mormons) and Catholic and Orthodox Christian churches are mostly likely to interpret selected scriptures with a patriarchal hermeneutic supporting benevolent sexism and promoting traditional gender roles. For instance, this verse from the King James Version of the Bible, "But I would have you know, that the head of every man is Christ; and the head of the woman is the man; and the head of Christ is God" (Corinthians 11:3;

BOX 8.6   *Two Fundamentalist Patriarchal Christian Movements (United States)*

Fundamentalist Church of Jesus Christ of Latter-Day Saints (FLDS)

The FLDS is essentially a Christian cult. Like other Christian cults, there is a male charismatic leader who claims to be a prophet. Followers are insulated from the outside world and secular influences. Not knowing what else to believe, they accept what they are told is God's truth. Nonconformity is punished with shunning or shaming, and sometimes with violence and expulsion.

The FLDS split from the LDS (the mainstream Mormon Church) in 1890. A polygamous sect of approximately 10,000 people, it is extremely patriarchal. All religious leaders are men, and they decide whom a woman (or girl) must marry and when. Women and girls may be married off to relatives, to older men, and to men with other wives. Girls and women are expected to submit to male authority at all times, to dress modestly, and to be "sweet," which means never questioning or rebelling. Due to the courage of several women, in 2006 leader Warren Jeffs was sentenced to life in prison for his role in forcing underage girls into marriage and rape, and for the sexual assault of two of his "wives," aged 12 and 15. Seen as their patriarch with a direct line to God, evidence indicates that he continues to lead the FLDS from prison, including directing sexual relationships between the remaining men and women.

The Christian Patriarchy Movement

This Evangelical Christian fundamentalist movement is based largely in the United States. The size of the movement is unknown but estimated to be in the low tens of thousands. The Duggar family, who had their own American reality show "Nineteen Kids and Counting," is an example. Due to sex scandals involving many of its leaders, the movement appears to have waned in recent years.

Although there are differences within the movement, a complementarian theology supporting clearly demarcated traditional gender roles is typical. Women do God's will by being mothers and submissive "helpmeets" to their husbands. They aren't supposed to cut their hair, wear pants, work outside the home, or question their husbands' authority. Men are the leaders, teachers, deciders, and providers serving in their God-appointed role as family patriarch. The movement also emphasizes the importance of women's sexual purity before marriage and her duty to satisfy all of her husband's sexual needs after marriage (so he can be a more effective leader).

The Quiverfull movement is an example. Adherents advocate a patriarchal, pronatalist, anti-birth control, anti-abortion form of Christianity supported by reading scriptures with a patriarchal hermeneutic. Psalm 127: 3–5 is a favorite and gives the movement its name. It says that "children are the heritage of the Lord" and "happy is the man that hath his quiver full of them." Trusting the Lord to determine family size, they have large families. They believe their children are not only a blessing, but part of an army for God that will ultimately increase Christians' political influence.

Sources: Blumberg, 2015; Joyce, 2010; Mattieu, 2015; Miller, 2020; Patterson, 2015; Wall & Pulitzer, 2009.

see also Ephesians 5: 22–25 and Colossians 3:18–19), is interpreted as meaning that God wants husbands to be the boss of their wives. This passage, "Wives, in the same way be submissive to your husbands so that, if any of them do not believe the word, they may be won over without words by the behavior of their wives, when they see the purity and reverence of your lives" (1 Peter 3:1–7; see also Proverbs 31:10–15, 28 and Titus 2:5), is converted into a divinely inspired gender norm that ties being a good Christian woman to being submissive to one's husband.

Feminist theologians see the Bible's book of Genesis as one of the most influential affecting women's status because it has so often been used to justify women's subordination to men. In Genesis (2:24), Eve is created as a companion ("help-meet")

"The Christian tradition is by no means bereft of elements which foster genuine experiences and intimations of transcendence. The problem is that their liberating potential is choked off in the surrounding atmosphere of the images, ideas, values, and structures of patriarchy."
Mary Daly, radical feminist theologian

"God transcends all our human perceptions and language expressions . . . If Christianity preaches a God of love who liberates every person for new possibilities and discipleship, then we have to speak of this God in non-patriarchal, non-sexist terms."
Elisabeth Schüssler Fiorenza, feminist theologian

"Women should keep silent in the churches, for they are not allowed to speak, but should be subordinate, as even the law says. But if they want to learn anything, they should ask their husbands at home. For it is improper for a woman to speak in the church."
I Cor. 14:34–25

to Adam from his rib. This is taken by some Christian religions to mean that woman was created from man and for men, and this justifies male supremacy. The story of Adam and Eve's fall from grace (Gen. 1:3) is often used to justify women's lower status and gendered burdens. Here, Eve is punished for eating from the tree of knowledge of good and evil. She is responsible for human's banishment from paradise, and because of her transgression, God tells her, "in sorrow thou shalt bring forth children; and thy desire shall be to thy husband" (Gen. 3:16). To support their claim that men and women are fundamentally different because God made them so, they turn to this verse, "And Adam said, this is now the bone of my bones, and the flesh of my flesh: she shall be called Woman, because she was taken out of Man. Therefore shall a man leave his father and his mother, and shall cleave unto his wife: and they shall be one flesh" (Genesis 2:24; see also Proverbs 5:18–20 and Ecclesiastes 9:9). Other Christian denominations, such as the Unitarian Church, the Episcopal Church, and United Methodist Church, do not look at the canon this way and are decidedly more progressive regarding women's roles.

In Christianity, gender-segregated religious practices are found mainly in religious leadership (most ministers, priests, deacons, church council and board members are men), although most conservative and evangelical churches see women's dedication to husband and family as women's religious practice. In many congregations, women are excluded formally or informally from decision-making leadership positions (Audette, Kwakwa, & Weaver, 2017). However, women commonly perform secondary religious duties consistent with the traditional female gender role, such as caring for elders and the sick, preparing food for church gatherings, singing in the choir, and cleaning the church. Protestant churches opposed to the ordination of women typically point to 1 Timothy 2:12, which states that women should not teach or have authority over men and 1 Corinthians 14:33–36, which says that women should be silent in church. All women in the Catholic Church are laity, including nuns, because ordination to the clerical state is denied to women. Pope John Paul II defended this on the grounds that Jesus had no women among his twelve apostles and that because Jesus is male, only another male may represent him. This argument is used by most Christian religions that deny women's ordination. The current pope, Pope Francis, says he stands behind Pope John Paul's declaration. However, nuns or female lay ministers lead approximately three percent of Catholic churches and are permitted to do everything but deliver the sacraments.

Christian and Catholic feminists sometimes refer to the formal and informal barriers in the way of women's progression through the church hierarchy as the "stained-glass ceiling." In the United States, about one in five mainline and African American Protestant churches are led by women, compared to only 3 percent of congregations within evangelical traditions. In the late 1960s and early 1970s, Christian feminists pointed out how males monopolized all visible roles in Christianity beyond singing in the choir, baking, and teaching young children (Gross, 1996). In some denominations, activism has led to the ordination of women and to the occupation by women of other church positions traditionally held by males, such as deacon. But change is uneven. For instance, the Catholic Church, the Orthodox Church, Southern Baptists, the Church of Jesus Christ of Latter-Day Saints (Mormon), Seventh Day Adventists, and some conservative branches of the Anglican Church do not ordain women. Protestant churches that ordain women include the Lutheran Church of America, the United Church of Christ, the United Methodist Church, the Church of England, the Presbyterian Church, and the Episcopal Church (most dioceses). According to the National Congregations study, by 2019 almost 14 percent of American Protestant congregations were led by women, 89 percent allowed women to serve as full members of main governing body, and 56 percent allowed women to be head clergyperson or primary religious leader (Chaves et al., 2020).

To support women's ordination, theologians and activists emphasize that women were major figures in the founding and spread of Christianity in its early years, and provide historical and scriptural evidence that women were among Jesus's disciples (French, 1992; Gerhart, 2003; Schüssler Fiorenza, 1995). They refer to the Bible to show that Jesus is portrayed as freely talking to women, assigning them roles in his parables, and thinking of them as good friends and followers (Gross, 1996). They point out that Jesus's role as the Son of God was first revealed to a woman, as was his resurrection. They point to passages such as the one where the apostle Paul said, "There is neither Jew nor Greek, there is neither slave nor free, there is neither male nor female; for you are all one in Christ Jesus" (Gal. 3:28). Activism includes a movement in the Catholic Church to ordain women, led by the Women's Ordination Conference and Roman Catholic Womenpriests. In defiance of the Vatican, Roman Catholic Womenpriests has ordained over 250 women worldwide since 2002; the ordained women and the bishops who ordained them have been excommunicated from the Church (Roman Catholic Women Priests, 2021). Another women's ordination movement is Ordain Women, an activist organization seeking gender equality and women's ordination to the priesthood in the Mormon faith.

Christian feminist theologians and religious leaders critique masculine God-language and imagery and rework prayers and liturgy to include female images of the divine (Slee, 2014; Ursic, 2015). They reexamine Christian texts and history and use feminist hermeneutics to challenge patriarchy and promote equality and well-being for all (Schüssler Fiorenza, 2015; Ruether, 1999). They translate and interpret ancient documents that provide less sexist versions of biblical stories (Arthur, 1987). They show how the story of Adam and Eve and the lives of female saints can be reread to empower women (McPhillips, 2017; Trible, 1973). "Mariologists" reclaim and redefine Mary, the mother of Jesus Christ, as a model of liberation, suffering, and struggle (Gebara & Bingemer, 1994).

Elizabeth Cady Stanton (1815–1902), one of the founders of the early American women's movement, wrote and lectured on a variety of women's issues, including religion. Her *Women's Bible*, published in 1895, was the major nineteenth-century feminist interpretation of the Bible.

"On any given Sunday, God is almost always named in male terms. Might our daughters conclude that God is male and they are not made in God's image? Might they conclude that they are secondary, derivative, less than men?"
A Church for Our Daughters

Intersectional Feminist Theologies

Most feminist theologies look at religion through the single lens of gender inequality, but many newer and lesser-known feminist theologies look at it through intersectional lenses (Kim & Shaw, 2018). Where women face multiple oppressions based on race, economics, and gender, feminist theologies are often liberation theologies focusing on justice and equality for all people and using religious texts as a means to empower the poor and oppressed (King, 1994; Lev, 2009). For them, feminist theology is not just about deconstructing religion as an agent of patriarchy but as an agent of racism, classism, heterosexism, and colonialism. Some African and Asian feminist theologies are **post-colonial theologies** that seek to rediscover nonpatriarchal religious traditions and interpretations common before colonization. Anti-colonialism and anti-imperialism are important parts of these theologies as they examine associations between religion and Western colonization and re-appropriate theological symbols for empowerment and resistance (Kim, 2020; Pui-lan, 2007; Schüssler Fiorenza, 2007). These theologies sometimes mix parts of the religion brought by missionaries and colonizers with native traditions and rely on oral storytelling as the source of indigenous religion (Oduyoye, 2001; Pui-lan, 2007).

Theologies developed by marginalized women in industrialized nations also address the intersection of gender, race, class, economics, and religion. For instance, **Womanist theology** is a women of color feminist liberation theology that began in the mid-1980s as a Protestant Christian African American endeavor but increasingly includes the voices of other Black women and women of color, and other religions (Razak, 2013; Townes, 2006). It is a liberation theology in that it emphasizes justice for women and the oppressed and is envisioned as an instrument for theological and social change. Womanists emphasize how women of color use their experiences of multiple oppressions as opportunities for transformative encounters with God that empower their hope and resilience (Prevot, 2018; Townes, 2006; Walker, 1983; Williams, 1994). It is not a denomination with a liturgy and formal leadership but is more of a spiritual framework or spiritually inspired social change perspective. Mitchem (2017) describes it as an "embodied spirituality" where Black women are in intimate relationships with other humans, nature, and God. For Christian womanists, the Bible is appropriated as a force supporting survival and quality of life, helping Black women "make a way out of no way." God is a real-time tool that helps marginalized Black women to feel loved and lovable in the face of negative stereotypes and prejudice. Black women's embodied spirituality includes the joy of song and physical movement in ritual and worship.

Mujerista theology, a Latin American feminist theology, is another example of an intersectional feminist theology that focuses on the relationships between race, class, and gender. This theology challenges theological understandings, religious teachings, and practices that oppress Latinas, although the ultimate goal is the liberation of all people (Isasi-Diaz, 2006). Mujerista theology emphasizes the discovery and affirmation of God in Latinas' daily lives and communities. The daily strategies used by Latinas to survive and pursue justice and liberation are sources of Mujerista theology (Medina, 2011). The concept of *la lucha,* or resisting suffering as a community activity, is central. For example, the fiesta is seen as a source of social resistance where Latinas support one another and make connections between their poverty, exploitation, and marginalization and the broader social implications of these problems (Flores, 2014).

Feminist Spirituality

Some feminists question that equality for women can be found through revision of the world's major religions. They believe that the essential core of the world's major religions and religious organizations are so fundamentally sexist that reform efforts are all but hopeless (Hampson, 1987). Separating their feelings about God and the Spirit from traditional religion, they work to create new traditions and to embrace ancient ones that value women's experience, past and present. Recurrent themes are women

---

"Womanist is to feminist as purple is to lavender."
Alice Walker, African American writer and womanist

"Womanism is a spirituality of life that calls me to remember that my life is a gift from God."
Emilie M. Townes, Dean of Vanderbilt University's Divinity School

---

"A mujerista is a Hispanic Woman who struggles to liberate herself not as an individual but as a member of the Hispanic community."
Ada Maria Isasi-Diaz, theologian

and nature, the significance of community with other women, women-centered stories and rituals, and the use of female imagery and symbolism (Christ & Plaskow, 1979). These efforts often embrace *paganism*, an umbrella term for a wide variety of pre- and nonbiblical religions that include female images of the divine (Aitamurto & Simpson, 2016; Feraro, 2017; Gross, 1996). These ancient religions are rich sources of positive female imagery and have the advantage of being rooted in tradition (Christ & Plaskow, 1979). Collectively, these groups are known as the **feminist spirituality movement** (Gross, 1996). However, others prefer the term **women's spirituality movement.** The feminist spirituality movement began in the 1970s and is mostly found in the United States, Australia, New Zealand, and Great Britain (Christ, 2006). These religions are among the few living religions created and led by women (Sered, 1994).

Many of these religions fall under the heading of **goddess spirituality** because the focus is on goddess worship, although there is a lot of variation in how these groups envision the goddess and the extent to which they include men (Aitamurto & Simpson, 2016; Griffin, 2003; King, 1987). Goddess spirituality is frequently based in the belief that humans lived in peace and harmony with nature during a goddess-worshipping prehistory (Braude, 2006). Writers such as Starhawk (1979), Eisler (1987), and Gimbutas (1991) point to archeological artifacts and myths showing the important role of the goddess in early religion and civilization. For instance, feminine sacred beings (goddesses) were popular in the Greco-Roman traditions that co-existed with early Christianity and remain common in many indigenous African and Native American traditions as well as in Hinduism (Gross, 1996). Visual images of the Goddesses stand in stark contrast to typical male God imagery that suggests that legitimate spiritual power is male (Christ, 1995).

According to Christ (1995, 2006), it is common for those who worship the Goddess to have an altar in their home that includes a reproduction of a full-figured ancient goddess statue, objects from nature (e.g., feathers, rocks, flowers) that represent women's connection to the "web of life," and family photos. Goddess rituals have no set form but are often conducted in groups called "goddess circles." They are held on the days or nights of the new and full moons and on eight seasonal holidays such as the winter solstice and are also conducted for special occasions such as birth, menopause, and healing. Rituals may involve singing, dancing, chanting, and meditation and are often playful and inventive. They are intended to connect people to a divinity that is found in nature and in the natural cycles of birth, death, and regeneration (Christ, 1995).

Within the Goddess movement is the religion of **Wicca,** *or* **witchcraft,** a form of spirituality based on ancient wiccan (witchcraft) traditions that involve both Gods and Goddesses. Witchcraft is a magical earth religion whose main tenet is harmony with the earth and all life (Covenant of the Goddess, 2009). This type of witchcraft is *not* associated with Satanism or devil worship; in fact, most witches do not even believe in the devil. Although some witches do cast spells, the laws of Wicca say that you can't cast a spell to "bend another person to your will," and you can't use a spell to harm another person.

There are many versions of Wicca. **Dianic witchcraft** is a feminist form that worships the feminine divine in mostly all-female covens. Dianic witches believe that before recorded history there were peaceful gender-egalitarian societies that

"There is no way to find any feminist value in the Qur'an. If people say it is found, then either they lie, or they try to interpret the verses differently to make it suitable with the present day."
Feminist Bengali physician and writer Taslima Nasrin

"Through the Goddess, we can discover our strength, enlighten our minds, own our bodies, and celebrate our emotions. We can move beyond narrow, constricting roles, and become whole."
Starhawk, founder of the Covenant of the Goddess

worshipped the Goddess but that these were displaced by patriarchal forces through violence (Wise, 2008). Dianic witchcraft arose during the 1970s, stimulated by Merlin Stone's *When God Was a Woman* (1976) and Zsuzsanna Budapest's *The Feminist Book of Lights and Shadows* (1976), which eventually became *The Holy Book of Women's Mysteries* (1989). These books became the foundations of the Dianic tradition of Wicca. Starhawk is another well-known leader in Dianic witchcraft who practices a version known as Reclaiming (Feraro, 2017). This type of witchcraft is an ecofeminist form emphasizing activism for peace and the environment.

Those who practice Wicca often emphasize that common stereotypes of witches as dangerous and self-serving were perpetrated by those who sought to eliminate this source of power for women. Negative stereotypes originated in an eradication campaign by the Christian Church in the years 1560–1760. Historian Anne Barstow (1994) says that approximately 100,000 women were killed in European witch hunts during this time period, and another 200,000 were accused of being witches. Old single women, seen as burdens, were especially likely to be accused, as were outspoken women and those who stepped out of the traditional female role. Barstow suggests that the European and American witch hunts had a number of effects on women's power. One is that fear of being accused of witchcraft kept women quiet and obedient. Another is that the campaign took away a source of power for women. Previously, witches had a lot of power as the village healers who delivered babies, performed abortions, set bones, and prescribed and administered herbal medicines. The attack on witchcraft had the effect of taking the practice of medicine away from women. The European and American witch hunts also essentially destroyed the religion of witchcraft.

Conclusion

"Human rights is a universal standard. It is a component of every religion and every civilization."
Shirin Ebadi

Throughout the book we have used a human rights framework as a basis for gender equality advocacy, and you may have noticed its absence in this chapter. That's because this framework presents special challenges when it comes to religion. Freedom of religion is affirmed as a human right in the UN Declaration on the Elimination of All Forms of Discrimination Based on Religion or Belief, but these religious rights may at times contradict the human rights of women. Indeed, conservative and fundamentalist religions often object to human rights instruments supporting women's rights and claim they are an infringement of religious freedoms. Some fundamentalists reject the concept of human rights altogether, viewing it as a Western strategy intended to eradicate their religious traditions or because they believe their scriptures are infallible and nothing can supersede them.

Many countries that ratified the Convention on the Elimination of Discrimination Against Women (CEDAW) did so with "reservations" based on religion (when governments enter a reservation to a treaty, it means that they will not be bound to those parts). In fact, 78 countries registered a total of 177 official reservations to CEDAW, most based on religious or cultural grounds. This is the highest number of reservations recorded for any international convention. For instance, Israel filed a reservation to Article 16, which states that parties undertake to eliminate discrimination against women in all matters relating to marriage and family relations (Shalev, 1995). Bangladesh, Egypt, Libya, and Tunisia all invoked Islam as the reason for their reservations to CEDAW (Mayer, 1995). Some of the CEDAW provisions that are most in conflict with freedom of religion are equality in protection before the law; the abolition of all laws and practices that discriminate against women; equality in all areas of economic and social life; equality in all manner before the law; and equal rights in family life (Boden, 2007).

As Boden (2007) points out, there is no easy solution to this issue. We don't want to subordinate women's rights to religious rights or vice versa. We have to honor women's rights and dignity while honoring the role of faith and faith-based communities to women. The best way to do this might be changing patriarchal religious ideology (Boden, 2007). This is something that is best done by those within a given religious tradition. Otherwise, charges of violating freedom of religion and disrespect are likely. Besides, it is those within a religion who best understand it; they are the ones that are most qualified to deconstruct and reinterpret it. Indeed, religious feminists seeking equality in their religions often find it more effective to promote change based on scriptural study and the religion's history rather than appealing to human rights frameworks, though it should be noted that many religious people believe that their religion is fundamentally compatible with human rights (Moghadam, 2003). As you saw in this chapter, deeply religious feminist women have brought the greatest changes.

This chapter, like those that preceded it, illustrates the multicultural, intersectional, contextual theme of global women's and gender studies. The ways that religion affects women's lives depend on where a woman lives and on other social categories such as her race, class, and sexual orientation. In contrast to the stereotype of religious women as passive, we saw that many devout women work for change and defy tradition. Once again there is evidence of positive results from women's activism. This activism theme is a major focus of the two remaining chapters, which center on women's political activities.

Glossary Terms and Concepts

Ambivalent sexism
Benevolent sexism
Bible
Buddhism
Canon
Christianity
Dianic witchcraft
Feminist hermeneutics
Feminist spirituality
  movement (women's
  spirituality movement)
Feminist theology

Gender-segregated
  religious practices
Goddess spirituality
Hadith
Hermeneutics
Hinduism
Hostile sexism
Islam
Islamists
Islamization
Judaism
Liberation theology
Masculine God-language

Mujerista theology
Post-colonial theologies
Qur'an
Religious
  fundamentalisms
Shari'ah
Talmud
Torah
Vedas
Womanist theology
Wicca (witchcraft)
Womanspaces

Study Questions

1. How can religion empower women? How can it disempower them?
2. Why is it important to contextualize the study of women and religion?
3. What are the features of religious fundamentalism? How do benevolent sexism and hostile sexism apply to conservative and fundamentalist religions?
4. What is feminist theology? What are the common feminist critiques of religion?
5. What are hermeneutics, and why do they matter in feminist theology? What feminist hermeneutics are outlined in the chapter?
6. What basic assumptions underlie reformist efforts in feminist theology? What are the four common reformist efforts?
7. Explain how the religious canons of the world's major religions are used to support patriarchy.
8. Review the gender-segregated religious rituals and practices in the world's major religions.
9. Briefly outline the gender equality efforts for each major world religion examined in the chapter.
10. What are the basic features of the intersectional feminist theologies described in the chapter? What are the features of Womanist theology and Mujerista theology?
11. What is the feminist spirituality movement? Why have some abandoned reformist efforts in favor of new traditions? What are some common features of these traditions?
12. What is goddess spirituality? What is the religion of Wicca (witchcraft)? What is Dianic witchcraft? How was the eradication of witchcraft accomplished prior to the eighteenth century, and how did it constitute an attack on women's power?
13. What challenges face the applications of a human rights framework to religion and women's human rights? Why do these challenges lead to the conclusion that it is usually best to promote change based on scriptural study and the religion's history?

Discussion Questions and Activities

1. Are traditional religions (Christianity, Islam, Hinduism, Judaism, and Buddhism) fundamentally sexist, or have they merely been misinterpreted? Is it feasible that traditional religions can be reconceived or reinterpreted in a way that permits gender equality? Or will it be necessary for women to develop their own religions in order to achieve equality?

2. Does the use of the pronoun "He" to refer to God and the exclusion of women from most religious hierarchies condition women to view themselves as inferior to men?

3. Make a list of masculine adjectives that describe God and another list of feminine adjectives that describe God. What does this tell you about your conceptions of God? Is God male?

4. Interview a woman minister or rabbi, a practitioner of feminist spirituality (for instance, a witch), or a traditional religious woman using questions developed from the chapter.

5. This chapter focused mostly on women in the world's major religions. Choose a lesser-known religion such as the Bahai, Sikh, or Jainism religions, a variant or denomination of a major religion like Sufism (Islam), or an intersectional feminist theology that wasn't covered in the chapter, like Native American feminist theology. Analyze the religion using chapter concepts.

6. Find a story from a religious text that features women and use Elizabeth Schüssler Fiorenza's feminist hermeneutics to interpret it in a way that empowers people that are marginalized by race, class, and gender.

7. Create your own goddess altar or invite a few friends over to do a ritual celebrating the feminine divine, the female body, a female rite of passage, or our connection with all things. See books by Starhawk or Zsuzsanna Budapest for ideas or create your own ritual. Or, see WATER (the Women's Alliance for Theology, Ethics, and Ritual; http://www.waterwomensalliance.org) for a variety of monthly prayers and rituals inspired by a variety of religious traditions.

Action Opportunities

1. If you worship regularly as part of an organized religion, lead a scripture study of passages suggestive of women's subordination to men. Be prepared to discuss their textual and historical context and whether they are otherwise consistent with the religion's conception of God. Introduce attendees to a few feminist hermeneutics to consider scriptures.

2. If you are a member of an organized religion and you are dissatisfied with the treatment of women within your tradition, lead a change effort. For instance, you can lead a petition drive in favor of women being allowed to hold positions such as deacon, minister, or bishop or to change liturgical language to be more gender neutral. You can also meet with your religious leaders and ask that they devote more time to presenting stories about women in the tradition and what they have to teach us, or that they encourage or recruit women for church leadership positions, such as deacon.

3. Check the chapter websites for feminist activist efforts specific to your religion. For example, if you are Jewish, Women of the Wall offers some exciting action opportunities. Bat Mitzvah girls in your synagogue can adopt the WOW cause

for their Bat Mitzvah project. You can empower young women by teaching about WOW and pluralism and women's rights in Israel and Judaism.

4. Go to http://www.Amnesty.org and http://www.HRW.org to participate in a letter-writing campaign for cases involving the persecution of women due to conservative Shari'ah.

5. Do something to counteract religious conservatives' assault on women's rights in your country or community. Write letters to editors and your representatives in Congress about a particular policy area of concern to you, such as the restriction of women's reproductive rights or the prohibition of sex education. Enlist progressive clergy to speak out to counter people who use religion to promote gender inequality. Create your own social media campaign to draw attention to fundamentalist religious attacks on women's rights; for example, by tweeting alarming quotes from fundamentalist religious leaders and politicians.

Activist Websites

A Church for Our Daughters http://achurchforourdaughters.org/resources

Christians for Biblical Equality http://www.cbeinternational.org/

Feminist Mormon Housewives www.feministmormonhousewives.org

Jewish Orthodox Feminist Alliance http://www.jofa.org/

Roman Catholic Women Priests http://www.romancatholicwomenpriests.org/

Sakyadhita (International Association of Buddhist Women) http://www.sakyadhita.org

WISE (*Women's Islamic Initiative in Spirituality and Equality*) https://www.wisemuslimwomen.org

Women of the Wall http://www.womenofthewall.org.il/

Women's Ordination Conference http://www.womensordination.org/resources/why-ordination/

Informational Websites

Asian Women's Resource Centre for Culture and Theology http://awrc4ct.org/about-us/

Feminist Studies in Religion http://www.fsrinc.org

Jewish Women's Archive https://jwa.org/aboutjwa

Musaweh https://www.musawah.org

Sufi Women's Organization http://www.sufiwomen.org/index.html

Starhawk's Homepage http://www.starhawk.org/

WATER (The Women's Alliance for Theology, Ethics, and Ritual) http://www.waterwomensalliance.org

References

Abraham, A. 2015, November 12. Interview with Nawal el Saadawi, Egypt's most fiery feminist. *Vice.* https://www.vice.com/en_us/article/nawal-el-saadawi -interview-activism-934. Retrieved on April 25, 2017.

Agadjanian V. 2015. Women's religious authority in a sub-Saharan setting: Dialectics of empowerment and dependency. *Gender & Society, 29,* 982–1008.

Agugideiri, H. 2014. Speaking from behind the veil: Does Islamic feminism exist? In *Faith and feminism: Ecumenical essays,* edited by B. D. Lipsett and P. Trible. Louisville, KY: Westminster John Knox Press.

Ahmed, L. 2002. Gender and literacy in Islam. In *Nothing sacred: Women respond to religious fundamentalism and terror,* edited by B. Reed. New York: Thunder's Mouth Press/Nation Books.

Aitamurto, K., and Simpson, K. 2016. The study of paganism and wicca. In *The Oxford handbook of new religious movements,* Vol. II, edited by J. R. Lewis and I. B. Tolleson. New York: Oxford University Press.

Angel, C. G. 2019. Nobel laureate Shirin Ebadi 'disappointed' by outcome of Iran's Islamic revolution. *France 24.* https://www.france24.com/en/20190213 -interview-shirin-ebadi-iran-islamic-revolution-ayatollah-khomenei-womens-rights. Retrieved on May 29, 2021.

Arthur, R. H. 1987. The wisdom goddess and the masculinization of western religion. In *Women in the world's religions, past and present,* edited by U. King. New York: Paragon House.

Audette, A. P., Kwakwa, M., and Weaver, C. L. 2017. Reconciling the god and gender gaps: The influence of women in church politics. *Politics, Groups, and Identities. 6.* DOI: 10.1080/21565503.2016.1273121

Avishai, O. 2008. Doing religion in a secular world: Women in conservative religions. *Gender and Society, 22,* 409–433.

Avishai, O. 2016. Theorizing gender from religion cases: Agency, feminist action, and masculinity. *Sociology of Religion, 77,* 261–279.

Baddorf, Z. 2017. Uganda ends its hunt for Joseph Kony empty-handed. *New York Times.* April 20.

Bancroft, A. 1987. Women in Buddhism. In *Women in the world's religions, past and present,* edited by U. King. New York: Paragon House.

Barlas, A. 2002. *Believing women in Islam: Unreading patriarchal interpretions of the Qu'ran.* Austin, TX: University of Texas Press.

Barnes, N. S. 1994. Women in Buddhism. In *Today's woman in world religions,* edited by A. Sharma. Albany, NY: State University of New York Press.

Barstow, A. L. 1994. *Witchcraze: A new history of the European witch hunts.* New York: HarperCollins.

BBC News. 2019a. Western Wall: Jewish women clash over prayer rights. *BBC News.* https://www.bbc.com/news/world-middle-east-47496456. Retrieved on May 30, 2021.

BBC News. 2019b. Sabarimala temple: India court to review ruling on women's entry. *BBC.* https://www.bbc.com/news/world-asia-india-50415356. Retrieved on May 31, 2021.

Bechmann, U. 2014. The women of Jericho: Dramatization of feminist hermeneutics. In *Faith and feminism: Ecumenical essays,* edited B. D. Lipsett and P. Trible. Louisville, KY: Westminster John Knox Press.

Begum, R. 2019. Iranian women rebel against dress code. https://www.hrw.org /news/2019/08/06/iranian-women-rebel-against-dress-code#. Retrieved on May 28, 2021.

Blumberg, A. 2015, May 26. What you need to know about the Quiverfull movement. *Huffpost.* http://www.huffingtonpost.com/2015/05/26/quiverfull -movement-facts_n_7444604.html. Retrieved on May 4, 2017.

Boden, A. L. 2007. *Women's rights and religious practice: Claims in conflict.* New York: Palgrave Macmillan.

Boucher, S. 2006. The way of the elders: Theravada Buddhism, including the Vipassana movement. In *Encyclopedia of women and religion in North America,* Vol. 2, edited by R. S. Keller, R. R. Ruether, and M. Canton. Bloomington, IN: Indiana University Press.

Braude, A. 2006. Religions and modern feminism. In *Encyclopedia of women and religion in North America,* Vol. 1. edited by R. S. Keller, R. R. Ruether, and M. Canton. Bloomington, IN: Indiana University Press.

Budapest, Z. 1976. *Feminist book of lights and shadows.* Venice, CA: Feminist Wicca.

Budapest, Z. 1989. *Holy book of women's mysteries: Feminist witchcraft, goddess rituals, spellcasting, and other womanly arts.* Berkeley, CA: Wingbow Press Book People.

Burn, S. M., and Busso, J. 2005. Ambivalent sexism, scriptural literalism, and religiosity. *Psychology of Women Quarterly, 29,* 412–418.

Callimachi, R. 2016. For women under ISIS, a tyranny of dress code and punishment. *New York Times.* https://www.nytimes.com/2016/12/12/world /middleeast/islamic-state-mosul-women-dress-code-morality.html?_r=0. Retrieved on April 25, 2017.

Cantor, A. 1995. *Jewish women, Jewish men: The legacy of patriarchy in Jewish life.* New York: Harper and Row.

Carmody, D. L. 1979. *Women and world religions.* Nashville, TN: Abingdon.

Carmody, D. L. 1989. *Women and world religions.* Englewood-Cliff, NJ: Prentice Hall.

Carmody, D. L. 1991. *Religious woman: Contemporary reflections on Eastern texts.* New York: Crossroad Publishing Company.

Carr, R. 2016. Orange revolution: Thailand's female monks fight for recognition. *Huffpost.* September 1.

Chaves, M., Roso, J., Holleman, A., and Hawkins, M. 2020. *National Congregations Study: Waves I-IV Summary Tables.* Duke University Department of Sociology, Durham, NC. https://sites.duke.edu/ncsweb/files/2020/11/NCS-IV_Summary -Tables_For- Posting.pdf. Retrieved on June 1, 2021.

Chernyak, E. 2016. What is woman created for? The image of women in Russia through the lens of the Russian Orthodox Church. *Feminist Theology, 24,* 299–313.

Chesler, P. 2008. The Women of the Wall: Twenty years on. *Jewcy,* November 30. http://www.jewcy.com/post/women_wall_twenty_years. Retrieved on August 29, 2009.

Chizhik-Goldschmidt, A. 2021. Is social media fueling a women's rights revolution in the Orthodox Jewish community? *Religion and Politics.* https://religionan dpolitics.org/2021/03/30/is-social-media-fueling-a-womens-rights-revolution-in-the -orthodox-jewish-community/. Retrieved on May 30, 2021.

Christ, C. P. 1995. *Rebirth of the Goddess: Finding meaning in feminist spirituality.* London: Routledge.

Christ, C. P. 2006. Rebirth of the religion of the Goddess. *Encyclopedia of Women and Religion in North America, 3,* 1200–1207.

Christ, C. P., and Plaskow, J. 1979. Introduction: Womanspirit rising. In *Womanspirit rising: A feminist reader in religion,* edited by C. P. Christ and J. Plaskow. San Francisco, CA: Harper and Row.

Cisneros, S. 1996. Guadalupe the sex goddess. In *Goddess of the Americas, La Diosa del las Americas,* edited by A. Castillo. New York: Riverhead Books.

CNN Editorial Research. 2020. ISIS fast facts. *CNN.* https://www.cnn.com /2014/08/08/world/isis-fast-facts/index.html. Retrieved on May 28, 2021.

Covenant of the Goddess. *About witchcraft.* http://www.cog.org/wicca/about.html. Retrieved on September 4, 2009.

Daly, M. 1973. *Beyond God the father.* Boston, MA: Beacon Press.

Daly, M. 1978. *Gyn/Ecology: The metaethics of radical feminism.* Boston, MA: Beacon Press.

Daly, M. 1985. *The church and the second sex,* 2nd ed. Boston, MA: Beacon Press.

Derris, K. 2008. When Buddha was a woman: Reimaging tradition in the Theravada. *Journal of Feminist Studies in Religion, 24,* 29–35.

Dhillon, A. 2019. Muslim woman receives death threats after leading prayers in Kerala. *The Guardian.* https://www.theguardian.com/world/2018/jan/30 /muslim-woman-receives-death-threats-leading-prayers-kerala-india. Retrieved on May 28, 2021.

Di, D. 2020. Are religious women more traditional? A cross-national examination of gender and religion. *Journal for the Scientific Study of Religion, 59,* 606–628.

Drury, C. 1994. Christianity. In *Women in religion,* edited by J. Holm. New York: St. Martin's Press.

Duderija, A. 2015. Toward a scriptural hermeneutics of Islamic feminism. *Journal of Feminist Studies in Religion, 31,* 45–64.

Eck, D. L., and Jain, D. 1987. Introduction. In *Speaking of faith: Global perspectives on women, religion, and social change,* edited by D. L. Eck and D. Jain. Philadelphia, PA: New Society Publishers.

Eisler, R. 1987. *The chalice and the blade.* San Francisco, CA: Harper & Row.

Estrin, D. 2020. Orthodox Jewish women take a new lead in Talmud study in Israel. *NPR.* https://www.npr.org/2020/02/02/794684710/orthodox-jewish -women-take-a-new-lead-in-talmud-study-in-israel. Retrieved on May 30, 2021.

Falk, M. L. 2008. Gender and religious legitimacy in Thailand. In *Gender politics in Asia: Women maneuvering within dominant gender orders,* edited by W. Burghoorn, K. Iwanga, C. Milwertz, and Q. Wang. Copenhagen, Denmark: NIAS Press.

Feraro, S. 2017. The politics of the Goddess: Racial/culture feminist influence of Starhawk's feminist witchcraft. In *Feminist leaders in new religious movements* (pp. 229–248), edited by B. Tollefsen and C. Giudice. New York: Palgrave MacMillan.

Findly, E. B. 2014. Women and Buddhism. In *The encyclopedia of psychology and religion,* edited by D. A. Leeming. New York: Springer US.

Flores, N. 2014. The personal is political: Toward a vision of justice in Latina Theology. In *Feminist Catholic theological ethics: Conversations in the world church,* edited by L. Hogan and A. Orobator. Maryknoll, NY: Orbis Books.

French, M. 1992. *The war against women.* New York: Simon and Schuster.

Gebara, I., and M. C. Bingemer. 1994. Mary—Mother of God, mother of the poor. In *Feminist theology from the Third World,* edited by U. King. New York: Orbis.

Gerhart, M. 2003. Christianity. In *Her voice, her faith,* edited by A. Sharma and K. K. Young. Boulder, CO: Westview Press.

Gibson, L. 2016, March 27. Shirin Ebadi shares her experience and a hug. *Harvard Magazine.* http://harvardmagazine.com/2016/03/shirin-ebadi-shares-her -experience-and-a-hug. Retrieved on April 25, 2017.

Gimbutas, M. 1991. *The civilization of the goddess: The world of Old Europe.* San Francisco, CA: Harper and Row.

Glick, P., and Fiske, S. T. (2001). An ambivalent alliance: Hostile and benevolent sexism as complementary justifications for gender inequality. *American Psychologist, 56,* 109-118.

Glick, P., Lameiras, M., and Castro, C. 2002. Education and Catholic religiosity as predictors of hostile and benevolent sexism toward women and men. *Sex Roles, 47,* 433–441.

Gold, A. G. 2008. Gender. In *Studying Hinduism: Key concepts and methods*, edited by S. Mittal and G. Thursby. New York: Routledge.

Goodwin J. 1994. *Price of honor: Muslim women lift the veil of violence on the Islamic world.* Boston, MA: Little, Brown.

Goonatilake, H. 1997. Buddhist nuns' protests, struggle, and the reinterpretation of orthodoxy in Sri Lanka. In *Mixed blessings: Gender and religious fundamentalism cross-culturally,* edited by J. P. Mencher and J. Brink. New York: Routledge.

Green, E. 2014, November 9. The warrior wives of evangelical Christianity. *The Atlantic.* https://www.theatlantic.com/national/archive/2014/11/the-warrior -wives-of-evangelical-christianity/382365/. Retrieved August 9, 2021.

Greenberg, B. 2000. Orthodox feminism in the next century. *Sh'ma: A Journal of Jewish Responsibility.* http://www.jofa.org/pdf/uploaded/962-QQQH9815.pdf. Retrieved on August 30, 2009.

Griffin, W. 2003. Goddess spirituality and wicca. In *Her voice, her faith,* edited by A. Sharma and K. K. Young. Boulder, CO: Westview Press.

Gross, R. M. 1979. Female God language in a Jewish context. In *Womanspirit rising: A feminist reader in religion,* edited by C. P. Christ and J. Plaskow. San Francisco, CA: Harper and Row.

Gross, R. M. 1993. *Buddhism after patriarchy: A feminist history, analysis, and reconstruction of Buddhism.* Albany, NY: State University of New York Press.

Gross, R. M. 1996. *Feminism and religion: An introduction.* Boston, MA: Beacon Press.

Gross, R. M. 1999. Strategies for a feminist revalorization of Buddhism. In *Feminism and world religions,* edited by A. Sharma and K. K. Young. Albany, NY: State University Press of New York.

Gross, R. M. 2003. Buddhism. In *Her voice, her faith,* edited by A. Sharma and K. K. Young. Boulder, CO: Westview Press.

Gross, R. M. 2009. *A garland of feminist reflections: Forty years of religious exploration.* Berkeley, CA: University of California Press.

Gupta, L. 1991. Kali the savior. In *After patriarchy: Feminist transformations of the world religions,* edited by P. Cooey, W. Eakin, and J. McDaniel. Maryknoll, NY: Orbis.

Halafoff, A., and Rajkobal, P. 2015. Sakyadhita International: Gender equity in ultramodern Buddhism. *Feminist Theology, 23,* 111–127.

Hamilton, M. C. 1988. Using masculine generics: Does generic *he* increase male bias in the user's imagery? *Sex Roles, 19,* 785–798.

Hamilton, M. C. 1991. Masculine bias in the attribution of personhood. *Psychology of Women Quarterly, 15,* 393–402.

Hampson, D. 1987. Women, ordination and the Christian Church. In *Speaking of faith: Global perspectives on women, religion, and social change,* edited by D. L. Eck and D. Jain. Philadelphia, PA: New Society Publishers.

Hannover, B., Gubernath, J., Schultze, M., and Zander, L. 2018. Religiosity, religious fundamentalism, and ambivalent sexism toward girls and women among adolescents and young adults living in Germany. *Frontiers in Psychology, 9.* https://www.frontiersin.org/articles/10.3389/fpsyg.2018.02399/full. Retrieved on May 26, 2021.

Hardin, C., and Banaji, M. R. 1993. The influence of language on thought. *Social Cognition, 11,* 277–308.

Hartman, T. 2007. *Feminism encounters traditional Judaism.* Walthan, MA: Brandeis University Press.

Hassan, R. 1991. Muslim women and post-patriarchal Islam. In *After patriarchy: Feminist transformations of the world religions,* edited by P. Cooey, W. Eakin, and J. McDaniel. Maryknoll, NY: Orbis.

Hassan, R. 1999. Feminism in Islam. In *Feminism and world religions,* edited by A. Sharma and K. K. Young. Albany, NY: State University Press of New York.

Hassan, R. 2003. Islam. In *Her voice, her faith,* edited by A. Sharma and K. K. Young. Boulder, CO: Westview Press.

Heschel, S. 2003. Judaism. In *Her voice, her faith,* edited by A. Sharma and K. K. Young. Boulder, CO: Westview Press.

Hidayyatullah, A. 2014. *Feminist edges of the Qu'ran.* UK: Oxford University Press.

Holm, J. 1994. Introduction. *Women in religion.* New York: St. Martin's Press.

Human Rights Watch. 2009. *Afghanistan: Law curbing women's rights takes effect.* http://www.hrw.org/en/news/2009/08/13/afghanistan-law-curbing-women-s-rights-takes-effect. Retrieved on August 28, 2009.

Human Rights Watch. 2017. *Iraq: Sunni women tell of ISIS detention, torture: Describe forced marriage, rape.* https://www.hrw.org/news/2017/02/20/iraq-sunni-women-tell-isis-detention-torture. Retrieved on April 25, 2017.

Hunsberger, B., Owusu, V., and Duck, R. 1999. Religious prejudice in Ghana and Canada: Religious fundamentalism, right-winged authoritarianism, and attitudes toward homosexuals and women. *The International Journal for the Psychology of Religion, 9,* 181–194.

Imam, A. 2016. *The devil is in the details: At the nexus of development, women's rights, and religious fundamentalisms.* Toronto: AWID.

Imam, A., Gokal, S., and Marler, I. 2017. The devil is in the details: A feminist perspective on development, women's rights, and fundamentalisms. *Gender and Development, 25,* 15–36.

Isasi-Diaz, A. M. 2006. Mujerista theology. In *Encyclopedia of women and religion in North America,* Vol. 3, edited by R. S. Keller, R. R. Ruether, and M. Canton. Bloomington, IN: Indiana University Press.

Jain, K. 2019. Good wives, good solidiers: Durga Vahini women take up arms to protect Hindu identity. *The World.* https://www.pri.org/stories/2019-11-14/good-wives-good-soldiers-durga-vahini-women-take-arms-protect-hindu-identity. Retrieved on May 31, 2021.

Jaskoll, S. K. 2021. Here's my plan to free women from get abuse. *The JC News.* https://www.thejc.com/comment/opinion/here-s-my-plan-to-free-women-from-get-abuse-1.512351. Retrieved on May 30, 2021.

Jewish Telegraph Agency. 2017. Orthodox Union bars women from serving as clergy in its synagogues. Februrary 2. http://www.jta.org/2017/02/02/top-headlines/ou-bars-women-from-serving-as-clergy-in-its-synagogues. Retrieved on April 26, 2017.

Joshee, R., and Sihra, K. 2013. Shakti as a liberatory and educative force for Hindu Women. In *Gender, religion and education in a chaotic postmodern world,* edited by L. Davies and A. Diab. Netherlands: Springer Netherlands.

Joyce, K. 2010. *Quiverfull: Inside the Christian patriarchy movement.* Boston, MA: Beacon Press.

Kaur, G. 2008. Indian city opens doorway to female Hindu priests. *Women's e-news.* http://www.womensenews.org/article.cfm/dyn/aid/3506/. Retrieved on September 1, 2009.

Kim, G. J. 2020. Post-colonial theology and intersectionality. *Journal of Ecumenical Studies, 55,* 595–608.

Kim, G. J., and Shaw, S. M. 2018. *Intersectional theology: An introductory guide.* Minneapolis, MN: Fortress Press.

King, U. 1987. Goddesses, witches, androgyny and beyond? Feminism and the transformation of religious consciousness. In *Women in the world's religions, past and present,* edited by U. King. New York: Paragon House.

King, U. 1994. Introduction. In *Feminist theology from the Third World,* edited by U. King. Maryknoll, NY: Orbis.

Kirkpatrick, L. 1993. Fundamentalism, Christian orthodoxy, and intrinsic religious orientation as predictors of discriminatory attitudes. *Journal for the Scientific Study of Religion, 32,* 256–268.

Kress, M. 2009. The state of Orthodox Judaism today. *Jewish Virtual Library.* http://www.jewishvirtuallibrary.org/jsource/Judaism/orthostate.html. Retrieved on August 30, 2009.

Lavine, A. 2006. Tibetan Buddhism. In *Encyclopedia of women and religion in North America,* Vol. 2, edited by R. S. Keller, R. R. Ruether, and M. Canton. Bloomington, IN: Indiana University Press.

Leamaster, R. J., and Einwohner, R. L. 2018. I'm not your stereotypical Mormon girl: Mormon women's gendered resistance. *Review of Religious Research, 60,* 161–181.

Lev, S. L. 2009. Liberation through the textual looking glass. *Journal of Feminist Studies in Religion, 25,* 170–180.

Lewis, C. 2019. BBC names Dhammananda Bhikkhuni Thailand's first woman monk. *Global Buddhist Door.* https://www.buddhistdoor.net/news/bbc -names-dhammananda-bhikkhuni-thailandrsquos-first-female-monk-among -100-influential-women-of-2019. Retrieved on July 27, 2021.

Lozano, A. 2009. Controversial Afghan law leaves Shiite women's rights in question. *Online News Hour.* http://www.pbs.org/newshour/updates/law /july-dec09/afghanwomen_08-21.html. Retrieved on August 28, 2009.

Lucia, A. Innovative gurus: Tradition and change in contemporary Hinduism. *International Journal of Hindu Studies, 18,* 221–263.

Maltby, L. E., and Hall, E. L. 2014. Religion and sexism. In *Encyclopedia of quality of life and well-being research,* edited by A. C. Michalos. Netherlands: Springer Netherlands.

Mangis, M. W. 1995. Religious beliefs, dogmatism, and attitudes toward women. *Journal of Psychology and Christianity, 14,* 13–25.

Mattieu, J. 2015. What it was like to grow up Quiverfull. *Cosmopolitan.* http://www .cosmopolitan.com/entertainment/books/q-and-a/a41047/growing -up-quiverfull-interview/. Retrieved on May 4, 2017.

Mayer, A. M. 1995. Cultural particularism as a bar to women's rights: Reflections on the Middle Eastern experience. In *Women's rights, human rights: International feminist perspectives,* edited by J. Peters and A. Wolper. New York: Routledge.

Mbon, F. M. 1987. Women in African traditional religions. In *Women in the world's religions, past and present,* edited by U. King. New York: Paragon House.

McMinn, M. R., Brooks, S. D., Triplett, M. A., Hoffman, W. E., and Huizinga, P. G. 1993. The effects of God-language on perceived attributes of God. *Journal of Psychology and Theology, 21,* 309–314.

McPhillips, A. 2017. Economies of sainthood: Disrupting the discourse of female hagiography. *Sophia Studies in Cross-cultural Philosophy of Tradition and Cultures, 17,* 57–68.

Medina, L. 2011. Taking La Luca to heart I. *Feminist Theology, 20,* 39–44.

Mernissi, F. 1987. *The veil and the male elite: A feminist interpretation of women's rights in Islam.* Reading, MA: Addison-Wesley.

Mikołajczak, M. and Pietrzak, J. 2014. Ambivalent sexism and religion: Connected through values. *Sex Roles, 70,* 387–399.

Miller, E. C. 2020. The price of white evangelical patriarchy. *Religion and Politics.* https://religionandpolitics.org/2020/07/07/the-price-of-white-evangelical-patriarchy/. Retrieved on June 1, 2021.

Misdary, R. 2021. The 'godmother' of Egyptian feminism has died: Remembering Nawal El Saadawi. *NPR.* https://www.npr.org/sections/goatsandsoda/2021/03/28/981250606/the-godmother-of-egyptian-feminism-has-died-remembering-nawal-el-saadawi. Retrieved on May 28, 2021.

Mitchem, S. Y. 2017. Black American women and the gift of embodied spirituality. *Sophia Studies in Cross-Cultural Philosophy of Tradition and Cultures, 17,* 159–172.

Moghadam, V. M. 2003. *Modernizing women: Gender and social change in the Middle East,* 2nd ed. Boulder, CO: Lynne Rienner Publishers.

Mostaghim, R., and Daragahi, B. 2009. Iranian Nobel Peace Prize winter Shirin Ebadi threatened in her home. *Los Angeles Times.* http://articles.latimes.com/2009/jan/03/world/fg-iran-ebadi3. Retrieved on August 28, 2009.

Nadell, P. S. 2009. Rabbis in the United States. *Jewish women: A comprehensive historical encyclopedia.* https://jwa.org/encyclopedia/article/rabbis-in-united-states. Retrieved on April 26, 2017.

Naidu, M. 2013. Transgressive subversions? Female religious leaders in Hinduism. *Journal for the Study of Religion, 26,* 44–57.

Nair, N. J. 2019. Kerala not to allow women to visit Sabarimala shrine. *The Hindu.* https://www.thehindu.com/news/national/kerala/govt-not-to-entertain-women-in-sabarimala/article29985595.ece. Retrieved on July 24, 2021.

Narayanan, V. 1999. Brimming with *Bhakti,* embodiments of *Shakti:* Devotees, deities, performers, reformers, and other women of power in the Hindu tradition.

In *Feminism and world religions,* edited by A. Sharma and K. K. Young. Albany, NY: State University Press of New York.

Narayanan, V. 2003. Hinduism. In *Her voice, her faith,* edited by A. Sharma and K. K. Young. Boulder, CO: Westview Press.

Narayanan, V. 2006. Hinduism in North America: Including emerging issues. In *Encyclopedia of women and religion in North America*, Vol. 2, edited by R. S. Keller, R. R. Ruether, and M. Canton. Bloomington, IN: Indiana University Press.

Nashrulla, T. 2014. A militant training camp in India is training young women to hate themselves and accept their weakness. *Buzzfeed.* https://www.buzzfeed .com/tasneemnashrulla/a-militant-hindu-camp-in-india-is-training-young-women -to-ha?utm_term=.dh2MXg4mK#.pb9PAY5wL. Retrieved on April 29, 2017.

Nawa, F., and Nomani, A. Q. 2015, March 15. Afghan women defy mullahs to bury murdered girl. *The Daily Beast.*

NCRI. 2016. Twenty bizarre bans on Iranian women by misogynistic mullahs' regime ruling Iran. http://www.ncr-iran.org/en/news/women/21310- twenty-bizarre-bans-on-iranian-women-by-misogynic-mullahs-regime-ruling-iran#. Retrieved on April 25, 2017.

Neumaier, E. K. 2016. Women in Buddhist tradition. In *Women in religious leadership: Buddhism and the ordination of women.* https://www.bc.edu/content/dam/files/centers /boisi/pdf/S16/Boisi%20Center%20Symposium%20Buddhism%20Reader.pdf. Retrieved on April 28, 2017.

Niditch, S. 1991. Portrayals of women in the Hebrew Bible. In *Jewish women in historical perspective*, edited by J. Baskin. Detroit, MI: Wayne State University Press.

Nobelprize.org. 2003. *Shirin Ebadi, Nobel Peace Prize 2003.* http://nobelprize.org /nobel_prizes/peace/laureates/2003/ebadi-lecture-e.html. Retrieved on August 28, 2009.

Oduyoye, M. A. 2001. *Introducing African women's theology.* Sheffield, England: Sheffield Academic Press.

Pagels, E. H. 1976. What became of God the Mother? Conflicting images of God in early Christianity. In *Womanspirit rising: A feminist reader in religion,* edited by C. P. Christ and J. Plaskow. San Francisco, CA: Harper and Row.

Pandey, G. 2016, February 18. Enough is enough: India women fight to enter temples. *BBC News.* http://www.bbc.com/news/world-asia-india-35595501. Retrieved on April 27, 2017.

Patterson, T. 2015. Polygamist sect limits sex to 'seed bearers' court documents say. *CNN.* http://www.cnn.com/2015/09/30/us/polygamist-flds-warren-jeffs -update/. Retrieved on May 4, 2017.

Peach, L. J. 2002. *Women and world religions.* Upper Saddle River, NJ: Prentice Hall.

Pew Research Center. 2014. *U.S. Catholics view Pope Francis as a change for the better.* http://www.pewforum.org/2014/03/06/catholics-view-pope-francis-as-a -change-for-the-better/. Retrieved on May 1, 2017.

Pew Research Center. 2017. The changing global religious landscape. http://www
.pewforum.org/2014/03/06/catholics-view-pope-francis-as-a-change-for-the
-better/. Retrieved on May 1, 2017.

Plaskow, J. 1979. The coming of Lilith: Toward a feminist theology. In *Womanspirit rising: A feminist reader in religion,* edited by C. P. Christ and J. Plaskow.
New York: Harper Collins.

Plaskow, J. 1987. Which me will survive all these liberations? In *Speaking of faith:
Global perspectives on women, religion and social change,* edited by D. Eck and
D. Jain. Philadelphia, PA.: New Society.

Plaskow, J. 1991. *Standing again at Sinai.* San Francisco, CA: HarperCollins.

Plaskow, J. 2005. *The coming of Lilith: Essays on feminism, Judaism, and sexual
ethics (1972-2003).* Boston, MA: Beacon Press.

Plaskow, J., and Christ, C. P. 2014. Two feminist views of Goddess and God.
Tikkun, 29, 29-34.

Poonam, S. 2019. Indian women did a remarkable thing: They formed a wall of
protest. *The Guardian.* https://www.theguardian.com/commentisfree/2019
/jan/03/gender-activism-india-womens-wall-sabarimala-temple-kerala. Retrieved
on May 31, 2021.

Prevot, A. 2018. Theology and race: Black and womanist theology in the United
States. *Theology, 2.2,* 1-79.

Pui-lan, K. 2007. *Postcolonial imagination and feminist theology.* Louisville,
KY: Westminster John Knox Press.

Raday, F. 2005. Women of the Wall. *Jewish Women's Archive.* http://jwa.org
/encyclopedia/article/women-of-wall. Retrieved on August 29, 2009.

Rasicot, C. 2021. To walk proudly as Buddhist women: An interview with
Dhammananda Bhikkhuni. *Lion's Roar.* https://www.lionsroar.com/to-walk
-proudly-as-buddhist-women-an-interview-with-dhammananda-bhikkhuni/.
Retrieved on July 27, 2021.

Ramshaw, G. 1995. *God beyond gender: Feminist Christian God-language.*
Minneapolis, MN: Argsburg Fortress.

Razak, A. 2013. Embodying Womanism: Notes toward a holistic and liberating
pedagogy. In *Ain't I a Womanist Too?,* edited by M. A. Coleman and
L. Maparyan. Minneapolis, MN: Augsburg Fortress Publishers.

Rezaiah, J. 2020. Why Iran's leading dissident is fighting for her life. *The Washington
Post.* https://www.washingtonpost.com/opinions/2020/09/22/why-irans-leading
-dissident-is-fighting-her-life/. Retrieved on May 28, 2021.

Rigby, J. 2017, January 8. Meet Burma's feminist Buddhist nun. *Trike Daily.*
https://tricycle.org/trikedaily/meet-burmas-feminist-nun/. Retrieved on April 30,
2017.

Robinson, S. P. 1985. Hindu paradigms of women: Images and values. In *Women,
religion, and social change,* edited by Y. Y. Haddad and E. B. Findly. Albany,
NY: State University of New York Press.

Roman Catholic Women Priests. 2021. *The ordained members.* https://www .romancatholicwomenpriests.org/meet-the-ordained/. Retrieved on June 1, 2021.

Ross, E. 2017. Women's largest gathering of female Muslim clerics issue fatwa against marital rape and child marriage. *Newsweek.* http://www.newsweek .com/gathering-female-muslim-clerics-issue-fatwa-against-child-marriage -rape-591442. Retrieved on May 7, 2017.

Ross, S. D. 2008. *Women's human rights: The international and comparative law casebook.* Philadelphia, PA: University of Pennsylvania Press.

Ruether, R. R. 1985. *Womanguides: Readings toward a feminist theology,* Boston, MA: Beacon Press.

Ruether, R. R. 1999. Feminism in World Christianity. In *Feminism and world religions,* edited by A. Sharma and K. K. Young. Albany, NY: State University Press of New York.

Ruether, R. R. 2002. The war on women. In *Nothing sacred: Women respond to religious fundamentalism and terror,* edited by B. Reed. New York: Thunder's Mouth Press/Nation Books.

Ruth, S. 1995. *Issues in feminism,* 3rd ed. Mountain View, CA: Mayfield.

Salih, Z. M. 2015. Outrage as nine Sudanese women face 40 lashes for wearing trousers. *The Guardian.* https://www.theguardian.com/world/2015/jul/14 /sudan-christian-women-40-lashes-trousers. Retrieved on April 24, 2017.

Samuel, S. 2014. Feminism in faith: Sara Hurwitz's road to becoming the first publicly ordained Orthodox Jewish Rabba. *Buzzfeed.* https://www.buzzfeed .com/sigalsamuel/feminism-in-faith-orthodox-judaism?utm_term=.bf0R2xe4Y# .vtJ5nk96B. Retrieved on April 26, 2017.

Schouten, L. 2016. Why Indian women weren't allowed to pray in a Hindu temple. *Christian Science Monitor.* http://www.csmonitor.com/World/Global-News /2016/0402/Why-Indian-women-weren-t-allowed-to-pray-in-a-Hindu-temple. Retrieved on April 27, 2017.

Schulman, G. B. 1974. View from the back of the synagogue. In *Sexist religion and women in the church,* edited by A. L. Hageman. New York: Association Press.

Schüssler Fiorenza, E. 1992. *But she said: Feminist practices of Biblical interpretation.* Boston, MA: Beacon Press.

Schüssler Fiorenza, E. 1995. *Bread not stone: The challenge of feminist biblical interpretation, 10th anniversary edition.* Boston, MA: Beacon Press.

Schüssler Fiorenza E. 2007. *The power of the Word: Scripture and the rhetoric of empire.* Minneapolis, MN: Fortress.

Schüssler Fiorenza, E. 2015. *Wisdom way: Introduction to feminist biblical interpretation.* Maryknoll, NY: Orbis Books.

Sered, S. S. 1994. *Priestess, mother, sacred sister.* Oxford: Oxford University Press.

Sered, S. S. 1999. *Women of the sacred groves: Divine priestesses of Okinawa.* Oxford, UK: Oxford University Press.

Shaaban, B. 1995. The muted voices of women interpreters. In *Faith and freedom: Women's rights in the Muslim world,* edited by M. Afkami. London: I. B. Tauris.

Shalev, C. 1995. Women in Israel: Fighting tradition. In *Women's rights, human rights: International feminist perspectives*, edited by J. Peters and A. Wolper. New York: Routledge.

Singh, K. C. 2016. In the Service of Nationalism: Women in the Hindu Nationalist Paradigm. *Fudan Journal of the Humanities and Social Sciences*, *9*, 493–515.

Slee, N. 2014. God-language in public and private prayer: A place for integrating gender, sexuality and faith. *Theology and Sexuality, 20*, 225–237.

Smith, A. 2009. Elisabeth Schüssler Fiorenza and the future of Native American theology. *Journal of Feminist Studies in Religion, 25*, 143–150.

Sommer, A. K., and Lithwick, D. 2013. The feminists of Zion. *New Republic.* https://newrepublic.com/article/114124/israels-orthodox-women -new-face-feminism. Retrieved on April 26, 2017.

Starhawk. 1979. Witchcraft and women's culture. In *Womanspirit rising: A feminist reader in religion,* edited by C. P. Christ and J. Plaskow. San Franciso, CA: Harper & Row.

Steinkopf-Frank, H. 2020. Women imams around the world challenge male-dominated Islam. https://worldcrunch.com/culture-society/women-imams-around-the-world -challenge-male-dominated-islam. Retrieved on May 28, 2021.

Stone, M. *When God was a woman.* San Diego, CA: Harcourt Brace Jovanovich.

Sugirtharajah, S. 1994. Hinduism. In *Women in religion,* edited by J. Holm. New York: St. Martin's Press.

Tanakasempipat, P. 2019. Thailand's rebel female Buddhist monks defy tradition. https://www.reuters.com/article/us-thailand-buddhism-women/thailands-rebel -female-buddhist-monks-defy-tradition-idUSKCN1OX1YP. Retrieved on July 27, 2021.

Taylor, L. 2018. The rise of the imama: Women-led mosques are growing. *Christian Science Monitor.* https://www.csmonitor.com/World/Europe/2018/0905/The-rise -of-the-imama-women-led-mosques-are-growing. Retrieved on May 28, 2021.

Taşdemir, N., and Sakalli-Uğurlu, N. 2010. The relationships between ambivalent sexism and religiosity among Turkish university students. *Sex Roles, 62*, 420–426.

Thiagarajan, K. 2019. Millions of women in India join hands to form a 385-mile wall of protest. *NPR.* https://www.npr.org/sections/goatsandsoda /2019/01/04/681988452/millions-of-women-in-india-join-hands-to-form-a-385 -mile-wall-of-protest. Retrieved on May 31, 2021.

Townes, E. M. 2006. Womanist theology. In *Encyclopedia of women and religion in North America,* Vol. 3, edited by R. S. Keller, R. R. Ruether, and M. Canton. Bloomington, IN: Indiana University Press.

Trible, P. 1973. Eve and Adam: Genesis 2–3 reread. In *Womanspirit rising: A feminist reader in religion,* edited by C. P. Christ and J. Plaskow. New York: Harper and Row.

Uchino, K. 1987. The status elevation process of Soto sect nuns in modern Japan. In *Speaking of faith: Global perspectives on women, religion, and social change,* edited by D. L. Eck and D. Jain. Philadelphia, PA: New Society Publishers.

Umanksy, E. M. 1999. Feminism in Judaism. In *Feminism and world religions,* edited by A. Sharma and K. K. Young. Albany, NY: State University Press of New York.

UN Special Rapporteur in the Field of Cultural Rights. 2017. *Report of the Special Rapporteur in the field of cultural rights.* https://documents-dds-ny.un.org/doc /UNDOC/GEN/G17/007/43/PDF/G1700743.pdf?OpenElement. Retrieved on April 23, 2017.

Ursic, E. 2015. *Women, ritual, and power: Placing female imagery of God in Christian worship.* New York: SUNY Press.

Wadud, A. 1999. *Qu'ran and women: Rereading the sacred text from a woman's perspective.* New York: Oxford USA.

Wadud, A. 2006. *Inside the gender jihad: Women's reform in Islam.* Oxford, UK: Oneworld.

Walker, A. 1983. *In search of our mothers' gardens: Womanist prose.* San Francisco, CA: Harcourt Brace.

Wall, E., and Pulitzer, L. 2009. *Stolen innocence.* New York: Harper.

Watson, N. K. 2003. *Feminist theology: A reader.* Grand Rapids, MI: Eerdmans Publishing.

Wemare, A. 2019. The rise of the female imam in France? *France 24.* https://www .france24.com/en/20190205-france-female-imam-islam-mosque-bahloul-fatima -muslim-paris. Retrieved on May 28, 2021.

Whitehead, A. L. 2012. Gender ideology and religion: Does a masculine image of God matter? *Review of Religious Research, 54,* 139–156.

Williams, D. S. 1994. Womanist theology: Black women's voices. In *Feminist theology from the Third World,* edited by U. King. Maryknoll, NY: Orbis.

Wise, C. 2008. *Hidden circles in the web: Feminist wicca, occult knowledge, and process thought.* Lanham, MD: Altamira Press.

Women of the Wall. 2017. *Timeline.* http://www.womenofthewall.org.il/timeline/. Retrieved on April 26, 2017.

Young, K. K. 1987. Hinduism. In *Women in world religions,* edited by A. Sharma. Albany, NY: State University of New York Press.

Design Element: Abstract floral frame: Telnov Oleksii/Shutterstock

9

Women and Politics

Political space belongs to all citizens, but men monopolize it.

—United Nations Human Development Report, 1995

Here are New Zealand Prime Minister Jacinda Arden and German Chancellor Angela Merkel on April 17, 2018. Although the number of women heads of state and national government has grown, they still occupy less than 10 percent of these powerful positions. The study of women and politics includes a focus on how women break through glass ceilings in politics. DPA Picture Alliance/Alamy Stock Photo

W omen and politics are the topic of this chapter. Although women's political rights are enshrined in many national constitutions and international agreements (see Box 9.1), the truth is that men dominate politics and have more political influence and status almost everywhere in the world (see Box 9.2). This matters because men's domination of the political sphere is both a symptom and a cause of women's lower status and power. In other words, it is an example of gender inequality at the same time that it perpetuates gendered disadvantage. This explains why one target of women's organizing worldwide is the transformation of politics, the shaping of public policymaking, and democratization of power relations (UNIFEM, 2009).

"There is no democracy in our beautifully democratic countries. Why? Women have not the same part in decision making as men have."
Vigdis Finnbogadottir, President of Iceland 1980–1996

BOX 9.1 *Some International Agreements Enshrining Women's Political Rights*

Convention on the Political Rights of Women (1954)

Article I Women shall be entitled to vote in all elections on equal terms with men, without any discrimination.

Article II Women shall be eligible for election to all publicly elected bodies, established by national law, on equal terms with men, without any discrimination.

Article III Women shall be entitled to hold public office and to exercise all public functions, established by national law, on equal terms with men, without any discrimination.

Convention on the Elimination of All Forms of Discrimination Against Women (1979)

Article 7 States Parties shall take all appropriate measures to eliminate discrimination against women in the political and public life of the country and, in particular, shall ensure to women, on equal terms with men, the right:

a. To vote in all elections and public referenda and to be eligible for election to all publicly elected bodies;

b. To participate in the formulation of government policy and the implementation thereof and to hold public office and perform all public functions at all levels of government;

c. To participate in nongovernmental organizations and associations concerned with the public and political life of the country.

Article 8 States Parties shall take all appropriate measures to ensure to women, on equal terms with men and without any discrimination, the opportunity to represent their Governments at the international level and to participate in the work of international organizations.

The Beijing Platform for Action (1995)

Women in Power and Decision Making (191–194) Reaffirms the importance of women's equal participation in politics; acknowledges women's low levels of representation in formal politics, their leadership in "community and informal organizations," and their work in grassroots movements and nongovernmental organizations; and identifies measures to "ensure women's equal access to and full participation in power structures and decision-making."

2030 Agenda for Sustainable Development (2015)

Target 5.5 Ensure women's full and effective participation and equal opportunities for leadership at all levels of decision-making in politics, economics, and public life.

BOX 9.2   *A Snapshot of Women's Formal Political Power*

In 2021, worldwide:

- There were 22 women heads of government or heads of state.

- Almost 26 percent of countries (50) have achieved a critical mass of 30 percent or more women in their congress or parliaments, and three have at least 50 percent.

- Women comprised about 25.5 percent of the membership of national legislatures (parliaments, national assemblies, and congresses).

- Countries with the highest percentages of women in national legislatures include: Rwanda (55.6%), Cuba (53.4%), New Zealand (48.3%), Mexico (48.4%), Nicaragua (47.3%), Sweden (47%), South Africa (45.9%), Andorra (46.4%), Bolivia (48%), and Finland (46%).

- Eritrea, Haiti, Micronesia, Papau New Guinea, Vanuatu, and Yemen have no women representatives in their national legislatures.

- The region with the higher proportion of women representatives is the Nordic region (44.4%), followed by the Americas (32.2%), followed by Europe (without Nordic countries; 29.3%), Sub-Saharan Africa (25%), the Pacific (20.9%), Asia (20.4%), and the Middle East and Northern Africa (17.7%).

Sources: Inter-Parliamentary Union (IPU), 2021a, 2021b; Vogelstein & Bro, 2021.

"The concept of democracy will only assume true and dynamic significance when political policies and national legislation are decided upon jointly by men and women with equitable regard for the interests and aptitudes of both halves of the population."
Inter-Parliamentary Union

But women, as you've almost certainly noticed in previous chapters, do act politically despite obstacles. These obstacles include traditional gender stereotypes and gender roles suggesting that political activity is more appropriate for men. Women's care labor responsibilities can also interfere with political engagement as well as men's control of political parties and organizations. Also, in many places, women have fewer of the resources that make political activity more likely, such as income, occupational prestige, and ties to trade unions (Kittleson, 2016). That so many women overcome the barriers to their participation is a testimony to their commitment to the ideals of political citizenship (Lister, 2003). This commitment is especially evident in the sphere of **informal politics** ("power from below"), which includes local community-based action and national and international social movements (Lister, 2003). This chapter begins with a consideration of women's participation in **formal politics** ("political power from above"), including voting, representation in parliaments and congresses, and women as heads of state and government. From there, it moves to a discussion of informal politics.

Women's Voting

Women's voting, or **women's suffrage,** was a major aim of the early feminist movement (first-wave feminism) from the mid-1880s through the first half of the twentieth century. Voting rights for women were hard-won, and women activists (suffragists) were arrested and harassed while demonstrating for this right. For example, in the United States, it took 72 years of activism to win women's right to vote.

BOX 9.3 *A Sampling of Women's Suffrage*

Year	Countries
1893–1919	Australia, Canada, Finland, Germany, Greenland, Iceland, New Zealand, Norway, Russia, Sweden, Turkey*
1920–1944	Brazil, Burma, Ecuador, France, Ireland, Lithuania, Philippines, Spain, Thailand, United Kingdom, United States
1945–1959	Argentina, Bolivia, Chad, Chile, China, Colombia, Costa Rica, El Salvador, Ethiopia, Guatemala, Honduras, India, Japan, Mali, Mexico, Morocco, Nicaragua, Niger, Pakistan, Portugal, Senegal, Venezuela, Vietnam
1960–1979	Algeria, Angola, Iran, Kenya, Libya, Nigeria, Paraguay, Peru, Sudan, Zaire, Marshall Islands
Since 1980	Hong Kong, Iraq, South Africa, Western Samoa, Vanuatu, Liechtenstein, Central African Republic
Since 1990	Bhutan, Western Samoa, Kazakhstan, Moldova, South Africa, Kuwait, United Arab Emirates, Saudi Arabia

*At that time the Ottoman Empire.

In 1916, members of the National Women's Party (NWP), led by Alice Paul, picketed in front of the White House continuously. For this they were imprisoned and abused. To draw attention to their cause, they staged a hunger strike. Media attention to the abuse of the activists led to increased popular support for their cause and to the passage of the nineteenth amendment in 1920.

See Box 9.3 for a list of countries and the year women's suffrage was attained in each. Keep in mind, though, that there were often restrictions on *which* women could vote. For example, Native American women were not allowed to vote until 1924, four years after other American women; in Australia, white women won the vote in 1902, but Aboriginal women had to wait until 1967; and in South Africa, white women won the vote in 1931, but Indian and Colored women waited until 1984 and Black women until 1994 (Seager, 2009). Available information indicates that in most cases, women vote at rates close or equal to the rates at which men vote, but there are national differences (Paxton & Hughes, 2016). For example, in Germany, the gender voting gap is nearly 8 percentage points in favor of men's turnout, but in the United States, the gap is 4 percentage points in favor of women's voter participation (CAWP, 2021; Kittleson, 2016). Unfortunately, less is known about voting differences among women based on race, ethnicity, religion, and class.

Not only did Alice Paul (1885–1977) act for American women's suffrage, she also began the fight for the Equal Rights Amendment, was instrumental in the UN including gender equality in its charter, and led a coalition that was successful in adding a sex discrimination clause to Title VII of the 1964 Civil Rights Act.

In 2011, the final holdout, Saudi Arabia, granted women the right to vote in and run for municipal local elections starting in 2015.

However, in the United States, the proportion of eligible white women that vote (69.6%) is somewhat higher than the voting of Black women (66.3%), Asian and Pacific Islander American women (61.3%), and Latina women (56.4%) (CAWP, 2021).

Gender gaps in voting behavior are a relatively new area of study with limited cross-cultural, comparative research. Most available evidence suggests that women, more than men, favor liberal or left-wing parties and have more liberal political attitudes (Bernauer, Giger, & Rosset, 2015). But this appears to depend on gender roles in a society, women's religiosity, and age (older and more religious women often vote more conservatively). Research in the United States and Western Europe indicates that as traditional gender roles wane in a country, women's voting patterns shift from being more conservative than men's, to aligning with men's, to becoming more liberal than men's in a process called **gender realignment** (Giger, 2009; Kittleson, 2016). It appears that as women become more educated and enter the labor force, they do not see conservative parties that support traditional gender roles as serving their interests. Gender differences in voting may also occur because women have more pro-environment, anti-military, and pro-social welfare political attitudes (Stevens, 2007). However, not all countries fit this profile. In post-Communist countries, the gender gap is in the other direction, with women more likely to favor conservative parties (Abendschön & Steinmetz, 2014).

Women Representatives in National Legislatures and Cabinets

Women's voting is only one form of formal political involvement. Governments are complex organizational structures including heads of government and state and other formal political actors such as members of **parliaments** and **congresses** (often called **national assemblies**) and **government cabinets.**

"A woman's place is in the house, and in the Senate."
American feminist proverb

"To achieve a more inclusive society, parliaments must be more proactive in addressing discrimination and eliminating violence against women and girls."
Abu Dhabi Declaration, Global Summit of Women Speakers of Parliament 2016

As is evident in Box 9.2, women remain significantly underrepresented in parliaments, national assemblies, and congresses. But there's good news: Although women occupy on average only 25.4 percent of seats in these national decision-making bodies, this is up from 11.3 percent in 1995 (Inter-Parliamentary Union, 2021b). There is no question that women's activism is partly responsible for this increase in women **MPs (members of parliament).** Rates vary internationally and, for reasons discussed later, high-income "developed" countries do not necessarily exhibit greater gender parity in legislatures. For example, in 2021, Japan had only 14.4 percent women representatives, the United States 26.6 percent, Hungary 12.1 percent, Ireland 27.2 percent, Bahrain 18.7 percent, Israel 24.2 percent, and the United Kingdom 30.5 percent. These countries lagged behind the low-income countries of Ethiopia (37.2%), Mozambique (42.4%), Rwanda (55.6%), and Senegal (43%) in the number of women MPs. The appendix includes the percentage of women MPs for each of the world's countries. A glass ceiling in national legislatures is also evident: Women head only 20.9 percent of national legislatures, but on the bright side, this represents a 6.35 percent increase from 2010 (Inter-Parliamentary Union, 2010, 2021c).

Women are even more rare as cabinet members, but like women in national legislatures, there's evidence of progress. Government cabinets consist of advisors to the head of government who frequently lead specific government agencies. Cabinets are often the originators of the policies considered by legislators and usually have control over spending and policies in their own department. In many countries, cabinet members are called *ministers* (as in Minister of Finance), but in some, such as the United States, they are called *secretaries* (as in Secretary of Labor). The number of women cabinet ministers is an indicator of gender equality in politics and provides evidence of the glass ceiling (O'Brien et al., 2015). The presence of women as cabinet members matters because cabinet members have power in the form of policy-making authority. Also, cabinet positions are sometimes a stepping-stone to executive political office. Globally, the percentage of cabinet positions held by women was 21.9 percent in 2021 (Inter-Parliamentary Union, 2021c).

> In 1986, Norway became the first country to have a cabinet with close to half of its members women.

Cabinet appointments differ in status and influence. They vary in respect to their influence within the cabinet, the media attention they receive, and the degree to which they provide a pathway to higher office (O'Brien et al., 2015). Women ministers are typically appointed to less powerful and less prestigious cabinet positions such as women's affairs and gender equality, or energy and environment. They are less likely to be appointed to powerful "inner cabinet" positions such as defense, foreign affairs, or finance positions (Inter-parliamentary Union, 2021d; Krook & O'Brien, 2012). Politically "left" governments (socialist or democratic socialist) not only appoint more women to cabinet positions but also are more likely to appoint women cabinet members to high-prestige posts (O'Brien et al., 2015).

> Women held only 17 percent of Cabinet positions under U.S. President Trump but this rose to 46 percent under President Biden.

Importance of Women Representatives in National Legislatures and Cabinets

Women's representation in these positions is of symbolic importance because it is consistent with the ideals of justice and equality at the heart of democracy. When we think about the true purpose of representative democracy, we should be alarmed that although women make up approximately half of the population, they constitute only 25.5 percent of legislatures, 21.9 percent of cabinet positions, and 20.9 percent of party leaders. Also concerning for representative democracy is that minority women's political representation has proceeded even more slowly than that of majority women and minority men (Paxton & Hughes, 2016). Women politicians are usually heterosexual and come from more educated, privileged backgrounds and may not represent the interests of other women in their societies (Joshi & Ochs, 2014; Paxton et al., 2007; Paxton & Hughes, 2016). Women politicians are also of symbolic importance because they shatter the gender stereotypes that politics are a masculine domain and that women do not have the capabilities for governance. Women's presence in governance improves both men's and women's assessments of women's capabilities and provides positive political role models for girls and women, leading to their greater political engagement (Hughes, 2009; Wolbrecht & Campbell, 2007).

> "Young girls in Liberia now can speak about wanting to be a minister or a President or a leader. I hope that motivation will just spread."
> *President Ellen Johnson Sirleaf of Liberia, Africa's first woman president, elected in 2006*

"Women will not simply be mainstreamed into the polluted stream. Women are changing the stream, making it clean and green and safe for all—every gender, race, creed, sexual orientation, age, and ability."
Bella Abzug (1920–1998), American congresswoman and women's rights advocate

Women political representatives are also of practical importance because they make a difference in law and policy. As Lister (2003) suggests, increasing women's political representation is particularly important because women have special interests, some in conflict with men's interests, that need to be articulated by women in political debate and decision-making. Cross-cultural research finds that women initiate more debates about women's issues, are more likely to support feminist and pro-equality policies, and are more likely than men to sponsor or co-sponsor bills addressing women's and children's issues (Atchison & Down, 2009; Joshi & Och, 2014; Paxton & Hughes, 2016; Swiss, Fallon, & Burgos, 2012). The number of women cabinet members is also positively associated with social policies benefiting women (Atchison & Down, 2009).

The United Nations estimates that women need to constitute at least 30 percent of a legislative body in order to exert a meaningful influence on politics; this is sometimes called **critical political mass.** The Beijing Platform for Action calls for a 30 percent minimum for women in representative politics. At this 30 percent point, women can form coalitions that can effectively influence policy, they are harder to marginalize, and the gender stereotyping of politicians will wane more quickly as women in politics becomes "normalized." By 2021, this critical mass was reached in 63 (33%) of the world's countries (Inter-Parliamentary Union, 2021c). Only 45 of the world's countries (23.3%) had one-third or more women congressional or parliamentary representatives, and only 13 (6.7%) achieved gender parity in their Cabinets (Nicaragua was the leader with 59% of Cabinet positions held by women). Twelve countries had no women in Cabinet positions (Inter-parliamentary Union, 2021c).

"It is only when there is a critical mass of women in all their diversity in every country of the world in both appointed and elected decision-making positions and in all international bodies, that gender issues will be addressed in the policy agenda and the goals of equality, development, peace and human rights for all can be realized in the 21st century."
Women's Environment and Development Organization (WEDO)

But having 30 percent women representatives does not magically lead to the introduction and passage of pro-women legislation. Not all women representatives promote women's causes, resistance from male politicians and marginalization of women can interfere, and sometimes even smaller minorities advance pro-women policies (Childs & Krook, 2008). The passage of pro-women's legislation is more likely when there is a well-organized parliamentary women's caucus crossing party lines and there is support for the policies from male colleagues and from the community (Wang, 2013; Weldon & Htun, 2013). A strong domestic feminist movement also makes a big difference in the success of women's issues advocacy by women parliamentarians (Johnson & Josefsson, 2016).

Explaining the Relatively Low Numbers of Women in National Legislatures

Figure 9.1 summarizes the many obstacles to women's election to parliaments and congresses. These also apply to women political executives, that is, as heads of state and government.

Traditional gender ideologies and culture are a large factor in women's exclusion from formal politics. It is no coincidence that the countries with the lowest rates of elected women parliamentarians and cabinet ministers are usually places where men's and women's roles are more rigidly segregated into the public (male) sphere of economics and politics and the private (female) sphere of home and family. As

Male politicians sometimes advocate for women's issues. Joe Biden introduced the Violence Against Women Act in 1990 when he was Senator and Chair of the Senate Judiciary Committee. It was signed into law four years later by President Bill Clinton.

FIGURE 9.1 *Obstacles to Women's Election to Parliaments and Congresses*

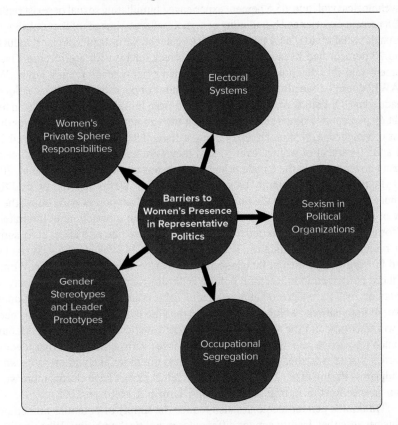

a public sphere activity, politics are seen as the domain of men, and this influences both demand for and the supply of women candidates and their election to office.

Gendered expectations of political leaders and leadership affect the supply and demand for women politicians. The archetypal political leader is male in appearance and gender and masculine in character traits (Sjoberg, 2014). Traditional gender stereotypes suggest that men, not women, are more naturally suited for these roles. As Peterson and Runyan (1999) suggest, women are socialized into domestic roles that are antithetical to public political sphere activities, and the traits associated with political efficacy (ambition, aggression, competitiveness, authority) are seen as distinctly *un*feminine. The result is that some people do not accept women as political agents and are less likely to support and vote for them (Krook & Norris, 2014; Peterson & Runyan, 1999).

Traditional gender ideologies sometimes lead to **violence against women in politics (VAWIP)**. According to the National Democratic Institute's campaign "Stopping the Violence Against Women in Politics" (#NotThe Cost), VAWIP has three characteristics: It targets political women because of their gender; it is usually a gendered form of violence; and its point is to discourage women from being or becoming active in politics.

> "Potential female aspirants may thus confront lingering stereotypes—within themselves, in the eyes of gatekeepers and among citizens—that politics is not a place for women."
> *Mona Krook and Pippa Norris, political scientists*

VAWIP is a global problem. A study of women parliamentarians in forty-two parliaments by the Inter-Parliamentary Union (2016) found that 81 percent experienced psychological violence, 65.5 percent experienced humiliating sexual or sexist remarks, 41.8 percent experienced humiliating or sexually charged images of themselves spread through social media, 44.4 percent were threatened with death, rape, or abduction, and 20 percent had been slapped, pushed, struck, or hit with a projectile. Over 60 percent said that defending human and women's rights made them a target. While VAWIP doesn't dissuade all women from pursuing or persisting in politics, it does dissuade some. One study of South Asian women from India, Nepal, and Pakistan found that 60 percent of women surveyed said that they do not participate in politics due to fear of violence (UN Women, 2014). In Australia, 60 percent of women aged 18 to 21 and 80 percent of women over 31 said they were less likely to run for office after seeing how negatively the female prime minister was treated (Krook & Sanín, 2016).

Political parties' support for women candidates is also affected by traditional gender ideologies. Without the financial and technical support of party elites, the supply of women candidates is reduced. Women are often unwelcome in the fraternity of formal politics. Concerns about voter bias against women also affect party support for running women candidates (Krook & Norris, 2014). What Chowdhury (1994) said in regard to politics in Bangladesh remains true so many years later: Women's reduced participation in electoral politics is illustrative of male control of party organizations; men have a greater ability to build viable constituency and party support in favor of nominations; women lack access to the kind of money and patronage needed to win elections; and the aggressive electioneering tactics often employed discourage women's entrance into the fray. However, parties with more egalitarian ideologies (parties that lean farther left in their ideologies) are more likely to promote women candidates (Paxton et al., 2007). Historically, leftist parties have elected more women than have centrist or rightist parties (Saint-Germain & Metoyer, 2008).

Traditional gender ideologies also reduce the supply of potential women politicians because they lead to gender differences in political ambition. When politics is stereotyped as a male domain, men are more likely to pursue formal politics than are women. Traditional gender roles and gender stereotypes reduce women's political interest and ambition as well as the likelihood they will have needed money, time, experience, and skills to run (Krook & Norris, 2014; Paxton et al., 2007). In many countries, the pool of qualified women is further reduced by gender occupational and educational segregation. The jobs leading to formal political office are customarily male-dominated (law, medicine, military, business), and women are less likely to receive the higher education often associated with office-holding (Peterson & Runyan, 1999; Saint-Germain & Metoyer, 2008). Moreover, in cultures with traditional gender roles, women's responsibilities as wife and mother do not provide the time to run for and hold political office. It is not only women's longer workday that interferes; it is their lack of control over when they will be available and whether (how) family obligations will interfere with political pursuits (Peterson & Runyan, 1999). Combining family responsibilities and political office is much more of an issue for women; men are not forced to make these choices (Norris & Lovenduski, 1995). Unlike men, many women who enter representative politics do not have children, or wait until their children are grown (Paxton & Hughes, 2016).

At Trump rallies during the 2016 U.S. presidential election, Trump supporters threatened to assassinate, hang, and shoot opponent Hillary Clinton (the first woman to be the presidential nominee of a major party). Some sported signs with images of her head on a spike and her face in the cross-hairs of a target.

"For parliament to play its role effectively, it must be elected and must be representative of all components of society."
Inter-Parliamentary Union

"But what is true I think is that women who want and need a life outside as well as inside the home have a much, much harder time than men because they carry such a heavy double burden."
Golda Meir, 1975, first and only woman to be Prime Minister of Israel

The structure of the political system, in particular, the electoral system, also affects women's presence in representative politics. It is far easier for women to run and win elections in some **electoral systems** than others (the electoral system consists of the procedures by which representatives are elected). There are three types of electoral systems, each with different effects on women's election to national legislative office: (1) In **party list/proportional representation systems** (PL/PR), three or more parties prepare lists of candidates for election from each district (party lists); seats are allocated roughly in proportion to the votes each party receives (e.g., if a party receives 30% of the votes, it gets 30% of the seats, and moves down its list until the party's seats are filled); and there are five or more representatives per district (multimember districts). In contrast are the (2) **single member district systems** (SMD) or **plurality/majority systems**. These nonparty list/nonproportional representation systems are "winner-take-all" systems where there is usually only one seat per district, and the person who gets the most votes wins. Some countries have (3) **mixed systems,** with PR systems in some regions of the country and a plurality/majority system in others.

The majority of the countries with the highest percentages of women legislators have a PL/PR system, and in "mixed" systems such as those in Australia and New Zealand, more women are elected from areas with PR systems (International IDEA, 2014; Paxton & Hughes, 2016). Under PL/PR systems, parties see an advantage in having some female candidates to attract more women voters and gain more seats, and when women run for office, it does not prevent men from running (Paxton & Hughes, 2007).

But the effect of PL/PR systems on women's representation is complicated by the fact that PL/PR systems vary considerably (Paxton & Hughes, 2016). For example, the size of the multimember district (district magnitude) makes a big difference—the higher the district magnitudes, that is, the more seats per district, the better for women. Party magnitude (the number of seats a party expects to win in a district) also makes a difference for women. This is because parties move down their lists in order. Party leaders tend to be men and tend to put themselves at the top of the lists to ensure their election. When women are placed lower on the lists, their odds of election are lower, especially if the party tends to win only a small number of seats (Paxton & Hughes, 2007). WEDO's "50/50 by 2005 Get the Balance Right" campaign to increase women's representation recommended alternating equal numbers of women and men on party electoral lists (the campaign ran from 2000 to 2007). Bolivia, Costa Rica, Ecuador, France, Kenya, the Republic of Korea, Lesotho, Libya, Nicaragua, Senegal, Tunisia, and Zimbabwe all require the names of female and male candidates on candidate lists to be alternated (International IDEA, 2014).

Women political representatives are fewer in SMD systems. Unsurprisingly, under these systems, parties will usually choose and support only those candidates believed capable of winning the required number of votes. Parties under these systems often believe that in a head-to-head contest between a male and female candidate, a male candidate gives them the best chance of winning the district (International IDEA, 2014). Another problem is that male domination of political parties increases reluctance to support women candidates over male candidates (male leaders want the few available spots to go to men) (Paxton & Hughes, 2016). SMD systems are one reason why nations like Canada, Japan, the United Kingdom, and the United States have relatively low numbers of women in their legislatures.

"We face many obstacles, but four of the more prevalent are stereotyping, the nature of the political beast, a rigid electoral system, and apathy." *Daisy Avance Fuentes, first woman deputy speaker in the Philippines House of Representatives*

Women parliamentarians in a 2008 IPU global survey said the major barriers to women's political careers were domestic responsibilities, cultural attitudes, lack of support from family and from political parties, and lack of confidence. *International IDEA, 2014*

FIGURE 9.2   *Strategies for More Women in Formal Political Positions*

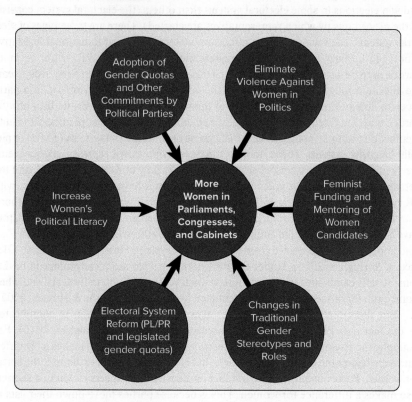

Increasing the Number of Women Representatives in National Legislatures with Electoral Reforms

Because women have a positive influence on policymaking regarding women's issues but their numbers remain relatively low, many feminist political scientists have studied how women gain greater power in representative democracies. Figure 9.2 summarizes strategies for promoting increased gender parity in formal politics.

Electoral reforms, changes to the electoral system, are one way to increase the number of women representatives. These reforms include the adoption of PL/PR systems and gender quotas. Many newly developing democracies chose PL/PR systems, with positive effects for women's representation. **Gender quotas** are rules that specify the minimum number of women (or women and men) that candidate lists should include, or designate the number of seats that should be allocated to women in legislatures. An effective electoral reform for increasing the number of women in formal political positions, they are intended to bring about change in the short-to-medium term and to be discarded when no longer needed. Studies indicate that quotas might be a greater influence on women's representation than type of electoral system (International IDEA, 2014; Tripp & Kang, 2008). Considered a "fast-track" model for bringing about greater gender equality in representative politics, gender quotas are designed to override cultural obstacles to women's political representation and motivate political parties to seriously consider and commit to women candidates. By 2021, 130 countries had some form of gender quota (International IDEA, 2021).

There are three types of gender quotas. The most common are *legislated candidate quotas* that specify the gender composition of candidate lists. *Legislated reserved seats* put aside a certain percentage of seats for women and are implemented through special electoral procedures. *Voluntary party quotas* are quotas adopted by political parties for their own candidate lists (International IDEA, 2014).[1] In 2021, fifty-seven countries had legislated or constitutional candidate gender quotas, twenty-six had reserved seats for women in the lower or single house, and fifty-six had political parties with voluntary gender quotas. Of the twenty-one countries with over 40 percent women in parliament, seventeen (81%) had at least one form of quota (International IDEA, 2021). The majority of these countries (90%) had PL/PR electoral systems (ACE Electoral Knowledge Network, 2021).

In 1991, Argentina, a PL/PR electoral system country, passed the first electoral law quota in the world. The law stipulated that women candidates must occupy 30 percent of the upper-level positions on party lists. Argentina's law resulted from a bill introduced by Senator Margarita Malharro and Representatives Norma Allegrone de Fonte and Florentina Gomez Miranda. On the day of the parliamentary debate, huge numbers of women from different social classes and different ideologies mobilized in the gallery, the Chambers, and in the streets and squares near the Congress (Bonder & Nari, 1995). The first election following implementation of the law made an immediate difference in the number of women federal district senators: Of the 54 senators elected, 19 (35%) were women (Molinelli, 1994). The quota law also increased women's representation in the Chamber of Deputies from 5.5 percent in 1991 to 12.8 percent in 1993 (Feijoo, 1998). In 2019, women comprised 42 percent of the Chamber of Deputies and 40 percent of the Senate (IPU, 2021a).

> "Those who oppose quotas hold women back in the name of old, traditional prejudices more worthy of a feudal era than of modern times."
> *Senator Margarita Malharro de Torres, Argentina*

New democracies often provide the opportunity to create a PL/PR electoral system with gender quotas, leading to dramatic increases in women's representation. For example, the new democracy of Namibia adopted a PL/PR system in 1989. A total of 14 women appeared on candidate lists, and women were elected to 6.9 percent of assembly seats. Although this may not seem significant, this was only the second election in which Namibian women were eligible to vote and run for office. Several different quotas were adopted beginning in 1992. By 2010, Namibian women representatives comprised 27 percent of the National Assembly, and by

---

[1]This is a bit of an oversimplification, as some countries use a variety of quotas to increase women's representation. There are even a few countries (like Burundi, Afghanistan, and Jordan) with quotas for women from marginalized groups. International IDEA (https://www.idea.int/data-tools/data/gender-quotas/country-overview) provides details on the quotas used by each country.

2021, this was up to 44 percent (the National Assembly's ruling party's adoption of a 50% quota in 2013 helped) (IPU, 2021). Rwanda is another example. In 2003, the newly formed democracy adopted a PL/PR system along with a multi-level quota system. As a result, Rwanda became the first country to come close to achieving gender parity in a national parliament (IPU, 2003, 2017). Rwanda has been ranked number one in the world for women's parliamentary representation ever since, and with each election, women's representation has grown. In 2021, 61.3 percent of the lower house and 38.5 percent of the senate was comprised of women representatives (IPU, 2021).

Quotas are not foolproof solutions to the problem of women's representation in elected politics, and their effects vary based on how they're structured and on levels of party compliance (Tripp & Kang, 2008). Success rates are highest in PR/PL countries with **zipper (zebra) systems.** These systems have legislated candidate quotas requiring a certain percentage of women on party lists, along with the alternation of male and female candidates (International IDEA, 2014). Sanctions for noncompliance also boost effectiveness. About 40 percent of countries with quotas have no sanctions for noncompliance (International IDEA, 2021). Some countries have not seen increases in women's representation following quotas because there are no penalties for noncompliance or parties prefer to pay fines rather than comply. France is an example of a country where gender quotas have contributed to very modest increases in women's representation because some parties prefer to pay the fines rather than comply (Paxton & Hughes, 2016). However, in 2017 France moved from 64th in world rankings of women's parliamentary representation to 17th when the country's winning political party (LREM) offered a gender equal party candidate list (Kelly, 2017).

The size of the quotas also varies, which is why countries with quotas can still have low numbers of women representatives. For example, Djibouti had a party list quota of 10 percent until 2018 when it was increased to 25 percent. Women's representation in the Djibouti National Assembly increased from 10 percent in 2017 to 26.2 percent in 2019 (International IDEA, 2021; IPU, 2021a). In Jordan, only 15 out of 130 seats must be reserved for women in the lower house. In 2021 Jordan had 15 women in the lower chamber and 8 in the upper chamber (International IDEA, 2021; IPU, 2021a). Also, under some systems, political parties can technically comply but still ensure that few women get elected. For example, they can run women in districts with unwinnable seats, place them low on a party list when party magnitude is low, or fail to support them (Tripp & Kang, 2008). This has been a problem in both Italy and France (Bryant, 2003; Gutierrez & Boselli, 2009).

Despite their overall effectiveness, quotas are not without controversy. Critics charge that that they promote the election of unqualified women, that "quota women" are blindly loyal to male party bosses, and that quotas may become a ceiling on women's participation (countries may not be motivated to pursue further strategies to ensure equal participation) (Franceschet & Piscopo, 2008; Paxton & Hughes, 2007). Some argue that quotas violate the principles of democracy because they force voters to elect women, give women preference over men, and push qualified men to the side (Dahlerup & Friedenvall, 2008). Many agree that quotas are a point of departure rather than a point of arrival and point out that we must continue efforts to eliminate the factors that led to the problem in the first place (Bonder & Nari, 1995; Chowdhury, 1994).

As you might expect, women's movements are instrumental in bringing about the legislative and constitutional changes that carve out new roles for women in government (Tripp et al., 2009). Indeed, strong women's groups and a national women's movement are associated with greater numbers of women in legislatures (Bystydzienski, 1995; Saint-Germain & Metoyer, 2008). In Mexico, women's activism and regional norms (by 2002 most Latin American countries had gender quotas) led to legislated gender quotas in 2008 and their strengthening in 2014. Now parties must field an equal number of male and female candidates, and a third of candidates on party lists must be women. The result: The percentage of women parliamentarians in the Chamber of Deputies rose from 23.2 percent in 2006 to 48 percent in the 2018 elections, while women's representation in the Senate increased from 18 percent to 49 percent (IPU, 2021).

International women's movements and international agreements, such as CEDAW and the Beijing Platform, foster new norms stressing the importance of women's political inclusion and encourage new democracies to pass gender equity laws and policies, including legislated, national-level gender quotas (Franceschet & Piscopo, 2008; Hughes, Krook, & Paxton, 2015). The idea is that to strengthen democracies, special measures are needed to promote the equal participation of women and men in political decision-making. International and local women's activism was responsible for the inclusion of quotas in the constitutions of the newly formed democracies of Afghanistan and Iraq in the mid-2000s. International IDEA (the Institute for Democracy and Electoral Assistance) provides support for the quota campaigns of NGOs, activists, and political representatives. Such campaigns have led to the adoption of quotas in Colombia, Ecuador, Ghana, Haiti, Kenya, Liberia, Namibia, Sierra Leone, and Senegal (International IDEA, 2014). However, while international pressure combined with national activism often spur quota adoption, resistance from male political elites sometimes thwarts quota campaigns (Hughes et al., 2015).

Women 50-50 is a Scottish NGO seeking legislative quotas for women on public boards, local councils, and in the Scottish parliament.

Other Strategies for Increasing Women's Representation in National Legislatures

Electoral reforms aren't the only way to increase the supply of and demand for women candidates. Box 9.4 summarizes the four other strategies for electing more women to public office. Getting elected is a complex, expensive, and bureaucratic process, and women have not always had the same access as men to information, money, and resources. And given that politics are stereotyped as a male domain, women may not feel inspired or equipped to run for office. That is why feminist efforts to increase the numbers of women political representatives include building the will of women to run and developing their political skills, and targeting the gender stereotypes that suggest politics are no place for women. Strategies include media campaigns, recruitment and outreach initiatives, increasing women's **political literacy** (their knowledge of politics and the political process), building women's public speaking and media skills, and helping them fund their campaigns.

BOX 9.4   **Non-Electoral System Strategies for Electing More Women to Public Office**

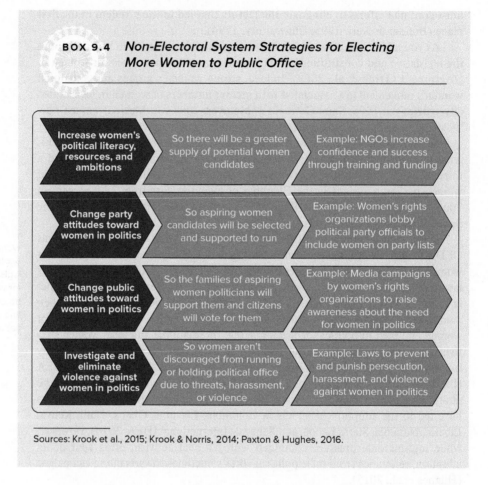

Increase women's political literacy, resources, and ambitions	So there will be a greater supply of potential women candidates	Example: NGOs increase confidence and success through training and funding
Change party attitudes toward women in politics	So aspiring women candidates will be selected and supported to run	Example: Women's rights organizations lobby political party officials to include women on party lists
Change public attitudes toward women in politics	So the families of aspiring women politicians will support them and citizens will vote for them	Example: Media campaigns by women's rights organizations to raise awareness about the need for women in politics
Investigate and eliminate violence against women in politics	So women aren't discouraged from running or holding political office due to threats, harassment, or violence	Example: Laws to prevent and punish persecution, harassment, and violence against women in politics

Sources: Krook et al., 2015; Krook & Norris, 2014; Paxton & Hughes, 2016.

"Our aim is simple: To inspire, equip, and inform women to run for political office."
Women for Election, Ireland

EMILY's List in the United States is one example. This NGO recruits and trains candidates and campaign professionals to effectively organize, fund-raise, and communicate their message. From 1985 to 2021, EMILY's List helped elect 16 women governors, 26 women to the U.S. Senate, 157 women to the U.S. House of Representatives, over 1,100 women to state and local political offices, and one Vice President. GRSOs (grassroots support organizations) like the Global Fund for Women; the Asia Pacific Forum on Women, Law, and Development (APWLD); and Development Alternatives with Women for a New Era (DAWN), as well as intergovernmental organizations like UN Women, also fund NGOs that recruit and train women to run for office.

Women's rights organizations also target political parties. In the 1970s in Norway, a coalition of women's groups mobilized women to run for office, worked through political parties, and taught voters how to use flexible voting rules (the system permits the writing in of names on ballots) (Bystydzienski, 1992, 1995).

Norwegian activists also convinced political parties to nominate women candidates and accept gender quotas. The result was the quadrupling of women's political representation locally and nationally in a period of two decades. A more recent example comes from Turkey. There the Association for the Support and Training of Women Candidates (KA-DER) lobbies political parties to run women for office (Paxton & Hughes, 2016). KA-DER also provides an example of an NGO that conducts media-based campaigns aimed at changing how citizens think about gender and politics (Krook & Norris, 2014).

Because violence and threats of violence are sometimes used to reinforce men's dominance in the political realm and to punish women that step into the political arena, specific laws and policies to prevent and punish all forms of persecution, harassment, and violence against women in politics are needed to reduce this potential cost to women candidates and representatives (Krook & Sanín, 2016). For example, in Bolivia, VAWIP is such a problem that only 9 percent of women run for reelection, and from 2004 to 2012, Bolivia's female politicians made more than 4,000 complaints of violence and harassment, many of them against their male colleagues (BBC News, 2014). Women's activism, spurred by the harassment and murder of politician Juana Quispe, who helped her female colleagues in the Bolivian parliament file harassment complaints, led Bolivia to become the first country to pass a specific law against VAWIP in 2012. The law was strengthened in 2014 and provides punishments ranging from 4 to 30 years for any physical, psychological or sexual aggression or any form of pressure, persecution, harassment, or threat toward a woman elected to or holding public office (BBC News, 2014; Krook & Sanín, 2016). International IDEA, the National Democratic Institute, ParlAmericas of the Organization of the American States (OAS), UN Women, and the Inter-Parliamentary Union are some of the organizations working to document and address VAWIP.

Women Heads of State and Government: Presidents and Prime Ministers

Although powerful female leaders like Cleopatra (Egypt), Catherine the Great (Russia), Yaa Asantewaa (Ghana), and Tz'u-Hsi (China) are found throughout history, women remain relatively rare as heads of state and government (political executives). The first three women political executives served in the 1960s; in the 1970s there were six, in the 1980s there were seven, in the 1990s there were twenty-six, and from 2000 to 2009 there were thirty-seven (Jalazai, 2017). Although progress is significant (75% of all women political executives have served in the last 20 years), this glass ceiling in politics is only cracked. Most countries have not had a woman heading their government.

In 2021, there were just twenty-six women presidents or prime ministers out of 262 executive posts, close to 10 percent of the world total (if we include Tsai Ing-wen, the first woman president of Taiwan, it is twenty-seven). Box 9.5 shows women heads of state and government in 2021 and designates whether the office holder is a **head of state** that represents her government in a symbolic, ceremonial

---

"My advice to women—you cannot afford to wait for anyone to give you rights. Women have to take the initiative and claim their rights. I plan to participate in the next municipal elections. I believe that I have the expertise, the willingness and also the strength to change our society for the better."
Raja Shahwan, member of the Women Local Committees in Gaza, Palestine, which helps women participate in local governance and community activities

---

"An alarming but uncounted number of women are specifically targeted because they are engaged in public life. It is a pervasive but often overlooked barrier that prevents women across the world from having their voices heard . . . When a woman participates in politics, she should be putting her hopes and dreams for the future on the line, not her dignity and not her life."
Madeline Albright, First woman U.S. Secretary of State, a founder of #NotTheCost

---

In 2009, Johanna Siguroadottir became the first woman prime minister in Iceland and the first openly lesbian head of government in the world.

BOX 9.5   *Women Heads of Government (HG) and Heads of State (HS) in 2021*

Prime Minister Sheikh Hasina (Bangladesh) HG

Prime Minister Mia Mottley* (Barbados) HG

Prime Minister Mette Frederiksen (Denmark) HG

President Kersti Kaljulaid*

Prime Minister Kaja Kallas* (Estonia) HS/HG

President Sahle-Work Zewde* (Ethiopia) HS

Prime Minister Sanna Marin (Finland) HG

Prime Minister Rose Christiane Ossouka Raponda* (Gabon) HG

President Salome Zourabichvili* (Georgia) HS

Chancellor Angela Merkel* (Germany) HG

President Katerina Sakellaropoulou* (Greece) HS

Prime Minister Katrín Jakobsdóttir (Iceland) HG

President Vjosa Osmani (Kosovo) HS

Prime Minister Ingrida Šimonytė (Lithuania) HG

Prime Minister Saara Kuugongelwa* (Namibia) HG

President Bidya Devi Bhandari* (Nepal) HS

Prime Minister Jacinda Ardern (New Zealand) HG

Prime Minister Erna Solberg (Norway) HG

Prime Minister Violeta Bermúdez (Peru) HG

President Maia Sandu* (Republic of Moldova) HS

Prime Minister Ana Brnabić* (Serbia) HG

President Halimah Yacob* (Singapore) HS

President Zuzana Čaputová* (Slovakia) HS

President Samia Suluhu Hassan* (Tanzania) HS/HG

Prime Minister Victoire Tomegah Dogbé* (Togo) HG

President Paula-Mae Weekes (Trinidad and Tobago) HS

*First woman to hold this position in this country.

---

fashion (the public face of the country or government) or a **head of government** that oversees daily executive and legislative activities of a country and is more powerful than a head of state (in some countries the role of prime minister or president requires both duties). Global analyses of women political executives find that women are more likely to be heads of state than government (Jalalzai, 2013), so this list is notable in that almost 60 percent of these leaders are heads of government.

Paths to Power

It is interesting to consider how women come to occupy these customarily male power positions and to ask how their leadership might differ from that of men. Unfortunately, the study of women political executives has received less attention than the study of women in legislative politics and so the answers to these questions are preliminary. The differing and complex political, economic, and cultural contexts specific to a given woman's trajectory and experience also make generalization difficult and study challenging. Let's begin with the first question: How do women get

In 2003, Finland became the first European country to have women as both president and prime minister.

BOX 9.6　*Recipe for Woman Head of State or Government*

One or more of these personal factors:

- Deceased husband or father who was a pro-nationalist or pro-democracy leader

- Served in national assembly, climbed party ladder

- Record of government service plus activism in a pro-democracy or anti-government corruption movement

- Educated and from upper class

One or more institutional/structural factors:

- Parliamentary system where prime minister or president isn't determined by the popular vote

- Dual executive system (both a president and a prime minister)

- Party structure with institutionalized leadership-selection processes

+

One or more sociohistorical factors:

- Government transition to democracy

- Society recovering from civil war, dictatorship, or political instability

- Recent history of government corruption

- Political party instability due to scandal, infighting, or death

- Active women's groups or movements

=

Woman Head of State or Government

to be president or prime minister of their country? Box 9.6 summarizes the many factors found to precipitate women's rise to executive office.

Historically, one of the most common paths to executive government office was kinship. About 29 percent of women heads of state or government have used kinship ties, as daughters or wives of political figures, to attain office (D'Amico, 1995; Jalalzai, 2017; Jalalzai & Rincker, 2018). This explains how women heads of state or government become president or prime minister in countries where women's status lags behind men's; they benefited from kinship ties to past political leaders (Jalalzai, 2008).

In the case of most **political surrogates**, the husband or father was assassinated and subsequently martyred by the citizenry as a persecuted leader of democratic change or national independence. When it appeared that the government was going in the direction of pre-struggle politics and there were no electable alternative candidates, political strategists sought the next best thing to the successful but now deceased challenger—his relatives. The wife or daughter was chosen when there were no male offspring to assume this role or when party leaders assumed that women would be more malleable and obedient than their male relatives (Jalalzai, 2008). During the campaign, references to the achievements and martyrdom of the husband/father were made repeatedly, and it was implied that the female candidate would serve as a stand-in for the cherished leader. Typically, these women were well educated and came from wealthy, political families. Although the first political surrogates had little political experience when drafted by a political party, this is less true of recent surrogates.

The surrogacy path is more common in Latin America and Asia, where 75 to 80 percent of women in executive office have had ties to a political family dynasty (Jalazai, 2017). Once the most common path for women to the executive office, of the twenty-six women heads of state and government in 2021, only three have hints of the surrogacy path to power (Sheikh Hasina of Bangladesh, Prime Minister Kaja Kallas of Estonia, and Prime Minister Mia Mottley of Barbados).

The first woman president of Taiwan, Tsai Ing-wen, elected in 2016, is the first woman in Asia elected to lead her country without having a husband or father in politics.

The world's first woman prime minister, Sirimavo Bandaranaike of Sri Lanka (1960-1965, 1970-1977, 1994-2000), took the "widow's walk to power." Her husband, Solomon Dias Bandaranaike, was a leader in the movement to gain independence from Britain. He became prime minister in 1956 only to be assassinated in September 1959. New elections were set for March 1960, and Sirimavo Bandaranaike was asked to campaign on behalf of her husband's political party, the Sri Lankan Freedom Party (SLFP). In May 1960, she reluctantly accepted headship of the SLFP, and the party won the majority of seats in the House of Representatives. As head of the party, she became prime minister. At the beginning she acted as a surrogate for her dead husband, carrying out his political plans, but over time she became a politician in her own right. In 1994, she was again appointed prime minister—this time by her daughter, President Chandrika Kumaratunga. Bandaranaike retired in 2000 at age 84 and died a few months later, only hours after voting in a public election.

Neither Dilma Rouseff, the first woman president of Brazil (elected in 2011 and impeached in 2016) or Laura Chinchilla, the first woman president of Costa Rica (2010–2014), were political surrogates.

In Latin America, the first women heads of government followed the widow's walk to power. They were political surrogates (stand-ins) for husbands killed by natural or political causes and were expected to act as their husbands would. The first woman president in Latin America, Isabel Peron (Argentina, 1974-1976), was poorly qualified, appointed president following the death of her president husband Juan while in office. Violeta de Chamorro (Nicaragua, 1990-1997), the first and only woman to be president of Nicaragua, was also unqualified, but she was the wife of assassinated political leader Pedro Chamorro. The first and only woman to be president of Panama, Mireya Moscoso (1999-2004), was the wife of deceased three-term president Arnulfo Arias. Like Peron and Chamorro, she did not have much political experience. Having served in Argentina's national assembly, Cristina Fernandez de Kirchner, Argentina's second woman president (2007–2015), had more legitimate political credentials than Peron, Chamorro, and Moscoso but probably would not have been elected were it not for her husband, President Nestor Kirchner, who served from 2003 to 2007 (he declined to run for another term and endorsed his wife, becoming an influential "First Husband").

In Asia, most women leaders have been the daughters of the country's founding fathers. Their political pedigree helped them to get their foot in the political party door, where they eventually became leaders in their own right. Benazir Bhutto, prime minister of Pakistan (1988–1990, 1993–1996) is an interesting example. It is unlikely she would have been elected in the gender-conservative country of Pakistan were it not for the popularity of her martyred father, Zulfikar Ali Bhutto. Following her father's political imprisonment and her brothers' political exile abroad, Bhutto carried on her father's struggle against the authoritarian regime of General Mohammad Zia. Eventually Zia executed her father and imprisoned Benazir. In time, international and domestic pressure led Zia to release Benazir and allow elections in 1988. Benazir used her father's image skillfully. She referred repeatedly to him in speeches and was photographed with his image in the background (Anderson, 1993). Zia was killed in a plane crash right before the election, and Benazir's party, the Pakistan People's Party (PPP), won the majority of seats in the National Assembly, and Benazir became prime minister. In 1990, President Izhaq Khan dismissed Bhutto on charges of nepotism and corruption. She ran for office and won again in 1993, but 3 years into her 5-year term, President Farooq Leghari dismissed her, again under charges of corruption. In 2007, Bhutto assumed leadership of the PPP and ran for parliament. A suicide bomber assassinated Bhutto during a campaign rally in December 2007. The terrorist group Al-Qaeda claimed responsibility, and it is widely speculated that then-President Musharraf deliberately provided inadequate security.

A second common path to power for female political executives is that of **political insider** or climber (D'Amico, 1995). Although D'Amico (1995) hypothesized that this is an infrequent path to power for women because women are statistically underrepresented in the professions that serve as political stepping-stones (that is, the law, military service, and business), this has changed. Today, most women heads of state or government are highly qualified. They are educated and many have policy relevant degrees such as law, finance, or economics. Most have extensive relevant experience as cabinet members, elected national representatives, or in the judiciary as judges on high courts. Many earned their prime minister or president position through dedicated service to their party and worked their way up their party's leadership ladder.

Indira Gandhi of India is one example of a leader who took the insider path, but her trajectory also has kinship/surrogate elements. She became a member of the Congress Party in 1948, was elected to its Working Committee in 1955, to its presidency in 1959, to the upper house of Parliament in 1964, and served an appointed position as Minister of Information and Broadcasting before assuming

"My father always would say, 'My daughter will go into politics. My daughter will become prime minister,' but it's not what I wanted to do. I would say, 'No, Papa, I will never go into politics.' As I've said before, this is not the life I chose; it chose me . . . But I accepted the responsibility and I've never wavered in my commitment."
Benazir Bhutto

"My father was a statesman, I am a political woman. My father was a saint. I am not."
Indira Gandhi

position of prime minister of India in 1966 (Carras, 1995). Although she certainly presented herself as a political surrogate early on (her father was leader in the movement to gain independence from Britain and the first prime minister following independence), her party granted her power in part because she had earned her status within the party hierarchy. Similarly, Margaret Thatcher of Great Britain began working for the Conservative Party in the 1950s, was elected to the House of Commons in 1959, became Parliamentary Secretary to the Ministry of Pensions and National Security in 1961, the Secretary of State for Education in 1970, leader of the Conservative Party in 1975, and finally, prime minister in 1979.

Golda Meir, the first and only woman prime minister of Israel, was clearly a political insider. Her government service to Israel began in the state's formative years. As a teenager in the United States, she became a Zionist, organizing and raising funds for an independent Jewish state in Palestine. In 1921, she moved to Palestine. For a time, she lived on a kibbutz, a communal experience dedicated to Zionism. In 1928, she took a position as secretary of the Women's Labor Council. Meir raised hundreds of millions of dollars for the fledging Israeli state. She spent a good part of the 1930s and 1940s traveling the world raising funds for the Jewish settlers in Palestine. She was active in the formation of the Mapai political party and served in many positions. She was responsible for settling the thousands of immigrants arriving from Europe in the late 1940s and orchestrated the building of thousands of homes. She served as the first Israeli ambassador to the Soviet Union, secretary of labor, foreign minister, head of the Mapai Party, and, finally, in 1970, as prime minister.

The first women who took the insider path to power appeared to function as "honorary males." They dismissed the relevance of gender to their leadership and saw themselves as one of the political "boys." Indira Gandhi once said, "As Prime Minister, I am not a woman. I am a human being" (quoted in Everett, 1993). Golda Meir (1975) said, "The fact is that I have lived and worked with men all my life, but being a woman has never hindered me in any way at all. It has never caused me unease or given me an inferiority complex or made me think that men are better off than women—or that it is a disaster to give birth to children. Not at all." Perhaps without these attitudes, these women would not have been able to rise through the party ranks.

Many women executives come to power under unique sociohistorical circumstances, entering office during transitions to national independence or democratic governance, party instability, or the opening of political opportunity due to the sudden removal, resignation, or death of an executive (Jalalzai, 2008). Many are compromise candidates in the case of a divided political party (D'Amico, 1995). For example, it is generally agreed that Indira Gandhi may not have come to power at all were it not for the unexpected death of Prime Minister Lal Bahadur Shastri, a divided political party, and a desire to prevent a particular individual (Morarji Desia) from becoming prime minister (Carras, 1995; Everett, 1993). Likewise, Margaret Thatcher became head of the Conservative political party because the person expected to run for the post refused to run, and there was a shortage of qualified competitors (Genovese, 1993). Like Thatcher, Golda Meir probably would not have become prime minister of Israel in 1970 were it not for some unusual circumstances. Israel's Prime Minister Levi Eskol died suddenly from a heart attack when Israel was on the verge of war with Egypt, and disagreements within Eskol's coalition cabinet prevented the selection of a leader from the cabinet. It made sense to appoint the steady Meir as an interim prime minister rather than engage in political infighting when Israel was on the verge of war.

Some recent examples of the tendency for women to come to power in cases of divided parliaments or parties include Han Myung-Sook and Angela Merkel. South Korea's first woman prime minister, Han Myung-Sook, elected by parliament in 2006, was a bipartisan compromise selected to mediate a bitter relationship between government and opposition parties (she served one year and was later convicted of receiving illegal donations). Merkel, the first female Chancellor of Germany (the head of Germany), was trained as a physicist and chemist. An East German, she got involved in German politics in 1989 after the fall of the Berlin Wall and the reunification of East and West Germany. She held a variety of elected and appointed positions in government and worked her way up her party's hierarchy. In 2005, she was elected by the majority of delegates in the Bundestag (Germany's parliament), where she was a compromise candidate following a major scandal in her political party that caused party leaders to step down. Considered one of the most powerful people in the world, she has served three terms and won a fourth term in 2017. Merkel chose not to run for a fifth term.

Some women come to power as their countries recover from brutal dictatorships and corrupt governments, or as their government transitions to democracy. These women seem to benefit from a combination of government service experience and a past history of activism in pro-democratic or anti-corruption movements. This seems to increase people's trust that they will serve democratic ends rather than use their power for personal gain and political repression. President Michelle Bachelet, the first woman president of Chile, is an example. First elected as president to serve from 2006 to 2010 and elected again in 2014, this pediatrician and epidemiologist with advanced education in military defense never served in Parliament. Her party chose her to run because of her popularity with the electorate, her visible and successful performance in both the Minister of Health and Defense Minister roles, her personal history as a political prisoner under the dictator Pinochet, and her expertise in the effects of trauma due to political oppression (helpful in a country still recovering from a brutal dictatorship). In Chile, where differences between women and men are taken for granted, the qualities attributed to women include generosity, a commitment to service, an interest in the common good, little ambition for power or wealth, incorruptibility, and closeness to citizens' concerns; these qualities appealed to the Chilean people who sought an incorruptible leader who was interested more in the nation than in petty party concerns (Rios Tobar, 2008). After her first term (2010), Bachelet served as the first executive director of the newly created UN Women and after her second term ended in 2018, she became the UN High Commissioner of Human Rights.

Like Bachelet, Ellen Johnson Sirleaf, elected by popular vote in 2005 as Liberia's first woman president and Africa's first woman elected head of state, also benefited from a combination of leadership experience and participation in the pro-democracy movement. Her election exemplifies that many women executives

"You can much better have an influence on the debate when you sit at the bargaining table and can give input."
Angela Merkel, Chancellor of Germany

"I think when women have equal qualifications, experience, capacities, they bring to the task a certain dimension that may be missing in men—a sensitivity to humankind. Maybe it comes from being a mother."
Ellen Johnson Sirleaf, President of Liberia and Africa's first elected woman president (2006)

No African women heads of state or government have traveled the surrogate path to power.

come to power following political instability and corruption. She came to power after Liberia experienced 23 years of political repression, corruption, and civil conflict. Johnson Sirleaf had served as Liberia's Finance Minister, worked for the UNDP, the World Bank, and for Citibank in senior positions. As Finance Minister, she became known for challenging the government's economic policies and corruption, and did prison time for speaking out. During the election, she capitalized on perceptions that women in Liberia were peacemakers rather than those responsible for sparking and prolonging the conflict, and she took a strong stance against corruption, building on the widespread view that women are less corrupt than men (Adams, 2008). Johnson Sirleaf served as Liberian president from 2006 to 2018. After her presidency, she went to work for the World Health Organization. She also founded the EJS Center, which promotes women's leadership roles in Africa.

Gender Differences in Leadership

"I don't think we should put the case for women's leadership on the foundation stone that women leaders are always better, because if we do that, we are baking the sexism in . . . And if we set up those differential hurdles, he's only got to be OK, but she's got to be amazing."
Julia Gillard, first woman Prime Minister of Australia (2010–2013), current Chairwoman of the Global Institute for Women's Leadership

People that believe aggressiveness and authoritarianism are male traits often assume that women world leaders will govern in a more peaceful and democratic way than do male leaders. Gender stereotypes that suggest that women are more selfless and other-centered have also led people to assume that women are less likely to abuse their power. However, none of this is necessarily true. Women heads of state and government vary, just as men leaders do. Their policy agendas and styles of leadership are diverse and often challenge gender-based notions of feminine values and behavior (D'Amico, 1995). Like some men leaders, some women leaders are aggressive and dominant. Also, contrary to our images of women as nurturers and peacemakers, women leaders are not less likely to use their militaries to resolve conflicts. Many of the women profiled in this chapter did not hesitate to use the military against domestic protesters or go to war to defend territorial interests. Indeed, Fraser (1988) suggests that many women leaders "have found in the crucible of war—if successfully survived—the fiery process which has guaranteed them passage into the realms of honorary men" (p. 10). Unfortunately, there are also corrupt or unethical women political leaders who did not use their power for the democratic good. Electing or appointing women to leadership positions won't necessarily clean up a government. Effective checks and balances on power are needed (democratic and transparent politics), whatever the gender of politicians.

"Women are not inherently passive or peaceful. We're not inherently anything but human."
Robin Morgan, global feminist and writer, a founder of the Women's Media Center

The world's first woman prime minister, Sirimavo Bandaranaike of Sri Lanka, increased defense spending, bought armaments from all over the world, and used them to control rebellion against her government. The military was used to squash ultra-leftists, who felt Bandaranaike was not moving quickly enough, and to combat the Tamils, a minority group that revolted when she decreed Buddhism the national religion and Sinhalese the national language. Indira Gandhi oversaw the most ambitious program of military buildup in India's history, presided over India's first underground nuclear explosion, built up the navy to become the principal naval power in the region, and went to war with Pakistan over East Pakistan's desire to become an independent state (Bangladesh).

Margaret Thatcher sent British forces to the Falkland Islands in 1982 to reclaim them from the Argentinean government. She did not hesitate to use the police in strike situations and showed little sympathy for the citizens injured (Genovese, 1993). Eugenia Charles, prime minister of Dominica, appealed to U.S. president Ronald Reagan for assistance in invading Grenada in 1983 following a political coup there. Golda Meir was quite willing to use force in conflicts with Israel's neighbors, seeing it as necessary to the establishment and preservation of a Jewish state in Palestine. As foreign minister, she was ready to use force against Egypt in 1956, and she supported the Six-Day War of 1967 with Egypt.

Tansu Ciller, the first female prime minister of Turkey (1993–1995), is yet another example that women leaders are often no more gentle, peaceful, and ethical than male leaders. While Ciller was prime minister, tensions between Greece and Turkey over the island of Cyprus escalated following the killing of a Greek protester who had tried to tear down a Turkish flag on the island. Ciller reportedly warned that anyone who tried to tear down the Turkish flag would have their hands broken. During her administration, human rights activists repeatedly called attention to the imprisonment and torture of political opponents and the evacuation and destruction of over 1,000 Kurdish villages. Ciller also introduced a law allowing the seizure and government sale of land that did not have a title issued since the last coup. Ciller personally benefited from such land seizures. Kurdish rebellion, economic instability, and charges of corruption led her to step down in 1996. Also contrary to the notion of women leaders as ethical is Benazir Bhutto, who lost her office amid charges of autocratic rule and corruption. Bhutto routinely bypassed parliament and awarded high positions in her administration to corrupt politicians, including her husband. In addition, many believe she was behind the death of her brother and political rival, who was ambushed and killed by police. In a country where the average person earned $1.18 a day, she proposed $1.1 billion in new taxes while she was in the process of purchasing a $4 million mansion in Britain (Dahlburg & Bearak, 1996).

Just as there are corrupt and unethical women leaders, there are women world leaders who fit the feminine image of peacemaker and ethical leader. For example, Corazon Aquino, president of the Philippines from 1986 to 1992 and a political surrogate for her martyred husband, Benigno Aquino, emphasized economic development and the peaceful resolution of long-standing internal conflicts (Boudreau, 1995). She granted amnesty to guerrillas, declared cease-fires with rebels, and released political prisoners (Col, 1993). Nicaragua's President Chamorro, much to the chagrin of the UNO party that ran her as a candidate, cooperated with the defeated yet powerful FSLN party. She did this by appointing General Humberto Ortega, a director of the FSLN, to be her senior military officer. By cooperating with the FSLN and the Contras, she undoubtedly quelled some civil strife. In a country torn for many years by civil war, she consistently advocated consensus and reconciliation over confrontation and vengeance (Williams, 1995).

A recent peacemaker head of state that has also done much to reduce government corruption is Ellen Johnson Sirleaf of Liberia. In a country scarred by 14 years of civil conflict (during which an estimated 200,000 people died) and a corrupt government, she created a national action plan for promoting lasting peace that focuses on the role of women as peacemakers and peacekeepers. She

"I have no experience in lying, stealing, or cheating like our male presidents have had. But then perhaps this better qualifies me to lead the nation well."
Corazon Aquino, the Philippines' first woman president, elected in 1986

"Having experienced personally and through my life the tragedy of Chile is something always present in my memory. I do not want events of that nature ever to happen again, and I have dedicated an important part of my life to ensuring that and the reunion of Chileans."
Michelle Bachelet

also emphasized the process of demilitarization, demobilization, and training and reintegration of ex-combatants. She was a founding member of the International Institute for Women in Political Leadership. Prior to her election to president, Johnson Sirleaf led the country's anti-corruption reform as Chairperson of the Governance Reform Commission. Sirleaf was awarded a Nobel Peace Prize in 2011 (along with Leymah Gbowee and Tawakkol Karman) for their peace-building work. Michelle Bachelet is also a peacemaker and brokered reconciliation between the military and victims of Pinochet's brutal dictatorship that lasted from 1973 to 1990. Over 40,000 Chileans were held as political prisoners and tortured. Bachelet's father was among the 3,065 citizens killed by Pinochet's military for political reasons, and she lived in exile in Australia and Germany. She returned to Chile in 1979 and in the 1980s fought for the reestablishment of democracy.

As the evidence currently stands, women leaders are also not more likely than men leaders to exhibit a democratic leadership style. Some are democratic leaders, but others are autocratic leaders. These leaders have strong convictions regarding the directions that their countries should take, and they believe that only they are qualified to lead their countries there. For instance, Turkey's Tansu Ciller (1993–1996) was described as combative, insensitive, arrogant, and power mad. In 2003, President Chandrika Kumaratunga of Sri Lanka suspended parliament and deployed troops around the capital while her prime minister and archrival Ranil Wickremesinghe was out of the country. She did this in part to signal her displeasure with his willingness to negotiate with Tamil rebels to end a 20-year civil conflict that had left 65,000 dead.

"Many women do not want to be mirror images of men in similar positions, but at the same time they must show authority or they will simply be swept aside."
Margaret Anstee, 1993, first woman to head a UN peacekeeping mission

Two best-known examples of women leaders who did not exhibit a democratic leadership style are Margaret Thatcher and Indira Gandhi, who shared the moniker of "Iron Lady." Their external gentle appearance was at odds with their shrewd and ruthless leadership style. Indira Gandhi, for instance, tolerated little dissent from political advisors and cabinet members. When threatened with public opposition, she imposed martial law and used the military against Indian citizens to repress dissent. For this she was ultimately killed. Gandhi authorized a military operation (resulting in at least 576 deaths) against a Sikh temple from which alleged terrorist activities were conducted. Several months later, she was assassinated by two of her Sikh security guards. Versions of the term "Iron Lady" are still used to describe women world leaders, who like Thatcher or Gandhi, are considered tough and assertive (Campus, 2013).

As the privileged and doted-upon daughter of a national hero, Benazir Bhutto was reputedly an arrogant and imperious leader who surrounded herself with family members who had proven their loyalty (Anderson, 1993). Margaret Thatcher was also known for an aggressive leadership style and chose cabinet members based on their loyalty to her. As Genovese (1993) says, Thatcher's style was highly personalized and imperious. She did not believe in listening to divergent viewpoints within her cabinet, nor did she believe in seeking consensus. She believed in getting her way and did it by arguing, bullying, intimidating, and threatening, and was unapologetic about it. Like Indira Gandhi, she chose her cabinet based on loyalty and obedience and regularly shuffled her ministers in order to maintain control. Although less extreme than Gandhi or Thatcher,

Golda Meir was known for toughness, especially in international relations. As an ardent international champion of Israeli interests, she became known for her confrontational style and her uncompromising opposition to concessions in the Arab-Israeli conflict.

In contrast, Corazon Aquino was clearly consensus-oriented and democratic in her leadership style. She came to power during a time when Filipinos were tired of the dictatorship of Ferdinand Marcos and longed for democracy. After 19 years of rule by Marcos, wealth and power were concentrated in the hands of a powerful few, and the people were angry. Cory Aquino represented human rights, civil liberties, ethics, and democracy. As leader of the Philippines, she sought to develop a political culture ruled by law, tolerance, and participation. In her commitment to democratic participation, she made decisions only after elaborate and lengthy consultations with as many people and groups as possible (Col, 1993). Although criticized as incompetent and indecisive, she remained committed to a democratic style of leadership.

Some people believe that there are no clear-cut gender executive leadership differences because women leaders are so aware of their precarious hold on power that they feel compelled to lead as men would. For instance, Carras (1995) points out that in time, this may change as the number of women leaders increases and as they feel less bound by the male rules of the current power game. Perhaps then the prediction that women leaders are more cooperative and community-oriented in their approaches will be borne out. However, the behavior of women world leaders may not be strikingly different from men's behavior because leadership, male or female, is more influenced by situational factors and personality than it is by gender. Similarly, the customary ways of gaining, wielding, and holding onto power may erroneously be believed to be male ways of power because males hold most power. If this is the case, the absence of a gender difference in world leader behavior is likely to persist regardless of women's increased presence in world politics. It may be that, regardless of gender, getting and maintaining political power often requires a certain ruthlessness and defensiveness.

Advocacy of Women's Issues

There is some evidence that adding women to existing power structures puts women's issues on policymaking agendas. However, this gender difference is unclear at the executive level, possibly because there is only so much women can do without the support of other political actors or because other issues, such as a poor economy or civil conflict, take precedence. Most women are also aware that being seen as a "women's leader" can quickly result in the loss of their already tenuous hold on power. Although Benazir Bhutto made women's rights a major theme of her campaign and in writings favored a feminist interpretation of Islam, she was nonetheless criticized by feminists as being more concerned with political power than with women's rights (Anderson, 1993). However, Islamic fundamentalism was on the rise at the time, and many were antagonistic to the idea of a woman leader—especially a Western-educated one. Furthermore, Bhutto's party did not have a majority in the congress, and there were laws

"And I know, in the depth of my being and in all my knowledge of history and humanity, I know women will struggle for a social order of peace, equality, and joy."
Joan Kelly, 1982

"I accept that women are gentler at the moment, but if they had the same amount of power as men, they wouldn't be more virtuous."
Lynne Segal, 1987

"As a woman leader, I thought I brought a different kind of leadership. I was interested in women's issues, in bringing down the population growth rate . . . as a woman I entered politics with an additional dimension—that of a mother."
Benazir Bhutto

"There is a special place in hell for women who do not help other women."
Madeleine K. Albright, first woman Secretary of State in the United States

limiting the prime minister's power. Given these constraints, she may have had little choice other than to soft-pedal her women's rights agenda.

Keep in mind that many women executives to come into office without "feminist consciousness" and that the political ideologies of women politicians vary (Montecinos, 2017). Some are members of conservative parties that place little emphasis on women's issues. Many are more loyal to their party than to their gender. Political insiders and "honorary men"—such as Indira Gandhi, Margaret Thatcher, Edith Cresson, and Golda Meir—advanced precisely because they proved to the party that they would advance a party line, not a feminist agenda. Margaret Thatcher once said, "The battle for women's rights has largely been won," and "The days when they were demanded and discussed in strident tones should be gone forever" (quoted in Harris, 1995). Her policies, which drastically decreased funding for education and social programs, disproportionately affected poor women and children, earning her the nickname "Maggie Thatcher the Milk Snatcher." As "honorary male" politicians, insider women seem no more likely than men politicians to encourage the appointment and election of women to political posts. For instance, Indira Gandhi appointed no women to her cabinet, and the number of women in the British cabinet decreased under Thatcher.

Hilda Heine, elected in 2016, is the first woman president of the Marshall Islands (and in the Pacific region). She founded Women United Together Marshall Islands, an NGO that worked to pass domestic violence legislation.

That said, it is increasingly common for women heads of state to come into office with a record of prior commitment to women's issues and organizations, and many have appointed record numbers of women to their cabinets. Women executives with ties to women's and feminist organizations and those that make campaign promises to women's groups and constituencies are more likely to promote women's rights and feminist policies (Schwindt-Bayer & Reyes-Householder, 2017). For instance, Michelle Bachelet kept a campaign promise to make her cabinet 50 percent women, a first for Chile. Han Myung-Sook, South Korea's first woman prime minister who served from 2006 to 2007 (she left to run for president but was not elected), was a feminist activist and pro-democracy leader before entering politics and is known as the founder of the Korean women's movement. Gro Harlem Brundtland, prime minister of Norway (1981, 1986–1989, and 1990–1996), appointed seven women of seventeen posts in her first cabinet and eight of eighteen in her second (D'Amico, 1995). She also extended maternity leave to 24 weeks, supported changing Norway's Constitution to include female inheritance of the throne, and was instrumental in the Labor Party's requirement that at least 40 percent of the party's candidates in any given election be women. Vignis Finnbogadottir, president of Iceland from 1980 to 1996, promoted feminist causes and had a long history with Iceland's feminist movements as a member of parliament (MP) and as a member of the Women's Alliance Party (Peterson & Runyan, 1999).

Women Political Executives and Gender Stereotypes

Women heads of state or government and women aspiring to these high-level government roles face unique challenges arising from traditional gender stereotypes. Viewed through gendered lenses, they may seem like a poor fit for the job because they do not fit the male leader prototype. As discussed in Chapter 5, "Women's Work," people often assume that in comparison to men, women lack the traits necessary for effective leadership. The traits associated with effective leadership, such as dominance, competitiveness, and decisiveness, are seen as natural for men and unnatural for women. However, evidence does not support the view that women political executives are less qualified for the job. Jalazai (2013) found that the educational credentials and political experience of modern women political executives are comparable to that of men executives. Despite this, women must often work much harder to overcome assumptions of their incompetence. Edith Cresson, prime minister of France for a mere 10 months in 1991 and 1992, could attest to this. Despite her credentials and experience, the French press repeatedly implied that she must have slept with President Mitterand to obtain the appointment. Gender stereotyped thinking may explain why women political executives are more likely to be appointed rather than elected, why they are more likely where there is dual headship of the government (both a president and a prime minister), and why historically many are found in relatively weak prime minister positions where they may be removed from office at any time by parliament or by the president (Jalazai, 2008, 2013; Paxton & Hughes, 2016).

Gender stereotypes often operate as social norms, so when women do demonstrate the "masculine" qualities associated with leadership, they are often subjected to gendered attacks and their ambition viewed as suspicious and unseemly. They must carefully demonstrate the masculine qualities associated with political leadership while asserting their femininity without confirming negative gender stereotypes (sometimes this is called a "gender double bind"). They must show strength and decisiveness without seeming too angry, emotional, or aggressive (Campus, 2013). Likewise, having violated their gender role by entering the public sphere of high-level politics, they are often resisted and undermined by gender stereotyped language and criticism (Yates & Hughes, 2017). Media coverage of women politicians reinforces the attitudes and beliefs that hinder women in politics (Yates & Hughes, 2017). Compared to male politicians, the personal lives, looks, clothing, hair, shoes, voices, weight, smiles, and make-up of women politicians are more often the subject of media coverage (Campus, 2013).

> "There were women who worked at the Prime Minister's Office with me who took all of the calls, and they would constantly get calls saying, 'I like the jacket she's got on today', 'I don't like the jacket', 'What on earth made her wear that necklace?' 'Don't tell me she's had her hair cut!"
>
> *Julia Gillard, first woman prime minister of Australia (2010–2013)*

Margaret Thatcher, the first woman prime minister of the United Kingdom, (1979-1990) was demeaned with such nicknames as "Attila the Hen," and slogans including "Ditch the Bitch" were used by those seeking to oust her (Geneovese, 1993). "Ditch the bitch" and "Ditch the witch" were also hurled at Julia Gillard, the first woman prime minister of Australia (2010-2013), and an opposing party's fund-raising dinner included the menu item "Julia Gillard Kentucky fried quail—small breasts, huge thighs, and a big red box" (Bates, 2015). Angela Merkel, head of government in Germany, has been called names including "man murdering power woman" (Paxton & Hughes, 2016). At the Republican National Convention in 2016, when Hillary Clinton was the Democratic Party presidential nominee, there were buttons for sale reading, "Don't be a pussy. Vote for Trump in 2016" and "Life's a bitch: don't vote for one" (Beinart, 2016). Donald Trump derided Carly Fiorina, his rival for the Republican nomination, by demeaning her looks—"Look at that face! Would anyone vote for that!" He called Democratic rival Hillary Clinton a "nasty woman" and tweeted, "If Hillary Clinton can't satisfy her husband, what makes her think she can satisfy America?" (Clinton's husband, former U.S. president Bill Clinton, had a widely publicized affair).

Women executives and aspiring executive candidates sometimes use gender to their advantage. For example, Ellen Johnson Sirleaf of Liberia campaigned with slogans like "All men have failed Liberia—let's try a woman" (Paxton & Hughes, 2016). Gender stereotypes suggesting that women are more ethical, honest, trustworthy, and caring than men can be political assets for women candidates in countries recovering from recent civil wars or authoritarian regimes (Yates & Hughes, 2017). But these same stereotypes seem to increase expectations of women's greater honesty and transparency such that they are held to higher ethical standards than their male colleagues (Jalazai, 2017). Many women leaders (and aspiring leaders) have faced charges of corruption and ethics scandals, and their mistakes are often magnified and distorted in an attempt to take their power. While this may be politics as usual and have nothing to do with gender, it may also result from resistance to women in these powerful political roles. The recent impeachments of Dilma Rouseff (Brazil) in 2016 and of Park Geun-hye (South Korea) in 2017, as well as Hillary Clinton's failed campaign for U.S. president, are interesting to consider in this regard.

Women in Informal Politics: Social and Protest Movements

"Everyone knows what a woman must suffer who undertakes to act against bad men. My reputation has been assailed, and it is done so cunningly, that I cannot prove it to be unjust."
Sarah Winnemucca, 1855, American Indian rights activist

Historians have often failed to record the important roles women have played in social protest, and women's informal political activity receives less scholarly attention from political scientists (West & Blumberg, 1990). But there's ample evidence of women's political activism, as you have seen throughout this book. Ordinary women act politically when they organize and put pressure on established power systems from the bottom up, and the results of these efforts are significant. Women all over the world are politically active and change world politics by their political agency (Peterson & Runyan, 1999). Sometimes women's informal political activity is an extension of their mother role (West & Blumberg, 1990). Traditional women feel justified in entering the public sphere of politics and often take political action when their families and communities are threatened (Lister, 2003). Although women participate in political violence as armed combatants and guerillas, more typically they are key actors and organizers of awareness campaigns and non-violent protests in the form of demonstrations, sit-ins, marches, strikes, petition drives, and boycotts (Murdie & Peksen, 2015; Yates & Hughes, 2017).

Unfortunately, violence as a consequence of women's social protest is well documented, and this punishment is frequently gendered in the sense that it may involve verbal sexual slurs, rape, sexual torture, and violence against their children (Amnesty International, 1990; Human Rights Watch, 2016). For example, in 2011 Egyptian women protestors during the Arab Spring (a wave of pro-democracy protests and demonstrations) were harassed, beaten, detained, shocked with stun guns, threatened with false charges of prostitution, and subjected to forced "virginity tests" by authorities (Rice, 2011). Within mixed-gender social protest groups, women also face sexism from their male counterparts, who often dominate decision-making and public speaking roles. For instance, although women were at least half of the Occupy Wall Street movement in the United States in 2011, they faced a daily battle for inclusion (McVeigh, 2011).

West and Blumberg (1990) suggest that there are four general types of issues that draw women into social protest: (1) issues linked to economic survival; (2) issues related to nationalist and racial/ethnic struggles; (3) issues addressing broad humanistic/nurturing problems (e.g., peace, environment); and (4) issues identified as women's rights issues. They also note that these might overlap—a protest of economic conditions may lead to a larger, nationalist struggle, as was the case when women's demands for food helped to spark both the French and Russian revolutions. Likewise, peace and environmental causes are often part of the agendas of feminist movements, and women's movements, particularly in the Global South, may connect their struggles as women to their struggles against racism.

The first three types of social protest described by West and Blumberg (1990) are examined next. The fourth type, political action for women's rights, is the focus of the next, final chapter of the book.

Women's Action Around Economic Issues

On April 30, 2008, more than 1,000 women gathered outside of Peru's Congress in Lima, banging pots and pans and demanding that their government do something about food shortages; similar protests occurred in thirty-four other countries (UNIFEM, 2009). In 2021 in India, thousands of women farmers held months-long protests near the capital. They demanded the repeal of new laws that eliminated minimum crop prices and benefited corporations at the expense of farmers. They also demanded recognition of their contributions to agriculture and inclusion in agricultural policy-making. As of this writing, the government suspended the laws but did not repeal them, and the protests continue (Bhowmick & Sonthalia, 2021). Women's protests in regard to economic conditions are one of the most durable and pervasive examples of women as political actors (Peterson & Runyan, 1999). Women have led and taken part in food riots, welfare protests, labor struggles, tenants' rights, and other similar actions (West & Blumberg, 1990). In Chapter 5, "Women's Work" and Chapter 7, "Women and Globalization," women's labor organizing around the world was noted.

Women also protest the profiteering of transnational corporations at the expense of their communities. For example, Nigerian women have staged a series of protests against multinational oil companies. Since 2002, they have taken over numerous oil facilities in their communities, refusing to leave until their demands are met. In one case in 2002, over 150 Nigerian women took over a Chevron facility for 8 days, resulting in a loss to the company of 500,000 barrels of oil a day (BBC News, 2002). They did not leave until Chevron promised to hire locals and build schools, water, and power facilities. In 2003, a group of eighty Nigerian village women, ranging from 25 to 60 years old, took over a Shell Oil pipeline station (Mbachu, 2003). Their action was precipitated by the company's moves to build a chainlink fence around the station—preventing the women from drying the vital local

"They said, 'you women activists and party members, you are all sharmuta [whores].' I said I work in what I believe. Then they started kicking me and one of them took his trousers off and started raping me." *Samia, who was picked up by Sudanese government security officers after handing out pamphlets calling for an election boycott*

. . . a political struggle that does not have women at the heart of it, above it, below it, and within it is no struggle at all. *Arundhati Roy, Indian women's activist*

"Every moment is an organizing opportunity, every person a potential activist, every minute a chance to change the world." *Dolores Huerta, Mexican-American labor rights organizer*

staple, manioc, in the heat of gas flares, an unwanted byproduct of oil. They called for employment opportunities, infrastructural development, and microcredit lending programs from the multinational corporation and accused the company of exploiting the environment and neglecting the country's poverty. The women occupied the pumping station after driving out employees and replacing the locks. Shell was forced to shut down facility operations, resulting in a daily loss of 40,000 barrels of crude oil, and eventually agreed to community improvements. In 2014, hundreds of women disrupted oil production to protest Shell's 2-year delay in implementing an agreement Shell made with the Peremabiri community (Vanguard, 2014).

Women's Action Around Nationalist and Racial/Ethnic Issues

"We are not myths of the past, ruins in the jungle, or zoos. We are people and we want to be respected, not to be victims of intolerance and racism."
Rigoberta Menchu Tum, Guatemalan indigenous rights activist and Nobel Peace Prize winner

Throughout history, women have initiated and joined protests and movements demanding liberation and equality (West & Blumberg, 1990). In the United States, for example, Harriet Tubman was a leader in the movement to free slaves. Black women were important organizers of civil rights actions, and Rosa Parks, famous for refusing to give up her bus seat for a white man, was a long-term activist in the NAACP, a major civil rights organization (West & Blumberg, 1990). Three American Black women, Alicia Garza, Patrisse Cullors, and Opal Tometi, created Black Lives Matter in 2012, an organization dedicated to anti-Black racism and reducing police brutality against African Americans. Women often organize Black Lives Matter marches, die-ins, protests, and other responses to incidents of police violence. In the 1980s and 1990s, Rigoberta Menchu Tum of Guatemala organized the politically marginalized Mayan population to resist military oppression and demand their rights. She also established the first indigenous-led political party in Guatemala.

Tawakkol Karman of Yemen, blogger and defender of democracy and freedom, and peace, leader of many struggles against tyranny and corruption, is the first Arab woman to win a Nobel Peace Prize, which she was awarded at the age of 32.

In many countries, women play key roles in organized resistance to authoritarian regimes and invading armies. Millions of women have participated in countless uprisings, guerrilla movements, and revolutions—ranging from the French, American, Russian, and Chinese revolutions to the more recent revolutionary struggles throughout Latin America, the Caribbean, Africa, and the Middle East. One example is the Argentinean group, Mothers of the Plaza de Mayo. A military junta took over the government in 1976 and began a terrorist regime in which an estimated 30,000 citizens (thought to be a political threat to the government) were kidnapped and killed (Feijoo, 1998; Navarro, 2001). People were taken without warning, and families were unable to obtain any information about the whereabouts of their loved ones, who came to be known as the "disappeared," or *desaparecidos.* The mothers (and grandmothers) marched defiantly and silently with photographs of their disappeared loved ones; they talked and made tapestries to share the truth about their loved ones; they used drama, speech, and other art forms to publicize their political message (West & Blumberg, 1990).

Iranian women were on the front lines of anti-government, pro-democracy protests in 2009. The face of an Iranian woman, Neda Agha Soltan, 27, who was captured on video dying of a gunshot wound from government forces, became the symbol of the opposition (Bazar, 2007). Thousands of women, including activists, housewives, and young women with no previous political involvement, participated (along with men) in citizen protests during the 2011 Arab Spring (Paxton & Hughes, 2017; Pedersen & Salib, 2013). Young women, like Esraa Abdul Fattah of Egypt, Libya's Danya Bashir, Lina Ben Mhenni of Tunisia, Tawakul Karman of Yemen, and Bahrain's Zainab al-Khawaja, played key roles as cyberactivists. They used social media to organize demonstrations, report on events, draw attention to the cause, and communicate with journalists.

Women's Action Around Humanistic/Nurturing Issues

Women have been leaders and mass participants in movements that address such issues as peace, environmentalism, public education, prison reform, mental health care, and hospices (West & Blumberg, 1990). Their actions in these arenas are sometimes extensions of their wife–mother roles. In Chapter 6, "Women, Development, and Environmental Sustainability," the role of women in the environmental sustainability movement was illustrated using the Chipko movement and the Greenbelt movement. In the United States, women like Lois Gibbs and Erin Brockovich have led campaigns against hazardous wastes dumped by corporations.

Women are the backbone of peace movements worldwide (Cockburn, 2007; West & Blumberg, 1990). In 1915, 1,500 women from twelve countries met at the International Congress of Women in The Hague to discuss women's role in ending World War I. They linked women's suffrage with peace, arguing that if women were allowed greater political participation, war would be less likely. After the meeting, envoys from the conference visited leaders in fourteen countries and called for peace and mediation by neutral countries. There is evidence that these women had a positive effect on the peace process (Stienstra, 1994). In the 1980s, women's activist antinuclear groups emerged in Australia, Canada, Holland, Italy, the United States, the United Kingdom, and West Germany (Cockburn, 2007; Peterson & Runyan, 1999). Their activism was often strongly connected to their maternal roles; you can't, they declare, "hug children with nuclear arms" (Strange, 1990).

Women's groups have also built pressure for peace talks and agreements in Sierra Leone, Liberia, Uganda, Sudan, Burundi, Somalia, Timor-Leste, the Democratic Republic of Congo, and the Balkans, although in many cases they had to demand inclusion in the peace process (Fleshman, 2003; Tripp et al., 2009). African women and women's groups have also engaged in grassroots peace activism, using a variety of tactics including rallies and boycotts and negotiating with rebels to release abducted child soldiers (Tripp et al., 2009). In 2002 and 2003, American women took a leading role in protesting the U.S. war in Iraq. Women in Black chapters held candlelight vigils all over the country to draw attention to the human costs of war. At protests, the women dressed in black to signify mourning for the war dead. Code Pink, a women's peace organization that uses the color pink in their demonstrations, staged creative demonstrations in many major U.S. cities and handed out "pink slips" to legislators who supported the war in Iraq. Some women's peace organizations seek the shifting of military and defense spending to social spending such as education and poverty reduction.

Women organize for peace in their communities and at the national and regional levels, but they are rarely a part of the official peace process from the start

"I believe the world gained lots of new insights from the Arab Spring. The first and most important lesson is that power lies in the hands of the people, not the rulers, even in a dictatorship. When people are angry, no one can face their anger. Women no longer see themselves as just housewives—they have rights for which they are going to fight."
Esraa Abdul Fattah, who used Facebook to organize a worker's strike now considered an important precedent for the Arab Spring protests

"What women want, God wants. Congolese women want peace."
Chant of Congolese women marching for peace in 2002

"Women more than men can strip war of its glamour and its out-of-date heroisms and patriotisms, and see it as a demon of destruction and hideous wrong."
Lillian Wald, reformer and peace activist, 1914

BOX 9.7 *Women Winners of the Nobel Peace Prize*

1905 – Bertha von Suttner (Austria) for her leadership in the European peace movement and her writings about the perils of nationalism and militarism

1931 – Jane Adams (United States) for her work in the international peace movement and on behalf of the poor in the United States

1946 – Emily Greene Balch (United States), founder of the Women's International League for Peace and Freedom

1976 – Betty Williams (Ireland), founder of the Northern Ireland Peace Movement

1976 – Mairead Corrigan (Ireland), founder of the Northern Ireland Peace Movement

1979 – Mother Teresa (India) for her work in bringing help to suffering humanity

1982 – Alva Myrdal (Sweden) for playing a central role in the United Nations' disarmament negotiations

1991 – Aung San Suu Kyi (Burma) for her nonviolent struggle for democracy and human rights

1992 – Rigoberta Menchu Tum (Guatemala) for her work on behalf of social justice and ethno-cultural

reconciliation based on respect for the rights of indigenous peoples

1997 – Jody Williams (United States) for her work with the International Campaign to Ban Landmines

2003 – Shirin Ebadi (Iran) for her efforts for democracy and human rights, especially the rights of women and children

2004 – Wangari Maathai (Kenya) for her contribution to sustainable development, democracy, and peace

2011 – Ellen Johnson Sirleaf (Liberia), Leymah Gbowee (Liberia), and Tawakkol Karman (Yemen) for their nonviolent struggle for the safety of women and for women's rights to full participation in peace-building work

2014 – Malala Yousafzai (Pakistan) for her struggle against the oppression of children and young people and for the right of all children to an education

2018 – Nadia Murad (Iraq) for her efforts to end the use of sexual violence as a weapon of war and armed conflict.

───────────

Source: http://nobelprize.org/nobel_prizes/lists/women.html.

"Shifting as little as 9.5 percent of global military spending to agriculture and infrastructure in poor communities could eliminate poverty and hunger by 2030."
UN Women

(WomenWarPeace.org, 2009). Although women's participation in conflict prevention and resolution improves outcomes, from 1992 to 2019, women were on average only 13 percent of mediators, 6 percent of negotiators, and 6 percent of signatories of major peace processes (Council on Foreign Relations, 2021). The UN notes that the marginalization of women from equal participation in peace negotiations denies half the population equal access to the political process and denies all people the benefits of having a female perspective in political decision-making. When women gain access, they often make a difference. For example, Mairead Corrigan and Betty Williams of Ireland won the Nobel Peace Prize in 1976 for their decade-long effort to stop the bloodshed between Protestants and Catholics; their work laid the foundation for a peace agreement (see Box 9.7 for other women winners of the prize).

The United Nations Security Council Resolution 1325 on women, peace, and security (adopted in 2000) is the first effort toward gender mainstreaming in the peace and security process. The resolution specifically addresses the impact of war on women and women's contributions to conflict resolution and sustainable peace. The Women's International League for Peace and Freedom (the world's oldest women's peace organization) coordinates the "PeaceWomen Project," which monitors and works toward the full implementation of Resolution 1325 and coordinates NGO efforts for including women in peace efforts. The group's web page includes contact information for hundreds of local grassroots women's peace organizations, national women's peace organizations, and international women's peace organizations.

Although some people assume that women's activism against war and for peace is because women are inherently more peaceful than men, their activism may result from the high costs of war they experience as civilians (Runyan & Peterson, 2014). These impacts of war include disease, hunger, being turned into refugees, and war rape. But worth noting is that while some women's activism against war and the military is associated with their maternal role, many mothers support the war effort. Not all women are maternalist pacifists opposed to war (Strange, 1990). Women, like men, are not innately peaceful and have always served militaries and supported wars (Peterson & Runyan, 1999). They also have a long history of fighting in wars, as women or covertly dressed as men (Sjoberg, 2013). Also, women take up arms and support national liberation struggles (Peterson & Runyan, 1999). In the first decade of the twenty-first century, women suicide bombers have killed themselves (and hundreds of others) for nationalist political causes in Lebanon, Turkey, Chechnya, Sri Lanka, Jordan, Iraq, Uzbekistan, Pakistan, Palestine/Israel, Kashmir, and Afghanistan (Rajan, 2016).

"Women's participation in formal peace negotiations (as mediators, negotiators, technical experts, and official observers) has a direct relationship to the content of the accords in terms of the inclusion of issues related to the rights and concerns of women."
PeaceWomen.org

Conclusion

Women's political rights have long been acknowledged in international human rights agreements, and although progress has been made, it remains true that in most places, men monopolize political space. Like other chapters, this chapter shows that the oppression of women is a sociohistorical and alterable phenomenon, affected by culture and context. Traditional gender stereotypes and gender roles affect both the demand and supply of women politicians. Political contexts, such as the structure of political systems and the development of new democracies, also affect women's political representation. The global women's and gender studies empowerment theme was also strongly evident in this chapter. Women have demanded their political rights and exercised them through social protest even when their numbers were low in representative politics. The ideas that the journey to gender justice is highly variable and a multicultural, contextual approach is needed were also in evidence. A country's history, culture, and political system greatly affect women's political participation and how they strengthen their political voices. Unfortunately, intersectionality remains a neglected topic in the study of women and politics. As noted by Paxton et al. (2007), research tends to compare women and men while ignoring distinctions among women. It is evident, for example, that in most countries, women from some economic and ethnic groups have more political rights than others.

The story of women in politics is a story of a glass "half-full" of remarkable progress, and "half-empty" with staggering disappointment. It is exciting that each year gives us a new first for women in politics—a country's first woman prime minister, first

"Women's equal participation in decision-making is not only a demand for simple justice or democracy, but can also be seen as a necessary condition for women's interests to be taken into account. Without the active participation of women and the incorporation of women's perspectives at all levels of decision-making, the goals of equality, development and peace cannot be achieved."
Beijing Platform for Action, 1995

woman defense minister, first national parliament over 50 percent female, and so on. In the last 15 years, many governments have pledged to reach a goal of 30 percent female representation. However, most governments and political parties have fallen far short in making changes that would fully include women. Gendered violence against women in politics is a problem. Also, too many women remain politically illiterate, unable to participate fully in politics and advocate for their rights. So, although there is room for cautious optimism, continued progress requires the transformation of the social structures and gender ideologies that interfere with women's full political participation. It also requires that women demand equality in the public sphere of politics.

Glossary Terms and Concepts

Critical political mass
Electoral reforms
Electoral system
Formal politics
Gender quotas
Gender realignment
Government cabinets
Head of state
Head of government

Informal politics
Mixed systems
MP (member of
  parliament)
National assembly
Party list/Proportional
  representation systems
  (PL/PR)
Political insiders

Political literacy
Political surrogates
Single member district
  systems (SMDs)/
  plurality majority system
Violence against women
  in politics (VAWIP)
Women's suffrage
Zipper (zebra) system

Study Questions

1. What are the main international agreements enshrining women's rights?

2. What are formal politics? What are informal politics?

3. What is women's suffrage? What was the first country to grant women voting rights? Which country most recently granted voting rights to women? How does women's voting differ from men's? What is gender realignment?

4. What is the global average of women's representation in national legislatures? What is the global average of women in government cabinets? What types of cabinet appointments are most common for women?

5. Why are women political representatives of symbolic importance? Why are they of practical importance? What is critical political mass? What factors increase the likelihood that more women MPs will translate into more pro-woman legislation?

6. How do cultural factors and traditional gender ideologies influence the supply of and demand for women political leaders?

7. How do the three types of electoral systems affect women's election? Why are more women elected under PL/PR systems? How do district magnitude and party magnitude affect women's election?

8. What are electoral reforms? Under what conditions are electoral systems changed to PL/PR systems? What role do gender quotas play in increasing women's representation? What are the three general types of gender quotas? How common are quotas? When do they arise? Under what conditions are they most effective? What criticisms are made of quotas?

9. What are the four non-electoral system strategies for electing more women to public office?

10. What is VAWIP? How does it affect women's pursuit of formal politics?

11. What role does feminist and women's organizing play in increasing women's representation?

12. How common are women heads of state and government? What kind of progress has been made in women's executive leadership? How much power do they have?

13. What are the paths to women's executive power? What personal factors are associated with women's executive leadership? What socio-historical circumstances are associated with women's executive leadership? What are the personal, socio-historical, and institutional factors that give rise to women heads of state and government?

14. Are women leaders more peaceful, ethical, and more democratic in their leadership style than men leaders?

15. How do gender stereotypes disadvantage women political executives? How are gender stereotypes sometimes used to their advantage?

16. What are some of the actions women take as social protesters? What four issues draw women into social protest? What are some examples of each?

Discussion Questions and Activities

1. Use the Inter-Parliamentary Union website to identify a country with low or high levels of women's representation in national legislatures. Conduct research to identify the ideological/cultural reasons and the structural/institutional reasons that explain the number of women MPs.

2. Quotas are one of the main means of getting women into political office worldwide. What is your position regarding the use of quotas to increase the number of women holding political office? Does your country have quotas? If so, what type and how did they arise? If not, why do you think they haven't been used to increase women's presence in national representative politics?

3. Do a biographical essay on a current woman president or prime minister. Analyze how she came to power using chapter concepts and explain whether she is an advocate for peace, ethics, and women's issues and whether she has a democratic leadership style. Answer questions such as how did she come to power? How much power does she have, that is, is she a head of state or

government? Is there any evidence that she experienced gendered political harassment or violence or extra scrutiny because of her gender?

4. Do you agree that were it not for the fact that women leaders must act like men to get and stay in office, gender differences in leadership would be more apparent? Why or why not?

5. The chapter suggested that many women political leaders (and aspiring leaders) routinely face gendered harassment and violence. Do some research to identify recent examples and to identify recent efforts to stop VAWIP.

6. Interview a woman politician or activist in your community. Develop questions based on the chapter. For example, ask her how being a woman influences the issues of concern to her, her leadership style, and others' response to her political activity.

7. This chapter focused on women's presence in national assemblies and as national executives. Do some research on women representatives in your local and state governments. How do the numbers compare to women in national office? How do you explain differences?

8. Minority women and women from culturally marginalized groups face even greater barriers to election to political office. Conduct research to discover whether this holds true for your government.

Action Opportunities

1. The online International Museum of Women showcases political women from all walks of life and across history. The site also includes a political action toolkit. Take one of the political actions suggested at http:/exhibitions .globalfundforwomen.org/exhibitions/women-power-and-politics/wpp-resources /toolkit

2. Do something to increase women's political literacy. For example, teach students how to use absentee ballots or help women run for campus elected offices by explaining the process. Or, share with your local or campus women's group different political tactics such as "tabling," petitions, and various forms of social protest that could be used to address an issue facing women in your community.

3. Participate in a campaign for a woman political candidate.

4. Women in social protest movements frequently face government persecution, such as imprisonment without due process. Participate in an Amnesty International letter-writing campaign on behalf of one or more female political prisoners (http://www.amnesty.org).

5. Become a political leader for an economic, racial, peace, or environmental issue. The political action toolkit mentioned above offers useful resources.

6. Help change the image of politics as a masculine domain by creating an educational display of women political leaders that is posted in a public place at your university or public library, or shared via social media.

Activist Websites

Amnesty International https://www.amnestyusa.org/our-work/cases/

Emily's List http://www.emilyslist.org/pages/get-involved

International Knowledge Network of Women in Politics (iKNOWpolitics) http://iknowpolitics.org/en

#NotTheCost https://www.ndi.org/not-the-cost

PeaceWomen http://peacewomen.org/why-WPS/what-can-you-do

She Should Run http://www.sheshouldrun.org

Women, Power, and Politics (online exhibition) http://exhibitions.globalfundforwomen.org/wpp

Informational Websites

Center for Women in American Politics (CAWP) http://www.cawp.rutgers.edu

Council of Women World Leaders http://www.councilwomenworldleaders.org/

Journal of Women, Politics, and Policy http://www.tandfonline.com/loi/wwap20

Inter-Parliamentary Union (IPU) https://www.ipu.org/our-impact/gender-equality

International Feminist Journal of Politics http://www.tandfonline.com/loi/rfjp20

International Institute for Democracy and Electoral Assistance (International IDEA) http://www.idea.int/our-work/what-we-do/gender-democracy

Politics and Gender (Research Journal) https://www.cambridge.org/core/journals/politics-and-gender

Quota Database http://www.quotaproject.org

Women Speakers of Parliament https://www.gsws.ae/speaker/

References

Abendschön, S., and Steinmetz, S. 2014. The gender gap in voting revisited: Women's party preferences in a European context. *Social Politics: International Studies in Gender, State and Society*, *21*, 315–344.

ACE Electoral Knowledge Network. 2021. *Country comparative data.* https://aceproject.org/regions-en/countries-and-territories/US/default?set_language=en. Retrieved on June 11, 2021.

Adams, M. 2008. Liberia's election of Ellen Johnson-Sirleaf and women's executive leadership in Africa. *Politics and Gender, 4,* 475–484.

Amnesty International. 1990. *Women in the front line: Human rights violations against women.* New York: Author.

Anderson, N. F. 1993. Benazir Bhutto and dynastic politics: Her father's daughter, her people's sister. In *Women as national leaders,* edited by M. A. Genovese. Newbury Park, CA: Sage.

Atchison, A., and Down, I. 2009.Women cabinet ministers and female friendly social policy. *Poverty and Public Policy, 1,* 1–23.

Bates, L. 2015, June 16. Julia Gillard's views on sexism in politics are about every women in every job. *The Guardian.* https://www.theguardian.com/lifeandstyle /womens-blog/2015/jun/16/julia-gillards-views-on-sexism-in-politics-are-about -every-woman-in-every-job. Retrieved on May 26, 2017.

Bazar, E. 2007, June 25. Iranian women take key role in protest; calls for equality during election energized many. *USA Today,* 4A.

BBC News. 2002, July 25. Nigerian women's oil protest ends. http://news.bbc .co.uk/1/hi/world/africa/2152264.stm. Retrieved on June 29, 2003.

BBC News. 2014, March 12. Bolivian women battle against culture of harassment. http:// www.bbc.com/news/world-latin-america-26446066. Retrieved on May 22, 2017.

Beinart, P. 2016. Fear of a female president. *The Atlantic.* https://www.theatlantic .com/magazine/archive/2016/10/fear-of-a-female-president/497564/. Retrieved on May 26, 2017.

Bernauer, J., Giger, N. and Rosset, J. 2015. Mind the gap: Do proportional electoral systems foster a more equal representation of women and men, poor and rich? *International Political Science Review, 36,* 78–98.

Bhowmick, N., and Sonthalia, K. 2021. 'I cannot be intimidated. I cannot be bought. The women behind India's farmer's protests. https://time. com/5942125/women-india-farmers-protests/. Retrieved on June 13, 2021.

Bonder, G., and Nardi, M. 1995. The 30 percent quota law: A turning point for women's political participation in Argentina. In *A rising public voice: Women in politics worldwide,* edited by A. Brill. New York: Feminist Press.

Boudreau, V. G. 1995. Corazon Aquino: Gender, class, and the people power president. In *Women in world politics: An introduction,* edited by F. D'Amico and P. R. Beckman. Westport, CT: Bergin and Garvey.

Bryant, E. 2003. Glass ceiling thrives in French politics. *United Press International,* 14 October.

Bystydzienski, J. M. 1992. Influence of women's culture on public policies in Norway. In *Women transforming politics: Worldwide strategies for empowerment,* edited by J. Bystydzienski. Bloomington, IN: Indiana University Press.

Bystydzienski, J. M. 1995. *Women in electoral politics: Lessons from Norway.* Westport, CT: Praeger.

Campus, D. 2013. *Women political leaders and the media.*United Kingdom: Palgrave MacMillan.

Carras, M. C. 1995. Indira Gandhi: Gender and foreign policy. In *Women in world politics: An introduction,* edited by F. D'Amico and P. R. Beckman. Westport, CT: Bergin and Garvey.

Center for American Women in Politics (CAWP). 2021. *Voting turnout by race.* https://cawp.rutgers.edu/facts/voters/turnout#NPGR. Retrieved on July 20, 2021.

Childs, S. and Krook, L.M. 2008. Critical mass theory and women's political representation. *Political Studies, 56,* 725–736.

Chowdhury, N. 1994. Bangladesh: Gender issues and politics in a patriarchy. In *Women and politics worldwide,* edited by B. J. Nelson and N. Chowdhury. New Haven, CT: Yale University Press.

Cockburn, C. 2007. *From where we stand: War, women's activism, and feminist analysis.* London: Zed.

Col, J. 1993. Managing softly in turbulent times: Corazon C. Aquino, President of the Philippines. In *Women as national leaders,* edited by M. Genovese. Newbury Park, CA: Sage.

Council on Foreign Relations. 2021. *Women's participation in peace processes.* https://www.cfr.org/womens-participation-in-peace-processes/. Retrieved on June 13, 2021.

D'Amico, F. 1995. Women as national leaders. In *Women in world politics: An introduction,* edited by F. D'Amico and P. R. Beckman. Westport, CT: Bergin and Garvey.

Dahlburg, J. T., and Bearak. B. 1996, November 6. Pakistani president sacks Bhutto and government. *Los Angeles Times,* A1, A26.

Dahlerup, D., and Freidenvall, L. 2008. *Electoral gender quota systems and their implementation in Europe.* Women in Politics Research Centre, Stockholm University.

Everett, J. 1993. Indira Gandhi and the exercise of power. In M. A. Genovese, *Women as national leaders.* Newbury Park, CA: Sage.

Feijoo, M. D. C. 1998. Democratic participation and women in Argentina. In *Women and democracy: Latin America and Central and Eastern Europe,* edited by J. S. Jaquette and S. L. Wolchik. Baltimore, MD: Johns Hopkins University Press.

Fleshman, M. 2003. African women struggle for a seat at the peace table. *Africa Renewal, 16,* 1.

Franceschet S., and Piscopo, J. M. 2008. Gender quotas and women's substantive representation: Lessons from Argentina. *Politics and Gender, 4,* 393–425.

Fraser, A. 1988. *The warrior queens: The legends and life of the women who have led their nations in war.* New York: Random House.

Genovese, M. A. 1993. Margaret Thatcher and the politics of conviction leadership. In *Women as national leaders,* edited by M. A. Genovese. Newbury Park, CA: Sage.

Giger, N. 2009. Towards a modern gender gap in Europe: A comparative analysis of voting behavior in twelve countries. *The Social Science Journal, 46,* 474–492.

Gutierrez, M., and Boselli, O. 2009, September 22. Politics-Italy: Where Are the Women? *IPS.*

Harris, K. 1995. Prime Minister Margaret Thatcher: The influence of her gender on her foreign policy. In *Women in politics: An introduction,* edited by F. D'Amico and P. R. Beckman. Westport, CT: Bergin and Garvey.

Hughes, M. M. 2009. Armed conflict, international linkages, and women's parliamentary representation in developing nations. *Social Problems, 56,* 174–204.

Hughes, M. M., Krook, M. L., and Paxton, P. 2015. Transnational women's activism and the global diffusion of gender quotas. *International Studies Quarterly, 59,* 357–372.

Human Rights Watch. 2016. *Good girls don't protest.* https://www.hrw.org/sites/default/files/report_pdf/sudan0316web.pdf. Retrieved on May 28, 2017.

International IDEA. 2014. *Atlas of electoral gender quotas.* http://www.idea.int/sites/default/files/publications/atlas-of-electoral-gender-quotas.pdf. Retrieved on July 20, 2021.

International IDEA (International Democracy and Electoral Assistance). 2021. *Gender quotas database.* https://www.idea.int/data-tools/data/gender-quotas/country-overview. Retrieved on June 11, 2021.

Inter-Parliamentary Union (IPU). 2003. *Women in national parliaments.* http://archive.ipu.org/wmn-e/arc/classif301203.htm. Retrieved on September 17, 2021.

Inter-Parliamentary Union (IUP). 2010. *Women in national parliaments.* http://www.ipu.org/wmn-e/classif.htm. Retrieved on April 13, 2010.

Inter-Parliamentary Union (IPU). 2016. *Sexism, harassment and violence against women parliamentarians.* https://www.ipu.org/resources/publications/issue-briefs/2016-10/sexism-harassment-and-violence-against-women-parliamentarians. Retrieved on September 17, 2021.

Inter-Parliamentary Union (IPU). 2021a. *Monthly ranking of women in national parliaments.* https://data.ipu.org/women-ranking?month=4&year=2021. Retrieved on June 8, 2021.

Inter-Parliamentary Union (IPU). 2021b. *Global and regional averages of women in national parliaments.* https://data.ipu.org/women-averages?month=4&year=2021&op=Show+averages&form_build_id=form-85fTupvKcZckS0JITjHyPLsuc2XEYwRmthkrd7oTgMY&form_id=ipu__women_averages_filter_form. Retrieved on June 8, 2021.

Inter-Parliamentary Union (IPU). 2021c. *Women in politics 2021.* https://www.ipu.org/women-in-politics-2021. Retrieved on June 8, 2021.

Inter-Parliamentary Union. 2021d. *Women in politics: New data shows growth but also setbacks.* https://www.ipu.org/news/women-in-politics-2021. Retrieved on June 9, 2021.

Inter-Parlimentary Union and UN Women. 2017. *Women in politics 2017.* https://beta.ipu.org/resources/publications/infographics/2017-03/women-in-politics-2017. Retrieved on May 13, 2017.

Jalalzai, F. 2008. Women rule: Shattering the executive glass ceiling. *Politics and Gender, 4,* 205–231.

Jalalzai, F. 2013. *Shattered, cracked, or firmly intact? Women and the executive glass ceiling worldwide.* New York, NY: Oxford University Press.

Jalalzai, F. 2017. Global trends in women's executive leadership. In *Women presidents and prime ministers in post-transition democracies*, edited by V. Montecinos. London: Palgrave MacMillan.

Jalalzai, F., and Rincker, M. 2018. Blood is thicker than water. *Historical Social Research, 43,* 54–72.

Johnson, N., and Josefsson, C. 2016. A New Way of Doing Politics? Cross-Party Women's Caucuses as Critical Actors in Uganda and Uruguay. *Parliamentary Affairs, 69,* 845–859.

Joshi, D., and Och, M. 2014, December. Talking about my generation and class? Unpacking the descriptive representation of women in Asian parliaments. In *Women's Studies International Forum, 47,* 168–179.

Kelly J. 2017. France elects record number of women to parliament. *Reuters.* https://www.reuters.com/article/us-france-election-women/france-elects-record-number-of-women-to-parliament-idUSKBN19911E. Retrieved on June 11, 2021.

Kittleson, M. C. 2016. Gender and political behavior. In *The Oxford Research Encyclopedia of Politics,* edited by W. R. Thompson. https://oxfordre.com/politics/view/10.1093/acrefore/9780190228637.001.0001/acrefore-9780190228637-e-71?print=pdf. Retrieved on June 8, 2021.

Krook, M. L., and Norris, P. 2014. Beyond quotas: Strategies to promote gender equality in elected office. *Political Studies, 62,* 2–20.

Krook, M. L., and O'Brien, D. Z., 2012. All the president's men? The appointment of female cabinet ministers worldwide. *The Journal of Politics, 74,* 840–855.

Krook, M. L., and Sanín, J.R. 2016. Gender and political violence in Latin America. *Política y gobierno, 23,* 125–157.

Lister, R. 2003. *Citizenship: Feminist perspectives,* 2nd ed. New York: New York University Press.

Mbachu, D. 2003, July 29. Women activists in peaceful takeover of Nigerian oil site. *Associated Press.*

McVeigh, K. 2011, May 30. Occupy Wall Street women struggle to make their voices heard. *The Guardian.* https://www.theguardian.com/world/2011/nov/30/occupy-wall-street-women-voices. Retrieved on May 28, 2017.

Meir, G. 1975. *My life.* New York: Putnam.

Molinelli, N. G. 1994. Argentina: The (no) ceteris paribus case. In *Electoral systems in comparative perspective: Their impact on women and minorities,* edited by W. Rule and J. F. Zimmerman. Westport, CT: Greenwood Press.

Montecinos, V. 2017. Introduction. In *Women presidents and prime ministers in post-transition democracies,* edited by V. Montecinos. London: Palgrave MacMillan.

Murdie, A., and Peksen, D. 2015. Women and contentious politics: A global event-data approach to understanding women's protest. *Political Research Quarterly, 68,* 180–192.

Navarro, M. 2001. Argentina: The long road to women's rights. In *Women's rights: A global view,* edited by L. Walter. Westport, CT: Greenwood Press.

Norris, P., and Lovenduski, J. 1995. *Political recruitment, gender, race, and class in the British Parliament.* Cambridge: Cambridge University Press.

O'Brien, D. Z., Mendez, M., Peterson, J. C., and Shin, J. 2015. Letting down the ladder or shutting the door: Female prime ministers, party leaders, and cabinet ministers. *Politics and Gender, 11,* 689–717.

Paxton, P., and Hughes, M.M., 2016. *Women, politics, and power: A global perspective,* 3rd ed. Washington, DC: CQ Press.

Paxton, P., Kunovich, P., and Hughes, M. M. 2007. Gender in politics. *Annual Review of Sociology, 33,* 263–284.

Pedersen, J., and Salib, M. 2013. Women of the Arab Spring: A conversation with Esraa Abdel Fattah and Lina Ben Mhenni. *International Feminist Journal of Politics, 15,* 256–266.

Peterson, V. S., and Runyan, A. S. 1999. *Global gender issues,* 2nd ed. Boulder, CO: Westview Press.

Rajan, V. J. 2016. Women suicide bombers (LTTE, Sri Lanka). *The Wiley Blackwell Encyclopedia of Gender and Sexuality Studies,* 1–2.

Rice, X. 2011. Egyptians protest over "virginity tests" on Tahir Square women. *The Guardian.* https://www.theguardian.com/world/2011/may/31/egypt-online -protest-virginity-tests. Retrieved on May 27, 2017.

Rios Tobar, M. 2008. Seizing a window of opportunity: The election of President Bachelet of Chile. *Politics and Gender, 4,* 509–519.

Runyan, A. S., and Peterson, V. S. 2014. *Global gender issues in the new millennium.* New York, NY: Westview Press.

Saint-Germain, M. A., and C. C. Metoyer. 2008. *Women legislators in Central America: Politics, democracy, and policy.* Austin, TX: University of Texas Press.

Schwindt-Bayer, L. A., and Reyes-Householder, C. 2017. Gender and institutions in post-transition executives. In *Women presidents and prime ministers in post-transition democracies,* edited by V. Montecinos. London: Palgrave MacMillan.

Seager, J. 2009. *The Penguin Atlas of women in the world,* 4th ed. New York: Penguin.

Sjöberg, L. 2013. *Gendering global conflict: Toward a feminist theory of war.* New York City: Columbia University Press.

Sjöberg, L. 2014. Feminism. In *The Oxford handbook of political leadership,* edited by R. A. Rhodes, and P. T. Hart. Oxford, United Kingdom: Oxford University Press.

Stevens, A. 2007. *Women, power, and politics.* New York: Palgrave Macmillan.

Stienstra, D. 1994. *Women's movements and international organizations.* New York: St. Martin's Press.

Strange, C. 1990. Mothers on the march: Maternalism in women's protest for peace in North America and Western Europe, 1900–1985. In *Women and social protest,* edited by G. West and R. L. Blumberg. Oxford, UK: Oxford University Press.

Swiss, L., Fallon, K. M., & Burgos, G. 2012. Does critical mass matter? Women's political representation and child health in developing countries. *Social Forces, 91,* 531–558.

Tripp, A. M., and Kang, A. 2008. The global impact of quotas: On the fast track to increased female legislative representation. *Comparative Political Studies, 41,* 338–361.

Tripp, A. M., Casimiro, I., Kwesiga, J., and Mungwa, A. 2009. *African women's movements: Changing political landscapes.* New York: Cambridge University Press.

UN Women. 2014. *Violence against women in politics: A study conducted in India, Nepal, and Pakistan.* http://www.unwomen.org/-/media/headquarters/attachments /sections/library/publications/2014/violence%20against%20women%20in%20 politics-report.pdf?vs=4441. Retrieved on May 17, 2017.

UNIFEM (United Nations Development Fund for Women). 2009. *Progress of the world's women 2008/2009. Who answers to women? Gender and accountability.* http://www.unifem.org/progress/2008. Retrieved on July 20, 2021.

Vogelstein, R. B., and Bro, A. 2021. Women's Power Index. *Council on Foreign Relations.* https://www.cfr.org/article/womens-power-index. Retrieved on June 8, 2021.

Vanguard. 2014, January 8. Half-nude women protest against Shell in Bayelse. http://www.vanguardngr.com/2014/01/half-naked-women-protest-shell-bayelsa/. Retrieved on May 27, 2017.

Wang, V. 2013. Women changing policy outcomes: Learning from pro-women legislation in the Ugandan Parliament. In *Women's Studies International Forum, 41,* 113-121. Pergamon.

Weldon, S. L., and Htun, M. 2013. Feminist mobilisation and progressive policy change: Why governments take action to combat violence against women. *Gender and Development, 21,* 231-247.

West, G., and Blumberg, R. L. 1990. Reconstructing social protest from a feminist perspective. In *Women and social protest,* edited by G. West and R. L. Blumberg. New York: Oxford University Press.

Williams, H. 1995. Violeta Barrios de Chamorro. In *Women in world politics: An introduction,* edited by F. D'Amico and P. R. Beckman. Westport, CT: Bergin and Garvey.

Wolbrecht, C., and D. E. Campbell. 2007. Leading by example: Female members of parliament as political role models. *American Journal of Political Science, 51,* 921-939.

WomenWarPeace.org. 2009. *Peace negotiations.* http://www.womenwarpeace.org /node/11. Retrieved on September 26, 2009.

Yates, E.A., and Hughes, M.M. 2017. Cultural explanations for men's dominance of national leadership worldwide. In *Women presidents and prime ministers in post-transition democracies*, edited by V. Montecinos. London: Palgrave MacMillan.

Design Element: Abstract floral frame: Telnov Oleksii/Shutterstock

10 Women's Movements

While gender subordination has universal elements, feminism cannot be based on a rigid concept of universality that negates the wide variation in women's experience. . . . There is, and must be, a diversity of feminisms, responsive to the different needs and concerns of different women, and defined by them for themselves.

—GITA SEN and CAREN GROWN of DAWN

Women's movements take many forms and employ many strategies, including public protests and marches. This protest in Istanbul, Turkey, in July 2020 was one of many protesting the high, increasing rate of femicide and government efforts to roll back legislation designed to protect women from gender-based violence. YASIN AKGUL/ AFP/Getty Images

Throughout the book, you have seen women's movements in action from the local to the global. By means of consciousness-raising and direct action, women's movements challenge and change gender-discriminatory laws, institutions, and cultural practices (Basu, 2017). By providing services and support, women's movement groups and organizations help and empower individual women and their families. This chapter takes a closer look at women's movements and how these vary cross-culturally and intra-culturally based on contextual factors such as history, politics, identity, and culture.

Diversity in Women's Movements

Women's movements are social and political movements characterized by the primacy of women's gendered experiences and women's issues, and in which women are the primary leaders and actors (Beckwith, 2013). They involve collective action by women and for women and use many tactics from the disruptive to the politically conventional (Kumar, 1995; Mazur, McBride, & Hoard, 2016; McBride & Mazur, 2005).

Women's movements are diverse because they are shaped by the time and place and the intersectional concerns of different groups of women. They emerge and develop under differing political, economic, and social conditions (Basu, 2017). Women's movements may be independently organized or affiliated with political parties; they may be of short or long duration; they may rest on a narrow social base or on multi-class coalitions; they may focus on one issue or multiple issues; and they may be local, national, or international (Basu, 1995). Women's movements arise in response to different issues and may focus on immediate needs or on gaining long-term rights. Movements arising out of **practical gender interests** develop in response to an immediate perceived need with the goal of reforming an existing system to address specific problems (Molyneaux, 1985; Peterson & Runyon, 2010). In contrast, some movements focus on **strategic gender interests** that arise out of an awareness of a generalized patriarchy and a desire to challenge and change it. However, a movement may begin based on practical interests only to turn into a struggle to defend women's strategic interests, and vice versa (Basu, 2017).

"Every country has women's rights groups."
Mahnaz Afkhami,
Iranian women's rights
advocate and scholar

Different Strands of Women's Movements

The women's movement is not a distinct organizational entity worldwide, nor in individual countries. In fact, women's movements show ideological variety and a range of organizational expressions (Katzenstein, 1987). There may be older, established branches accepted as the mouthpiece for women's rights and a younger, noninstitutionalized branch made up of small, loose groups outside of the mainstream, which build alternatives outside of government systems (Bystydzienski, 1992a). Even within a country, women's movements take many forms, employ many strategies, focus on women in general or specific groups of women, and vary in the issues they target. Consider this example from Alvarez (1994) describing the Brazilian women's movement of the 1970s and 1980s:

> Women spearheaded protests against the regime's human rights violations; poor and working-class women crafted creative solutions to meet community needs in response to gross government neglect of basic urban and social services; women workers swelled the ranks of Brazil's new trade union movement; rural women struggled for their rights to land that were increasingly being usurped by export-agribusiness; Afro-Brazilian women joined the United Black Movement and helped forge other organized expressions of a growing antiracist, Black-consciousness movement; Brazilian lesbians joined gay *dalitales* to launch a struggle against homophobia; young women and university students enlisted in militant student movements; some took up arms against the military regime, and still others worked in legally sanctioned parties of the opposition. By the 1980s, thousands of women involved in these and other struggles had come to identify themselves as feminists (p. 13).

Three major "strands" of women's movements (see Figure 10.1) are found in many countries: (1) women's rights activist groups that raise women's issues at the legal and policy level; (2) women's research and advocacy organizations that raise awareness; and (3) nongovernmental organizations that work to raise women's awareness, provide services, and mobilize women. These different types of groups often build coalitions to create change. Jahan (1995) describes these

FIGURE 10.1 *Three Strands of Women's Movements*

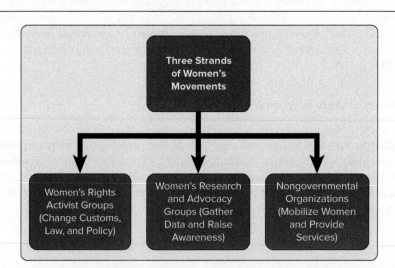

three major strands in Bangladesh in her discussion of campaigns to eliminate violence against women in Bangladesh from the late 1970s to early 1980s. Researchers documented violence against women, grassroots groups started intervention programs, and women's organizations pressured the government to enact laws against that violence.

Large, national organizations focused on legislative change are perhaps the most obvious women's movements, but despite their visibility, the vitality of women's movements lies primarily in small, local-level activist groups (Basu, 1995; Katzenstein, 1987). Recall that women's grassroots organizations (GROs) include small, local-level groups that provide services such as shelter to women experiencing intimate partner violence and groups that engage in local protests or awareness campaigns. Grassroots support organizations (GRSOs) are another type of nongovernmental organization characteristic of women's movements worldwide. GRSOs are nationally or regionally based assistance organizations, usually staffed by professionals, which channel funds and information to grassroots organizations. In every chapter, you have encountered examples of GROs and GRSOs that respond to women's issues.

Due to the diversity of women's movements, it is far more accurate to speak of women's movement*s* than *a* women's movement. Box 10.1 provides a sense of this variety. But while there are many differences between women's movements, there are also similarities. In particular, there is a common core of interests addressed by women's movements. These include reproductive, sexual, and maternal rights; violence against women and girls; and women's civil and political rights (Beckwith, 2013). Contemporary women's movements also share a focus on coalition building and intersectionality. They are most successful when they join with other movements and groups to contest unfair laws and policies and advocate for women's issues while maintaining their own objectives and identities (Basu, 2017).

BOX 10.1 *Diversity in Women's Rights Activism*

- In 1978 in Spain, as part of a national campaign in support of women on trial for having abortions, 1,000 women publicly proclaimed in a written document that they too had had abortions and should be tried. In a second document, both men and women stated that they had participated in abortions and insisted that they too be judged. Abortion became legal in 1985. Efforts to change the law in 2014 (making abortion legal only in cases of rape or if two physicians testified that

the mother's life was at risk) resulted in massive protests and led the government to abandon the proposed changes.

- Since 1991, the U.S.-based Center for Women's Global Leadership (CWGL) has coordinated the annual campaign "16 Days of Activism to End Gender-Based Violence," which runs from

continued

Box 10.1 Diversity in Women's Rights Activism continued

November 25th to December 10th. The first 16 Days Campaign was a successful worldwide petition drive demanding that the United Nations recognize gender-based violence as a human rights issue. Each year, the campaign has a different theme and offers an action toolkit. Over 6,000 NGOs in 187 countries and a variety of UN bodies have participated in the campaign.

- The National Women's Lobby Group (NWLG), formed in Zambia in 1991, aims to promote the end of laws and customs that discriminate against women, to increase women's education and political participation, and to put women in political decision-making positions. The NWLG intensely campaigns to get women's issues on the government agenda, forms alliances with other NGOs, and does outreach to educate women on their legal and human rights.

- The Sri Lanka Federation of University Women (SLFUW) was formed almost 80 years ago by a handful of graduate women. Today the organization's focus is on helping women graduates and undergraduates and on training programs to enhance women's employment opportunities. The organization networks with a number of other organizations both nationally and internationally.

- In Saudi Arabia, women protested for the right to drive and an end to male guardianship. It began in 1990, when forty-seven Saudi Arabian women protested the law prohibiting women from cars by

driving on the King Abdul Aziz Highway in Riyadh. By 2017, the campaign included social media (#resistancebywalking), online petitions, and videos where women are playing basketball, singing, and dancing, activities women are not allowed to do in public. In September 2017, the Saudi King announced the driving ban would be lifted in 2018. Women's rights activists' next plan is to target the remaining male guardianship laws that give males power over their female relatives and prevent women's independence.

- The Bahamas Crisis Centre (BCC), opened in 1982 by Dr. Sandra Dean Patterson, is an NGO based in Nassau, Bahamas. The BCC offers free counseling and legal assistance to victims of domestic and sexual violence. The BCC also works to sensitize the community to the effects of abuse and targets the beliefs that perpetuate gender-based violence.

- On January 21, 2017, over 5 million people (mostly women) in over 550 cities and towns in the United States and more than 100 cities in other parts of the world, including Kenya, Brazil, the Netherlands, Macau, Mexico, the United Kingdom, Georgia, Canada, Serbia, Australia, India, France, and Peru, participated in women's marches for reproductive rights, LGBTQ rights, and other social justice and human rights issues. In the United States alone, an estimated 3 million people participated, making the protests the largest in American history.

Not All Women's Movements Are Feminist Movements

In most countries, there are women's movement actors and organizations that identify as feminist. Although their feminisms differ, feminist-identifying women's movements are found all over the world. Box 10.2 summarizes some key characteristics of feminist social movements identified by the AWID, the Association for Women in Development.

But many women's movements are *not* **feminist movements** because they do not frame their work using feminist ideas and language (Beckwith, 2013). There

BOX 10.2   *Characteristics of Feminist Women's Movements*

Feminist movements:

- Have agendas built from a gendered analysis of the problem or situation they are confronting or seeking to change.

- Have a critical mass of women that form the movement's membership or constituency.

- Embrace feminist values and ideology, including gender equality, social and economic equality, the full body of human rights, tolerance, inclusion, peace, nonviolence, respectful spaces and roles for all, and so on.

- Systematically build women's leadership.

- Have gendered political goals (change that transforms gender and social power relations).

- Use gendered strategies building on women's own mobilizing and negotiating capacities, and involving women at all stages.

- Create feminist organizations with transparent systems and structures, consciously addressing the distribution of power and responsibility across roles.

Source: Adapted from S. Batliwala (2012).

are many reasons for this. One is that "feminist" is not always an important identity to women's movement actors and is sometimes seen as irrelevant to the work they do. Another reason many women's movements, organizations, and actors do not identify as feminist is that feminism has a negative connotation in many cultures. In some places, it is perceived as anti-male and anti-family (Chinchilla, 1994). In China, many young activists openly identify as feminist, but some women's advocates prefer the term "womanism" or "women's rights/power-ism" to "feminism" because it is seen as representing a less antagonistic view of gender relations (Xu, 2009; Zheng, 2017). Until the 2000s, African women's movements generally avoided the feminist label because due to the media and politicians, it was perceived as anti-male and a product of Western influence. Today, however, many African women, especially younger women, have embraced and redefined feminism for the African context (Tripp, 2017).

Feminist labels are sometimes avoided because they are considered politically unwise (Moghadam, 2015). They are also potentially dangerous (see the next section). In countries with a history of colonization (many African countries) or other antagonistic relationships with the West (many Muslim countries), the effectiveness of openly feminist organizations may be compromised by the public perception that feminism is a Western, imported notion (Keddie, 2007; Moghadam, 1991; Tohidi, 2017). Many women's movements also avoid the feminist label because the term *feminism* is associated with a narrow, Western view of women's issues and strategies. Western feminism historically ignored

"By naming ourselves Feminists, we politicize the struggle for women's rights, we question the legitimacy of the structures that keep women subjugated, and we develop tools of transformatory analysis and action. We have multiple and varied identities as African feminists."
From the first African Feminist Forum, Ghana 2006

"In its various guises and disguises, feminism continues to be the most avid manufacturer of gender consciousness and gender categories, inevitably at the expense of local categories such as ethnicity, seniority, race, and generation that may be more locally salient." *Oyeronke Oyewumi, Nigerian sociologist, author of The Invention of Women: Making an African Sense of Western Gender Discourses*

"This demonization of feminism as Western totally ignores the fact that for more than two decades, women of Asia, Africa, Latin America, and the Middle East have been creating their own contextualized forms of feminism and speaking about their rights and demands in their own voices."
Rosemary Ruether, American feminist scholar and theologian

"Power is not something people give away. It has to be negotiated, and sometimes wrested from the powerful." *Devaki Jain, Indian feminist economist, writer, and activist*

intersectionality, and to many Southern women, it was too singularly focused on the struggle against gender discrimination when their oppression cannot be limited to gender alone (Ghodsee, 2004; Johnson-Odim, 1991; Sekhon & Bystydzienski, 2001). Non-Western women may distance themselves from Western feminism for other reasons as well. They are often aware, for example, that Western women participated in the oppression of Southern women (Johnson-Odim, 1991; Kemp et al., 1995). It is sometimes difficult for them to think of these feminists as their sisters when these women received privileges on the backs of non-white women (Oyěwùmí, 2003). Some women's movements of minority women and women of color in Western countries eschew the feminist label for similar reasons.

Forces Operating Against Women's Activism

People are sometimes puzzled that women put up with gendered abuses and inequalities. They proclaim that it could all be stopped if women would just join together and stand up for themselves. There is a small truth in this—the system of patriarchy can function only with the cooperation of women. However, as Lerner (1986) points out, this cooperation is secured by a variety of means: gender indoctrination, educational deprivation, denying women their history of struggle and achievement, dividing women from one another, restraints and outright coercion, discrimination in access to economic resources and political power, and awarding class privileges to conforming women. In other words, standing up for women's rights is not such a simple matter after all.

It is important to understand the perils of women's activism and to acknowledge the courage of women who challenge gender inequality. One danger in speaking out is the possible loss of social belongingness and social approval (people may not like you, and may reject and shun you). The social costs of speaking out are especially severe in collectivist cultures that emphasize the subordination of individual goals for the sake of the community. In collectivist cultures, people's identity is strongly rooted in family and community. Speaking out for gender equality is that much harder in these cultures because individuals do not want to bring shame upon their family or community. However, even in Western, individualistic countries such as the United States, fears of social rejection sometimes inhibit people from identifying themselves as feminist or calling attention to sexism and gender inequalities.

Another reason why women often do not resist is that they do not see much point in defiance. Women often lack **self-efficacy** (the belief that their efforts will be effective) in regard to challenging the traditional gender order. Self-efficacy matters because if you are skeptical about your chances of success, then you are unlikely to try or to persist if your efforts are not immediately fruitful (Bandura, 1986). Self-efficacy is fostered by personal success experiences with the task, seeing people like you succeed at the task (role models), and receiving social support and encouragement (Bandura, 1986). Looked at this way, it is unsurprising that women sometimes put up with gender inequality. Many girls and women learn early that efforts to rebel are unlikely to be successful. This is especially true in cultures with rigid gender roles, and in countries where freedom of speech (including a free press) and freedom of political assembly (e.g., political meetings, organizations, and rallies) are limited or disallowed by the government. Also in some societies, there are few successful role models of resistance. Instead, women see women rebels ostracized and punished. We must also consider that when there are few economic options for women outside of conformity to traditional roles, and punishment is the likely result of deviation, the loved ones of potential "rebels" encourage conformity. Women's NGOs and GRSOs often foster self-efficacy by providing advocacy and activism skills training as well as examples of successful activism and activists.

Also remember that because women's rights activists challenge traditional notions of family and gender roles, they are often targeted with violence and harassment (UNOHCHR, 2020). They are regularly detained, interrogated, slandered, attacked, beaten, jailed, and killed. Examples are found throughout this book but here are a few more:

- A few weeks prior to the lifting of the ban on women driving (in 2018), the Saudi government arrested, jailed, and abused the women's activists that campaigned against the ban. Some activists remain in jail (Zayadin & Youseff, 2020).
- In 2021, women's rights advocacy groups in Poland received death and bomb threats for protesting government efforts to restrict reproductive and LGBT+ rights and the government's plans to withdraw from a European treaty focused on reducing violence against women. Police declined to investigate (Human Rights Watch, 2021).
- Tens of thousands of women protested in Mexico in 2020 and 2021 demanding government action to end unchecked violence against women and girls. Police harassed protesters with violent and sexualized language. Some of those arrested were threatened and subjected to physical and sexual violence. Thousands also protested by going on strike, their absences intended to remind people of the murdered women that "disappear" every year. Meanwhile, the President tried to discredit the protesters (Amnesty International, 2021; Villegas, 2020).
- AWID (Association for Women in Development) provides biographies of some of the women's rights advocates murdered every year.
- Box 10.3 highlights Malala Yousafzai, who was shot in Pakistan for advocating for the education of girls.

The amazing thing, then, is not that women don't always protest gender injustice, but that *they often do.* Indeed, in every society, in every generation, there have been efforts by women to fight their lower status. For instance, in nineteenth-century Persia (now Iran), Fatimah Umm Salamih fought for the equality of women. Murdered in 1852, thrown in a well, and covered with rocks, her last words were recorded as "You can kill me as soon as you like, but you cannot stop the emancipation of women" (Tomasevski, 1993).

"Believe not those who say the upward path is smooth,

Lest thou should stumble on the way

And faint before the truth."

Anne Brontë (1820–1849), British writer

"Self-belief does not necessarily ensure success, but self-disbelief assuredly spawns failure."
Albert Bandura, American psychologist

"Our hands are empty, our homes are made of glass; there is a knot in our throats and no time to cry; our sisters are in jail; our days are filled with danger, and yet forever, until these laws change, we will leave traces of even more signatures on the campaign's petition."
Nafiseh Azad, Campaign for Equality activist (the petition demands equal rights for women in Iran)

BOX 10.3 *Activist Profile: Malala Yousafzai*

By now it is likely that you've heard of Malala Yousafzai. Malala is an example of how advocates for girls' and women's rights face danger for their advocacy, and how they persist despite it.

Born in 1997 in Mingora, Pakistan, Malala's parents believed girls should have the same educational opportunities as boys and provided her an education (many parents and authorities in rural Pakistan do not share this belief). But in 2008, when she was eleven, the Taliban took control of her village and banned the education of girls. Malala began her activism soon after. She began blogging for the BBC in 2009, writing about the Taliban's efforts to deny girls the right to education. Her advocacy led to accolades, including Pakistan's Youth Peace Prize in 2011. But in 2012, she was shot in the face by a Taliban agent as she returned from school. She was airlifted to England in critical condition, and after several surgeries and a lengthy recovery, she and her family made a new home in the United Kingdom.

In 2013, nine months after the shooting, Malala gave a speech to the United Nations, saying that, "The terrorists thought they would change our aims and stop our ambitions, but nothing changed in my life except this: Weakness, fear, and hopelessness died. Strength, power, and courage were born . . . They are afraid of women . . . Let us pick up our books and pens. They are our most powerful weapons." She also published her first book in 2013, *I Am Malala,* which became a best-seller.

In the years that followed, Malala completed high school and college at Oxford, where she majored in philosophy, politics, and economics. She wrote two more books, and a film was made about her life.

Today Malala promotes education for girls through the Malala Fund. But she still stirs controversy in her native Pakistan where some do not see her as a feminist hero but as a stooge for the West who denigrates religious values. In 2021, the hashtag #ShameOnMalala trended after she gave an interview where she questioned the need for marriage.

_____

Sources: Hadid, 2021; Kettler, 2014; Malala Fund, 2021; NobelPrize.org, 2014.

Contextual Influences on Women's Movements

"Because of cultural and historical differences, it would be naïve to assume that Indian women fight for change in the same ways American and European women did."
Mangala Subramaniam, sociologist

Scholars from the United States, Canada, and Western Europe were the first to study women's movements, and they focused on the Global North and rarely on movements in postcolonial countries (Basu, 1995). Using the more visible women's movements in their own countries as their guide, their analyses of women's movements often overemphasized the role of middle-class women, the role of economic development, and particular types of activities such as a focus on reproductive rights. Today's scholars recognize the long history of struggle for women's equality in the Middle East; Latin America; Asia; Africa; and Central, Eastern, and South Eastern Europe (Basu, 2017; Bystydzienski, 1992a; de Haan, Daskalova, & Loutfi, 2006; Tripp, 2017). They understand that women's movements are diverse not only due to intersectionality, but also because they arise in a variety of circumstances and are affected by unique cultural and political contexts.

Local Political and Economic Conditions

Local political and economic conditions affect women's movements, both positively and negatively, and as these conditions change, women's movements change also. On the positive side, women's movements frequently arise out of other political struggles. These include working-class struggles, movements opposing state repression, fights against colonialism or neocolonialism, and civil rights struggles. For instance, Nigeria's first women's activist association, the National Women's Union, was founded in 1947 by Funmilayo Ransome-Kuti and represented over 100,000 women who protested the colonial power's taxation policies and those prohibiting assembly (Tripp, 2017; Tripp et al., 2009). What initially motivates many women to organize is not necessarily a belief in the distinctive nature of their problems but rather a sense of shared oppression with other groups that have been denied their rights (Basu, 1995). West and Blumberg (1990) suggest that women's consciousness is also raised when they begin to see the contradictions in ignoring their own oppression while fighting other injustices. They add that in the course of participating in these other struggles, women also gain valuable leadership training, skills, and confidence.

On the negative side, gender equality is often subordinated to other political and economic issues. Reforms intended to promote gender equality are often given a low priority while other pressing social and economic matters are attended to. Women's rights can seem like a luxury when the majority of people are struggling for basic survival (Margolis, 1993; Matynia, 1995). For example, Chowdhury (1994) states that women's issues are not perceived as major issues in Bangladesh, hidden as they are behind the country's poverty and underdevelopment. In Eastern Europe, the transition to market economies created inflation and unemployment for both genders, and many women's issues are subordinated to these economic concerns (Aulette, 2001; Ghodsee, 2004; Gottlick, 2001).

War also typically causes struggles for women's rights to be put on hold. To illustrate, from the early 1900s until 1937, the women's movement was strong in Japan. Women such as Kishida Toshiko, Fukuda Hideko, Ishimoto Shizue, and Ichikawa Fusae spoke against the oppression of women, advocated for women's rights, organized women's groups, and joined political parties (Ling & Matsumo, 1992). However, when Japan invaded China, the Japanese women's movement was prohibited, feminist leaders were forced to cooperate with the war effort, and those who persisted in feminist organizing were arrested and some got killed (Fujieda, 1995; Ling & Matsumo, 1992). Likewise, during times of political turmoil and repression, women's issues activism is often marginalized and subordinated to the cause of national liberation (Acosta-Belen & Bose, 1995). For example, in Iran, in the late 1970s through the 1980s, women's demands for equal rights coincided with anti-colonial and nationalist discourses; any criticism of the patriarchal aspects of Muslim culture were seen as betrayals (Mir-Hosseini, 2001).

In repressive states where the vast majority of men also experience oppression, it is difficult for women to present a case that they are particularly oppressed (Bystydzienski, 1992b). Under Soviet communism, Polish, Hungarian, Czech,

> "This is a common story in many women. We began with the social struggle, and little by little we moved toward the struggle of women." *Gilda Rivera, one of the founders of the Honduran Women's Organization Centre de los Derechos de la Mujer*

"Carving a shared
feminist space often
puts us at a difficult
position with respect
to our primordial tribal
affiliations. If we strive
to build effective
women's movements,
we cannot escape the
challenge of facing
our communities with
harsh truths about
the exclusion of,
discrimination against
and oppression of
women, all women."
*Samah Salaime,
Palestinian Feminist,
founder of NGO
Women in the Center*

"*Hum Bharat ki nari
hain, phool nahin,
chingari hain.*" ("We,
the women of India, are
not flowers, but fiery
sparks.")
Indian feminist slogan

and Slovak women *and* men felt equally repressed by the state, and the energies of every social movement were directed toward activities with the potential for large-scale change (Matynia, 1995). Kemp and colleagues (1995) describe a similar phenomenon in regard to Black South African feminism in the twentieth century. The state's systemic attack on Black people meant that the debate over issues of gender and women's oppression had to wait until the battle for national liberation was won. The Palestinian women's movement is currently hampered due to the Israeli Occupation of Palestine (Jad, 2017). It is nearly impossible for Palestinian women to advocate for women's rights when Palestinians are granted few civil rights by Israel and Palestinian statehood is the priority. It is also common for feminists to put their women's issues activism on hold to join nationalist or demo-cratic movements under the assumption that women's liberation will follow. This was the case in the Philippines from the 1950s until the 1970s as many feminists joined the movement against dictator Ferdinand Marcos (Santiago, 1995).

Women's Movements Arising from Class Struggles

India in the 1970s shows how women's movement organizations can arise from political movements focused on class inequalities. These include the Self-Employed Women's Association (SEWA), founded in 1970 in Gujarat by trade unionist Ela Bhatt; the Progressive Organization of Women (POW) of Hyderabad and the Stree Mukti Sangathana (Women's Liberation Organization) of Bombay (both of which arose out of the Maoist communist movement), and Mahila Samta Sainik Dal (League of Women Soldiers for Equality) of Maharashtra, which was associated with the anticaste *dalit* movement (Kumar, 1995).[1] In many Latin American countries, the origins of women's movements are easily traced to efforts by the working class to organize, unionize, and struggle for better wages and working conditions. In Chile, for example, women workers began organizing around both class and gender issues in the early 1900s (Frohmann & Valdes, 1995).

Women's Movements Arising from Nationalist Struggles

Women's movements sometimes arise in tandem with nationalist struggles. Historically, women have played important roles in movements for national liberation, and women's activists frequently promote women's rights in tandem with other nationalist struggles for freedom. One early example is Huda Sha'rawi, an important Egyptian feminist of the twentieth century who actively involved women in the nationalist debate against the British in 1919. Women's public participation in a nationalist march empowered women to take a more public stand on women's rights, including the formation of feminist organizations and political activities on behalf of women (Sherif, 2001). Sha'rawi founded the Egyptian Feminist Union, one of many Egyptian women's rights organizations

---

[1] Those born into the *dalit* or untouchable social class have the lowest status in India's caste system.

working in the first half of the twentieth century whose activism led to significant progress for women (Keddie, 2007).[2] Likewise, the rise of women's activism in India is traced to women's involvement in the nationalist campaign against British colonialism (Desai, 2001). In Egypt and India, women learned the language of political rights in the nationalist movement and insisted that the full economic and political equality of women be guaranteed by the new constitution (Desai, 2001; Sherif, 2001).

The involvement of women in nationalist struggles stimulates women's activism in yet another way. When women work hard in the battle for liberation only to discover the patriarchy within the very liberation movement in which they are working, their feminist consciousness is often raised. For example, Elaine Salo, of the South African United Women's Congress (UWC), recalls how the UWC was called upon to provide the tea and snacks at a national conference on the media instead of being a full participant (Kemp et al., 1995). Likewise, many leaders of the Bangladeshi women's movement became aware of gender discrimination as a result of the war for independence from Pakistan. Despite their role in the national independence movement, the new government marginalized women. They responded by organizing the first autonomous women's research organization in Bangladesh (Women for Women). Their reports on the status of women provided the basis for much of women's activism from the mid-1970s onward (Jahan, 1995).

Women's Movements and Democratization

The transition to democracy (democratization) often opens up new spaces for political participation, including women's rights and issues activism. Women often mobilize to ensure that new government laws, policies, and structures promote gender equality and address specific women's needs. But this is not always the case and, unsurprisingly, it depends on contextual factors.

Spain is an example of a country where democratization went hand-in-hand with a strong women's movement. The modern Spanish women's movement coincided with the 1975 end of a long struggle for democratic rule (Threlfall, 1996). Most of the movement leaders at that time were members or ex-members of leftist political and women's groups who had struggled against the authoritarian rule of General Franco. Under Franco, women were allowed to form "Housewives Associations," and these were used as covers by women's rights and democracy advocates (Threlfall, 2013). Following the death of the dictator in 1975, Spanish feminists pressured the newly developing government to include women's liberation as part of the task of building democracy and socialism. They encouraged the eradication of discriminatory legislation and the passing of legislation favorable to women. Women's organizations emerged throughout the country.

"If particular care and attention is not paid to the ladies, we are determined to foment a rebellion and will not hold ourselves bound by any laws in which we have no voice or representation."
Abigail Adams, wife of U.S. President John Adams, and one of America's first feminists

---

[2] Egypt's vibrant women's movement was suppressed following the assassination of Anwar Sadat in the early 1980s. Many of the gains resulting from the movement have since been reversed.

The developing movement was protected and encouraged by the fact that 1975 was the United Nations' International Women's Year (Threlfall, 2013). In 1983, the government set up the Instituto de la Mujer (Institute of Women), one of the largest women's public administrations in Europe, although it appears more effective in representing women's movement goals when a left-wing party is in office (Valiente, 2005).

South Africa is yet another example of how feminism may emerge in the space created by national liberation. The British and the Dutch colonized South Africa. By 1948, the Dutch-descended Afrikaners controlled the government and the country. The Afrikaans government restricted the rights and movements of all non-white citizens under a system called *apartheid*. All Black opposition parties were banned, and individuals who violated this ban were arrested. The majority of Black South Africans were forced to live in desolate "home-lands" called *bantustans*. They were not allowed to own property, and when in white areas, were required to carry passes proving they had permission to be there. It wasn't until 1992, following years of national and international protest, that apartheid was outlawed and a new constitution granted equal rights to all South Africans. Like the case in Spain, women's organizations in South Africa played an important role in the struggle for national liberation from the beginning. They organized protests and other grassroots challenges to the state.

As South African women's level of political awareness and experience grew, they demanded that women's issues be addressed in the national agenda. Having taken on co-responsibility for waging the political struggle, for sustaining and conserving it when it was really embattled, women expected to be included as equals in the new democracy (Kemp et al., 1995). Following the fall of apartheid, new women's organizations formed and old ones emerged from hiding. In 1992, the Women's National Coalition (WNC), representing eighty-one diverse women's organizations, was formed to ensure that women's rights were represented in the new constitution. The WNC successfully advocated for the addition of women's issues to the national agenda of the post-apartheid government. In 1996, the new South African Constitution, which provides equality between women and men as well as protection for lesbian and gay rights, was ratified.

The Philippines also fit this model of the newly liberated country sympathetic to women's issues. Like Chile, Spain, and South Africa, Filipino women played important roles in labor and liberation movements from the beginning (Santiago, 1995). Philippine suffragists campaigned in the Philippine Assembly, in the media, in schools, and at gatherings, and in 1937 they became the first women in Asia to win the right to vote. During the liberation movement of the 1970s and 1980s, *feministas* became an integral part of the struggle and insisted that a feminist perspective be part of the national agenda. In 1984, they founded a feminist political party and the feminist coalition GABRIELA. In 1985, when dictator Ferdinand Marcos declared victory in the national elections, feminist organizations were central in challenging the election results and affirming Corazon Aquino as president. The Filipino women's movement today consists of many women's organizations working on an array of issues, including reproductive rights, eliminating violence against women, protections for women working abroad, and the dismantling of

National Women's Day, a public holiday in South Africa, commemorates the 1956 march of 20,000 South African women who protested the extension of "pass laws" to Black women and their children.

"Twenty years are but the wink of an eye in the vast historical terrain of womankind's struggle for emancipation and liberation. The next 20 years will be another wink of an eye. But if we find the southward-flowing river, we can likely make the way easier and achieve the dreamt-of society sooner, with no backward sliding."
Ninotchka Rosca, GABRIELA activist

U.S. military bases. However, traditional gender attitudes, the Catholic Church, and poor economic conditions remain barriers to social reforms addressing women's issues.

Although the fall of oppressive governments may lead to the adoption of reforms favorable to women and to climates supportive of feminist activism, this is not always true. The countries of the former Soviet Union demonstrate this. The new "masculine democracies" that arose in countries of the former Soviet Union in the 1990s gave little space to women's needs, interests, civil rights, and organizations in the policy process (Molyneaux, 1996). In Russia, for instance, an independent women's movement began almost immediately following the break-up of the Soviet Union, but politicians (and the Russian Orthodox Church) favored a Russia based on traditional patriarchal values. Women that speak out about gender inequalities and violence against women are threatened and harassed. *Anna,* the association of women's shelters profiled in Chapter 2, was recently labeled a "foreign agent" by the Russian government. Meanwhile, the government supports "faux-feminist" events and organizations to give the appearance of caring about women's issues (Azhgikhina, 2017).

Initially, it is puzzling that the fall of oppressive governments in Spain, the Philippines, and South Africa led to positive developments for women's movements but not in the former Soviet republics. However, there are important differences. First, women's post-transition movements benefit from women's pretransition activism because there is a base of experienced activists and networks, and this prior activism legitimates present-day a feminist demands (Vitema & Fallon, 2008). This was true in Spain, the Philippines, and South Africa, where politically active feminists played key roles in the nationalist struggle. There were already a fairly strong feminist consciousness and a familiarity with political advocacy that was used to advocate for women's rights during the transition to democracy. This was not true in the majority of the Eastern bloc countries. Soviet communism collapsed unexpectedly in 1989, the collapse was not the result of a democratic movement of the people, and the Communist Party stifled women's pretransition mobilizations (Ghodsee, 2004; Vitema & Fallon, 2008). Indeed, the countries with the most active women's movements during the democratic transition (such as Poland) had a longer history of organized rebellion against the Soviet Union (Waters & Posadskaya, 1995).

Second, democratic transitions introduce new ideologies, and to the extent that these are compatible with women's rights, women's movements will have greater influence in the "design" of the new state (Vitema & Fallon, 2008). For example, unlike the Spanish democracy that arose during the International Decade for Women and the South African transition that arose out of a movement emphasizing equality for all, the new democracies of the 1980s and 1990s arose in a climate emphasizing free markets (neoliberalism) and minimal government protections (Molyneaux, 1996). Additionally, other countries (typically Western industrialized nations) with masculinist political systems often guide transitions, and the importation of these systems may not leave space for women's inclusion (Fallon, 2008). This was true in Eastern Europe, where new governments were not designed around an ideology of equality but rather around

Meena (1957–1987)
of Kabul, Afghanistan
dangerously
campaigned against
the occupying Soviet
forces, began a
feminist women's
magazine, founded
the Afghan feminist
organization RAWA,
advocated against
Islamic fundamentalist
views of women, and
established schools for
Afghanistan refugee
children in Pakistan and
microenterprises for
their parents. She was
assassinated in 1987
by the Soviet secret
service (KGB) and
their fundamentalist
accomplices.

"Men are used to the
old lifestyle so they
cannot tolerate that
women can stand up
to them. If women
stand and ask for their
rights, men think it is
shamelessness."
*Malfuza Folad,
executive director
of the Afghan NGO
Justice for All*

an ideology of the free market shaped by Western Europe and the United States (Ghodsee, 2004). Furthermore, in the former Soviet republics, much of the language of feminist ideology—emancipation, equality, and oppression—resembled the propaganda of the Communist regime (Cravens, 2006). Consequently, the very fact that the Soviet regime espoused the idea of women's equality was enough to bring it under suspicion (Molyneaux, 1996; Waters & Posadskaya, 1995). Many women even favored a return to traditional roles because "Soviet-style" gender equality forced women into the workplace without providing any relief at home and because the pre-Soviet past was romanticized (Matynia, 1995; Cravens, 2006).

Successful nationalist struggles may also interfere with women's equality when the ideology of the "winning" regime is a conservative religious one, incompatible with gender equality. This type of nationalism often seeks inspiration from an imaginary past and usually advocates redomesticating women and controlling their sexuality (Basu, 1995). Religious states and traditional women's roles are presented as necessary to preserve centuries-old cultures in the face of globalization and the importation of Western values and culture. The battle between those who desire a secular modernist state and those favoring a traditional religious state continues to be waged in many countries, including Algeria, Morocco, Iran, Iraq, Saudi Arabia, Syria, and Afghanistan. Who wins will greatly affect women's lives.

The traditional religious state won for a time in Afghanistan, where a nationalist religious movement succeeded in ending 10 years of Soviet occupation. Prior to that, chaos reigned for almost 9 years as the freedom fighters turned against one another. It was the nationalist Taliban group that brought peace. However, as you may recall, the ruling Taliban government enforced an extreme version of Islam that prohibited women from working outside the home, prevented girls from going to school, and required that women in public be completely covered. The Taliban was overthrown following U.S. intervention in 2001, but by the end of the decade, it regrouped and resurged. In 2003, the Loya Jirga's (Grand Council) draft constitution did not recognize women's rights as equal to men's, nor did it grant women the right to vote. Due to the activism of women's rights advocates in Afghanistan and internationally, the final version passed in January 2004 explicitly states that men and women have equal rights under the law, pledges to promote education for women, and guarantees women a place in government. However, the Constitution also states, "no law can be contrary to the beliefs and provisions of the sacred religion of Islam." Government officials and elected male politicians resist raising the minimum age of marriage, punishments for domestic violence, funding for women's shelters, and changing laws that imprison women for "morality crimes," including those who run away from their families or from forced marriages (Human Rights Watch, 2017). Forced virginity tests of women reporting rape or domestic violence or suspected of sex outside of marriage are still ordered by officials although they are supposedly banned (Nader & Mashal, 2017). Legal and cultural change occurs at a slow pace in Afghanistan due to entrenched patriarchy and concerns that women's rights are "un-Islamic."

In a recent significant setback for the rights of girls and women, the Taliban regained power. After 20 years, the United States withdrew its troops from

Afghanistan in August 2021, and the Taliban took over the government within days. They immediately rolled back women's and girls' rights in Afghanistan by restricting their education, and women's participation in government and professional work. Protesters calling for a gender-equal society are met with violence from Taliban security forces.

Iran is yet another case in which women's rights were significantly curtailed following a nationalist religious revolution. In Iran, a 1979 revolution led to an Islamist state. The new government restricted women's activities and rights, and Iranian women fought to regain the ground they lost (Mir-Hosseini, 2001). They did this by anchoring their arguments in favor of women's rights in the teachings of Islam (Afshar, 1996). They referred to parts of the Qur'an that favor respect for women and support for females' education and training, and to educated and powerful female role models such as Muhammad's wives Khadija (politician and businesswoman) and A'isha (politician and religious expert). By the 1990s, Iranian women successfully argued for the removal of many of the barriers placed upon educating women, women practicing medicine and law, and women owning and running businesses. They also successfully sought representation in parliament. Unfortunately, women still face pervasive gendered discrimination in law and practice. Iranian women's rights defenders are beaten by police at public rallies, detained and interrogated, arrested and tortured, and sentenced to prison (Amnesty International, 2017; Human Rights Watch, 2020a).

"Whenever women protest and ask for their rights, they are silenced with the argument that the laws are justified under Islam. It is an unfounded argument. It is not Islam at fault, but rather the patriarchal culture that uses its own interpretations to justify whatever it wants."
Shirin Ebadi, first person from Iran to win a Nobel Peace Prize

After the overthrow of Saddam Hussein by U.S. forces in 2003, Iraq struggled to design a government that would satisfy those preferring a progressive democratic government enshrining the rights of women and those desiring a government based on the precepts of a conservative interpretation of Islam. Initially, the U.S.-backed Governing Council passed a resolution that put family law under shari'ah (recall that shari'ah is Islamic religious law and is often interpreted in ways that promote gender inequality). Iraqi women's activists lobbied the Bush administration not to approve the interim constitution with this provision (Wong, 2005). Eventually, the Governing Council agreed to tone down the language to say that Islam would be *a* source of legislation, rather than *the* source. While women's organizations like Women for a Civil Iraq and the Organization of Women's Freedom in Iraq (OWFI) work for women's rights and assist women victims of trafficking and ISIS (ISIL), and the constitution requires that 25 percent of parliamentary seats be held by women, the situation for women in Iraq has barely improved. Entrenched patriarchy and fundamentalist religious influences create continued resistance to women's empowerment. In 2014, the government's ministers proposed a law to legalize polygamy, lower the age of marriage for girls to age 9, reduce women's rights in regards to divorce, and give married men the right to have sex with their wives whenever they wanted to (the law was protested and was not passed). Women cannot get a passport or leave the country without a male relative's permission. Iraq still has no laws against domestic violence, and charges are dropped against rapists that agree to marry their victims (Human Rights Watch, 2017, 2020b).

American Fern Holland, a women's activist who worked for the U.S.-led Coalition setting up women's centers across south-central Iraq and who helped draft the women's rights section of the interim constitution, was assassinated in March 2004, two weeks after the constitution was signed.

Box 10.4 summarizes the conditions under which women's rights are more likely to be part of new democracies.

> **BOX 10.4**   *Factors Increasing the Likelihood That Women's Rights Are Included in New Democracies*
>
> • The ideology of the new democracy emphasizes equality.
>
> • The new state is not a religious state, or one strongly influenced by conservative religious leaders.
>
> • Women were active in the fight for democracy.
>
> • There is feminist consciousness, experience with feminist organizing, and existing feminist networks that exert pressure for women's rights.
>
> • Other countries or international organizations aiding the democratic transition emphasize the need to incorporate gender equality in new government constitutions, policies, and structures.

Women's Movements and State Feminism

"Women hold up half the sky."
Chinese saying

State feminism refers to activities of government structures that are formally charged with furthering women's status and rights (Stetson & Mazur, 1995). The feminist bureaucrats who sometimes work as part of these government structures are referred to as **"femocrats"** (Stetson & Mazur, 1995). State feminism assumes a variety of forms at many levels of government, ranging from temporary advisory commissions to permanent ministries (Mazur, 2001). Ideally, women's policy agencies (WPAs) are government allies of women's movement actors and ensure that women's movement goals are translated into government policy and action (Haussman & Sauer, 2007). Many governments have added offices, commissions, agencies, ministries, committees, and advisors to deal with women's issues and gender equality. This development was stimulated in part by the 1995 Beijing Platform for Action of UN Fourth World Conference on Women. The Platform called upon governments to eliminate gender-based discrimination and incorporate gender equality at all stages of policymaking; in other words, to practice gender mainstreaming (Tripp et al., 2009). Box 10.5 provides a synopsis of the modern Chinese women's movement and the movement's primary WPA, the All-China Democratic Women's Federation (ACDWF).

"We do not want a piece of the pie; we want to change the basic recipe of the pie."
Birgit Brock-Utne, Norwegian professor and politician

Norway serves as an example of an effective state feminism with centralized government offices that have integrated gender equity principles into policy and fostered the empowerment of women's groups (Stetson & Mazur, 1995). Although the Equal Status Council (ESC) remains the main agency responsible for gender equality, gender has been mainstreamed into most state agencies. The state actively promotes women's equality through childcare subsidies, generous parental leave policies, quotas, and publicly appointed boards, committees, and councils. Although Norway's state feminism is due in part to Norway's commitment to the values of equality and justice and the belief that it is the state's role to promote equality, Norway's active women's movement played a large role in

BOX 10.5 *The Modern Chinese Women's Movement*

The modern Chinese women's movement began as a state policy following the Communist Revolution. The Chinese Communist Party (CCP), which has ruled the country since 1949, believed that women's emancipation would increase the state's productivity. In addition to abolishing forced marriage, concubinage, child marriage, and bride price, they created the All-China Democratic Women's Federation (ACDWF) to mobilize and represent the interests of Chinese women.

For a long time, the only feminism allowed in China was the state feminism of the ACDWF. But in the 1980s and 1990s, stimulated by the UN's Women's World Conferences and contact with transnational feminists, Chinese women began developing independent women's NGOs. Women's studies as an academic discipline, along with women's publications and literature, have grown. Although women's status has improved, workplace discrimination, reproductive rights, son preference, the "second shift," and violence against women are still problems. Some say that more attention needs to be paid to the difficulties faced by rural Chinese women.

Although the ACDWF has supported many women's NGOs with funding and worked with feminist NGOs for passage of China's first domestic violence law (passed in 2015 after 20 years of advocacy), the Chinese government still stifles independent Chinese women's organizations. Women's NGOs are sometimes raided and feminist activists detained. A 1995 law restricted international funding for women's NGOs and increased monitoring and state control. A 2016 law further limited the work of many women's rights NGOs. In 2015, the government detained five feminist activists planning a peaceful protest against sexual harassment on public transportation (intended for March 8, International Women's Day). Young social media savvy feminists publicized the detention of the "Feminist Five" (#freethefive) after it was left out of the mainstream media. Domestic and international pressure led to their release after 37 days. The growth of social media, the transnational women's movement, and the popularity of feminism among young women make the suppression of the Chinese women's movement more difficult. Nonetheless, activists face challenges from government authorities. For example, the government deleted #MeToo posts and then banned the most popular and influential feminist social media accounts.

Sources: Fincher, 2019; Hu, 2016; Kaiman, 2016; Yuan, 2005; Xu, 2009; Zheng, 2017.

creating a state responsive to women's needs (Bystydzienski, 1992b, 1995). One particular goal of the feminist coalition that significantly impacted state feminism was to increase the number of women in public office (as discussed in Chapter 9). As more women entered government, the state became more responsive to women's demands from below, and women began to participate in forming state policy. For example, in 2002, the government ordered companies to ensure that at least 40 percent of their board members are women (Seager, 2009).

Debate About the Role of the State

In theory, women's policy agencies and bureaucracies represent women's interests in state decision-making (Lovenduski, 2008). But whether these agencies and bureaucracies promote a feminist agenda and advance women's interests varies. Some governments undermine change by co-opting women's organizations and weakening them such that they become part of the system rather than a challenge to it. Other

"The feminist movement is about women's everyday concerns and building a community, rather than just having one or two famous individuals who can enlighten everybody else. Chinese women feel very unequal every day of their lives, and the government cannot make women oblivious to the deep injustice they feel."
Lü Pin, the founding editor of Feminist Voices

governments create women's organizations to control women's activism and depo-
liticize women (Basu, 1995; Tripp, 2017). In some countries, such as Egypt and
Uganda, independent women's movements are restricted or forbidden and government commissions and government-sponsored women's organizations do almost all
women's issues advocacy (Keddie, 2007; Sekhon & Bystydzienski, 1999). In Uganda
and South Africa, national gender machineries are frequently undermined through
political appointments of people with little expertise and commitment to women's
issues (Fester, 2014; Tripp, 2017). The result is the appearance of progress despite
the fact that key women's issues are ignored and traditional gender relations and
gender power differentials remain largely intact.

Feminist-government alliances are also somewhat risky because when governments change, state feminist machineries may be dismantled or weakened and government funding for women's NGOs reduced or eliminated. As Stetson and Mazur
(1995) caution, "If interests become overly dependent on the state, not only is their
autonomy threatened, but their own fortunes become intertwined with those of the
policy offices, and these are often linked to the fate of a governing party coalition"
(p. 276). The United States is a typical example. There, feminist organizations have
stronger alliances with the Democratic Party. When the Democrats are in power,
more feminist policies are made and the federal government's women's policy
machinery is strengthened. Under Democrat President Obama, the Department of
Labor's Women's Bureau was well funded, and the White House Council on Women
and Girls was created and pursued an ambitious agenda. However, under Republican
President Trump, the budget of the Women's Bureau was slashed, the White House
Council on Women and Girls lay dormant, the Global Gag rule reinstated, and an
anti-abortion, anti-contraception advocate put in charge of federal family planning
programs. Trump lost to Democrat Joe Biden in 2020 and in his first few months,
President Biden reversed these Trump administration actions.

Nicaragua is another good example. As was the case in many Latin American countries, a nationalist struggle for independence from a dictatorship
stimulated the growth of the women's movement. Nicaraguan women played
an important role in the overthrow of the Somoza dictatorship and, in the
process, honed their political skills and confidence and earned the right to inclusion in the new Sandinista government. AMNLAE (Asociación de Mujeres
Louisa Amanda Espinosa) became the Sandinista-affiliated women's organization, and by 1985, played an aggressive role in educating Nicaraguan society
about women's issues. The Sandinista government also funded many significant feminist research projects and created a Women's Legal Office, located
in the president's office, to participate in strategic planning. But in 1990, the
Sandinistas lost the election to the conservative UNO party, and the women's
movement lost traction due to its association with the FSLN, the Sandinista
party. Violeta de Chamorro became president, and her government advocated
traditional gender roles and the rhythm method as the only acceptable form
of birth control and cut services that benefited women (Chinchilla, 1994). To
regain and retain power, the FSLN aligned itself more closely with the Catholic
Church. Once again in power, they outlawed all abortion (in 2006), prevented demonstrations by women's organizations, and raided the offices of the

"There are no feminist
prisoners, threatened
with death, murdered
for being feminists,
but there is enormous
hostility on the part
of governmental and
party structures toward
feminists."
*María Teresa Blandón,
Nicaraguan feminist,
2017*

Nicaraguan Autonomous Women's Movement, a vocal critic of the government's policies (Booth, 2008; Lacey, 2008). Although state feminism is now weak, an independent women's movement has grown as a consequence.

Factors Affecting the Success of State Feminism

Without an independent women's movement, the potential dangers of state feminism are greater. These dangers include the state co-opting women's movements, losing ground when political administrations change, and superficial attention to women's issues. A robust, independent women's movement can exert continued pressure on government so that it cannot break gender-equality promises. A diverse movement of women's groups focused on a variety of women's issues and sensitive to the needs of different groups of women also prevents governments from responding to only a narrow range of women and issues. If state feminism is weak, an independent women's movement often provides services to women through GROs and pressures government to respond to women's issues and needs. Basu (2017) concludes that the most effective forms of state feminism entail close links and open communication between femocrats and strong and independent women's organizations.

Tripp and colleagues (2009), in a discussion of state feminism in Africa, note a variety of factors influencing the effectiveness of state machineries in promoting women's interests. These include: (1) how much authority they have to make and enforce policy; (2) whether they have a clear mandate and are given adequate resources to meet it; (3) whether the leaders of the agency or ministry are true femocrats or simply government bureaucrats or political appointees without gender consciousness; (4) whether they are part of strategic government units or marginalized; and (5) whether they coordinate and collaborate with women's NGOs or actively weaken them. Others have noted that state feminism does the most for women when the state is defined as the site of social justice, has the structural capacity to institutionalize demands for equality, and supports feminist organizations and reform politics in unions and political parties. In sum, state feminism seems to work best when the agency or bureau is a separate ministry (rather than subsumed under another); when they have a clear mandate; when they have adequate (and technically trained) staff and money; when they are run by true femocrats rather than bureaucrats; and when they have a strong, positive relationship with women's movement GROs and GRSOs, letting them help set the agenda and providing them with funding (Haussman & Sauer, 2007; Waylen, 2008).

Transnational Feminist Movements and Networks

A key feature of modern women's movements is their focus on coalition building and intersectionality (Basu, 2017). This is well demonstrated by **transnational feminist movements** that span multiple nations. These movements share the belief that women are entitled to the same rights as men, regardless of where women

"Women are taking the lead and making a huge contribution to defining the international agenda in terms of human rights, macroeconomics, conflict/peace, and sustainable development. We have a valuable and unique perspective on these issues as women and as human beings. We recognize that feminism in one country is not sustainable—we need feminism on a global scale."
WIDE (Women in Development Europe)

"Another world is possible, but only when women and men confront the fundamental injustice of a system that privileges one experience of humanity, and one that seeks to dominate and control all those it constructs as "Other" – whether the Otherness is based on class, political affiliation, race, ethnicity, religion, country or gender. That system is patriarchy, and it robs men of their humanity as much as it robs women of their agency."
Peggy Antrobus, member of DAWN from Barbados

live and their ethnicity, sexual orientation, religion, and social class. However, diversity and difference remain central values in transnational feminisms, values to be acknowledged and respected, not erased in the building of alliances (Mohanty, 2003). The modern transnational women's movement has grown due to globalization and advances in information and communication technologies (Baksh & Harcourt, 2015). In addition to regional and international conferences, websites, ListServs, social media, and email are used to protest, advocate, educate, organize, collaborate, and network. By building regional and international linkages, women's ability to develop effective political and legal strategies for their local struggles is enhanced (Human Rights Watch, 1995; Tripp et al., 2009).

Transnational feminist networks (TFNs) are the organizational expression of the transnational feminist movement. These transnational coalitions of women's organizations operate across national borders to resist inequalities created or aggravated by globalization, to influence policymaking, support specific grassroots struggles, and to insert a feminist perspective in transnational advocacy and activism (Baksh & Harcourt, 2015; Moghadam, 2005). Some TFNs ensure that United Nations' treaties and organizations address women's rights and issues and practice gender mainstreaming; some work to stop the trafficking of women and gender-based violence; some focus on environmental sustainability; some focus on peace and the effects of war and conflict on women; some resist patriarchal nationalism and fundamentalisms; and others monitor, document, and protest the gendered effects of globalization and neo-liberalism. Initially, liberal feminists from the North dominated the transnational feminist movement, but this ended with the founding of South-based Development Alternatives with Women for a New Era in 1984 (DAWN; Antrobus, 2015). Figure 10.2 summarizes the many activities of TFNs.

Throughout the book you have seen the impacts of successful transnational feminist organizing on the UN and international agreements. International laws and agreements strengthen feminism worldwide by placing pressure on governments to respond to women's movements (Basu, 1995). Successful TFN actions include not only the acknowledgment that women's rights are human rights, but also the addition of war rape as a crime to be prosecuted by the International Criminal Court; gender mainstreaming in UN organizations and development programs; a UN focus on women's reproductive health as key to poverty reduction; acknowledgment of the importance of women's unpaid labor and their labor in the informal economy to economies; the inclusion of sexual and reproductive rights in human rights protections; gender responsive budget analysis; attention to the role of women in environmental sustainability; actions to stop war rape, sweatshop labor, and sex trafficking; and actions to increase women's representation in formal politics. A 3-year effort by a coalition of over 300 organizations in 80 countries (led by WEDO and the Center for Women's Global Leadership) resulted in the creation of UN Women in 2009. The high-level agency replaced four small, poorly funded UN women's agencies (UNIFEM, DAW, INSTRAW, and the Office of Special Advisor on Gender Issues). The inclusion of women's issues targets in the UN's Millennium Development Goals and Sustainable Development Goals also

FIGURE 10.2 *Transnational Feminist Networks' (TFNs) Activities*

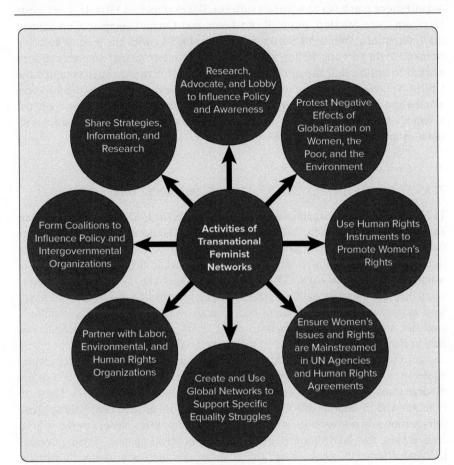

resulted from TFN activism. Women from the North and the South also worked together to get the UN Security Council to pass Resolution 1325 in 2000, which requires that women be included in peace negotiations and peacekeeping missions (Tripp, 2006a).

Transnational feminist networks are not new. The first transnational feminist organization, *Association Internationale des Femmes,* was founded in 1868 in Geneva, Switzerland (Tripp, 2006a). In 1887, American suffragists Elizabeth Cady Stanton and Lucretia Mott called a meeting of the International Council of Women to be held the following year in Washington, DC. They expressed the hope that the international council would "devise new and more effective methods for securing the equality and justice of women" and would help them realize their power in combining together to these ends (Fraser, 1987). The 1888 meeting resulted in the first formal international women's organization, the International

"Transnational women's groups have demystified the idea that women's issues are narrow; they have shown how gender matters in macroeconomic issues, in trade and finance. It is an accomplishment that the World's Bank president announced that gender justice is a worthy goal."
Zenebeworke Tadesse, founder of AAWORD (a TFN based in Ethiopia)

March 8 is International Women's Day (IWD). Celebrated since 1901, it was originally intended to highlight the struggles of working-class women and to promote women's suffrage. The idea is that on this day, every year, women would speak together with one voice. In many countries, IWD is a day for rallies and marches to call attention to women's economic, political, and reproductive rights.

"The women's movement, not only here in the U.S., but worldwide, is bigger and stronger than ever before and in places where it has never been. It has arms. It has legs. And most importantly, it has heads."
Bella Abzug, U.S. Congresswoman and cofounder of Women's Environment & Development Organization (WEDO)

Congress of Women (ICW) (Stienstra, 1994). Many early international women's organizations emphasized women's suffrage. For example, in 1904, U.S. feminists Elizabeth Cady Stanton, Susan B. Anthony, and Carrie Chapman Catt formed the International Women's Suffrage Alliance (IWSA) with the goal of securing women's right to vote. Following World War I, international women's groups worked to ensure that the newly forming League of Nations (later renamed the United Nations) included women's representatives and addressed issues affecting women and children. Other early international feminist organizations include the Women's International League for Peace and Freedom (1905) and the International Alliance of Women (1926).

TFNs and the United Nations' Four World's Women's Conferences

TFNs pushed the UN General Assembly to declare 1976–1985 as the *United Nations Decade for Women* (Bunch, 2007; Dairiam, 2015). The decade stimulated transnational feminism by creating national and international forums for action, including three world women's conferences. These international conferences on the status of women (1975–Mexico City; 1980–Copenhagen, Denmark; 1985–Nairobi, Kenya) catapulted the international connections among women to a qualitatively different level as women from very different backgrounds worked together on committees, caucuses, and networking (Chowdhury et al., 1994). A fourth world conference was held in Beijing, China, in 1995.

NGO forums at the four UN conferences and the numerous preparatory conferences that preceded them were central to the formation and growth of the modern transnational women's movement (Desai, 2007; Porter, 2007). These forums allowed thousands of NGO representatives from around the world to share information and network. In contrast to the formal political spaces of the official conferences, the NGO forums were "counter-political spaces," mixing serious political discussion, networking, and coalition building with women's cultural events and shopping (West, 1999). This, combined with feminist resistance to the negative effects of economic globalization and conservative religious and political forces, fostered the development of a new global feminist identity and solidarity (Moghadam, 2005).

Agreements forged at the four UN women's conferences also resulted in national commitments to increase the status of women. These include the **Nairobi Forward Looking Strategies for the Advancement of Women** (from the third women's conference in 1985) and the **Beijing Platform for Action (BPFA),** the product of the Fourth World Conference on Women (FWCW). The BPFA, referred to throughout the book, is considered the most comprehensive agenda ever negotiated for women's empowerment. Negotiated by 5,000 delegates from 189 countries, it identifies twelve "critical areas of concern" (see Box 10.6). It is called the *Platform for Action* because for each critical area of concern, it specifies strategic objectives and specific actions to be undertaken by governments. For example, violence against women is one critical area of concern and includes three strategic objectives: (1) take integrated measures to prevent and eliminate

BOX 10.6 *The Beijing Platform for Action: Twelve Critical Areas of Concern*

The Platform for Action is an agenda for women's empowerment. It aims to accelerate the implementation of the Nairobi Forward-Looking Strategies for the Advancement of Women, and to remove all obstacles to women's active participation in all spheres of public and private life through a full and equal share in economic, social, cultural, and political decision-making. Governments are called upon to take strategic, specified actions in regard to twelve critical areas of concern:

1. The persistent and increasing burden of poverty on women.

2. Inequalities and inadequacies in and unequal access to education and training.

3. Inequalities and inadequacies in and unequal access to health care and related services.

4. Violence against women.

5. The effects of armed or other kinds of conflict on women, including those living under foreign occupation.

6. Inequality in economic structures and policies, in all forms of productive activities, and in access to resources.

7. Inequality between men and women in the sharing of power and decision-making at all levels.

8. Insufficient mechanisms at all levels to promote the advancement of women.

9. Lack of respect for and inadequate promotion and protection of the human rights of women.

10. Stereotyping of women and inequality in women's access to and participation in all communication systems, especially in the media.

11. Gender inequalities in the management of natural resources and in the safeguarding of the environment.

12. Persistent discrimination against and violation of the rights of the girl child.

_____

Source: UN Women, 2018.

violence against women (thirty recommended actions); (2) study causes and consequences of violence against women and the effectiveness of prevention measures (four recommended actions); and (3) eliminate trafficking in women and assist victims of violence due to prostitution and trafficking (five recommended actions). Activists from all over the world have used the Platform to lobby governments and call for women's empowerment (Moghadam, 2007). The **Commission on the Status of Women (CSW),** the main UN body dedicated to the promotion of gender equality and the empowerment of women, is responsible for monitoring and reviewing progress and problems in the implementation of the Beijing Declaration and Platform for Action (UN Women, 2017).

There is agreement among transnational feminist scholars that the UN women's conferences enabled the growth of the transnational feminist movement, but there is also agreement that the movement cannot rely on the UN to provide this type of forum. Although specialized NGOs working on the implementation of CEDAW are part of the annual meetings of the Commission on the Status of Women (CSW) and the follow-ups to Beijing, the women's "megaconferences" have probably come to

"The obstacles to the equality of women created by stereotypes, perceptions of and attitudes towards women should be totally removed. Elimination of these obstacles will require, in addition to legislation, education of the population at large through formal and informal channels, including the media, non governmental organizations, political party platforms and executive action."
Nairobi Forward-Looking Strategies for the Advancement of Women, from the Third Women's World Conference in 1985

"Unless the human rights of women, as defined by international human rights instruments, are fully recognized and effectively protected, applied, implemented and enforced in national law as well as in national practice in family, civil, penal, labour and commercial codes and administrative rules and regulations, they will exist in name only."
Beijing Platform for Action, from the Fourth Women's World Conference in 1995

"Women's rights are human rights."
Slogan of women's human rights movement popularized at the UN's 1993 Vienna Conference

an end. Many question whether additional UN women's conferences would have positive results given the influential voices of the Vatican, fundamentalist Christians, and Islamists on UN women's platforms and declarations (Basu, 2017; Porter, 2007). Alternative forums held by organizations including AWID (Association for Women in Development), the International Interdisciplinary Congress on Women, the World Social Forum, and the International Feminist Dialogues (held prior to the World Social Forums) have to some extent taken the place of the UN women's conference NGO forums (Basu, 2017; Porter, 2007).

Transnational Feminist Movements and Women's Rights as Human Rights

As shown throughout this book, contemporary transnational feminism relies on the women's rights as human rights framework. Transnational feminists work to link women's rights to the inalienable human rights identified in the 1948 Universal Declaration of Human Rights. Various forms of gender discrimination are framed as violations of internationally recognized human rights. TFN activism ensures that women's rights and issues are explicitly included in international documents and agreements. Women's movements, from the local to the global, use international laws and agreements such as the Convention on the Elimination of Discrimination Against Women (CEDAW), the Beijing Platform for Action (BPFA), the Millennium Development Goals (MDGs), and the Sustainable Development Goals (SDGs) to legitimize their struggles and provide mechanisms for change. Women's international NGOs in Africa, Latin America, and Asia lead in the use of human rights frameworks and in the building of transnational coalitions and networks. These include Women Living Under Muslim Laws (WLUML) and Women in Law and Development in Africa. Box 10.7 profiles TFN leader Charlotte Bunch, a scholar and founder of the Center for Women's Global Leadership.

Although CEDAW (the 1979 Convention on the Elimination of Discrimination Against Women) is an early and important women's human rights treaty, transnational feminists view the 1993 United Nations World Conference on Human Rights (often called the Vienna Conference) as a turning point in the effort to link women's rights to human rights (Moghadam, 2005). Women's rights advocates from all over the world organized and cooperated to get the Vienna Conference to include discussions of women's human rights. The conference organizers initially excluded women's human rights from the agenda, but two women's TFNs (the Center for Women's Global Leadership and the International Women's Tribune Center) orchestrated a petition drive to demand that the conference address women's human rights. Signatures were garnered from over 500,000 people in 123 countries.

A major goal of activists for the conference was the UN affirmation of the rights of women as universal human rights and, in particular, that all forms of violence against women be recognized as violations of human rights (Bunch, 2007). Success came in the form of the **Vienna Declaration and Programme of Action,** which documents women's rights abuses in five areas: (1) abuse within the family, (2) war crimes against women, (3) violations of women's bodily integrity, (4) socioeconomic

> **BOX 10.7** *Activist Profile: Charlotte Bunch of the Center for Women's Global Leadership*
>
> Charlotte Bunch of the United States has been advocating for women's rights for over 45 years. As a young feminist in the 1960s, she was one of the first American feminists to work for lesbian rights. In 1989, she founded the Center for Women's Global Leadership (CWGL), an organization dedicated to including gender and sexual orientation on the international human rights agenda. Under her leadership, CWGL organized TFNs and individuals to successfully demand the inclusion of women's rights at the 1993 Vienna Human Rights Conference. CWGL remains one the world's leading women's human rights organizations and is a presence at most UN conferences.
>
> CWGL promotes networking internationally for women's rights, provides training, and organizes international campaigns such as CWGL's 16 Days of Activism Against Gender Violence (during this annual campaign, women all over the world take action to protest gender violence). In 2000, Bunch was a lead organizer of the Women's International War Crimes Tribunal on Japan's Military and Sexual Slavery, which presented evidence of the sexual slavery of over 200,000 women by the Japanese military. Results from the tribunal were used to influence the International Criminal Court to include the prosecution of war rape as part of war crimes. CWGL also worked for adoption of the new UN women's agency. Bunch is the author of many books and reports on women's rights as human rights and is the recipient of many awards.

abuses, and (5) political participation and persecution abuses (Friedman, 1995). At the conference, TFNs also successfully advocated for the UN appointment of a Special Rapporteur on Violence Against Women. The Special Rapporteur provides annual thematic reports to the UN's Human Rights Council, seeks and receives information on VAW, and recommends local, regional, and international actions to reduce VAW (UN Human Rights Office of the High Commissioner, 2018). TFN advocacy at the Vienna Conference also led to the definition of practices such as sati, dowry deaths, domestic violence, and FGC as "violence against women." Previously these practices were considered "cultural customs and traditions" and were not considered to be human rights violations (Jain, 2005; Tripp, 2006b).

Challenges to Women's Rights as a Human Rights Approach

Transnational women's organizing has resulted in impressive gains, particularly in regard to the inclusion of women's human rights in international human rights agendas and agreements—agendas and agreements that local and national activists then use as a basis upon which to further gender equality. But the global movement for women's human rights faces many challenges, including the complexities of international politics and cooperation regarding women's rights. In the United States, for example, many politicians favor a unilateral approach to foreign relations and claim a multilateral approach will give the UN too much power over U.S. laws. The result is that the United States often resists international agreements, including those focused on women's rights, such as CEDAW.[3]

The UN women's conferences illustrate the complexities of arriving at international agreements. Language issues and the fact that the UN uses a consensus model of decision-making made agreement more difficult. For instance, at the Fourth World Conference, voting on the 149-page "Platform for Action" was delayed by wording difficulties. There were translation problems with the word *gender,* which does not exist in some languages, as well as terms such as *gender-neutral* and *feminization.* Some countries had problems with the phrase "universal human rights," arguing that human rights are relative to the culture. Ultimately this issue was resolved by dropping the word *universal.* Likewise, it took 16 hours of debate before a subcommittee could accommodate the contrary views of countries who believe that sex education encourages risky youth sexual behavior and those who insist such education reduces youth risk.

An "accountability problem" is yet another challenge to the women's rights as human rights endeavor. While many UN agreements now declare the rights of women and outline the states' responsibilities, the UN only monitors and encourages compliance. This problem is worsened by the fact that women's rights are frequently enshrined in agreements that are not legally binding (like declarations or "goals") rather than in "treaties" that technically are (although treaties are often unenforced because this piece of international law remains underdeveloped). This choice is often an indicator of resistance to women's rights; it is harder to ratify treaties, which in the case of women's rights, often have to be relatively weak before member states agree to ratify them.

Another problem is that although the UN documents relevant to women's rights clearly imply that gender equality is a desirable value, this universal value is not so universal after all. Indeed, local customs and national and religious laws often contradict the treatment of women required by UN conventions and declarations. This is glaringly evident in regards to the **Convention on the Elimination of Discrimination Against Women (CEDAW).** CEDAW is an international bill of rights for women requiring ratifying nations to eliminate discrimination against women in employment, education, law, and politics, and to provide proof of progress. "Cultural reservations" allow countries to ratify a treaty or agreement while rejecting parts they believe are contrary to their cultural or religious practices, and CEDAW breaks the record for the most reservations recorded for a human rights instrument. Most of these reservations are incompatible with the treaty's goal of eliminating gender discrimination.

"The Holy See cannot accept ambiguous terminology concerning unqualified control over sexuality and fertility particularly as it could be interpreted as a societal endorsement of abortion and homosexuality."
One of the Holy See's Reservations on the Beijing Platform for Action (the Holy See is the home of the Pope and the central administration of the Roman Catholic Church)

---

[3] A unilateral approach to foreign affairs involves acting individualistically, without consulting or involving other nations. A multilateral approach emphasizes transnational cooperation and agreements.

Another challenge to the women's human rights agenda is embracing both universal human rights and cultural difference. We must continue to work and organize for an inclusive women's human rights agenda so that the interests of diverse women worldwide are represented (Thomas, in Friedman, 1995). While the heart of the women's rights as a human rights endeavor is universalism—the idea that all humans share the same inalienable rights—the truth is that the needs and interests of women often vary based on intersectionality and local and national contexts. In the early history of the modern transnational feminist movement (1975–1985), Western feminist conceptions of feminism and feminist concerns dominated, and northern and southern feminists clashed. Transnational feminist organizations like DAWN, Women Living Under Muslim Laws, and Women in Law and Development in Africa successfully engaged in their own activism within the transnational feminist movement so they could have a leadership role and create a more inclusive agenda.

We also must remember that the formal acknowledgment of women's rights as human rights by governments does not in and of itself resolve problems of inequality (Charlesworth et al., 1991). That will require economic and cultural change that is unlikely to occur without women's activism. As Bunch and Fried (1996) point out, the UN documents that affirm women's equal rights (such as CEDAW and the Beijing Platform for Action) are only tools. The potential of these tools can only be realized through vigorous leadership, difficult political dialogue among different groups of women, and women's political activity at all levels—from the global to the local.

Conclusion

This chapter illustrates the many ways, from the local to the global, in which women collectively work to change gender ideologies, policies, and structures; advocate and empower women and girls; and serve individual women's needs. The array of contextual factors that influence how women's movements arise and whether they succeed illustrates that the path to gender equality in one place is likely to be different than the path in another place. While a core of shared interests unites women and often forms the basis for building coalitions, the diversity of women translates into diversity in women's movements. A multicultural approach to global women's studies requires that we respect the rights of women to initiate their own movements in ways that work for them in their countries. Ethnocentrism in regard to women's movements is foolhardy—the strategies of women in one country often fail to translate to another, and believing that the path taken by women in one's country is the only path leads to an incomplete understanding of women's movements.

As we end the final chapter of *Women Across Cultures: A Global Perspective,* it is appropriate to consider the impact of women's movements. After reading this book, you will probably agree that while significant gains have been made, women's movements have not achieved many of their goals. Millions of women still face preventable death and disability due to pregnancy. Early and forced marriages are still problems. Violence against women remains endemic. Occupational gender

"I don't know how we have survived so many years by thinking of women as a separate chapter. We are not a separate chapter, we are half the book."
Rosario Green, 1996, Assistant Secretary for UN Political Affairs

Maryam Rajavi is president-elect of the National Council of Resistance of Iran. Rajavi uses UN women's human rights documents to critique what she calls the "gender apartheid" of Iran. Now living in exile, Rajavi continues to give speeches refuting the fundamentalists' use of the Qur'an to support their oppression of women. Rajavi emphasizes that democracy and world peace depend on the advancement of women.

segregation, the gender pay gap, and the glass ceiling persist. Women still perform the majority of care labor even when they work for pay, and women's unpaid labor is still undervalued. The sexual harassment and sexual objectification of women remain common. Although improved, women's representation in formal politics lags far behind men's, and men dominate most decision-making bodies. In many places, women continue to fight for their reproductive and sexual rights, and in some places, for their basic civil, legal, and property rights. Non heterosexual and transwomen still experience significant discrimination. Progress has been greater for some groups of women over others, and in some places more than others. Many women still experience multiple, overlapping forms of discrimination. Contesting gender inequalities remains fraught with social disapproval, and in many places results in harassment, detention, imprisonment, or violence. Religious fundamentalisms try to confine women to the private sphere of the home and limit their religious practice and leadership. Constant vigilance is necessary to keep steps forward from being followed by steps backward.

Many explanations have been offered for the uneven success of women's movements. One is that countermovements against feminism, usually led by religious and conservative organizations, often challenge and weaken women's movements. As Basu (1995) points out, the opposition to women's equal rights is often better funded and better organized and often has the weight of the state, and tradition, behind it. Another explanation is that many middle-class women's movements have failed because they did not mobilize poor women or were too narrowly focused on women's interests without considering how these interact with nationalism, class, or other important identities (Basu, 1995). Women's movements also sometimes face significant challenges from within, as feminist groups differ about what they see as critical issues and how to solve them. Conflicts and schisms within and between groups, partly due to competition for limited resources, sometimes interfere with the cooperation needed to bring real change (Batliwala, 2012).

Does this mean that women's movements have failed? The many successes of women's movements suggest otherwise. In the last 25 years, life expectancies for women have improved, maternal morbidity and mortality have dropped, child marriage has declined, and women have greater access to contraception. Women's literacy approaches that of men's, and girls' enrollment in primary and secondary education has increased significantly. There are more laws that address violence against women, national constitutions that include gender equality, and international agreements that include women's issues and call for gender equality. State feminism is more common, and gender is mainstreamed in many governments and in UN agencies. SOGI rights are more widely acknowledged. Women's shelters and other services and programs for women are far more common than they once were. Media more frequently cover women's rights violations, women's issues, and women's rights activism. Women's representation in formal politics has markedly grown as has women's participation in the formal labor force. The glass ceiling, while not shattered, is cracked, and while the gender pay gap remains, it has been reduced in many places. The number and variety of women's NGOs, GRSOs, and WINGOs have grown. Diversity in the needs and interests of different groups of women and intersectionality are increasingly recognized.

"Feminism in Mexico, as elsewhere, is not expressed in a single voice."
Victoria Rodriquez

"We need to learn from each other. To use the Constitution as a bridge that connects us. The State oppresses us equally, yet we on the bottom fight over who has more rights. When the people gain consciousness, nobody can stop us."
Dolene Miller, women's human rights defender, Nicaragua

Due to women's activism, many women and girls have more rights and opportunities than past generations. The thing to keep in mind is that thousands of years of patriarchy (the social order of male rights and privilege) have deeply affected attitudes, beliefs, norms, roles, and institutions. This means that change is inevitably a long-term process requiring continued advocacy and activism. All things considered, we have made significant gains in a relatively short period of time. There is reason for hope if our hope leads to action.

Glossary Terms and Concepts

Commission on the Status of Women (CSW)

Convention on the Elimination of Discrimination Against Women (CEDAW)

Beijing Platform for Action (BPFA)

Feminist movements

Femocrats

Nairobi Forward Looking Strategies for the Advancement of Women

Practical gender interests

Self-efficacy

State feminism

Strategic gender interests

Transnational feminist movements

Transnational feminist networks (TFNs)

United Nations Decade for Women

Vienna Declaration and Programme of Action

Women's movements

Study Questions

1. What are women's movements? Why is it more accurate to speak of women's movement*s* rather than *a* women's movement?

2. What are the ways in which women's movements vary? Despite their differences, what commonalities do they share?

3. What are the three major strands of women's movements?

4. How do feminist movements differ from other women's movements? Why don't some women's movement actors and organizations identify as feminist?

5. What forces operate against women's activism? Why do some women lack self-efficacy when it comes to asserting their rights?

6. What are the four categories of contextual influences on women's movements identified in the chapter? How do these affect the diversity of women's movements?

7. How can local political and economic conditions affect the development of women's movements, both positively and negatively?

8. What are some specific examples of how women's movements can arise out of nationalist struggles for liberation? Why does women's involvement in nationalist struggles often stimulate women's movements and activism?

9. What are some examples of women's movements arising in new democracies? What are some examples where democratization didn't benefit women's movements? What factors seem to explain these differences?

10. What is state feminism? What is a femocrat? What are some of the concerns about state feminism? What are some examples of state feminism not doing much to help women's equality and some examples of it helping? What accounts for the difference?

11. What characterizes transnational feminist movements? What are transnational feminist networks, and what do they do? How have TFNs influenced the UN?

12. What are the four international UN women's world conferences? How did the UN conferences contribute to the growth of transnational feminist movements? What is the Beijing Platform for Action, and why is it important?

13. What is the Vienna Declaration, and why is it important?

14. What are the main features of the women's rights as human rights framework? What challenges face the women's rights as human rights endeavor?

15. How have women's movements both succeeded and failed? What explanations are given for the uneven success of women's movements?

Discussion Questions and Activities

1. Considering the broad definition of women's movements given at the beginning of the chapter, identify the various women's GROs and GRSOs in your community and explain what they do.

2. Would you recommend that groups working on women's issues in your culture use the feminist label? Why or why not?

3. What state feminism structures exist in your national government and your state government? To what extent do these serve women's interests, and how does that depend on the party in office? To what extent do they reflect a feminist perspective?

4. Women's movements vary depending on the cultural context and on intersectionality, and outsider perspectives are not always relevant or welcome. If this is true, how can feminists in one culture assist feminists in another culture, or can they?

5. The chapter discussed the cases of Iran, Iraq, and Afghanistan. In 2021, in all the three countries, women's rights were uncertain as those favoring an Islamist government and traditional gender roles conflicted with those favoring a more progressive government and society. What has happened since? What is the current status of women's rights in those countries?

6. Research the women's movements in a country not covered in this chapter, framing your report using chapter concepts.

7. Using examples from Chapters 1 to 9, illustrate the diversity of women's movements. Show how they take many forms, employ many strategies, vary in the issues they target, range from the local to the global, and how they are shaped by intersectionality.

8. Write a report on the status of the CEDAW in your country using concepts from the chapter section on challenges to women's rights as human rights.

Action Opportunities

1. Volunteer your time to help a women's organization in your community. If you don't want to make a long-term commitment, many can use occasional office help or assistance with fund-raising efforts.

2. There are many specific types of women's movement groups and organizations that reflect the intersectional interests of particular groups of women. Identify and explore one that reflects you from an intersectional perspective.

3. Identify a women's movement organization in your country that advocates for women at a national level and participate in one of their campaigns.

4. Create your own campaign on a women's issue of your choice. Organize women (and men) to take action on a women's issue in your local or university community (for example, is women's safety an issue on your campus? Is drug-facilitated sexual assault a problem at fraternity parties? Is emergency contraception available at your university's health center?). Or take action on a national or international women's issue. Remember women's activists use a range of tactics— you can do a "teach-in," a rally, a petition drive, a letter-writing campaign, fund-raising drives, or organize a picket, a social media campaign, etc. You can also use art, music, theater, and other creative means to increase awareness.

5. Participate in a transnational feminist movement such as the Global Fund for Women (https://www.globalfundforwomen.org/champions-of-equality/).

Activist Websites

Center for Women's Global Leadership http://www.cwgl.rutgers.edu

CLADEM (Latin American and Caribbean Committee for the Defense of Women's Rights) https://cladem.org/

Equality Now https://www.equalitynow.org

European Women's Lobby http://www.womenlobby.org

Feminist Majority (US) http://www.feminist.org

Global Fund for Women https://www.globalfundforwomen.org

Human Rights Watch (Women) https://www.hrw.org/topic/womens-rights

International Women's Day https://www.internationalwomensday.com

International Women's Media Foundation http://www.iwmf.org/get-involved /advocacy/

Jahajee Sisters (Indo-Caribbean) http://www.jahajeesisters.org

National Organization for Women (US) http://www.now.org

All India Democratic Women's Association http://aidwaonline.org

OWFI (Women's Organization for Freedom in Iraq) http://www.owfi.info/EN /category/campaigns/

Solidarity for African Women's Rights https://www.soawr.org/

Women for Women International http://www.womenforwomen.org

Women's International League for Peace and Freedom http://wilpf.org

Informational Websites

ARROW (Asian-Pacific Resource and Research Centre for Women) http://arrow .org.my/our-work/

AWID (Association for Women in Development) research reports https://www .awid.org/publications

Commission on the Status of Women http://www.unwomen.org/en/csw

Institute for Women's Policy Research (US) https://iwpr.org

International Alliance of Women (Alliance Internationale Des Femmes) http:// womenalliance.org

International Council for Research on Women http://www.icrw.org

International Justice Resource Center http://www.ijrcenter.org/thematic-research -guides/womens-human-rights/

UN Conventions and Declarations relevant to women's rights http://www.unesco.org /new/en/unesco/themes/gender-equality/resources/conventions-and-declarations/

UN Research guides on women and gender equality http://libraryresources.unog .ch/women

UN Women Beijing +20 http://beijing20.unwomen.org/en/in-focus/human-rights

References

Acosta-Belen, E., and Bose, C. E. 1995. Colonialism, structural subordination, and empowerment: Women in the development process in Latin America and the Caribbean. In *Women in the Latin American development process,* edited by C. E. Bose and E. Acosta-Belen. Philadelphia, PA: Temple University Press.

Afshar, H. 1996. Islam and feminism: An analysis of political strategies. In *Feminism and Islam: Legal and literary perspectives,* edited by M. Yamani. New York: New York University Press.

Alvarez, S. E. 1994. The (trans)formation of feminism(s) and gender politics in Brazil. In *The women's movement in Latin America: Participation and democracy,* 2nd ed., edited by J. S. Jaquette. Boulder, CO: Westview Press.

Amnesty International. 2017. *International report: The state of the world's human rights.* London: Amnesty International.

Amnesty International. 2021. *Mexico: Authorities use illegal force and sexual violence to silence women protesting against gender-based violence.* https://www .amnesty.org/en/latest/news/2021/03/mexico-autoridades-usaron-violencia -sexual-para-silenciar-mujeres/. Retrieved on June 17, 2021.

Antrobus, P. 2015. DAWN, the Third World Feminist Network: Upturning hierarchies. In the *Oxford handbook of transnational feminist movements*, edited by R. Baksh and W. Harcourt. New York: Oxford University Press.

Aulette, J. R. 2001. New roads to resistance: Polish feminists in the transition to democracy. In *Democratization and women's grassroots movements,* edited by J. M. Bystydzienski and J. Sekhon. Bloomington, IN: Indiana University Press.

Azhgikhina, N. 2017, March 29. In Russia, are fake feminist groups back in action? *The Nation.* https://www.thenation.com/article/archive/in-russia-are -fake-feminist-groups-back-in-action/. Retrieved on July 20, 2021.

Baksh, R., and Harcourt, W. 2015. Introduction. In *The Oxford handbook of trans-national feminist movements*, edited by R. Baksh and W. Harcourt. New York: Oxford University Press.

Bandura, A. 1986. *Social foundations of thought and action.* Englewood Cliffs, NJ: Prentice-Hall.

Basu, A. 1995. *The challenge of local feminisms: Women's movements in global perspective.* Boulder, CO: Westview.

Basu, A. 2017. Introduction. In *Women's movements in the global era: The Power of local feminisms,* edited by A. Basu. Philadelphia, PA: Westview.

Batliwala, S. 2012. *Changing their world: Concepts and practices of women's movements.* Toronto: AWID.

Beckwith, K. 2013. The comparative study of women's movements. In *The Oxford handbook of gender and politics,* edited by G. Waylen, K. Cellis, J. Kantola, and Weldon, S.L. New York: Oxford University Press.

Booth, W. 2008, November 20. Democracy in Nicaragua in peril. *Washington Post,* A2.

Bunch, C. 2007. *Women and gender: The evolution of women specific institutions and gender integration at the United Nations.* http://www.cwgl .rutgers.edu /globalcenter/charlotte/UNHandbook.pdf. Retrieved on October 28, 2009.

Bunch, C., and Fried, S. 1996. Beijing '95: Moving women's human rights from margin to center. *Signs: Journal of Women in Culture and Society, 22,* 200–204.

Bystydzienski, J. M. 1992a. Introduction. In *Women transforming politics: Worldwide strategies for empowerment,* edited by J. Bystydzienski. Bloomington, IN: Indiana University Press.

Bystydzienski, J. M. 1992b. Influence of women's culture on public policies in Norway. In *Women transforming politics: Worldwide strategies for empowerment,* edited by J. Bystydzienski. Bloomington, IN: Indiana University Press.

Bystydzienski, J. M. 1995. *Women in electoral politics: Lessons from Norway.* Westport, CT: Praeger.

Charlesworth, H., Chinkin C., and Wright, S. 1991. Feminist approaches to international law. *The American Journal of International Law, 85,* 613–645.

Chinchilla, N. S. 1994. Feminism, revolution, and democratic transitions in Nicaragua. In *The women's movement in Latin America: Participation and democracy,* edited by J. S. Jaquette. 2nd ed. Boulder, CO: Westview Press.

Chowdhury, N., Nelson, B. J., Carver, K. A., Johnson, N. J., and O'Loughlin, P. L. 1994. Redefining politics: Patterns of women's political engagement from a global perspective. In *Women and politics worldwide,* edited by B. J. Nelson and N. Chowdhury. New Haven, CT: Yale University Press.

Chowdhury, N. 1994. Bangladesh: Gender issues and politics in a patriarchy. In *Women and politics worldwide,* edited by B. J. Nelson and N. Chowdhury. New Haven, CT: Yale University Press.

Cravens, C. S. 2006. *The culture and customs of the Czech Republic and Slovakia.* Westport, CT: Greenwood Press.

Dairiam, M. S. 2015. CEDAW, gender, and culture. In *The Oxford handbook of transnational feminist movements*, edited by In R. Baksh and W. Harcourt. New York: Oxford University Press.

de Haan, F., Daskalova, D., and Loutfi, A. 2006. *Biographical dictionary of women's movements and feminisms: Central, Eastern, and South Eastern Europe, 19th and 20th centuries.* Budapest and New York: Central European University Press.

Desai, M. 2001. India: Women's movements from nationalism to sustainable development. In *Women's rights: A global view,* edited by L. Walter. Westport, CN: Greenwood Press.

Desai, M. 2007. The messy relationship between feminisms and globalizations. *Gender and Society, 21,* 797–804.

Fallon, K. M. 2008. *Democracy and the rise of women's movements in Sub-Saharan Africa.* Baltimore, MD: Johns Hopkins University Press.

Fester, G. 2014. The South African revolution: Protracted or postponed? In S. Nazeen and M. Sultan (Eds.), *Voicing demands: Feminist activism in transitional contexts.* London: Zed.

Fincher, L. H. 2019. China's women's movement has not only survived an intense crackdown, it's grown. *The Guardian.* https://www.theguardian.com/world/commentisfree/2019/mar/07/chinas-womens-movement-has-not-only-survived-an-intense-crackdown-its-grown. Retrieved on June 16, 2021.

Fraser, A. S. 1987. *The U.N. Decade for Women: Documents and dialogue.* Boulder, CO: Westview Press.

Friedman, E. 1995. Women's human rights: The emergence of a movement. In *Women's rights, human rights: International feminist perspectives,* edited by J. Peters and A. Wolper. New York: Routledge.

Frohmann, A., and Valdes, T. 1995. Democracy in the country and in the home: The women's movement in Chile. In *The challenge of local feminisms: Women's movements in global perspective,* edited by A. Basu. Boulder, CO: Westview Press.

Fujieda, M. 1995. Japan's first phase of feminism. In *Japanese women: New feminist perspectives on the past, present, and future,* edited by K. Fujimura-Fanselow and A. Kameda. New York: Feminist Press.

Ghodsee, K. 2004. Feminism-by-design: Emerging capitalisms, cultural feminisms, and women's non-governmental organizations. *Signs: A Journal of Culture and Society, 29,* 728–752.

Gottlick, J. F. B. 2001. From the ground up: Women's organizations and democratization in Russia. In *Democratization and women's grassroots movements,* edited by J. M. Bystydzienski and J. Sekhon. Bloomington, IN: Indiana University Press.

Hadid, D. 2021. Malala Yousafzai's interview in 'British Vogue' sparks anger in her native Pakistan. https://www.npr.org/sections/goatsandsoda/2021/06/04 /1003236671/malala-yousafzais-interview-in-british-vogue-sparks-anger-in-her -native-pakistan. Retrieved on June 16, 2021.

Haussman, M., and Sauer, B. 2007. Introduction: Women's movements and state restructuring in the 1990s. In *Gendering the state in the age of globalization: Women's movements and state feminism in postindustrial democracies,* edited by M. Haussman and B. Sauer. New York: Rowman and Littlefield.

Hu, A. C. 2016, August 22. Half the sky, but not yet equal: China's feminist movement. *Harvard International Review.* https://www.jstor.org/stable/26445831. Retrieved on June 17, 2021.

Human Rights Watch. 1995. *The Human Rights Watch global report on women's human rights.* New York: Human Rights Watch.

Human Rights Watch. 2017. *World report 2017.* https://www.hrw.org/world -report/2017/. Retrieved on June 22, 2017.

Human Rights Watch. 2020a. *Iran: Events of 2019.* https://www.hrw.org/world -report/2020/country-chapters/iran#1de7c4. Retrieved on June 16, 2021.

Human Rights Watch. 2020b. *Iraq: Events of 2019.* https://www.hrw.org/world -report/2020/country-chapters/iraq#0ed443. Retrieved on June 17, 2021.

Human Rights Watch. 2021. *Poland: Escalating threats to women's human rights defenders.* https://www.hrw.org/news/2021/03/31/poland-escalating-threats -women-activists. Retrieved on June 16, 2021.

Jad, I. 2017. The Palestinian women's movement. In *Women's movements in the global era: The Power of local feminisms,* edited by A. Basu. Philadelphia, PA: Westview.

Jahan, R. 1995. Men in seclusion, women in public: Rokeya's dream and women's struggles in Bangladesh. In *The challenge of local feminisms: Women's movements in global perspective,* edited by A. Basu. Boulder, CO: Westview Press.

Jain, D. 2005. *Women, development, and the UN: A sixty-year quest for equality and justice.* Bloomington, IN: Indiana University Press.

Johnson-Odim, C. 1991. Common themes, different contexts: Third World women and feminism. In *Third world women and the politics of feminism,* edited by C. T. Mohanty, A. Russo, and L. Torres. Bloomington, IN: Indiana University Press.

Kaiman, J. 2016, June 15. In China, feminism is growing and so is the backlash. *Los Angeles Times.* http://www.latimes.com/world/asia/la-fg-china-feminist -activists-20160614-snap-story.html. Retrieved on June 20, 2017.

Katzenstein, M. F. 1987. Comparing the feminist movements of the United States and Western Europe: An overview. In *The women's movements of the United States and Central Europe: Consciousness, political opportunity, and public policy,* edited by M. F. Katzenstein and C. M. Mueller. Philadelphia, PA: Temple University Press.

Keddie, N. R. 2007. *Women in the Middle East: Past and present.* Princeton, NJ: Princeton University Press.

Kemp, A., Madlala, N, Moodley, A., and Salo, E. 1995. The dawn of a new day: Redefining South African feminism. In *The challenge of local feminisms: Women's movements in global perspective,* edited by A. Basu. Boulder, CO: Westview Press.

Kettler, S. 2014. *Malala Yousafzai Biography* (last updated October 15, 2020). https:// www.biography.com/activist/malala-yousafzai. Retrieved on June 16, 2021.

Kumar, R. 1995. From Chipko to Sati: The contemporary Indian women's movement. In *The challenge of local feminisms: Women's movements in global perspective,* edited by A. Basu. Boulder, CO: Westview Press.

Lacey, M. 2008, November 24. Sandinista fervor turns sour for former comrades of Nicaragua's president. *New York Times,* A6.

Lerner, G. 1986. *The creation of patriarchy,* Vol. 1. New York: Oxford.

Ling, Y., and A. Matsumo. 1992. Women's struggle for empowerment in Japan. In *Women transforming politics: Worldwide strategies for empowerment*, edited by J. Bystydzienski. Bloomington, IN: Indiana University Press.

Lovenduski, J. 2008. State feminism and women's movements. *West European Politics, 31,* 169–194.

Malala Fund. 2021. Malala's story. https://malala.org/malalas-story. Retrieved on June 16, 2021.

Margolis, D. R. 1993. Women's movements around the world: Cross-cultural comparisons. *Gender and Society, 7,* 379–399.

Matynia, E. 1995. Finding a voice: Women in post-communist Central Europe. In *The challenge of local feminisms: Women's movements in global perspective,* edited by A. Basu. Boulder, CO: Westview Press.

Mazur, A. G. 2001. Introduction. *State feminism, women's movements, and job training.* London: Routledge.

Mazur, A. G., McBride, D. E., and Hoard, S. 2016. Comparative strength of women's movements over time: conceptual, empirical, and theoretical innovations. *Politics, Groups, and Identities, 4,* 652–676.

McBride, D. E., and Mazur, A. G. 2005. *Comparative study of women's movements: Conceptual puzzles and RNGS solutions.* Paper presented at the annual meeting of the American Political Science Association, Marriott Wardman Park, Omni Shoreham, Washington Hilton, Washington, DC. http://www .allacademic.com/meta/p41943_index.html. Retrieved on October 2, 2009.

Mir-Hosseini, Z. 2001. Iran: Emerging women's voices. In *Women's rights: A global view,* edited by L. Walter. Westport, CT: Greenwood Press.

Moghadam, V. M. 1991. Islamist movements and women's responses in the Middle East. *Gender and History, 3,* 268–284.

Moghadam, V. M. 2005. *Globalizing women: Transnational feminist networks.* Baltimore, MD: Johns Hopkins University Press.

Moghadam, V. M. 2007. An introduction and overview. In *From Patriarchy to empowerment,* edited by V. M. Moghadam. Syracuse, NY: Syracuse University Press.

Moghadam, V. M. 2015. Transnational feminist activism and movement building. In *The Oxford handbook of transnational feminist movements*, edited by R. Baksh and W. Harcourt. New York: Oxford University Press.

Mohanty, C. 2003. *Feminism without borders: Decolonizing theory, practicing solidarity.* Durham, NC: Duke University Press.

Molyneaux, M. 1985. Mobilization with emancipation? Women's interests, the state, and revolution in Nicaragua. *Feminist Studies, 11,* 227–255.

Molyneaux, M. 1996. Women's rights and international context in the post-communist states. In *Mapping the women's movement: Feminist politics and social transformation in the North,* edited by M. Threlfall. London: Verso and New Left Review.

Nader, Z., and Mashal, M. 2017, January 6. Despite ban, invasive virginity tests remain prevalent in Afghanistan. *New York Times.*

NobelPrize.org. 2014. *Malala Yousafzai - Facts.* https://www.nobelprize.org/prizes /peace/2014/yousafzai/facts/. Retrieved on June 16, 2021.

Oyěwùmí, O. 2003. *African women and feminism: Reflecting on the politics of sisterhood.* Trenton, NJ: Africa World Press.

Peterson, V. S., and Runyan, A. S. 2010. *Global gender issues in the new millennium,* 4th ed. CO: Westview Press.

Porter, M. 2007. Transnational feminism in a globalized world: Challenges, analysis, and resistance. *Feminist Studies, 33*, 43–63.

Santiago, L. Q. 1995. Rebirthing *Babaye:* The women's movement in the Philippines. In *The challenge of local feminisms: Women's movements in global perspective,* edited by A. Basu. Boulder, CO: Westview Press.

Seager, J. 2009. *The Penguin Atlas of women in the world,* 4th ed. New York: Penguin.

Sekhon, J., and J. M. Bystydzienski. 2001. Conclusion. In *Democratization and women's grassroots movements,* edited by J. M. Bystydzienski and J. Sekhon. Bloomington, IN: Indiana University Press.

Sherif, B. 2001. Egypt: Multiple Perspectives on Women's Rights. In *Women's rights: A global view,* edited by L.Walter. Westport, Connecticut: Greenwood Press.

Stetson, D. M., and A. G. Mazur. 1995. Introduction. In *Comparative state feminism,* edited by D. M. Stetson and A. G. Mazur. Newbury Park, CA: Sage.

Stienstra, D. 1994. *Women's movements and international organizations.* New York: St. Martin's Press.

Threlfall, M. 1996. Feminist politics and social change in Spain. In *Mapping the women's movement: Feminist politics and social transformation in the North,* edited by M. Threlfall. London: Verso and New Left Review.

Threlfall, M. 2013. Women's movements in Spain. *Wiley-Blackwell encyclopedia of social and political movements,* 1400–1402. Hoboken, NJ: Wiley-Blackwell.

Tohidi, N. 2017. The women's movement and feminism in Iran: Revisiting a global perspective. In *Women's movements in the global era: The Power of local feminisms,* edited by A. Basu. Philadelphia, PA: Westview.

Tomasevski, K. 1993. *Women and human rights.* London: Zed.

Tripp, A. M. 2006a. The evolution of transnational feminisms: Consensus, conflict, and new dynamics. In *Global feminism,* edited by M. M. Ferree and A. M. Tripp. New York: New York University Press.

Tripp, A. M. 2006b. Challenges in transnational feminist mobilization. In *Global feminism,* edited by M. M. Ferree and A. M. Tripp. New York: New York University Press.

Tripp, A. M. 2017. Women's movements in Africa. In *Women's movements in the global era: The Power of local feminisms,* edited by A. Basu. Philadelphia, PA: Westview.

Tripp, A. M., Casimiro, I., Kwesiga, J., and Mungwa, A. 2009. *African women's movements: Changing political landscapes.* New York: Cambridge University Press.

UN Human Rights Office of the High Commissioner. 2018. Special Rapporteur on violence against women, its causes and consequences. http://www.ohchr.org/EN/Issues/Women/SRWomen/Pages/SRWomen/Pages/SRWomenIndex.aspx. Retrieved on January 16, 2018.

UN Women. 2017. *Commission on the Status of Women.* http://www.unwomen.org/en/csw. Retrieved on June 25, 2017.

UN Women. 2018. The United Nations Fourth World Conference on Women Beijing China 1995: Platform for Action. http://www.un.org/womenwatch/daw/beijing/platform/. Retrieved on January 16, 2018.

UN Office of the High Commissioner on Human Rights (UNOHCHR). 2020. *Women human rights defenders.* https://www.ohchr.org/documents/issues /women/wrgs/sexualhealth/info_whrd_web.pdf. Retrieved on June 16, 2021.

Valiente, C. 2005. The women's movement, gender equality agencies, and central-state debates on political representation in Spain. In *State feminism and political representation,* edited by J. Lovenduski. New York: Cambridge University Press.

Vitema, J., and Fallon, K. M. 2008. Democratization, women's movements, and gender-equitable States: A framework for comparison. *American Sociological Review, 73,* 668–688.

Villegas, P. 2020. In Mexico, women go on strike to protest violence. *New York Times.* https://www.nytimes.com/2020/03/09/world/americas/mexico-women -strike-protest.html?action=click&module=RelatedLinks&pgtype=Article. Retrieved on June 17, 2021.

Waters, E., and Posadskaya, A. 1995. Democracy without women is no democracy: Women's struggles in postcommunist Russia. In *The challenge of local feminisms: Women's movements in global perspective,* edited by A. Basu. Boulder, CO: Westview Press.

Waylen, G. 2008. Enhancing the substantive representation of women: Lessons from transitions to democracy. *Parliamentary Affairs, 61,* 518–534.

West, G., and Blumberg, R. L. 1990. Reconstructing social protest from a feminist perspective. In *Women and social protest,* edited by G. West and R. L. Blumberg. New York: Oxford University Press.

West, L. 1999. The United Nations women's conferences and feminist politics. In *Gender politics in global governance,* edited by M. K. Meyer and E. Prugl. Lanham, MD: Rowman and Littlefield.

Wong, E. 2005, July 20. Iraqi constitution may curb women's rights. *New York Times.*

Xu, F. 2009. Chinese feminisms encounter international feminisms: Identity, power, and knowledge production. *International Journal of Politics, 11,* 196–215.

Yuan, L. 2005. *Reconceiving women's equality in China: A critical examination of models of sex equality.* Oxford, UK: Lexington.

Zayadin, H., and Youseff, A. 2020. Saudi Arabia to host women's summit while women's activists sit behind bars. *Human Rights Watch.* https://www.hrw.org /news/2020/10/20/saudi-arabia-host-womens-summit-while-women-activists -sit-behind-bars. Retrieved on June 16, 2021.

Zheng, W. 2017. In *Women's movements in the global era: The Power of local feminisms,* edited by A. Basu. Philadelphia, PA: Westview.

Design Element: Abstract floral frame: Telnov Oleksii/Shutterstock

Appendix: Statistical Indicators
of Women's Status by Country

This appendix provides data by country for the following:

1. **Country's relative geographic location** from the *CIA Factbook*: https://www.cia.gov/the-world-factbook/.

2. A **country's ranking on the Global Gender Gap Index** from the World Economic Forum. This index uses benchmarks of national gender gaps on economic, political, education, and health criteria to rank countries on gender-based gaps in access to resources and opportunity. The score may range from 1 (complete equality/parity between women and men) to 0 (complete inequality/imparity between women and men). Data reported here is from World Economic Forum's *Global Gender Gap Report 2021*: https://www.weforum.org/reports/global-gender-gap-report-2021.

3. **Life expectancy for women at birth** from UNDP *Human Development Report 2020*: http://www.hdr.undp.org/sites/default/files/hdr2020.pdf.

4. **Average years of schooling for women** from UNDP *Human Development Report 2020*: http://www.hdr.undp.org/sites/default/files/hdr2020.pdf.

5. **Average age at marriage for females** from the World Bank's Data Bank /Gender Statistics: https://databank.worldbank.org/reports.aspx?source =283&series=SP.DYN.SMAM.FE.

6. **Fertility rate** (average births per woman) from the World Bank's Data Bank/ Gender Statistics: https://data.worldbank.org/indicator/SP.DYN.TFRT.IN.

7. **Adolescent birth rate** (births per 1,000 women ages 15 to 19) from UNDP *Human Development Report* 2020: http://www.hdr.undp.org/sites/default/files /hdr2020.pdf.

8. **Maternal Mortality Ratio** (deaths per 100,000 live births) from UNDP *Human Development Report 2020*: http://www.hdr.undp.org/sites/default/files /hdr2020.pdf.

9. **Abortion Law** from Center for Reproductive Rights, https://maps .reproductiverights.org/worldabortionlaws.

10. **Women % of Total Labor Force** (ages 15 and older) from the World Bank's *Gender Portal:* https://data.worldbank.org/indicator/SL.TLF.TOTL.FE.ZS.

11. **Adjusted Gender Wage Gap** (the factor-weighted mean gender pay gap after statistically controlling for education, age, full/part-time work, private/public sector work) from ILO's *Global Wage Report 2018–2019:* https://www.ilo.org /wcmsp5/groups/public/—dgreports/—dcomm/—publ/documents/publication /wcms_650553.pdf. Note that data is not available for all countries.

12. **Proportion of Women in Managerial Positions** from *ILOSTAT SDG Indicator 5.5.2:* https://ilostat.ilo.org/data/ and *2020: Trends and Statistics:* https://worlds -women-2020-data-undesa.hub.arcgis.com/datasets/undesa::proportion -of-women-in-managerial-positions/explore.

13. **Share of Seats in Parliament Held by Women** (% held by women) from the Inter-parliamentary Union (includes National Assemblies and Congresses): https:// data.ipu.org/women-ranking?month=4&year=2021.

Notes and Suggestions for Obtaining Current Statistics

1. Many countries lack the human and economic resources to reliably collect and analyze data on women's issues and status, so data is unavailable for some countries on some indicators. Also, Appendix data may be outdated due to changes in abortion laws and recent elections or due to a lack of current data. Keep in mind that abortion laws are often more detailed than presented here; for example, the Appendix indicates whether abortion is criminalized but does not indicate the criminal penalties for those obtaining or performing abortions.

2. For country data on "Lifetime Physical and/or Sexual Intimate Partner Violence and Lifetime Non-Partner Sexual Violence," see UN Women's *Global Database on Violence Against Women:* http://evaw-global-database.unwomen.org/en/countries.

3. The World Bank's *Gender Portal* (https://www.worldbank.org/en/data/datatopics /gender) also has data on a variety of other indicators, including contraceptive prevalence; banking; education; laws on domestic violence, sexual harassment, and equality at work; and women's power to make decisions regarding purchases, their health care, and visiting family.

4. UN Women and the UNDP publish updated figures almost annually. Check for the most recent *Human Development Report and Progress of the World's Women.*

Country	Location	Global Gender Gap Index	Life Expectancy Women	Mean Years of Schooling (Women)	Average Age at Marriage for Females	Fertility Rate (births per woman)	Adolescent Birth Rate	Maternal Mortality Ratio (per 100,000 live births)	Abortion Law (Whether and under what conditions it is allowed)	Women % of Total Labor Force	Adjusted Gender Pay Gap	Proportion of Women in Managerial Positions	Percent of Seats in Parliament Held by Women
Afghanistan	Southern Asia, north and west of Pakistan, east of Iran	0.444	66.4	1.9	21.5	4.3	69.0	638	Criminalized except to save the woman's life	21.6	No data	4.9	27.2
Albania	Southeastern Europe, bordering the Adriatic Sea and Ionian Sea, between Greece and Serbia and Montenegro	0.770	80.2	9.7	24.2	1.6	19.6	15	Without restriction as to reason; parental authorization/notification required; gestational limit of 12 weeks	43.0	13.8	34.1	29.5
Algeria	Northern Africa, bordering the Mediterranean Sea, between Morocco and Tunisia	0.633	78.1	7.7	28.2	3.0	10.1	112	To save the woman's life; preserve health	19.9	No data	8.4	21.2
Andorra	Southwestern Europe, Pyrenees mountains, on the border between France and Spain	No data	No data	10.4	No data	1.3	No data	No data	Criminalized except to save the woman's life	No data	No data	No data	46.4
Angola	Southern Africa, bordering the South Atlantic Ocean, between Namibia and Democratic Republic of the Congo	0.657	64.0	4.0	21.5	5.4	150.5	241	Criminalized except to save the woman's life; preserve health	50.3	No data	19.7	29.6
Antigua and Barbuda	Caribbean islands between the Caribbean Sea and the North Atlantic Ocean, east-southeast of Puerto Rico	No data	78.1	No data	No data	2.0	42.8	42	Criminalized except to save the woman's life	No data	No data	45.1	31.4

Country	Location	Global Gender Gap Index	Life Expectancy for Women	Mean Years of Schooling (Women)	Average Age at Marriage for Females	Fertility Rate (births per woman)	Adolescent Birth Rate	Maternal Mortality Ratio (per 100,000 live births)	Abortion Law (Whether and under what conditions it is allowed)	Women % of Total Labor Force	Adjusted Gender Pay Gap	Proportion of Women in Managerial Positions	Percent of Seats in Parliament Held by Women
Argentina	Southern South America, bordering the South Atlantic Ocean, between Chile and Uruguay	0.752	80.0	11.1	No data	2.2	62.8	39	Without restriction as to reason; gestational limit of 14 weeks	43.3	20.3	31.6	41.9
Armenia	Southwestern Asia, east of Turkey	0.673	78.5	11.3	24.2	1.8	21.5	26	Without restriction as to reason; parental authorization/notification required; gestational limit of 12 weeks	44.2	29.7	26.2	22.7
Australia	Oceania, continent between the Indian Ocean and the South Pacific Ocean	0.731	85.4	12.8	29.9	1.7	11.7	6	Without restriction as to reason; law determined at state level	46.6	19.2	37.8	37.9
Austria	Central Europe, north of Italy and Slovenia	0.777	83.9	12.2	27.1	1.5	7.3	5	Without restriction as to reason; gestational limit of 90 days	46.4	No data	32.8	38.9
Azerbaijan	Southwestern Asia, bordering the Caspian Sea, between Iran and Russia, with a small European portion north of the Caucasus range	0.688	75.5	10.2	24.2	1.8	55.8	26	Without restriction as to reason; gestational limit of 12 weeks	48.6	No data	35.8	18.2
Bahamas	Caribbean chain of islands in the North Atlantic Ocean, southeast of Florida, northeast of Cuba	0.725	76.1	11.7	27.4	1.7	30.0	70	Criminalized with some exceptions to save the woman's life; preserve health	48.2	No data	51.6	21.8

Country	Location	Global Gender Gap Index	Life Expectancy for Women	Mean Years of Schooling (Women)	Average Age at Marriage for Females	Fertility Rate (births per woman)	Adolescent Birth Rate	Maternal Mortality Ratio (per 100,000 live births)	Abortion Law (Whether and under what conditions it is allowed)	Women % of Total Labor Force	Adjusted Gender Pay Gap	Proportion of Women in Managerial Positions	Percent of Seats in Parliament Held by Women
Bahrain	Middle East, archipelago in the Persian Gulf, east of Saudi Arabia	0.632	78.4	9.1	No data	2.0	13.4	14	Criminalized except to save the woman's life	20.1	No data	10.6	18.8
Bangladesh	Southern Asia, bordering the Bay of Bengal, between Burma and India	0.719	74.6	5.7	18.8	2.0	83.0	173	Criminalized except to save the woman's life	30.5	2.2	10.7	20.9
Barbados	Caribbean, island in the North Atlantic Ocean, northeast of Venezuela	0.769	80.5	11.0	No data	1.6	33.6	27	With physician consent up to 13 weeks to save the woman's life; rape or incest; fetal impairment; preserve health; socioeconomic grounds; parental authorization/ notification required	49.3	No data	45.9	29.4
Belarus	Eastern Europe, east of Poland	0.758	79.6	12.2	22.5	1.4	14.5	2	Without restriction as to reason; gestational limit of 12 weeks	49.0	No data	49.1	34.7
Belgium	Western Europe, bordering the North Sea, between France and the Netherlands	0.789	83.9	11.9	26.3	1.6	4.7	5	Without restriction as to reason; gestational limit of 14 weeks	46.2	6.3	34.5	42.9
Belize	Central America, bordering the Caribbean Sea, between Guatemala and Mexico	0.699	77.8	9.9	20.5	2.3	68.5	36	"Broad Social or Economic Grounds"; permitted in cases of fetal impairment	38.8	No data	56.7	19.6

Country	Location	Global Gender Gap Index	Life Expectancy for Women	Mean Years of Schooling (Women)	Average Age at Marriage for Females	Fertility Rate (births per woman)	Adolescent Birth Rate	Maternal Mortality Ratio (per 100,000 live births)	Abortion Law (Whether and under what conditions it is allowed)	Women % of Total Labor Force	Adjusted Gender Pay Gap	Proportion of Women in Managerial Positions	Percent of Seats in Parliament Held by Women
Benin	Western Africa, bordering the Bight of Benin, between Nigeria and Togo	0.653	63.3	2.4	20.7	4.8	86.1	397	To preserve health	49.2	No data	No data	8.4
Bhutan	Southern Asia, between China and India	0.639	72.2	3.3	23.8	2.0	20.2	183	Criminalized except to save the woman's life; rape or incest; grounds related to woman's age or capacity to care for a child	40.8	No data	18.5	15.3
Bolivia	Central South America, southwest of Brazil	0.722	74.5	8.3	24.0	2.7	64.9	155	To preserve health	44.3	No data	30.1	48.2
Bosnia-Herzegovina	Southeastern Europe, bordering the Adriatic Sea and Croatia	0.713	79.9	8.9	25.7	1.3	9.6	10	Without restriction as to reason; parental authorization/notification required; gestational limit of 12 weeks	40.6	No data	24.3	24.6
Botswana	Southern Africa, north of South Africa	0.716	72.4	9.5	22.9	2.8	46.1	144	To preserve health	48.9	No data	54.5	10.8
Brazil	Eastern South America, bordering the Atlantic Ocean	0.695	79.6	8.2	23.1	1.7	59.1	60	Criminalized except to save the woman's life; rape; grounds related to woman's age or capacity to care for a child	43.9	27.2	38.2	14.8
Brunei Darussalam	Southeastern Asia, bordering the South China Sea and Malaysia	0.678	77.1	9.1	26.1	1.8	10.3	31	Criminalized except to save the woman's life	41.6	No data	33.0	9.1

Country	Location	Global Gender Gap Index	Life Expectancy for Women	Mean Years of Schooling (Women)	Average Age at Marriage for Females	Fertility Rate (births per woman)	Adolescent Birth Rate	Maternal Mortality Ratio (per 100,000 live births)	Abortion Law (Whether and under what conditions it is allowed)	Women % of Total Labor Force	Adjusted Gender Pay Gap	Proportion of Women in Managerial Positions	Percent of Seats in Parliament Held by Women
Bulgaria	Southeastern Europe, bordering the Black Sea, between Romania and Turkey	0.746	78.7	11.5	32.6	1.6	39.9	10	Without restriction as to reason; gestational limit of 12 weeks	46.1	18.9	41.3	27.1
Burkina Faso	Western Africa, north of Ghana	0.651	62.3	1.1	20	5.1	104.3	320	To preserve health	44.7	No data	58.1	6.3
Burundi	Central Africa, east of Democratic Republic of the Congo	0.769	63.4	2.6	22.8	5.3	55.6	548	To preserve health	51.9	No data	32.4	38.9
Cambodia	Southeastern Asia, bordering the Gulf of Thailand, between Thailand, Vietnam, and Laos	0.684	71.9	4.2	21.6	2.5	50.2	160	Without restriction as to reason; gestational limit of 14 weeks; parental authorization/ notification required	48.9	No data	24.1	19.8
Cameroon	Western Africa, bordering the Bight of Biafra, between Equatorial Guinea and Nigeria	0.692	60.6	4.7	22.2	4.5	105.8	529	To preserve health	47.1	No data	49.3	31.1
Canada	Northern North America, bordering the North Atlantic Ocean on the east, North Pacific Ocean on the west, and the Arctic Ocean on the north, north of the U.S.	0.772	84.4	13.4	27.2	1.5	8.4	10	Without restriction as to reason	47.2	17.9	35.5	33.8

Country	Location	Global Gender Gap Index	Life Expectancy for Women	Mean Years of Schooling (Women)	Average Age at Marriage for Females	Fertility Rate (births per woman)	Adolescent Birth Rate	Maternal Mortality Ratio (per 100,000 live births)	Abortion Law (Whether and under what conditions it is allowed)	Women % of Total Labor Force	Adjusted Gender Pay Gap	Proportion of Women in Managerial Positions	Percent of Seats in Parliament Held by Women
Cape Verde (Cabo Verde)	Western Africa, group of islands in the North Atlantic Ocean, west of Senegal	0.716	76.2	6.0	24.6	2.2	73.8	58	Without restriction as to reason; gestational limit of 12 weeks	44.2	19.2	46.0	26.4
Central African Republic	Central Africa, north of Democratic Republic of the Congo	No data	55.5	3.0	17.9	4.6	129.1	829	To preserve health; rape or incest; fetal impairment note: law unclear	45.8	No data	No data	8.6
Chad	Central Africa, south of Libya	0.593	55.7	1.3	18.8	5.6	161.1	1,140	To preserve health; rape or incest	45.6	No data	No data	15.4
Chile	Southern South America, bordering the South Pacific Ocean, between Argentina and Peru	0.716	82.4	10.5	27.4	1.6	41.1	13	Criminalized except when a woman's life is in danger, a fetus is unviable, or pregnancy results from rape	42.4	26.1	27.5	23.7
China	Eastern Asia, bordering the East China Sea, Korea Bay, Yellow Sea, and South China Sea, between North Korea and Vietnam	0.682	79.2	7.7	25.4	1.7	7.6	29	Without restriction as to reason; spousal authorization required; sex selective abortion prohibited	43.6	22.1	No data	24.9
Colombia	Northern South America, bordering the Caribbean Sea, between Panama and Venezuela, and bordering the North Pacific Ocean, between Ecuador and Panama	0.725	80.0	8.6	22.7	1.8	66.7	83	To preserve health	42.7	No data	53.4	19.6

Country	Location	Global Gender Gap Index	Life Expectancy for Women	Mean Years of Schooling (Women)	Average Age at Marriage for Females	Fertility Rate (births per woman)	Adolescent Birth Rate	Maternal Mortality Ratio (per 100,000 live births)	Abortion Law (Whether and under what conditions it is allowed)	Women % of Total Labor Force	Adjusted Gender Pay Gap	Proportion of Women in Managerial Positions	Percent of Seats in Parliament Held by Women
Comoros	Southern Africa, group of islands at the northern mouth of the Mozambique Channel, about two-thirds of the way between northern Madagascar and northern Mozambique	No data	66.1	4.0	22.6	4.1	65.4	273	To preserve health	37.7	No data	25.6	16.7
Congo	Western Africa, bordering the South Atlantic Ocean, between Angola and Gabon	No data	66.0	6.1	21.9	4.4	112.2	378	Prohibited altogether	49.1	No data	No data	13.6
Congo, Democratic Republic of	Central Africa, northeast of Angola	0.576	62.2	5.3	20.9	5.8	124.2	473	To preserve health; rape or incest; fetal impairment	48.5	No data	20.2	14.3
Costa Rica	Central America, bordering both the Caribbean Sea and the North Pacific Ocean, between Nicaragua and Panama	0.786	82.9	8.9	26.4	1.7	53.5	27	To preserve health (not save life)	40.5	17.4	41.0	45.6
Cote d'Ivoire	Western Africa, bordering the North Atlantic Ocean, between Ghana and Liberia	0.637	59.1	4.2	23.0	4.6	117.6	617	Criminalized except to save the woman's life or in cases of rape	41.0	No data	56.9	14.7
Croatia	Southeastern Europe, bordering the Adriatic Sea, between Bosnia and Herzegovina and Slovenia	0.733	81.6	11.1	27.4	1.5	8.7	8	Without restriction as to reason; parental authorization/ notification required; gestational limit of 10 weeks	46.2	No data	28.4	31.1

Country	Location	Global Gender Gap Index	Life Expectancy for Women	Mean Years of Schooling (Women)	Average Age at Marriage for Females	Fertility Rate (births per woman)	Adolescent Birth Rate	Maternal Mortality Ratio (per 100,000 live births)	Abortion Law (Whether and under what conditions it is allowed)	Women % of Total Labor Force	Adjusted Gender Pay Gap	Proportion of Women in Managerial Positions	Percent of Seats in Parliament Held by Women
Cuba	Caribbean, island between the Caribbean Sea and the North Atlantic Ocean, 150 km south of Key West, Florida	0.746	80.8	11.2	22.1	1.6	51.6	36	Without restriction as to reason; parental authorization/ notification required; gestational limit of 12 weeks	38.8	No data	38.1	53.4
Cyprus	Middle East, island in the Mediterranean Sea, south of Turkey	0.707	83.0	12.1	26.4	1.3	4.6	6	Without restriction as to reason; gestational limit of 12 weeks	45.8	14.3	24.2	21.4
Czech Republic	Central Europe, between Germany, Poland, Slovakia, and Austria	0.711	81.9	12.5	32.4	1.7	12.0	3	Without restriction as to reason; parental authorization/ notification required; gestational limit of 12 weeks	44.7	19.6	27.8	20.6
Denmark	Northern Europe, bordering the Baltic Sea and the North Sea, on a peninsula north of Germany (Jutland)	0.768	82.9	12.8	31.9	1.7	4.1	4	Without restriction as to reason; parental authorization/ notification required; gestational limit of 12 weeks	47.1	No data	27.9	39.7
Djibouti	Eastern Africa, bordering the Gulf of Aden and the Red Sea, between Eritrea and Somalia	No data	69.4	No data	29.9	2.7	18.8	248	To preserve health	39.9	No data	12.3	26.2

Country	Location	Global Gender Gap Index	Life Expectancy for Women	Mean Years of Schooling (Women)	Average Age at Marriage for Females	Fertility Rate (births per woman)	Adolescent Birth Rate	Maternal Mortality Ratio (per 100,000 live births)	Abortion Law (Whether and under what conditions it is allowed)	Women % of Total Labor Force	Adjusted Gender Pay Gap	Proportion of Women in Managerial Positions	Percent of Seats in Parliament Held by Women
Dominica	Caribbean, island between the Caribbean Sea and the North Atlantic Ocean, about halfway between Puerto Rico and Trinidad and Tobago	No data	No data	No data	No data	1.9	No data	No data	Criminalized unless to save the woman's life	No data	No data	48.4	34.4
Dominican Republic	Caribbean, eastern two-thirds of the island of Hispaniola, between the Caribbean Sea and the North Atlantic Ocean, east of Haiti	0.699	77.4	8.8	21.5	2.3	94.3	95	Prohibited and criminalized	40.9	No data	40.4	25.7
Ecuador	Western South America, bordering the Pacific Ocean at the Equator, between Colombia and Peru	0.739	79.8	8.7	22.0	2.4	79.3	59	To preserve health	41.0	15.5	38.6	38.0
Egypt	Northern Africa, bordering the Mediterranean Sea, between Libya and the Gaza Strip, and the Red Sea north of Sudan, and includes the Asian Sinai Peninsula	0.639	74.4	6.8	22.3	3.3	53.8	37	Prohibited altogether	20.6	27.9	7.1	22.7
El Salvador	Central America, bordering the North Pacific Ocean, between Guatemala and Honduras	0.738	77.8	6.6	22.6	2.0	69.5	46	Prohibited and criminalized	42.0	16.3	44.3	27.4

Country	Location	Global Gender Gap Index	Life Expectancy Women	Mean Years of Schooling (Women)	Average Age at Marriage for Females	Fertility Rate (births per woman)	Adolescent Birth Rate	Maternal Mortality Ratio (per 100,000 live births)	Abortion Law (Whether and under what conditions it is allowed)	Women % of Total Labor Force	Adjusted Gender Pay Gap	Proportion of Women in Managerial Positions	Percent of Seats in Parliament Held by Women
Equatorial Guinea	Western Africa, bordering the Bight of Biafra, between Cameroon and Gabon	No data	59.9	4.2	20.5	4.4	155.6	301	To preserve health	36.7	No data	No data	20.3
Eritrea	Eastern Africa, bordering the Red Sea, between Djibouti and Sudan	No data	68.6	No data	No data	4.0	52.6	480	To preserve health; rape or incest	46.0	No data	No data	22.0
Estonia	Eastern Europe, bordering the Baltic Sea and Gulf of Finland, between Latvia and Russia	0.733	82.7	13.6	33.6	1.7	7.7	9	Without restriction as to reason; gestational limit of 12 weeks	48.5	25.2	37.4	25.7
Eswatini	Southern Africa, between Mozambique and South Africa	0.729	64.8	6.3	26.5	3.0	76.7	437	To preserve health; rape or incest; fetal impairment	48.0	No data	43.4	18.4
Ethiopia	Eastern Africa, west of Somalia	0.691	68.5	1.7	21.3	4.1	66.7	401	Criminalized except to save the woman's life; rape or incest; fetal impairment; preserve health; grounds related to woman's age or capacity to care for a child	46.6	No data	26.5	37.3
Fiji	Oceania, island group in the South Pacific Ocean, about two-thirds of the way from Hawaii to New Zealand	0.674	69.3	11.0	No data	2.8	49.4	34	Criminalized except to save the woman's life; rape or incest; fetal impairment; preserve health; socioeconomic grounds; parental authorization/notification required	32.9	No data	38.9	21.6

Country	Location	Global Gender Gap Index	Life Expectancy Gap for Women	Mean Years of Schooling (Women)	Average Age at Marriage for Females	Fertility Rate (births per woman)	Adolescent Birth Rate	Maternal Mortality Ratio (per 100,000 live births)	Abortion Law (Whether and under what conditions it is allowed)	Women % of Total Labor Force	Adjusted Gender Pay Gap	Proportion of Women in Managerial Positions	Percent of Seats in Parliament Held by Women
Finland	Northern Europe, bordering the Baltic Sea, Gulf of Bothnia, and Gulf of Finland, between Sweden and Russia	0.861	84.7	13.0	30.7	1.4	5.8	3	To save the woman's life; rape or incest; fetal impairment; preserve health; grounds related to age of woman or capacity to care for a child; socioeconomic grounds	48.0	19.5	37.5	46.0
France	Western Europe, bordering the Bay of Biscay and English Channel, between Belgium and Spain, southeast of the UK; bordering the Mediterranean Sea, between Italy and Spain	0.784	85.5	11.3	32.0	1.9	4.7	8	Without restriction as to reason; gestational limit of 14 weeks	48.1	12.5	35.5	38.6
Gabon	Western Africa, bordering the Atlantic Ocean at the Equator, between Republic of the Congo and Equatorial Guinea	No data	68.7	7.8	22.9	3.9	96.2	252	To save the woman's life; rape or incest; fetal impairment	40.0	No data	No data	18.7
Gambia	Western Africa, bordering the North Atlantic Ocean and Senegal	0.644	63.5	3.3	21.5	5.2	78.2	597	Criminalized unless to save the woman's life; fetal impairment	44.0	16.1	17.4	8.6
Georgia	Southwestern Asia, bordering the Black Sea, between Turkey and Russia	0.732	78.1	13.2	22.8	2.1	46.4	25	Without restriction as to reason; parental authorization/notification required; gestational limit of 12 weeks	46.4	No data	36.1	20.7

Country	Location	Global Gender Gap Index	Life Expectancy for Women	Mean Years of Schooling (Women)	Average Age at Marriage for Females	Fertility Rate (births per woman)	Adolescent Birth Rate	Maternal Mortality Ratio (per 100,000 live births)	Abortion Law (Whether and under what conditions it is allowed)	Women % of Total Labor Force	Adjusted Gender Pay Gap	Proportion of Women in Managerial Positions	Percent of Seats in Parliament Held by Women
Germany	Central Europe, bordering the Baltic Sea and the North Sea, between the Netherlands and Poland, south of Denmark	0.796	83.7	13.9	31.7	1.5	8.1	7	Without restriction as to reason; gestational limit of 14 weeks	46.3	No data	28.1	31.9
Ghana	Western Africa, bordering the Gulf of Guinea, between Cote d'Ivoire and Togo	0.666	65.2	6.6	23.7	3.8	66.6	308	To preserve health; rape or incest; fetal impairment; preserve health; grounds related to woman's age or capacity to care for a child	46.7	No data	33.8	14.6
Greece	Southern Europe, bordering the Aegean Sea, Ionian Sea, and the Mediterranean Sea, between Albania and Turkey	0.689	84.7	10.3	29.2	1.4	7.2	3	Without restriction as to reason; parental authorization/notification required; gestational limit of 12 weeks	43.8	No data	29.4	21.7
Grenada	Caribbean, island between the Caribbean Sea and Atlantic Ocean, north of Trinidad and Tobago	No data	75.0	No data	No data	2.0	29.2	25	To preserve health	No data	No data	No data	32.1
Guam	Oceania, island in the North Pacific Ocean, about three-quarters of the way from Hawaii to the Philippines	No data	No data	No data	No data	2.3	No data	No data	No data	40.7	No data	No data	No data

Country	Location	Global Gender Gap Index	Life Expectancy for Women	Mean Years of Schooling (Women)	Average Age at Marriage for Females	Fertility Rate (births per woman)	Adolescent Birth Rate	Maternal Mortality Ratio (per 100,000 live births)	Abortion Law (Whether and under what conditions it is allowed)	Women % of Total Labor Force	Adjusted Gender Pay Gap	Proportion of Women in Managerial Positions	Percent of Seats in Parliament Held by Women
Guatemala	Central America, bordering the North Pacific Ocean, between El Salvador and Mexico, and bordering the Gulf of Honduras (Caribbean Sea) between Honduras and Belize	0.655	77.2	6.6	22.7	2.8	70.9	95	Criminalized except to save the woman's life	33.5	No data	36.8	19.4
Guinea	Western Africa, bordering the North Atlantic Ocean, between Guinea-Bissau and Sierra Leone	0.660	62.1	1.5	19.8	4.6	135.3	576	To preserve health	54.5	No data	23.4	16.7
Guinea-Bissau	Western Africa, bordering the North Atlantic Ocean, between Guinea and Senegal	No data	60.2	No data	24.1	4.4	104.8	667	Without restriction as to reason	47.7	No data	No data	13.7
Guyana	Northern South America, bordering the North Atlantic Ocean, between Suriname and Venezuela	0.728	73.1	8.9	19.2	2.4	74.4	169	Without restriction as to reason; gestational limit of 8 weeks	39.2	No data	40.5	35.7

Country	Location	Global Gender Gap Index	Life Expectancy for Women	Mean Years of Schooling (Women)	Average Age at Marriage for Females	Fertility Rate (births per woman)	Adolescent Birth Rate	Maternal Mortality Ratio (per 100,000 live births)	Abortion Law (Whether and under what conditions it is allowed)	Women % of Total Labor Force	Adjusted Gender Pay Gap	Proportion of Women in Managerial Positions	Percent of Seats in Parliament Held by Women
Haiti	Caribbean, western one-third of the island of Hispaniola, between the Caribbean Sea and the North Atlantic Ocean, west of the Dominican Republic	No data	66.2	4.3	24.9	2.9	51.7	480	Prohibited altogether	48.0	No data	24.0	0.0
Honduras	Central America, bordering the Caribbean Sea, between Guatemala and Nicaragua and bordering the Gulf of Fonseca (North Pacific Ocean), between El Salvador and Nicaragua	0.716	77.6	6.6	21.2	2.4	72.9	65	Prohibited and criminalized	38.3	No data	49.3	21.1
Hong Kong	Eastern Asia, bordering the South China Sea and China	No data	87.7	11.9	29.9	1.1	2.7	No data	Two doctors must confirm fetal impairment or that having the child would seriously harm the woman's physical or mental health; counseling required for those under 26	49.3	No data	No data	No data
Hungary	Central Europe, northwest of Romania	0.688	80.3	11.7	32.9	1.5	24.0	12	Without restriction as to reason; gestational limit of 12 weeks	45.2	12.7	39.2	12.1

Country	Location	Global Gender Gap Index	Life Expectancy for Women	Mean Years of Schooling (Women)	Average Age at Marriage for Females	Fertility Rate (births per woman)	Adolescent Birth Rate	Maternal Mortality Ratio (per 100,000 live births)	Abortion Law (Whether and under what conditions it is allowed)	Women % of Total Labor Force	Adjusted Gender Pay Gap	Proportion of Women in Managerial Positions	Percent of Seats in Parliament Held by Women
Iceland	Northern Europe, island between the Greenland Sea and the North Atlantic Ocean, northwest of the United Kingdom	0.892	84.5	12.6	32.4	1.8	6.3	4	Without restriction as to reason; gestational limit of 22 weeks	47.2	No data	38.6	39.7
India	Southern Asia, bordering the Arabian Sea and the Bay of Bengal, between Burma and Pakistan	0.625	71.0	5.4	21.4	2.2	13.2	133	Permitted in cases of rape or fetal impairment; gestational limit of 24 weeks; parental authorization notification required	20.3	No data	14.6	13.4
Indonesia	Southeastern Asia, archipelago between the Indian Ocean and the Pacific Ocean	0.688	74.0	7.8	22.4	2.3	47.4	177	Criminalized except to save the woman's life; rape; fetal impairment; spousal authorization required	39.5	23.1	32.7	21.0
Iran	Middle East, bordering the Gulf of Oman, the Persian Gulf, and the Caspian Sea, between Iraq and Pakistan	0.582	77.9	10.3	23.1	2.1	40.6	16	To save the woman's life; fetal impairment	19.4	No data	18.9	5.6
Iraq	Middle East, bordering the Gulf of Oman, the Persian Gulf, and the Caspian Sea, between Iraq and Pakistan	0.535	72.7	6.0	22.7	3.6	71.7	79	Prohibited altogether	13.4	No data	18.9	26.4

Country	Location	Global Gender Gap Index	Life Expectancy for Women	Mean Years of Schooling (Women)	Average Age at Marriage for Females	Fertility Rate (births per woman)	Adolescent Birth Rate	Maternal Mortality Ratio (per 100,000 live births)	Abortion Law (Whether and under what conditions it is allowed)	Women % of Total Labor Force	Adjusted Gender Pay Gap	Proportion of Women in Managerial Positions	Percent of Seats in Parliament Held by Women
Ireland	Western Europe, occupying five-sixths of the island of Ireland in the North Atlantic Ocean, west of Great Britain	0.800	83.9	12.9	32.4	1.7	7.5	5	Without restriction as to reason; gestational limit of 12 weeks	45.8	No data	36.4	27.3
Israel	Middle East, bordering the Mediterranean Sea, between Egypt and Lebanon	0.724	84.5	13.1	26.2	3.0	9.6	3	To preserve health	47.6	No data	34.5	24.2
Italy	Southern Europe, a peninsula extending into the central Mediterranean Sea, northeast of Tunisia	0.721	85.5	10.2	32.2	1.3	5.2	2	Without restriction as to reason; gestational limit of 90 days	42.7	16.2	27.3	35.3
Jamaica	Caribbean, island in the Caribbean Sea, south of Cuba	0.741	76.1	10.2	25.3	2.0	52.8	80	Prohibited altogether	45.9	No data	56.7	31.0
Japan	Eastern Asia, island chain between the North Pacific Ocean and the Sea of Japan, east of the Korean Peninsula	0.656	87.7	13.1	29.2	1.4	3.8	5	No restrictions if before 22 weeks; some exceptions to save the woman's life	44.3	No data	14.8	14.4

Country	Location	Global Gender Gap Index	Life Expectancy for Women	Mean Years of Schooling (Women)	Average Age at Marriage for Females	Fertility Rate (births per woman)	Adolescent Birth Rate	Maternal Mortality Ratio (per 100,000 live births)	Abortion Law (Whether and under what conditions it is allowed)	Women % of Total Labor Force	Adjusted Gender Pay Gap	Proportion of Women in Managerial Positions	Percent of Seats in Parliament Held by Women
Jordan	Middle East, northwest of Saudi Arabia	0.638	76.3	10.3	24.6	2.7	25.9	46	To preserve health	18.3	16.5	62.0	11.8
Kazakhstan	Central Asia, northwest of China; a small portion west of the Ural (Zhayyq) River in eastern-most Europe	0.710	77.7	10.9	22.4	2.9	29.8	10	Without restriction as to reason; gestational limit of 12 weeks	48.0	No data	37.0	24.5
Kenya	Eastern Africa, bordering the Indian Ocean, between Somalia and Tanzania	0.692	69.0	6.0	21.9	3.4	75.1	342	To preserve health	49.3	No data	49.6	23.2
Kiribati	Oceania, group of 33 coral atolls in the Pacific Ocean, straddling the Equator; the capital Tarawa is about halfway between Hawaii and Australia	No data	72.3	No data	21.5	3.5	16.2	92	Criminalized except to save the woman's life	No data	No data	40.2	6.7
Korea, North	Eastern Asia, northern half of the Korean Peninsula bordering the Korea Bay and the Sea of Japan, between China and South Korea	No data	75.7	No data	No data	1.9	0.3	89	Without restriction as to reason	47.1	No data	No data	17.6

Country	Location	Global Gender Gap Index	Life Expectancy for Women	Mean Years of Schooling (Women)	Average Age at Marriage for Females	Fertility Rate (births per woman)	Adolescent Birth Rate	Maternal Mortality Ratio (per 100,000 live births)	Abortion Law (Whether and under what conditions it is allowed)	Women % of Total Labor Force	Adjusted Gender Pay Gap	Proportion of Women in Managerial Positions	Percent of Seats in Parliament Held by Women
Korea, South	Eastern Asia, southern half of the Korean Peninsula bordering the Sea of Japan and the Yellow Sea	0.687	86.0	11.4	31.5	0.9	1.4	11	Without restriction as to reason	42.6	28.3	15.7	19.0
Kuwait	Middle East, bordering the Persian Gulf, between Iraq and Saudi Arabia	0.621	76.6	8.0	25.7	2.1	8.2	12	To preserve health; fetal impairment; preserve health; parental/spousal authorization required	25.1	No data	13.6	1.5
Kyrgyzstan	Central Asia, west of China	0.681	75.6	11.2	21.2	3.3	32.8	60	Without restriction as to reason; gestational limit of 12 weeks	38.5	No data	37.8	17.1
Laos	Southeastern Asia, northeast of Thailand, west of Vietnam	0.750	69.7	4.9	20.7	2.6	65.4	185	Prohibited altogether	49.1	No data	59.0	22.0
Latvia	Eastern Europe, bordering the Baltic Sea, between Estonia and Lithuania	0.778	80.0	13.4	30.4	1.6	16.2	19	Without restriction as to reason; parental authorization/ notification required; gestational limit of 12 weeks	50.0	21.7	46.9	29.0
Lebanon	Middle East, bordering the Mediterranean Sea, between Israel and Syria	0.638	80.9	8.5	No data	2.1	14.5	29	Criminalized except to save the woman's life; requires approval from two physicians	24.5	No data	21.2	4.7

Country	Location	Global Gender Gap Index	Life Expectancy for Women	Mean Years of Schooling (Women)	Average Age at Marriage for Females	Fertility Rate (births per woman)	Adolescent Birth Rate	Maternal Mortality Ratio (per 100,000 live births)	Abortion Law (Whether and under what conditions it is allowed)	Women % of Total Labor Force	Adjusted Gender Pay Gap	Proportion of Women in Managerial Positions	Percent of Seats in Parliament Held by Women
Lesotho	Southern Africa, an enclave of South Africa	0.698	57.6	7.2	22.2	3.1	92.7	544	To preserve health (not save life); rape or incest; fetal impairment	45.4	No data	33.8	22.9
Liberia	Western Africa, bordering the North Atlantic Ocean, between Cote d'Ivoire and Sierra Leone	0.693	65.5	3.5	22.6	4.2	136.0	661	To preserve health; rape or incest; fetal impairment; approval from two physicians required	47.5	No data	20.0	8.7
Libya	Northern Africa, bordering the Mediterranean Sea, between Egypt and Tunisia	No data	76.0	8.5	No data	2.2	5.8	72	Prohibited and criminalized with some exceptions to save the woman's life	34.1	No data	No data	16.0
Liechtenstein	Central Europe, between Austria and Switzerland	No data	No data	No data	29.9	1.5	No data	No data	To preserve health; rape; parental authorization/notification required	No data	No data	No data	28.0
Lithuania	Eastern Europe, bordering the Baltic Sea, between Latvia and Russia	0.804	81.4	13.1	32.7	1.6	10.9	8	Without restriction as to reason up to 12 weeks; up to 22 weeks for medical reasons; parental authorization/notification required	50.5	16.6	37.9	27.7
Luxembourg	Western Europe, between France and Germany	0.726	84.3	12.0	30.7	1.3	4.7	5	Without restriction as to reason; gestational limit of 14 weeks	45.2	7.8	26.3	31.7

Country	Location	Global Gender Gap Index	Life Expectancy for Women	Mean Years of Schooling (Women)	Average Age at Marriage for Females	Fertility Rate (births per woman)	Adolescent Birth Rate	Maternal Mortality Ratio (per 100,000 live births)	Abortion Law (Whether and under what conditions it is allowed)	Women % of Total Labor Force	Adjusted Gender Pay Gap	Proportion of Women in Managerial Positions	Percent of Seats in Parliament Held by Women
Macau SAR	Eastern Asia, bordering the South China Sea and China	No data	No data	No data	30.3	1.2	No data	No data	No data	48.3	No data	No data	No data
Macedonia	Southeastern Europe, north of Greece	0.715	77.8	9.4	25.5	1.5	15.7	7	Without restriction as to reason; parental authorization/notification required ; gestational limit of 12 weeks	40.7	No data	19.9	39.2
Madagascar	Southern Africa, island in the Indian Ocean, east of Mozambique	0.725	68.7	6.4	19.8	4.0	109.6	335	Prohibited altogether	48.9	25.6	31.8	17.2
Malawi	Southern Africa, east of Zambia	0.671	67.4	6.9	20.4	4.1	132.7	349	Prohibited and criminalized except to save the woman's life	48.9	19.2	15.6	22.9
Malaysia	Southeastern Asia, peninsula bordering Thailand and northern one-third of the island of Borneo, bordering Indonesia, Brunei, and the South China Sea, south of Vietnam	0.676	78.3	10.3	25.1	2.0	13.4	29	To preserve health	38.6	No data	23.3	14.6
Maldives	Southern Asia, group of atolls in the Indian Ocean, south-southwest of India	0.642	80.8	7.0	22.5	1.8	7.8	53	Without restriction as to reason; gestational limit of 120 days	20.2	No data	80.8	4.6

Country	Location	Global Gender Gap Index	Life Expectancy for Women	Mean Years of Schooling (Women)	Average Age at Marriage for Females	Fertility Rate (births per woman)	Adolescent Birth Rate	Maternal Mortality Ratio (per 100,000 live births)	Abortion Law (Whether and under what conditions it is allowed)	Women % of Total Labor Force	Adjusted Gender Pay Gap	Proportion of Women in Managerial Positions	Percent of Seats in Parliament Held by Women
Mali	Western Africa, southwest of Algeria	0.591	60.1	1.7	18.8	5.8	169.1	562	Criminalized with exceptions to save the woman's life; rape or incest	42.2	No data	17.4	27.3
Malta	Southern Europe, islands in the Mediterranean Sea, south of Sicily (Italy)	0.703	84.3	11.1	28.0	1.1	12.9	6	Prohibited and criminalized	41.9	10.9	28.5	13.4
Marshall Islands	Oceania, two archipelagic island chains of 29 atolls, each made up of many small islets, and five single islands in the North Pacific Ocean, about halfway between Hawaii and Australia	No data	No data	10.7	24.2	4.0	No data	No data	Only to save a woman's life; spousal consent and counseling required	No data	No data	33.2	6.1
Mauritania	Northern Africa, bordering the North Atlantic Ocean, between Senegal and Western Sahara	0.606	66.5	3.8	21.8	4.5	71.0	766	Prohibited altogether	31.1	No data	No data	20.3
Mauritius	Southern Africa, island in the Indian Ocean, east of Madagascar	0.679	78.5	9.4	23.9	1.4	25.7	61	To preserve health; incest	39.6	No data	30.2	20.0

Country	Location	Global Gender Gap Index	Life Expectancy for Women	Mean Years of Schooling (Women)	Average Age at Marriage for Females	Fertility Rate (births per woman)	Adolescent Birth Rate	Maternal Mortality Ratio (per 100,000 live births)	Abortion Law (Whether and under what conditions it is allowed)	Women % of Total Labor Force	Adjusted Gender Pay Gap	Proportion of Women in Managerial Positions	Percent of Seats in Parliament Held by Women
Mexico	Middle America, bordering the Caribbean Sea and the Gulf of Mexico, between Belize and the United States and bordering the North Pacific Ocean, between Guatemala and the United States	0.757	77.9	8.6	23.2	2.1	60.4	33	Decriminalized in 2021; nationally allowed in cases of rape and incest; laws determined at the state level	38.5	22.5	38.5	48.4
Micronesia	Oceania, island group in the North Pacific Ocean, about three-quarters of the way from Hawaii to Indonesia	No data	69.6	No data	No data	3.0	13.9	88	Prohibited except to save the woman's life; laws also determined at state level	No data	No data	20.3	0.0
Moldova	Eastern Europe, northeast of Romania	0.768	76.2	11.8	25.0	1.3	22.4	19	Without restriction as to reason; parental authorization/notification required; gestational limit of 12 weeks	48.6	No data	42.3	24.8
Monaco	Western Europe, bordering the Mediterranean Sea on the southern coast of France, near the border with Italy	No data	No data	No data	29.2	No data	No data	No data	Only permitted to preserve the women's physical health	No data	No data	No data	33.3
Mongolia	Northern Asia, between China and Russia	0.716	74.1	10.7	23.0	2.9	31.0	45	Without restriction as to reason; gestational limit of 3 months	45.1	19.5	49.8	17.3

Country	Location	Global Gender Gap Index	Life Expectancy for Women	Mean Years of Schooling (Women)	Average Age at Marriage for Females	Fertility Rate (births per woman)	Adolescent Birth Rate	Maternal Mortality Ratio (per 100,000 live births)	Abortion Law (Whether and under what conditions it is allowed)	Women % of Total Labor Force	Adjusted Gender Pay Gap	Proportion of Women in Managerial Positions	Percent of Seats in Parliament Held by Women
Montenegro	Southeastern Europe, between the Adriatic Sea and Serbia	0.732	79.3	10.9	26.3	1.7	9.3	6	Sex selective abortion prohibited; parental authorization required; gestational limit of 12 weeks	44.0	No data	32.2	24.7
Morocco	Northern Africa, bordering the North Atlantic Ocean and the Mediterranean Sea, between Algeria and Western Sahara	0.612	77.9	4.7	24.4	2.4	31.0	70	To preserve health	24.3	No data	12.8	18.4
Mozambique	Southeastern Africa, bordering the Mozambique Channel, between South Africa and Tanzania	0.758	63.7	2.7	18.7	4.8	148.6	289	Without restriction up to 12 weeks; up to 16 in cases of rape	52.3	No data	24.3	42.2
Myanmar (Burma)	Southeastern Asia, bordering the Andaman Sea and the Bay of Bengal, between Bangladesh and Thailand	0.681	70.1	5.0	22.9	2.1	28.5	250	Criminalized except to save the woman's life	40.2	No data	32.3	15.0
Namibia	Southern Africa, bordering the South Atlantic Ocean, between Angola and South Africa	0.809	66.5	7.3	30.3	3.3	63.6	195	To preserve health; rape or incest; fetal impairment	49.2	21.1	43.6	35.6
Nauru	Oceania, island in the South Pacific Ocean, south of the Marshall Islands	No data	No data	No data	No data	No data	No data	No data	To preserve health; rape or incest; fetal impairment	No data	No data	36.1	10.5

Country	Location	Global Gender Gap Index	Life Expectancy for Women	Mean Years of Schooling (Women)	Average Age at Marriage for Females	Fertility Rate (births per woman)	Adolescent Birth Rate	Maternal Mortality Ratio (per 100,000 live births)	Abortion Law (Whether and under what conditions it is allowed)	Women % of Total Labor Force	Adjusted Gender Pay Gap	Proportion of Women in Managerial Positions	Percent of Seats in Parliament Held by Women
Nepal	Southern Asia, between China and India	0.683	72.2	4.3	20.1	1.9	65.1	186	Sex selective abortion prohibited; gestational limit of 12 weeks	55.8	26.7	13.2	33.6
Netherlands	Western Europe, bordering the North Sea, between Belgium and Germany	0.762	84.0	12.2	32.4	1.6	3.8	5	Without restriction as to reason	46.4	15.0	26.2	39.1
New Caledonia	Oceania, islands in the South Pacific Ocean, east of Australia	No data	No data	No data	32.8	1.9	No data	No data	Without restriction as to reason; gestational limit of 12 weeks	45.6	No data	No data	No data
New Zealand	Oceania, islands in the South Pacific Ocean, southeast of Australia	0.840	84.0	12.7	29.2	1.7	19.3	9	Without restriction as to reason; gestational limit of 20 weeks	47.9	No data	40.0	48.3
Nicaragua	Central America, bordering both the Caribbean Sea and the North Pacific Ocean, between Costa Rica and Honduras	0.796	78.0	7.2	21.1	2.4	85.0	98	Prohibited and criminalized	38.5	No data	35.2	47.3
Niger	Western Africa, southeast of Algeria	0.629	63.6	1.4	17.2	6.8	186.5	509	To preserve health; fetal impairment	42.5	No data	49.3	25.9
Nigeria	Western Africa, bordering the Gulf of Guinea, between Benin and Cameroon	0.627	55.6	5.7	21.2	5.3	107.3	917	Criminalized except to save the woman's life	43.1	No data	30.3	4.5

Country	Location	Global Gender Gap Index	Life Expectancy for Women	Mean Years of Schooling (Women)	Average Age at Marriage for Females	Fertility Rate (births per woman)	Adolescent Birth Rate	Maternal Mortality Ratio (per 100,000 live births)	Abortion Law (Whether and under what conditions it is allowed)	Women % of Total Labor Force	Adjusted Gender Pay Gap	Proportion of Women in Managerial Positions	Percent of Seats in Parliament Held by Women
Norway	Northern Europe, bordering the North Sea and the North Atlantic Ocean, west of Sweden	0.849	84.4	13.0	32.1	1.5	5.1	2	Without restriction as to reason; parental authorization/notification required; gestational limit of 12 weeks	47.0	10.2	34.1	44.4
Oman	Middle East, bordering the Arabian Sea, Gulf of Oman, and Persian Gulf, between Yemen and UAE	0.608	80.3	10.6	No data	2.8	13.1	19	Criminalized except to save the woman's life	15.4	No data	11.1	9.9
Pakistan	Southern Asia, bordering the Arabian Sea, between India on the east and Iran and Afghanistan on the west and China in the north	0.556	68.3	3.8	23.2	3.5	38.8	140	To preserve health	20.1	43.8	4.9	19.9
Palau	Oceania, group of islands in the North Pacific Ocean, southeast of the Philippines	No data	No data	No data	28.5	2.2	No data	No data	Prohibited; law unclear	No data	No data	29.9	6.9
Palestine	In the Middle East, on the eastern coast of the Mediterranean, bordered by Jordan, Lebanon, and Egypt; includes the West Bank and Gaza Strip claimed by Israel	No data	75.8	8.9	22.1 (West Bank and Gaza)	3.6 (West Bank and Gaza)	52.8	27	Criminalized except to save the woman's life (West Bank and Gaza)	20.3 (West Bank and Gaza)	No data	21.7	No data

Country	Location	Global Gender Gap Index	Life Expectancy for Women	Mean Years of Schooling (Women)	Average Age at Marriage for Females	Fertility Rate (births per woman)	Adolescent Birth Rate	Maternal Mortality Ratio (per 100,000 live births)	Abortion Law (Whether and under what conditions it is allowed)	Women % of Total Labor Force	Adjusted Gender Pay Gap	Proportion of Women in Managerial Positions	Percent of Seats in Parliament Held by Women
Panama	Central America, bordering both the Caribbean Sea and the North Pacific Ocean, between Colombia and Costa Rica	0.737	81.8	11.2	21.0	2.4	81.8	52	Criminalized except to save the woman's life; rape; fetal impairment; a health commission's approval required; parental authorization/notification required	41.0	12.7	45.8	22.5
Papua New Guinea	Oceania, group of islands including the eastern half of New Guinea between the Coral Sea and the South Pacific Ocean, east of Indonesia	0.635	65.8	4.0	21.4	3.5	52.7	145	Criminalized except to save the woman's life	48.7	No data	18.1	0.0
Paraguay	Central South America, northeast of Argentina	0.702	76.4	8.5	21.9	2.4	70.5	84	Criminalized except to save the woman's life	40.7	21.1	37.9	16.0
Peru	Western South America, bordering the South Pacific Ocean, between Chile and Ecuador	0.721	79.5	9.1	23.3	2.2	56.9	88	To preserve health	45.8	20.3	26.7	26.2
Philippines	Southeastern Asia, archipelago between the Philippine Sea and the South China Sea, east of Vietnam	0.784	75.5	9.6	23.4	2.5	54.2	121	Prohibited altogether	39.4	16.2	50.5	28.0

Country	Location	Global Gender Gap Index	Life Expectancy for Women	Mean Years of Schooling (Women)	Average Age at Marriage for Females	Fertility Rate (births per woman)	Adolescent Birth Rate	Maternal Mortality Ratio (per 100,000 live births)	Abortion Law (Whether and under what conditions it is allowed)	Women % of Total Labor Force	Adjusted Gender Pay Gap	Proportion of Women in Managerial Positions	Percent of Seats in Parliament Held by Women
Poland	Central Europe, east of Germany	0.713	82.6	12.5	26.6	1.4	10.5	2	To preserve health; rape or incest; fetal impairment; parental authorization/notification required	44.5	23.5	43.3	27.5
Portugal	Southwestern Europe, bordering the North Atlantic Ocean, west of Spain	0.775	84.9	9.4	30.1	1.4	8.4	8	Without restriction as to reason; parental authorization/notification required; gestational limit of 10 weeks	49.2	23.1	35.7	40.0
Puerto Rico	Caribbean, island between the Caribbean Sea and the North Atlantic Ocean, east of the Dominican Republic	No data	No data	No data	23.8	1.0	No data	No data	Without restriction as to reason	43.6	No data	No data	No data
Qatar	Middle East, peninsula bordering the Persian Gulf and Saudi Arabia	0.624	82.0	11.3	No data	1.8	9.9	9	To preserve health; fetal impairment	13.6	No data	14.0	9.8
Romania	Southeastern Europe, bordering the Black Sea, between Bulgaria and Ukraine	0.700	79.5	10.8	25.9	1.8	36.2	19	Without restriction as to reason; gestational limit of 14 weeks	42.9	12.5	35.0	18.5

Country	Location	Global Gender Gap Index	Life Expectancy for Women	Mean Years of Schooling (Women)	Average Age at Marriage for Females	Fertility Rate (births per woman)	Adolescent Birth Rate	Maternal Mortality Ratio (per 100,000 live births)	Abortion Law (Whether and under what conditions it is allowed)	Women % of Total Labor Force	Adjusted Gender Pay Gap	Proportion of Women in Managerial Positions	Percent of Seats in Parliament Held by Women
Russia	Northern Asia (the area west of the Urals is considered part of Europe), bordering the Arctic Ocean, between Europe and the North Pacific Ocean	0.708	77.8	11.9	No data	1.5	20.7	17	Without restriction as to reason	48.6	27.4	44.7	16.1
Rwanda	Central Africa, east of Democratic Republic of the Congo	0.805	71.1	4.0	24.3	4.0	39.1	248	To preserve health; rape or incest; forced marriage; grounds related to age	51.7	No data	28.6	55.7
Saint Kitts and Nevis	Caribbean, islands in the Caribbean Sea, about one-third of the way from Puerto Rico to Trinidad and Tobago	No data	No data	No data	No data	2.1	No data	No data	To preserve health	No data	No data	No data	25.0
Saint Lucia	Caribbean, island between the Caribbean Sea and North Atlantic Ocean, north of Trinidad and Tobago	No data	77.6	8.8	21.9	1.4	40.5	117	To preserve health	48.5	No data	57.3	20.7

Country	Location	Global Gender Gap Index	Life Expectancy for Women	Mean Years of Schooling (Women)	Average Age at Marriage for Females	Fertility Rate (births per woman)	Adolescent Birth Rate	Maternal Mortality Ratio (per 100,000 live births)	Abortion Law (Whether and under what conditions it is allowed)	Women % of Total Labor Force	Adjusted Gender Pay Gap	Proportion of Women in Managerial Positions	Percent of Seats in Parliament Held by Women
Saint Vincent & the Grenadines	Caribbean, islands between the Caribbean Sea and North Atlantic Ocean, north of Trinidad and Tobago	No data	75.1	8.9	21.2	1.9	49.0	68	Broad social or economic grounds; rape or incest; fetal impairment	41.6	No data	49.3	18.2
Samoa	Oceania, group of islands in the South Pacific Ocean, about halfway between Hawaii and New Zealand	No data	75.5	No data	23.8	3.8	23.9	43	To preserve health	34.4	No data	43.1	10.0
San Marino	Southern Europe, an enclave in central Italy	No data	No data	No data	31.3	1.3	No data	No data	Prohibited altogether	No data	No data	No data	33.3
Sao Tome & Principe	Southern Europe, an enclave in central Italy	No data	72.8	5.8	21	4.3	94.6	130	Without restriction as to reason; gestational limit of 12 weeks	36.3	No data	24.4	23.6
Saudi Arabia	Middle East, bordering the Persian Gulf and the Red Sea, north of Yemen	0.603	76.8	9.8	26.6	2.3	7.3	17	To preserve health; parental/spousal authorization required; approval of three physicians required	15.8	No data	16.4	19.9

Country	Location	Global Gender Gap Index	Life Expectancy Women	Mean Years of Schooling (Women)	Average Age at Marriage for Females	Fertility Rate (births per woman)	Adolescent Birth Rate	Maternal Mortality Ratio (per 100,000 live births)	Abortion Law (Whether and under what conditions it is allowed)	Women % of Total Labor Force	Adjusted Gender Pay Gap	Proportion of Women in Managerial Positions	Percent of Seats in Parliament Held by Women
Senegal	Western Africa, bordering the North Atlantic Ocean, between Guinea-Bissau and Mauritania	0.684	69.9	1.9	22.2	4.6	72.7	315	Prohibited altogether	40.5	No data	23.2	43.0
Serbia	Southeastern Europe, between Macedonia and Hungary	0.780	78.6	10.8	26.6	1.5	14.7	12	Without restriction as to reason; parental authorization/notification required; gestational limit of 12 weeks	44.7	No data	31.5	39.2
Seychelles	Archipelago in the Indian Ocean, northeast of Madagascar	No data	77.4	9.9	No data	2.3	62.1	53	To preserve health; rape or incest; fetal impairment; additional grounds, including mental health	No data	No data	47.7	22.9
Sierra Leone	Western Africa, bordering the North Atlantic Ocean, between Guinea and Liberia	0.655	55.5	2.9	23.1	4.2	112.8	1,120	Prohibited altogether	49.9	No data	37.9	12.3
Singapore	Southeastern Asia, islands between Malaysia and Indonesia	0.727	85.7	11.2	26.5	1.1	3.5	8	Without restriction as to reason; gestational limit of 24 weeks	41.7	No data	38.9	29.8
Slovakia	Central Europe, south of Poland	0.712	81.0	12.6	31.0	1.6	25.7	5	Without restriction as to reason; parental authorization/notification required; gestational limit of 12 weeks	45.4	17.9	35.5	22.7

Country	Location	Global Gender Gap Index	Life Expectancy for Women	Mean Years of Schooling (Women)	Average Age at Marriage for Females	Fertility Rate (births per woman)	Adolescent Birth Rate	Maternal Mortality Ratio (per 100,000 live births)	Abortion Law (Whether and under what conditions it is allowed)	Women % of Total Labor Force	Adjusted Gender Pay Gap	Proportion of Women in Managerial Positions	Percent of Seats in Parliament Held by Women
Slovenia	Central Europe, eastern Alps bordering the Adriatic Sea, between Austria and Croatia	0.741	84.0	12.6	34.0	1.6	3.8	7	Without restriction as to reason; parental authorization/notification required; gestational limit of 12 weeks	46.4	14.2	40.1	21.5
Solomon Islands	Oceania, group of islands in the South Pacific Ocean, east of Papua New Guinea	No data	74.9	No data	22.4	4.4	78.0	104	Criminalized except to save the woman's life; approval of two physicians, spouse or next of kin	48.6	No data	25.7	8.0
Somalia	Eastern Africa, bordering the Gulf of Aden and the Indian Ocean, east of Ethiopia	No data	59.1	No data	No data	6.0	100.1	829	To save the woman's life	23.5	No data	No data	24.3
South Africa	Southern Africa, at the southern tip of the continent of Africa	0.781	67.7	10.0	27.2	2.4	67.9	119	Without restriction as to reason; gestational limit of 12 weeks	45.3	31.1	31.4	45.9
South Sudan	East-Central Africa; south of Sudan, north of Uganda and Kenya, west of Ethiopia	No data	59.4	3.9	24.1	4.6	62.0	1,150	To save the woman's life or in case of fetal death	49.4	No data	No data	26.6
Spain	Southwestern Europe, bordering the Bay of Biscay, Mediterranean Sea, North Atlantic Ocean, and Pyrenees Mountains, southwest of France	0.788	86.2	10.2	27.7	1.2	7.7	4	Without restriction as to reason; gestational limit of 14 weeks; parental authorization/notification required	46.4	13.9	35.0	42.6

Country	Location	Global Gender Gap Index	Life Expectancy for Women	Mean Years of Schooling (Women)	Average Age at Marriage for Females	Fertility Rate (births per woman)	Adolescent Birth Rate	Maternal Mortality Ratio (per 100,000 live births)	Abortion Law (Whether and under what conditions it is allowed)	Women % of Adjusted Total Labor Force	Gender Pay Gap	Proportion of Women in Managerial Positions	Percent of Seats in Parliament Held by Women
Sri Lanka	Southern Asia, island in the Indian Ocean, south of India	0.670	80.3	10.6	23.9	2.2	20.9	36	Criminalized except to save the woman's life	33.7	27.3	26.0	5.4
Sudan	Northern Africa, bordering the Red Sea, between Egypt and Eritrea	No data	67.2	3.3	21.9	4.3	64.0	295	Criminalized except to save the woman's life; rape	30.6	No data	No data	No data
Suriname	Northern South America, bordering the North Atlantic Ocean, between French Guiana and Guyana	0.729	75.1	9.4	29.3	2.4	61.7	120	Prohibited altogether	38.4	No data	43.3	31.4
Sweden	Northern Europe, bordering the Baltic Sea, Gulf of Bothnia, Kattegat, and Skagerrak, between Finland and Norway	0.823	84.6	12.7	31.0	1.7	5.1	4	Without restriction as to reason; gestational limit of 18 weeks	47.7	8.6	42.3	47.0
Switzerland	Central Europe, east of France, north of Italy	0.798	85.6	12.7	30.9	1.5	2.8	5	Without restriction as to reason; gestational limit of 12 weeks	46.9	9.6	33.3	39.0
Syria	Middle East, bordering the Mediterranean Sea, between Lebanon and Turkey	0.568	78.1	4.6	No data	2.8	38.6	31	Criminalized except to save the woman's life; parental/spousal authorization required	16.7	No data	9.0	11.2

Country	Location	Global Gender Gap Index	Life Expectancy for Women	Mean Years of Schooling (Women)	Average Age at Marriage for Females	Fertility Rate (births per woman)	Adolescent Birth Rate	Maternal Mortality Ratio (per 100,000 live births)	Abortion Law (Whether and under what conditions it is allowed)	Women % of Total Labor Force	Adjusted Gender Pay Gap	Proportion of Women in Managerial Positions	Percent of Seats in Parliament Held by Women
Tajikistan	Central Asia, west of China	0.650	73.4	10.2	20.7	3.6	57.1	17	Without restriction as to reason; gestational limit of 12 weeks	36.9	No data	14.8	23.4
Tanzania	Eastern Africa, bordering the Indian Ocean, between Kenya and Mozambique	0.707	67.2	5.8	21.0	4.8	118.4	524	Criminalized except to save the woman's life	48.3	13.6	23.3	36.9
Thailand	Southeastern Asia, bordering the Andaman Sea and the Gulf of Thailand, southeast of Burma	0.710	80.9	7.7	22.5	1.5	44.9	37	Without restriction as to reason; gestational limit of 12 weeks	45.7	11.3	39.2	13.9
Timor-Leste	Southeastern Asia, northwest of Australia in the Lesser Sunda Islands at the eastern end of the Indonesian archipelago	0.720	71.6	3.8	23.0	3.9	33.8	142	Criminalized except to save the woman's life; parental authorization/notification required	45.7	No data	24.5	38.5
Togo	Western Africa, bordering the Bight of Benin, between Benin and Ghana	0.683	61.9	3.5	21.3	4.3	89.1	396	To preserve health; rape or incest; fetal impairment	48.3	No data	70.1	18.7
Tonga	Oceania, archipelago in the South Pacific Ocean, about two-thirds of the way from Hawaii to New Zealand	No data	72.9	11.3	25.3	3.5	14.7	52	Prohibited altogether	41.5	No data	41.6	7.4

Country	Location	Global Gender Gap Index	Life Expectancy Women	Mean Years of Schooling (Women)	Average Age at Marriage for Females	Fertility Rate (births per woman)	Adolescent Birth Rate	Maternal Mortality Ratio (per 100,000 live births)	Abortion Law (Whether and under what conditions it is allowed)	Women % of Adjusted Total Labor Force	Gender Pay Gap	Proportion of Women in Managerial Positions	Percent of Seats in Parliament Held by Women
Trinidad & Tobago	Caribbean, islands between the Caribbean Sea and the North Atlantic Ocean, northeast of Venezuela	0.749	76.2	11.1	29.2	1.7	30.1	67	To preserve health	42.4	No data	44.5	32.4
Tunisia	Northern Africa, bordering the Mediterranean Sea, between Algeria and Libya	0.649	78.7	6.5	28.2	2.2	7.8	43	Without restriction as to reason; gestational limit of 3 months	27.4	16.9	14.8	26.3
Turkey	Southeastern Europe and Southwestern Asia bordering the Black Sea, between Bulgaria and Georgia, and bordering the Aegean Sea and the Mediterranean Sea, between Greece and Syria	0.638	80.6	7.3	23.4	2.1	26.6	17	Without restriction as to reason; gestational limit of 10 weeks; parental/spousal notification required	33.3	15.9	18.2	17.3
Turkmenistan	Central Asia, bordering the Caspian Sea, between Iran and Kazakhstan	No data	71.7	No data	23.5	2.7	24.4	7	Without restriction as to reason; gestational limit of 12 weeks	39.4	No data	No data	25.6
Tuvalu	Oceania, island group consisting of nine coral atolls in the South Pacific Ocean, about halfway from Hawaii to Australia	No data	No data	No data	No data	No data	No data	No data	Criminalized except to save the woman's life	No data	No data	35.9	6.3

Country	Location	Global Gender Gap Index	Life Expectancy for Women	Mean Years of Schooling (Women)	Average Age at Marriage for Females	Fertility Rate (births per woman)	Adolescent Birth Rate	Maternal Mortality Ratio (per 100,000 live births)	Abortion Law (Whether and under what conditions it is allowed)	Women % of Total Labor Force	Adjusted Gender Pay Gap	Proportion of Women in Managerial Positions	Percent of Seats in Parliament Held by Women
Uganda	Eastern Africa, west of Kenya	0.717	65.6	4.9	20.7	4.8	118.8	375	Criminalized except to save the woman's life	49.5	No data	31.8	32.9
Ukraine	Eastern Europe, bordering the Black Sea, between Poland, Romania, and Moldova in the west and Russia in the east	0.714	76.8	11.3	23.0	1.2	23.7	19	Without restriction as to reason; gestational limit of 12 weeks	47.3	20.7	41.3	20.8
United Arab Emirates	Middle East, bordering the Gulf of Oman and the Persian Gulf, between Oman and Saudi Arabia	0.716	79.3	11.7	No data	1.4	6.6	3	Criminalized except to save the woman's life; fetal death; parental/spousal authorization required	17.5	No data	21.5	50.0
United Kingdom	Western Europe, islands including the northern one-sixth of the island of Ireland between the North Atlantic Ocean and the North Sea, northwest of France	0.775	83.0	13.2	27.0	1.6	13.4	7	To save the woman's life; fetal impairment; preserve health; socioeconomic grounds; approval of two physicians required	47.0	18.1	36.8	30.6
United States	North America, bordering both the North Atlantic Ocean and the North Pacific Ocean, between Canada and Mexico	0.763	81.4	13.5	28.4	1.7	19.9	19	Without restriction as to reason; many laws determined at state level include restrictions	46.2	19.0	41.1	26.6

Country	Location	Global Gender Gap Index	Life Expectancy for Women	Mean Years of Schooling (Women)	Average Age at Marriage for Females	Fertility Rate (births per woman)	Adolescent Birth Rate	Maternal Mortality Ratio (per 100,000 live births)	Abortion Law (Whether and under what conditions it is allowed)	Women % of Total Labor Force	Adjusted Gender Pay Gap	Proportion of Women in Managerial Positions	Percent of Seats in Parliament Held by Women
Uruguay	Southern South America, bordering the South Atlantic Ocean, between Argentina and Brazil	0.702	81.5	9.2	23.0	2.0	58.7	17	Without restriction as to reason; parental authorization/ notification required; gestational limit of 12 weeks	45.5	23.1	35.7	26.2
Uzbekistan	Central Asia, north of Afghanistan	No data	73.8	11.6	21.6	2.8	23.8	29	Without restriction as to reason; gestational limit of 12 weeks	40.1	No data	No data	28.7
Vanuatu	Oceania, group of islands in the South Pacific Ocean, about three-quarters of the way from Hawaii to Australia	0.625	72.2	No data	No data	3.7	49.4	72	To preserve health	43.6	No data	37.4	0.0
Venezuela	Northern South America, bordering the Caribbean Sea and the North Atlantic Ocean, between Colombia and Guyana	0.699	76.0	10.6	22.9	2.3	85.3	125	Criminalized except to save the woman's life	37.2	No data	32.8	22.2
Vietnam	Southeastern Asia, bordering the Gulf of Thailand, Gulf of Tonkin, and South China Sea, alongside China, Laos, and Cambodia	0.701	79.5	8.0	22.8	2.0	30.9	43	Without restriction as to reason	47.9	12.5	26.3	26.7

Country	Location	Global Gender Gap Index	Life Expectancy for Women	Mean Years of Schooling (Women)	Average Age at Marriage for Females	Fertility Rate (births per woman)	Adolescent Birth Rate	Maternal Mortality Ratio (per 100,000 live births)	Abortion Law (Whether and under what conditions it is allowed)	Women % of Total Labor Force	Adjusted Gender Pay Gap	Proportion of Women in Managerial Positions	Percent of Seats in Parliament Held by Women
Yemen	Middle East, bordering the Arabian Sea, Gulf of Aden, and Red Sea, between Oman and Saudi Arabia	0.492	67.8	2.9	22.8	3.7	60.4	164	To save the woman's life; spousal authorization required	7.9	No data	4.1	0.97
Zambia	Southern Africa, east of Angola	0.726	66.9	6.3	21.8	4.6	120.1	213	Criminalized except to save the woman's life; fetal impairment; preserve health; socioeconomic grounds; approval from three medical practitioners required	48.4	No data	40.5	16.8
Zimbabwe	Southern Africa, between South Africa and Zambia	0.732	62.9	8.1	21.1	3.5	86.1	458	To preserve health (not save life); rape or incest; fetal impairment; approval from two physicians required	50.9	No data	33.7	34.6

Glossary

Abortion (Induced) Surgical or chemical means of terminating a pregnancy.

Agenda for Sustainable Development for 2030 A 2015 UN member agreement to seventeen goals, each with multiple targets.

Ambivalent sexism The coexistence of both benevolent and hostile sexism.

Barrier contraceptive methods Reversible birth control methods, such as condoms, diaphragms, or sponges, that prevent pregnancy by keeping sperm from reaching the ovum.

Behavioral contraceptive methods Contraceptive methods including abstinence, outercourse, withdrawal, and the rhythm method.

Beijing Platform for Action (BPFA) An agreement from governments and NGOs at the 1995 UN Fourth World Conference on Women that identifies twelve critical areas of concern and specifies strategic objectives and specific actions for each area.

Benevolent sexism A type of sexism that includes protective paternalism, complementary gender differentiation, and heterosexual intimacy and is more subtle than overt, hostile sexism.

Bible The primary text of the Christian religion containing both Old and New Testaments; the Old Testament is an important text in Judaism.

Bilateral aid Country-to-country development aid.

Biphobia Fear and hatred of bisexual people; often used to refer to prejudice and bias toward bisexual people.

Bisexual invisibility The tendency for bisexual women to hide their sexuality and for people to ignore or deny their existence.

Bride kidnapping The practice of kidnapping a woman for purposes of forced marriage.

Bride price (bridewealth or *lobala*) A practice wherein the groom gives money, goods, or livestock to the family of the bride in return for her hand in marriage.

Buddhism A nontheistic religion based on the teachings of the Prophet Buddha in the fifth or sixth century; found throughout the world, especially in Asia.

Canon A religion's scriptures and texts.

CEDAW A 1979 international treaty affirming women's rights that requires ratifying nations to eliminate discrimination against women in employment, education, and politics.

CEDAW committee The group comprised of twenty-three women's rights experts who monitor countries' compliance with CEDAW and issue recommendations.

Child marriage Marriage that occurs before the age of eighteen.

Chipko movement A grassroots movement originating in India that uses passive resistance methods to stop environmentally destructive logging and mining.

Christianity The Christian faith based on the life, death, and resurrection of Jesus Christ and on the Bible.

Cisgender A person whose gender identity matches their birth-assigned gender.

Climate change Long-term changes in the Earth's climate arising from a build-up of greenhouse gases in the atmosphere.

Climate justice Demands that responses to climate change are fair to all and that people be empowered to participate in climate change mitigation and adaptation.

Clitoridectomy A type of female genital mutilation where the clitoris is partially or totally removed; also known as *sunna*.

Coercive antinatalism When a government concerned about overpopulation discourages childbearing with policies that infringe on reproductive and human rights.

Coercive pronatalism When a government limits contraceptive and/or abortion access in order to increase the population.

Commission on the Status of Women (CSW) The main UN body dedicated to the promotion of gender equality and the empowerment of women, including monitoring the implementation of the Beijing Declaration and Platform for Action.

Comparable worth   The use of detailed classification systems to compare different jobs on skill, effort, responsibility, and working conditions to address gender pay gaps.

Compulsory heterosexuality   The idea that societies "require" heterosexuality by giving women few economic options outside of marriage and by hiding nonheterosexuality.

Concrete ceiling   The dual burden of racism and sexism in organizations that leads to low numbers of minority women in managerial and leadership positions.

Conflict-related sexual violence   Includes rape, sexual slavery, forced prostitution, forced pregnancy, and other types of sexual violence directly or indirectly linked to war.

Contextualize   When analyzing something, to consider how it is situated within multiple contexts (cultural, social, political, historical, economic).

Contrapower sexual harassment   When men harass women of equal or greater formal power than themselves.

Contributing family workers   Those that work in the informal employment sector in family-run enterprises.

Convention on the Elimination of Discrimination Against Women (CEDAW)   The 1979 international bill of rights for women signed by the majority of UN member nations that defines gender discrimination and sets up an agenda for national action to end it.

Critical political mass   The estimated 30 percent minimum for women in a legislative body necessary to exert a meaningful influence on politics.

Cultural globalization   The transnational migration of people, information, and consumer culture.

Cultural relativism   The notion that right and wrong are matters of culture and that there is no universal right or wrong.

Debt bondage   When people are trapped in exploitative work due to the debt they owe to those whom recruited or transported them.

Development   The process of economic, political, or social growth in a nation.

Development programs and projects   Projects and programs intended to promote economic and social development and reduce poverty.

Dianic witchcraft   A feminist form of wicca that worships the female divine, mostly in all-female covens.

Domestic violence or intimate partner violence (IPV)   Violence that may include bodily harm,

verbal threats, stalking, harassment, emotional abuse or the destruction of property as means of coercion, control, revenge, or punishment on a person with whom the abuser is in an intimate relationship.

Double jeopardy   Refers to how minority women are at an increased risk for multiple forms of harassment because of their multiple minority status.

Dowry   Money or goods given to the groom or his family by the bride's family.

Dowry murder (dowry death)   The staged death of wives by husbands or in-laws so that the husband can remarry, also called *bride burnings* and *dowry deaths*.

Dowry violence   A type of IPV that occurs in the Southeast Asian countries of Bangladesh, India, and Pakistan when husbands or in-laws use emotional, physical, or sexual violence to get a wife to extract more dowry from her family.

Economic globalization   The integration and rapid interaction of economies through production, trade, and financial transactions by banks and multinational corporations.

Electoral system   The procedures by which representatives are elected (PR, SMD, or mixed).

Electoral reforms   Changes in the procedures by which representatives are elected such as quotas or the adoption of PL/PR systems.

Empowerment   The process by which women are able to advocate for their rights and have decision-making power in their public and private lives.

Empowerment approach   See *Gender and development approach (GAD)*.

Equal Remuneration Convention   ILO convention that requires states to ensure equal pay for men and women for work of equal value through laws, wage setting, and collective bargaining agreements between employers and employees.

Ethnocentric   When people think their culture is superior to other cultures, and are quick to judge and reject other cultures' practices and beliefs.

Excision   A type of female genital mutilation involving partial or total removal of the clitoris and the labia minora, with or without excision of the labia majora.

Export processing zones (EPZs)   Industrial zones with incentives (usually a relaxing of labor and environmental laws and tax breaks) to attract foreign investors; also known as free trade zones.

Family responsibility discrimination   When an employer makes employment decisions about employees or prospective employees based on their assumed or real caregiving responsibilities.

Female genital mutilation (FGM) Partial or total removal of external female genitalia or other injury to the female genital organs for cultural or other nonmedical reasons.

Feminism A variety of theories and approaches all committed to understanding and changing the structures that keep women lower in status and power.

Feminist economics An economics framework emphasizing gender analyses, including the economic value of unpaid domestic and care work, the use of human well-being as a measure of an economy's success, and intersectionality in economics.

Feminist hermeneutics Interpretations of religious texts and scriptures using feminist and liberation lenses instead of patriarchal ones.

Feminist movements Women's movements that frame their work using feminist ideas and language.

Feminist spirituality movement Variety of nonbiblical religions that include female images of the divine; also known as *women's spirituality movement*.

Feminist theology Reconsiderations of the traditions, practices, scriptures, and theologies of religion from a feminist perspective with a commitment to transforming religion for gender equality.

Femocrats Feminist bureaucrats that work for governments.

Forced marriage When girls or women are forced by their parents to marry against their will or when they are kidnapped and raped so that they will have to marry.

Formal labor sector Official labor sector where people get a paycheck and pay taxes.

Formal politics Institutionalized politics such as voting, parliaments and congresses, and heads of state and government.

Gender The socially constructed roles, behavior, activities, and attributes a given society considers appropriate for girls/women and boys/men.

Gender and development approach (GAD) Development approach that focuses explicitly on improving women's status, also called the *empowerment approach*.

Gender binary The perception that "female/femininity" and "male/masculinity" are clear-cut, mutually exclusive categories.

Gender expression The way you express your gender through such things as your clothing, name, haircut, behavior, and body characteristics.

Gender harassment Type of sexual harassment characterized by verbal and nonverbal behavior that conveys insulting, hostile, and degrading attitudes toward women.

Gender health disparities The ways in which health risks, experiences, and outcomes are different for girls and women relative to boys and men.

Gender identity A person's psychological sense of being male or female, one's deeply held sense of gender.

Gender inequality Women and girls' disadvantage relative to men and boys.

Gender job segregation (gender occupational segregation) Refers to the fact that employed women and men tend to work in different jobs and employment sectors and men hold the higher positions compared to women in the same job category.

Gender mainstreaming The inclusion of a gender perspective in all development activities; requires women's active participation in the development process.

Gender norms Societal expectations and rules that vary based on gender.

Gender perspective on unpaid domestic and care work Suggests that gendered divisions of unpaid care labor reflect traditional gender roles and stereotypes; unpaid care labor is viewed as "women's work."

Gender quotas Rules that specify the minimum number of women (or women and men) that candidate lists should include or the number of seats that should be allocated to women in legislatures (reserved seats for women).

Gender realignment The process whereby women's voting patterns shift from being more conservative than men's, to aligning with men's, to becoming more liberal than men's.

Gender roles Divisions of labor and social roles according to gender.

Gender socialization The processes by which gendered societal beliefs and expectations are instilled in us.

Gender stereotypes Beliefs about how females and males are different.

Gender wage discrimination The practice of paying women in the same jobs as men less just because they are women, because the skills associated with "women's jobs" are devalued, because it is assumed that a woman's income is supplemental to her husband's, or to maximize profits.

Gender wage gap The common gap between male and female earnings, with women generally receiving less pay.

Gender-biased sex selection The use of prenatal or postnatal practices for purposes of having a son rather than a daughter.

Gender-responsive budget analysis Policy analyses examining how national budgets impact women and girls differently than men and boys.

Gender-segregated religious practices The notion that in most religions, women and men are expected to show their devotion to God differently; public religious roles and rituals are often designated as male.

Genocidal rape The practice of using rape to destroy an ethnic or political group perceived as the enemy.

Girl neglect When son preference leads girl children to receive less care, food, attention, and resources than boy children; sometimes a form of postnatal gender biased sex selection.

Glass ceiling The various barriers that prevent women from advancing upward in their organizations into management power positions.

Glass walls When gender segregation in management functions contributes to the leaky pipeline by reducing women's qualifications for top executive and CEO positions.

Global care chains (GCCs) A series of links between people across the globe based on the work of care.

Global feminism A feminism recognizing women's connectedness but emphasizing diverse meanings of feminism and feminist activism based on culture, region, and other intersectional variables.

Global gag rule (Mexico City policy) A United States policy where family planning monies are denied to family planning NGOs that provide abortion services or abortion information.

Global North The industrialized (developed) nations located in the northern hemisphere.

Global South The non-industrialized (developing) nations located in the southern hemisphere.

Global supply chains (GSCs) Complex manufacturing and production systems spread across multiple countries with many suppliers and subcontractors.

Global women's studies The interdisciplinary, cross-cultural study of women's issues and gender equality that emphasizes how intersectionality and context impact women's issues and activism.

Globalization The integration of the world's economies, cultures, and societies through a global network of trade and communication.

Goddess spirituality Pagan religions focused on goddess worship and based in the belief that humans lived in peace and harmony during a goddess-worshiping pre-history.

Government cabinets The group of ministers (advisors) to the head of government who lead specific government agencies and often wield considerable policy-making power.

Grassroots organization (GRO) A locally based NGO that works to develop and improve the community.

Grassroots support organization (GRSO) A nationally or regionally based NGO providing development assistance and funding to grassroots organizations.

Greenbelt movement A Kenya-based GRSO that organizes women to plant and manage trees for sustainable forestry use.

Hadith In Islam, the report of the Sunna, the collective sayings attributed to Muhammad and what he approved of; a single report is *a hadith*.

Head of government A political executive that oversees daily executive and legislative activities of a country (more powerful than a head of state).

Head of state A political executive that represents the government in a symbolic, ceremonial fashion (the public face of the country or government).

Hermeneutics The theory and practice of interpretation for the sacred texts of a religion.

Heteronormativity The assumption that only heterosexuality is acceptable and normal.

Heteropatriarchy Social structures, including laws, religion, and justice systems, that reinforce heterosexuality and traditional gender roles and make living as a nonheterosexual difficult.

Heterosexism Bias in favor of heterosexuals and against nonheterosexuals.

Hinduism A 6,000-year-old religion originating in India with numerous male and female deities.

HIV/AIDS The Human Immunodeficiency Virus that may lead to the potentially fatal autoimmune disease Acquired Immune Deficiency Syndrome.

Homophobia Fear of gay and lesbian people; often used to refer to prejudice and bias against gay and lesbian people.

Honour-based violence (HBV) A form of IPV occurring in cultures where a woman's virtuous behavior is believed to affect the honor and prestige of her male relatives who are in charge of her.

Honour killing An extreme form of honour-based violence where it is seen as morally justifiable to kill a wife, daughter, or sister for doing something that brings shame on her family or male relatives.

Horizontal occupational segregation The tendency for women and men to work in different occupations with higher status and higher pay occupations more likely to be occupied by men.

Hormonal contraceptive methods   Forms of reversible birth control using hormones to suppress ovulation or thicken cervical mucus to prevent fertilization.

Hostile sexism   The perception of women as enemies or adversaries and as inferior in ways that justify men's control of them.

Human capital approach   Suggests that the gender pay gap occurs because women are less skilled, less educated, or less experienced workers than men are.

Infibulation   A type of FGM/FGC where cutting and stitching of the labia minora or labia majora are used to almost completely cover the vaginal opening; may also involve clitoridectomy.

Informal labor sector   The part of the economy that includes "under the table" and "off the books" employment such as small enterprises and trading and selling at markets; often uncounted by governments.

Informal politics   Politics from below, with citizen actions including grassroots protests and citizen movements.

International Labour Organization (ILO)   United Nations agency that develops and monitors international labor laws and agreements and promotes gender equality in work.

Intersectionality   The interplay of different social categories; gender is intersectional because the way it is enacted and experienced depends on the way it interacts with other social categories and identities.

Intersex   People with both male and female chromosomal and anatomical features.

Intrauterine device (IUD)   A type of reversible birth control where a small device is placed in the uterus.

Islam   Religion founded in the eighth century C.E., and based on the Prophet Muhammad's teachings.

Islamists   Muslim fundamentalists who use strict scriptural interpretations that restrict women and favor a state governed by religious law.

Islamization   The process by which states become governed by conservative forms of Islam.

Job prestige   The valuing of some types of work over others.

Judaism   The Jewish faith, which is based on study of the Torah and ritual practice as described in the Talmud.

Lack of fit model   Proposes that the communal gender stereotype of females is incompatible with the agentic male stereotype believed necessary for success in powerful organizational positions; this leads to the perception that women are ill-equipped for leadership.

Leaky pipeline   Refers to how women managers are more often in lower and middle management positions, and do not advance to top leadership positions.

Least developed countries (LDCs)   Countries with a gross national annual income per capita under US$1,018, and where maternal and child mortality rates are higher than average, and literacy rates and secondary school enrollments are lower.

Legal literacy   Knowledge of one's legal rights and how to exercise them.

Lesbian baiting/sexuality baiting   Accusing nonconforming women and women's activists of being lesbian to disempower them.

Lesbian feminism   A variety of beliefs and practices connecting lesbianism to political resistance to patriarchy.

Lesbian invisibility   The tendency for lesbians to lead quiet hidden lives and for cultures to deny or hide their existence.

Lesbian separatism   A rare type of lesbian feminism emphasizing a complete rejection of patriarchy; may involve all-women communities and the avoidance of any relationship with men.

LGBTIQ rights   Human rights related to sexual orientation and gender identity; also known as SOGI rights.

Liberation theology   An activist theology focused on justice and equality that uses religious texts as a means to empower the poor and oppressed.

Marriage migrants   Women with so few economic opportunities that they choose migration to marry a virtual stranger; often aided by international marriage brokers who market women to men seeking traditional wives.

Masculine God-language   Religious language in scriptures, prayers, and liturgy that suggests God is male.

Materialist explanations for gender inequality   Suggest that family and social institutions arising from material forces such as the ownership of private property led to and maintain gender inequality.

Maternal morbidity (disability)   Serious disease, disability, or physical damage such as fistula and uterine prolapse caused by pregnancy-related complications.

Maternal mortality   The death of a woman while pregnant or within 42 days of termination of pregnancy from any cause related to or aggravated by the pregnancy or its management.

Maternity leave policies   Maternity protection measures providing time off for mothers following the birth of a child.

Maternity Protection Convention   International labor standard on maternity protection stipulating at least 14 weeks of paid maternity leave and other maternity protections.

Maternity protections   Policies and laws ensuring that expectant and nursing women will not face employment discrimination or be exposed to health hazards, that they will have time off to have children and return to the job without discrimination, and that they will be permitted breast-feeding breaks.

Microcredit   The extension of small loans to women in poverty for small-scale economic enterprises.

Migrant domestic workers   International migrants whose main job is work performed in or for a household.

Millennium Development Goals (MDGs)   A 2000 commitment by UN member nations and leading development organizations to eight goals focused on ending poverty by 2015.

Mixed system   An electoral system with PR systems in some regions of the country and a plurality/majority system in others.

Modernization theory   A traditional development approach focused on economic growth and a conversion to capitalist market economies.

Mononormativity   Acting as though gay and straight are the only normal sexual orientations.

Monosexism   Placing greater value on romantic and sexual attractions to one sex; valuing heterosexuality or homosexuality over bisexuality.

Motherhood penalty   The penalty paid by working mothers who, compared to working fathers and (male or female) childless workers, experience discrimination in recommendations for hiring, salary, training, opportunities, and promotion.

Motherhood wage gap   Pay gap associated with motherhood; employed mothers earn less than other women and men experience a fatherhood wage bonus.

MP (member of parliament)   A minister of parliament, a person who serves as a parliamentary representative.

Mujerista theology   A Latin American feminist theology challenging theological understandings, religious teachings, and practices that oppress Latinas.

Multiculturalism   A perspective that emphasizes helping people to understand, accept, and value the cultural differences among groups, with the ultimate goal of reaping the benefits of diversity.

Multilateral aid   Development aid funded by international agencies such as the UNIFEM, the IMF, and the World Bank.

Nairobi Forward Looking Strategies for the Advancement of Women   The document adopted by governments and NGOs at the 1985 Third World Conference on Women that reviewed progress from the UN Decade for Women and provided an action blueprint for the next decade.

National Assembly   Sometimes called a parliament or congress, this legislative body of citizen-elected representatives designs and enacts a country's national laws.

Neo-liberal economic policies   Economic policies emphasizing free trade, social services cuts, privatization of government services, and balanced government budgets.

Neocolonialism   When northern countries treat southern countries as pseudo-colonies, using them for raw materials and cash crops and controlling them through business corporations and lending.

Non-normative rape   Rape that is in violation of social norms for expected behavior.

Nongovernmental organizations (NGOs)   Local, regional, national, or international not-for-profit.

Normative rape   Rape supported by social norms, often not investigated or punished; may include marital rape, punitive rape, war rape.

Objectifying gaze   Visual inspection of a woman's body by another person, including "leering," or looking a person "up and down."

Obstetric fistula   A maternal disability arising from prolonged and obstructed labor; tears between the vaginal wall and bladder or rectum result in incontinence, infections, and ulcerations.

Own-account workers   Self-employed women without employees.

Palermo Protocol   An international agreement where governments pledge to prevent and combat the trafficking of women and children; to assist victims; and cooperate with other governments to achieve these objectives.

Party list/proportional representation system (PL/PR)   Electoral system wherein parties receive seats in proportion to the votes they receive and party lists and multimember districts are common.

Patriarchy   When gender inequality is embedded in economic, political, cultural, and legal structures; a society in which men have greater power and status is **patriarchal.**

Political insiders   Candidates that are loyal to a party and work their way up the party hierarchy.

Political literacy   Knowledge of the processes required for political participation.

Political surrogates   Women politicians who "stand-in" for a father or husband who was a national leader.

Post-colonial theologies   Theologies that examine associations between religion and colonization, rediscover indigenous religions common before colonization, and reappropriate religion for empowerment and resistance.

Postnatal sex selection   A form of gender-biased sex selection where poor care of girl children leads to their higher mortality rates, leaving the family able to try again for a boy while limiting family size.

Practical gender interests   A motivation for women's movements that arises out of concerns about an immediate issue facing women.

Prenatal (antenatal) care   Health care provided during pregnancy for maternal and child health.

Prenatal sex selection   A form of gender-biased sex selection where prenatal technologies such as ultrasound or IVF are used.

Private sphere   The domestic domain of the home.

Prostitution   The selling of sexual services.

Public sphere   The public domain outside of the home.

Plurality majority system   See *Single member district system*

Quid pro quo sexual harassment   Legal term for *sexual coercion,* when a person requires sex as a condition of providing employment or job rewards.

Qur'an   The primary text of the religion of Islam (also spelled **Koran**).

Queer   An inclusive, unifying term for LGBTI people.

Queer theory   A theory opposing sexuality classifications as artificial, limiting, and inaccurate.

Racialized sexual harassment   A type of sexual harassment combining racial and sexual harassment and experienced mostly by ethnic and migrant women; also called *double jeopardy* and *sexualized racism.*

Rape   A form of sexual violence involving penetration of a person's body without their consent.

Rape cultures   Cultures where rape is accepted, promoted, ignored, or minimized.

Relative resources perspective on unpaid care work   Idea that women do more household labor to make up for their smaller monetary contribution to the household.

Religious fundamentalisms   Religions that are committed to the infallibility of scriptures, that see traditional gender roles as divinely mandated, and are antagonistic toward feminism.

Remittances   The money earned by migrants that is sent back home to help family.

Reproductive control   The extent of women's control over their fertility, sexuality, and reproductive health.

Reproductive health   Health topics including family planning, reproductive tract infections and cancers, infertility, maternal mortality, morbidity, abortion, and female genital mutilation/cutting.

Reproductive rights   The right to reproductive health care and the right to reproductive self-determination.

Role congruity theory   The idea that we are less likely to assign people to roles that call for qualities associated with the other gender.

Second shift   Refers to the fact that employed women frequently work one shift in paid work and another shift doing unpaid care labor before or after paid work.

Self-efficacy   A person's belief that he or she can perform actions to reach a goal and that efforts to reach a goal will be effective.

Sex   A person's biological maleness or femaleness as determined by chromosomes and sex organs.

Sex tourism   A type of tourism or tourism industry that facilitates commercial sexual relationships between tourists and residents at the travel destination.

Sex trafficking   The recruitment, transport, harboring, or receipt of persons by means of threat, deception, coercion, abduction, fraud, or abuse of power with the purpose of victim exploitation.

Sexual assault   Any unwanted or forced sexual contact or acts including rape, sexual harassment, and incest.

Sexual coercion   A type of sexual harassment that occurs when a person requires sex as a condition of providing employment or job rewards. *See also* **quid pro quo sexual harassment.**

Sexual double standard   Norms and beliefs regarding women's sexuality, such as monogamy and virginity, that are opposite of expectations for men.

Sexual exploitation   The use of women as sexual objects for financial gain or pleasure without regard to them as people.

Sexual harassment   Unwelcome sexual advances or verbal or physical conduct of a sexual nature that has the purpose or effect of unreasonably interfering with the individual's work performance or creating an intimidating, hostile, abusive or offensive working environment.

Sexual health   A state of physical, emotional, mental and social well-being in relation to sexuality.

Sexual minority stress   The stress and strain experienced by LGBTQI people due to stigma and discrimination.

Sexual objectification The reduction of women to their bodies.

Sexual orientation Whether a person feels sexual desire for people of the other gender (heterosexual), the same gender (homosexual), or both genders (bisexual).

Sexual rights Human rights related to sexuality, such as the rights of people to make personal decisions about their sexuality and LGBTQI rights/SOGI rights.

Sexual violence Any type of sexual contact or behavior without explicit consent of the recipient.

Sexualized racism A type of sexual harassment combining racial and sexual harassment and experienced mostly by ethnic and migrant women; also called *double jeopardy* and *racialized sexual harassment.*

Shari'ah (or sharia) The collectivity of laws that Muslims govern themselves by based on sayings attributed to Muhammad; often conservative and supportive of traditional gender roles.

Single-member district system (SMDs) Electoral system in which the winning candidate is the one with the most votes and there is only one seat per district.

Sociocultural explanations (social constructivist) Explanations emphasizing that gendered power relations are socially constructed and maintained.

SOGI rights Human rights related to sexual orientation and gender identity.

Son preference Valuing male children over female children.

State feminism Government structures such as bureaus and agencies that are charged with addressing women's issues and equality.

Sterilization In women, blocking or cutting the fallopian tubes to prevent fertilization of the ovum and in men, cutting the vas deferens so that sperm cannot mix with the seminal fluid; A permanent form of birth control.

Strategic gender interests A motivation for women's movements that arises out of a desire to bring about large-scale gender social change.

Street harassment A form of sexual harassment involving unwanted sexualized comments, gestures, and actions forced on women in public places.

Survival sex When women are forced to trade sex for services or goods in order to survive.

Sustainable development Development that meets the needs of the present without compromising the ability of future generations to meet their own needs.

Sustainable Development Goals (SDGs) The seventeen global goals created by the UN General Assembly as a blueprint for a better and sustainable future; created in 2015 to be achieved by 2030.

Sweatshops Businesses that do not provide a living wage, require excessively long work hours, and provide poor working conditions with many health and safety hazards; common in EPZs.

Talmud Sixty-three volumes of legal and theological teachings centering on the meaning of the Torah and the practice of Judaism; in addition to the Torah, one of the most important Jewish texts.

Time availability perspective on unpaid care work Explains gendered divisions of household labor by suggesting that women have more time to perform household tasks due to less time in the paid workforce.

Time-use surveys Labor surveys providing gender-disaggregated information on how people spend their time in both market and nonmarket work.

Torah In the Jewish faith, an important religious source comprised of the first five chapters of the Bible's Old Testament.

Trafficking of women and girls The recruitment, transportation, harboring, or receipt of women and girls for purposes of slavery, forced labor, and servitude.

Trans girls/women People that identify as girls or women although they were labeled male at birth.

Transgender (trans) People whose gender identity and/or expression differs from what is typically associated with their birth-assigned sex.

Transnational feminisms Feminisms that cut across cultures and unite women's struggles from many parts of the world.

Transnational feminist movements Women's movements spanning multiple nations built on common interests yet emphasizing diversity and difference.

Transnational feminist networks (TFNs) Coalitions operating across national borders to resist gender inequalities, to influence policymaking, support specific grassroots struggles, and to insert a feminist perspective in transnational advocacy and activism.

Transphobia Fear of transgender people; often used to refer to prejudice and bias against transpeople.

Tripartite model of sexual harassment Identifies the three behavioral dimensions of sexual harassment: gender harassment, unwanted sexual attention, and sexual coercion.

United Nations (UN)   An international organization with 192 participating countries. Its purposes are international peace and security; human rights; and the correction of international economic, social, environmental, and humanitarian problems.

United Nations Decade for Women   Period from 1976 to 1985 when transnational feminist networking grew and international women's rights agreements were forged at three United Nations Women's Conferences.

Universal Declaration of Human Rights (UDHR)   The 1948 UN member agreement affirming that all humans are born free and equal in dignity and rights; a cornerstone of human rights law and practice.

Universal human rights   A perspective based on the belief that by virtue of being human, and regardless of culture, we are all entitled to full and equal rights.

Unmet need for family planning   Defined as the percentage of women who don't want to become pregnant but don't use contraception.

Unpaid domestic and care labor   The daily routine household labor and primary caregiving of children, elders, and sick family members.

Unwanted sexual attention   A type of sexual harassment where a person makes suggestive comments about another's body or makes unsolicited and unreciprocated sexual advances such as repeated requests for a kiss, a date, or sex.

Uterine prolapse   A condition in which the supporting pelvic structure of muscles, tissue, and ligaments gives way, and the uterus drops into or even out of the vagina.

Vedas   The primary Hindu scriptures.

Vertical occupational segregation   How women tend to be in the lower-ranked, lower-paid positions than men with the same occupation; explains part of the gender wage gap.

Victim blaming   Holding women responsible for the violence against them.

Vienna Declaration and Programme of Action   Outcome of the 1993 UN human rights conference (the Vienna Conference) that affirms women's rights are human rights and that VAW is a human rights violation.

Violence against women and **Violence against women and girls** (**VAW** and **VAWG**)   Any act of gender-based violence resulting in, or likely to result in, physical, sexual, or mental harm or suffering to women or girls.

Violence against women in politics (VAWIP)   A gendered form of violence targeting women with the intent of discouraging women's participation in politics.

Vulnerable employment   Economically precarious employment, which lacks in labor protections and benefits.

Wicca   Form of earth-based, magical, feminist spirituality based on wiccan (witchcraft) traditions.

WINGOs   Women's international nongovernmental organizations.

Womanist theology   A feminist liberation theology reflecting women of color's social, religious, and cultural experiences.

Womanspaces   The "female-only" spaces provided by traditional religions; potentially a source of power, sharing, and integrity for women.

Women in development (WID)   Development approach that includes women through income-generating projects, labor-saving technologies, and improving women's local resource access.

Women's micro-and-small-scale enterprises (WMSEs)   Small-scale businesses run by women in the informal labor sector.

Women's movements   Social movements characterized by the primacy of women's gendered experiences and women's issues and in which women are the primary leaders and actors.

Women's rights as human rights perspective   A perspective emphasizing that regardless of culture, women and men are equally deserving of rights and freedoms; views abuses against women as human rights violations.

Women's spirituality movement   See *Feminist spirituality movement.*

Women's suffrage   A name for women's voting rights.

Zipper (zebra) systems   Electoral systems with legislated candidate quotas designating the number of women on party lists and the alteration of women and men candidates on party lists.

Index

Key terms and the pages on which they are defined are boldfaced.

A

Aassve, A., 130
Abaya, 32, 257
Abdolmanafi, A., 102
Abendroth, A. K., 148, 149
Abendschön, S., 300
Abma, J., 72
Abortion, 75–77, 343. *See also*
    Reproductive health and rights
Abraham, A., 259
Abrahamson, P., 223
Abramsky, T., 104
Abstinence, 74
Abuse, sexual, 31, 45. *See also* Rape
Abzug, Bella S., 196, 302, 362
Acosta-Belen, E., 176, 349
Action opportunities
    development and environmental
        sustainability, 200
    globalization, 234
    political power, 329
    religion, women and, 281–282
    reproductive rights and health,
        87–88
    sexual rights, 118
    status and power, women, 51
    women's movements, 371
    work, women and, 160–161
Activist websites. *See* Websites
Adams, Abigail, 351
Adams, G., 83
Adams, Jane, 328
Adams, John, 351
Adams, M., 223, 224, 318
Addams, Jane, 106
Adiche, Chimanda, 10
Adidas, 213
Adusei-Asante, K., 185
Afghanistan
    activism, by women, 354–355
    religion, 258
    sexual rights, 103

status, gender difference, 29, 32,
    33, 34
women as property, 33
work, women and, 148
Afkhami, Mahnaz, 341
Afkir, Nawal, 32
Africa. *See also* specific country
    names
    activism, by women, 196, 352, 367
    development, 182
    environmental activism, 196
    HIV/AIDS, 104
    maternal mortality and morbidity,
        64, 65
    maternity leave, 136
    political power, 305, 326
    religion, 256, 271, 274, 275, 276
    status, gender difference, 33, 38
    women as property, 33
    work, women and, 136, 139, 155
Afro-Brazilian religions (Brazil), 246
Afshar, H., 355
Agadjanian V., 245
Agarwal, B., 191
**Agenda for Sustainable Development
    for 2030, 65**
Agenjo, C. A., 131
Agrawal, P., 66
Agugideiri, H., 259
Agunah, 263
Ahmed, L., 252, 259
Ailes, Roger, 154
Aitamurto, K., 277
Ajtún, Maria, 150
Akeredolu, M., 178
Akute, W., 196
Al-Dayel, N., 79
al-Khawaja, Zainab, 327
Albright, Madeline, 311, 322
Alexander, A. C., 17
All-China Women's Democratic
    Federation (ACDWF), 356, 357

Allen, A., 178
Allen, P. G., 107
Alliances, feminist-government, 358
Allison, R., 102
Alonso-Villar, O., 140
Alvarez, S. E., 342
Ambivalent sexism, 249
American Psychiatric Association
    (APA), 106
Amnesty International, 347, 355
Anand, A., 177
Anand, E., 34
Anderson, K. J., 8
Anderson, N. F., 315, 320, 321
Angel, C. G., 260
ANNA (Association No to Violence),
    39, 40, 353
Anstee, Margaret, 320
Antenatal care, 65
Anthony, Susan B., 362
Anthropology, 4, 5
Anti-harassment policies, 153
Antrobus, P., 24, 360
Apartheid, 352
Aquino, Benigno, 319
Aquino, Corazon, 319, 321
Aran, M., 190
Aranda, Beatriz, 149
Ardern, Jacinda, 312
Arekapudi, N., 153
Arias, Arnulfo, 314
Aristotle, 107
Arreola-Ornelas, H., 190
Arthur, R. H., 275
Ashford, L. S., 72, 80
Asia, 61, 64–65. *See also* specific
    country names
    development, 174, 182, 183
    globalization and, 215, 218, 221,
        223
    intimate partner violence, 37–40

migration, 219–221, 223–226
political power, 314
religion, 256, 275
reproductive health and rights, 66, 80, 82
sex tourism, 226
sex trafficking, 228, 231
son preference, 28–31
sweatshop labor, 214–218
women's movement, 348, 352, 364
work, women and, 136, 149, 155
Asia Pacific Forum on Women, Law, and Development (APIWLD), 310
Asociación de Mujeres Louisa Amanda Espinosa (AMNLAE), 358
Assifi, A, 76
Association for Women in Development (AWID), 187, 344, 347
Astell, Mary, 252
Atchison, A., 302
Atun, R., 190
Atuyambe, L., 80
Audette, A. P., 252, 274
Aulette, J. R., 349
Australia
  abortion laws, 76
  migration, 224, 226
  political power, 299, 304, 305, 320, 323
  religion, 264, 270, 277
  work, women and, 128, 131
Australian Human Rights Commission, 151
Autorino, T., 82
Avishai, O., 245, 249
AWID (Association for Women in Development), 347
Azad, Nafiseh, 347
Azad, Nikita, 11
Azhgikhina, N., 352

B

Bachelet, Michelle, 296, 317, 320, 322
Bachofen, J. J., 6
Baddorf, Z., 272

Bae, G., 225
Bahamas Crisis Centre (BCC), 344
Baker, C. N., 150
Baksh, R., 360
Balbus, J., 191
Balch, Emily Greene, 328
Bales, K., 79
Banaji, M. R., 251
Bancroft, A., 269
Bandaranaike, Sirimavo, 314, 318
Bandaranaike, Solomon Dias, 314
Bandura, A., 346, 347
Banerjee, A., 182
Bangladesh
  development, 174, 190
  global sex trade, 226
  globalization and, 215, 219, 226
  migration, 219, 222, 226
  political power, 304, 312, 314
  Rana Plaza industrial disaster, 215
  religion, 256, 279
  status, gender difference, 29, 39, 41
  women as property, 343, 349, 351
Bangura, Zainab Hawa, 48
Bantustans, 352
Baral, S. D., 106
Barlas, A., 256, 259
Barnes, N. S., 269
Barot, S., 30, 80
Barrier contraceptive methods, 74
Barry, K., 32, 33, 225
Barstow, A. L., 278
Barstow, Anne, 278
Bas, N. F., 218
Bashir, Danya, 327
Bashir, N. Y., 8
Basile, K. C., 42
Basu, A., 110, 338, 341, 343, 349, 354, 358, 359, 360, 364, 368
Bates, K., 133, 178
Bates, L., 323
Batliwala, S., 345, 367
Baum, T., 226
Baun, Aleta (Mama Aleta), 194
Baxter, J., 131
Bay-Cheng, L. Y., 102
Bazar, E., 326
Bearak, B., 319
Bearak, J., 76

Beavin, C., 76
Bechmann, U., 255
Beckwith, K., 341, 343, 344
Bedi, A. S., 30
Begum, R., 260
Behavioral contraceptive methods, 74
Beijing Platform for Action
  activism, by women, 356, 362–364
  environment and sustainable development, 183, 185
  human rights, 14
  political power, women, 309
  work, women and, 154
Beinart, P., 323
Bemba, Jean-Pierre, 47
Bendavid, E., 80
Benería, L., 132, 176, 180, 185
Benevolent sexism, 248–249
Benjamin, M., 218
Bennett, K., 107
Berg, R. C., 68
Bergh, S., 179
Berik, G., 132, 180
Bermúdez, Violeta, 312
Bernardino, Minerva, 13
Bernauer, J., 300
Bernstein, S., 79
Bessey, Sarah, 271
Beyrer, C., 106
Bhandari, Bidhya Devi, 312
Bhatt, E., 156, 350
Bhikkhu (monks), 269
Bhikkhuni, Dhammananda, 271
Bhikkhuni (nuns), 269
Bhowmick, N., 325
Bhutto, Benazir, 315, 319, 319–320, 321
Bhutto, Zulfikar Ali, 315
Bianchi, S., 128, 129, 130
Bible, 270, 273
Biden, Joe, 80, 301, 302, 358
Bilateral aid, 175
Bindel, J., 114
Bingemer, M. C., 275
Biphobia, 114
Birth control pills, 75
Bisexual feminists, 114
Bisexual women, 104–105
Black Carib religion (Central America), 246

Black Lives Matter, 326
Blackstone, A., 152, 153
Blackwood, E., 107, 108, 113, 115
Blandón, María Teresa, 358
Blau, F. D., 140, 141, 143
Blomberg, M., 216
Blumberg, A., 273
Blumberg, R. L., 127, 130, 134, 182, 209, 211, 324–325, 326, 327, 349
Boden, A. L., 279
Bolton, Sharon, 148
Bonder, G., 307, 309
Bongaarts, J., 29, 30
Bonnet, F., 155
Bonvillian, N., 6
Boonstra, H. D., 78
Booth, W., 359
Bornstein, R. F., 39
Bose, C. E., 176, 349
Boselli, O., 308
Boserup, E., 175, 176
Boserup, Ester, 176
Boucher, S., 270
Boudreau, V. G., 319
Brahme, D., 30
Brallier, S. A., 109
Brandiotti, R., 191
Brands, Raina, 28
Braude, A., 245, 277
Braun, S., 146, 148
Brennan, D., 226
Brenner, M., 81
Brewis, K., 28
Bride deficits, 223
Bride kidnappings, 33
Bride price, 33
Bridewealth, 33
Brisbane, J., 184
Brnabić, Ana, 312
Brock-Utne, Birgit, 356
Brontë, Anne, 347
Brooks, N., 80
Brooks, S. D., 251
Browne. N., 103
Brownmiller, S., 44
Brundtland, Gro Harlem, 180, 322
Bryant, E., 308
Bryceson, D. F., 177, 178, 180, 181
Buchanan, N. T., 152

Budapest, Zsuzsanna, 278, 281
Buddhism, 268-270
Buddig, M. J., 144
Bullough. V., 107, 112
Bunch, C., 5, 12, 108, 362, 364, 365, 367
Burgos, G., 302
Burke, Tarana, 153
Burmese Nat religion (Upper Burma), 246
Burn, S. M., 15, 16, 112, 151, 153, 248
Burqa, 32
Bush, G.W., 225
Busso, J., 248
Butler, S., 214
Bystydzienski, J. M., 309, 310, 338, 341, 346, 349, 357, 358

C

Cabezas, A. L., 226, 231
Cabinets, government. *See* Political power
Cabral, H., 64
Càceres, Bertha, 194
Cadinu, M., 32
Callimachi, R., 259
Cambodia, 216
Cammaer, Patrick, 45
Campbell, D. E., 301
Campus, D., 320, 323
Canada, gender wage gaps in, 139
Canetto, S. S., 15, 16
Canon, religious, **255**
Cantor, A., 262-263
Capello, O., 76
Čaputová, Zuzana, 312
Cardoso, L. F., 11
Caribbean Association for Feminist Research and Action (CAFRA), 24
Carillo, R., 39
Carli, L. L., 146, 147
Carmody, D. L., 254, 261, 265, 266
Carmona, Magdalena Sepuilveda, 131
Carr, R., 270
Carraro, E., 102
Carras, M. C., 316, 321

Carta, A., 102
Carver, K. A., 16, 349, 362
Casimiro, I., 309, 327, 349, 356, 359, 360
Castro, C., 247
Catherine the Great, 311
Catt, Carrie Chapman, 362
Cavin, S., 107, 108, 112
CEDAW Committee, 14
Center for Reproductive Rights, 76
Center for Women's Global Leadership (CWGL), 343, 365
Central American Free Trade Agreement (CAFTA), 217
Cervical cap, 74
Cha, Y., 149
Chafetz, J. S., 4, 127
Chalasami, S., 130
Chamorro, Pedro, 314
Chamorro, Violeta de, 314, 319
Chang, G., 209, 210
Chang, J. C., 218
Chant, S., 102, 110, 182, 185, 211
Charkiewicz, E., 191
Charles, Eugenia, 319
Charles, M., 141
Charlesworth, H., 15, 145, 184, 185, 367
Chasteen, A. L., 8
Chaves, M., 275
Chavkin, W., 82
Chen, J., 42
Chen, K., 78
Chen, M., 155
Chernyak, E., 272
Cheryan, S., 147
Chesler, P., 41, 264
Chesters, J., 130, 131
Cheung, H. K., 153
Cheung, S. F., 153
Chi, D. Q., 214
Child marriage, 33
in the United States, 34
Childs, S., 302
Chile, gender wage gaps in, 139
China, activism, by women, 356, 357
Chinchilla, Laura, 314
Chinchilla, N. S., 345, 358
Chinery-Hesse, Mary, 126

Chinkin C., 367
Chinkin C. M., 15
Chipko movement, 194–195, 327
Chizhik-Goldschmidt, A., 263
Choi, C., 219
Chopra, Deepta, 177
Chou, D., 66
Chow, E. N., 78
Chowdhury, N., 16, 41, 304, 349, 362
Christ, C. P., 250, 255, 277, 278
Christian Science (United States), 246
Christianity, 270–275
Chuang, J., 32
Chung, W., 31
Ciller, Tansu, 319, 320
Cimons, M., 195
Cisgender, 105
Citro, B., 30, 31
The City of Ladies, 6
Clancy, K. B, 151
Clark, E., 213
Clarke, V., 105, 114
Class inequalities, women's movement, 350
Cleopatra, 311
Climate change, 188, 189
Climate justice, 192
Clinton, Bill, 302, 324
Clinton, Hillary, 26, 304, 323, 324
Clitoridectomy, 68
Coalition Against Trafficking in Women (CATW), 225, 230
Cobble, D. S., 157
Cockburn, C., 327
Code Pink, 327
Coercive antinatalism, 78
Coercive pronatalist policies, 78
Cohen, P. N., 129, 137
Cohen, S. A., 80
Col, J., 319, 321
Cole, E. R., 9
Collyns, D., 79
Colombia, gender wage gaps in, 139
Colverson, K., 178
Combahee River Collective, 9, 113
Commission on the Status of Women (CSW), 363

Comparable worth, 144
Compulsory heterosexuality, 111
Concrete ceiling, 145
Condom use, 74, 103
Conflict-related sexual violence, 45–48
Congresses, 300
Conley, T. D., 102
Contemporary woman-centered religions, 246
Contextualization
overview, 10
Contraception, 72–75. *See also* Reproductive health and rights
Contraceptive implant, 75
Contraceptive injection, 75
Contraceptive patch, 75
Contraceptive ring, 75
Contraceptive sponge, 74
Contrapower sexual harassment, 152–153
Contributing family workers, 155
Convention on the Elimination of Discrimination Against Women (CEDAW), 13–15, 136, 154, 178, 363, 364, **366**
Coomaraswamy, R., 15
Coomaraswamy, Radhika, 100
Coontz, Stephanie, 149
Copelon, R. J., 46
Copelon, Rhonda, 15
Cornwall, A., 183, 185
Corrigan, Mairead, 328
Cortina, L. M., 152, 153
Costa, Antonio Maria, 32
Costa Rica, gender wage gaps in, 139
COVID-19 pandemic, 81, 84, 173, 214, 216
Cox, J. Jr., 145
Cravens, C. S., 354
Cresson, Edith, 322, 323
Critical political mass, 302
Cuadrado, I., 146
Cullors, Patrisse, 326
Cultural globalization, 209
Cultural imperialism, 10
Cultural relativism, 12
Cummings, N., 31, 32

Currier, A., 110, 113
Cyber-brides, 223–225
Czech Republic, gender wage gaps in, 139

D

Dahan, Y., 217
Dahlburg, J. T., 319
Dahlerup, D., 308
Dairiam, M. S., 362
Dalit movement, 350
Daly, M., 245, 247, 250, 251, 274
Dalziel, P., 132
D'Amico, F., 315, 316, 318, 322
Daniluk, J. C., 103
Danuser, B., 137
Dara, M., 216
Daragahi, B., 260
Das Gupta, M., 31
Daskalova, D., 348
D'Augelli, A. R., 110
Daughters of Rabia, 7
Davidson, J. O., 226
Davies, C., 84
Davis, A., 79
Davis, D., 147
Davis, G., 76
Davis, R., 217
Dawson, R., 78
de Fonte, Norma Allegrone, 307
de Haan, F., 348
de la Cruz, Sor Juana Inés, 4
de Pizan, Christine, 6
Debt bondage, 219
Declercq, E., 64
Dekovic, M., 102
Del Río, C., 140
Dellepiane, L., 129, 130, 133, 178
Democratization, women's movements and, 351–356
Denmark, gender wage gaps in, 139
Derris, K., 270
Desai, M., 209, 231, 351, 362
Desai, Trupti, 266
Desaparecidos (disappeared), 326
Desia, Morarji, 316
Developed countries, 176. *See also* Global North

Developing nations, 172–207. *See also*
   Global South; Least developed
   countries (LDCs); Women and
   Development
Development. *See also* **Globalization**
   defined, 175
   **development programs and projects,
   175**
   environmental sustainability and,
      187–194
   feminist concerns, 176–179
   gender and development approach
      (GAD), 183–187
   overview, 173–175
   traditional development programs,
      177–179
   women in development (WID),
      180–182
Development with Women for a New
   Era (DAWN), 24
Devine, P. G., 9
Devries, K., 104
Dharma, 265, 270
Dhillon, A., 257
Dhingra, N., 29
Di, D., 249
Dianic witchcraft, 278
Diaphragm, 74
Dickinson, Emily, 106
Diduk, S., 175
Diner, H., 6
Disney, 213
Ditsie, Palesa Beverly, 98
Diversity
   climate change policy, 191
   global women's studies, 3, 6, 9, 10,
      12, 15–17
   lesbian, 112, 115
   religion, 245–249
   reproductive rights, 85
   SOGI rights, 104, 105, 115
   women's movements, 341–346
Diviners, 245
Dixon-Mueller, R., 64, 72, 78
Dobash, M., 194
Dogbé, Victoire Tomegah, 312
Dolker, T., 187
Domestic violence, 26, 27, 28, 35,
   37–41, 62, 103, 105, 343. *See
   also* Intimate partner violence

The Domestication of Women, 179
Donovan, M., 76
Dorf, J., 110
Double jeopardy, 152
Down, I., 302
Downey, J. C., 109
Dowry, 29–30
Dowry death, 39
Dowry murder, 39
Dowry violence, 39
Dreier, P., 214
Driving ban, 344
Drury, C., 271
Duck, R., 247
Duderija, A., 254, 255
Duff, Nancy, 144
Dukureh, Jaha, 70
Duley, M. I., 175
Durga, 267
Dworkin, A., 102

E

Eagly, A. H., 5, 145, 146, 147, 149
Ebadi, Shirin, 260, 278, 328, 355
Eck, D. L., 252
Economic globalization, 209
Economic power, 25–26. *See also*
   Work, women and
   domestic violence and, 39
   women's action around, 325–326
   women's movements and,
      349–350
Edlund, L., 30
Education for girls, 348
Egalitarian culture, 6
Ehrenberg, M., 6
Ehrenreich, B., 214
Einwohner, R. L., 249
Eisler, R., 277
El Saadawi, Nawal, 4, 5, 244
Elders, J., 80
Electoral reforms, 306–309
Electoral systems, 305
Elks, S., 153
Elliot, L., 191
Elliott, B., 114
Elliott, C. J., 148
Ellis, S. J., 111, 112, 113
Ellison, M., 33
Elsayegh, N., 8

"Embodied spirituality," 276
Emergency contraceptive pills, 75
EMILY's List, 310
Emmett, B., 210
Empowerment, overview, 6
Endendijk, J. J., 102
ENDTHEBACKLOG project, 43
Engstrom, D., 229
Enloe, C., 226
Entrepreneurs, women as, 155
Environmental defenders, of global
   women's, 191–194
Environmental sustainability, women
   in, 190–191
**Equal Remuneration Convention,
   140**
Equal Status Council (ESC), 356
Eskol, Levi, 316
Esquerra, A., 82, 83
Estrin, D., 265
Ethnocentric, 10
Evangelical Christian fundamentalist
   movement, 273
Everett, J., 316
Excision, 68
**Export processing zones (EPZs),
   212–213**
Ezeonu, P. O., 80

F

Faderman, L., 106
Faderman, Lillian, 106
Falk, M. L., 270
Fallon, K. M., 302, 353
Family balancing, 31
**Family responsibility discrimination,
   148**
Farhana, K., 215
Fattah, Esraa Abdul, 327
Fatwas, 258
Fehr, C. P., 105
Feijoo, M. D. C., 307, 326
Female condom, 74
**Female genital mutilation (FGM),
   67–72**
Feminism
   global women's studies, 6, 8, 9, 16
   lesbian feminism, 111–114
   sexual orientation and feminism,
      110–111

state feminism, 356–359

transnational feminist movements, 360–367

women's movements, 341–346, 350, 352

The Feminist Book of Lights and Shadows, 278

Feminist critiques of religion, 249–253

Feminist economics, 131

Feminist hermeneutics, 255

Feminist movements, 344–346, 350, 352, 357

Feminist spirituality, 246, 276–278

Feminist spirituality movement, 276–278

Feminist theology
   Christian, 274–275
   common critiques, 250–251
   common reforms, 253–256
   definition, 250
   Jewish, 262–265
   Muslim, 258

Feministas, 352

Femocrats, 356

Feraro, S., 278

Ferber, M. A., 143

Ferdman, B., 9

Ferguson, A., 111

Ferrant, G., 211

Fertility awareness, 74

Fester, G., 358

Fincher, L. H., 357

Findly, E. B., 270

Finnbogadottir, Vigdis, 297, 322

Fiorenza, Elisabeth Schüssler, 274

Fiorina, Carly, 323

Firoz, T., 66

Fisher, J., 197

Fiske, S. T., 248, 249

Fitzgerald, L. F., 150, 152, 153

Fitzgerald, T., 62

Flaherty, G. T., 226

Flanders, C. E., 109

Fleshman, M., 327

Flores, N., 276

Floro, M., 132, 180

Folad, Malfuza, 354

Forced marriage, 33

Forced prostitution, 229

Formal labor sector, 154–155

Formal politics, 27, 297, 300
   women heads of state and government, 311–324
   women's representation in parliaments and congresses, 300–314
   women's voting, 298–300

Forrester, A., 182

Fourth World Conference on Women (FWCW), 2, 14, 185, 356, 362–363, 364, 367

Francheschet, S., 309

Frederiksen, Mette, 312

Frankson, J. R., 47

Fraser, A., 318

Fraser, A. S., 361

Free trade zones, 212

Freidenvall, L., 308

French, M., 275

French, Marilyn, 3

Fretheim, A., 68

Fried, S., 367

Friedman, E., 12, 365, 367

Friedman, R. C., 109

Frohmann, A., 350

Frost, S., 12

Frye, J., 153

Fuentes, A., 214

Fuentes, Daisy Avance, 305

Fuentes, L., 79

Fujieda, M., 349

Fukuda Hideko, 349

Fukuda-Parr, Sakiko, 132

Fundamentalist Church of the Latter Day Saints (FLDS), 273

Funk, C., 151

Fuochi, G., 130

Fuwa, M., 129, 130, 137

G

GABRIELA, 352

Galambos, N. L., 129, 130

Galdi, S., 32

Gálvez, M. L., 131

Ganatra, B., 76

Gandhi, Indira, 315, 316, 318, 320, 322

Garcia, L., 195

García-Ael, C., 146

García-Moreno, C., 102

Garcia-Retamero, R., 146

Garza, Alicia, 326

Gautam, A., 30

Gebara, I., 275

Genat, A. E., 151

Gender, 4

Gender and development approach (GAD), 183–187
   vs. WID, 184

Gender-biased sex selection, 28

Gender binary, 105

Gender-egalitarian cultures, 6

Gender expression, 105

Gender gap, in unpaid care work, 131–134

Gender harassment, 150, 150–151

Gender health disparities, 62

Gender identity, 105–106

Gender inequality, 3, 25–48
   biological differences, 4
   climate change and, 192
   employment, 134–154
   materialist explanations, 3–4
   politics, 256–275
   religion, 250–275
   sociocultural explanations, 4–5
   unpaid domestic and care labor, 128–131

Gender job/occupational segregation, 140

Gender mainstreaming, 183, 191, 194

Gender norms, 5

Gender perspective on unpaid care work, 130–131

Gender quotas, 306–310

Gender realignment, 300

Gender-responsive budget analysis, 132

Gender roles, 5

Gender-segregated religious practices, 252, 252–253, 255–257, 262–266, 268–270, 274–275

Gender socialization, 5

Gender stereotypes, 5
   employment, 143, 146, 149
   politics, 300, 303–306, 309, 318–324, 329

Gender wage discrimination, 143

Gender wage gap, 26, 140–144

General Agreement on Tariffs and Trade (GATT), 217

Genesis Rabbah, 261

Genocidal rape, 46

Genovese, M. A., 316, 319, 320

Gerdts, C., 76

Gerhart, M., 270, 275

Gerstner, D. A., 114

Ghanim, D., 102

Gharib, M., 103

Ghodsee, K., 346, 349, 353, 354

Ghorban, R., 102

Gibson, L., 260

Giger, N., 300

Gildersleeve, Virginia, 13

Gillard, Julia, 323

Gilroy, H., 34

Gilson, J., 30, 31

Gimbutas, M., 6, 277

The Girl Generation: Together to End FCM, 71

Girl neglect, 29

GirlsNotBrides.org, 35

Glass ceiling, 145–150, 152

Glass walls, 148

Glick, P., 247, 248, 249

Glick, Peter, 149

Global Alliance Against Trafficking in Women (GAATW), 225

Global Alliance Against Trafficking in Women (GATW), 225

Global feminism, 6

Global Gender and Climate Alliance (GGCA), 194

Global North (developed or industrial countries)**, 175**

Global South (developing nations)**, 175**

Global supply chains (GSCs), 213–215

Global women's and gender studies, 6

activism and empowerment, 6–8

human rights, 12–17

inequality, overview, 3–6

multicultural approach, overview, 8–9

Globalization

action opportunities, 234

cultural, **209**

"dark underside," 219

defined, **209**

economic, **209**

effects on women, 209–212

migration and, 210–211, 218–225

sex trade, 225–231

transnational (multinational) corporations, 214–218

websites, 235

Goddess spirituality, 277

Gokal, S., 248

Gold, A. G., 266

Goldberg, A. E, 108

Goldberg, C. B., 153

Goldenberg, S. M., 229

Goldenstein, J. M., 62

Goldsmith, J., 213

Goodwin, J., 259

Goonatilake, H., 270

Gottlick, J. F. B., 349

Government cabinets, 300, 301. *See also* Political power

Graham, E., 221

Granryd, M., 211

Grant, J. M., 152

Grassroots organizations (GROs), 7, 19, 27, 194, 196, 297, 327, 329, 343, 352

Grassroots support organizations (GRSOs), 7, 196, 310, 343

Green, E., 272

Green, Rosario, 367

Green Wave, 84

Greenbelt movement, 327

Greenberg, B., 264, 265

Greene, B., 107, 108, 110, 113

Griffin, W., 277

Griffith, K. A., 152

Grimshaw, D., 142

Grosh, O., 225

Gross, R. M., 6, 10, 245, 247, 251, 252, 253, 254, 262, 265, 269, 270, 274, 275, 277

Grown, C., 175, 177, 183

Grown, Caren, 340

Grusky. D. B., 141

Guadamuz, T. E., 106

Gubernath, J., 247

Guiding principles, 217

Guilmoto, C. Z., 29, 30

Gunewardena, N., 212

Gupta, L., 267

Gutierrez, E. R., 79

Gutierrez, M., 308

Guttmacher Institute, 76

H

Hadid, D., 348

Halafoff, A., 269, 270

Halim, D., 155

Hall, E. L., 245, 248

Halliwell, E., 105, 114

Hamilton, M. C., 251

Hampson, D., 276

Han Myung-Sook, 317, 322

Hancock, P., 185

Handron, C., 147

Hannover, B., 247

Harcourt, W., 360

Hardin, C., 251

Haredi, 261, 265

Harris, E. C., 148

Harris, K., 322

Hartman, T., 253, 261, 264

Hartmann, B., 72, 78

Hasina, Sheikh, 312, 314

Hassan, R., 259

Hassan, Samia Suluhu, 312

Hausler, S., 191

Haussman, M., 356, 359

Hawke, A., 226

Hawkesworth, M. E., 14, 15

Hawkins, B. W., 105

Hawkins, M., 275

Hayashi-Panos, N., 33

Hayashino, D. S., 152

Hayfield, N., 105, 114

Head of government, 27, **312,** 313–324

Head of state, 27, **312**, 313–324

Healers, 245

Heilman, M. E., 146, 147, 149

Heine, Hilda, 322

Heise, L., 41

Hemmings, S., 229

Hennessy-Fiske, M., 76

Henrichs-Beck, C., 152

Hequembourg, A. L., 109

Herdt, G., 106, 108

Herek, G. M., 107

Hermeneutics, 254-255, 259, 270, 273, 275

Hernandez, S., 157

Heschel, S., 261, 262

Hesketh, T., 29

Heston, L. V., 224

Heteronormativity, 113

Heteropatriarchy, 111, 114

Heterosexism, 110

Heterosexual marriage and romance, 107

Hidayyatullah, A., 250, 251, 254, 259

Hijab, 32, 260

Hinchliffe, E., 145

Hinduism, 265-268

HIV/AIDS, 61-62, 73-74, 81
  contributors, 103-104
  facts about, 104
  reduction of, 104
  trafficking of women and girls, 229
  transgender women and, 106

Hoang, L., 221

Hoard, S., 341

Hochschild, A., 129

Hochschild, A. R., 221, 231

Hoerl, K. E., 102

Hoerl, Kristen, 102

Hoffman, W. E., 251

Hogan, C., 84

Holdcroft, J., 213

Holland, Fern, 355

Holland, K. J., 152, 153

Holleman, A., 275

Hollingsworth, J., 225

Holm, J., 251

Holmes, A., 226

The Holy Book of Women's Mysteries, 278

Homophobia, 110

"Honorary male" politicians, 322

Honour-based violence (HBV), 40-41

Honour killing, 40-41

Hook, J., 137

Hook, J. L., 130

Horizontal occupational segregation, 140

Hormonal methods, birth control, 75

Horne, R. M., 129, 130

Hostile sexism, 249

Howard, L. M., 229

Htun, M., 302

Hu, A. C., 357

Huang, J., 153

Hudson, L., 147

Huerta, Dolores, 325

Huffman, M. L., 148

Hughes, M. M., 299, 302, 305, 308, 309, 323, 327

Hui, K., 110, 112

Huizinga, P. G., 251

Human capital approach, 143

Human rights
  child marriage and, 34
  female genital mutilation and, 69-70, 82, 85
  globalization and, 210, 216-219, 223-224, 230-231
  labor rights as, 140, 157
  overview, 12-17
  political rights as, 297, 309, 328
  reproductive rights as, 61-62, 72, 78-79, 82, 85
  sexual rights as, 99-101
  transnational women's movements and, 345, 358, 359, 364-367
  violence against women and, 35, 344

Human Rights Watch, 27, 150, 222, 227, 229

Human trafficking, 33
  child marriage and, 34
  HIV/AIDS infection, 229
  marriage migrants, 223-225
  migration and, 210, 217, 219-221
  sex trafficking, 227-231
  sexual violence and, 35, 42, 45, 47
  son preference and, 30

Humanistic issues, action around, 327-329

Hundley. T., 82

Hunsberger, B., 247

Hurwitz, Sara, 263

Huso, Y., 106

Hussain, R., 72, 80

Hussein, Lubna, 260

Hussein, Saddam, 355

Hwang, M. C., 219

Hymen restoration surgeries, 102

I

I Am Malala (2013), 348

Ichikawa Fusae, 349

ICPD. *See* International Conference on Population and Development (ICPD)

Imam, A., 232, 248, 249, 267

Imams, 257

Income-generating projects, 180

India
  activism, by women, 338, 350-351
  child marriage, 12
  Chipko movement, 194-195
  migration, 219, 222, 224
  politics, 299, 315, 320
  religion, 265-266, 267, 268
  sexual rights, 102, 108, 110
  son preference, 29, 30
  traditional development programs, 175
  violence against women, 38, 39, 40
  women as property, 34
  work, women and, 148, 156

Industrialized countries, 175

Inequality, overview, 3-6

Infibulation, 68

Informal labor sector, 154-156

Informal politics, 298, 324-329

Inter-Parliamentary Union (2016), 152

International Alliance of Women, 362

International Center for Research on Women (ICRW), 7, 26, 34

International Conference on Population and Development (ICPD), 61

International Criminal Court (ICC), 47

International Gay and Lesbian Human Rights Commission (IGLHRC), 99

International Labour Organization (ILO), 26, 28, 126, 131, **136**, 137, 140, 144, 145, 148, 149, 154, 155, 157, 212, 213, 216, 217, 221, 223

International League for Peace and Freedom, 329
International marriage, 223–225
International marriage brokers (IMBs), 224
International Planned Parenthood Federation, 100
International Trade Union Congress (ITUC), 154
International Women's Day (IWD), 362
International Women's Development Agency (IWDA), 184
International Women's Suffrage Alliance (IWSA), 362
Internet brides, 223–225
Intersectionality, 9–11
    contraception and, 73
    effects of globalization and, 212
    gender pay gap and, 140
    glass ceiling and, 145
    politics and, 329
    SOGI-related discrimination and, 104–105, 113
    violence against women and, 35
    women's health and, 62
    women's movements and, 343, 345–346, 359, 367, 368
Intersex, 105
Intimate partner violence (IPV), 26, 27, 28, 35, **37**–41, 62, 103, 104, 343
Intrauterine devices (IUDs), 75
Iran
    activism, by women, 345, 347, 353
    CEDAW, 13
    politics, 299, 326
    religion, 26, 258
    reproductive rights, 64, 78
    sexual violence, 38
    sexuality, 102, 103, 107, 108
Iraq
    politics, 299, 309, 327, 329
    reproductive rights and health, 68, 78, 79
    sexual violence, 38, 41, 45, 48
    women's rights, 258, 352, 353
Iregui-Bohórquez, A. M., 134
"Iron Lady," 320
Isasi-Diaz, A. M., 276

Ishimoto Shizue, 349
Ishino, S., 112
Ishizaka, S., 195
ISIS (ISIL), 47, 48, 79, 258, 355
Islam, 244, 246, 250, 251, 252, 254, 267, 279, 321, 338, 354, 355
Islamists, 7, 16, 27, 79, 258, 355, 364
Islamization, 258
Israel, gender wage gaps in, 139
Iyoke, C. A., 80

J

Jacobsen, J. P., 143
Jacobson, J., 78
Jad, I., 338
Jagsi, R., 152
Jahan, R., 197, 342, 351
Jain, D., 13, 252, 346, 365
Jain, Devaki, 132, 344
Jain, K., 267
Jaising, I., 15
Jakobsdóttir, Katrín, 312
Jalalzai, F., 312, 313, 314, 316
Japan, gender wage gaps in, 139
Jaquette, J. S., 176, 180
Jaskoll, S. K., 263
Jeffs, Warren, 273
Jeglic, E. L., 226
Jennings, L., 80
Jewish Orthodox Feminist Alliance (JOFA), 264
Jha, P., 29
Jilani, Hina, 41
Jiyu Kennett Roshi, 269
Job prestige, 28
Johnson, B. R. Jr., 76
Johnson, M. D., 129, 130
Johnson, N., 302
Johnson, N. J., 16, 349, 362
Johnson, N. L., 178
Johnson, P. A., 62
Johnson-Odim, C., 346
Johnson Sirleaf, Ellen, 301, 317, 318, 319, 320, 324, 328
Jokhio, A. H., 66
Jonas, Regina, 263
Jones, J., 72
Jones, R., 152
Josefsson, C., 302

Joshee, R., 266, 268
Joshi, D., 301, 302
Joyce, K., 273
Joyful Heart Foundation, 43
Judaism, 246, 254, **261**–265
Julios, C., 71

K

Kabagenyi, A., 80
Kadlec, K., 112
Kafala (sponsorship) system, 222
Kagan, S., 222
Kahn, L.M., 140, 141, 143
Kaiman, J., 357
Kakoko, D., 78, 79
Kakuyama, T., 153
Kalantry, S., 30, 31
Kali, 267
Kaljulai, Kersti, 312
Kallas, Kaja, 312, 314
Kandiyoti, Deniz, 132
Kang, A., 307, 308
Kanner, M., 8
Karau, S. J., 147
Karides, M., 231
Kark, R., 145, 149
Karlan, D., 182
Karlsson, J., 81
Karma, 265
Karman, Tawakul, 326, 327
Katsulis, Y., 227
Katsura, Masika, 47
Katumba, R., 196
Katzenstein, M. F., 341, 343
Kaur, G., 266
Kavanagh, A., 77
Keddie, N. R., 345, 351, 358
Kelley, Casey, 102
Kelly, C. R., 102
Kelly, Joan, 321
Kelly, Kate, 252
Kelly J., 308
Kemp, A., 346, 350, 351, 352
Kende-Robb, C., 182
Kettler, S., 348
Khan, Izhaq, 315
Khan, T. S., 3, 41
Kilbourne, J., 102
Kim, G. J., 275, 276

Kincaid, E., 149
King, E. B., 153
King, M. A., 110, 112
King, Ursula, 253, 275, 277
Kingsolver, A., 212
Kirchner, Cristina Fernandez de, 315
Kirchner, Nestor, 315
Kirkpatrick, L., 247
Kirui, D., 196
Kishida Toshiko, 349
Kiss, L., 104
Kittleson, M. C., 298, 299, 300
Kittony, Zipporah, 68
Klugman, J., 131, 133, 178
Kmec, J. A., 148
Knaul, F. M., 190
Koenig, A.M., 146
Kony, Joseph, 272
Korea, gender wage gaps in, 139
Korean household religion, 246
Koss, M. P., 41
Kosuri, M. D., 226
Koval, C. Z., 147
Kovarik, C., 178
Krahn, H. J., 129, 130
Kresnow, M., 42
Kress, M., 265
Krief, P., 137
Krook, L.M., 302
Krook, M. L., 302, 309
Krook, Mona, 301
Kumar, R., 29, 341, 350
Kumar, S., 30
Kumaratunga, Chandrika, 314, 320
Kunovich, P., 301, 304, 329
Kuugongelwa-Amadila, Saara, 312
Kuwait
  migrant women domestic workers,
    220, 222, 299
  political rights in, 27
Kwakwa, M., 252, 274
Kwesiga, J., 309, 327, 349, 356, 359,
  360
Kwok, L., 77
Kyegombe, N., 104

L

La Barbera, M. C., 71
Labor-saving technologies, 181

Laboy, M. M., 106
Lacey, M., 359
Lack of fit model, 147
Lakshmi, 265
Lam, T., 221
Landor, A. M., 103
Langer, A., 190
Larsen, S. E., 152
Latt, S. M., 77
Lavine, A., 270
Lawani, L. O., 80
LBT (lesbian, bisexual, and
  transgender) women, 104
Leadership, gender differences in,
  145–150, 315–318
Leaky pipeline, 145
Leamaster, R. J., 249
Least developed countries (LDCs),
  174, 176
Leck, J. D., 148
Lee, K., 151
Legal literacy, 28
Legal power
  gender inequality, 26–28
Leghari, Farooq, 315
Leitman, L., 82
Lemery, J., 191
Lennox, Annie, 11
Lerner, G., 39, 346
Lerner, Gerda, 4, 5
Lerner, H., 217
**Lesbian and bisexual invisibility,
  106–**110
**Lesbian-baiting/sexuality-baiting,
  110**
Lesbian feminism, 111–114
Lesbian Herstory Archives (LHA),
  106–107
Lesbian separatism, 112
Lesbianism, 107–110
Lev, S. L., 275
Levtov, R., 129, 130, 131, 133
Lewis, C., 271
LGBT+, 106, 110
LGBTI (lesbian, gay, bisexual,
  transgender, intersex), 106
LGBTQIA rights, 99. *See also* SOGI
  rights
Li, H., 30
Liberation theology, 255, 275, 276

Lim, L. Y. C., 211
Lindau, R., 112
Lindee, K. M., 225
Lindgreen, A., 218
Line jobs, 148
Linea Aborto Libre, 85
Ling, Y., 349
Lips, H. M., 48
Lister, R., 298, 302, 324
Liturgy, 261
Livingston, G., 149
Livingston, R., 147
Lobala, 33
Local women environmental
  defenders, 194–196
Lockwood, P., 8
López-Sáez, M., 147
López-Zafra, E., 146
Lorber, J., 105
Lorde, A., 111, 113
Lorde, Audre, 9
Lorentzen, L. A., 209
Louie, M. C. Y., 214
Loutfi, A., 348
Lovenduski, J., 304, 357
Lozano, A., 258
Lu, L., 29
Lu, T. S., 226
Lucia, A., 265, 268
Lund-Thomsen, P., 218
Lustgarten, A., 185
Lutz, Bertha, 13

M

Ma, A., 147
Maass, A., 32
Maathai, Wangari, 187, 196, 328
Macdonald, F., 145
MacGregor, S., 194
MacKay, J. M., 105
Maddox, J., 34
Madlala, N., 346, 350, 351, 352
MADRE, 40, 46, 48
Mae chii (female monks), 259
Magley, V. J., 150, 152, 153
Mahayana tradition, 271
Mahayana (Zen) Buddhism, 268,
  269

Mahila Samta Sainik Dal (League of Women Soldiers for Equality), 350
Mak, A., 110, 112
Mala, Keta, 269
Malala Fund, 348
Male condom, 74
Malharro, Margarita, 307
Maltby, L. E., 245, 248
Manfre, C., 178
Mangis, M. W., 247
Manzi, F., 146
Maphisa, Kunyalala, 146
Maquila Solidarity Network (MSN), 217
Marcos, Ferdinand, 321, 350, 352
Margolis, D. R., 349
Marin, Sanna, 312
Marler, I., 248
Marriage Broker Regulation Act of 2005, 225
Marriage migrants, 18, 209, **223**–225
Martin, D., 156
Martini, S.A., 102
Masculine God-language, 250–251
Mashal, M., 354
Materialist explanations, gender inequality, 3–4
Maternal morbidity, 66–67
Maternal mortality, 64–66
Maternity leave policies, 136–137
Maternity Protection Convention, 136
Maternity protections, 135–138
Matriarchies, 6
Matsui, T., 153
Matsumo, A., 349
Matteazzi, E., 131
Mattieu, J., 273
Mattioli, F., 82
Matynia, E., 349, 350, 354
Mayer, A. M., 15, 16, 279
Mazur, A. G., 341, 356, 358
Mbachu, D., 325
Mbon, F. M., 245
McArthur, C., 66
McBride, D. E., 341
McCann, D., 150
McFarlane, J., 34
McLaughlin, H., 152, 153
McMinn, M. R., 251

McPhillips, A., 272, 275
McVeigh, K., 325
Medina, L., 276
Meinzen-Dick, R., 178
Meir, Golda, 304, 316, 319, 321, 322
Meleis, A., 190
Melnikova, T., 131, 178
Members of parliament (MPs), 300
MenCare, 133–134
Mencarini, L., 82, 130
Mendez, M., 301
Menstrual hygiene management (MHM), 11
Menstruation
  gender-role and, 4
  menstrual hygiene management (MHM), 11
  as taboo, 11
Mercier, M. P. P., 137
Merkel, Angela, 296, 312, 317, 323
Mermel, A., 173
Mernissi, F., 102, 259
Merrick, M. T., 42
Meszaros, J., 223
#MeToo movement, 43, 153
Metoyer, C. C., 304, 309
Mexico, 347
  gender wage gaps in, 139
Meyer, I., 109, 110
Mhenni, Lina Ben, 327
Michaelson, R., 70
Micro-and-small-scale enterprises (WMSEs), 155
Micro-lending, 182
Microcredit, 182
Migraine-George, T., 110, 113
Migrant domestic workers, 219–223
Migration, 210–211, 218–225
Milkie, M. A., 128, 129, 130
Millennium Development Goals (MDGs), 65, 185, 364
Miller, E. C., 273
Miller, G., 80
Milman-Sivan, F., 217
Milner, A., 77
Ministers, 301
Minyan, 261, 262
Mir-Hosseini, Z., 349, 355
Miranda, Florentina Gomez, 307

Misdary, R., 259
Misra, J., 144
Mitchell, A. A., 146
Mitchem, S. Y., 276
Mitzvot, 261
Mixed systems, 305
Mlambo-Ngcuka, Phumzile, 35, 144, 192
Mmari, K., 11
Modernization theory, 176
Moghadam, V. M., 211, 259, 279, 345, 360, 362, 363, 364
Mohammed, L., 76
Mohanty, C., 9, 16, 360
Moineddin, R., 29
Mojaheds, 257
Molero, F., 146
Molinelli, N. G., 307
Moller, A., 76
Moloney, A., 79
Molyneaux, M., 341, 353, 354
Momsen, J., 180
Mononormativity, 114
Monosexism, 114
Montanari, B., 179
Montecinos, V., 322
Moodley, A., 346, 350, 351, 352
Moors, A. C., 102
Moran, T. H., 217
Morgan, Robin, 318
Mortensen, A., 40
Morton, C., 64
Moscoso, Mireya, 315
Moser, C., 178, 183
Mosha, I., 78, 79
Mosher, W., 72
Mosse, J. C., 176, 178, 180, 181, 182, 183
Mostaghim, R., 260
Mother Teresa, 328
Motherhood penalty, 148
Motherhood wage gap, 142
Motherhood wage penalty, 142
Mothers of the Plaza de Mayo, 326
Mott, Lucretia, 3
Mottet, L. A., 152
Mottley, Mia, 312, 314
Mu, Z., 223
Mujerista theology, 276
Mullahs, 257

Multiculturalism, 8-9
challenge of, 10-12
Multilateral aid, 175
Multinational corporations, 214-218
Mumford, A., 79
Mungwa, A., 309, 327, 349, 356, 359, 360
Murad, Nadia, 328
Murdie, A., 324
Murray, V., 191
Musaweh, 261
Muteshi, J., 71, 72
Myrdal, Alva, 328

N

Nadasen, P., 157
Nadell, P. S., 262
Nader, Z., 354
Nadolny, D., 8
Naide, S., 76
Naidu, M., 266
Nair, N. J., 267
Nairobi Forward Looking Strategies for the Advancement of Women, 362
Nakano, Hiromi, 37
Nakiganda, Betty, 155
Nakuti, J., 104
Nalwadda, G., 80
Nanda, P., 30
Napasri, T., 148
Naples, N. A., 212
Nardi. M., 307
Nardi, M., 309
Nash, E., 76
Nashrulla, T., 267
Nasrin, Taslima, 277
National assemblies, 300
National Crime Records Bureau, 40
National legislatures, 298-300. *See also* Parliaments
National Women's Lobby Group (NWLG), 344
Nava, A., 34
Navaratri, 265
Navarro, M., 326
Nawa, F., 258

Neal, M., 227
Nelson, B. J., 16, 349, 362
Nelson, M. R., 102
Neocolonialism, 188
Neoliberal economic policies, 209-210
Neumaier, E. K., 270
Newport, F., 28
Ng, Vivien, 106
Nguyen, Amanda, 43
Nguyen, F., 150
Niarchos, C. N., 44
Nicaragua
activism, by women, 358-359
Niddah, 262
Niditch, S., 262
Nike Corporation, 213, 218
Niqab, 259
Njuki, J., 178
Nkomo, S. M., 145
"No Means No" campaign, 43
Nobel Peace Prize winners, 328
Nobre, P., 102
Nomani, A. Q., 258
Nomoto, Ritsuko, 39
Non-normative rape, 41-42
Nongovernmental organizations (NGOs), 7
Noone, C., 226
"Nordic Model," 230
Normative rape, 42
Norris, P., 304, 311
Norris, Pippa, 303
North American Free Trade Agreement (NAFTA), 217
Norway, 130, 137, 145, 227, 230, 299, 301, 312, 322, 356-357
gender wage gaps in, 139
Noyes, I., 8
Ntozi, J., 80
Nugent, Julie, 147
Nur, R., 110
Nurturing issues, action around, 327-329
Nyukuri, E., 191

O

Oba, A. A., 71
Obama, Barack, 6, 106

Obama, Michelle, 6
Objectifying gaze, 32
O'Brien, D. Z., 301
Obstetric fistula, 66
Occupational gender role segregation, 152
Och, M., 301, 302
O'Connor, L. T., 148
Oduyoye, M. A., 276
Of Woman Born, 111
Okimoto, T., 147, 149
Oliveira, M., 185
Olney, Shauna, 131
O'Loughlin, P. L., 16, 349, 362
Olson, R. M., 102
Oman, migrant domestic workers in, 222
Onda, T., 77
Onglatco, M. L., 153
OpenDemocracy, 40
Oral contraceptives, 75
Oram, S., 229
Organization of Women's Freedom in Iraq (OWFI), 48, 355
Ortega, Humberto, 319
Ortega, Irene, 129
Osmani, Vjosa, 312
Osotimehin, Babatunde, Dr., 34
O'Sullivan, D., 76
Otobe, N., 213, 214
Ottisova, L., 229
Outercourse, 74
OutRight Action International, 99-100
Own-account workers, 155
Owusu, V., 247
Oxfam, 131, 177, 178
Oyewumi, O., 346
Oyewùmí, Oyeronke, 346

P

Paek, H., 102
Pagels, E. H., 250
Paid labor, 134-154. *See also* **Unpaid domestic and care labor**
Pakekh, S., 209, 211, 212
Pakistan
activism, by women, 348
education for girls, 348

Pala-Okeyo, Achola, 16
Palermo Protocol, 230
Palet, L. S., 226
Panday, G., 11
Pandey, G., 267
Pangestu, M. E., 211
Parental rights of women, 7
Park Geun-hye, 324
Parker, K., 151
Parks, Rosa, 326
Parliaments, 4, 27, 300
   women's representation in, 300,
   301
Parpart, J. L., 183, 185
Parreñas, R. S., 218, 219
Parrot, A., 32
Parrot, Andrea, 31
**Party list/proportional representation
   systems (PL/PR), 305**
Pativratya, 266
Paton, E., 216
Patriarchal, social systems, **4**. *See
   also* Patriarchy
Patriarchy, 3, 4, 5, 16. *See also*
   heteropatriarchy
   religion and, 245, 250, 251, 258,
   259, 270, 272, 273, 274, 275, 278
   SOGI rights and, 107, 108, 127
   women's movements and, 338, 341,
   346, 351, 355, 360, 369
   women's reproductive rights and,
   63, 80
Patterson, C. J., 108
Patterson, Sandra Dean, Dr., 344
Patterson, T., 273
Paul, Alice, 299
Paustian-Underdahl, S. C., 146
Paxton, P., 299, 301, 302, 304, 305,
   308, 309, 310, 311, 323, 324,
   327, 329
Pay gap, 140–144. *See also* Gender
   wage gap
p'Bitek, Okot, 180
Peace movements, 327–328
"PeaceWomen Project," 329
Peach, L. J., 249, 252, 256, 257, 261,
   262, 268
Pearson, Elaine, 39
Pedersen, J., 327
Peel, E., 111, 112, 113

Peksen, D., 324
Penelope, J., 110, 111
Perasso, G., 102
Perez, G. C., 110
Period poverty, 11
Peron, Isabel, 315
Peron, Juan, 315
Perumalswami, C. R., 152
Peterson, C., 108
Peterson, J. C., 301
Peterson, V. S., 304, 324, 325, 327,
   329, 341
Pettit, B., 137
Pharr, S., 110
Pietrzak, J., 248
Pinochet, 317, 320
Piscopo, J. M., 308, 309
Pisklakova, Marina, 39, 40
Plaskow, J., 250, 252, 255, 262,
   277
Play, V. C., 147
Plurality/majority systems, 305
Poland, 347
   abortion laws, 76
Polin, K., 82
Politi, D., 84
Political insider, 315–316
Political literacy, 309
Political power
   action opportunities, 332
   congress, cabinet, 300–314
   heads of government, women as,
   311–324
   increasing women's, 306–311
   international agreements, 297
   Kuwait, 27
   men's greater, 26–28, 300–314
   overview, 297–298
   paths to power, 312–318
   social and protest movements,
   324–329
   violence against women in politics,
   304, 308, 309
   voting, 298–300
   websites, 333
Political surrogates, 319
Poonam, S., 267
Poone, J., 110, 112
Poonia, M., 195
Pope Francis, 274

Pope John Paul II, 274
Popinchalk, A., 76
Porter, M., 9, 362, 364
Portnoy, J., 34
Posadskaya, A., 353, 354
Post-colonial theologies, 275
Postnatal sex selection, 29
Poteat, T., 106
Powell, J. M., 211
Practical gender interests, 341
Prajnaparamita, 269
Prell, E., 109
Premarital sex, 103
Premarital virginity, 102
Prenatal care, 65
Prenatal sex selection, 29, 31
Presidents, women as
   advocacy of women's issues,
   321–322
   gender differences, leadership,
   318–321
   overview, 311–312
   paths to power, 312–318
Prevot, A., 276
Prime ministers, women as
   advocacy of women's issues,
   321–322
   gender differences, leadership,
   318–321
   overview, 311–314
   paths to power, 312–318
Private sphere, 4
"Pro-family values," 272
Probst, I., 137
Progressive Organization of Women
   (POW), 350
Prostitution, 32, 228–229
Protest movements, 324–328
Prugl, E., 185
Public sphere, 4
Puertas, S., 147
Pui-lan, K., 276
Pulitzer, L., 273
Purdah, 190, 266

Q

Queen, C., 114
Queer, 113
Queer theory, 113

Quid pro quo sexual harassment, 151
Quisumbing, A., 178
Qur'an, 256. *See also* Islam

R

"Rabba," 263
Rabelo, V. C., 152
Rachels, J., 15, 16
Racial/ethnic issues, 326–327
Racialized sexual harassment,
    151–152
Raday, F., 264
Radwin, M., 77
Rahman, A. K., 190
Rajan, V. J., 329
Rajavi, Maryam, 367
Rajkobal, P., 269, 270
Ramayana, 266
Ramdas, K. N., 195
Ramírez-Giraldo, M. T., 134
Ramshaw, G., 250
Rana Plaza industrial disaster (2013),
    215
Ransome-Kuti, Funmilayo, 349
Rao, A., 16
Rape
    abortion and, 76, 82, 83
    conflict (war)-related, 45–48, 176,
        360, 365
    early and forced marriage and, 33,
        34
    fistula and, 66
    form of violence against women,
        35, 36, 37, 41–45
    honour-violence and, 40
    as a human rights violation, 13
    ISIS, 79
    laws, 26, 27, 37, 42–43, 47, 343,
        360. *See also* the Appendix
    menstruation and, 11
    women in politics, 304, 324, 354
    at work, 216, 222
Rape cultures, 33, 45
Raphael, A., 226
Raponda, Rose Christiane Ossouka,
    312
Rashtriya Swayamsevak Sangh
    (RSS), 266
Rasicot, C., 271

Rassemblement Algerien des
    Femmes Democrates (RAFD),
    260
Razak, A., 276
Reagan, Ronald, 319
Recavarren, I. S., 153
Rees, C., 217
Reid, A., 80
Relative resources perspective on
    unpaid care work, 129-130
Religion
    action opportunities, 281–282
    Buddhism, **268**-270
    Christianity, **270**-275
    critiquing and deconstructing,
        249–253
    diversity and study of, 245–249
    feminist spirituality, 276–278
    Hinduism, **265**-268
    intersectional feminist theologies,
        275–276
    Islam, **256**-261
    Judaism, **261**-265
    reforming and reconstructing,
        253–255
    religious fundamentalism,
        246–249
    sexism in texts, 251
    websites, 282
Religious fundamentalism
    Christian, 103, 272, 273, 362
    general, 246–249, 251, 254, 279,
        360, 368
    Hindu, 265, 266
    Islamic, 7, 27, 103, 257, 258, 260,
        261, 321, 354, 355, 364, 368
    Jewish, 262, 263
Remez, L., 77
Remittances, 219
Reproductive control, 61
Reproductive health and rights
    abortion, 75–77
    activism, by women, 83–85
    contraception and choice, 72–75
    factors affecting, 63
    female genital cutting, 67–72
    global economy and corporations,
        81
    government controls, 77–80
    human rights key to, 62

men, control by, 80–81
    overview, 61–63
    religious organizations and, 81–83
Reproductive tourism, 31
Revolutionary Association of Women
    in Afghanistan (RAWA), 7
Rexer, R., 112
Reyes-Householder, C., 322
Rezaiah, J., 260
Rice, X., 324
Rich, A., 108, 111
Richey, C., 151
Rigby, J., 270
Rincker, M., 313
Rios Tobar, M., 317
Risman, B. J., 102
Ristikari, T., 146
Rivas, A. M., 183, 185
Rivera, Gilda, 349
Rizvi, R. M., 66
Robbins, C. P., 80
Robinson, J. P., 128, 129, 130
Robinson, M., 109
Robinson, S. P., 264, 266
Rockwell, B. V., 148
Rodgers, E. M., 151
Roehling, M. V., 153
Rogers, B., 179
Roldan, M., 176
Role congruity theory, 147
Rolon, M. L., 229
Rondon, E., 110
Roosevelt, Eleanor, 106
Rosaldo, M. Z., 28
Rosaldo, Michelle Zimbalist, 4, 28
Rosca, Ninotchka, 352
Rose, Amber, 102
Roselli, F., 102
Rosenthal, R., 5
Rosette, A. S., 147
Roso, J., 275
Ross, E., 258
Ross, L. E., 105
Ross, S.D., 266
Rosset, J., 300
Rossier, C., 76
Rost, L., 129, 130, 133, 178
Rouseff, Dilma, 314, 324
Roy, Arundhati, 325
Ruan, F. F., 107, 112

Ruben, R., 78, 79
Rubery, J., 142, 144
Rubin, D., 178
Rubin, D. B., 5
Ruether, R. R., 188, 246, 251, 275
Ruether, Rosemary, 346
Ruggie, J. G., 217
Runyan, A. S., 304, 324, 325, 327, 329, 341
Rupp, L. J., 106, 111, 113
Ruppanner, L., 130
Russia
    domestic violence and, 40
Russo, N. F., 41
Ruth, S., 245, 250
Ryabov, I., 223

S

Sadat, Anwar, 351
Sadik, Nafis, Dr., 2
Saint-Germain, M. A., 304, 309
Sáinz, M., 147
Sakalli-Ugurlu, N., 248
Sakellaropoulou, Katerina, 312
Sakyadhita, 270
Salaime, Samah, 350
Salamih, Fatimah Umm, 347
Salganicoff, A., 62
Salib, M., 327
Salih, Z. M., 258
Salim, S., 109
Salo, E., 346, 350, 351, 352
Salo, Elaine, 351
Salway, T., 105
Salzinger, L., 214
Samuel, S., 263
Sanchez-Hucles, J. V., 147
Sanday, P. R., 4, 6
Sande secret society (West Africa), 246
Sandfort, T., 106
Sandu, Maia, 312
Sanín, J. R., 311
Santiago, L. Q., 350, 352
Sarasvati, 265
Sass, J., 71, 72
Sati, 266
Sattar, A., 43
Sauer, B., 356, 359

Saunders, C., 132
Sayer, L. C., 128, 129, 130
Scherer, S., 131
Schouten, L., 267
Schroeder, T. M., 211
Schulman, G. B., 262
Schultze, M., 247
Schüssler Fiorenza, E., 250, 254, 255, 274, 275, 276
Schwartz, M., 81
Schwindt-Bayer, L. A., 322
Scothern, A., 184
Scott, L., 177
Seager, J., 149, 194, 299, 357
Sebastian, C., 40
Second shift, 129
Secretaries, 301
Sedgh, G., 72, 76, 77, 80
Segal, Lynne, 321
Sekhon, J., 346, 358
Self-efficacy, 346–347
Self-Employed Women's Association (SEWA), 156, 350
Sen, G., 6, 175, 177, 183, 340
Seo, Y., 225
Sepúlveda Carmona, M., 131
Sered, S. S., 245, 246, 252, 277
Sethna, C., 76
Settles, I. H., 152
Sex, 4
Sex selection, 28–31
Sex tourism, 226–227
Sex trade, 225–231
Sex trafficking, 35, 36, 42, 45, 47, 209, 225, 227–231
Sexism, 104
    in politics, 301, 302, 325
    in religious texts, 251
    in the workplace, 141, 143, 145, 147, 152
Sexual assault, 34–35, 36, 101, 114, 152
Sexual coercion, 151
Sexual double standard, 102, 103
Sexual exploitation, 32
Sexual harassment, 150–154, 213, 216, 219, 304, 355, 366
Sexual minority stress, 109
Sexual objectification, 32
Sexual orientation, 106–107, 110–114

Sexual orientation and gender identity (SOGI), 99, 104–110
Sexual purity of girls and women, 102
Sexual rights
    defined, **99**
    gender identity, **105**–106
    as human rights, 99–101
    important, 100
    LBT women, 104
    lesbian feminism, **111**–114
    sexual double standard, **102**, 103
    sexual orientation, 110–114
    sexuality, ownership of, 101–104
    SOGI rights, **99**, 104–110
    websites, 118–119
Sexual violence, 41–48. *See also* Rape; Sexual assault; Violence against women in politics
Sexuality of women, 103
Sexualized racism, 151–152
Sexually transmitted disease (STD), 73
Sexually transmitted infections (STI), 73
Shaaban, B., 257
Shaheen, Jeanne, 44
Shahwan, Raja, 311
Shakti, 266
Shalev, C., 264, 279
#ShameOnMalala, 348
Shapiro, D. N., 108
Sharafeldin, Marwa, 178
Shari'ah, 39, **256**, 257, 258, 260, 261, 355
Sharma, M., 110
Shastri, Lal Bahadur, 316
Shaw, S. M., 275
Sherif, B., 350, 351
Sherman, J., 217
Shetti, S., 217
Shin, J., 301
Shiva, Vandana, 172, 194
Sholkamy, Hania, 182
Siguroadottir, Johanna, 311
Sihra, K., 266, 268
Silverman, J. G., 229
Silvey, R., 218
Simanowitz, Stephan, 48
Simons, J., 173

Simons, L. G., 103
Simons, M., 226
Šimonytė, Ingrida, 312
Simpson, K., 277
Singh, Betu, 109
Singh, J., 34
Singh, K. C., 267
Singh, S., 77
Single member district systems (SMD), 305
Sjöberg, L., 303, 329
Sjöberg, O., 134
Slee, N., 251, 275
Smith, A., 251, 254
Smith, B., 113
Smith, S. G., 42
Social and protest movements, 324–328
Social constructivist, 4
Social conventions, 14, 15
Social norms, FGM/FGC, 70–71
Social roles theory, 5
Sociocultural explanations, inequality, **4**
SOGI rights, 99, 104–110
Sojo, V. E., 151
Solberg, Erna, 312
Soltan, Neda Agha, 326–327
Sommer, A. K., 255
Sommer, M., 11
Son preference, 28–31
Songdammakalayani monastery, 271
Songdammakalayani Temple, 271
Sonthalia, K., 325
Sorensen, C., 191
South African Domestic Workers' Union (SADWU), 156
South Korea, son preference in, 31
Special economic zones, 212
Special Rapporteur on Violence Against Women, 365
Spiritual diversity, 245. *See also* Religion
Sri Lanka, 271
Sri Lanka Federation of University Women (SLFUW), 344
Sri Lankan Freedom Party (SLFP), 314
Srinivasan, S., 30
"Stained-glass ceiling," 274

Stankiewicz, J. M., 102
Stanton, Elizabeth Cady, 254, 275, 362
Starhawk, 277, 278, 281
Starmann, E., 104
Starr, E., 223, 224
State feminism, 356–359
Status and power, gender difference, 24–48
  domestic violence, 37–41
  economic power, 25–26
  as objects and property, 31–35
  political and legal power, 26–28
  sex selection, 28–31
  sexual violence, 41–48
  VAWG, 35–41
Staudt, K., 176, 180
Staying Alive: Women, Ecology and Development, 194
Steinkopf-Frank, H., 257
Steinmetz, S., 300
Sterilization, 75
Stetson, D. M., 356, 358
Stevens, A., 146, 300
Stewart, A., 108, 152
Stienstra, D., 327, 362
Stone, Merlin, 278
Stop Rape Now campaign, 47
StopStreetHarassment.org, 32
Strange, C., 327, 329
Strategic gender interests, 341
Strathdee, S. A., 229
Stree Mukti Sangathana (Women's Liberation Organization), 350
Street harassment, 32
Stricker, K., 30, 31
Strikes, 215
Strömdahl, S., 106
Sturgis, S. M., 114
Subramaniam, Mangala, 338
Sugirtharajah, S., 267
Summerfield, G., 178
Sunna, 68
Supreme Sangha Council, 271
Survival sex, 47
Sustainable development, 173, 187–194
Sustainable Development Goals (SDGs), 61, 65, 70, 134, 140, 192, 223, 224, 230, 361, 364

Suu Kyi, Aung San, 328
Swann, S., 150, 152, 153
Sweatshop labor, 214–218
Sweetman, C., 182, 185
Sweis, R. F., 182
Swiss, L., 302
Symbolic circumcision, 68
Sztokman, Elana, Dr., 262
Szymanski, D. M., 152

T

Ta Tao Fa Tzu, 271
Tadesse, Zenebeworke, 361
The Tahirih Justice Center, 34
Tai, T., 131
Talmud, 262
Tanaka, K., 149
Tanakasempipat, P., 271
Tanis, J., 152
Tarasoff, L. A., 105
Tasdemir, N., 248
Tayah, M., 220, 221
Taylor, L., 257
Taylor, V., 111
Teggarty, N., 76
Thai Theravada tradition, 271
Thailand, 271
Tharoor, Shashi, 267
Thatcher, Margaret, 316, 320, 322, 323
Theravada (Hinayana) Buddhism, 269
Therigatha, 270
Thiagarajan, K., 267
Thiruchelvam, D., 29
Threlfall, M., 351, 352
Thurnell-Reid, T., 227
Tilley, T. J. M., 102
Time availability perspective on unpaid care work, 128–129
Time-use surveys, 127–128
Tinker, I., 134, 183
Tohidi, N., 345
Tomasevski, K., 14, 347
Tometi, Opal, 326
Tonstol, Geir, 142
Torah, 26
Torres, Margarita Malharro de, 307

Townes, E. M., 276
Tracy, Carol, 42
Traditional development programs, 177–179
Traditional gender roles, 152
Traeen, B., 109
Trafficking of women and girls, 227.
    See also Sex trafficking
HIV/AIDS infection, 229
mail-order brides, 223–225
overview, 33, **227–231**
prostitution, 228–229
status, gender difference, 33–34
Tran, T., 225
Trans girls, 105
Trans women, 105
Transfeminine, 105
Transgender, 105
Transnational feminist movements, 9, 19, 211, **359–367**
United Nations and, 362–364
women's rights as human rights, 364–367
Transnational feminist networks (TFNs), 360–362
Transnational feminist organizations, 261
Transnational (multinational) corporations, 214–218
Transphobia, 105–106
Travis, Dnika, 147
Treas, J., 148
Tribín-Uribe, A. M., 134
Trible, P., 275
Tripartite model of sexual harassment, 150
Triplett, M. A., 251
Tripp, A. M., 12, 17, 307, 308, 309, 327, 338, 345, 349, 356, 358, 359, 360, 361, 365
Trujillo, C., 111
Trump, Donald, 301, 304, 323, 358
Tsai Ing-wen, 214, 311, 314
Tsuzuki, Y., 153
Tubal ligation, 75
Tubman, Harriet, 113, 326
Tuccio, M., 211
Tum, Rigoberta Menchu, 326, 328

Tunçalp, O., 66, 76
Turpin, J., 209
2030 Agenda for Sustainable Development, 192
Tyc, A., 217
Tz'u-Hsi, 311

U

Ubel, P., 152
Uchino, K., 269
Uggen, C., 152, 153
Ulema, 257–258
Umanksy, E. M., 262
Unchained At Last, 34
Underland, V., 68
United Nations (UN), 13, 65
Action Against Sexual Violence in Conflict, 47
activism, by women, 360, 362–364
Beijing Platform for Action, 14, 183, 309, 356, 362–364
Children's Fund (UNICEF), 26
Commission on the Status of Women, 192
Commission on the Status of Women (CSW), 363
Conference on Economic Development (UNCED), 191
Conference on Women in Beijing, 99
Convention on Elimination of All Forms of Discrimination Against Women (CEDAW), 13–15, 136, 154, 178, 363, 364, 366
Decade for Women, 362
Declaration on the Elimination of Violence Against Women, 35
Four World's Women's Conferences, 362–365
Framework Convention on Climate Change (UNFCC), 193
International Women's Year, 352
Office on Drugs and Crime (UNODC), 227–228, 230
Population Fund (UNFPA), 29, 64, 66
UN Women, 26, 362

UNFPA, 29
UNICEF, 26
Universal Declaration of Human Rights, 13
World Conference on Human Rights, 364
World Tourism Organization (UNWTO), 226
United States
abortion laws, 76
activism, by women, 344, 358, 365–366
AIDS/HIV, 104
CEDAW, 15
child marriage in, 34
contraception and choice, 72
globalization and, 212, 218, 224, 225, 230
maternity leave, 137
migration, 224–225
political power, 194–196, 310, 325, 326, 327
religion, 249, 261, 262–263, 268, 269, 274
sexual rights, 103, 104–105, 106–107, 112, 113, 115
voting, 298–300
work, women and, 128, 131, 137, 140, 142, 145, 153, 155–156
United Women's Congress (UWC), 351
Universal Declaration of Human Rights (UDHR), 12–13, 99, 100, 217
Universal human rights, 12
Unmet need for family planning, 72–73
Unpaid domestic and care labor, 127–134. *See also* **Paid labor**
gender gap, 131–133
gender perspective on, **130**–131
relative resources perspective, 129–130
time availability perspective on, 128–129
Unpaid labor, 18
Until We Are Free: My Fight for Human Rights in Iran, 260
Unwanted sexual attention, 150, 151

Upanishads, 267
Ursic, E., 275
Uterine prolapse, 66

V

"Vacation cutting," 70
Valdes, T., 338, 350
Valenti, J., 102, 103
Valenti, Jessica, 44, 102
Valiente, C., 352
van Baar, A. L., 102
Van Dam, A., 144
van den Broek, D., 214
Vanderkruik, R., 66
Vanek, J., 155
Varghese, Winnie, 272
Vasa, P., 29
Vedas, 265, 266, 267
Verma, R., 30
Vertical occupational segregation, 142
Victim blaming, 42
Vienna Conference, 364
Vienna Declaration and Programme of Action, 364-365
Villegas, P., 347
Violence against women and girls (VAWG), 25, 28, 32, **35**-48, 62, 69, 99, 100, 102, 103, 104, 105, 106, 108, 109, 111, 114
Violence against women in politics (VAWIP), 303, 311
Violence against women (VAW)
  mail-order brides, **223**-225
  overview, **35**-48
  reproductive rights and health, 61, 62, 68, 69
  sexual violence and exploitation, 32, 102, 150-154, 227-231
  women's movements, 343-344, 346, 352, 360, **365**, 367-368
  women's sexuality and, 40, 99, 100, 102, 103, 104, 105, 106, 108, 109, 110, 111, 114
Violence and Harassment Convention, 154
Virginity, 102, 103
Virginity tests, 102-103, 324
Vist, G. E., 68

Vitema, J., 351
Voluntary party quotas, 307
Von Dadelszen, P., 66
Von Suttner, Bertha, 328
Voramai Kabilsingh, 271
Voting power, 298-300
Vulnerable employment, 155

W

Waddud, Amina, 257
Wakabayashi, N., 112
Wald, Lillian, 327
Walker, A., 276
Walker, L. S., 146
Walker, Madam C. J., 155
Wall, E., 273
Walter, L., 16
Wang, J., 42
Wang, V., 302
War
  women's movements and, 349
Waring, M., 131, 132
Waters, E., 353, 354
Watson, N. K., 249
Waylen, G., 359
Weaver, C. L., 252, 274
Weekes, Paula-Mae, 312
Weinstein, Harvey, 153
Weiss-Wolf, J., 11
Weldon, S. L., 302
Welzel, C., 17
Wemare, A., 257
West, G., 324, 325, 326, 327, 349
West, L., 362
West Coast Lesbian Collections, 107
The Western Wall (or HaKotel) in Jerusalem, 264
When God Was a Woman, 278
#WhereIsMyName, 7
Whitehead, A. L., 250, 251
Wicca (witchcraft), 278
Wickremesinghe, Ranil, 320
Wieringa, S., 108, 113, 115, 191
Wilcox, S., 209, 211, 212
Wilkinson, S., 114
Williams, Betty, 328
Williams, D. S., 276
Williams, H., 319
Williams, Jody, 328

Wilshire, Roshina, 176
Winnemucca, Sarah, 324
Winter, S., 102
Wirtz, A. L., 106
Wise, C., 278
Withdrawal, 74
Wittig, Nancy Hatch, 255
Woehr, D. J., 146
Wolbrecht, C., 301
Womanist theology, 276
Womanspaces, 253
Women Environmental Programme (WEP), 192
Women in Development Europe (WIDE), 360
Women in development (WID) approach, 180-182
  vs. GAD, 184
Women in Europe for a Common Future (WECF), 192
Women in Law and Development in Africa, 364
Women Living Under Muslim Laws (WLUML), 261, 364
Women Migrant Workers (WMWs), 218-225
Women of the Wall, 264, 265
Women on Waves, 85
Women's Collection, 107
Women's Earth and Climate Action Network International (WECAN), 193
Women's Environment and Development Organization (WEDO), 184, 191, 208
Women's grassroots support organizations (GRSOs), 196, 310, 343
Women's International League for Peace and Freedom, 362
Women's international nongovernmental organizations (WINGOs), 7-8, 184, 191, 368
Women's Islamic Initiative in Spirituality and Equality (WISE), 261
Women's Major Group (WMG), 191-192
Women's micro- and small-scale enterprises (WMSEs), 155

Women's movements
action opportunities, 371
assumptions about, 344–346
contextual factors and, 338–356
democratization and, 351–356
forces operating against, 346–348
human rights, 364–365
overview, **341**
state feminism, **356–359**
strands of, 341–344
success, evaluating, 359
transnational movements, **359–367**
United Nations and, 362–364
websites, 371–372
Women's National Coalition (WNC),
352
Women's policy agencies (WPAs), 356
*Women's Role in Economic
Development*, 176
**Women's spirituality movement,
276–278**
Women's suffrage, 27, 298–300
WomenWarPeace.org, 328
Wong, E., 355
Wood, R. E., 151
Wood, S. F., 62
Work, women and. *See also*
Globalization
action opportunities, 160–161
development programs and,
177–179

glass ceiling, 145–150
informal labor sector, 154–156
maternity protections, 135–138
paid labor, overview, 134–138
pay gap, 140–144
sex trade, 225–231
sexual harassment, 150–154
sexual orientation, 110
status and power, 25–26
sweatshop labor, **214–218**
trafficking and, 33, **227–231**
transnational corporations, 214–218
unpaid domestic and care labor,
127–134
unpaid labor, **127**–134
websites, 161
Wright, S., 367
Wu, H. C., 152
Wu Yi-Fang, 13

X

Xu, F., 345, 357

Y

Yacob, Halimah, 312
Yates, E. A., 323, 324
Yeates, N., 221
Yeoh, B., 221
Yeung, W. J., 223

Yi, J., 30
Yoshimi, Yoshiaki, 46
Young, K. K., 267
Yousafzai, Malala, 328, 347,
348
Youseff, A., 347
Yuan, L., 357
Yukongdi, V., 148

Z

Za-r, 246
Zacharias-Walsh, A., 148, 149
Zambia, Heifer, 185
Zander, L., 247
Zayadin, H., 347
Zellweger, A., 137
Zerwick, P., 76
Zewde, Sahle-Work, 312
Zhang, J., 30
Zhang, X., 42
Zheng, W., 345, 357
Zhu, W. X., 29
Zia, Mohammad, 315
Ziegler, A., 102
Zimmerman, C., 229
Zinman, J., 182
Zionism, 316
Zipper (zebra) systems, 308
Zourabichvili, Salome, 312
Zucker, A. N., 102